1/0

 St. Louis Community College

Forest Park
Florissant Valley
Meramec

Instructional Resources
St. Louis, Missouri

SECOND EDITION

Counseling and Psychotherapy

Theories and Interventions

David Capuzzi
Portland State University

Douglas R. Gross
Professor Emeritus, Arizona State University

Merrill,
an imprint of Prentice Hall
Upper Saddle River, New Jersey ■ *Columbus, Ohio*

Library of Congress Cataloging-in-Publication Data

Counseling and psychotherapy theories and interventions / [edited
  by] David Capuzzi, Douglas R. Gross—2nd ed.
       p.   cm.
   Includes bibliographical references and index.
   ISBN 0-13-569955-X
   1. Counseling.   2. Psychotherapy.   3. Counseling—Case studies.
4. Psychotherapy—Case studies.   I. Capuzzi, Dave.   II. Gross,
Douglas R.
BF637.C6C634   1999
158'.3—dc21   98-8649
                                                               CIP

Cover art: © Superstock Private Collection/Diana Ong
Editor: Kevin M. Davis
Production Editor: Linda Hillis Bayma
Design Coordinator: Diane C. Lorenzo
Text Designer: Rebecca Bobb
Cover Designer: Ceri Fitzgerald
Production Manager: Laura Messerly
Illustrations: Carlisle Communications, Ltd.
Director of Marketing: Kevin Flanagan
Marketing Manager: Suzanne Stanton
Advertising/Marketing Coordinator: Krista Groshong

This book was set in Garamond Light by Carlisle Communications, Ltd. and was printed and bound
by R.R. Donnelley & Sons Company. The cover was printed by Phoenix Color Corp.

Printed in the United States of America

10 9 8 7 6 5 4 3 2

ISBN: 0-13-569955-X

Reprinted with corrections September, 1999.

Prentice-Hall International (UK) Limited, *London*
Prentice-Hall of Australia Pty. Limited, *Sydney*
Prentice-Hall of Canada, Inc., *Toronto*
Prentice-Hall Hispanoamericana, S. A., *Mexico*
Prentice-Hall of India Private Limited, *New Delhi*
Prentice-Hall of Japan, Inc., *Tokyo*
Prentice-Hall Asia Pte. Ltd., *Singapore*
Editora Prentice-Hall do Brasil, Ltda., *Rio de Janeiro*

Meet the Authors

Meet the Editors

David Capuzzi, Ph.D., N.C.C., L.P.C., is past president of the American Counseling Association (formerly the American Association for Counseling and Development) and is professor of counselor education in the School of Education at Portland State University in Portland, Oregon.

From 1980 to 1984, Dr. Capuzzi was editor of *The School Counselor.* He has authored a number of textbook chapters and monographs on the topic of preventing adolescent suicide and is coeditor and author, with Dr. Larry Golden, of *Helping Families Help Children: Family Interventions With School-Related Problems* (1986) and *Preventing Adolescent Suicide* (1988). In 1989 and 1996 he coauthored and edited *Youth at Risk: A Prevention Resource for Counselors, Teachers, and Parents;* in 1991 and 1997, *Introduction to the Counseling Profession;* and in 1992 and 1998, *Introduction to Group Counseling* with Douglas R. Gross. He has authored or coauthored articles in a number of ACA and related journals.

A frequent speaker and keynoter at professional conferences and institutes, Dr. Capuzzi has also consulted with a variety of school districts and community agencies interested in initiating counseling and intervention strategies for adolescents at risk for suicide. He has facilitated the development of suicide prevention, crisis management, and postvention programs in communities throughout the United States; provides training on the topic of "youth at risk;" and serves as an invited adjunct faculty member at other universities as time permits. He is the first recipient of ACA's Kitty Cole Human Rights Award.

Douglas R. Gross, Ph.D., N.C.C., C.P.C., is professor emeritus of Arizona State University in Tempe, where he was a faculty member in the counseling program for 29 years. His professional work history includes public school teaching, counseling, and administration. He has been president of the Arizona Counselors Association, president of the Western Association for Counselor Education and Supervision, chairperson of the Western Regional Branch Assembly of the American Counseling Association (formerly the American Association for Counseling and Development), president of the Association for Humanistic Education and Development, and treasurer and parliamentarian of ACA.

In addition to his work on this textbook, Dr. Gross has contributed chapters to nine other texts: two editions of *Youth at Risk: A Prevention Resource for Counselors, Teachers, and Parents* (1989 and 1996); two editions of *Introduction to the Counseling Profession* (1991 and 1997); two editions of *Introduction to Group Counseling* (1992 and 1998); *Foundations of Mental Health Counseling* (1986); *Counseling: Theory, Process, and Practice* (1977); and *The Counselor's Handbook* (1974). His research has appeared in *The Jour-*

nal of Counseling Psychology; The Journal of Counseling and Development; The Association for Counselor Education and Supervision Journal; The Journal of Educational Research, Counseling, and Human Development; The Arizona Counselors Journal; The Texas Counseling Journal; and *The AMHCA Journal.*

Dr. Gross currently serves as a consultant to several alcohol and drug programs in the state of Arizona and conducts training on the topic of grief and loss.

Meet the Contributors

Valerie E. Appleton, Ed.D., is an associate professor of applied psychology at Eastern Washington University in Spokane. She is the director of counselor education at Eastern. Dr. Appleton is a Licensed Marriage, Family, and Child Counselor and a Registered Art Therapist (ATR). She worked for 10 years on an intensive care burn unit providing art therapy to patients and their families. Recently, she was the principal investigator for a federal grant serving rural secondary students at risk for school failure. She is serving as the president of the Washington Association for Counselor Educators and Supervisors and past president of the Evergreen Art Therapy Association. Dr. Appleton is a member of the Education Board of the American Art Therapy Association and the author of numerous book chapters and peer-reviewed journal articles.

G. Miguel Arciniega, Ph.D., is an associate professor in the Division of Psychology in Education at Arizona State University in Tempe. Dr. Arciniega has been director of minority counseling projects and institutes, teacher corps, and centers for bilingual and bicultural education. He has consulted extensively with federal, state, and local agencies about counseling minorities, and has also consulted with Aid for International Development (AID) in Central and South America. He has published several articles concerning multicultural counseling.

Loretta J. Bradley, Ph.D., is a professor of counselor education and chair of the Division of Educational Psychology and Leadership at Texas Tech University in Lubbock. Dr. Bradley is president of the American Counseling Association and a past president of the Association for Counselor Education and Supervision. She teaches graduate-level counseling classes, including counseling practicum, counseling theories, dysfunctional behavior, and counseling diverse populations. Dr. Bradley received her Ph.D. from Purdue University. She has written more than 75 articles published in professional journals, authored or coauthored four books, and given more than 80 presentations at professional conferences. Dr. Bradley was the co-recipient of the 1987 ACA Research Award, the 1985 ACES Research Award, and the 1990 ACES Best Publication Award. In addition to serving as chairperson of the ACA Media Committee, she has served on the editorial boards of *The American Counselor, The Journal of Counseling and Development, Counselor Education and Supervision,* and *The Journal of Humanistic Education and Development.*

Larry D. Burlew, Ed.D., is an associate professor of counseling at the University of Bridgeport. His teaching experience has mostly been with urban universities, while his counseling experience has been with employee assistance programs, college students, midlife adults, AIDS clients, and gay men. He has developed an appreciation for alternative forms to Western therapy through work and study on spiritual development, Shamanism, past-life therapy, and Eastern philosophies. He believes that traditional "talk" therapy is important for some clients, but that it is only the "tip of the onion." Alternative forms of therapy may be necessary to help each individual pull back the "onion skin layers" to reach her or his potential as a human being, only one of the many life-forms on planet earth.

Leonard R. Corte, Ph.D., is a psychoanalyst in private practice. He is a member of the Los Angeles Institute and Society for Psychoanalytic Studies and an associate member of the International Psychoanalytic Association. In addition, Dr. Corte is the president of the Southwest Center for Psychoanalytic Studies and a member of the teaching faculty at the center. He is also an adjunct faculty member at the Arizona State University School of Social Work.

Cass Dykeman, Ph.D., is an associate professor of applied psychology at Eastern Washington University in Spokane, where he serves as the director of the school counseling program. Dr. Dykeman is a National Certified Counselor and Master Addictions Counselor. He received his master's degree in counseling from the University of Washington and a doctorate in counselor education from the University of Virginia. He was the principal investigator for a $1.5 million federal school-to-work research project. In addition, he is the author of numerous books, book chapters, and peer-reviewed journal articles. Dr. Dykeman is a past president of both the Washington State Association for Counselor Education and Supervision and the Western Association for Counselor Education and Supervision. He is also a past chair of the School Counseling Interest Network of the Association for Counselor Education and Supervision. His current research interests include the role of couples and families in addictive behavior counseling.

Jacqueline M. Elliott, received her B.S. in English in secondary education from the University of Wisconsin–Milwaukee. She is a counselor for Disability Services for students at Portland State University. Ms. Elliott has also taught women's studies issues and contributed feminist articles to newspapers and newsletters. She is currently a member of NOW and is pursuing graduate studies in the community counseling specialization in the master's program in counselor education at Portland State University.

Mary Lou Bryant Frank, Ph.D., received her training as a family therapist and a counseling psychologist at Colorado State University. At Arizona State University in Tempe she coordinated the eating disorders program, co-coordinated the master's and doctoral practicum training program, and concurrently taught in the counseling department. She contributed a chapter to Capuzzi and Gross's *Introduction to Group Counseling* (first and second editions) and has published articles in the *Journal of Counseling and Development* and *Psychological Reports*. Dr. Frank received a Distinguished Service Provider Award in Counseling for 1989–90. She has been a consultant and speaker at eating disorders conferences, private hospitals, and universities. She has served as the assistant academic dean and an associate professor of psychology at Clinch Valley College of the University of Virginia. Currently she serves as a professor and the head of the Psychology Department at North Georgia College and State University.

L. J. Gould, M.A., is a doctoral candidate in counseling in the Division of Educational Psychology and Leadership at Texas Tech University. Ms. Gould's previous publications include coauthoring four book chapters and three journal articles. She has served as the

ACES program committee student chairperson and has presented programs at national ACA and ACES conferences. Her major research interests include gender bias, stereotyping, multicultural counseling, and gay/lesbian issues.

Richard J. Hazler, Ph.D., is a professor of counselor education at Ohio University in Athens. He earned his Ph.D. at the University of Idaho. Previously he worked professionally as an elementary school teacher, school counselor, prison counselor, counselor in the military, and counselor in private practice. Dr. Hazler is editor of the *Student Focus* column for the American Counseling Association's *Counseling Today,* is on the editorial board of the *Journal of Counseling and Development,* and has published numerous articles on a variety of counseling and human development topics. His most recent books are *Helping in the Hallway: Advanced Strategies for Enhancing School Relationships* (1998), *What You Never Learned in Graduate School: A Survival Guide for Therapists* (1997), with Jeffrey Kottler, and *Breaking the Cycle of Violence: Interventions for Bullying and Victimization* (1996). He has been a leader in the development of numerous youth programs, including those for gifted and remedial education, school violence, and the Youth Conservation Corps.

Cynthia R. Kalodner, Ph.D., is associate professor of counseling psychology in the Department of Counseling, Rehabilitative Counseling, and Counseling Psychology at West Virginia University. She received her doctorate in counseling psychology from Pennsylvania State University in 1988. Previously, she was an assistant professor in the counseling psychology program at the University of Akron. Dr. Kalodner spent a year in a postdoctoral fellowship studying public health at Johns Hopkins University. She currently studies the interface between psychology and health. Her present research focuses primarily on cognitive-behavioral approaches to understand and treat women with eating disorders.

Rolla E. Lewis, Ed.D., is an assistant professor of counselor education in the School of Education at Portland State University where he serves as coordinator of the school counseling specialization for the masters program in counselor education. Dr. Lewis has taught, led groups, and counseled students in alternative and public school settings for more than 15 years. He is a past president of the Oregon Association for Counselor Education and Supervision and is author of a number of book chapters and journal articles. His current research interests focus upon fostering resiliency and using structured narrative in the schools.

Mary Finn Maples, Ph.D., is a former president of the American Counseling Association (then the American Personnel and Guidance Association) and the Association for Spiritual, Ethical and Religious Values in Counseling. She is professor of counseling and educational psychology at the University of Nevada, Reno. Dr. Maples also serves as an adjunct faculty member for the National College of Juvenile and Family Law, located in Reno, and as a consultant in business and industry. Her areas of specialization include organizational development, team building, values and attitudes in decision making, spirituality in adult development, effective interpersonal communication, and gracious confrontation.

Betty J. Newlon, Ed.D., is professor emeritus of the University of Arizona in Tucson, where she served as head of the counseling and guidance program. Dr. Newlon was responsible for training and supervising graduate students in the mental health and community counseling program at the university.

Gregory J. Novie, Ph.D., has been in private practice as a psychologist since 1985. His areas of research interest include countertransference with borderline and narcissistic patients and the therapeutic action of psychotherapy. Dr. Novie received his master's degree in rehabilitation counseling from Southern Illinois University and his doctorate in educational psychology from Arizona State University in Tempe. He received his psychoanalytic training from, and is a member of, the Southwest Center for Psychoanalytic Studies. He is also a member of the division of psychoanalysis of the American Psychological Association.

Gerald Parr, Ph.D., is a professor of counselor education and associate dean of graduate education and research in the College of Education at Texas Tech University in Lubbock. He received his Ph.D. from the University of Colorado in 1974. His experience includes secondary school teaching and counseling. Dr. Parr currently teaches group counseling, theories of counseling, and testing. He has received a President's Excellence in Teaching Award during his tenure at Texas Tech University. He was co-recipient of the 1988 Texas Association of Counseling and Development's Professional Writing Award.

Catherine B. Roland, Ed.D., is a counselor educator at the University of Arkansas, Fayetteville. She received her Ed.D. in 1977 from the University of Cincinnati and has lived in New York, Philadelphia, and New Orleans, where she had a full-time private practice for many years. She has been active in the American Counseling Association as a former board member and committee chair. Her interests include gender and diversity issues in counseling, counseling and spirituality, and research on women and nontraditional, non-talk counseling approaches. She is advisor to Chi Sigma Iota at the University of Arkansas and fully enjoys working with and mentoring her students.

Susan E. Schwartz, Ph.D., is a Jungian analyst trained at the C. G. Jung Institute in Zurich, Switzerland; she also has a doctorate in clinical psychology. She is a senior analyst, teacher, and secretary of the C. G. Jung Institute of Santa Fe, New Mexico. Dr. Schwartz is also a member of the International Association of Jungian Analysts, the American Psychological Association, and the National Association for Advancement of Psychoanalysis. She has given lectures and workshops on various aspects of Jungian analytical psychology in the United States, Europe, Canada, South Africa, Australia, and New Zealand, and has a private practice in Scottsdale, Arizona, and Las Vegas, Nevada.

Conrad Sieber, Ph.D., completed a postdoctoral fellowship in the counselor education program at Portland State University, where he taught courses on program evaluation in educational and social service agencies and supervised counseling practicum students and interns. He also pursued interests in treating post-traumatic stress disorder, in person-centered psychology, and in developing educational/counseling programs for disadvantaged youth. Dr. Sieber received his doctoral degree from Colorado State University and completed an internship at The Ohio State University. He has 5 years of professional experience in university counseling centers where he coordinated and developed group therapy programs, evaluated clinical services, and was actively involved in training graduate students. Currently, he maintains a private practice in Portland, Oregon; evaluates educational and counseling programs; and consults with public schools and institutions of higher education. Dr. Sieber has authored counseling book chapters and articles for professional publications.

Mary E. Stafford, Ph.D., is a faculty member in the school psychology program in the Division of Psychology in Education at Arizona State University in Tempe. She teaches child counseling to school and counseling psychology doctoral students and masters-level counselor education students. Previously, she has worked with children in public school and residential treatment center settings as a teacher, counselor, evaluator, and school principal. Dr. Stafford received her doctorate in educational psychology with an emphasis in school psychology from the University of Texas at Austin in 1994. Her research and writing have focused on psychometric issues of personality and vocational tests, children's counseling issues, children's achievement and adjustment in schools, and cultural issues in mental health.

Thomas J. Sweeney, Ph.D., is professor emeritus of counselor education in the College of Education of Ohio University in Athens, Ohio. Dr. Sweeney earned his bachelor's degree from the University of Akron, his master's degree in school counseling from the University of Wisconsin–Madison, and his Ph.D. in counselor education from The Ohio State University. Since taking early retirement from Ohio University in 1992, he remains a faculty member at that institution and teaches full-time one quarter per year. In addition to authoring books, monographs, chapters in books, research reports, and articles, Dr. Sweeney has had both training videos and an award-winning telecourse, *Coping With Kids,* distributed worldwide and broadcast on local, state, and regional television. He recently finished the fourth edition of *Adlerian Counseling.* He is a keynote speaker, presenter, workshop director, and consultant in this country and abroad.

Robert E. Wubbolding, Ed.D., received his bachelor of arts degree from the Athenaeum of Ohio and his doctorate in counseling from the University of Cincinnati. As director of training for the William Glasser Institute, he monitors the 18-month reality therapy training program. He is also assistant director and full professor in the counselor education department at Xavier University as well as the director of the Center for Reality Therapy in Cincinnati. Author of seven books on reality therapy, Dr. Wubbolding has taught reality therapy in North America, Europe, and the Pacific Rim. He currently studies cross-cultural applications of reality therapy.

Preface

Counseling and Psychotherapy: Theories and Interventions provides a collection of conceptual frameworks for understanding the parameters of the helping relationship. These parameters can include models for viewing personality development; explaining past behavior; predicting future behavior; understanding the current behavior of the client; diagnosing and treatment planning; assessing client motivations, needs, and unsolved issues; and identifying strategies and interventions of assistance to the client. Theories help organize data and provide guidelines for the prevention and intervention efforts of counselors and therapists. They direct a professional helper's attention and observations and offer constructs, terminology, and viewpoints that can be understood by colleagues and used during supervision and consultation sessions. Theory directly influences the interventions used by counselors and therapists to promote a client's new insight, new behavior, and new approaches to relationships and problem solving. The greater a counselor's or therapist's awareness of the strengths and possibilities inherent in numerous theoretical frames of reference, the greater the potential for understanding the uniqueness of a particular client's life space.

This book is unique in both format and content. All the contributing authors are experts who provide state-of-the-art information about theories of counseling and psychotherapy (see the "Meet the Authors" section for their backgrounds). In addition, each chapter discusses applications of a theory as it relates to one particular case study: a hypothetical client named Maria, whom we are introduced to on page 68. The book also includes information that is sometimes not addressed in other counseling and psychotherapy textbooks, such as a chapter that focuses on the importance of achieving a personal and professional identity before beginning work with clients, a chapter on feminist theory, and a chapter on Eastern approaches to counseling and psychotherapy. The book's unique approach enhances its readability and should increase reader interest in the material.

Features of the Text

This book is designed for students who are beginning their study of individual counseling and psychotherapy. It presents a comprehensive overview of each of the following theories: psychoanalytic, Jungian, Adlerian, existential, person-centered, feminist, Gestalt, cognitive-behavioral, reality, family, brief, and Eastern. Each theory is addressed from the perspective of background, human nature, major constructs, applications (which includes a discussion of the goals of counseling and psychotherapy, the process of change, and intervention strategies), evaluation (which evaluates both the supporting research and the limitations of the theory), a summary chart, and a case study consistent with the theoretical model under discussion.

We know that one text cannot adequately address all the factors connected with a given theory; entire texts have been written discussing each of the theories in this book. We have, however, attempted to provide readers with a consistent approach to analyzing each theory and have included examples of how to apply a theory in a case study.

The format for this text is based on the contributions of the coeditors, who conceptualized the content and wrote the first three chapters, as well as the contributions of 22 authors selected for their expertise in various theories. Each chapter contains theoretical and applied content. The text is divided into the following three parts: "Foundations for Individual Counseling and Psychotherapy," "Theories of Counseling and Psychotherapy," and "Integrative Theoretical Applications."

Part I, "Foundations for Individual Counseling and Psychotherapy" (Chapters 1 through 3), begins by offering general information about the helping relationship and individual counseling. That foundation is followed by chapters titled "Achieving a Personal and Professional Identity" and "Ethical and Legal Issues in Counseling and Psychotherapy."

Part II, "Theories of Counseling and Psychotherapy" (Chapters 4 through 12), presents information on the nine theories selected for inclusion in this portion of the text. Each of these chapters—"Psychoanalytic Theory," "Jungian Analytical Theory," "Adlerian Theory," "Existential Theory," "Person-Centered Theory," "Feminist Theory," "Gestalt Theory," "Cognitive-Behavioral Theories," and "Reality Therapy Theory"—presents a theory and then applies the theory to the case study of Maria.

Part III, "Integrative Theoretical Applications" (Chapters 13 through 18), involves a discussion of theoretical approaches that are integrative in nature and draw upon many of the previously discussed theoretical systems ("Family Theory," "Brief Theories," "Counseling and Psychotherapy With Children," and "Counseling and Psychotherapy: An Integrative Perspective"), theoretical approaches that stem from Eastern philosophy ("Eastern Theories), and multicultural concepts and issues that have application across all theoretical systems ("Counseling and Psychotherapy: Multicultural Considerations").

New to This Edition

This edition of our text includes some additional topics that we think will be of high interest to the readership. A chapter on feminist theory presents an excellent overview of the evolution of feminist theory and its relationship to psychoanalysis, object relations, Jungian, cognitive-behavioral, and family systems perspectives, as well as addressing human nature, major constructs, applications, evaluation, and the case of Maria. The chapter on family theory is new to this edition and is included to sensitize the reader to the fact that counselors and therapists engaging clients in individual work must keep in mind the systemic variables influencing clients and the fact that some clients may need family counseling and psychotherapy as part of a comprehensive treatment plan. The chapter on brief theories is included because of the influence of managed care on the provision of mental health services in almost all settings. This chapter also provides information on systematic treatment selection because of its relationship to brief approaches.

In response to the increasing interest in alternative approaches to counseling and psychotherapy, this edition includes a chapter on Eastern theories and is focused on Morita therapy. Few textbooks of this nature address conceptual frameworks that are nontraditional or external to the "mainstream" models usually adopted by practitioners and academicians in Western cultures. Finally, since most of the theories in use today were not originally developed with minors as clients as the primary focus, we have added a chapter on counseling and psychotherapy with children.

Readers of the second edition will find the *Instructor-Student Handbook to Accompany Counseling and Psychotherapy* helpful in the process of mastering the content of the text. This handbook is designed to assist the reader in a variety of ways. For each chapter the following information is provided: a chapter pre-inventory, a chapter outline, a chapter overview, lists of key terms and key people, suggested classroom exercises designed to enhance instruction as well as to provide experiential components to the learning experience, individual exercises that can be completed between class sessions, questions for study and discussion, suggested readings, a chapter post-inventory, an answer key for the pre- and post-inventories, and, in some instances, a subsection containing supplementary materials. It is possible that professors adopting this text may tie some of the course assignments and requirements to the contents of this handbook.

We, the coeditors, and the 22 other contributors have made every effort to give the reader current information and content focused on both theory and application. It is our hope that the second edition of *Counseling and Psychotherapy: Theories and Interventions* will provide the foundation that students need to make decisions about follow-up study of specific theories as well as development of their own personal theory of counseling and psychotherapy.

Acknowledgments

We would like to thank the other 22 authors who contributed their time and expertise to the development of this textbook for professionals interested in individual counseling and psychotherapy. We also thank our families, who supported and encouraged our writing and editing efforts, as well as the counselor education faculties at Portland State University and Arizona State University. Thanks go out to our editors and the other staff members at Prentice Hall for their collaborative and thorough approach to the editing and production of this textbook. We would like to give special recognition to Diane Unck, graduate assistant and student in the rehabilitation counseling specialization of the counselor education program at Portland State University, for her assistance in meeting publication deadlines. Without the dedicated efforts of this group of colleagues, we know this book could not have been published.

We are also grateful to the reviewers of this manuscript for their comments and suggestions: Margery A. Neely, Kansas State University; Beverly B. Palmer, California State University at Dominquez Hills, and Toni R. Tollerud, Northern Illinois University. We also want to acknowledge the reviewers of the first edition: Virginia Allen, Idaho State University; Martin Gerstein, Virginia Tech; Samuel T. Gladding, Wake Forest University; Larry Golden, University of Texas at San Antonio; Richard J. Hazler, Ohio University; Don C. Locke, North Carolina State University; Don W. Locke, Northeast Louisiana University; Donald L. Mattson, University of South Dakota; Eugene R. Moan, Northern Arizona University; and Nancy L. Murdock, University of Missouri at Kansas City.

David Capuzzi
Douglas R. Gross

Brief Contents

Contents

6 Adlerian Theory   113

Thomas J. Sweeney

11   Cognitive-Behavioral Theories   261
Cynthia R. Kalodner

16 Counseling and Psychotherapy With Children   413
Mary E. Stafford

17 Counseling and Psychotherapy: Multicultural Considerations   435
G. Miguel Arciniega and Betty J. Newlon

18 Counseling and Psychotherapy: An Integrative Perspective   459
Loretta J. Bradley, Gerald Parr, and L. J. Gould

Foundations for Individual Counseling and Psychotherapy

Counseling and psychotherapy encompass a number of relationship modalities in which the counselor or therapist needs to be proficient. Achieving a personal and professional identity is also fundamental to facilitating the process of counseling and psychotherapy. In addition to being able to create some essential core conditions that are prerequisite to change on the part of the client, the counselor or therapist, before choosing a particular frame of reference from which to operate, must possess knowledge about ethical and legal issues pertinent to the practice of counseling or psychotherapy. This section of the text provides foundational information pertinent to individual work with clients.

The helping relationship is the foundation on which the process of counseling and psychotherapy is based. It is not possible to use the concepts and associated interventions of a specific theory unless such applications are made in the context of a relationship that promotes trust, insight, and behavior change. Chapter 1, "Helping Relationships in Counseling and Psychotherapy," is designed to aid students in both the development of and the presentation of the helping relationship. To achieve this purpose, the helping relationship is presented in terms of definitions and descriptions, stages, core conditions and personal characteristics, and helping strategies. A brief case study is also presented.

Chapter 2, "Achieving a Personal and Professional Identity," discusses why the personal and professional identity of the helping professional must be addressed before and during the process of studying and applying individual approaches to counseling and psychotherapy. The chapter addresses the importance of health and wellness for the helping professional, recognition of values and cultural bias in theory and practice, awareness of the daily world of the practitioner, and achieving perspective and balance between the individual as a person and the individual as a professional. Brief comments about the importance of developing a personal theory are also provided.

For both the novice and the experienced practitioner, determining what is or is not ethical behavior is often a perplexing dilemma. While the numerous specialties that comprise the helping professions have provided practitioners with a plethora of guidelines and codes of ethical behavior, confusion still exists. The purpose of Chapter 3, "Ethical and Legal Issues in Counseling and Psychotherapy," is to discuss the definition and rationale for ethical codes, models for ethical decision making, dimensions of ethical behavior, dimensions of unethical behavior, procedures utilized in the processing of complaints of unethical behavior, and legal issues. No counselor or therapist should initiate individual work with a client, from any theoretical frame of reference, prior to becoming familiar with the information in this chapter.

As these chapters indicate, practitioners must achieve high levels of competence, effectiveness, and expertise to create a helping relationship beneficial to clients. They must also develop the ability to know themselves from both personal and professional perspectives, and understand the ethical and legal aspects of working with clients prior to adopting, modifying, or integrating the theory and interventions options for individual counseling and psychotherapy. We have made every attempt to introduce the readers to these topics in the chapters included in this section of the text. Readers are encouraged to do additional reading and follow-up course work and to commit to personal counseling or therapy to achieve the purposes we have outlined in these chapters.

Helping Relationships in Counseling and Psychotherapy

Douglas R. Gross
Professor Emeritus
Arizona State University

David Capuzzi
Portland State University

T he following scenario depicts a student, much like you, who has taken the preparatory classes leading to enrollment in practicum. Jean has completed course work in testing, analysis, careers, groups, human development, personality theory, ethics, cultural diversity, and counseling strategies. In her work with clients in practicum, she will be asked to integrate the knowledge gained from this course work with both her personal dynamics and her life experiences. Such integration is the foundation on which the process of counseling and psychotherapy rests—a foundation defined for our purposes as the **helping relationship.** The information contained in the scenario serves as an introduction to our discussion of this relationship.

Jean maneuvered her car through the heavy traffic at the entrance to the university parking area. She was annoyed that it was taking her so long to park this morning. She had left home early so that she would have plenty of class time to prepare to meet her first client in practicum. Already 10 minutes behind her timeline and concerned that she would not have time to review all the material before beginning her first client meeting, she parked her car and caught the tram into the main part of the campus. She was oblivious to the various classroom buildings she passed and to the other people on the tram. Her thoughts centered on the fact that she would see her first client this morning. Would she be able to work effectively with this person?

Jean's supervisor had reviewed basic helping conditions and strategies, such as empathy, respect, genuineness, rapport building, active listening skills, session planning, and a myriad of other operational procedures, during the early meetings of her practicum group.

He then asked members of the practicum group to explain their theoretical approach to working with clients. During her time, Jean discussed the appeal of the Gestalt approach and also her fear that she would not be able to translate this into action once she sat down face-to-face with another person. The supervisor assured her that he would work with her in helping translate knowledge into action steps. The supervisor had cautioned all members of the practicum group to remain open to other theoretical approaches. He said that the purpose of practicum was to experiment with various approaches and to see what worked best for both the student and the client. Jean thought the supervisor's cautions made sense. She had practiced other approaches in role-playing sessions, but none felt as comfortable to her as the Gestalt approach. She remembered that she had received a good deal of positive feedback the day she had presented this particular role-play. Today, however, was not a role-play. She would meet a client, not a peer, and she had many reservations—not about the theory, but about her ability to apply it. She was frightened, because she knew that people would be watching from the adjoining room, and by the fact that she would be evaluated directly after the session. Jean was a good student, and she wanted to be a good practitioner. But she was not sure that the two necessarily went together. This was the first time she had been called upon to demonstrate her knowledge and skill in what she saw as the "real" setting.

When the tram reached the stop closest to her building, Jean raced to the fourth-floor practicum training center. Carolyn, the center receptionist, told her that her client had arrived early and was completing the necessary paperwork. Jean was instructed to get the room ready and then return to the waiting area to meet her client. She felt her heart beat a little faster as she returned to the waiting room. She had checked in with her supervisor, arranged the chairs in the room where she would meet the client, put a tape in the recorder, and made sure that nothing was blocking the two-way mirror. She was ready for the most exciting yet frightening experience of her educational program.

This scenario plays itself out each semester when students are confronted with their first client contacts in either practicum or internship. All of the classes you have taken to this point have been preparing you for this encounter. It is often the first time you are called upon to integrate the learned knowledge and skills into a counseling or therapeutic relationship—a helping relationship. The fact that you must demonstrate this untried relationship for both peers and supervisors in the fishbowl environment called **practicum** or **internship** adds both excitement and anxiety. The excitement stems from being able to put your knowledge and skills to a practical test. The anxiety stems from a lack of experience of trying this relationship outside the safety of the role-play situations in structured classes. You should expect such personal reactions—perhaps they are necessary as you move from a position of inexperience to one of experience.

This chapter will aid you in understanding the various factors that affect the helping relationship: definitions and descriptions, stages, core dimensions, and strategies. We hope the information presented in this chapter will help you realize that your excitement and anxiety can be natural and productive. We also hope you will be able to incorporate this information into effective models of the helping relationship.

Helping Relationships: Definitions and Descriptions

The helping relationship appears to be the cornerstone on which all effective helping rests (Combs & Gonzalez, 1994; Dixon & Glover, 1984; Miars, Burden, & Pedersen, 1997; Purkey & Schmidt, 1987; Terry, Burden, & Pedersen, 1991). Words such as *integral, necessary,* and *mandatory* are used to describe this relationship and its importance in the ultimate effectiveness of the **helping process.** Even though different theoretical systems use different words to describe this relationship (see Chapters 4 through 12), each addresses the significance of the helping relationship in facilitating client change. Kottler and Brown (1992), in their *Introduction to Therapeutic Counseling,* made the following comments regarding the significance of this relationship:

> Regardless of the setting in which you practice counseling, whether in a school, agency, hospital, or private practice, the relationships you develop with your clients are crucial to any progress you might make together. For without a high degree of intimacy and trust between two people, very little can be accomplished. (p. 64)

In further support of the significance of the helping relationship, Brammer and MacDonald (1996) said:

> The helping relationship is dynamic, meaning that it is constantly changing at verbal and nonverbal levels. The relationship is the principal process vehicle for both helper and helpee to express and fulfill their needs, as well as to mesh helpee problems with helper expertise. Relationship emphasizes the affective mode, because relationship is commonly defined as the inferred emotional quality of the interaction. (p. 52)

The ideas expressed in these two statements describe the essential value of the helping relationship in the process of counseling or psychotherapy and the significant role that the counselor or therapist plays in developing this relationship. Through this relationship, client change occurs. Although the creation of this relationship is not the end goal of the process, it certainly is the means by which other goals are met. It serves as the framework within which effective helping takes place.

Although agreed-upon definitions and descriptions of the helping relationship should be easy to find, such is not the case. Despite the importance of this relationship in the overall helping process, a perusal of textbooks and articles dealing with counseling and psychotherapy shows the lack of a common definition. Rogers (1961), for example, defined a helping relationship as one "in which at least one of the parties has the intent of promoting the growth, development, maturity, improved functioning and improved coping with life of the other" (p. 39). Okun (1992) stated that "the development of a warm, trustful relationship between the helper and the helpee underlies any strategy or approach to the helping process and, therefore, is a basic condition for the success of any helping process" (p. 14). Purkey and Schmidt (1987) described the helping relationship as an "inviting relationship" and defined it as "the incorporation of compatible theories, systems, and techniques of human service into a therapeutic 'stance' for professional helping" (p. 3).

It is easy to see the difficulty in categorically stating an accepted definition or description of the helping relationship, regardless of which of these statements you choose to embrace. Yet despite the differences, each carries with it directions and directives aimed at a single goal: the enhancement and encouragement of client change. The following definitive characteristics of the helping relationship embrace this goal and describe our conceptualization of this relationship:

- A relationship initially structured by the counselor or therapist but open to cooperative restructuring based upon the needs of the client
- A relationship that begins with the initial meeting and continues through termination
- A relationship in which all persons involved perceive the existence of trust, caring, concern, and commitment and act accordingly
- A relationship in which the needs of the client are given priority over the needs of the counselor or therapist
- A relationship that provides for the personal growth of all persons involved
- A relationship that provides the safety needed for self-exploration of all persons involved
- A relationship that promotes the potential of all persons involved

The major responsibility in creating this relationship rests initially with the counselor or therapist, with increasing demands for client involvement and commitment over time. It is a shared process, and only through such shared efforts will this relationship develop and flourish. This development evolves in stages that take the relationship from initiation to closure. The stages in this evolving process are the subject of the following section.

Helping Relationships: Stages

The helping relationship is a constant throughout the counseling or psychotherapeutic process. The definitive characteristics we have already presented indicate that the relationship must be present from the initial meeting between the client and the counselor or therapist and continue through closure. Viewing the helping relationship as a constant throughout the helping process leads to visualizing this process from a developmental perspective. This development can best be viewed in terms of a narrow path whose limits are established by the client's fear, anxiety, and resistance. Such client reactions should not be seen as lack of commitment to change; rather, they need to be understood in terms of the unknown nature of this developing alliance and the fact that this may be the first time the client has experienced this type of interaction. These reactions are often shared by the counselor or therapist, based upon his or her level of experience. The path broadens through the development of trust, safety, and understanding as this relationship develops. The once narrow path becomes a boulevard along which two persons move courageously toward their final destination—change.

The movement along this broadening path is described by various authors in terms of stages or phases. Osipow, Walsh, and Tosi (1980), in discussing the stages of the helping relationship, stated:

> Persons who experience the process of personal counseling seem to progress through several stages. First, there is an increased awareness of self and others. Second, there is an expanded exploration of self and environment (positive and negative behavioral tendencies). Third, there is increased commitment to self-enhancing behavior and its implementation. Fourth, there is an internalization of new and more productive thoughts and actions. Fifth, there is a stabilization of new behavior. (p. 73)

Brammer (1985) divided this developmental process into two phases, each with four distinctive stages. Phase one is entitled "Building Relationships" and includes preparing the client and opening the relationship, clarifying the problem or concern of the client, structuring the process, and building a relationship. Phase two is entitled "Facilitating Positive Action" and involves exploration, consolidation, planning, and termination.

Purkey and Schmidt (1987) set forth three stages in building the helping relationship, each containing four steps. Stage one, "Preparation," includes having the desire for a relationship, expecting good things, preparing the setting, and reading the situation. Stage two is "Initiating Responding" and includes choosing caringly, acting appropriately, honoring the client, and ensuring reception. The third and final stage, "Follow-up," includes interpreting responses, negotiating positions, evaluating the process, and developing trust.

Authors such as Corey and Corey (1993), Egan (1994), Hackney and Cormier (1996), and Patterson and Eisenberg (1994) provide other models of the developmental nature of the stages of the helping relationship. Although the terms used to describe these stages may differ, there seems to be a consistency across these models: The reader moves from initiation of the relationship through a clinically based working stage to a termination stage. The following developmental stages show our conceptualization of this relationship-building process and are based on the consistency found in our research and our clinical experience:

- *Stage 1: Relationship development.* This stage includes the initial meeting of client and counselor or therapist, rapport building, information gathering, goal determination, and informing the client about the conditions under which counseling will take place (e.g., confidentiality, taping, counselor/therapist/client roles).

- *Stage 2: Extended exploration.* This stage builds on the foundation established in the first stage. Through selected techniques, theoretical approaches, and strategies, the counselor or therapist explores in depth the emotional and cognitive dynamics of the person of the client, problem parameters, previously tried solutions, decision-making capabilities, and a reevaluation of the goals determined in stage 1.

- *Stage 3: Problem resolution.* This stage, which depends on information gained during the previous two stages, is characterized by increased activity for all parties involved. The counselor or therapist's activities include facilitating, demonstrating, instructing and providing a safe environment for the development of change. The client's activities focus on reevaluating emotional and cognitive dynamics, trying out new behaviors (both inside and outside of the sessions), and discarding those that do not meet goals.

- *Stage 4: Termination and follow-up.* This stage is the closing stage of the helping relationship and is cooperatively determined by all persons involved. Methods and procedures for follow-up are determined prior to the last meeting.

It is important to keep in mind that people do not automatically move through these identified stages in a lockstep manner. The relationship may end at any one of these stages based upon decisions made by the client, the counselor or therapist, or both. Nor is it possible to identify the amount of time that "should" be devoted to any particular stage. With certain clients, much more time will need to be devoted to specific stages. Brown and Srebalus (1988), in addressing the tentative nature of these relationship stages, have the following caution for their readers:

> Before we describe a common sequence of events in counseling, it is important to note that many clients, for one reason or another, will not complete all the stages of counseling. The process will be abandoned prematurely, not because something went wrong, but because of factors external to the counselor-client relationship. For example, the school year may end for a student client, or a client or counselor may move away to accept a new job. When counseling is in process and must abruptly end, the participants will feel the incompleteness and loss. (p. 69)

Viewing the helping relationship as an ongoing process that is composed of developmental stages provides counselors and therapists with a structural framework within which they can function effectively. Inside this framework fit the core conditions and strategies that serve the goals of movement through the relationship process and enhancement and encouragement of client change. We discuss these core conditions and strategies in the following two sections.

Helping Relationships: Core Conditions

The concept of basic or **core conditions** related to the helping relationship has its basis in the early work of Rogers (1957) and the continued work of such authors as Carkhuff and Barenson (1967), Combs (1986), Egan (1994), Ivey (1988), Patterson (1974), and Truax and Carkhuff (1967). The concept incorporates a set of conditions which, when present, enhance the effectiveness of the helping relationship. These conditions vary in terminology from author to author but generally include the following: **empathic understanding, respect and positive regard, genuineness and congruence, concreteness, warmth,** and **immediacy.** We also add **cultural awareness** to this list. Our rationale for this inclusion stems from our belief that counselors and therapists must be culturally aware, culturally sensitive, and appreciative of cultural diversity in order to provide the other six core conditions. Support for this belief is found in Mathews and Atkinson (1997), Newlon and Arciniega (1992), Sue and Sue (1990), and Wehrly (1991). It should be obvious in reviewing this listing that the concept of core or basic conditions relates directly to various personal characteristics or behaviors that the counselor or therapist brings to and incorporates into the helping relationship. It is difficult to pinpoint with any exactness how such characteristics or behaviors develop. Are they the result of life experiences, classroom instruction, or some combination of both? Our experience in education favors the last explanation: Core conditions or behaviors must already be present to some degree in our students for our instruction to enhance or expand them.

The remainder of this section deals with the core conditions and relates these directly to personal characteristics or behaviors of counselors or therapists that should enhance their ability to effectively utilize these conditions in the process of helping. Although definitions, emphases, and applications of these conditions differ across theoretical systems, there appears to be agreement about their effectiveness in facilitating change in the overall helping relationship (Brammer, Abrego, & Shostrom, 1993; Fox, 1993; Gladding, 1996; Sexton & Whiston, 1994; Thompson, 1996).

Empathic Understanding

Empathic understanding is the ability to feel *with* clients as opposed to feeling *for* clients. It is the ability to understand feelings, thoughts, ideas, and experiences by viewing them from the client's frame of reference. The counselor or therapist must be able to enter the client's world, understand the myriad aspects that make up that world, and communicate this understanding so that the client perceives that he or she has been heard accurately.

Egan (1994) identified both primary and advanced levels of empathic understanding. At the primary level, it is the ability to understand, identify, and communicate feelings and meanings that are at the surface level of the client's disclosures. At the advanced level, it is the ability to understand, identify, and communicate feelings and meanings that are buried, hidden, or beyond the immediate reach of a client. Such feelings and meanings are more often covert rather than overt client expressions.

Personal characteristics or behaviors that enhance a counselor's or therapist's ability to provide empathic understanding would include, but not be limited to, the following:

- The knowledge and awareness of one's own values, attitudes, and beliefs and the emotional and behavioral impact they have on one's own life
- The knowledge and awareness of one's own feelings and emotional response patterns and how they manifest themselves in interactive patterns
- The knowledge and awareness of one's own life experiences and one's personal reactions to those experiences
- The capacity and willingness to communicate these personal reactions to one's clients

Respect and Positive Regard

Respect and positive regard are defined as the belief in each client's innate worth and potential and the ability to communicate this belief in the helping relationship. This belief, once communicated, provides clients with positive reinforcement relative to their innate ability to take responsibility for their own growth, change, goal determination, decision making, and eventual problem solution. It is an empowering process that delivers a message to clients that they are able to take control of their lives and, with facilitative assistance from the counselor or therapist, foster change. Communicating and demonstrating this respect for clients takes many forms. According to Baruth and Robinson (1987), it "is often communicated by what the counselor does not do or say. In other words, by not offering to intervene for someone, one is communicating a belief in the individual's ability to 'do' for himself or herself" (p. 85).

Personal characteristics or behaviors that enhance a counselor's or therapist's abilities to provide respect and positive regard include, but are not limited to, the following:

- The capacity to respect oneself
- The capacity to view oneself as having worth and potential
- The capacity to model and communicate this positive self-image to clients
- The capacity to recognize one's own control needs, and the ability to use this recognition in a manner that allows clients to direct their own lives

Genuineness and Congruence

Genuineness and congruence describe the ability to be **authentic** in the helping relationship. The ability to be real as opposed to artificial, to behave as one feels as opposed to playing the role of the helper, and to be congruent in terms of actions and words are further descriptors of this core condition. According to Boy and Pine (1982),

> The counselor's genuineness is imperative if the client is to achieve genuineness. If the counselor is truly genuine, he or she engages in counseling attitudes and behaviors that influence clients to be genuine. The authentic counselor feels compelled to be involved in facilitative behaviors that have meaning and relevance for clients rather than to adopt superficial and mechanical behaviors that have little or no value. (p. 8)

Implicit in this statement is the idea of the counselor's ability to communicate and demonstrate this genuineness, not only for relationship enhancement but also to model this core condition so that clients can develop greater authenticity in their interactions with others.

Personal characteristics or behaviors that enhance a counselor's or therapist's ability to provide genuineness and congruence would include, but are not limited to, the following:

- The capacity for self-awareness and the ability to demonstrate this capacity through words and actions
- The understanding of one's own motivational patterns and the ability to use them productively in the helping relationship
- The ability to present one's thoughts, feelings, and actions in a consistent, unified, and honest manner
- The capacity for self-confidence and the ability to communicate this capacity in a facilitative way in the helping relationship

Concreteness

Concreteness is the ability not only to see the incomplete picture that clients paint with their words, but also to communicate to clients the figures, images, and structures that will complete the picture. In the process of exploring problems or issues, clients often present a somewhat distorted view of the actual situation. Concreteness enables the counselor or therapist to help clients identify the distortions in the situation and fit them together in such a way that clients are able to view the situation in a more realistic fashion. This concreteness helps clients clarify vague issues, focus on specific topics, reduce degrees of ambiguity, and channel their energies into more productive avenues of problem solution.

Personal characteristics and behaviors that enhance a counselor's or therapist's ability to provide degrees of concreteness include, but are not limited to, the following:

- The capacity for abstract thinking and the ability to "read between the lines"
- The willingness to risk being incorrect as one attempts to fill in the empty spaces
- The belief in one's own competence in analyzing and sorting through the truths and partial truths in clients' statements
- The ability to be objective while working with clients in arriving at the reality of clients' situations

Warmth

Warmth is the ability to communicate and demonstrate genuine caring and concern for clients. Using this ability, counselors and therapists convey their acceptance of clients, their desire for clients' well-being, and their sincere interest in finding workable solutions to the problems that clients present. The demeanor of the counselor or therapist is often the main avenue for communicating and demonstrating warmth, for it is often through nonverbal behaviors—a smile, a touch, tone of voice, a facial expression—that genuine caring and concern are communicated. The counselor's or therapist's capacity for transmitting concerns and caring to clients, either verbally or nonverbally, enables clients to experience, often for the first time, a truly accepting relationship.

Personal characteristics or behaviors that enhance a counselor's or therapist's ability to demonstrate warmth include, but are not limited to, the following:

- The capacity for self-care and the ability to demonstrate this capacity in both actions and words
- The capacity for self-acceptance, basing this acceptance on one's assets and liabilities
- The desire for one's own well-being and the ability to demonstrate this desire through both words and actions
- The desire to find, and successful personal experience in finding, workable solutions to one's own problems, and the ability to communicate this desire through words and actions

Immediacy

Immediacy is the ability to deal with the here-and-now factors that operate within the helping relationship. These factors are described as overt and covert interactions that take place between the client and the counselor or therapist. A client's anger at a counselor or therapist, the latter's frustration with a client, and the feelings of the client and the counselor or therapist for each other are all examples of factors that need to be addressed as they occur and develop. Addressing such issues in the safety of the helping relationship should help participants in two ways: to gain insight into personal behavioral patterns that may be conducive and not conducive to growth, and to use this insight in relationships outside the helping relationship.

Dealing with these factors can be threatening, as it is often easier to deal with relationships in the abstract and avoid personal encounters. A counselor or therapist needs to be able to use this factor of immediacy to show clients the benefits that can be gained by dealing with issues as they arise. According to Egan (1994), immediacy not only clears the air but also is a valuable learning experience.

Personal characteristics or behaviors that enhance a counselor's or therapist's ability to use immediacy effectively include, but are not limited to, the following:

- The capacity for perceptive accuracy in interpreting one's own feelings for, thoughts about, and behaviors toward clients
- The capacity for perceptive accuracy in interpreting clients' feelings for, thoughts about, and behaviors toward the counselor or therapist
- The capacity for and willingness to deal with one's own issues related to clients on a personal as opposed to an abstract level
- The willingness to confront both oneself and clients with what one observes to be happening in the helping relationship

Cultural Awareness

Cultural awareness addresses the counselor's or therapist's openness and motivation to understand more about one's own cultural diversity as well as the cultural diversity that clients bring to the helping relationship. Such understanding is the cornerstone on which all the core conditions rest. This understanding, based upon both education and life experiences, should enable culturally aware counselors or therapists to increase their sensitivity to the issues that confront clients. It should enable them to develop insight into the many variables that affect clients and should enable them to place clients' issues, problems, and concerns in their proper perspective. The key word in these last three statements is *should*. Experience indicates that the key factor in the development of cultural awareness is the individual's receptiveness, openness, and motivation to gain such awareness. Without these characteristics, education and experience will have little value. The combination of these characteristics with both education and experience enhances the chances of changing the *should* to *will*.

Personal characteristics or behavior that enhance a counselor's or therapist's ability to become culturally aware include, but are not limited to, the following:

- The need and the personal motivation to understand one's own cultural heritage as well as that of others
- The need to seek out both education and life experiences that will afford one the opportunity to gain greater cultural awareness
- The need to be open to new ideas and differing frames of reference as they relate to cultural diversity

- The need for self-assurance to admit what one does not know about the cultural diversity of clients and the willingness to learn from clients
- The need to be aware of one's own cultural stereotypes and biases and be open to changing them through education and experience

Helping Relationships: Strategies

The previous sections identified the core conditions that need to be present for the effective development of the helping relationship. The difference between these core conditions and the **strategies** are the subject of this section.

The core conditions relate to specific dynamics present in the personality and behavioral makeup of counselors or therapists that they are able to communicate to clients. The term *strategies* refers to skills gained through education and experience that define and direct what counselors or therapists do within the relationship to attain specific results and to move the helping relationship from problem identification to problem resolution.

Varying terms have been used to address this aspect of the helping relationship. Some authors prefer the term *strategies* (Combs & Avila, 1985; Cormier and Cormier, 1991; Gilliland, James, & Bowman, 1989; Hackney & Cormier, 1994); others prefer *skills* (Hansen, Rossberg, & Cramer, 1994; Ivey, 1988; Terry et al., 1991); still others prefer the term *techniques* (Belkin, 1980; Brown & Pate, 1983; Osipow et al., 1980). The terms, however, are interchangeable.

We have decided to use the term *strategies,* which denotes not only deliberative planning but also action processes that make the planning operational. We feel that both factors are necessary. For the purpose of the following discussion, we have grouped the strategies into the following categories:

- Strategies that build rapport and encourage client dialogue
- Strategies that aid in data gathering
- Strategies that add depth and enhance the relationship

Note that specific strategies, such as those stemming from various theoretical systems, are not included in this section. They will be presented in Chapters 4 through 12, which deal with specific theories. It is also important for you to understand that there is much overlap between these arbitrary divisions. Strategies designed to build rapport and encourage client dialogue may also gather data and enhance relationships. With this caveat in mind, we present the following strategies.

Strategies That Build Rapport and Encourage Client Dialogue

This group of strategies includes the active listening strategies that enhance the listening capabilities of counselors and therapists. When used effectively, these strategies should provide an environment in which clients have the opportunity to talk and to share their feelings and thoughts with the assurance that they will be heard. By using such strategies, counselors and therapists enhance their chances of providing such an environment.

This set of strategies includes **attending** and **encouraging, restating, paraphrasing, reflecting content** and **reflecting feeling, clarifying** and **perception checking,** and **summarizing.** The following paragraphs present explanations and examples of these strategies.

Attending and Encouraging.   These strategies use the counselor's or therapist's posture, visual contact, gestures, facial expressions, and words to indicate to clients not only that they are being heard but also that the counselor or therapist wishes them to continue sharing information.

Example

Encouraging	COUNSELOR/THERAPIST: (smiling) Please tell me what brought you in today.
	CLIENT: I'm having a hard time trying to put my life in order. I'm very lonely and bored, and I can't seem to maintain a lasting relationship.
Attending/	COUNSELOR/THERAPIST: (leaning forward) Please tell me more.
Encouraging	CLIENT: Every time I think I have a chance of developing a relationship, I screw it up by saying or doing something dumb.
Encouraging	COUNSELOR/THERAPIST: (nodding) This is helpful, please go on.

Restating and Paraphrasing.   These strategies enable a counselor or therapist to serve as a sounding board for the client by feeding back thoughts and feelings that clients verbalize. Restating involves repeating the exact words used by the client. Paraphrasing repeats the thoughts and feelings of the client, but the words are those of the counselor or therapist.

Example

	CLIENT: I don't know why I do these dumb things. It's almost as if I didn't want a relationship.
Restating	COUNSELOR/THERAPIST: You don't know why you do dumb things. It may be that you don't want a relationship.
	CLIENT: I *do* want a relationship, but each time I get close I seem to do everything in my power to destroy it.
Paraphrasing	COUNSELOR/THERAPIST: You are very sure that you want a relationship, but each time you have the opportunity, you sabotage your chances.

Reflecting Content and Reflecting Feeling.   These strategies enable the counselor or therapist to provide feedback to the client regarding both the ideas (content) and the emotions (feelings) that the client is expressing. By reflecting content, the counselor or therapist shares his or her perceptions of the thoughts that the client is expressing. This can be done either by using the client's words or by changing the words to better reflect the counselor or therapist's perceptions. By reflecting feelings, a counselor or therapist goes beyond the ideas and thoughts expressed by the client and responds to the feelings or emotions behind those words.

Example

CLIENT: "Sabotage" is a good word. It's like I see what I want, but instead of moving toward it, I take a different path that leads me nowhere.

Reflecting COUNSELOR/THERAPIST: You have a good idea of what you want,
Content   but when you see it developing, you turn and walk the other way.

CLIENT: I am not sure "walk" is the right word. "Run" is more descriptive of what I do, and all the time I'm looking back to see if anyone is following.

Reflecting COUNSELOR/THERAPIST: You're afraid of getting close to someone, so
Feeling   you put as much distance between the other person and yourself as possible. I also hear that you're hoping that someone cares enough about you to run after you and stop you from running away.

Clarifying and Perception Checking.   These strategies enable a counselor or therapist to either ask the client to define or explain words, thoughts, or feelings (clarifying) or to request confirmation or correction of perceptions he or she has drawn regarding these words, thoughts, or feelings (perception checking).

Example

CLIENT: If what you say is true, I'm a real jerk. What chance do I have to be happy if I run away every time I get close to someone else?

Clarifying COUNSELOR/THERAPIST: You say you want to be happy. What does "happy" mean to you?

CLIENT: (long pause) I would be happy if I could let someone care for me, get to know me, want to spend time with me, and allow me to just be me and stop pretending.

Perception COUNSELOR/THERAPIST: Let me see if I'm understanding
Checking   you. Your view of happiness is having someone who cares enough about you to spend time with you and to allow you to be yourself. Am I correct?

Summarizing.   This strategy enables the counselor or therapist to do several things: first, to verbally review various types of information that have been presented to this point in the session; second, to highlight what the counselor or therapist sees as significant information based on everything that has been discussed; and third, to provide the client with an opportunity to hear the various issues that he or she has presented. Therefore, summarizing provides both the client and the counselor or therapist with the opportunity not only to review and determine the significance of information presented but also to use this review to establish priorities.

Example

CLIENT: Yes, I think that's what I'd like to have happen. That would make me happy. I would be in a relationship, feel cared about, and yet be able to be myself without having to either run or pretend.

Summarizing   COUNSELOR/THERAPIST: We've talked about many things today. I'd like to review some of this and make plans for our next meeting. The parts that stick out in my mind are your loneliness, boredom, desire to have a lasting relationship, your behaviors that drive you away from building such a relationship, and your need for caring and the freedom to be yourself. Am I missing anything?

CLIENT: Only that I want someone who wants to spend time with me. I think that's an important factor.

Summarizing   COUNSELOR/THERAPIST: So now we have a more complete picture that includes loneliness, boredom, desire for a relationship, desire for someone to spend time with, desire for someone who cares, and the need to be yourself. On the other side of the picture, we have your behaviors that keep this from happening. Where do you think we should begin next week?

Strategies That Aid in Data Gathering

This group of strategies includes all of the active listening strategies plus three strategies designed to extract specific information and gain greater depth of information in areas that are significant in the client's statements. As with active listening strategies, a counselor or therapist who uses the following strategies enhances his or her chances of gaining significant information. This set of strategies includes **questioning, probing,** and **leading.** The following paragraphs present explanations and examples of these strategies.

Questioning.   This strategy, when done in an open manner, enables the counselor or therapist to gain important information and allows the client to remain in control of the information presented. Using open questioning, the counselor or therapist designs these questions to encourage the broadest client responses. Open questions, as opposed to closed questions, generally cannot be completely answered by either a yes or no, nor can they be answered nonverbally by the shaking of the head. This type of questioning places responsibility with clients and allows them a degree of control over what information will be shared.

Example

CLIENT: I've thought a lot about what we talked about last week, and I feel I have to work on changing my behavior.

Open Questioning   COUNSELOR/THERAPIST: Would you tell me what you think needs to be done to change your behavior?

	CLIENT: (short pause) I need to stop screwing up my chances for a relationship. I need to face whatever it is that makes me run away.
Open Questioning	COUNSELOR/THERAPIST: Would you please talk more about the "it" that makes you run away?
	CLIENT: (long pause) I can't tell you what it is. All I know is that I hear this voice saying, "Run, run."

Probing and Leading.   These strategies enable a counselor or therapist to gather information in a specific area related to the client's presented concerns (probing) or to encourage the client to respond to specific topic areas (leading). Each of these enables the counselor or therapist to explore at greater depth areas that are seen as important to progress within the session.

Example

Probing	COUNSELOR/THERAPIST: I want you to be more specific about this "voice." Whose voice is it? What does it say to you?
	CLIENT: (very long pause) I guess it's my voice. It sounds like some thing I would do. I'm such a jerk.
Leading	COUNSELOR/THERAPIST: You told me whose voice it is, but you didn't tell me what the voice says. Would you talk about this?
	CLIENT: (raising his voice) It says, "Get out or you're going to get hurt. She doesn't like you and she'll use you and drop you just like the rest."

Strategies That Add Depth and Enhance the Relationship

This group of strategies is used to enhance and expand the communicative and relationship patterns that are established early in the counseling or therapeutic process. When used effectively, these strategies should open up deeper levels of communication and strengthen the relationship patterns that have already been established. Counselors or therapists using these strategies model types of behaviors that they wish their clients to emulate. Such behaviors include, but are not limited to, **risk taking, sharing of self, demonstrating trust,** and **honest interaction.** This set of strategies includes **self-disclosure, confrontation,** and **response to nonverbal behaviors.** The following paragraphs present explanations and examples of these strategies.

Self-Disclosure.   This strategy has implications for both clients and counselors or therapists. In self-disclosing, the counselor or therapist shares with the client his or her feelings, thoughts, and experiences that are relevant to the situation presented by the client. The counselor or therapist draws upon situations from his or her own life experiences and selectively shares these personal reactions with the client. It is important to note that self-disclosure could have both a positive and negative impact on the helping relationship, and care must be taken in measuring the impact it may have. From a positive perspective, it carries with it the possibility of modeling self-disclosure for the client or helping the client gain a different perspective on the presenting problems. From a negative perspective, self-disclosure might place the focus on the counselor's or therapist's issues rather than on those of the client. When used appropriately, gains are made by all persons involved, and the relationship moves to deeper levels of understanding and sharing.

Example

Self-disclosure	COUNSELOR/THERAPIST: (aware of the client's agitation) The anger I hear in your voice and words triggers anger in me as I think of lost relationships in my own life.
	CLIENT: (smiling) I am angry. I'm also glad you said that. Some times I feel like I'm the only one who ever felt this way.
Self-disclosure	COUNSELOR/THERAPIST: (smiling) I am very pleased with what you just said. At this moment, I also do not feel alone with my anger.

Confrontation.   This strategy enables the counselor or therapist to provide the client with feedback in which discrepancies are presented in an honest and matter-of-fact manner. A counselor or therapist uses this strategy to indicate his or her reaction to the client, to identify differences between the client's words and behaviors, and to challenge the client to put words and ideas into action. This type of direct and honest feedback should provide the client with insight as to how he or she is perceived, as well as indicate the degree of counselor or therapist caring.

Example

	CLIENT: (smiling) I feel angry at myself a great deal. I want so much to find a person and develop a relationship that lasts.
Confrontation	COUNSELOR/THERAPIST: You've said this several times in our sessions, but I'm not sure I believe you, based on what you do to keep it from happening. Make me believe you really want this to happen.
	CLIENT: What do you mean, you don't believe me? I just told you, didn't I? What more do you want?
Confrontation	COUNSELOR/THERAPIST: Yes, I've heard your words, but you haven't convinced me. I don't think you've convinced yourself, either. Say something that will convince both of us.

Responding to Nonverbal Cues.   This strategy enables a counselor or therapist to go beyond a client's words and respond to the messages that are being communicated by the client's physical actions. Care must be taken not to overgeneralize regarding every subtle body movement. The counselor or therapist is looking for patterns that either confirm or deny the truth in the words the client uses to express him- or herself. When such patterns become apparent, it is the responsibility of the counselor or therapist to share these patterns with the client. It becomes the client's responsibility to confirm or deny the credibility of the perception.

Example

	CLIENT: (turning away) Yes, you're right. I'm not convinced that this is what I want. (smiling) Maybe I was just never meant to be happy.
Nonverbal Responding	COUNSELOR/THERAPIST: What I said made you angry and, I would suspect, hurt a little. Did you notice you turned away before you began to speak? What were you telling me when you turned away?
	CLIENT: (smiling) What you said did hurt me. I was angry, but I'm also embarrassed not to be able to handle this part of my life. I don't like you seeing me this way.
Nonverbal Responding	COUNSELOR/THERAPIST: I've noticed that on several occasions when you talk about your feelings such as anger, embarrassment, or hopelessness, you smile. What does the smile mean?
	CLIENT: (long pause) I guess I want you to believe that it isn't as bad as it sounds, or that I'm not as hopeless as I think I am.
	COUNSELOR/THERAPIST: It is bad, or you wouldn't be here, and "hopeless" is your word, not mine. Our time is up for today. Between now and next week I want you to think about what we've discussed. See you next week?

The strategies we have outlined in this section enable a counselor or therapist to achieve more effectively both the process and outcome goals related to counseling or psychotherapy. Choosing which strategy to use, when to use it, and its impact in the helping relationship is based upon the education, experience, and personal dynamics that a counselor or therapist brings to the helping relationship.

Conclusions

The helping relationship is the foundation on which the process of counseling or psychotherapy rests. It is best viewed in terms of developmental stages, the first of which begins with the initial meeting of the client and the counselor or therapist and is characterized by rapport building, information gathering, goal determination, and information sharing. Building on the foundation established in the first stage, later stages address extended exploration and problem resolution, then lead to the final stage in this process, termination and follow-up.

The helping relationship, when viewed from this developmental perspective, progresses from stage to stage due to the presence of certain components that the counselor or therapist brings to the relationship. The first of these are the core conditions of empathic understanding, respect and positive regard, genuineness and congruence, concreteness, warmth, immediacy, and cultural awareness. These conditions are personality characteristics of a counselor or therapist which he or she is able to incorporate into the helping relationship.

The second component is a set of strategies aimed at building rapport and encouraging client dialogue, data gathering, and relationship enhancement. These conditions are skills and techniques that a counselor or therapist gains through education and experience and is able to use effectively within the helping relationship. In combination, the developmental nature of the helping relationship, the presence of the core conditions, and the implementation of the various strategies create a facilitative environment in which both the client and the counselor or therapist have the strong potential for positive growth. *The potential exists; guarantees do not.* Achieving the true potential of the helping relationship depends upon what the client and the counselor or therapist bring to the relationship and what each takes from it.

In closing, we return to Jean as she begins her practicum experience. She appears to have concern for the client and the desire to be an effective counselor or therapist. These qualities should aid her as she attempts to provide the core conditions. Her education has provided her with both a theoretical foundation and some practice in the helping process. This background should aid her as she begins to apply helping strategies. Her practicum experience should assist her to reduce her anxiety and fear by enhancing her ability to apply both the core conditions and the strategies in a theoretical system of her choosing. Her excitement should increase as she enters the complex and challenging arena of the helping relationship.

References

Baruth, L. G., & Robinson, E. H. (1987). *An introduction to the counseling profession.* Upper Saddle River, NJ: Prentice Hall.

Belkin, G. S. (1980). *An introduction to counseling.* Dubuque, IA: Wm. C. Brown.

Boy, A. V., & Pine, G. J. (1982). *Client centered counseling: A renewal.* Boston: Allyn & Bacon.

Brammer, L. M. (1985). *The helping relationship: Process and skills* (3rd ed.). Upper Saddle River, NJ: Prentice Hall.

Brammer, L. M., Abrego, P., & Shostrom, E. (1993). *Therapeutic counseling and psychotherapy* (6th ed.). Upper Saddle River, NJ: Prentice Hall.

Brammer, L. M., & MacDonald, G. (1996). *The helping relationship: Process and skills* (6th ed.). Needham Heights, MA: Allyn & Bacon.

Brown, D., & Srebalus, D. J. (1988). *An introduction to the counseling profession.* Upper Saddle River, NJ: Prentice Hall.

Brown, J. A., & Pate, R. H. (1983). *Being a counselor: Direction and challenges.* Monterey, CA: Brooks/Cole.

Carkhuff, R. R., & Barenson, B. G. (1967). *Beyond counseling and psychotherapy.* New York: Holt, Rinehart & Winston.

Combs, A. W. (1986). What makes a good helper? A person-centered approach. *Person-Centered Review, 1,* 51–61.

Combs, A. W., & Avila, D. (1985). *Helping relationships: Basic concepts for the helping professions.* Boston: Allyn & Bacon.

Combs, A. W., & Gonzalez, D. M. (1994). *Helping relationships: Basic concepts for the helping profession* (4th ed.). Needham Heights, MA: Allyn & Bacon.

Corey, M. S., & Corey, G. (1993). *Becoming a helper* (2nd ed.). Pacific Grove, CA: Brooks/Cole.

Cormier, W. H., & Cormier, L. S. (1991). *Interviewing strategies for helpers: A guide to assessment, treatment, and evaluation* (3rd ed.). Pacific Grove, CA: Brooks/Cole.

Dixon, D. N., & Glover, J. A. (1984). *Counseling: A problem solving approach.* New York: Wiley.

Egan, G. (1994). *The skilled helper* (5th ed.). Pacific Grove, CA: Brooks/Cole.

Fox, R. (1993). *Elements of the helping process: A guide for clinicians.* Binghamton, NY: Haworth Press.

Gilliland, B. E., James, R. K., & Bowman, J. T. (1989). *Theories and strategies in counseling and psychotherapy* (2nd ed.). Upper Saddle River, Merrill NJ: Prentice Hall.

Gladding, S. T. (1996). *Counseling: A comprehensive profession* (3rd ed.). Upper Saddle River, NJ: Merrill/Prentice Hall.

Hackney, H., & Cormier, L. S. (1994). *Counseling strategies and interventions* (4th ed.). Upper Saddle River, NJ: Prentice Hall.

Hackney, H. J., & Cormier, L. S. (1996). *The professional counselor: A process guide to helping* (3rd ed.). Needham Heights, MA: Allyn & Bacon.

Hansen, J. C., Rossberg, R. H., & Cramer, S. H. (1994). *Counseling: Theory and process* (5th ed.). Needham Heights, MA: Allyn & Bacon.

Ivey, A. E. (1988). *Intentional interviewing and counseling: Facilitating client development.* Monterey, CA: Brooks/Cole.

Kottler, J., & Brown, R. (1992). *Introduction to therapeutic counseling* (2nd ed.). Pacific Grove, CA: Brooks/Cole.

Mathews, L. G., & Atkinson, D. R. (1997). Counseling ethnic minority clients. In D. Capuzzi & D. Gross (Eds.), *Introduction to the counseling profession* (pp. 433–462). Needham Heights, MA: Allyn & Bacon.

Miars, B. D., Burden, C. A., & Pedersen, M. M. (1997). The helping relationship. In D. Capuzzi & D. Gross (Eds.), *Introduction to the counseling profession* (pp. 64–84). Needham Heights, MA: Allyn & Bacon.

Newlon, B. J., & Arciniega, M. (1992). Group counseling: Cross cultural. In D. Capuzzi & D. Gross (Eds.), *Introduction to group counseling* (pp. 285–306). Denver: Love.

Okun, B. (1992). *Effective helping: Interviews and counseling techniques* (4th ed.). Pacific Grove, CA: Brooks/Cole.

Osipow, S. H., Walsh, W. B., & Tosi, D. J. (1980). *A survey of counseling methods.* Homewood, IL: Dorsey.

Patterson, C. H. (1974). *Relationship counseling and psychotherapy.* New York: Harper & Row.

Patterson, L. E., & Eisenberg, S. (1994). *The counseling process* (4th ed.). Boston: Houghton Mifflin.

Purkey, W. W., & Schmidt, J. J. (1987). *The inviting relationship: An expanded perspective for professional counseling.* Upper Saddle River, NJ: Prentice Hall.

Rogers, C. R. (1957). The necessary and sufficient conditions of therapeutic personality change. *Journal of Consulting Psychology, 21,* 95–103.

Rogers, C. R. (1961). *On becoming a person: A therapist's view of psychotherapy.* Boston: Houghton Mifflin.

Sexton, T. L., & Whiston, S. C. (1994). The status of the counseling relationship: An empirical review, theoretical implications, and research directions. *Counseling Psychologist, 22,* 6–78.

Sue, D. W., & Sue, D. (1990). *Counseling the culturally different: Theory and process.* New York: Wiley.

Terry, A., Burden, C., & Pedersen, M. (1991). The helping relationship. In D. Capuzzi & D. R. Gross (Eds.), *Introduction to counseling: Perspectives for the 1990's* (pp. 44–68). Boston: Allyn & Bacon.

Thompson, R. A. (1996). *Counseling techniques.* Washington, DC: Accelerated Development—Taylor and Francis.

Truax, C. B., & Carkhuff, R. R. (1967). *Towards effective counseling and psychotherapy: Training and practice.* Chicago: Aldine.

Wehrly, B. (1991). Preparing multicultural counselors. *Counseling and Human Development, 24,* 1–23.

Achieving a Personal and Professional Identity

David Capuzzi
Portland State University

Douglas R. Gross
Professor Emeritus
Arizona State University

How well do I really know myself, and how effective will I be with clients? Do I really understand my chosen profession and the stressors involved? These are just two of the questions we believe each of you should continually ask yourself as you progress through your graduate education and clinical supervision experience. Some careers can be pursued without a high level of self-awareness, but the profession of counseling or psychology is not one of them. Knowledge of theory and research and expertise in translating that knowledge into strategies and interventions can be delivered only through the being and personhood of the provider. Each member of the helping professions is given an enormous amount of responsibility every time client interactions occur. This responsibility can be upheld only if each counselor or therapist maintains a sense of **health and wellness** to ensure that the understanding and support, assessment, and treatment planning that a client receives are the best they can possibly be. The more a counselor or therapist has developed, integrated, and accepted an identity as a person and as a professional, the better that individual is at giving the incredible gift of helping another human being develop a unique sense of self.

Personal and **professional identity** must be addressed before and during the process of studying and applying individual approaches to counseling and psychotherapy. It is not easy, for example, for the beginning graduate student to be receptive to peer and supervisor feedback as it relates to individual work with clients. The student must have enough self-awareness and a great enough sense of well-being to be receptive to suggestions for changes that are needed to maximize therapeutic effectiveness. As we noted in

Chapter 1, on-site observations of individual sessions and required videotaping and playback for supervisory purposes escalate the stress level of any graduate student. If students can develop high levels of self-acceptance and self-understanding, they will receive more benefit from the supervision process and have greater potential for developing clinical skills.

Many students are enrolled in graduate programs that require participation as a client in either individual or group counseling for the purpose of facilitating their continued personal growth. This requirement helps students avoid the confusion that arises when client issues are similar to unresolved personal issues. Such personal issues often surface during the practicum or internship experiences required of students. For this reason, many graduate programs expect enrollees to complete requirements for counseling or therapy prior to initiating practicum and internship courses and placements. At times, supervisors may recommend that students seek additional counseling or therapy at the same time they are enrolled in practicum or internship.

Because of the stresses and complexities of the helping professions, faculties in counseling and psychology departments are becoming more definitive and assertive about expectations for the wellness and functionality of potential counselors and therapists. Many educators and clinical supervisors are stressing the need for counselors and therapists to involve themselves in consultation and counseling or psychotherapy after graduation in order to maintain personal growth, wellness, and treatment-planning ability. Many experienced professionals stress the importance of involving significant others in ongoing couples or family counseling so that as the counselor or therapist grows and changes, friends and family members can participate in and understand that process of change.

This chapter addresses the importance of health and wellness for the counselor or therapist, as well as the importance of recognizing values and cultural bias in theory and practice, becoming aware of the daily world of the practitioner, and achieving perspective and balance between personal and professional roles. It also includes some brief comments about developing a personal theory.

The Importance of Health and Wellness

The personal qualities, traits, and characteristics of the counselor or therapist have long been recognized as an extremely important component of the helping relationship (Carkhuff & Berenson, 1977; Egan, 1975; Evans, 1997; Rogers, 1961). As noted by Okun (1987), a continually increasing database supports the concept that counselors and therapists are effective only if they are self-aware and able to use themselves as the instruments through which change occurs. One way of conceptualizing this role in the relationship is to compare the contribution the counselor or therapist makes to a client's growth and maturation to that of a painter working on a canvas, an architect designing a building, or a sculptor chiseling a statue. The client presents possibilities and options, which are much like the raw materials of canvas and paint, building site and construction materials, or chisels and stone. The artist approaches the task with a database of information and the expertise to translate a concept or mental image into something beautiful or functional. Whether the database and expertise of the artist can be fully accessed most often depends on the mental, emotional, physical, and spiritual sensitivities with which the artist approaches the work. Creativity can be compromised or never actualized if the being of the creator is impaired, tired, or dysfunctional, because everything the artist has to contribute is conveyed through the person of the artist.

The counselor or therapist is the conveyer of possibilities and potentials to the client. If the being or personhood of the counselor or therapist is impaired at the time of an encounter with a client, it may be difficult to see the client's potential and use those possibilities for engaging in a mutually rewarding relationship to achieve desirable outcomes. The health and wellness of the counselor or therapist have much to do with the art form inherent in the helping relationship.

Approaches to Health and Wellness

There are a number of approaches to health and wellness that are described, researched, and prescribed by those wishing to sensitize counselors and therapists to the importance of self-care as a prerequisite to caregiving. We have identified three commonly discussed models for presentation: the **personal characteristics model,** the **psychological health model,** and the **multidimensional health and wellness model.** Each model provides counselors and therapists with concepts that are helpful and applicable to the maintenance of their own sense of well-being and the ability to cope successfully with both personal and professional responsibilities.

The Personal Characteristics Model.   Person-centered counseling theory offers a well-researched analysis of how counselors and therapists might work with clients. The person-centered school identifies accurate **empathy,** nonpossessive **warmth, positive regard,** and **genuineness** as the "necessary and sufficient conditions" for therapeutic change (Rogers, 1957; Truax & Carkhuff, 1967). *Empathy*—often defined as the capacity to view and understand the world through another person's frame of reference (Egan, 1975)—is one of the most extensively studied personal characteristics or variables in process-outcome research. Most reviews of studies that analyze the relationships between empathy and outcome show positive relationships in one half to two thirds of the research under scrutiny (Orlinsky & Howard, 1978, 1986). *Genuineness*—described as consistency in values, attitudes, and behaviors on the part of the counselor or therapist—is also the focus of therapeutic process research and is generally related positively to therapeutic outcomes (Orlinsky & Howard, 1986).

Counselor or therapist **affirmation**—the ability to communicate positive regard, warmth, and acceptance to the client—is also significantly associated with positive therapeutic outcomes (Orlinsky & Howard, 1978). In addition, Carkhuff and his associates have stressed the importance of concreteness or specificity of expression (Carkhuff & Berenson, 1977). As we noted in Chapter 1, *concreteness* means that the practitioner's response serves to clarify the meaning the client is communicating so that the client's self-understanding is actually enhanced.

The personal characteristics model for addressing the health and wellness of the counselor or therapist has been discussed from perspectives other than that of Carl Rogers. A number of writers and researchers focus on the importance of the personal characteristics of the counselor or therapist on the outcome of counseling or psychotherapy

(Goldfried, Greenberg, & Maramar, 1990; Hanna & Bemak, 1997; Hanna & Ottens, 1995; Whiston & Sexton, 1993). Combs and his colleagues (1969) conducted a series of studies resulting in the conclusion that the personal beliefs and traits of the counselor or therapist differentiated between effective and ineffective helping. Effective helpers seem to perceive others as able, rather than unable, to solve their own problems and manage their own lives. Effective helpers also perceive others as dependable, friendly, worthy, able to cope, and able to be communicative and self-disclosing. In general, effective helpers maintain a positive view of human nature and approach family, friends, colleagues, and clients in a trusting, affirming way. A **composite model of human effectiveness** was suggested by George and Cristiani (1990) as a means of analyzing the personal characteristics of effective helpers. The elements of this composite model included openness to and acceptance of experiencing, awareness of values and beliefs, ability to develop warm and deep relationships with others, willingness to be seen by others as one actually is, willingness to accept personal responsibility for one's own behaviors, and development of realistic levels of aspiration.

The literature about the personal characteristics model that is available to counselors or therapists is voluminous. Characteristics such as assertiveness, flexibility, tolerance of ambiguity, honesty, emotional presence, goal-directedness, and self-respect have all been addressed to the point that the beginning counselor or therapist may find the suggested profile somewhat overwhelming and threatening. The important thing to remember is that it would never be possible to achieve the perfection that such idealized models suggest. All of us have flaws and imperfections that can obstruct our ability as helpers, just as all of us have unique strengths and capabilities that enable us to influence others positively. We believe that effective counselors and therapists are able to maintain a sense of personal well-being and happiness despite flaws or inadequacies, and we stress the importance of a perspective that ensures that personal issues do not diminish the capacity to engender personal growth on the part of clients.

The Psychological Health Model.   The following provocative scenario (Kinnier, 1997) can be used to introduce some of the dilemmas inherent in suggesting criteria for psychological health:

> Imagine a psychological health contest between the John Wayne persona of the 1950s silver screen and the Leo Buscaglia persona of the 1990s lecture circuit. Which "persona" would win? Among John Wayne's celluloid traits were his stoicism and his readiness to fight. He rarely displayed any weaknesses or "shared his feelings" with anyone. In contrast, Leo Buscaglia's most salient public traits have been his readiness to cry and "share his feelings" with everyone. Is "strong and silent" healthier than "vulnerable and expressive"? For males? For females? Does the answer depend entirely upon the biases of the judges and the context of a specific time and place? (p. 48)

To cope with dilemmas such as the one posed by Kinnier, the majority of mental health practitioners have focused upon identifying symptoms of psychopathology instead of criteria for mental health. It has been easier to identify undesirable behaviors and emotions than it has been to identify and agree upon behavior and emotions indicative of mental health. Cross-cultural differences have further complicated attempts to delineate the traits of a psychologically healthy client. It is difficult to establish acceptable criteria for psychological health because such criteria are intricately woven into a particular cultural and temporal background. Nevertheless, a number of theoreticians and practitioners have emphasized psychological health models as approaches to promoting the health and well-ness of clients.

More than four decades ago, Jahoda (1958) proposed six criteria for mental health: a positive attitude toward self, continual movement toward self-actualization, purpose or meaning in life, the ability to function independently and autonomously, an accurate per-ception of reality, and mastery of the environment. Basic self-esteem was viewed as es-sential by luminaries such as Allport (1961), Erikson (1968), Jung (1954), Maslow (1970), Rogers (1961), and Sullivan (1953). Personal autonomy and competence were emphasized by Fromm (1955), Horney (1950), Maslow (1970), and Rogers (1961). The capacity to give and receive love as a criterion for psychological health has also been endorsed by Adler (1978), Allport (1961), Erikson (1968), Freud (1930), Fromm (1955), Maslow (1970), and Sullivan (1953).

Following a survey of psychological literature to determine what criteria for psy-chological health had been identified by theoreticians and researchers, Kinnier (1997) pro-posed nine criteria for psychological health. We believe these criteria apply to counselors and therapists as well as to their clients.

1. *Self-acceptance.* Self-esteem seems to be a prerequisite for developing other im-portant components of psychological health. Psychologically healthy individuals experi-ence strong feelings of self-acceptance and self-love. Individuals who love and respect themselves have the capacity to love and respect others and possess the foundation for becoming self-actualized.

2. *Self-knowledge.* The importance of self-exploration and self-knowledge cannot be overemphasized. Psychologically healthy individuals know themselves well and stay aware of their feelings, motivations, and needs. They are introspective and committed to understanding themselves.

3. *Self-confidence and self-control.* Individuals who are psychologically healthy have confidence in themselves and can function independently of others. They have appropri-ate skills for assertive behavior but do not unnecessarily impose their views or will on oth-ers. Such individuals have an internal locus of control, believe that they can exert rea-sonable control over their lives, and feel capable of achieving their goals.

4. *A clear (though slightly optimistic) perception of reality.* Perceptions of the people, events, and objects around us are always subjective, but there is usually enough societal consensus about the nature of reality to provide beneficial comparisons with our own point of view. Psychologically healthy individuals have a clear perception of reality and an optimistic view of life. They view themselves, their present circumstances, and their fu-tures accurately and positively, which enhances possibilities and potentials.

5. *Courage and resilience.* Danger and risk surround the daily lives and decision-making opportunities of most individuals; therefore failures, crises, and setbacks are in-evitable. Psychologically healthy individuals are aware of this reality, adapt well to chal-

lenges and changed circumstances, and can bounce back from disappointments and setbacks. As Kinnier notes, "psychologically healthy individuals bravely confront their fears and accept their responsibility. They are prepared to take risks when appropriate. They accept setbacks and failures as part of life, and as the popular song says, after a fall they 'pick themselves up, dust themselves off, and start all over again'" (1997, p. 55).

6. *Balance and moderation.* The theme of balance and moderation is one that recurs in psychological literature. Psychologically healthy individuals work and play, laugh and cry, enjoy planned and spontaneous time with family and friends, and are not afraid to be both logical and intuitive. They are rarely extremists or fanatics, and usually they do not do anything in excess.

7. *Love of others.* The capacity to care deeply about the welfare of another person or the condition of humanity in general is another characteristic of the psychologically healthy person. Mental health professionals from a number of theoretical orientations believe that the ability to give and receive love, the desire to develop close ties to another person or persons, and the need to belong to another person, family, or group are fundamental to mental health. Psychologically healthy individuals are not reticent about loving and caring for others. They need to experience close interpersonal relationships and are intimate with at least one other person.

8. *Love of life.* The psychological benefits of humor, spontaneity, and openness have been touted by numerous professionals. People who are active, curious, spontaneous, venturesome, and relaxed have traits that promote their capacity to partake of and enjoy life. Psychologically healthy people embrace the opportunities that life presents, do not take themselves too seriously, and look forward to the unexpected with the vitality to cope, problem-solve, and move on to the future with a positive perspective.

9. *Purpose in life.* Individuals vary in their choice of the most meaningful aspects of life. Work, love, family, intellectual or physical accomplishment, or spirituality may become the primary focus for one individual or another. While variation among individuals is bound to exist, the important achievement for each person is to develop a purpose—an investment—that creates a sense of meaning and satisfaction. The joy and sense of exhilaration and accomplishment that result from finding meaning and purpose in life are prime factors in the maintenance of psychological health.

The Multidimensional Health and Wellness Model.   As noted by Myers (1991), several different wellness models have been proposed for use by counselors and therapists. One of the most common models defines wellness holistically by considering it from spiritual, mental, and physical aspects of functionality. Other models describe dimensions such as spirituality, physical fitness, job satisfaction, relationships, family life, nutrition, leisure time, and stress management (Ardell, 1988). Quite often, physical wellness is given more attention than other dimensions of wellness because physical illness cannot be as easily ignored (Evans, 1997). Most systemic models of wellness, however, suggest that all the identified dimensions of wellness interact and that they must all be evaluated in the process of assessing a person's state of wellness. In 1984 Hettler proposed six dimensions of wellness—intellectual, emotional, physical, social, occupational, and spiritual—as components of a lifelong paradigm to promote health and wellness. Health has been defined as the absence of illness; wellness goes far beyond the absence of illness and incorporates a zest and enthusiasm for life which results when the dimensions of wellness (intellectual, emotional, physical, social, occupational, spiritual) have been addressed, developed, and integrated. "With a holistic focus, wellness incorporates not just the whole person, but the whole person throughout the totality of the life span" (Myers, 1991, p. 185). A person can be "well" even when undergoing treatment for physical illness because the physical dimension is just one dimension of the wellness model.

The importance of this brief discussion of the multidimensional health and wellness model should be understood by all those undertaking the study of theories of counseling and psychotherapy. The counselor's role in facilitating the wellness of clients creates a natural link between counseling and wellness; however, the emphasis in the link is on counselors helping clients. Little emphasis has been placed on the importance of counselors helping themselves, and even less attention is given to counselors' wellness behaviors (Evans, 1997). In addition to the fact that counselors need to address wellness with respect to both their clients and themselves, it is important that counselors and therapists assess what the various theories of counseling and psychotherapy offer with respect to the dimensions of health and wellness. Some of the theories and approaches included in Part II of this book do not encourage the counselor or therapist to approach clients from a multidimensional health and wellness perspective, nor do they encourage the practitioner to engage in personal care from a holistic frame of reference. One of the tasks of a beginning counselor or therapist is to think about developing a theory or approach to the helping relationship. This may entail the adoption of one of the theories presented in this textbook, the development of an integrated model, or the conceptualization of a personalized theory or approach based on the study of theory and research as well as experience with clients. We encourage you to consider a number of perspectives before conceptualizing a personal theory of counseling and psychotherapy, for no single theory provides a perspective that could be described as multidimensional.

Values and Cultural Bias in Theory and Practice

As you read the theory chapters in Part II of this book, you should think about the way the values and cultural biases of the chief proponents of each theory may have influenced the development of the theory. In addition, you should assess personal values and understandings of cultural differences. In this section of the chapter, we introduce you to a discussion of values and cultural bias in theory and practice. After presenting Chapters 4 through 16, we reintroduce the topic of cultural differences and further refine the subject in Chapter 17.

Values in Theory and Practice

Everyone has a set of beliefs that guides decisions, determines one's ability to appreciate the people and things in the environment, governs conscience, and influences perceptions of others (Belkin, 1984). Because the **values** of a counselor or therapist are an integral part of what is brought to a relationship with a client, we think it is important to consider the role values play in theory and practice and in achieving a personal and professional identity.

One of the key issues to consider is whether, during the process of counseling or psychotherapy, counselors or therapists can avoid conveying their values to their clients (George & Cristiani, 1990). Some maintain (especially professionals associated with the orthodox **psychoanalytic** point of view) that a counselor or therapist must remain neutral with clients and avoid communicating value orientations. In such circumstances a counselor or therapist would strive to appear nonmoralizing, ethically neutral, and focused on the client's values. If topics such as pro-choice versus pro-life, religion, euthanasia, or gay or lesbian orientation were to arise during the counseling or psychotherapy process, the counselor or therapist would not take a position. The reason for such neutrality is the belief that it is important for clients to move from an external to an internal locus of control during the counseling or psychotherapy process. Values introduced by the counselor or therapist would be detrimental to such an objective.

As early as 1958, however, Williamson voiced an opposing position and promoted the idea that counselors and therapists cannot avoid letting clients know about their values and should be open and explicit about the nature of those values. Williamson reasoned that counselor or therapist neutrality may be interpreted by clients to mean that the professional is supporting client behavior that is not acceptable by social, moral, or legal standards. Samler (1960) went further and encouraged counselors and therapists to develop an awareness of their own values and how these values relate to and influence the development of client values. He further believed that assisting clients to change their values is a legitimate goal and a necessary component of the helping relationship. As early as 1958 and as recently as 1989, Patterson pointed out that the values of the counselor or therapist influence the ethics of the helping relationship and the goals, techniques, and interventions employed in the context of helping. Eugene Kelly's (1995) study focused upon the value orientations of counselors in the domains of universal values, mental health values, individualism-collectivism values, and religious-spiritual values to identify values that characterize counselors and may represent values taught to clients during the counseling or psychotherapy process.

We believe it is imperative for counselors and therapists to be aware of their own values and to consider the influence that these values have upon clients. The following questions may prove useful to the helper in the process of examining values issues:

- Am I completely cognizant of my own values?
- Do my values influence my preference for particular theoretical frameworks (such as rational-emotive behavior theory or Jungian concepts) and associated techniques and interventions?
- How will I resolve dilemmas that arise when my values and those of my client are opposed?
- What is my belief about whether a counselor or therapist can remain neutral and avoid communicating value orientations to clients?
- What is my role in helping clients delineate their values more clearly?

Cultural Bias in Theory and Practice

In 1962, C. Gilbert Wrenn was one of the first to suggest that practitioners were providing counseling and psychotherapy from a narrow cultural perspective. He encouraged counselors and therapists to broaden their **monocultural** perspectives and be more responsive to clients from different cultural backgrounds. By the mid-1970s, more emphasis on the issue of **cultural bias** in theory and practice began to appear in the literature. For example, Sue (1997), Katz (1985), and Pedersen (1987) pointed out that traditional counseling is based exclusively on white culture and fails to meet the needs of culturally diverse client populations. Today it is widely acknowledged that current theories are derivatives of Western culture and are not universally applicable to cross-cultural counseling and psychotherapy situations (McFadden, 1988; Richardson & Molinaro, 1996; Vontress, 1988).

Because the United States is becoming increasingly diversified, recognition of the cultural bias that exists in theories and techniques of counseling and psychotherapy becomes even more important in the process of achieving a personal and professional identity. Christopher (1996) addresses diversity issues through the concept of **moral visions.** He notes that moral visions are constellations of cultural values and assumptions that shape our experience of life and the stances we take toward life. He points out that different cultures provide different moral visions. The ideal person in traditional Confucian China was first and foremost characterized by filial loyalty and being a dutiful son or daughter. In contrast, in the American culture, attributes such as authenticity and autonomy are reinforced. Moral visions both prescribe and describe what a person should be or become, and they influence the development of theories of counseling and psychotherapy. Most Western counseling theories are moral visions that presuppose the importance of individualism. For example, **behaviorist, cognitive-behavioral,** and **reality** theories emphasize utilitarian individualism. They stress rationality, control over emotions, enhanced human liberty, the importance of achieving self-defined goals, and opposition to irrational authority. **Humanistic** theories, such as **person-centered** and **Gestalt** theories, promote the importance of turning inward, of making contact with inner experiencing, and of identifying and expressing feelings. Such emphases may not be congruent with the moral visions of clients from other cultures.

Usher (1989) provided some helpful guidelines for assessing the cultural bias inherent in theories of counseling and psychotherapy. We include those guidelines here to extend the discussion of cultural awareness that we began in Chapter 1 and to alert the reader to some of the pitfalls associated with attempts to apply Western frames of reference to all clients irrespective of their cultural identity and experience. We do not intend to discourage counselors and therapists from making appropriate use of current theory; rather, we want to sensitize practitioners to the importance of cultural differences as determiners of approach selection and the development of a personal theory of counseling and psychotherapy.

Assumptions About Normal Behavior.   A very real source of cultural bias is the assumption that *normal* means the same thing to members of various social, political, economic, and cultural backgrounds. Although some clients may believe that being reasonably assertive or responsibly individualistic is a normal goal, such traits may be considered inappropriate in other cultures. Pedersen (1987) argued that "what is considered normal behavior will change according to the situation, the cultural background of a person or persons being judged, and the time during which a behavior is being displayed or observed" (p. 16). He pointed out the danger of diagnostic errors when using definitions of normality grounded in the perspective of the culture in which a particular theory or conceptual frame of reference was developed.

Emphasis on Individualism.   A number of theories (e.g., person-centered and **rational-emotive behavior theory**) emphasize the welfare and centrality of the individual and deemphasize the importance of obligation and duty to family, organizations, and society. Because such themes are central to some cultures' value systems, it would be a mistake for the counselor or therapist to promote individualism on the part of a client for whom such a focus would be contrary to cultural or ethnic identity. For example, an Asian-American client might not return to a counselor or therapist who did not respect what the client communicated about deference to the wishes of parents or other older members of the extended family.

Fragmentation by Academic Disciplines.   Many theories of counseling and psychotherapy have been developed without considering the potential contributions of other academic disciplines such as sociology, anthropology, theology, and medicine. A counselor or therapist who uses a theory that has been developed from a narrow perspective may be handicapped in attempts to facilitate the helping relationship with a client who is culturally different. It is important for all counselors and therapists to take courses or participate in training experiences offered by other disciplines or by those who maintain a different cultural perspective.

Dependence on Abstract Words.   Counselors and therapists with a Western frame of reference live in a low-context (i.e., less emphasis on how the meaning of a statement is affected by the context) culture, and they may depend on abstract words associated with theory and practice and assume that these abstractions will be understood by others—including clients—in the same way they are understood by the professional. Such abstractions may have little meaning, or take on different meanings, when used outside the cultural context in which they were initially developed. For example, would all clients understand the concepts of *self-actualization* or *fictional finalism*? Many clients are not receptive to abstractions or conceptualizations, which, in a culture not based on Western values, worldviews, or protocols, may seem removed from the reality of life.

Overemphasis on Independence.   Usher (1989) cited Pedersen (1987), who criticized theories and practices that devalue necessary dependencies inculcated by certain cultures. Because most counselors and therapists in this country view the independence of the client as desirable and neglect the function of healthy dependencies in some cultures, many of the theories used by counselors and therapists do a disservice to clients who have grown up and continue to function in a different cultural context. There are many cultural groups that value a person's capacity to subjugate individual desire to the overall welfare of the family, community, or organization. It is important for counselors and therapists to be both sensitive to and respectful of such a perspective.

Neglect of Client Support Systems.   Many theoretical orientations do not recognize the role that family and peers play in providing support for a troubled client to the same extent that they recognize the role of the professionally prepared counselor or therapist. (Neither do the proponents of many approaches to counseling and psychotherapy.) It may be necessary for counselors and therapists to incorporate the client's natural support system into a treatment plan. In some cultures, talking with family members or friends may be more acceptable than talking with a trained professional who is usually a total stranger.

Dependence on Linear Thinking.   Most theories make the assumption that clients relate to linear thinking. Linear thinking emphasizes cause-and-effect relationships, whereas the nonlinear or circular thinking characteristic of some cultures does not separate cause and effect, does not follow a singular stream of thought, and invites free association. It is important for counselors and therapists to realize that for some clients, conversation about topics seemingly unrelated to counseling or psychotherapy may be an essential element of a productive helping relationship.

Focus on Changing the Individual Rather Than the System.   Quite often, counselors and therapists who use Western theory as the sole basis for practice assume that their role is to make the client more congruent with the system. Such a role can be quite problematic when Western culture-bound paradigms, such as the *DSM-IV,* are used to assess the behavior of clients who are culturally different (Lewis-Fernandez & Kleinman, 1995). If counselors or therapists do not question whether the "system" is in the best interests of a culturally different client, are they simply serving as agents of the status quo?

Neglect of History.   Some counselors and therapists minimize the relevance of a client's personal and cultural history, focusing more intensively on present behavior, the current problem, and immediate events. Clients from some cultures, such as Native American cultures, see themselves as closely connected to their ancestors. Their current problems cannot be fully understood without consideration of their history. Such clients might not return to a counselor or therapist who did not provide opportunities to explore the present in terms of past experience as well as present needs.

Cultural Encapsulation.   It is important for counselors and therapists to guard against the possibility of becoming **culturally encapsulated** by the mainstream group with which they are associated. When such encapsulation occurs, assumptions and beliefs may not be questioned, and clients from diverse cultural backgrounds may not be treated effectively because of the operation of certain biases on the part of the professional. The more counselors and therapists can experience and learn about other cultural groups, the less likely they will be to approach clients with biases that prevent effective helping.

The Daily World of the Practitioner

There is no doubt that there is a complex relationship between elements of the therapeutic process and the demands experienced by the counselor or therapist on a daily basis. The clients with whom one works, the setting, the expectations of colleagues and supervisors, one's personal life, and significant others are constantly interacting and, at times, reciprocally influencing outcomes. We believe that an important part of developing a personal and professional identity is becoming as aware as possible of the daily world of the practitioner and the stresses that sometimes impede the counselor or therapist's well-being and the services provided to clients.

The demands inherent in just about any work environment (school, college, university, mental health center, hospital, private practice, rehabilitation clinic, etc.) are tremendous. Concerns about having enough clients, students, supervisees, research funds, publications, involvements in professional and community organizations, collected fees, malpractice, and liability insurance are just a few examples of the kinds of demands that converge on counselors and therapists. As Freudenberger (1983) notes, the very nature of the therapeutic personality often makes it difficult to say no, and many people engaged in counseling and psychotherapy find themselves overextended, tired, and overly involved with work. For some professionals, the drive to develop a reputation for excellence, coupled with the needs for success, must be monitored carefully to avoid chronic discontent and eventual **burnout.**

The demands that clients place upon counselors and therapists are a significant factor in a practitioner's daily world. In the span of just a few days, many counselors and therapists find themselves confronted with the problems of the chronically mentally ill, the terminally ill, the physically or sexually abused, the suicidal, the eating disordered, the substance abuser, and clients with a host of other concerns and issues. Most research to date (e.g., Finch & Krantz, 1991; Hellman & Morrison, 1987; Pines & Maslach, 1978) indicates that counselors and therapists in settings that serve large numbers of seriously disturbed clients experience higher rates of personal depletion, less career satisfaction, and more impaired working relationships with colleagues. This information is quite pertinent for those planning to place themselves in settings in which there is a high probability of working with challenging clients.

The ominous shadow of malpractice hovers all too often over the daily world of the practitioner. Rates for liability insurance have risen as clients have become more litigious and counselors and therapists have become fair game. Because many clients enter the counseling or psychotherapy process with expectations about becoming better, perhaps in an unrealistically short period of time, counselors and therapists are vulnerable to having client disappointments or frustrations worked out in court rather than in a therapeutic environment. More and more lawyers have chosen to specialize in personal injury and malpractice cases and actively seek clients who are discontented with the results of counseling and psychotherapy (Kaslow & Schulman, 1987). Even when the counselor or therapist is innocent, the insurance carrier or one's own legal counsel may suggest an out-of-court settlement in order to avoid the trauma of a trial, the possibility of a guilty verdict, the accompanying censure by professional organizations, and the possibility of losing required state licensing. To the beginning—and even to the experienced—counselor or therapist, such a settlement can seem like an admission of guilt, yet preparing for and going through a trial can pose an even greater ordeal and create a high level of stress. In addition, such trials may attract a great deal of unwelcome media attention. Because counselors and therapists believe in the sanctity and privacy of the therapeutic encounter, such public exposure can be a bitter experience, with negative impacts on personal well-being as well as on the lives of family members.

More than any other professional, the counselor or therapist must continually deal with the reality of terminations. Whether the treatment process has been successful or not, the ending of a helping relationship may be experienced as another separation and, quite often, as a permanent loss. Despite the fact that counselors and therapists are prepared during their educational and supervisory experiences for the inevitability of terminating with clients, endings may be difficult and force the counselor or therapist to deal with unresolved personal losses (departure of adult children, death of significant others, divorce).

Terminations can also become transformations when clients appear in different roles in the life of the counselor or therapist. Examples of these roles include former clients who may later reenter as trained mental health professionals or, as is often the case in small communities, become part of the social milieu of the counselor or therapist. The reality of termination or transformation can be a source of satisfaction or stress depending upon how the counselor or therapist views the nature of the posttreatment void or the posttreatment relationship.

In many ways, the daily world of the counselor or therapist may threaten relationships outside the workplace. For example, in the process of striving to improve working relationships with co-therapists, colleagues, and supervisors, counselors or therapists may share much of their inner selves and, in so doing, develop satisfying relationships built on trust, respect, and mutual understanding. These relationships may supplant or replace other significant relationships outside the workplace. As a result, a marriage or long-term relationship may begin to seem less interesting and rewarding unless some steps are taken to prevent this from happening.

In addition to the impact that relationships with colleagues may have on the personal life of a counselor or therapist, the expression of admiration by clients, trainees, and colleagues may also result in some unexpected fallout. Significant others outside the workplace may begin to resent the attention that the counselor or therapist receives from clients and colleagues, or the counselor or therapist may begin to expect the same level of admiration from significant others. In either situation, resentment, frustration, and anger may result. Again, counselors and therapists need to take steps to prevent this from occurring.

Finally, the basic principle of confidentiality may create problems for the counselor or therapist in relationships outside the workplace. Counselors and therapists cannot talk about their clients except in the context of receiving supervision or consultation or in situations when the best interests of the client or society are at stake. Significant others may feel shut out, especially when they know that others have access to information unavailable to them.

Achieving Perspective and Balance

Our previous discussion of the daily world of the counselor or therapist is necessarily limited in scope, yet we believe the discussion does convey the fact that counselors and therapists deal with demands and stresses that can place them at risk for burnout (Schulz, Greenley, & Brown, 1995) and personal depletion. Because it is important to maintain a high level of personal health and wellness, we think the following guidelines may prove useful to individuals in training as well as to other members of the profession.

Know the Warning Signs for Burnout

How do graduate students or practicing counselors or therapists know they are heading for difficulty when striving to develop and maintain a high level of professional competence? Kaslow (1986) lists some of the signs of burnout:

- Not wanting to go to work
- Constantly complaining about disliking practice or feeling overwhelmed by it
- Experiencing a sense of foreboding or imminent doom
- Viewing life as dull, heavy, and tedious
- Experiencing an increasing number of negative countertransference reactions to patients or students
- Being extremely irritable, withdrawn, depressed, or intolerant at home
- Suffering frequent illnesses of inexplicable origin
- Wanting to run away from it all or having periodic suicidal ideation

Kaslow (1986) notes that when two or more of these indicators appear periodically and with gradually increasing frequency, intensity, and duration, a counselor or therapist has entered a warning zone and should seek personal counseling and psychotherapy, take a vacation, cut back on obligations, and so on until he or she reexperiences perspective and balance.

Consider Networking Options

It is not always necessary to enter a counseling or psychotherapy relationship to achieve balance and perspective. Counselors and therapists have a number of beneficial protections that they can use to renew and revitalize their ability to function in a positive way. They can establish a network of professional contacts to provide different options for support and continued professional development. For example, working with a co-therapist, asking a colleague to view a client session through a one-way mirror and then offer feedback, or seeking clarification and assistance from a supervisor can provide invaluable support and ideas for treatment options when working with a difficult client. Any one of these networking options can help a counselor or therapist to share the burden of providing counseling or psychotherapy or to break through an impasse in a client/practitioner relationship (Kaslow & Schulman, 1987).

Most communities provide opportunities for professionals to join a support group to share personal or professional concerns. Often there are local opportunities to attend workshops and training sessions to enhance expertise or develop new skills. Such workshops also allow practitioners to meet and talk with other counselors and therapists who share similar interests. It is always important to participate in some combination of local, state, regional, or national professional organizations such as the American Counseling Association, the American Psychological Association, or the American Association of Marriage and Family Therapists. Professional organizations provide a myriad of opportunities for continued learning and networking with other members of the helping professions. An excellent source for graduate students is involvement with a local chapter of Chi Sigma Iota, an international honor society for students, alumni, and supporters of counselor education programs and departments.

Refer Clients When Appropriate

Another way to maintain perspective and balance is to be amenable to the possibility of referring clients who are difficult or chronic or whose issues fall outside your ability to provide adequate care. A referral can be done in a positive way from the vantage point of a client, and colleagues will view it as a sign of professional integrity and wisdom. Sometimes, when a client is struggling with issues too close to those of the counselor or therapist, referral of the client is preferable to undertaking or prolonging work in which one becomes overly involved.

Disengage from the Professional Role

The experienced counselor or therapist knows how to disengage from the role of being a professional so that time with friends and family members, social engagements, vacations, and avocational interests can be enjoyed. Disengaging provides opportunities for rest, relaxation, and rejuvenation while relieving the practitioner from obligations. It is important for counselors and therapists to experience nurturing interpersonal relationships, just as it is important for clients to spend time with significant others. At times, counselors and therapists can become so enmeshed in the demands of the profession that it becomes difficult to enjoy opportunities for fun and relaxation.

Consider Possible Options for Renewal

We began our careers in the 1960s as members of the profession of counseling and human development. At that time the daily world of the practitioner was quite different from the way it is today. Standards for credentialing, education, and supervision, although reasonably demanding, were not as specific, time-consuming, and exacting as they are currently. As the profession has matured, the expectations for graduate work, **credentialing,** practice, and **continuing education** have become decidedly more demanding and stress-producing. Because of these demands, many professionals develop a pattern of overload that can be traced back to graduate education and, quite often, to some inherent needs and predispositions that make overload seem acceptable as a way of life.

We do not believe that it is possible to continue indefinitely as an effective counselor or therapist unless options for renewal are considered and pursued. These options are unique for each counselor or therapist and can only be identified on an individual basis. Exercise, time with friends, participation in a choral group, leaves of absence or sabbaticals, travel, gardening, white-water rafting, massages, time with significant others, and time alone are examples of the hundreds of options, and combinations of options, that may have appeal as well as potential for practitioner renewal.

In a very interesting study, Richard and Eileen Mackey (1994) analyzed the impact of personal therapy on the outlook of the practicing professional. Results indicated that counselors and therapists emerged from the experience with new ideas for therapeutic techniques, enhanced empathy, better understanding of the therapeutic process, higher levels of self-awareness, and greater ability to set limits, establish boundaries, and maintain an appropriate balance between closeness and distance in professional relationships. All of these outcomes are pertinent to "renewal" and to the avoidance or overcoming of burnout.

It is not possible to nurture others unless we provide the self-nurturance and renewal that maintains and restores our capacity as helpers. As we have already mentioned, the health and wellness of the helper has much to do with the art form inherent in the helping relationship. Readers are referred to Coster and Schwebel (1997) and Dupree and Day (1995) for additional information about avoiding burnout.

The Importance of a Personal Theory

After you finish reading the next chapter of this book, you will begin a fascinating exploration of theories of counseling and psychotherapy. Some theories will have more personal appeal than others; all of them will present some stimulating perspectives about human nature and about providing help to those seeking assistance. In addition, each will suggest a variety of theory-congruent strategies or applications designed to help clients achieve desired changes in behavior, outlook, motivation, and so on. We want the contents of this book to help you continue to think about a personal theory of counseling and psychotherapy.

Which theory you decide to adopt or develop will be gradually identified as you accumulate knowledge about theory, research, and practice and build experiences with clients through practicum, internships, and volunteer and paid positions. A personal theory will also relate to values, culture, experience with diverse client populations, and a view of human growth and development throughout the life span. We encourage you to begin thinking about the conceptual frame of reference with which you plan to approach clients, but we discourage you from adopting a position until you carefully explore possibilities and participate in a variety of clinical opportunities with associated one-to-one and group supervision experience.

As you read Chapters 4 through 15, notice that each theory is consistently addressed in terms of a six-point paradigm: background, human nature, major constructs, applications, evaluation, and a case study based on the description of Maria, a divorced, single parent of two elementary-aged children. These six elements may form the basis for beginning to formulate a personal theory. It is important to realize, however, that there are other paradigms that could be developed with additional elements or components. In addition, it is beneficial to read the last three chapters of this book, which address theories of counseling and psychotherapy from the perspectives of working with children and adolescents, diverse clients, and integrative paradigms, before formulating a frame of reference for working therapeutically with others.

Conclusions

This chapter has stressed the importance of achieving a personal and professional identity as you begin to study theories of counseling and psychotherapy and gain experience in translating theory into practice. We believe that personal identity and professional identity are interrelated and fundamental to being able to understand, evaluate, and apply the theories presented in this text. Because the health and wellness of the counselor or therapist is a prerequisite to effectiveness, we addressed this topic through descriptions of personal characteristics, psychological health, and multidimensional health and wellness models.

The values and cultural biases of each counselor or therapist do have an impact on the use and application of theory as well as the structuring of the helping relationship. We hope you will make personal assessments of your values and sensitivity to culturally diverse client populations as well as evaluate the values and cultural biases upon which the theories presented in subsequent chapters are based.

At times, students enroll in college and university programs for preparing counselors and therapists without being totally aware of the demands they will encounter. By describing the daily world of the counselor or therapist and the importance of achieving perspective and balance, this chapter provided an initial overview of the stresses and expectations as well as the importance of learning how to cope with professional demands. We believe each person needs to develop a realistic understanding of the profession and that this knowledge is an essential component for the development of personal and professional identity.

Finally, this chapter stressed the importance of thinking about the conceptual frame of reference with which clients are approached. Although some practitioners may adopt an existing theory, many will develop integrative or other perspectives based upon a number of professional and life experiences. We want you not only to obtain the benefits provided by the information in this book, but also to develop the analytic and evaluative skills that will enable you to apply this information effectively to client populations. Effective application will result when a practitioner is able to find a compatible balance between theoretical tenets and the personal and cultural characteristics that serve as a basis for his or her uniqueness. At that point you will have answers to the two questions that began this chapter.

References

Adler, A. (1978). Cooperation between the sexes. In H. L. Ansbacher & R. R. Ansbacher (Eds.), *Writings on women, love, and marriage, sexuality and its disorders*. Garden City, NY: Doubleday.

Allport, G. W. (1961). *Pattern and growth in personality*. New York: Holt, Rinehart & Winston.

Ardell, D. B. (1988). The history and future of the wellness movement. In J. P. Opatz (Ed.), *Wellness promotion strategies: Selected proceedings of the eighth annual National Wellness Conference*. Dubuque, IA: Kendall/Hunt.

Belkin, G. (1984). *Introduction to counseling* (2nd ed.). Dubuque, IA: Brown.

Carkhuff, R. R., & Berenson, B. G. (1977). *Beyond counseling and therapy* (2nd ed.). New York: Holt, Rinehart & Winston.

Christopher, J. C. (1996). Counseling's inescapable moral visions. *Journal of Counseling and Development, 75*, 17–25.

Combs, A., Soper, D., Gooding, C., Benton, J., Dickman, J., & Usher, R. (1969). *Florida studies in the helping professions*. Gainesville: University Press of Florida.

Coster, J. S., & Schwebel, M. (1997). Well-functioning in professional psychologists. *Professional Psychology: Research and Practice, 28*, 5–13.

Dupree, P. I., & Day, H. D. (1995). Psychotherapists' job satisfaction and job burnout as a function of work setting and percentage of managed care clients. *Psychotherapy in Private Practice, 14,* 77–93.

Egan, G. (1975). *The skilled helper.* Monterey, CA: Brooks/Cole.

Erikson, E. H. (1968). *Identity: Youth and crisis.* New York: Norton.

Evans, K. M. (1997). Wellness and coping activities of African American counselors. *Journal of Black Psychology, 23*(1), 24–35.

Finch, E. S., & Krantz, S. R. (1991). Low burnout in a high-stress setting: A study of staff adaption at Fountain House. *Psychological Rehabilitation Journal, 14,* 15–26.

Freud, S. (1930). *Civilization and its discontents* (J. Strachey, Trans. & Ed.). New York: Norton.

Freudenberger, H. (1983). Hazards of psychotherapeutic practice. *Psychotherapy in Private Practice, 1*(1), 83–89.

Fromm, E. (1955). *The sane society.* New York: Rinehart.

George, R. L., & Cristiani, T. S. (1990). *Counseling theory and practice* (3rd ed.). Upper Saddle River, NJ: Prentice Hall.

Goldfried, M. R., Greenberg, L. S., & Maramar, C. (1990). Individual psychotherapy: Process and outcome. *Annual Review of Psychology, 41,* 659–688.

Hanna, F. J., & Bemak, F. (1997). The quest for identity in the counseling profession. *Counselor Education and Supervision, 36,* 194–206.

Hanna, F. J., & Ottens, A. J. (1995). The role of wisdom in psychotherapy. *Journal of Psychotherapy Integration, 5,* 195–219.

Hellman, I. D., & Morrison, T. L. (1987). Practice setting and type of caseload as factors in psychotherapist stress. *Psychotherapy, 24*(3), 427–432.

Hettler, B. (1984). Wellness: Encouraging a lifetime pursuit of excellence. *Health Values, 8*(4), 13–17.

Horney, K. (1950). *Neurosis and human growth.* New York: Norton.

Jahoda, M. (1958). *Current concepts of positive mental health.* New York: Basic Books.

Jung, C. G. (1954). *The development of personality.* Princeton: Princeton University Press.

Kaslow, F. W. (1986). Therapy with distressed psychotherapists: Special problems and challenges. In R. R. Kilburg, P. E. Nathan, & R. W. Thoreson (Eds.), *Professionals in distress: Issues, syndromes,* *and solutions in psychology* (pp. 187–210). Washington, DC: American Psychological Association.

Kaslow, F. W., & Schulman, N. (1987). How to be sane and happy as a family therapist, or the reciprocal impact of family therapy teaching and practice and therapists' personal lives and mental health. *Journal of Psychotherapy and the Family, 3*(2), 79–96.

Katz, J. H. (1985). The sociopolitical nature of counseling. *The Counseling Psychologist, 13,* 615–624.

Kelly, E. W., Jr. (1995). Counselor values: A national survey. *Journal of Counseling and Development, 73,* 648–653.

Kinnier, R. T. (1997). What does it mean to be psychologically healthy? In D. Capuzzi & D. R. Gross (Eds.), *Introduction to the counseling profession* (2nd ed.) (pp. 48–63). Boston: Allyn & Bacon.

Lewis-Fernandez, R., & Kleinman, A. (1995). Cultural psychiatry: Theoretical, clinical, and research issues. *Psychiatric Clinics of North America, 18,* 433–448.

Mackey, R. A., & Mackey, E. F. (1994). Personal psychotherapy and the development of a professional self. *Families in Society: The Journal of Contemporary Human Services, 75,* 490–499.

Maslow, A. H. (1970). *Motivation and personality* (2nd ed.). New York: Harper.

McFadden, J. (1988). Cross-cultural counseling: Caribbean perspective. *Journal of Multicultural Counseling and Development, 16,* 36–40.

Myers, J. E. (1991). Wellness as the paradigm for counseling and development: The possible future. *Counselor Education and Supervision, 30*(3), 183–193.

Okun, B. F. (1987). *Effective helping: Interviewing and counseling techniques* (3rd ed.). Monterey, CA: Brooks/Cole.

Orlinsky, D. E., & Howard, K. I. (1978). The relation of process to outcome in psychotherapy. In S. L. Garfield & A. E. Bergin (Eds.), *Handbook of psychotherapy and behavior change* (2nd ed.) (pp. 283–330). New York: Wiley.

Orlinsky, D. E., & Howard, K. I. (1986). Process and outcome in psychotherapy. In S. L. Garfield & A. E. Bergin (Eds.), *Handbook of psychotherapy and behavior change* (3rd ed.) (pp. 311–381). New York: Wiley.

Patterson, C. H. (1958). The place of values in counseling and psychotherapy. *Journal of Counseling Psychology, 5,* 216–223.

Patterson, C. H. (1989). Values in counseling and psychotherapy. *Counseling and Values, 33,* 164–176.

Pedersen, P. (1987). Ten frequent assumptions of cultural bias in counseling. *Journal of Multicultural Counseling and Development, 15,* 16–22.

Pines, A., & Maslach, C. (1978). Characteristics of staff burnout in mental health settings. *Hospital and Community Psychiatry, 29,* 233–237.

Richardson, T. Q., & Molinaro, K. L. (1996). White counselor self-awareness: A prerequisite for developing multicultural competence. *Journal of Counseling and Development, 74,* 238–242.

Rogers, C. R. (1957). The necessary and sufficient conditions of therapeutic personality change. *Journal of Consulting Psychology, 21,* 95–103.

Rogers, C. R. (1961). *On becoming a person: A therapist's view of psychotherapy.* Boston: Houghton Mifflin.

Samler, J. (1960). Change in values: A goal in counseling. *Journal of Counseling Psychology, 7,* 32–39.

Schulz, R., Greenley, J. R., & Brown, R. (1995). Organization, management, and client effects on staff burnout. *Journal of Health and Social Behavior, 36,* 333–345.

Sue, S. (1997). Community mental health services to minority groups: Some optimism, some pessimism. *American Psychologist, 32,* 616–624.

Sullivan, H. S. (1953). *The interpersonal theory of psychiatry.* New York: Norton.

Truax, C. B., & Carkhuff, R. R. (1967). *Toward effective counseling and psychotherapy: Training and practice.* Chicago: Aldine.

Usher, C. H. (1989). Recognizing cultural bias in counseling theory and practice: The case of Rogers. *Journal of Multicultural Counseling and Development, 17,* 62–71.

Vontress, C. (1988). An existential approach to cross-cultural counseling. *Journal of Multicultural Counseling and Development, 16,* 73–83.

Whiston, S. C., & Sexton, T. L. (1993). An overview of psychotherapy outcome research: Implications for practice. *Professional Psychology: Research and Practice, 24,* 43–51.

Williamson, E. (1958). Value orientation in counseling. *Personnel and Guidance Journal, 36,* 520–528.

Wrenn, C. G. (1962). The culturally encapsulated counselor. *Harvard Educational Review, 32,* 444–449.

Ethical and Legal Issues in Counseling and Psychotherapy

Douglas R. Gross
Professor Emeritus
Arizona State University

David Capuzzi
Portland State University

The following scenario depicts students much like you, who are enrolled in a required course entitled "Ethics and Legal Issues in Counseling and Therapy." Courses such as this are now required in all educative programs for counselors or therapists and are one of the core requirements for national and state **certification, credentialing,** or **licensing** of counselors and therapists. This chapter is intended to increase your knowledge of ethical and legal issues related to counseling and therapy, and the information contained in the following scenario serves as our way of introducing you to the subject.

As Dr. James ended her class for the evening, she said, "Keep in mind that the codes of ethics we are reviewing are only guidelines and offer directives rather than hard-and-fast answers for situations that arise in counseling or therapy. The answers rest with you as you review the situation and attempt to apply the guidelines and directives. We'll discuss this more fully next week."

While she gathered her materials and erased the board, she noticed that several students were huddled together in the back of the room. The voice level of the participants indicated that they were involved in a heated discussion. When Dr. James crossed to the door, one of the students asked if she could spare a moment to answer a question.

"I will if I can," she said as she approached the group. "What's the question?" She drew up a chair to join the group.

John, the student who had stopped her, explained that he and some other students were very concerned because all they were getting in class were guidelines and directives. They had hoped for clear-cut answers regarding what should and should not be done in counseling or therapy. He explained that the students wanted the type of information that would enable them to behave ethically, information they would need when they took professional positions.

Dr. James thanked John for asking her to join the group. "You raise an issue that has been raised in every section of this course I've taught," she said. She explained that she saw it as a very important issue and that the group should compliment itself.

"It usually takes students longer to voice this concern," she said. "Ethical codes seldom provide specific answers for specific situations. They are designed to guide practitioners as they evaluate the various aspects of the helping relationship and enable them to make decisions regarding appropriate behaviors. I know it would be nice to have specific answers for the situations that each of you will face as you assume professional positions, but neither I nor the codes of ethics presented in this class will provide those answers. As a professional, it will be your responsibility both to interpret and apply the information contained in these codes to assure that your behaviors in the helping relationship are ethical. This class cannot give you the answers you seek, but it should equip you to interpret and apply the ethical guidelines more effectively."

As she stood up and moved toward the door, she asked, "Will one of you bring up this issue at next week's class? I feel that all the students in class could benefit from this discussion."

After Dr. James left the room, the group asked John if he would bring up the issue at the next class. He agreed; and after gathering up their materials, the students left the classroom.

We hope that you are able to identify with the concerns of the class members as they attempt to translate ethical principles into operational procedures that they will be able to apply. **Ethics,** as an area of professional investigation, is both confusing in definition and frustrating in application. The confusion stems from the generalized terminology used in established codes to cover a broad professional population. The frustration stems from attempting to translate this generalized terminology into specific behaviors that are operational within the helping relationship.

Determining what is or is not ethical behavior often creates a perplexing dilemma for both the novice and the experienced practitioner. While the helping professions have offered practitioners a plethora of guidelines and codes of ethical behavior, confusion still exists (Gross & Robinson, 1987). These codes include *Code of Ethics* (1989) published by the National Board of Certified Counselors (NBCC); *AAMFT Code of Ethics* (1991) adopted by the American Association for Marriage and Family Therapy; *Code of Ethics for Mental Health Counselors* (1987) adopted by the American Mental Health Counselors Association (AMHCA) and supported by the National Academy for Certified Clinical Mental Health Counselors (NACCMHC); *Ethical Guidelines for Group Counselors* (1989) approved by the Association for Specialists in Group Work (ASGW); *Ethical Principles of Psychologists and Code of Conduct* (1992) adopted by the American Psychological Association (APA); *Code of Ethics and Standards of Practice* (1995) adopted by the American Counseling Association (ACA); *Ethical Standards for School Counselors* (1992) adopted by the American School Counselors Association (ASCA); *Ethical Code for the International Association for Marriage and Family Counselors* (1993) adopted by the International Association for Marriage and Family Counselors (IAMFC); and the *Ethical Guidelines for Counseling Supervisors* (1993) adopted by the Association of Counselor Educators and Supervisors (ACES).

Not only have these national professional groups provided ethical guidelines for their members, but also many state counseling and psychological associations have adopted their own versions of ethical standards.

Although intended to be helpful, these **codes, standards, principles,** and **guidelines** result in more questions than answers. This is particularly true if one examines the documents for parameters of ethical conduct in light of the various roles and functions that practitioners perform. According to Gross and Robinson (1987), "Most counselors consider direct service to individuals, to groups, or to families as their primary role. Secondary role responsibilities might include consultation, supervision of counselor trainees or subordinates, and research attempting to evaluate service or to answer clinical questions. Regardless of the role being performed, counselors must be cognizant of ethical responsibilities to clients or client systems and to the profession" (pp. 5–6).

The variety of codes and the diversity of practitioner roles add directly to the confusion inherent in definition and the frustration involved in application. This chapter addresses these problems in relation to the following topics: the definition and rationale of ethical codes, models for ethical decision making, dimensions of ethical behavior, dimensions of unethical behavior, procedures for processing unethical behavior, and legal issues. We place major emphasis on the ACA's *Code of Ethics and Standards of Practice* (1995) and the APA's *Ethical Principles of Psychologists and Code of Conduct* (1992). We selected these sets of standards because they are widely used in educational course work for counselors and therapists.

Ethical Codes: Definition and Rationale

As an area of inquiry, ethics is a branch of philosophy that focuses on morals and morality as they relate to decision making. Studies in this area concentrate on the standards of morality found in various cultures, societies, and professional groups and how these standards translate into directives aimed at regulating the behaviors of members of these various groups.

According to *Merriam-Webster's Collegiate Dictionary* (1993), the word *ethic* can mean "the discipline dealing with what is good and bad and with moral duty and obligation," "a set of moral principles or values," or "the principles of conduct governing an individual or a group" (p. 398). Of the three definitions, the one that most closely captures the subject of this chapter is the one dealing with "principles of conduct governing an individual or a group." The other two definitions, which address concepts of good and bad, **moral duty** and obligation, and values, are inherent in these "principles of conduct" and provide the context around which professional codes of ethics were developed. **Ethical behavior,** therefore, deals with the application of concepts of morality, values, and good and bad to situations that individuals encounter in life. Ethical behavior related to counseling or therapy deals with the application of these same concepts to situations that counselors and therapists encounter in the context of the helping relationship.

The terms *ethics* and *ethical behavior* can be addressed from both an individual and a group perspective. It is obvious that areas such as morality and values are best understood in terms of the attitudes and behaviors of the individual. People develop their moral and value orientations based upon a wide array of variables. These orientations often govern not only the interactive patterns of people, but also their views of the world. Human diversity would make it extremely difficult for people to develop agreed-upon standards of ethical behavior for each individual in every part of the world. But such standards are possible for specific cultures, societies, and professional groups when they are based upon shared values, views of morality, and accepted concepts of good and bad. These shared beliefs and the group's desire to have its members behave according to these beliefs are the foundation on which codes of ethics are developed. According to Allen (1986), "One of the beliefs of every professional organization is that its members must perform their professional duties according to an established code of ethics. Without an established ethical code, a group of people with similar interests cannot actually be considered a professional organization" (p. 293). This statement provides a rationale for the development of codes of ethics by professional groups and indicates that such codes are one of the unifying factors that designate disciplines such as medicine, psychology, and counseling as professional organizations. Support for this proposition can be found in the writings of Corey, Corey, and Callanan (1993); Gibson and Pope (1993); Huber (1994); and Robinson-Kurpius (1997).

Besides providing a professional identity, what other purposes do such codes serve? Van Hoose and Kottler (1985) identified the following:

1. Provide guidelines for ethical decision making.
2. Regulate the behavior of members of the profession.
3. Demonstrate the willingness of an organization to police itself and provide a method of self-regulation.
4. Regulate intermember interactions such as referral of clients, consultation, and client recruitment.
5. Protect the profession by setting standards of practice that are used in the adjudication of liability suits.

We support all of these purposes as appropriate rationales for the development of codes of ethics. Each code of ethics attempts to provide the profession, its members, and its public with guidelines and directives aimed at assuring the group that basic ethical standards will be practiced. Such assurance also serves a protective function for each group. The profession itself is protected because it is able to police its membership and suspend members who are in violation of the code; members who operate within these ethical standards are protected to some degree from malpractice adjudication; and the public is served when the profession provides a degree of protection, through legal recourse, against violations of these standards.

The importance of codes of ethics to professional groups and their various publics seems obvious. We would present an unbalanced picture, however, if we did not also discuss various limitations of these codes (Corey et al., 1993; Ibrahim & Arredondo, 1990). One such limitation deals with the general nature of the codes and the fact that the types of situations encountered by members attempting to operate within them are seldom as clearcut as those addressed in the codes. This leaves the final determination of ethical versus unethical behavior with an individual and his or her ability to make the correct decision.

A second limitation stems from the lack of adequate coverage for certain areas within the codes. Examples include consultation and group work. The ACA and APA codes of ethics deal with these topics in a cursory manner. Members must seek out special codes of ethics, developed by associations that specialize in these areas, to be aware of all of the ethical parameters that surround them.

A third limitation stems from differences that exist among various codes of ethics. This limitation exists when an individual is a member of more than one professional group. If such a situation exists (and it often does with persons who are members of both the ACA and the APA), which code do members follow? How do they decide which code best governs their behavior? In addressing this limitation, Kitchener (1986) notes that "these codes may not always be in agreement" and that "compliance with the ethical code of one association may be judged as unethical by another association" (p. 306).

A fourth limitation exists when ethical codes are in conflict with institutional policies and procedures. A person who is both a member of a professional association and an employee of an institution may discover that the policies and procedures supported by the two are in conflict.

A fifth limitation exists due to the **cultural diversity** of the public and the need for adaptation when dealing with specific cultures.

There are no easy answers to the questions posed by these limitations. If answers do exist, they will be found in the counselor's or therapist's ability to interpret the information presented in the codes and to make appropriate decisions. To aid you in this interpretive and decision-making process, we direct your attention to the following section where we present three models for ethical decision making.

Models for Ethical Decision Making

Kitchener's Model for Ethical Decision Making

Kitchener (1984, 1986) approached ethical decision making from an integrative perspective combining moral and ethical viewpoints. She identified the following five moral principles that are viewed as the foundation on which ethical decision making is based:

- *Autonomy:* individual freedom of choice and action
- *Nonmaleficence:* not causing harm to others
- *Beneficence:* contributing to welfare of client
- *Justice:* treating equals equally and unequals unequally in proportion to their relevant differences
- *Fidelity:* loyalty, faithfulness, and honoring commitments

These moral principles and the values placed on them by counselors and therapists aid the counselor or therapist to better understand the conflicting issues surrounding **ethical dilemmas.** For example, the moral principle "autonomy" deals with the value the counselor or therapist places on a client's freedom of choice and action. If a counselor or therapist places high value on this principle, an ethical dilemma occurs whenever he or she is faced with limiting this freedom due to possible negative outcomes or when a client (e.g., a child or an individual with a mental disability) is not capable of making competent choices.

Kitchener (1986) believes that "ethics involves making decisions of a moral nature about people and their interaction in society" (p. 306). The moral principles she presents serve as "thinking tools" that allow counselors and therapists to critically analyze, interpret, and evaluate the various ethical dilemmas that arise, along with their feelings related to these dilemmas, in the light of the ethical codes they have agreed to uphold. The five moral principles provide the counselor or therapist with the tools for this type of critical examination.

Forester-Miller and Davis's Model for Ethical Decision Making

Forester-Miller and Davis (1996) developed *A Practitioner's Guide to Ethical Decision Making* under the auspices of the ACA's Ethics Committee. Using Kitchener's (1984) five moral principles as a basis for their work, they set forth a seven-step ethical decision-making model to be used in conjunction with the ACA *Code of Ethics and Standards of Practice* (1995). The model contains the following steps:

1. Identify the problem.
2. Apply the ACA *Code of Ethics and Standards of Practice.*
3. Determine the nature and dimensions of the dilemma.
4. Generate possible courses of action.
5. Consider the potential consequences of all options.
6. Evaluate the selected course of action.
7. Implement the course of action.

These steps are cumulative, and each step provides questions, directions, and courses of action that enable the practitioner to move from problem identification to action implementation. In each step the practitioner is encouraged to evaluate problem identification, application of the code, nature and dimensions of the dilemma, courses of action, and implementation in terms of Kitchener's (1984) moral principles. Forester-Miller and Davis (1996) suggest that simply examining the ethical situation in the light of the five moral principles may "clarify the issues enough that the means for resolving the dilemma will become obvious" (p. 3). (*A Practitioner's Guide to Ethical Decision Making* is available through the ACA, Alexandria, Virginia.)

Capuzzi and Gross's Model for Ethical Decision Making

The third and final model of ethical decision making for your consideration grew out of our research and experience and is set forth in a series of seven directive guidelines. The guidelines that follow provide direction rather than answers, have application to a wide range of situations, and should help you answer the question, "What should I do if I think an ethical or legal issue exists because of my behavior or the behavior of others?"

- *Guideline 1:* When confronted with a situation that may have ethical or legal ramifications, review the ethical standards of your professional group to determine if the situation is addressed and if guidelines and directives exist. If not, review codes of ethics of professional groups that may deal more specifically with the special situation you face.

- *Guideline 2:* If you cannot find answers or if you need more information, review the *Ethical Standards Casebook* (Herlihy & Corey, 1996), which was designed to clarify the intent of the ACA *Code of Ethics and Standards of Practice* (1995). Also review the *Casebook of Ethical Principles of Psychologists* (APA, 1987). In addition, it might be helpful to review *Policies and Procedures for Processing Complaints of Ethical Violations* (ACA, 1994).

- *Guideline 3:* If you cannot find satisfactory answers, talk with colleagues and ask them for assistance in both interpretation and decision making. The decision must be yours, but make that decision only after you have investigated all possible sources of information.

- *Guideline 4:* If you believe that the situation has legal parameters, review the legal statutes that have implications for counseling or psychotherapy, not only within your state but also from a national perspective.

- *Guideline 5:* To better understand the legal parameters, talk with members of the legal profession who have expertise in the area of member-client rights. Review the material presented in *The Counselor and the Law* (Anderson, 1996) that explores the permissible bounds of conduct within which counselors or therapists can perform their job legally. Also review the material in *The ACA Legal Series* (ACA, 1992a). This seven-volume monograph series covers a wide range of ethical and legal issues for counseling and psychotherapy. Swenson's (1997) *Psychology and the Law: For the Helping Professions* provides yet another source in aiding practitioners to achieve a balance between protecting the interests of their clients and complying with the law.

- *Guideline 6:* If the situation stems from differences between organizational and professional requirements, review the various policies and procedures that operate within your work environment. In most settings, these policies are available in printed form; you are responsible for understanding them and operating within them. If questions arise, check with your supervisor to gain appropriate clarification.

- *Guideline 7:* If the situation stems from questions of professional competence or personal issues that may negatively affect the counseling or therapeutic relationship, review the situation with a colleague or supervisor. Based upon the results of this review, either continue with the client or make an appropriate referral.

These three models are designed to help you initiate the interpretive and decision-making processes of ethical behavior. We will refer to them later in this chapter. One final note on ethical decision making. As you become familiar with the ethical codes emphasized in this chapter, please note that section H of the ACA *Code of Ethics and Standards of Practice* (1995) and section 8 of the APA *Ethical Principles of Psychologists and Code of Conduct* (1992) both deal with resolving ethical issues.

Dimensions of Ethical Behavior

Codes of ethics are composed of both general and specific categories that describe the various dimensions of ethical behavior. These categories or major topical areas establish the ethical dimensions or parameters within which members of a profession operate. A review of the two ethical codes that are the primary focus of this chapter reveals the similarities and differences within these categories or major topical areas. Each category discussed in the codes contains specific principles that not only explain and define the category, but also show the differing degrees of emphasis that the two professional groups place on the category. These differences, for the most part, are based on the fact that each code was developed to address a specific professional population. Therefore, each professional association places its emphasis on what is most appropriate for its members.

Regardless of differences in terminology and emphasis, there are also striking similarities in the two codes. Both deal with (1) counselors' and psychologists' ethical responsibilities to both the profession and to clients, (2) their integrity, (3) their respect for diversity, (4) their competence to perform stated services, (5) their attention to **clients' welfare** as it relates to relationship variables, (6) their need not to meet personal needs at clients' expense, (7) their respect for **human rights** and dignity, (8) their need to avoid **dual relationships,** (9) their respect for **clients' privacy** and confidentiality, (10) their respect for **clients' rights,** (11) their responsibility to their publics and other professionals, (12) their appropriate use of assessment and research, (13) their need for continued education and growth, (14) their willingness to confront unethical behavior in others, and (15) their willingness to adhere to their respective codes of ethics. Each of these principles carries with it behavioral directives for the counselor or therapist.

Because this book deals with theories related to individual counseling and psychotherapy, this chapter will focus on specific dimensions in the two codes that have the greatest significance to the individual counselor or psychologist in a one-to-one or **multiple-client relationship** or therapeutic relationship. These dimensions include **member responsibility, member competence,** and **member-client relationships.** Basing our decision on the language of the codes and the fact that they deal with both counselors and psychologists, we have chosen the term *member* to designate either one.

Member Responsibility

Member responsibility is central to all ethical behavior. Members are responsible for determining what ethical conduct means both philosophically and behaviorally, and for incorporating this meaning into their professional practice. Members are responsible for continually evaluating not only their own behavior but also that of their colleagues. All of the principles in the codes hold members responsible for understanding the principles and the ethical application of the intent of the principles. Even though the codes address the tenets of ethical behavior, the responsibility for putting those tenets into practice rests squarely in the hands of the member.

The breadth of members' responsibility is obvious: Each member is expected to understand and apply the behaviors outlined in the codes. This would not seem like a difficult task if the member were responsible only to self and clients. In reality, however, a member's responsibility goes beyond self and clients.

After reviewing five sets of ethical standards, Gross and Robinson (1987) discovered that members "are found to be responsible not only to the client but also to society, the community in which the service is provided, the institution which employs the counselor, the referral agency, the parents of the client, the more extended family of the client, colleagues and professional associates, state statutes which impact on counseling practices as these relate to working with minors, professional boards which set counseling policies, and self" (p. 6). The list clearly mentions a larger public to or for whom members are responsible. Even if one were to discuss major and minor degrees of responsibility or to prioritize according to "most responsible for, least responsible for," the answer as to member responsibility remains confusing.

Even more confusion results when the member works with a multiple-client system. In discussing member responsibility, Section A.8 of the ACA *Code of Ethics and Standards of Practice* (1995) states: "When counselors agree to provide counseling services to two or more persons who have a relationship (such as husband and wife, or parents and children), counselors clarify at the outset which person or persons are clients and the nature of the relationships they will have with each involved person" (p. 33).

The area of marriage and family counseling presents yet another dimension in the complex issue of member responsibility. According to Margolin (1982), "difficult ethical questions confronted in individual therapy become even more complicated when a number of family members are seen together in therapy" (p. 788). The area of **multiple-client systems** brings into play a myriad of issues that are addressed only superficially in the two sets of ethical standards that serve as the primary focus for this chapter. Even the *Ethical Code for the International Association for Marriage and Family Counselors* (IAMFC, 1993) and the *AAMFT Code of Ethics* (AAMFT, 1991) lack specificity. According to the latter, "Marriage and family therapists are dedicated to advancing the welfare of families and individuals, including respecting the rights of those persons seeking their assistance, and making reasonable efforts to ensure that their services are used appropriately" (p. 1).

How does one resolve these complex issues? Where do members turn to find the direction and guidance that will lead them through this ethical maze? To paraphrase the words of Dr. James, our hypothetical instructor in the opening scenario, helping professionals have the responsibility both to interpret and to apply the information contained in the established codes of ethics to ensure that their behaviors in the helping relationship are ethical. In other words, they must gain knowledge regarding acceptable ethical standards, develop the ability to interpret these standards in the light of the situations they face, and develop decision-making skills that will allow them to put these standards into practice. Moreover, members' responsibility does not end with an awareness of the many publics or the ability to interpret, make decisions, and apply the codes. They must also take responsibility for their own mental health to ensure that personal difficulties do not have a negative impact on clients or the helping relationship.

Although specific answers do not exist to questions surrounding member responsibility, we direct your attention to the models of ethical decision making presented earlier in this chapter. Be aware of the following considerations as you identify areas where member responsibility may be an issue:

1. Age of the clients
2. Individual versus multiple-client systems
3. Legal statutes that address member responsibilities
4. Policies and procedures of the employing agency or institution that address member responsibilities
5. Ethical standards of the profession that address member responsibilities
6. Referral sources that require member responsibility not only to the clients but also to the referral source (i.e., insurance companies, managed care)
7. Client rights that prescribe member responsibilities

When in doubt, follow the directives of the models we presented earlier in the chapter and seek answers from those who can assist you. Both the clients' interests and your professional welfare depend on your appropriate use of decision-making skills.

Member Competence

Member competence centers on the member's provision of only those services and techniques for which he or she is qualified by training or experience. Member competence is also central to all ethical behavior. In reviewing the ethical codes that serve as the main focus of this chapter, we identified such competence as encompassing five basic areas:

1. Accurately representing one's professional qualifications
2. Growing professionally through continuing education
3. Providing only those services and techniques which one is qualified to provide
4. Maintaining accurate knowledge and expertise in specialized areas
5. Seeking assistance in solving personal issues that impede effectiveness

Robinson (1991) adds to these a sixth element: "your responsibilities as counselors-in-training to learn basic skills, to integrate academic study with supervised practice, to develop self-understanding, to seek continual evaluation and appraisal, and to become intimately familiar with ethical guidelines" (p. 451).

A review of these areas and the fact that they consistently appear in statements of professional standards leads one to assume that this aspect of ethical behavior has been clearly defined and that evaluation of member competence is a relatively simple task. In reality, however, this is not the case. Ethical review boards and licensing committees spend a large percentage of their time and financial resources attempting to determine the degree of competence of the practitioner.

It is interesting to note that of the six areas defining member competence, only the first four are subject to formal review and evaluation. The fifth and sixth, which deal with the personal aspects of the member, are seemingly left to the member's discretion. If the member has personal issues that impede effectiveness or if he or she does not integrate study and practice, develop self-understanding, seek continual evaluation, or become familiar with ethical guidelines, the ethical standards recommend that the member seek assistance in resolving these issues. Such a directive seems somewhat weak when compared with the strong evaluative measures for the other areas of competence.

The concept of member competence must be viewed from both internal and external frames of reference. From an internal perspective, members do all they can to gain the skills and knowledge basic to the profession. Each member takes full responsibility for adhering to the rules and regulations of the profession that address the concepts of proper representation of professional qualifications, for providing only those services for which he or she has training and experience, and for making every effort to seek assistance with personal issues that stand in the way of providing effective service.

From an external perspective, it is important for members to realize that processes such as reviewing, evaluating, examining, and screening will continue to be handled by external forces such as licensing boards and professional groups. The best advice that can be given to members in dealing with this situation is to exercise the responsibilities and controls from an internal perspective, to develop confidence in their own degree of competence, and to be alert to the established criteria used in external evaluations. If members conscientiously attend to these aspects of competence, the end result should be positive.

Specific answers to questions surrounding competence do not exist. If questions persist, follow the directives of the models presented earlier in this chapter and seek answers from those who can assist you. The following list can also alert you to situations when member competence may be an issue:

1. Statements made in advertising your services
2. Not keeping current in your field
3. Dealing with clients' problems about which you have little education or training
4. Legal statutes dealing with required competencies
5. Ethical standards dealing with required competencies
6. Agency or institutional requirements related to required competencies
7. Personal problems that impede the effective use of competencies in the helping relationship
8. Lack of familiarity with the existing codes of ethics

Member-Client Relationships

A third central factor related to ethical behavior deals with relationship dynamics between the member and his or her clients. This is a broadly defined area and includes provision for or prohibition of such relationship variables as clients' freedom of choice; clients' accessibility regardless of ethnicity, race, religion, disability, and socioeconomic group; **confidentiality; informed consent;** dual relationships; sexual involvement; other professional relationships; and **technology.** Due to the interrelatedness of these variables, we will discuss them in terms of their applicability to the more generic term **client welfare.**

Client welfare serves as the focal point around which all codes of ethics revolve. It is present both overtly and covertly in the various sections and principles that make up the codes. It serves as the goal of the helping process, and the developers of the codes of ethics designed the codes to meet this goal through their emphasis on the maintenance and protection of the welfare of clients. Principle E of the APA *Ethical Principles of Psychologists and Code of Conduct* (1992) contains the following statement related to client welfare:

Psychologists seek to contribute to the welfare of those with whom they interact professionally. In their professional actions, psychologists weigh the welfare and rights of their patients or clients, students, supervisees, human research participants, and other affected persons, and the welfare of animal subjects of research. When conflicts occur among psychologists' obligations or concerns, they attempt to resolve these conflicts and to perform their roles in a responsible fashion that avoids or minimizes harm. (p. 4)

Whether a member is a counselor or a psychologist, the directive regarding the promotion and protection of client welfare is central to the helping relationship. To comply with this directive, the member must pay special attention to the following issues.

Freedom of Choice.   Members must recognize the need for clients to be free to choose as that choice relates to the helping relationship. Such choices include but are not limited to the following:

- Counseling or therapy as a treatment modality
- Counselor or psychologist selection
- Treatment selection
- Types of information provided by the client
- Testing procedures
- The involvement of others in the treatment process
- Length of treatment
- Access to the client's records and information
- Sharing client information with others

Under those circumstances where freedom of choice may not be possible (e.g., **involuntary treatment,** working with minors, agency or institution rules and regulations, state statutes), members must apprise clients of the restrictions that may limit their freedom of choice. For further information regarding freedom of choice, read section A.3.b ("Freedom of Choice") in the ACA *Code of Ethics and Standards of Practice* (1995), and principle D ("Respect for People's Rights and Dignity") of the general principles of the APA *Ethical Principles of Psychologists and Code of Conduct* (1992).

Client Accessibility.   Members must do all they can to ensure that the services they provide are available to all clients regardless of ethnicity, race, religion, sex, sexual orientation, disability, or socioeconomic status. If the member finds that such barriers exist within the work setting, he or she must take steps to alleviate such barriers. For further information regarding clients' accessibility, read principles D ("Respect for People's Rights and Dignity") and F ("Social Responsibility") of the general principles of the APA *Ethical Principles of Psychologists and Code of Conduct* (1992), and sections A.2.a and C.5.a ("Nondiscrimination") of the ACA *Code of Ethics and Standards of Practice* (1995).

Confidentiality.   According to Schwitzgebel and Schwitzgebel (1980), the principle of confidentiality protects clients from unauthorized disclosures of information given in confidence without their expressed consent. The concept of confidentiality has been used by professional associations to establish parameters applied to information shared by clients during the helping process.

It is important to distinguish confidentiality from **privileged communication,** which is a legal term that indicates that the client's communications cannot be disclosed in a court of law without the client's consent. This privilege belongs to the client, not the member, and under most circumstances only the client can waive the privilege. Privileged communication is usually granted by states to clients of legally certified mental health professionals such as psychologists, certified professional counselors, and certified marriage and family counselors.

Confidentiality is best viewed as a client right. Codes of ethics assure clients that the information they present in the helping relationship will not be shared with others. It is important to note that, in working with groups, confidentiality is requested, not guaranteed. Exceptions to this right do exist, as stated in section 5.05(a) ("Disclosures") in the APA *Ethical Principles of Psychologists and Code of Conduct* (1992):

> Psychologists disclose confidential information without the consent of the individual only as mandated by law, or where permitted by law for a valid purpose, such as (1) to provide needed professional services to the patient or the individual or organizational client, (2) to obtain appropriate professional consultations, (3) to protect the patient or client or others from harm, or (4) to obtain payment for services, in which instance disclosure is limited to the minimum that is necessary to achieve the purpose. (p. 10)

A statement in section B.1.c ("Exceptions") of the ACA *Code of Ethics and Standards of Practice* (1995) also addresses this issue of disclosure: "The general requirement that counselors keep information confidential does not apply when disclosure is required to prevent clear and imminent danger to the client or others or when legal requirements demand that confidential information be revealed" (p. 34).

Confidentiality has application to more than just the verbal communication between the member and clients. It also applies to client records. Section B.4.b ("Confidentiality of Records") of the ACA *Code of Ethics and Standards of Practice* (1995) states that "Counselors are responsible for securing the safety and confidentiality of any counseling records they create, maintain, transfer, or destroy whether the records are written, taped, computerized, or stored in any other medium" (p. 34). Similar statements appear in section 5.04 ("Maintenance of Records") of the APA *Ethical Principles of Psychologists and Code of Conduct* (1992).

Informed Consent.   The term *informed consent* appears in both sets of the ethical standards. Informed consent has a direct relationship to clients' freedom of choice, as discussed earlier. The choices that clients have relative to the helping process are based, first, on their being provided with all significant information relevant to the helping process, and second, on their being provided with the opportunity to agree or to consent based upon this information. Such information includes the procedures to be used in the helping relationship, the member's responsibilities, and the client's rights. Such consent may be given orally, but it is a much better practice in certain situations to have the client's written consent. According to Calfee (1997), "In most jurisdictions, this informed consent discussion does not, by law, need to be put in writing. However, wisdom would suggest otherwise" (p. 115).

In discussing the legality of informed consent, Everstine et al. (1980) propose the following three conditions that must be present for informed consent to be legal: First, the individual granting the consent must be competent to engage in rational thought; second, the individual must be supplied with all relevant information so that the consent is based in fact, not fiction; and third, the individual must give the consent voluntarily without the presence of coercion.

As with other ethical standards, there are exceptions. If the client is under the age of 18, informed consent must be secured from the parent or legal guardian. Even in such situations, however, it is suggested that consent also be secured from the client (see section 4.02 ["Informed Consent to Therapy"] in the APA *Ethical Principles of Psychologists and Code of Conduct* [1992]).

Dual Relationships.   The term *dual relationships* refers to a member's involvement with a client in a capacity other than that of a professional helper. These relationships may impair the member's judgment and his or her ability to work effectively with the client. Such relationships are found when the member has an administrative, supervisory, instructional, or evaluative relationship with an individual seeking his or her services for counseling or therapy. The codes caution against such a dual relationship and suggest referral of the individual to another professional. Only in situations where such an alternative is unavailable and where delaying counseling or therapy could be harmful to the individual should the member enter into or maintain such a relationship.

Providing counseling or therapy to one's family members or friends is another example of a dual relationship that reduces the member's ability to be objective and in turn may be harmful to a client. Such dual relationships are discouraged by the codes for obvious reasons.

For further information on this issue, read section A.6 ("Dual Relationships") in the ACA *Code of Ethics and Standards of Practice* (1995) and section 1.17 ("Multiple Relationships") in the APA *Ethical Principles of Psychologists and Code of Conduct* (1992).

Sexual Involvement.   There is strong agreement between the two sets of ethical standards under discussion in this chapter that sexual involvement with current clients or any form of sexual harassment emanating from the member is unethical. Section A.7.a ("Sexual Intimacies With Clients") in the ACA *Code of Ethics and Standards of Practice* (1995) states, "Counselors do not have any type of sexual intimacies with clients and do not counsel persons with whom they have had a sexual relationship" (p. 33). Sections 4.05 ("Sexual Intimacies With Current Patients or Clients") and 4.06 ("Therapy With Former Sexual Partners") in the APA *Ethical Principles of Psychologists and Code of Conduct* (1992) state, respectively, "Psychologists do not engage in sexual intimacies with current patients or clients" and "do not accept as therapy patients or clients persons with whom they have engaged in sexual intimacies" (p. 1605). Both codes further advise both counselors and psychologists not to engage in sexual intimacies with former clients or patients for at least two years after the termination of the professional relationship.

For information relating to sexual harassment, see section C.5.b of the ACA *Code of Ethics and Standards of Practice* (1995) and section 1.11 in the APA *Ethical Principles of Psychologists and Code of Conduct* (1992).

Other Professional Relationships.   The member may find that a client seeking his or her service is currently in another helping relationship. In such cases, the member considers the treatment issues and the client's welfare, discusses these issues with the client to reduce the risk of confusion and conflict, and, with the client's consent, consults with the other provider, where appropriate, in order to establish a cooperative and positive relationship. For further information, read sections A.4 and C.6.c ("Clients Served by Others") in the ACA *Code of Ethics and Standards of Practice* (1995), and section 4.04 ("Providing Mental Health Services to Those Served by Others") in the APA *Ethical Principles of Psychologists and Code of Conduct* (1992).

Technology.   Because computer use in the fields of counseling and psychotherapy is a growing phenomenon, it is important that members be aware of the possible impact it may have on ensuring client welfare. **Electronic data storage** of client files, assessments, and test results places such information at the disposal of any person who can tap into such data systems. The issue of confidentiality of client records is included in both codes of ethics under discussion. According to section B.4.b ("Confidentiality of Records") in the ACA *Code of Ethics and Standards of Practice* (1995), "Counselors are responsible for securing the safety and confidentiality of any counseling records they create, maintain, transfer, or destroy whether the records are written, taped, computerized, or stored in any other medium" (p. 34). Section 5.07.(a) ("Confidential Information in Databases") in the APA *Ethical Principles of Psychologists and Code of Conduct* (1992) further informs members on their responsibility to maintain confidentiality of client records.

Other Issues

Prior to completing this section on member responsibility, we will consider the area of managed care and the possible ethical dilemmas it creates for many counselors and therapists. The rapid proliferation of the **managed care industry,** together with its conditions for participation, often places members in an ethically conflicting situation. On one side of this conflict are the codes of ethics that stress members' responsibility in such areas as client confidentiality, informed consent, and **conflict of interest** as this relates to clients' welfare. On the other side are managed care companies, which often base their approval or denial of service and payment on the disclosure of client information, financial and therapeutic efficiency, **capitation** versus fee-for-service, increased paperwork, and specific criteria for preferred provider status. Ethical conflicts arise when members address such questions as the following: How much client information can I disclose without violating client confidentiality? How do I protect the client's right to informed consent and at the same time comply with the managed care company's need to know? What responsibility do I have to the client to challenge the managed care company's decision to terminate treatment, knowing that such action could endanger my preferred provider status?

Again, questions are more prevalent than answers. What is known, however, is that as more and more clients are funded through managed care systems, counselors and therapists are called upon to find an ethical balance between, on the one hand, their clients' rights to competent treatment and care, privacy, informed consent, and protection from situations that may stem from conflicts of interest, and, on the other hand, the realities and constraints of a managed care environment.

The member-client relationship is very complex, and, as with other issues addressed by the standards, guidelines—not answers—exist. The models for ethical decision making that we presented earlier in this chapter should aid you. In addition, the following client situations may help you identify areas in which the member-client relationship may be an issue:

- Clients have no choice regarding what is taking place in the helping relationship
- Clients have difficulty availing themselves of the service due to issues of ethnicity, race, religion, sex, sexual orientation, disability, or socioeconomic status
- Client information, presented in the privacy of the individual or group relationship, is known outside the relationship
- Clients are not asked either orally or in writing to agree to certain aspects of the treatment process
- Parents of clients who are under the age of 18 are not given the opportunity to consent to the treatment
- Clients are involved in relations with the member outside the professional helping relationship
- Clients are being approached sexually or are being sexually harassed by the member
- Clients are in helping relationships with other professionals who are providing the same type of service
- Client information in the electronic data storage system is not protected
- Clients' rights are compromised based upon demands and constraints of their managed care provider

Dimensions of Unethical Behavior

Any discussion of ethical behavior would be incomplete without a consideration of trends in unethical behavior. Both the ACA and the APA, through their respective ethics committees, report to their memberships both categories and frequency of ethical complaints. The following is a listing of the most frequently reported ethical complaints as reported by the ACA between 1991 and 1996 (ACA, 1992b; Garcia, Salo, & Hamilton, 1995; Garcia, Smith, & Glossoff, 1994; Salo, Forester-Miller, & Hamilton, 1996; Smith, 1993):

- Failure to maintain high standards of professional conduct
- Violation of confidentiality
- Dual relationship with clients
- Exceeding one's level of competence
- Sexual intimacies with clients
- Meeting personal needs at clients' expense
- Inaccurate representation of professional qualifications
- Discriminatory employment or educational administration practices
- Unethical research procedures

Processing of Complaints of Unethical Behavior

Most beginning counselors and therapists, and even those with several years of experience, are often confused or uninformed as to the procedures followed in the processing of complaints of unethical behavior by licensing and certification boards. Although it is difficult to address this issue with great specificity due to the myriad of state laws that affect such boards, there does seem to be a degree of similarity as to the general procedures utilized. The following steps are designed to take the reader from the initial filing of the complaint through to its final adjudication. It is important to keep in mind that "confidentiality" plays a major role in the following process. Boards—except in the presence of state laws to the contrary—treat all aspects of this adjudication process as confidential. Please read Chauvin and Remley's (1996) article "Responding to Allegations of Unethical Conduct" for a more detailed explanation of this process. According to Chauvin and Remley, the following steps should be taken:

STEP 1: Once a complaint is received by the board, it must determine if it has jurisdiction over the accused. Boards only have jurisdiction over those persons licensed, certified, or granted membership by the board. If the board lacks jurisdiction, the person filing the complaint is notified and may be given instruction about appropriate board filing.

STEP 2: If the board does have jurisdiction over the accused, then it must determine if an ethical violation has occurred based upon the complainant's written statement. If the board determines that an ethical violation has not occurred, all parties are notified and the complaint is dismissed.

STEP 3: If the board determines that an ethical violation has occurred, it may institute an investigation. The accused will be notified prior to the investigation unless such notification would jeopardize the board's investigation.

STEP 4: Upon notification, the accused is provided an opportunity to present his or her side of the story in writing to the board.

STEP 5: A hearing may be held at this point, or the board may make a decision based upon the written documentation from all involved parties. If a hearing is held, the complainant, witnesses, and the accused are given an opportunity to present their cases and are questioned by board members or by delegates appointed by the board.

STEP 6: At the conclusion of the hearing, the board, acting as a jury, makes a decision regarding the complaint. If no violation has occurred, the charges are dismissed and the record of the accused is cleared. If it is determined that a violation has occurred, the board may impose sanctions ranging from a reprimand to revocation of the license or certification.

STEP 7: If the decision is in favor of the complainant, an appeal process to the board is available to the accused.

STEP 8: If the appeal process fails to bring the desired results, the accused may sue the board in court to seek a reversal of the earlier decision.

Legal Issues

Legal issues have become a major concern for today's practitioner. They are closely allied with issues of ethical behavior already discussed in this chapter. According to Brown and Srebalus (1988):

> Twenty-five years ago this chapter would have been unnecessary. Today, legal concerns stand as one of the most serious issues confronting counselors. The dramatic rise in the importance attached to legal concerns can be attributed to two factors: the status of the counseling professional and the "legalizing" of American society. Even the most casual observer of current news events is aware that civil liability is of great concern to professionals, corporations, municipalities, and private citizens. This is primarily because juries have awarded increasingly larger sums of money to plaintiffs when physicians, psychologists, or others have been found liable for damages in malpractice cases. (p. 210)

Regarding the developing importance of legal issues for the practitioner, Robinson (1991) stated, "Because the relationship between a counselor and a client is a fiduciary relationship, one which fosters great trust and confidence, the legal system becomes involved when this trust is violated and the client does not receive what he or she believes is a reasonable standard of care" (p. 465).

These two statements show an intensified emphasis on the part of practitioners to be aware of the legal ramifications of their behaviors. Because of the complexity of state laws, it is difficult to discuss such ramifications with great specificity. The information that follows was selected, not because it encompasses all of the areas in which legal issues play a part, but because it is representative of the growing impact that legal interpretations have on professional practice. We present information about the following topics: duty to warn and due care.

Duty to Warn

According to the codes of ethics, counselors and psychologists have a duty to maintain confidentiality and not to disclose matters unless there is clear and imminent danger to clients or others, or if they are required to do so by law. It is the second part of this statement that speaks directly to the concept of **duty to warn.** *Tarasoff v. Regents of the University of California* (1976) is perhaps the most well-known example. In this situation, legal action was taken regarding the responsibility of a university psychologist to warn the Tarasoff family regarding the possible actions of Prosenjit Poddar, a client at the University of California Hospital. The client informed the psychologist that he planned to kill an unnamed girl, readily identifiable as Tatiana Tarasoff, when she returned home after spending the summer in South America. The psychologist informed the university police department and requested that the client be detained. The client was taken into custody but was soon released after he promised to stay away from Ms. Tarasoff. Shortly after her return from South America, the client went to her home and killed her. Her parents brought suit against the university regents, the police, and doctors in the university hospital, charging that they had not been warned of the danger.

The lower court decided in favor of the defendants. Following that decision, the Tarasoff family filed an appeal, and the Supreme Court of California reversed the judgment and found the defendants guilty of negligence. The state supreme court held that "once a therapist does in fact determine, or under applicable professional standards reasonably should have determined, that a patient poses a serious danger of violence to others, he bears a duty to exercise reasonable care to protect the foreseeable victims of that danger" (*Tarasoff v. Regents,* 1976).

We agree with Corey et al. (1993), Pope and Vetter (1992), and Robinson-Kurpius and Gross (1996) when they advise practitioners, through the use of informed consent forms, to tell clients before the beginning of the helping relationship that confidentiality does not exist in certain situations. The clients are then able to make informed decisions regarding the type of information they are willing to share. We also recommend that practitioners inform clients of the action that they will be taking, in order to protect clients and others before taking the action. This step tries to involve clients as much as possible in the process.

Due Care

Because of the special relationship that exists between practitioners and clients, members must do everything within their power to place the care of the clients foremost on their list of priorities. This demonstration of care is exemplified in the provision of skilled services and treatment and by not placing the clients in compromising situations that will either detract from the treatment or cause physical or psychological harm to the clients. The concept of **due care** is inherent in the various standards of the codes of ethics, and it serves as a major directive governing the ethical behavior of members.

A legal interpretation of the principle of due care is exemplified in the case of *Roy v. Hartogs* (1975). Client Julie Roy sought damages through a malpractice suit from her therapist, Dr. Hartogs, claiming she had experienced deleterious effects from a sexual relationship lasting several months that had developed between the two during therapy. In defending himself, Dr. Hartogs claimed that their sexual relationship had nothing to do with the therapeutic process. He said it was outside their professional relationship; therefore, he was not guilty of malpractice. The court, in deciding the case, ruled in favor of Ms. Roy and gave the opinion that Dr. Hartogs had not used due care in his professional relationship with the client.

Van Hoose and Kottler (1985), in discussing due care as it relates to the helping relationship, have this advice for the practitioner: "The courts seem to be saying to the helping professions that close relationships involving trust and mutual caring between therapist and client are understood and are, in fact, necessary for effective treatment. Such intimacies are permitted as long as the therapist does not use the relationship for personal advantage and as long as he maintains due regard for professional propriety and community conscience" (pp. 55–56).

Most areas of counseling and psychotherapy have witnessed the involvement of the law and its interpretation as they relate to ethical practice. Legislation such as P.L. 94-142, the Education for All Handicapped Children Act, and P.L. 93-380, the Family Educational Rights and Privacy Act, both of which were passed in the 1970s, are further examples of this involvement. The decision-making models mentioned earlier in this chapter may help you make decisions about legal issues as well.

Conclusions

This chapter has discussed the ethical and legal aspects that affect the helping relationship through its presentation of the definition and rationale of ethical codes, models for ethical decision making, dimensions of ethical behavior, dimensions of unethical behavior, and procedures utilized in the processing of complaints of unethical behavior. It has addressed the complexity of the issues involved and provided the reader with models and guidelines, not answers. Dr. James, the professor in the opening scenario, may wish to offer her students the models for ethical decision making as well as the information that follows, which should aid them in the difficult process of ethical interpretation and decision making:

- *Ethical standards of the profession.* Review the ethical standards of your professional group to determine if the responsibility issue in question is addressed and if guidelines and directives exist. If not, review codes of ethics of professional groups that may deal more specifically with the special situation you face. Review the *Ethical Standards Casebook* (Herlihy & Corey, 1996), which was designed to clarify the intent of the ACA's *Code of Ethics and Standards of Practice* (1995). Review the APA's *Casebook of Ethical Principles of Psychologists* (1987). It might also be helpful to review the ACA's *Policies and Procedures for Processing Complaints of Ethical Violations* (1994). If you cannot find satisfactory answers, talk with colleagues and ask them for assistance in both interpretation and decision making. In the last analysis, the decision must be yours, but make that decision only after you have investigated all possible sources of information.

- *Legal statutes.* Become familiar with the legal statutes that have implications for counseling and therapy, not only for your state but also from a national perspective. Talk with members of the legal profession who have expertise in the area of member-client rights. Review the material presented in *The Counselor and the Law* (Anderson, 1996), which explores the bounds of conduct within which counselors and therapists can perform their job legally; *The ACA Legal Series* (ACA, 1992a), which covers a wide range of ethical and legal issues; and *Psychology and Law: For the Helping Professionals* (Swenson, 1997).

- *Agency's or institution's policies and procedures.* Be knowledgeable about the various policies and procedures that operate within your work environment. They are usually available in printed form, and it is your responsibility to understand them and operate within them. If questions arise, please check with your supervisor for clarification.

Even though Dr. James's hypothetical students do not have the specific answers they had hoped for, the information, models, guidelines, directives, and situations in this chapter should enable them to enter the professions of counseling and psychotherapy feeling more assured of their ability to make informed and intelligent ethical decisions.

References

Allen, V. B. (1986). A historical perspective of the AACD Ethics Committee. *Journal of Counseling and Development, 64*(5), 293.

American Association for Marriage and Family Therapy. (1991). *AAMFT code of ethics.* Washington, DC: Author.

American Counseling Association. (1992a). *ACA legal series* (T. Remley, Ed.). Alexandria, VA: Author.

American Counseling Association. (1992b). Report of the ACA Ethics Committee: 1991–1992. *Journal of Counseling and Development, 71*(2), 252–253.

American Counseling Association. (1994). *Policies and procedures for processing complaints of ethical violations.* Alexandria, VA: Author.

American Counseling Association. (1995). *Code of ethics and standards of practice.* Alexandria, VA: Author.

American Mental Health Counselors Association. (1987). *Code of ethics for mental health counselors.* Alexandria, VA: Author.

American Psychological Association. (1987). *Casebook of ethical principles of psychologists.* Washington, DC: Author.

American Psychological Association. (1992). Ethical principles of psychologists and code of conduct. *American Psychologist, 47*(12), 1597–1611.

American School Counselors Association. (1992). *Ethical standards for school counselors.* Washington, DC: Author.

Anderson, B. S. (1996). *The counselor and the law* (4th ed.). Alexandria, VA: ACA Press.

Association for Specialists in Group Work. (1989). *Ethical guidelines for group counselors.* Alexandria, VA: Author.

Association of Counselor Educators and Supervisors. (1993). *Ethical guidelines for counseling supervisors.* Alexandria, VA: Author.

Brown, D., & Srebalus, D. J. (1988). *An introduction to the counseling profession.* Upper Saddle River, NJ: Prentice Hall.

Calfee, B. E. (1997). Lawsuit prevention techniques. In *The Hatherleigh guide to ethics in therapy* (pp. 109–125). New York: Hatherleigh Press.

Chauvin, J., & Remley, T. P., Jr. (1996). Responding to allegations of unethical conduct. *Journal of Counseling and Development, 74*(6), 563–568.

Corey, G., Corey, M. S., & Callanan, P. (1993). *Issues and ethics in the helping professions* (4th ed.). Monterey, CA: Brooks/Cole.

Everstine, L., Everstine, D. S., Heymann, G. M., True, R. H., Frey, D. H., Johnson, H. G., & Seiden, R. H. (1980). Privacy and confidentiality in psychotherapy. *American Psychologist, 35*(9), 828–840.

Forester-Miller, H., & Davis, T. E. (1996). *A practitioner's guide to ethical decision making.* Alexandria, VA: American Counseling Association.

Garcia, J., Salo, M., & Hamilton, W. M. (1995). Report of the ACA Ethics Committee: 1994–1995. *Journal of Counseling and Development, 74*(2), 221–224.

Garcia, J., Smith, J., & Glossoff, H. (1994). Report of the ACA Ethics Committee: 1993–1994. *Journal of Counseling and Development, 73*(2), 253–256.

Gibson, W. T., & Pope, K. S. (1993). The ethics of counseling: A national survey of certified counselors. *Journal of Counseling and Development, 71*(3), 330–336.

Gross, D. R., & Robinson, S. E. (1987). Ethics in counseling: A multiple role perspective. *TACD Journal, 15*(1), 5–16.

Herlihy, B., & Corey, G. (1996). *Ethical standards casebook* (5th ed.). Alexandria, VA: ACA Press.

Huber, C. H. (1994). *Ethical, legal, and professional issues in the practice of marriage and family therapy* (2nd ed.). Upper Saddle River, NJ: Merrill/Prentice Hall.

Ibrahim, F. A., & Arredondo, P. M. (1990). Ethical issues in multicultural counseling. In B. Herlihy & L. B. Golden (Eds.), *Ethical standards casebook* (4th ed.) (pp. 137–145). Alexandria, VA: ACA Press.

International Association for Marriage and Family Counselors. (1993). *Ethical code for the International Association for Marriage and Family Counselors.* Alexandria, VA: Author.

Kitchener, K. S. (1984). Intuition, critical evaluation, and ethical principles: The foundation for ethical decisions in counseling psychology. *Counseling Psychologist, 12*(3), 43–55.

Kitchener, K. S. (1986). Teaching applied ethics in counselor education: An integration of psychological processes and philosophical analysis. *Journal of Counseling and Development, 64*(5), 306–310.

Margolin, G. (1982). Ethical and legal considerations in marital and family therapy. *American Psychologist, 37*, 788–801.

National Board of Certified Counselors. (1989). *Code of ethics.* Alexandria, VA: Author.

Pope, K. S., & Vetter, V. A. (1992). Ethical dilemmas encountered by members of the American Psychological Association. *American Psychologist, 47*, 397–411.

Robinson, S. E. (1991). Ethical and legal issues related to counseling: Or it's not as easy as it looks. In D. Capuzzi & D. Gross (Eds.), *Introduction to counseling: Perspectives for the 1990s* (pp. 445–468). Boston: Allyn & Bacon.

Robinson-Kurpius, S. E. (1997). Ethical and legal considerations in counseling: What beginning counselors should know. In D. Capuzzi & D. Gross (Eds.), *Introduction to counseling* (2nd ed.) (pp. 85–101). Boston: Allyn & Bacon.

Robinson-Kurpius, S. E., & Gross, D. R. (1996). Professional ethics and the mental health counselor. In W. J. Weikel and A. J. Palmo (Eds.), *Foundations of mental health counseling* (2nd ed.) (pp. 353–377). Springfield, IL: Charles C Thomas.

Roy v. Hartogs, 366 N.Y. S.2d 297 (1975).

Salo, M., Forester-Miller, H., & Hamilton, M. W. (1996). Report of the ACA Ethics Committee: 1995–1996. *Journal of Counseling and Development, 75*(2), 174–176.

Schwitzgebel, R. L., & Schwitzgebel, R. K. (1980). *Law and psychological practice.* New York: Wiley.

Smith, J. (1993). Report of the ACA Ethics Committee: 1992–1993. *Journal of Counseling and Development, 72*(2), 220–222.

Swenson, L. (1997). *Psychology and law: For the helping professions* (2nd ed.). Pacific Grove, CA: Brooks/Cole.

Tarasoff v. Regents of the University of California, 551, Cal. P.2d 334 (1976).

Van Hoose, W. H., & Kottler, J. A. (1985). *Ethical and legal issues in counseling and psychotherapy* (2nd ed.). San Francisco: Jossey-Bass.

Theories of Counseling and Psychotherapy

In Part I of this text we examined three basic areas that are significant to the individual counseling process and to the person of the counselor or therapist. We discussed the helping relationship, the issues surrounding the counselor's or therapist's personal and professional identity, and ethical and legal issues. We believe that this foundation was necessary before introducing you to the theories of counseling and psychotherapy that are the subject of Part II.

Part II contains nine chapters, each of which addresses a selected theoretical system that has direct application to the counseling or therapy process. We selected these particular theoretical systems because of their current use in the field, and we chose the chapter authors based upon their expertise and their current application of the theoretical system in their work with clients. To provide the reader with a consistent format, each chapter contains information dealing with the following areas:

- *Background.* Historical information related to the development of the theoretical system and the individual(s) responsible for its development.
- *Human nature: A developmental perspective.* The process of individual development over time, as defined by the theoretical system.
- *Major constructs.* The structural components that comprise the theoretical system.
- *Applications.* This section of each chapter includes the following subsections:

    Overview. An introduction to the three areas that follow.

    Goals of counseling and psychotherapy. A description of desired client outcomes based upon the tenets of the theory.

    The process of change. The factors within the theory that address what brings about change in the individual.

    Intervention strategies. Techniques for implementing the process of change.

- *Evaluation.* This section of each chapter includes the following subsections:

    Overview. An introduction to the three areas that follow.

    Supporting research. Current research studies that form the bases for continued use of the theoretical system.

    Limitations. A description of the factors that limit the use of this theoretical system with clients and types of presenting problems.

    Summary chart. A chart that summarizes the information in the chapter.

- *Case study.* The application of the theoretical system to the development of a treatment or counseling plan for a client. The same case study information was used by all authors.

The first three chapters in Part II deal with the theoretical systems, often classified as *analytical,* which were developed by Freud, Jung, and Adler. Chapter 4, "Psychoanalytic Theory," provides background information relative to counseling and psychotherapy within a psychoanalytic framework and emphasizes current use of this framework for individual counseling and psychotherapy. Chapter 5, "Jungian Analytical Theory," takes the reader from the development and definition of the major constructs of Jungian psychology to their application in the case of Maria, the subject of our hypothetical case study. We think readers will find this journey both intriguing and enlightening. Chapter 6, "Adlerian Theory," highlights the contributions of Alfred Adler and demonstrates the application of his major constructs in current approaches to counseling and psychotherapy.

Chapter 7, "Existential Theory," sets forth the philosophical underpinnings of existential counseling and psychotherapy and demonstrates how this philosophy translates into approaches that can be used by the counselor or therapist in working with clients. Chapter 8, "Person-Centered Theory," deals specifically with the work of Carl Rogers and highlights the continual development of this theoretical system from Rogers's work in the early 1940s to the last years of his life, when he traveled to the most troubled places in the world and used his person-centered approach to promote peace among warring groups. Chapter 9 discusses "Feminist Theory," which has evolved gradually over time as a response to women's rejection of traditional psychotherapies. This chapter addresses some of the sexist, oppressive aspects of many of the currently used theories of counseling and psychotherapy and encourages counselors and therapists not to apply theories based on male developmental models to women. Chapter 10, "Gestalt Theory," emphasizes the pioneering work of Frederick Perls and his development of Gestalt counseling and psychotherapy. Major concepts and interventions are presented in combination with their current use in counseling and psychotherapy.

The final two chapters in Part II deal with the theoretical systems, often classified as *behavioral* or *cognitive-behavioral,* which were developed by Ellis, Beck, Meichenbaum, and Glasser. Chapter 11, "Cognitive-Behavioral Theories," provides the reader with a general background about the behavioral and cognitive-behavioral theoretical views and discusses how the cognitive-behavioral approach developed from the behavioral point of view. Emphasis is given to the work of Albert Ellis, Aaron Beck, and Donald Meichenbaum. Chapter 12, "Reality Therapy Theory," highlights the work of William Glasser and places special emphasis on a system he developed to provide a delivery system for reality therapy in helping clients remediate deficiencies, make better choices, and become more fully self-actualized.

We think that the theoretical systems discussed here provide the reader with a comprehensive and current review of major counseling and psychotherapy approaches to working with individuals. Our conviction is strengthened by our selection of authors, who not only have expertise in the specific theoretical systems, but also practice these approaches in working with clients.

We asked each author or set of authors to address the following case study information in the development of a treatment or counseling plan that is consistent with the theoretical system. This approach gives readers the opportunity to view the theoretical systems from a comparative perspective as they search for the theoretical system that is most appropriate for their future work as counselors or therapists.

The Case of Maria

Client Demographics

The client, Maria, is a 32-year-old Hispanic female. The oldest of five children, she was raised in a culturally encapsulated Hispanic neighborhood in a large metropolitan area in the Southwest. She attended Catholic schools, and religion remains a very significant part of her life. She is a single parent raising two children: a 6-year-old son and an 8-year-old daughter. Maria, who is bilingual, graduated from college with honors, has a degree in education, and for the past four years has taught math and science in a middle school. She and her husband of five years divorced three years ago. She receives no financial assistance from her ex-husband, and the only knowledge the children have of their father is through communication with their paternal grandparents.

Presenting Problem

Accompanied by her children, Maria arrived 15 minutes early for her initial appointment. She related easily and expressed herself well, but her body appeared tense and her voice was strained. She expressed appreciation for getting an early appointment because she felt that she could not have waited much longer. Maria had been referred to the mental health agency by her physician because of insomnia and frequent unexplained crying spells. During the intake process she stated that she was depressed, unable to sleep because of recurring nightmares, not eating, losing control of her children, and having difficulty dealing with family members. She said that she has thought about suicide but feels guilty at the prospect of abandoning her children. She has difficulty concentrating, and this is having a negative impact on her teaching. She has frequently been absent from work, and her principal is recommending that she take a leave of absence. This situation is causing her great distress, as she needs the income to support her children and would be forced to move back to live with her family if she left her teaching position. She is unable to maintain meaningful relationships with various males she has been dating, and views her future very negatively.

Family Background

During the intake process, Maria described her family of origin as very close-knit, held together by both cultural and religious values. She was raised to be proud of her Hispanic heritage, her language, and her culture's traditions. She has three younger brothers and one younger sister, all of whom looked to her for advice and support while growing up. Education was stressed in her home, and her academic success brought much pride to the family. She was touted as a model to her siblings and was expected to perform in an exemplary way not only in school but also in other aspects of her life.

Maria's parents were self-educated and operated a small business near their home. Because the business demanded a large time commitment from both parents, during her adolescence Maria often found herself taking care of both the house and her siblings. Most of the family activities centered around their local parish and special events generated in the community. Maria's social life was very much tied to her immediate family and to contacts she made at either the Catholic school or church youth groups. She was encouraged to bring her friends to her home and to date young men within the community. Cultural pride and the parameters of the local Hispanic community affected much of her formative development.

Early Adult Years

Maria's first true exposure to other cultures came upon her leaving home to attend a state university. She had received scholarships from two of the state's three universities, and even though her parents wanted her to stay at home and attend a local university, she decided to attend a school approximately 200 miles from home. Her decision caused conflict within her family, and she reported that it strained her relationships with both parents. Her sister supported her actions, but her brothers felt that she was abandoning the family.

Maria was very successful at the university, and it was there that she met Mark, her future husband, who was the first person she had ever dated outside of her religion and culture. Mark was a student in the college of engineering, caucasian, and seemed to have no specific religious affiliation. It wasn't until their graduation that Maria introduced Mark to her family and at the same time announced their plans to be married.

Maria's family, with the exception of her sister, was deeply opposed to the marriage and made their opposition known not only to Maria, but also to Mark. Maria and Mark also received opposition from his parents. In order to avoid further confrontations, they eloped and were married by a justice of the peace in another state.

After their marriage they returned to their home area, secured jobs, and began to build a life together. It was not until after their first child was born that contact with both families was renewed. By the time their second child was born, both families were much more involved with both their children and their grandchildren.

The second child put a strain on the marriage, and within two years, Maria and Mark separated. They were divorced a year later. Mark left the state and has had no contact with his children in two years. The paternal grandparents do, however, continue to have contact with their grandchildren.

Post-Divorce Years

Since the divorce three years ago, Maria has been able to discuss the physical and psychological abuse that she received from Mark. He became physically abusive when drinking, and he constantly demeaned both her profession and her culture. He withdrew from Maria and the children and spent more and more time away from home. Turning to her family for support, Maria met with indifference and reminders of their opposition to the marriage. Her sister, once supportive, now blames Maria for a great deal of the disunity within the family. Mark's parents refuse to believe that he was abusive and are very critical of the manner in which Maria is raising their grandchildren.

With the lack of support from her family, Maria turned to friends for help. One friend suggested that Maria needed to date and get "back into circulation." She found that she had difficulty relating to men, was afraid to trust, and felt that all they wanted was sex. She felt that when they found out she had two children, the relationships cooled down rapidly.

She turned next to her work and poured all of her energy into her students. This left very little for her own children, and the mother-child relationships grew very strained. It was at this time that she began to have disturbing dreams that kept her from sleeping. Maria offered the following description:

> I am always running, and there are shadowy figures behind me. I am in a large warehouse-type structure with lots of boxes and crates. The boxes and crates are all marked with arrows reading "Exit." The problem is that the arrows are all going in different directions. Therefore, I never find the exit, and the figures keep getting closer and closer. I wake up in a cold sweat, breathing rapidly, heart pounding, and a scream stuck in my throat. I lie there trying to calm down, knowing that I am too afraid to go back to sleep. In a little while I get up and spend the rest of the night sitting at the kitchen table drinking coffee.

The more often the dreams occurred, the more depressed Maria became. She fought sleep because of her fear of dreaming, and at times she found herself crying uncontrollably. Her eating habits have also changed drastically, and she finds herself buying fast food for the children so that she won't have to cook. She seldom eats and has lost 15 pounds—weight she can't afford to lose.

The depression has kept her away from work and away from people. She began spending more and more time alone. In Maria's words, "I have nothing to live for. No one cares about me. I've ruined my life and the lives of two families, and I'm currently hurting my children." Upon the advice of her priest, she sought the help of her physician, who recommended that she seek psychological help.

Psychoanalytic Theory

Gregory J. Novie
Southwest Center for Psychoanalytic Studies
Phoenix, Arizona

Leonard R. Corte
Southwest Center for Psychoanalytic Studies
Phoenix, Arizona

This chapter provides a brief outline of psychoanalytic theory and technique. It has been written for the beginning clinician and is intended as an introduction to a complex psychotherapeutic process. Its goal is to interest the student in further exploring psychoanalysis as a treatment option.

Beginning with the work of Sigmund Freud, the chapter reviews a history of psychoanalysis and then divides and presents the psychoanalytic movement from the perspective of three historical periods. The first period is dominated by Freud and covers his early work through the end of World War I. The second period, which follows the end of World War I, is dominated by the establishment of training institutions and the emergence of the American Psychoanalytic Association. The third period begins with the end of World War II, continues into the present, and deals with the expansion of psychoanalysis worldwide.

Building on this historical background, the chapter presents a developmental perspective of human nature that emphasizes unconscious dynamics and the processes involved in change. These dynamics include psychic determinism or causality, consciousness as an exceptional rather than a regular attribute of the psychic process, displacement, condensation, psychosexual stages, and defense mechanisms. The developmental theory espoused by Freud is used to explain not only the etiology of human behavior but also the etiology of human neuroses and psychoses. This developmental perspective both explains client dynamics and provides a framework for the intervention strategies used by the counselor or therapist.

Material from Maria's case study is woven into an explanation of theoretical concepts, and we have invented a session involving dream material in order to demonstrate a clinical application of psychoanalytic theory and technique. The chapter also includes a discussion of the limitations of the psychoanalytic approach and a summary of the significant material presented.

Background

The history of psychoanalysis begins with **Sigmund Freud** (1856–1939). Freud had collaborated with his mentor, Josef Breuer, to write the first psychoanalytic paper, *Studies in Hysteria,* in 1895. This paper was about the "founding case" (Gay, 1988, p. 63) of psychoanalysis, a patient referred to as Anna O. Before Freud, the field of psychology was considered a speculative philosophy on one hand and an empirical study of psychophysiological processes on the other, and the study of the human mind was limited to religious and magical thought. With psychoanalysis, psychology took a definite first step in the direction of scientific thinking about human motivation. As Fenichel (1945) observed, "An understanding of the multiplicity of everyday human mental life, based on natural science, really began only with psychoanalysis" (p. 4).

Fine (1979) divides the history of psychoanalysis into three periods. The first period is dominated by Freud and covers his early work through the end of World War I. During this period Freud drew adherents to his cause, many of whom became the early pioneers of the psychoanalytic movement. The context of Western European and Viennese society during this period involved strict social norms and mores regarding sexuality. In such a Victorian setting, sexuality—and particularly female sexuality—was permitted very limited expression. It was the blocking or **repression** of such sexuality that led to Freud's (and Breuer's) conception of hysteria. In hysteria, patients presented vague complaints of paralysis and pain without organic causes—the present-day psychosomatic disorders. The first psychoanalytic society was formed in Vienna after the turn of the century; a few years later, as psychoanalysis gained recognition, the International Psychoanalytical Association was founded. This period led to the emergence of psychoanalysis, which has since evolved into a dynamic psychology and a philosophy of great cultural importance.

The second period, which dates from 1918 to 1939, was dominated by the establishment of training institutions and the emergence of the American Psychoanalytic Association. With the organization of many new psychoanalytic societies in democratic countries, specific regulations were adopted for the training of psychoanalysts. The training system that is now almost universally standard involves a tripartite model, the foundation of which includes the candidate's personal analysis. "It may be assumed that since about 1930 every practicing analyst has been through a training analysis" (Fine, 1979, p. 3). The training also includes theoretical instruction that lasts about four years and control analyses in which the candidate in training is supervised in the conduct of several analyses. Candidates are typically drawn from the mental health professions, especially in the United States, which has the largest membership of psychoanalysts belonging to the International Psychoanalytical Association. The significance of this second historical period is marked by not only the proliferation of psychoanalytic education worldwide, but also by the expansion of psychoanalytic thought through the creation of a sizable body of scientific literature. Such literature typically utilizes the case study method of one or a few patients.

The third period begins with the end of World War II and continues into the present. This period is marked by the further expansion of psychoanalysis worldwide. The 1992–93 roster of the International Psychoanalytical Association lists 8,197 members, 45 component and provisional societies, and one regional society (the American Psychoanalytic Association). The roster includes 18 societies in Europe, 16 in Latin America, 3 in the Middle and Far East, 1 in Australia, and 8 in North America. This third historical period is also marked by the expansion of psychoanalytic theory beyond classical Freudian metapsychology. Pine (1985) enumerates four distinct psychoanalytic psychologies that have developed within psychoanalytic metapsychology: Freud's **drive theory,** and the newer theories of **ego, object relations,** and **self psychology.**

Recent developments in American health care are also affecting the perception of modern psychoanalysis. The contemporary psychotherapeutic scene has been greatly influenced by modern health care marketing. Rising health care costs have engendered the development and promotion of a variety of abbreviated psychotherapeutic strategies. Managed care programs such as health maintenance organizations, preferred provider agreements, and employee assistance programs typically rely on interventions designed to keep costs to a minimum. Accordingly, the field of psychotherapy has become a veritable "convenience market" in which reducing the total number of contacts between the counselor or therapist and the client is a priority. Similarly, the choices available to persons who decide to get help are limited by the health care option to which they subscribe. It is not surprising, therefore, that a precise definition of psychotherapy has been further obscured by rapidly expanding methods designed to limit costs. Wolberg (1977) lists no fewer than 36 definitions that "generally do not agree on the techniques employed, the process included, the goals approximated or the personnel involved" (p. 14).

Amidst these "innovations," psychoanalysis has lost favor as a treatment option, except perhaps in a few urban areas. Because it is recognized as a depth psychology, and because the analytic method involves multiple weekly sessions over an extended period of time, it has little short-term economic advantage in the contemporary marketplace of managed health care. Nevertheless, despite the predicted demise of psychoanalysis, new training institutes continue to form in major metropolitan areas, indicating a continued interest in psychoanalysis on the part of professional counselors and therapists. In part, this may be the result of dedication to a dynamic theory and method that seeks to understand and change psychopathology as well as the forces operative in the therapeutic process. It may also reflect counselors' and therapists' dissatisfaction with technique-oriented strategies and their wish to increase the use of self as a tool in the therapeutic process. (Personal analysis is a requirement for psychoanalytic training.)

What distinguishes psychoanalysis as a psychotherapeutic theory and method? Wolberg (1977) divides the varieties of psychotherapy into three main groups: **supportive therapy, reeducative therapy,** and **reconstructive therapy.** His schema depicts a gradation from lesser to greater complexity in the perceived objectives of each therapeutic strategy. For example, whereas in supportive therapy the object "is to bring the patient to an emotional equilibrium as rapidly as possible" (p. 68), reeducative therapy attempts to achieve more extensive goals through an "actual remodeling of the patient's attitudes and behavior in line with more adaptive life integration" (p. 101). The difference is in the specific therapeutic technique employed. In supportive strategies, reassurance, suggestion, relaxation, and persuasion may be used. In contrast, reeducative approaches rely more on reconditioning. The counselor or therapist introduces behavioral reinforcers or the therapeutic relationship (approval/disapproval) to modify, liberate, or promote self-growth.

The objectives of reconstructive therapies offer the greatest complexity. The goal of reconstructive psychotherapy is to bring the client to an awareness of crucial unconscious conflicts, their derivatives, and how these limit his or her daily life. In contrast, supportive efforts toward this kind of insight are minimal, and the reeducative emphasis is less on searching for unconscious causes than on promoting new and better forms of conscious behavior through conscious action. Counselors or therapists who direct their efforts toward reconstructive changes within the client have typically turned toward psychoanalytic methods and theories because of their emphasis on bringing unconscious conflicts to awareness.

Human Nature: A Developmental Perspective

The Freudian Unconscious

In the late nineteenth century, medically oriented approaches assumed that neuroses were caused by some unknown organic factor, and therapeutic measures were limited to electric shock and hypnotism (Fine, 1979). Freud isolated himself from this mainstream position, as Fine observes, and in the process made his first major discovery: "The key to neuroses lies in psychology, and all neuroses involve a defense against unbearable ideas" (1979, pp. 21–25). In an attempt to understand clinical data, Freud arrived at two fundamental hypotheses concerning mental development and functioning, hypotheses that can apply to normal as well as pathological activity. According to Brenner (1974), these two hypotheses, "which have been abundantly confirmed, are the principle of psychic determinism or causality, and the proposition that consciousness is an exceptional rather than a regular attribute of psychic processes" (p. 2).

According to the first principle, **psychic determinism,** mental activity is not meaningless or accidental; nothing in the mind happens by chance or in a random way, and all mental phenomena have a causal connection to the psychic events that precede them. An example of this principle can be drawn from the case study of Maria. The presenting information and the client's childhood history are organized in such a way as to develop a context of continuity between early psychic experiences and the symptoms we assume to be a consequence of these experiences. We ask ourselves, "What caused this?" and we organize our data around this question because we are confident that a coherent answer exists that is connected to the rest of the client's psychic life. We assume that each neurotic symptom is caused by other mental processes. For example, Maria complains of insomnia and difficulty concentrating and perhaps feels these are signs of some spiritual problem; hence her first effort at seeking help is with her priest. As counselors or therapists, however, we presume that there are psychological causes outside of the client's conscious awareness.

Freud first noted the principle of psychic determinism in relation to dreams. He discovered that "each dream, indeed each image in each dream, is the consequence of other psychic events, and each stands in coherent and meaningful relationship to the rest of the dreamer's psychic life" (Brenner, 1974, p. 3). This principle contrasts with the notion that dreams are products of random brain activity during sleep, an idea popularly held by neurologists and psychiatrists seventy years ago and by some organic theorists today.

The second principle, that of **unconscious mental processes,** is closely linked to the first. This principle accounts for the apparent discontinuities in the client's perception of symptom and cause, for the causal connection has become part of the unconscious process. In the case study, Maria has repressed her mental conflicts into the unconscious, thereby causing her symptoms. It follows, then, that if the unconscious cause or causes can be discovered through the therapeutic process, the causal sequence becomes clear and the client's insight leads to cure. It should be noted that this brief explanation is a rather simplified version of what in actuality is a long and complex treatment process in which the client examines through free association a variety of unconscious mental processes. This simplified explanation also ignores the role of interpersonal influence— that of the client-therapist relationship—as a mutative factor in psychoanalysis.

Freud (1938/1940) argued that "the governing rules of logic carry no weight in the unconscious; it might be called the Realm of the illogical" (pp. 168–169). He also declared: "We have found that processes in the unconscious or in the Id obey different laws from those in the preconscious ego. We name these laws in their totality the primary process, in contrast to the secondary process, which governs the course of events in the preconscious ego" (p. 164). In other words, Freud called attention to the fact that a portion of the mind, which is particularly active in our dreams, our emotional life, and our childhood, works within a framework of timelessness, spacelessness, and the coexistence of opposites. For example, timelessness is implied in our clinical work when we take for granted the simultaneous presence of an adult client and his or her expressions of infancy. Freud's notions of **displacement** (an idea's emotional emphasis becomes detached from it and is superimposed on some other ideas) and **condensation** (several ideas are expressed through a single idea) exemplify spacelessness. We recognize in clinical work that feelings expressed toward an uncaring employer may be an unconscious replication of childhood feelings felt toward a parent in the past or toward the counselor or therapist in the present. These feelings are displaced onto the employer as a defense against a painful memory or onto the counselor or therapist against the threat of awareness. Displacement is essentially a disconnecting of some feeling toward someone and a reconnecting of it to someone else (who had nothing to do with the original feeling), without being aware of it. Usually we displace such affect onto people who bear some resemblance to the original person. For example, if a man goes through a bitter divorce, he may displace onto the next woman he dates the resentment he feels toward his ex-wife.

Condensation is a more difficult and abstract concept. Think of it as a mosaic in which many parts are put together in a disorganized way, so that the end product becomes an amalgam of images, shapes, and colors. The mechanism of condensation is the mind's way of unconsciously keeping from awareness disturbing affects and thoughts by rendering them confusing and distorted. It is perhaps similar to an abstract artwork in which the themes depicted by the author are blended together in a strange and logic-defying way. Freud and his followers identified a number of defensive strategies, or **defense mechanisms,** unconsciously employed by the mind; these defy normal logic but act to protect the subject from awareness of unwanted feelings.

In *The Ego and the Mechanisms of Defense* (1966), Anna Freud specified ten such defense mechanisms: **regression, repression, reaction formation, isolation, undoing, projection, introjection, turning against the self, reversal,** and **displacement.** Repression and projection, commonly seen in clinical practice, are unconscious defensive processes. Repression refers to "an operation whereby the subject attempts to repel, or to confine to the unconscious, representations (thoughts, images, memories) which are bound to an instinct" (Laplanche & Pontalis, 1973, p. 390). Projection is an "operation whereby qualities, feelings, wishes or even 'objects,' which the subject refuses to recognize or rejects in himself, are expelled from the self and located in another person or thing" (p. 349). The other mechanisms operate similarly by unconsciously protecting the subject from awareness of repressed conflict and subsequent anxiety.

Prejudice, for example, represents a culturally defined projection of one group's disavowed aspects of itself onto another (usually subordinate) group. For example, in American culture blacks were seen as overly sexual, dishonest, and lazy, projections of unwanted traits of the dominant cultural group. Groups of young men attacking male homosexuals would also be a refusal of these young men to accept loving or tender feelings toward other men—finding it too threatening to consider such feelings and hence needing to defend by projecting them onto others and then attacking. Reaction formation is a process whereby an individual will take the opposite stance (unconsciously) to protect from awareness one's gratification in the abhorred position. For example, a man may become a preacher and rail against "sins of the flesh" as a way to defend against his own sexual impulses. What is often a sign of a reaction formation is the zeal with which someone embraces a position and simultaneously attacks the opposite—expressed in Shakespeare's words "he doth protest too much."

Freud's Developmental Theory

"In psychoanalytic treatment, the client regresses and recapitulates, in a modified form, early developmental phases. Both neuroses and psychoses are based on a series of fixations on and regressions to these past ego stages and orientations" (Giovacchini, 1987, p. 87). Freud postulated the **psychosexual stages** of infantile sexuality as oral, anal, and phallic, which linked developmental theory with sexual impulses. This meant that Freud believed sexual expression went beyond what is ordinarily considered sexual, for he postulated infantile activities as erotic.

In essence, psychosexual stages refer to a sequential acquisition of progressively sophisticated modes of gratification from various bodily zones that are necessary for growth and development. The term **libido** describes instinctual energy that belongs to the sexual drive. The discharge of this energy leads to pleasure, and the part of the body that leads to such pleasure is referred to as an **erogenous zone.** Erikson (1963) elaborated on these erogenous zones: "oral-sensory, which includes the facial apertures and the upper nutritional organs; anal, or the excretory organs; and the genitalia" (pp. 73–74). He posited modes of functioning within each zone. These included modes of incorporation, retention, elimination, and intrusion. The following examples show how modes may interplay with each zone.

Orality represents a method of relating to the external world. The infant's smiling is an indication of ability to recognize objects in the external world as separate from the self. The first mode of approach in the oral zone is incorporation, that is, to "take in" in a dependent fashion what is offered by the mother. Modes of incorporation dominate this stage, yet other modes are also expressed. According to Erikson (1963), "There is in the first incorporative stage a clamping down with jaws and gums; there is spitting up and out (eliminative mode); and there is a closing up of the lips (retentive mode). In vigorous babies even a general intrusive tendency of the whole head and neck can be noticed, a tendency to fasten itself upon the nipple and, as it were, into the breast (oral intrusive)" (p. 73).

In clinical work, one might refer to orally dependent clients. This indicates that extreme dependence is the result of a predominance of oral elements in adult functioning. This functions as a metaphor to describe a fixation at the oral stage of development, wherein the overly dependent adult client tends to relate to the world in terms of a need to be nurtured. While the child actually requires this nurturing to survive, the adult client is seen as wanting to be taken care of, to be soothed and nurtured in a psychological sense. A client described as an oral character may use any or all of the modes described previously: spitting out what the counselor or therapist offers, or intrusively penetrating into the counselor or therapist's space, demanding to be "fed." Erikson saw the primary conflict at this level as one of developing the sense of basic trust versus the sense of mistrust.

To Freud, control of the anal sphincter initiates the anal stage of development and is seen as an important contributor to adult structure. Control of the sphincter, which is part of the total muscle system activated at this stage, places an emphasis on the duality of rigidity and relaxation, flexion and extension. As noted by Erikson (1963),

> The development of the muscle system gives the child a much greater power over the environment in the ability to reach out and hold on, to throw and to push away, to appropriate things and to keep them at a distance. This whole stage, then, which the Germans called the stage of stubbornness, becomes a battle for autonomy. For as he gets ready to stand more firmly on his feet the infant delineates his world as "I" and "you," "me" and "mine." Every mother knows how astonishingly pliable a child may be at this stage, if and when he has made the decision that he wants to do what he is supposed to do. (p. 82)

Accordingly, the conflict at this stage involves the antithesis of letting go and holding on, of autonomy versus shame and doubt.

The **Oedipus complex,** which is one of the most controversial and best-known of Freud's theories, dominates the phallic stage. At this stage the child has moved away from a two-person system of mother-child interaction to a triangular relationship with both mother and father. The Oedipus legend, from Greek mythology, assumes the child's wish to possess the parent of the opposite sex, which creates a conflict with the parent of the same sex. In more graphic terms, and truer to the original legend, incestuous feelings are combined with patricidal impulses.

In the case of the boy who wishes to possess his mother, he fears retaliation by the father and fantasizes the father's revenge of castration (i.e., the father's retaliation will be directed at the boy's penis), which is termed castration anxiety. This complex is necessary for later development because the threat of castration leads the child to internalize, as a permanent part of his psychic structure, a prohibiting, controlling superego that is the foundation of morality. In the case of a girl, the unconscious wish is to marry the father and to take care of him in a much better way than she imagines the mother is capable of doing. While these theories remain controversial today and are seriously questioned by modern developmental theorists, they continue to be used as important metaphors in understanding clinical material.

Post-Freudian Psychoanalytic Theory

According to Pine (1990), it was Fairbairn (1941) who coined the term **object relations theory** and focused attention not on the pleasure-seeking motivation (Freud's drive theory) but on the *object-seeking* nature of motivation. Pine went on to describe how it was a new *method* of clinical work—infant and child observation—that added momentum to this shift in emphasis from an internal drive based on instinct to seeking an object (person). Others contributing to this shift and expansion of knowledge and theory included Melanie Klein, Donald Winnicott, and Heinz Kohut. Kohut (1977) developed a theory and technique that came to be known as **self psychology,** which emphasized the concept of self as the organizing construct of experience, rather than innate drives and instincts.

These post-Freudian theorists, taken together, can be seen as expanding psychoanalytic theory from Freud's one-person system to a two-person system. Rather than seeing the individual as a closed and separate system attempting to negotiate a balance between inner needs striving for gratification on the one hand and the constraints of society (the reality principle) on the other, the scope has widened to include another person (the analyst). Freud's metaphor for psychoanalytic treatment was the surgeon removing a tumor (repressed memory). In addition, Freud conceived the analyst as a mirror (non-reactive, non-contributory) reflecting back only those unconscious desires and fears emanating from the client. Winnicott (1958), who was a pediatrician before becoming a psychoanalyst, saw therapy as more like the relationship between a mother and an infant, where there is a highly attuned emotional sensitivity, first on mother's part and then, as the infant develops, of a more reciprocal nature. To underscore how important the object relation is in development and in psychotherapy, Winnicott would say there is no such thing as an infant. These object relations theorists did not discard Freud's drive theory but tended to add to it the significance of interaction with important others in the formation of personality and pathology.

Rabin (1995) described a recent paradigm shift in psychoanalysis that can be characterized by a number of different terms such as *intersubjectivity theory* (Stolorow, Brandshaft, & Atwood, 1987), *relational theorizing* (Mitchell, 1988), and *social constructivism* (Hoffman, 1991). Rabin argued that this shift is "from the positivistic belief that there are ultimate truths to be found within the intrapsychic structure of the patient, with the analyst as the arbiter of reality, to the 'postmodern' perspective, where all knowledge is perspectival, contextual and nonuniversal. *The analyst and the patient together create or construct* what is clinically useful" (p. 467) (emphasis added). This paradigm shift is away from Freud's metaphor of analyst as archeologist, sifting through strange symbols (dreams, slips of the tongue, symptoms) to decipher these meanings and present them to the client

Table 4.1
Comparison of Theoretical Approaches

	Drive	Ego	Object Relations	Self
Motivating Force	Instincts	Instincts and growth	Seeking object to satisfy instincts	Feelings of inadequacy
Goal of Therapy	Uncovering unconscious conflicts	Uncovering methods of defending against conflicts, developing inherent potential	Uncovering the way one relates to others in getting needs met	To enable clients to better meet their needs for feeling worthwhile
Role of Counselor	Mirror	Mirror	Participant observer	Participant observer
Central Agent of Change	Interpretation	Interpretation	Experience of therapeutic relationship	Experience of therapeutic relationship

via an interpretation. This shift has also entailed a greater awareness of and use of the therapist's feelings and thoughts during a therapy session, data referred to as **countertransference.** Freud viewed such reactions as contaminating therapy and saw them as a function of unrecognized neurotic conflicts within the analyst. However, recent trends are toward the recognition and use of countertransference as a tool to facilitate therapy (Lecours, Bouchard, & Normandin, 1995). Table 4.1 compares the drive, ego, object relations, and self theories we have discussed.

Major Constructs and Processes of Change

The assumptions upon which the system of psychoanalytic theory rests are referred to as **metapsychology** (Rapaport & Gill, 1959). As noted by Greenson (1967), "The clinical implications of metapsychology intimate that in order to comprehend a psychic event thoroughly, it is necessary to analyze it from six different points of view—the topographic, dynamic, economic, genetic, structural and adaptive" (p. 21).

The **topographic** point of view is the first major construct. It contrasts unconscious versus conscious mental processes. The deeper layer of the mind, the unconscious, has only the aim of discharging impulses. Both conscious and unconscious expressions are present in clinical material and can be described as manifest and latent. In order to illustrate this construct, we will use the dream material noted in Maria's clinical study. The client reports recent occurrences of dreams such as the following:

> I am always running, and there are shadowy figures behind me. I am in a large warehouse-type structure with lots of boxes and crates. The boxes and crates are all marked with arrows reading "Exit." The problem is that the arrows are all going in different directions.

Therefore, I never find the exit, and the figures keep getting closer and closer. I wake up in a cold sweat, breathing rapidly, heart pounding, and a scream stuck in my throat. I lie there trying to calm down, knowing that I am too afraid to go back to sleep. In a little while I get up and spend the rest of the long night sitting at the kitchen table drinking coffee.

In psychoanalytic clinical work, it is essential to have the client's association to a dream in order to verify our assumptions about the latent, or unconscious, meaning of a symbol or the dream itself. To interpret the meaning of a dream without these associations would be to impose our own thoughts onto the client, a process derogatorily called **wild analysis.** Because we do not have Maria's associations in this case, we will guess at some possible associations in order to illustrate the metapsychological points of view. We might assume, for example, that the **manifest symbol** of the *warehouse* would unconsciously represent (i.e., have a latent meaning of) a place that holds things, as could the boxes and crates. A large warehouse gives the feeling of much open space, perhaps emptiness. The structures that could hold things (comfort as in being held) are all marked in different directions. She has turned to numerous people for support and has found no way out of the emptiness/depression (warehouse). While the conscious representation of a warehouse with labeled boxes and crates represents order and control, the unconscious representation stands for chaos without exit. Both stand in topographical relation to the other: one conscious, the other unconscious. A further elaboration, and much more presumptive, is that the warehouse is not only symbolic of her depression and emptiness but also at a deeper level of intestine and bowel. We might assume that at this level Maria's not eating is about control versus chaos, a desperate attempt to deny her need to put something into her, be it need for food or for relationships and sexual intimacy.

Dynamic and **economic** points of view are the second and third major constructs of psychoanalytic metapsychology. In order to understand these two points of view, it is necessary to explore Freud's idea of the **psychoeconomic hypothesis.** This hypothesis requires a construct of **psychic energy,** much like physical energy, with principles of pleasure-pain and constancy. We will explain the idea of psychic energy briefly before we define the dynamic and economic points of view.

For Freud, the development of instincts necessitated conflict. For example, when the two primary instincts of sexual and aggressive drives strive toward expression, they clash with the reality principle, leading to states of pent-up tension. As noted by Giovacchini (1987),

> Psychoanalysis requires a concept of psychic energy to explain the various movements of the psychic apparatus, those involved in action, problem solving, reestablishment of emotional equilibrium, and growth. A hypothesis of psychic energy must be based on certain general principles that dictate the distribution and production of energy and how it is to be used. (p. 62)

Giovacchini further noted:

> Freud relied on two principles on which he built his concepts of psychic energy, the *principle of constancy* and the pleasure principle, more specifically, the *pleasure-pain principle.* The constancy principle is based on the hypothesis that the function of the nervous system and the psychic apparatus is to keep the level of excitation at its lowest point. The pleasure principle is related to the constancy principle in that it asserts that lowering the level of excitation, which connotes release and relief, leads to pleasure, whereas increased excitation creates tension and disruption and is experienced as pain. (p. 63)

This **tension-discharge hypothesis** supports the dynamic point of view, which assumes that mental phenomena are the result of the interaction of psychic forces seeking discharge. This was based in part on the theories of hydraulic systems in physics during Freud's time. Greenson (1967) tells us that "this assumption is the basis for all hypotheses concerning instinctual drives, defenses, ego interests, and conflicts. Symptom formation, ambivalence, and over-determination are examples of dynamics" (p. 23).

The way in which psychic energy is distributed, transformed, or expended defines the economic point of view. To illustrate these points of view, we might assume that Maria was in a state of dammed-up instinctual tension before the recent outbreak of her depressive symptoms. However, her ego was beginning to lose the ability (in the dream the shadowy figures are getting closer and closer) to carry out defensive operations so that she could function without such obvious debilitating symptoms. These operations seemed to be consistent with a compulsion for activity such as was exemplified by her pouring all of her energy into her students. We would expect that her need for activity and control was bolstered by a variety of stereotypical rituals and repetitions, not only as they concerned herself (i.e., her thoughts and her body, as in not eating) but also as they involved her interpersonal interactions (not letting men get close). This coping style would be necessary to contain instinctual forces—such as intense rage and fear of abandonment—from explosive expression. The client's strained relationship with her children precipitated the most recent outbreak of symptoms such as nightmares and insomnia.

Maria's ego has lost the ability to cope with this influx of affect seeking discharge, and she didn't think she could have waited much longer for an appointment. The impulse to rage is frozen in its attempt for expression as in her dream "a scream is stuck in my throat." This reflects the conflict around intentionally holding onto and involuntarily letting go of something from within. In this instance the something within happens to be a scream, which unconsciously could be equated with her sense of self, a self she struggled to find in the midst of family and cultural pressures to be what was expected of her.

This brings us to the fourth major construct of psychoanalytic metapsychology, the **genetic** point of view, which concerns an understanding of the origin and development of psychic phenomena. It explains how the past is being brought to the present and why a certain compromise solution has been adopted. To return again to our case example, Maria's history and associations in analytic sessions would no doubt highlight the importance her mother played in her adopting a particular defensive style as well as those psychic conflicts already noted.

The fifth major metapsychological construct is the **structural** point of view, which assumes that the psychic apparatus can be divided into several persisting functional units. "The concept of the psychic apparatus as consisting of an ego, id, and superego is derived from the structural hypothesis" (Greenson, 1967, p. 25). The id is the agency from which all instincts derive, while the ego is the agency that mediates these drives with the external environment. Based on a signal of anxiety, the ego brings a number of defensive operations into play. It works as an agency of adaptation with functions such as control over perception, voluntary motility, and the setting up of affective memory traces, to name just a few. The superego is the agency of the personality within which develops a framework of conscience, self-observation, and the formation of ideals. It acts as a judge or censor for the ego.

To illustrate the structural point of view as it applies to Maria, we could assume that the ego's defensive functions have weakened under the pressure of her divorce and her family's criticism and shunning of her. Her pouring herself into her students to the neglect of her children has mobilized the conflict she likely experienced as a child when her parents "poured" themselves into the family business to the neglect of Maria (as she became mother to her younger siblings). This conflict centers in part around the expression of anger (the trapped scream, the depressive shutting down). We might further assume that as she progresses in analysis she will no longer regress in this way when confronted with similar situations, for her ego functions will have replaced inadequate defenses with new insight and greater freedom of choice in responding.

Thus far, all the examples we have used from the case study reflect attempts at **adaptation,** the last major metapsychological construct. A person's relationship to his or her environment, objects of love and hate, and society are based on the adaptive point of view.

Applications

Overview

The following sections present information dealing with the goals and intervention strategies that have application to psychoanalytic theory. The goals of psychoanalytic theory stress changing the personality and character structure of the individual through resolving unconscious conflicts and developing more effective ways of dealing with problems, particularly in relationships. The intervention strategies that are part of psychoanalytic theory place special emphasis on free association, dream analysis, analysis of transference, analysis of resistance, interpretation, and the interactions that take place between the client and the counselor or therapist. The goals and intervention strategies that follow are designed to enhance the change process for the individual.

Goals of Counseling and Psychotherapy

The goals of psychoanalysis place emphasis on the resolution of clients' problems to enhance the clients' ability to cope with life changes (to make their way of relating to self and important others more meaningful and enriching), their working through unresolved developmental stages, and their ability to cope more effectively with the demands of the society within which they live. Although these goals vary with the client and with the psychoanalytic approach (drive theory, ego psychology, object relations, self psychology), each approach seeks the attainment of its goals through the exploration of unconscious material particularly as it relates to the client-analyst relationship.

Intervention Strategies

Freud's technique for uncovering hidden psychic processes evolved over a period of several years, and despite some relatively minor variations it is still in use today. The classical technique entails a process of **free association** (letting thoughts drift over events of daily life, past history, and dreams) on the part of the client, who is typically in a recumbent position with the counselor or therapist sitting behind and out of sight. The practitioner maintains a position of neutrality, referred to as the **rule of abstinence,** based on denying the client's wish for gratification of instinctual demands, such as wanting to have a more personal relationship with the analyst by asking about his or her personal life, or for the analyst to agree with the client. These techniques minimize the actual presence of the counselor or therapist and allow the client to focus more freely on intrapsychic matters such as fantasies, dream analysis, childhood-based conflicts, and defensive or resistive operations that block awareness of unconscious processes. More important, they facilitate the development of the **transference,** defined by Laplanche and Pontalis (1973) as "infantile prototypes that re-emerge and are experienced with a strong sensation of immediacy and are directed toward the analyst within the analytic situation. This is the terrain on which all the basic problems of a given analysis play themselves out: the establishment, modalities, interpretation and resolution of the transference are in fact what define the cure" (p. 455).

In other words, transference involves the client's reliving—in the presence of the counselor or therapist—the repetitious and rigid defenses of the past. It is the analysis and the eventual understanding of these defenses within the transference that make change possible. For example, if a client says something and the analyst is silent, the client might feel that the analyst is critical of what was said, and not only feel but also be convinced that this is what the analyst thinks. We would likely find that one or both parents often reacted with indifference to the client and that this pattern was being reactivated as a "here and now" experience for the client. The early pattern of experience with the parent was being "transferred" onto the analytic relationship. It is strategic on the part of the analyst to maintain enough of a neutral and anonymous presence—sort of like a blank screen—onto which the client can project these transferences. The analyst would then help the client become aware of such patterns (expecting criticism or needing approval) and how these cause problems in living.

The aim of the analytic technique, primarily through the analysis of transference, is to increase the clients' insight into themselves. The analysis also seeks to strengthen ego functions, such as being able to look at oneself realistically, that are required for gaining understanding. The most important analytic procedure is **interpretation**—making unconscious phenomena conscious. Strachey (1934) stated in a classic paper that interpretation modifies existing psychic structure, where structure is conceived as stable and enduring ways of relating to oneself and others. Greenberg (1996), however, wrote that the client-therapist *interaction* is mutative "because structure itself consists of internalized interactions represented in a particular way" (p. 36).

Empathy, intuition, and the counselor or therapist's own unconscious and theoretical knowledge all contribute to the construction of an interpretation. Other analytic procedures include confrontation, clarification, and working through. This latter procedure is of great significance because it involves the continued analysis of resistances brought about after an insight has been achieved. It refers to the broadening and deepening of insight that leads to permanent change. An example of a resistance would be a client who takes great pains in coming to sessions exactly on time, not a minute before or after. This would be thought of as a resistance to whatever experience the client might fear in being late or early. Being late could represent aggression toward the therapist (making him or her wait), and being early a feeling of need of the therapist and fear the therapist will be disapproving. Working through in this case would involve confronting the client with this

behavior and helping him or her sort through feelings, thoughts, and fears about the behavior. As such resistance often continues for some time, this process takes several weeks
or months to work through to the point where the client does not act (or freezes oneself
from acting in this case) but can put his or her feelings into words and perhaps fantasies
(images or daydreams) and arrive at an understanding that would then obviate the necessity of that particular resistance.

Gill (1996) described what he believes to be a major shift in conceptualizing therapeutic action or change. This shift is away from the emphasis on interpretations to an emphasis on what he calls the "experiential factor." What he means is that the experience between the client and the counselor or therapist is what is mutative. This shift has meant a
greater awareness of and appreciation for how the therapist experiences the therapeutic
interaction and how this experience (which includes countertransference) influences the
course of change (or lack thereof). In training analysts this shift is seen in a drifting away
from supervising analysts' trying to help the analyst trainee find the "right" interpretation
to trying to understand what is happening in the experience of a therapy session, not only
with the client but also within the analyst trainee. Interpretations would then be less about
the "there and then" and more about the "here and now."

Evaluation

Overview

This section of the chapter presents information dealing with research supporting psychoanalytic theory and its application to counseling and therapy and also the limitations
that surround the use of this theoretical approach. Thousands of research studies have
been conducted on the scientific status of psychoanalysis, and this research is ongoing.
We will show that limitations exist in terms of both cost of treatment and geographical
setting.

Supporting Research

Psychoanalysis shares with other fields of study in the social sciences the problem of
demonstrating itself as scientific. In addition, because it is a method of therapy, research
limitations are imposed upon it that do not exist in other fields. For example, a simple research design of treating one person analytically while using a similar person as a control
would be unethical. Therefore, the empirical value of psychoanalysis has to be founded
on clinical investigations—that is, the empirical testability of psychoanalytic theory must
be demonstrated in the treatment situation. As Grunbaum (1984) notes, "The naturalistic
setting or 'psychoanalytic situation' is purported to be the arena of experiments in situ., in
marked contrast to the contrived environment of the psychological laboratory with its superficial, transitory interaction between the experimental psychologist and his subject"
(p. 100). The following information is a cursory review of research findings from studies
of the psychoanalytic theory and method.

In *The Scientific Credibility of Freud's Theories and Therapy,* Fisher and Greenberg (1977) compiled a synthesis of almost 2,000 individual studies on the scientific status of psychoanalysis. They concluded that Freudian theory had been subjected to more scientific appraisal than any other theory in psychology and that results had borne out Freud's expectations. Similarly, Luborsky and Spence (1978) emphasize that the psychoanalytic session has epistemic superiority over validity obtained from the more artificially controlled conditions of an experiment and supports Freud's general theory of unconscious motivation.

Despite these affirmations, particularly as they relate to the clinical observation of the major motivational forces of mental life, current criticism of psychoanalysis focuses on its use of multiple sessions and overall length of treatment. Opponents of psychoanalysis point to the efficacy of briefer models of treatment, especially in contemporary health care settings where cost of care is a major concern. They argue that brief, technique-oriented psychotherapy may be just as effective in alleviating a specific symptom without uncovering unconscious dynamics. This debate is not so much about the empirical testability or value of psychoanalysis as it is about the economics of treatment.

Limitations

Psychoanalysis in the United States has traditionally been limited to educated middle- to upper-class clients who are able to afford the cost of treatment. Likewise, counselors or therapists using psychoanalysis have tended to practice mainly in areas of large urban populations. Therefore, the urban and rural poor, as well as the rural middle and upper class, have not had access to psychoanalytic services. Even if this limitation were alleviated by a national health care plan, the overall cost of educating a counselor or therapist, as well as the personal sacrifices involved in analytic training, automatically tend to limit the availability of practitioners certified in psychoanalysis. It is a rigorous training method that severely taxes interested candidates both financially and emotionally. The unfortunate outcome of this last limitation is that it restricts the pool of psychotherapists, whose training includes—in fact, mandates—personal therapy of considerable duration.

It is not surprising that counselors and therapists, on occasion, harbor disturbing feelings toward their clients. These strong passions of both love and hate can skew how well the therapy is conducted. Sometimes a practitioner is aware of these strong emotions, but sometimes they are buried in the unconscious, making an understanding of the source and usefulness of these feelings unavailable as a means of improving the therapeutic process. In this regard, psychoanalytic training provides an advantage that could be offered to any counselor or therapist who wishes to go beyond a method of brief or technique-limited therapy. Those who do not have an understanding of the source and rationale for emotions experienced in therapeutic situations may be shortchanging themselves and their clients.

The limitations of psychoanalytic methods, as applied to large populations of both rural and urban poor, may never be alleviated. Yet, greater strides may be made toward offering counselors and therapists, through psychoanalytic training, a sound procedure for better understanding themselves and their clients, thereby improving their overall therapeutic skill.

Summary Chart—Psychoanalytic Theory

Human Nature

Human nature is dynamic, based upon the flow and exchange of energy within the personality. This view is based on two fundamental hypotheses concerning mental development and functioning: psychic determinism, or causality (nothing happens by chance or in a random way, and all mental phenomena have a causal connection to the psychic events that precede them); and unconscious mental processes (a portion of the mind works within a framework of timelessness, spacelessness, and the coexistence of opposites).

Major Constructs

- The topographic hypothesis means that there exists a conscious and unconscious mind.
- The dynamic hypothesis sees the mind as a closed energy system where every effect has a cause.
- The economic hypothesis entails the pleasure-pain and constancy principles.
- The structural hypothesis divides the mind into id, ego, and superego.
- The adaptive hypothesis describes how the individual attempts to cope with societal demands.

Goals

The goals of psychoanalysis place emphasis on the resolution of clients' problems so as to enhance clients' personal adjustment, their working through unresolved developmental stages, and their ability to cope more effectively with the demands of the society within which they live.

Change Process

The changing of the personality and character structure of the individual involves resolving unconscious conflicts, working through unresolved developmental issues, and developing skills to cope with particular societal relationship demands.

Interventions

- Free association means encouraging the client to say whatever comes to mind.
- Analysis of dreams is important because dreams reflect the status of the analytic relationship.
- Analysis of transference is an attempt to state what is happening between client and analyst.
- Analysis of resistance involves putting into words what is blocking the patient's awareness.
- Interpretation refers to the analyst's formulation of what is taking place in the analysis.

Limitations

- More than any other treatment, psychoanalysis requires the client's commitment in terms of time, money, and personal effort.
- Psychoanalysis is a long-term treatment.
- Psychoanalysis is generally available only in urban areas due to the availability of trained analysts.
- A rigorous training program requiring time, money, and emotional commitment of practitioners is a formidable obstacle.

The Case of Maria: A Psychoanalytic Approach

In order to continue to illustrate the psychoanalytic method and theory outlined in the pre-ceding pages, it is necessary to invent a session as we might imagine it unfolding. As we have already noted, the research material of psychoanalysis is drawn from the productions of clients in therapeutic settings—that is, free association, dream analysis, and so on. This material is used to substantiate psychoanalytic theories regarding mental functions. Ac-cordingly, this section provides clinical material as it might unfold in order to serve as an example as well as to explain our ideas about unconscious processes.

We begin by assuming that the client, Maria, has been in analysis for several months and is being seen for four sessions weekly. The counselor or therapist is using a classical technique (Maria is in a recumbent position with the practitioner out of sight), it having been determined that the client was capable of working in the psychoanalytic situation.

Before the session begins, the counselor or therapist recalls that the client had re-ported a dream in the previous session. The dream involved the client's being at a library or a bookstore, she wasn't sure which. In the dream she knew that whichever it was, it was hers; that is, she owned it. A faceless person, a woman or a man, was there rear-ranging the order of the books. Maria concluded that this person was critical of her arrangement. She was afraid.

Her associations to the dream took her to her need for order and the somewhat rit-ualized way in which she followed directions. She recalled being touted as a model to her siblings and that she was expected to perform in an exemplary way in all aspects of her life. She thinks the person in the dream could be her mother. Here is an excerpt from the session following the dream.

> CLIENT: I went to the doctor and I told him my insomnia is not getting any better. I need to take my medication regularly, yet I don't want to be dependent on it. I agreed to take it, though, and I guess I'm taking it because someone said I should. I'm still crying a lot. It makes me think of a water tank that could ex-plode under pressure. I shouldn't fight it because it could get much worse. Sometimes I imagine I'll never stop crying. Something in the back of my head says "I told you so," as if the doctor were saying it. For some reason I think of coming here. I've had thoughts of ending therapy, but I've made a commitment to do this. It's like unless I make a strong commitment to someone else, I won't do it on a regular basis. I guess I need the structure. If I stop doing something over and over, I won't do it at all. Like there's a destructive part of me.
>
> COUNSELOR/THERAPIST: You need to imagine that I'm making you do this; other-wise, you feel you wouldn't do it at all.

The dream and the clinical material reflect the developing transference, in which the counselor or therapist is seen as both the doctor and the critical mother or father inside her library. The library possibly signifies the inside of the client's body, which incorpo-rates the faceless person, both man and woman, who is critical of her arrangement. Her anxiety in the dream is assumed to be a reaction to her growing rage at the critical parent/practitioner whom she has internalized and on whom she feels dependent.

In the session, Maria continues with this theme. Here she imagines that she must do something according to formula or repetition or her initiative would fail the faceless person. This compulsion suggests that she cannot derive pleasure from an acquired control during the anal phase because she is not the initiator of action; that is, she is not in control of what is inside of her. It also suggests a defensive measure to block explosive expression of her anger. The defense is her compulsive adherence to repetition. The conflict of holding onto or letting go of her anger is experienced somatically as insomnia and unexplained crying, the latter being a somewhat involuntary, out-of-control discharge of internal contents.

In order to be a "good girl," Maria must depend on her absolute commitment and dependency on someone else's regimen. The result is a somatic experience of pressure mounting within, along with a fantasy of permanent physical damage—that is, never being able to stop crying. Her need for the parent/practitioner to provide structure, however, thereby defending herself and the counselor or therapist from her anger, seems evident, even though she experiences this as suicide, damaging the faceless person physically, and provocative of destructive urges.

The counselor or therapist chooses to interpret within the transference, calling attention to the general nature of the client's defense. We might assume that the counselor or therapist selected this alternative over other possible interpretations because Maria is still in the early months of the analysis and is learning to think in terms of displacing thoughts and feelings onto the counselor or therapist. Other aspects of the dream or the clinical material are open to interpretation, such as the unconscious connection between mother and director, between anger and not eating, and between medication and the counselor or therapist's prescription of words and sessions. The latter interpretation would be of particular importance because the material reflects the client's growing anger at the counselor or therapist (analogous to the doctor), whose medication does not seem to be effective. In fact, the client feels that it is provoking discomfort, and her thoughts turn to retreat from her therapy. In other words, the very conflict that we imagine brought Maria to therapy—holding on to wakefulness or involuntarily letting go of her tears and her self-destructiveness—is not being mobilized in her analysis and directed at the counselor or therapist. Although the client is as yet unaware of this development, it is nonetheless surfacing in her dreams and in her associations.

References

Brenner, C. (1974). *An elementary textbook of psychoanalysis*. New York: Doubleday.

Erikson, E. (1963). *Childhood and society*. New York: Norton.

Fairbairn, W. R. D. (1941). A revised psychopathology of the psychoses and psychoneuroses. *International Journal of Psychoanalysis, 22,* 250–279.

Fenichel, O. (1945). *The psychoanalytic theory of neurosis*. New York: Norton.

Fine, R. (1979). *A history of psychoanalysis*. New York: Columbia.

Fisher, S., & Greenberg, R. (1977). *The scientific credibility of Freud's theories and therapy*. New York: Basic Books.

Freud, A. (1966). *The ego and the mechanisms of defense*. New York: International Universities Press.

Freud, S. (1940). *An outline of psychoanalysis* (Vol. 23). Standard Edition (J. Strachey, Trans.). London: Hogarth Press. (Original work published 1938).

Gay, P. (1988). *Freud: A life for our time*. New York: Norton.

Gill, M. (1996). Discussion: Interaction III. *Psychoanalytic Inquiry, 16*(1), 118–135.

Giovacchini, P. (1987). *A narrative textbook of psychoanalysis*. London: Aronson.

Greenberg, J. (1996). Psychoanalytic interaction. *Psychoanalytic Inquiry, 16*(1), 25–39.

Greenson, R. (1967). *The technique and practice of psychoanalysis*. New York: International Universities Press.

Grunbaum, A. (1984). *The foundations of psychoanalysis: A philosophical critique*. Berkeley: University of California Press.

Hoffman, I. (1991). Discussion: Toward a social-constructivist view of the psychoanalytic situation. *Psychoanalytic Dialogues, 1,* 74–105.

Kohut, H. (1977). *The restoration of the self*. New York: International Universities Press.

Laplanche, J., & Pontalis, J. B. (1973). *The language of psychoanalysis*. New York: Norton.

Lecours, S., Bouchard, A.-M., & Normandin, L. (1995). Countertransference as the therapist's mental activity: Experience and gender differences among psychoanalytically oriented psychologists. *Psychoanalytic Psychology, 12*(2), 259–281.

Luborsky, L., & Spence, D. P. (1978). Quantitative therapy. In S. L. Garfield & A. E. Bergin (Eds.), *Handbook of psychotherapy and behavior change* (2nd ed.). New York: Wiley.

Mitchell, S. (1988). *Relational concepts in psychoanalysis*. Cambridge: Harvard University Press.

Pine, F. (1985). *Developmental theory and clinical process*. New Haven: Yale University Press.

Pine, F. (1990). *Drive, ego, object, and self*. New York: Basic Books.

Rabin, H. (1995). The liberating effect on the analyst of the paradigm shift in psychoanalysis. *Psychoanalytic Psychology, 12*(4), 467–483.

Rapaport, D., & Gill, M. M. (1959). The points of view and assumptions of metapsychology. *International Journal of Psychoanalysis, 40,* 153–162.

The roster of the International Psychoanalytical Association. (1992–93). London: Broomhill's.

Stolorow, R., Brandshaft, B., & Atwood, G. (1987). *Psychoanalytic treatment: An intersubjective approach*. Hillsdale, NJ: The Analytic Press.

Strachey, J. (1934). The nature of therapeutic action in psychoanalysis. *International Journal of Psychoanalysis, 15,* 127–159.

Winnicott, D. W. (1958). *Collected papers*. New York: Basic Books.

Wolberg, L. (1977). *The technique of psychotherapy*. New York: Harcourt Brace Jovanovich.

Jungian Analytical Theory

Susan E. Schwartz

C. G. Jung Institute of Santa Fe, New Mexico

Everything good is costly, and the development of personality is one of the most costly of all things. It is a matter of saying yea to oneself, of taking oneself as the most serious of tasks, of being conscious of everything one does, and keeping it constantly before one's eyes in all its dubious aspects—truly a task that taxes us to the utmost. (Jung, 1967, p. 24)

Background

Jungian analytical psychology originated with the Swiss psychiatrist **Carl Gustav Jung.** An early member of Freud's psychoanalytic circle, Jung had at one point been designated by Freud to head the psychoanalytic movement. However, through a series of events, dreams, and interactions with Freud it became clear to Jung that he could not agree with Freud concerning the primacy of the sexual trauma theory and Freud's approach to psychological phenomena. Their differences were accentuated in Jung's book *Symbols of Transformation.* The ideas Jung articulated in this book were pivotal to his being ostracized by Freud and the psychoanalytic organization, as he made different interpretations of psychological processes.

After resigning from teaching psychiatry at the University of Zurich and leaving his position at the Burkholzi Psychiatric Clinic in Zurich, Jung spent six years with no outer production but his private analytical practice. All his energy was absorbed in a psychological crisis, a personal and professional journey precipitated by the break with Freud. Through deepening psychological work involving journaling and dialoguing with dreams, constructing figures and cities in sand, drawing, chiseling in stone, researching myth, Eastern religions, and ancient cultures, Jung developed the concepts later appearing in his writings and methodology of personality transformation, which he called the **process of individuation.**

Jung's work at the Burkholzi Clinic, under Eugen Bleuler (famous for his studies in schizophrenia), included his development of the word association test. This psychological test revealed the **complexes** with their **archetypal core** and confirmed the influence of the unconscious on conscious life. The research brought Jung and Freud together because both were unearthing evidence about the existence and effects of the unconscious. Jung also discovered what he later termed the **collective unconscious** from working with schizophrenic patients. The dreams and actions of these patients reflected the images and symbols found in ancient religions, alchemy, myths, and tales of the world. Jung says,

> At a time when all available energy is spent in the investigation of nature, very little attention is paid to the essence of man, which is his psyche, although many researches are made into its conscious functions . . . yet deciphering these communications seems to be such an odious task that very few people in the whole civilized world can be bothered with it. Man's greatest instrument, his psyche, is little thought of, if not actually mistrusted and despised. "It's only psychological" too often means: "it is nothing." (1964, p. 102)

Jung's basic premise resonated with his belief in the reality of the psyche.

Jung, born in 1875, descended from a heritage of clergymen. His father was a minister in a small town outside of Basel, Switzerland. During preparation for his confirmation in the Protestant church, Jung was dismayed by his father's lack of faith and inability to convey his spirituality. This lacuna led to Jung's lifelong search for spiritual components within the psyche (*spiritual* refers to a connection to the meaning of one's life and also to whatever is beyond us). This and other disappointing experiences with his father contributed to Jung's projection of the father image onto Freud, twenty years his senior. On their trip to America to lecture at Clark University in 1907, Freud refused to share his dreams and interpreted Jung's dreams in personalistic modes. From the disappointment in this experience Jung began the eventual severance of their friendship, propelling him on a different path. The psychological struggles in their relationship portray aspects of the initiation process when a son separates from his father.

Jung was significantly influenced by observing the two personalities of his mother. He perceived her outward compliance with social rubrics, while under her breath she expressed contrasting individual opinions. Jung later used this concept in his theoretical distinction between the personal unconscious and collective unconscious and the ego and Self. His mother and father, whose relationship was emotionally distant, represented the dichotomies of spirit and matter, anima and animus, persona and shadow.

Jungian analytical psychology derived from Jung's life, and its theories and substantiations came from his clinical work. He said, "My life is what I have done, my scientific work; the one is inseparable from the other. The work is the expression of inner development" (1963, p. 211). Jung found parallels to his psychological explorations in the various religions and symbols of the world, the medieval science of alchemy, and in myths and fairy tales. They all delineated the classic psychological patterns evident in his clinical practice and supported two of Jung's contributions to psychology—the collective unconscious and the process of individuation.

Prior to a discussion of the various tenets of Jungian analytical theory, Figure 5.1 is presented to aid the reader in better understanding the special terminology used by Jung in explaining various aspects of his theory.

Anima: the constellation of feminine qualities in a man.

Animus: the masculine side of a woman.

Archetype: all typical, universal human manifestations of life—whether biological, psychological, or spiritual. They reflect instinctive reactions which have an inherited mode of psychic functioning and arise from the collective unconscious.

Complex: an energic constellation composed of a cluster of images with a similar feeling tone, presenting as more or less well-organized and autonomous parts of the personality.

Ego: the center of the field of consciousness. Its role is to maintain relation with other psychological contents. It establishes boundaries between a person and others.

Persona: the person's presentation put forth to the world. It is structured from parental introjects, social role expectations, and peer expectations.

Psyche: the essence of a person, the totality of all psychic processes. It is composed of the conscious and unconscious.

Self: the Self provides the blueprint of life and is the center and guide to the personality. It expresses the unity of the personality and encompasses the experiencable as well as the not yet known. The Self contains the uniqueness of each person entwined with the entirety of life—human, plant, animal, inorganic matter, and the cosmos.

Shadow: the "not I" subpersonality. It symbolizes the other or dark side that is an invisible but inseparable part of the psychic totality. It has both positive and negative forms and can be manifest in both personal and collective figures.

Figure 5.1
Jungian Vocabulary

Human Nature: A Developmental Perspective

The psyche, the essence of a person, is composed of the conscious and unconscious, and is the matrix from which consciousness arises. The personal unconscious is composed of the forgotten, repressed, and subliminally perceived events and reactions in one's life. The collective unconscious includes symbols, images, and **archetypes** common to all peoples. The foundation of every individual contains these deposits of human reactions to universal situations occurring since primordial times. The personality is composed of the ego, persona, shadow, anima, animus, and Self.

Ego

The **ego** is the center of the field of consciousness, and its role is to maintain relation with other psychological contents. It is personally oriented with the task of developing subjective identity and self-worth and establishes boundaries between a person and others. The ego must be functional for the inner gifts to be actualized.

The ego's archetypal core is the Self, the director of the whole personality. The first half of life involves the ego separation from the Self. In the second half of life, ego and self reunite and assimilate alienated aspects of the personality. The process of individuation requires giving up the will of the ego for a resilient relationship with the Self.

Persona

In Jungian psychology the word *persona* (from the Greek, meaning "sounding through a mask") denotes the presentation put forth to the world. The **persona** is structured from parental introjects, social role responsibilities, and peer expectations. Although the genuine nature of a person comes through the public face, the persona can be a cover for personality weaknesses and conjoin with the need for protection and acceptance. The persona either prevents the inner conflicts and insecurities from attaining visibility, or its creative aspects lead to growth.

The persona is like a skin mediating the inside and outside and functioning in dynamic and compensatory relation to the ego, shadow, anima and animus, and Self. The persona bridges the gap between the ego and the outside world, while the animus and anima, the inner masculine and feminine images, mediate between the ego and the core of the Self. The persona corresponds and is compensatory to the habitual outer attitude, and the animus or anima reflects the habitual inner attitude. If rigid, the persona severs a person from the natural instincts, and the anima and animus remain undifferentiated and the shadow repressed. In this situation, the ego lacks flexibility and adaptation.

There are problems when the individuality of a person is suppressed or neglected to fit **collective ideals**—outer expectations substitute for one's individual standpoint. If external values are artificially adapted, a person acts in false and mechanistic conduct to him- or herself and others. Inordinate dependence on the persona denotes self-distrust and inauthenticity.

Shadow

The **shadow,** or "not-I" subpersonality, and its differentiation from the ego are part of the movement into personality awareness. Jung says,

> The shadow . . . usually presents a fundamental contrast to the conscious personality. This contrast is the prerequisite for the difference of potential from which psychic energy arises. Without it, the necessary tension would be lacking. . . . One is flat and boring when too unsullied and there is too much effort expended in the secret life away from the eyes of the others. Without its counterpart virtue would be pale, ineffective, and unreal. Their impact on consciousness finally produces the uniting symbols. (1963, p. 707)

The shadow confronts a person with dilemmas arising from being a part of the collective consciousness. Jungian psychology warns of the danger of blind obedience to the collective, resulting in neglect of the individual. Jung brought attention to the shadow because he lived through two world wars where the **collective shadow** brutally ruled. Facing the shadow promotes reflection on human nature and reveals individual values. Living the shadow consciously implies taking responsibility for oneself and others, owning talents and problems, and taking back projections. The moral obligation to live one's potential appears in dream figures that signify repressed personality aspects.

We are often ambivalent about the shadow, which contains the worst and best in the personality. The dark side gains strength when potential is denied. Although it is bitter to accept the shadow—the black, the chaos, the melancholia—doing so can be the start of psychological work. Jung thought of the shadow as the first complex to personalize in analysis. It also contains material with the potential for healing.

The shadow is difficult to confront and assimilate due to the ease of unconsciously projecting it onto others. We prefer to entertain idealized images of ourselves rather than acknowledge weaknesses or shame. Recognizing the shadow means giving up the ideal or perfect. The shadow gives dimensionality to life, makes one real, and allows the ego to use its strength. Owning one's shadow makes it easier to solve relationship and family problems rather than projecting the unwanted or rejected contents. By taking back projections, the personality attains definition, style, and inner unity.

Integration of the personal shadow provides a bridge from the ego to the **contrasexual** part of the personality. Jung says that a person "will have every opportunity to discover the dark side of his personality, his inferior wishes and motives, childish fantasies and resentments, etc.: in short, all those traits he habitually hides from himself. He will be confronted with his shadow, but more rarely with the good qualities, of which he is accustomed to make a show anyway. He will learn to know his soul, his anima" (1963, p. 673). (Please note Jung's use of the masculine pronoun reflects the bias of his era.)

Anima

In Jungian psychology the **anima** (from the Greek, meaning "soul") connotes the constellation of feminine qualities in a man. It personifies his relation to these aspects, the image of woman inside himself, and his projections onto females. In each era the feminine image changes. The anima initially is experienced from a male's psychological life with his mother or the primary female figure in his life and is influenced by his personal and archetypal experience of the feminine. Becoming conscious of this sexual polarity is essential for personality completeness and psychological union of the masculine and feminine aspects. This concept applies to all people, regardless of sexual orientation.

The anima is an archetype, and, like all archetypes, is never wholly comprehended. It is discovered with inner work. If separate from his feminine nature, a man can become uneasy, uncommitted, avoid conflict, and drift. Disconnected from the feminine and his emotions, he pays sparse attention to his psyche, and this constricts inner and outer freedom. Flat and monotonous moods signify anima neglect and cause various reactions such as depression, impotence, and even suicide. When out of touch with this aspect of his personality, a man might use drivenness, accomplishment, or physical performance to avoid inner reflection. Fearing the feminine, he becomes distant from inner and outer relationships, and the anima cannot sufficiently function as the bridge to the ego and the self.

The inner feminine becomes known through images from the unconscious, which are associated with the instinctual part of life, the flow of emotion, the rhythm of nature, and the physicality of pleasure. The anima can take the forms of the creative muse, lover, caregiver, and so on. Jung defines the anima as implying the "recognition of the existence of a semiconscious psychic complex, having partial autonomy of function" (1953a, p. 302). He describes the anima as expressing spiritual values and being close to nature. As the anima becomes increasingly differentiated, a man assumes an active rather than a passive role in relation to the feminine. In reference to this, Jung describes consciousness arising from the anima: "it lives of itself, makes one live, and cannot be fully part of consciousness" (1959, par. 57). This statement refers to the transcendent and archetypal aspects that extend the personality beyond ego consciousness.

Animus

The **animus** (from the Greek, meaning "spirit" or "breath") refers to the masculine side of a woman. It is influenced by the collective image of man that woman inherits, her experience of masculinity from contact with her father or other primary male figures, and the masculine principle in the culture. If the animus is undeveloped, without sufficient room for expression or growth, it hinders the feminine through internal castigations and sufferings, undermining her participation in life. Classically interpreted, the animus signifies woman's feeling relationship to man, culture, and spiritual life, reflecting the predominance of the masculine deity in Western culture.

Feminine nature is pushed into the background by the negative animus. Unassimilated, unacknowledged, or projected, the negative animus causes chronic self-esteem problems, power struggles, and self-alienation. The negative animus manifests in a voice of critical commentary or issues excessive commands and prohibitions. Drawn to a destructive fascination with the animus, a person may sever contact with the world, give up her or his soul, be dreamy and without focus, or be driven to accomplishment.

There are problems if a father has no limits and is either all-giving or a rigid disciplinarian. If he is encased in a distant and foreboding authority structure, a daughter is not personally affected in a positive way. If his emotion is absent or he is physically unavailable, a negative father complex forms. Activating the masculine principle brings courage, determination, force, and authority. These qualities from a positive father complex enable a person to be effective and competent in the world.

The anima and animus together form a **heiros gamos,** or an internal union of opposites in the personality, appearing in dreams, ancient symbols like yin and yang, and relationships. In current Jungian thought, the anima and animus characteristics are found in both males and females to different degrees depending on the person.

Self

Behind all psychological patterns lies the **Self,** the blueprint of life and the unfolding center and guide for the personality. The Self contains the uniqueness of each person entwined with the entirety of life—human, plant, animal, inorganic matter, and the cosmos. The Self is a synthesis for personality emergence, a cohesive force establishing balance and well-being and guiding the whole personality. It causes us to be what we are and is based on the innate drive toward self-realization.

The Self is personal, yet its striving nature affects the progress of humanity. The empirical symbols of the Self are identified with an aura of numinosity, and its images have strong emotional value. They appear in dreams in many forms such as animals, hermaphroditic figures, jewels, flowers, and geometric concentrically arranged figures known as **mandalas.** *Mandala* is a Sanskrit word meaning "magic circle," and is one of the oldest religious symbols. Jung discovered the mandala in the dreams of his patients, where it functioned as a creator and preserver of development and pushed the personality through chaos toward potential wholeness.

The question is not how the Self is created during the course of life, but the extent of its attaining consciousness. The Self is a **temenos,** a center for the source and ultimate foundation of our being, transcending personal vision. It is a metapsychological concept referring to the entirety of the psyche and containing the whole range of psychic phenomena. The Self, composed of archetypes and instincts, is supraordinate to the conscious ego. This center of the personality, the midpoint that embraces the conscious and the unconscious psyche, is also the whole circumference. "The beginnings of our whole psychic life seem to be inextricably rooted in this point and all our highs and ultimate purposes seem to be striving toward it" (Jung, 1967, p. 67). The Self is without bounds, an illimitable and indeterminable unconscious where one is simultaneously oneself and connected beyond the personal.

We are born with the Self as the matrix of potential faculties waiting to be actualized. "In the last analysis," Jung says, "every life is the realization of a whole, that is, of a self, for which reason this realization can also be called individuation" (1953b, p. 330). The Self is paradoxical, containing both positive and negative polarities for the organizing of experiences, operating through the ego, and having continuity throughout time.

Major Constructs

When **psychic energy,** or **libido,** is lost from consciousness, it passes into the unconscious and activates the contents of the archetypes and complexes. Jung's concept of **enantiodromia,** a term he borrowed from the Greek philosopher Heraclitus, means "flowing into the opposite." The psyche is a dynamic self-regulating system governed by opposition, based on complementary or compensatory factors pulsing through all psychological constructs. The point is not to radically convert from one side to the other, but to integrate personality aspects.

Jungian psychology is teleologically oriented, based on a philosophy of human development as proceeding from childhood though adulthood. Each stage of life requires new attitudes, renewed orientation, and reanchoring to different contexts. The major constructs that undergird this development are **psychological types, complexes,** archetypes, symbols, and the personal and collective unconscious.

Psychological Types

Jung's notion of typology orients itself toward conscious life. The terms *introvert* and *extravert* originated with Jung. They represent the two attitudes for perceiving the world and one's relationship to it. An **extravert** looks at the world and then to him- or herself, whereas an **introvert** uses the perspective of the inner world and then perceives the outer. The extravert is influenced by collective norms, the introvert by subjective factors. Jungian analysts are predominantly introverts, as are often those who come for this kind of counseling or psychotherapeutic treatment. The work emphasizes the mix of conscious and unconscious and appeals to people searching the psychological depths to find their way.

In addition to the two attitudes, there are four functions that determine a person's psychological perception of the conscious world: **sensation,** perceiving through the senses; **thinking,** giving order and understanding; **feeling,** which weighs and values; and **intuition,** the leap to future possibilities. In each person, one function, called the **superior function,** predominates and takes its particular form according to social and cultural influences. Another function, called the **inferior function,** remains mostly unconscious and is connected to the shadow. The functions are limited to four, a number regarded throughout cultural history as designating wholeness and totality.

The main or superior function becomes the most developed and the two accessory functions reasonably so, leaving the fourth or inferior function undifferentiated, primitive, impulsive, and out of conscious control. Since human nature is not simple, we rarely find an absolutely pure type. The functions change in dominance depending on the activities at different life stages. The attitudes do not change but are realized as a person progresses through life. For example, a child may appear to be an introvert in a quiet and withdrawn family, but later in life he or she may uncover this adaptation and release the pent-up extraversion.

Each attitude can be paired with each function, making eight psychological combinations in all. For example, a person may be introverted sensation thinking, extraverted sensation feeling, and so on. The complementary or compensatory relation between the opposite functions is a structural law of the psyche. In the second half of life the inferior function gains attention as the psychological situation naturally alters to round out the personality.

A sensation-type person takes life as it comes, focusing on the conscious daily perception of physical stimuli. Intuition and sensation are called irrational functions—the rational and logical are associated with thinking and feeling. Intuition is the opposite function to sensation, and the person of this type is imbued with creative capacities and inspirations. Intuitive types perceive possibilities, but can be so removed from the present and the senses that they forget the physical world. Thinking is apparent in persons ruled by intellectual motives; their life actions are based on objective data. Such people prefer logic and order, and emotion and feeling are repressed. A thinking person tends to be cold and has difficulty understanding human relationships. In contrast to this, a feeling type is especially concerned with human relationships, but feeling is not to be confused with emotion. Any function can lead to emotional reactions. A feeling person weighs, accepts, or refuses by evaluating what something is worth.

The Myers-Briggs Type Indicator is a popularized adaptation of Jung's principles of **typology.** It is not taught in Jungian institutes because it is solely oriented to conscious functioning, and is not Jung's original conception.

Complex

A **complex** is an energic **constellation** with varying degrees of autonomy, ranging from hardly disturbing ego functioning to attaining predominance over the personality. It is composed of a cluster of images or ideas with a similar feeling tone, presenting as a well-organized and autonomous part of the personality. The psyche's inherent tendency to split into complexes brings dissociation, multiplicity, and the possibility of change and differentiation.

Jungian counseling or psychotherapy aims to separate the complexes from the unconscious into conscious awareness. Jung says we all have complexes and the real issue is whether or not they are controlling us. Complexes either repress or promote consciousness, inhibit or inspire, hinder development or provide the seeds for new life. Complexes are like magnets, drawing psychological and archetypal experience into a person's life. They occur where energy is repressed or blocked, point to unresolved problems and weaknesses, and develop from emotional wounds. When a complex is touched, it is accompanied by exaggerated emotional reactions and may also be experienced physically.

A complex does not completely disappear, but the arrangement of energy changes with awareness. The psychic energy caught in the complex is accessed for personality development. No complex should entirely control the personality, but the ego complex dominates during waking life. The particular makeup of a complex is apparent through images pertaining to the unconscious psychological situation occurring in dreams and the synchronous events of waking life. One's destiny can be adversely affected by a complex, and psychological issues can remain unresolved for generations. For example, a woman with a negative father complex transfers a limited purview onto everything male and operates from negatively biased perceptions.

Archetype

The personal unconscious consists of complexes, and the collective unconscious is composed of **archetypes.** The word *archetype* originated with Plato, and means "ideal form" or "first imprint." The archetype is at the core of the complex. It is imbued with the tendency to form images rich in emotional content with infinite possibilities for analysis. The repetitions and clustering of archetypes are called **motifs.**

The archetype is a formless structure with infinite varieties, enmeshed in history, and more or less pertinent to a time or place in the evolution of the psyche. The archetype is expressed and comprehended through mythological and sacred images in cultural and personal life. Jung comments on this when he says that "it is only possible to come to a right understanding and appreciation of a contemporary psychological problem when we reach a point outside our own time from which to observe it. This point can only be some past epoch that was concerned with the same problems, although under different conditions and in other forms" (1954, p. viii).

We inherit a tendency to structure experiences of psyche and **soma** in typical and predictable ways called archetypes. These archetypes have a basic form, express the human psyche, and define a pattern of development. Yet Jung states, "No archetype can be reduced to a simple formula. It is a vessel which can never empty and never fill. It has a potential existence only, and when it takes shape in matter it is no longer what it was. It persists throughout the ages and requires interpreting anew. The archetypes are imperishable elements of the unconscious, but they change their shape continually" (1959, p. 301).

These building blocks of the psyche operate in basic psychological instinctual patterns that are counterparts to the biological instincts. Instincts are impulses of action without conscious motivation. Like a snake appearing in a dream, instincts are collective, universal, and regularly occurring phenomena, without individuality yet having personal significance. Jung describes the archetype as composed of two poles. The "psychic infrared," or the biological psyche of one end, gradually passes into the "psychic ultra-violet" on the psychic end. The archetype describes a field both psychic and physical. The essence of the archetype forms a bridge where spirit and matter meet.

Jung says that the archetype "represents or personifies certain instinctive data on the dark, primitive psyche, the real but invisible roots of consciousness" (1959, p. 271). An archetype cannot be described but is circumscribed by the opposites of its spectrum. Archetypes are impersonal personifications of human potential encompassing the deeper currents of life. Their images in dreams, mythology, religions, and fairy tales gain relevance with personal application. The remembrance of a favorite fairy tale or myth and its archetypal journey help a person glean meaning from life's sorrows and joys. Archetypes inform everyday life. They are at work in relationships, organizations, family systems, and the way life is experienced and interpreted.

Symbol

The Jungian definition of **symbols** includes the personal and collective, conscious and unconscious. A symbol is felt, often viscerally, as in an important dream. Jung describes this feeling as "numinous," giving significance and depth to life, and connecting with the transcendent.

Each symbol has two sides, one related to the conscious ego and one turned toward the archetypal contents of the collective unconscious. The unconscious produces answers to psychological problems through its symbolic images, which are compensatory to the conscious mind. A symbol takes energy from the unconscious and transforms it to resolve conflicts and channel self-expression. It unfolds as a working metaphor throughout life. Symbols are spontaneous psychic manifestations pertinent for individual and societal change.

It seems understandable that if people are biologically related, they are psychologically related, especially on collective and archetypal levels. Jung studied myths, the fundamental symbolic expressions of human nature, as representing typical psychic phenomena. The mythological patterns reflect the distinctive psyche of a given culture or religion and contain universal symbolic relevance. Myths and their symbols help bring order out of psychological chaos.

The word *symbol* derives from the Greek *symbolon,* which means "coming together." A symbol arises from conflict or disorientation, joins two separate elements, and mobilizes energy. Symbols spontaneously arise from the unconscious psyche, transform it into conscious experience, and energize the ego. Signals in the form of symbols are received through dreams every night.

Psychic contents not yet conscious express themselves in symbolic ways. Because the unconscious contains the germs of future psychological situations and ideas, Jung calls the transmutation of libido or energy through symbols the **transcendent function.** Conscious and unconscious confront each other, and the symbol provides a bridge to a third possibility which is transcendent. It is activated after an experience of disintegration, when the personality is jarred by psychological threats to the status quo.

Because the psyche is as real as the body and encompasses the spiritual and biological realms, the unconscious is the matrix of psychogenic symptoms signaling disharmony with conscious life. To the extent that we are unaware of the symbolic dimension of existence, the problems of life are experienced as symptoms. The ability to recognize the symbolic images behind the symptoms transforms the experience.

Collective Unconscious

The **collective unconscious** encompasses all previous aspects of the psyche. This concept distinguishes Jungian analytical psychology from other approaches. The unconscious is not only personal, but also collective and impersonal. The collective unconscious consists of the sum of the instincts and their correlates, the archetypes. This storehouse of potentially energizing, enriching, and also abhorrent material brings the understanding and knowledge that furthers development of each human being. The complexity of the psyche means that our comprehension of it is, at the most, partial because there is no finite knowledge of its boundaries or complete nature.

The collective unconscious goes beyond the individual ego, and its nature is revealed through cultural myths, religious images and symbols, dreams, drawings, active imagination, dance, or any creative work. The collective unconscious contains the deposit of human reactions to universal situations, initiations, and rites of passage through the stages of life operating since primordial time.

Applications

Overview

The following sections present information dealing with the goals, process of change, and intervention strategies that apply to Jungian analytical psychology. The goals of Jungian psychology stress the processes of individuation, personality unity, and transcendence. The transformation of personality depends on the potential for growth inherent in each person. The intervention strategies that follow are designed to both meet the goals and enhance the change process for an individual, with concurrent ramifications for society.

Goals of Counseling and Psychotherapy

Individuation and personality unification are central to Jungian psychology. Individuation, the differentiation of the various components of the psyche, addresses the development of the unique elements of an individual. As a person gains knowledge of the various personality aspects, they synthesize into what Jung termed the transcendent function. Transcendence involves a constant striving for wholeness, integration of the personality, and realization of the self.

The Process of Change

Jungian psychology is conceptually broad and attempts to address the isolation and confusion of modern times. The uneasy ambience and aimlessness of our age impels the search for fulfillment. The illnesses of society—the boredom, joylessness, and inability to love—adversely affect interpersonal and intrapersonal relationships.

The transformation of character follows the potential for growth inherent in the human psyche. When the conscious attitude is at an impasse, psychic energy is drawn into the unconscious and emerges in dreams, images, and synchronous events. Jung's concept of **synchronicity** involves the acausal and meaningful coincidences that impart order in the world, opening the way toward experiencing the Self. For example, the *I Ching,* the ancient book of Chinese wisdom, is based on synchronicity. Asking a question and throwing yarrow sticks or coins provides a symbolic answer to the presenting problem.

Over a lifetime, psychic energy transforms. The individuation process, or the way a person comes into his or her uniqueness, requires the differentiation and reintegration of the unconscious. The process reflects the archetypal, spiritual, and religious activities of the psyche. Jungian counseling or psychotherapy is a method encompassing the phases of education, catharsis, rebirth, and transformation. The process recaptures developmental difficulties where growth is stopped. Renewal comes with initiatory experiences reactivating the psyche.

Jung found the individuation process repeated in history, religious rituals, tribal ceremonials, and initiatory practices. He studied Eastern religions and mystical wisdom literature, the spiritual disciplines of the Kaballah, gnosticism, Kundalini yoga, and so on, as analogous methods to the individuation process. He extensively researched alchemy, a medieval science and precursor to modern-day chemistry. The symbols and goals of alchemical work, or symbolically turning lead into gold, parallel the individuation process, the stages of psychological development, dream symbols, and issues of the transference and countertransference.

A person can proceed, often until midlife, functioning reasonably well, but part of the personality remains undeveloped and dormant. A crisis comes, relationships alter, and life becomes tumultuous. Beliefs become challenged, a terminus is reached, and change must occur, some new direction taken. The energy stored in the unconscious pushes to be known. The prospective, or forward-moving, function of the psyche leads to further development and finding a sense of purpose in life. Jung is noted for recognizing the significance of the second half of life as a time for deepening the personality.

Jungian analysts use the chair and/or couch. People are seen weekly, and preferably two or more times a week. A higher frequency of sessions encourages depth, concentration, and activation of the unconscious influence upon conscious functioning. Because the process of individuation plays out differently for each person, there are no prescribed techniques, no formal treatment goals set by the Jungian counselor or therapist, nor reliance on the traditional pathological categorizing.

Problems develop due to an ossified approach to life and disunity with oneself. The disorder is not only painful, but also becomes an impetus for personality growth. The issue is not whether one has difficulties, but the way they are handled. The psychological illness is simultaneously a warning and a natural attempt at healing. The process of change is not quick or easy. Consciously suffering the psychic pain of the past allows it to transform so that the person gains a more satisfying present and future life. This approach is applicable to people of all ages, including children.

Intervention Strategies

Dreams.   Dreams are a natural way to discover and unravel the mysterious workings of the personality. More than just bizarre images that come with sleep, they are as real as waking life. Dreams address core issues, and throughout history they have been recognized as a source of inspiration.

The belief that dreams are a means of divine communication or an occult way of discerning the future was pervasive in the ancient Near East. In biblical times dreams were considered the agents of God's word, announcing his will to the dreamer. Dream interpretation was an important part of the spiritual life of the ancient Greeks and Egyptians, whose word for *dream* was derived from the verb "to awaken." In all races and at all times, dreams were regarded as truth-telling oracles.

Attending to dreams is a way to obtain information about unknown and untapped psychological areas. Dream information enhances the day world and shines a light on the repressed qualities and contents robbing the individual of actualizing potential. Big dreams occur at significant life markers or crisis times, with dream messages providing inroads to the psyche. Dream books do not suffice as ready-made guides for interpretation because the dream and its symbols cannot be separated from the dreamer. Following dreams leads to recovery of oneself as dreams weave together current experiences with those from the past and future.

Dreams keep us from straying from the truths of the body. Their images are symbolic portrayals of an actual unconscious situation, bringing its potency to life and triggering emotional reactions. Physical disorders in dreams express psychological issues and may serve as an early warning system for illness. Dreams often suggest treatment, contain methods and tools for psychological and physical healing, and crystallize a problem into something workable and understandable.

The Jungian form of counseling or psychotherapy involves not only the treatment of a symptom, but also the reconstruction of an individual and the restoration of human dignity. As Jung writes, "One should never forget that one dreams in the first place, and almost to the exclusion of all else, of oneself" (1964, p. 312). What the dream has to say is always seen in light of the attitude of the conscious mind of the dreamer. When inner potential is negated or ignored, pathology appears; when the gold of the personality becomes stuck and repressed into the unconscious, things go badly.

Recurring dreams, nightmares, and childhood dreams are all crucial expressions of the unconscious and relate to factors primary in the life of the individual and his or her culture. Through personal associations, the dreamer is led deeper into the psyche and finds similar motifs repeated in religions, legends, myths, and fairy tales. Although we have lost the formal rites of initiation, all people have a psychological need to access the spirit which cultural lore imparts. These initiatory processes are stored in the unconscious and emerge through dreams and fantasy material to replenish the personality.

The dream is not merely the ego reflecting on itself but a communication from the unconscious—beyond, yet in relation to the ego. To concern oneself with dreams is a way of accessing one's true nature and gaining knowledge to free the complexes. Children are easily in touch with their dreams because they are psychologically closer to the unconscious. For adults, work is needed to get back to this state. Too often the rational world takes over and the inner life is negated.

The dream is like a play with an opening scene, statement of the problem, action, climax, and resolution. The dream characters represent compensatory expressions of the personality. Awareness of the projection of one's qualities onto dream figures is a way to reclaim them. On the subjective level, the figures in dreams are personified features of the dreamer's personality. On the objective level, they represent an actual person or someone in close relation, such as a partner, child, or parent. It is worth noting in the dream where the dreamer stands, the position and action of the dreaming ego, and whether one is an observer, a participant, or not present. There is meaning in the sequential order of events, the people who appear, and those named or unnamed. The latter represent qualities remote from consciousness and, therefore, less identifiable. A dream placed in a foreign or familiar country or not on earth reveals the distance of the psychological information from conscious awareness. Holding the living relationship between the conscious and unconscious, called by Jung the **"tension of the opposites,"** helps sustain and organize a person while he or she pursues the psychological "treasure hard to attain" in the unconscious.

The dream is an important means of facilitating inner work and addressing the blind spots of one's personality. Dream images arise from involuntary psychological processes not controlled by the ego or will. In working with the dream, one stays consonant with the facts and does not distort or change the information. By sticking to the dream images, the reasons for psychological blocking and resistance gradually emerge. The Jungian counselor or therapist uses theory to create a flow of information without distorting the dream into an intellectual venture.

In dreams, nothing is absolute; not everything is analyzable at the time of the dream, and clarification may emerge with later dream material. Personality definition develops through its aspects being named, while the dream retains a mystery by keeping some things hidden. Dreams are self-regulating and depict the psyche's forward and regressive movements. Dreams are more or less synchronous with daily life, and they parallel or anticipate actual occurrences. Dreaming is growth-producing by synthesizing psychological aspects. When understood, this natural process reinforces reliance on the psyche and its wisdom. Concentration and value placed on the dream world fosters personality integration and individuation.

Transference and Countertransference.   Jungian analytical psychology reweaves the personality through the container, or temenos, of the counseling or psychotherapeutic relationship. The transference relates to past personal dramas as well as the archetypal struggle of each person on the path toward self-realization.

During a Jungian session, a client discusses dreams, active imagination, personal relationships, current problems, childhood development, transference, synchronous occurrences, and so forth. All of these are worked on additionally outside of the sessions through journaling feelings, emotions, and thoughts and by engaging in creative endeavors that make the unconscious conscious. Presenting problems vary, and treatment usually goes beyond the initial symptoms. People naturally become intrigued with themselves as they awaken to the meaning of their existence.

Addressing transference and countertransference is part of the art of Jungian counseling or psychotherapy. "The unrelated human being lacks wholeness, for he can achieve wholeness only through the soul, and the soul cannot exist without its other side, which is always found in a 'you' " (Jung, 1966, p. 454). Through the attention and reflection of the Jungian counselor or therapist, clients learn to regard themselves psychologically and to comprehend and honor the reality of the psyche. The discourse between two individuals is actually a discourse among four. Present are the Jungian counselor or therapist and his or her anima or animus, as well as the client and his or her anima or animus. Treatment involves exploring how all the characters interact within the therapeutic vessel as the archetypal process of individuation unfolds.

Transference portrays the inner situation, expectations, complexes, fantasies, and feelings of the client. Part of the psyche looks for a bridge from the past into present reality. Transference is defined by its phenomenon of **projection,** or seeing oneself in an other, and occurs in all relationships. Split-off or unintegrated parts of the client are projected onto the counselor or therapist, who embodies the family, the unused aspects of the personality, and the potential of the client—until the client begins to take back the projections. The relationship enacts the unconscious drama holding the client through exploring current and past issues, discovering what archetype colors the person, and finding the hints at solution present in dreams and fantasies. The counselor or therapist needs emotional clarity to differentiate the client's projections from his or her own. The treatment relies on the totality of the psyche of both participants.

In order to be aware of his or her complexes and psychological composition, a Jungian counselor or therapist has intensive personal analysis prior to and during formal training at a Jung Institute. One must engage in his or her own psychological work to facilitate psychological transformation with others. Countertransference reflects the counselor or therapist's reacting to the client and gives useful information. The nonverbal communication, timing, and sensitivity of the counselor or therapist relies on the psychological and physical signals received from the client. The counselor or therapist's personality corresponds to the unconscious of the client in this shared interactive space. Each counselor or therapist must ask whether feelings about the client stem from his or her unconscious and unintegrated conflicts, or whether the reaction is to the unconscious drama of the client. The mutual transformation occurring through this process demands honesty and perseverance of both participants. Jung says, "The doctor is therefore faced with the same task which he wants the patient to face" (1954, p. 167).

Jung comments about the transformative process, "I have no ready made philosophy of life to hand out . . . I only know one thing: when my conscious mind no longer sees any possible road ahead and consequently gets stuck, my unconscious psyche will react to the unbearable standstill" (1954, p. 84). Jung describes the counselor or therapist as a wounded healer, reminiscent of the shaman or medicine man in various cultures who can activate the healing powers of the sick.

Active Imagination.   In a state of "abaissement du niveau mental" (a lowering of consciousness), the ego loses energy and a person receives information from the unconscious. One approaches active imagination with the intent to accept whatever arises from the psyche, and without the ego assuming control. From this state people create or make sense of the unknown material that floats up from the unconscious by writing, drawing, dancing, and so forth. A person takes the symbols and images and communes with them without the pressure of producing something rational.

Evaluation

Overview

The following section presents information dealing with research supporting Jungian analytical psychology, as well as the limitations that surround the use of this approach. It is important for the reader to understand that, based upon the nature of Jungian analytical psychology, little traditional research has been done with this approach to counseling and psychotherapy. However, clinical results, gleaned from a heuristic perspective, provide support for the continued use of Jungian analytical psychology. The limitations addressed in this section occur according to choice of the client who seeks to embark on this journey of self-discovery.

Supporting Research

There is little statistical research about Jungian analytical psychology. The process is non-replicable, confidential, and based on individual and archetypal processes. Tests are not usually administered in this depth approach to the psyche. The heuristic approach from personal and archetypal research validates this transformative process. Jung claimed the scientific proof resided in his empirical researches into myth themes, world tales, primitive cultures, and religious ceremonies and rituals. The growing popularity of Jungian psychology correlates with the cultural need to compensate emptiness and loss of meaning by reconnecting with unconscious realms.

Jung made significant contributions to the fields of sand play therapy, art therapy, and psychology. He advocated analysts' coming from a wide background, the crucial point being that they have a personal analysis. His interest in Eastern philosophy, mystical religions, and mythology brought him in contact with many of the great thinkers of the twentieth century. Jungian counselors and therapists lecture and write on topics ranging from classical Jungian thought to music, mathematics, philosophy, Eastern and Western religion, and modern psychological developments.

Limitations

Jungian analytical psychology has limitations in the sense that most people who embark on this path are often of an intellectual bent, have reached a certain level of accomplishment, and are looking not only for crisis intervention but also to enhance the meaning of their lives. Their outer functioning may look sufficient to others, but they know they are living below their level of satisfaction and must plumb the psychological depths to stretch their personality. This is not an elitist approach, but some people have an impetus for deeper psychological development, as well as more time, money, and personal effort to expend. It requires more than a cursory look at oneself, and the psyche is rigorous in its demand for attention once it is discovered. So although the approach is useful for all ages and backgrounds, the internal desire and the ability for strenuous work are requirements and set the limitations. Often people do not know at the beginning what is entailed in this process, yet some part of their psychological makeup agrees to take a long and arduous internal look. Sometimes it is surprising to discover who remains in the work and who finds it inappropriate.

Essentially, this approach is useful for those who want to invest in themselves over time and not for the short term, and for those who wish to go beyond the symptoms and proceed into the psyche. These people have wonder, fear, and a need to work out their underlying malaise, depression, anxiety, or other presenting problem through discovering what lies in the unconscious. Those who fit this approach will naturally find this way.

Summary Chart—Jungian Analytical Theory

Human Nature
The foundation of every individual contains deposits of human reactions to universal situations occurring since primordial times. This foundation is reflected in the concepts of the ego, persona, shadow, anima, animus, and self.

Major Constructs
The complex is a cluster of impressions with similar feeling tones having an autonomous functioning. The archetype, or inherited mode of psychic functioning, is at the core of the complex. It becomes known through symbols arising from the collective unconscious. The symbols contain answers to psychological problems. The collective unconscious contains the deposits of the human psyche from the beginning of time. The psychological types are oriented to conscious life. People are introverted, taking the world from a subjective standpoint, or extraverted, which means they look outward before registering their inner reactions. The four functions are the ways libido, or psychic energy, manifests: sensation, what is happening now; intuition, future leap of ideas; thinking, intellect and logic; and feeling, the valuing of a person or thing.

Goals
Individuation is the unification of the personality by incorporating the conscious and unconscious realms.

Change Process
The transformation of character follows the potential for growth inherent in the human psyche. When the current conscious attitude is at an impasse, psychic energy is drawn into the unconscious and emerges in dreams, images, and synchronous events. The individual process, or the way a person comes into his or her uniqueness, requires the differentiation and reintegration of unconscious psychological complexes.

Interventions
Dream analysis provides an important way to understand the unconscious and its impact on conscious life. Transference and countertransference are part of the dynamic process occurring in the therapeutic relationship. Active imagination and other creative productions support the movement of the psyche from problems to solutions.

Limitations
This approach requires the client's serious and usually long-term commitment in terms of time, money, and personal effort. Clients, based on personality makeup, are self-selecting of this theoretical approach.

The Case of Maria: A Jungian Approach

Psychological problems call attention to one-sided attitudes—and create possibilities for movement. This happens when personality disunity activates the unconscious. Conflictual needs and values serve as touchstones for growth and for the development of authentic self-definition. Being involved in Jungian work equips people to become their own interpreters of life and to decipher the meaning in their experiences.

The beginning paragraph of the case study informs us about the importance of Maria's spiritual life and her family connections. She appeals to the church for assistance, a place where the symbols and rituals can provide support during times of distress. Her anxiety represents dissonance with family values that previously held meaning, as well as the current lack of family support. Although she is suffering and unable to comprehend the meaning of her pain, an aspect of her personality is embarking on psychological exploration.

Childhood issues, conflicts, and the present situation signal Maria's ineffective patterns which are operating autonomously and taking over her ego functioning. The initial information about Maria shows her ego lacking sufficient connection to the self, or core of her being, signified by the decomposition of her persona. This damaged ego-self axis negatively affects confidence, ability to function, and access to internal support.

We develop an image of self as an infant initially through body experiences. Maria displays denial of her physical existence, and her not eating symbolizes a refusal of emotional and physical nourishment. The treatment will explore her history with food in childhood and in crisis times during adulthood. Jung says,

> But if we can reconcile ourselves with the mysterious truth that the spirit is the life of the body seen from within, and the body an outer manifestation of the life of the spirit—the two being really one—then we can understand why the striving to transcend the present level of consciousness through acceptance of the unconscious must give the body its due, and why recognition of the body cannot tolerate a philosophy that denies it in the name of the spirit. (1968, Par. 2142)

Part of Jungian counseling or psychotherapy involves exploring childhood, recurrent, and present dreams. The dream emanates from the unconscious and is compensatory to consciousness for personality adjustment and rectification. Taken alone, a dream is ambiguous and contains a multiplicity of meanings; a series of dreams, however, shows an arrangement around a particular problem, a circumambulation (or "walking around") to gain different perspectives. Few or no associations demonstrates repression and difficulty accessing the material due to resistance.

Rather than the counselor or therapist supplying brilliant associations, a correct interpretation is what fits for the dreamer. Later on, as a therapeutic relationship is established, Maria can begin dialoguing with the dream figures, drawing them, and/or writing her reactions and amplifications. The first session is a time to establish rapport and build a place where she can begin to share her material. Her efforts along with the Jungian counselor or therapist aim to translate the upset in her life into a developing consciousness.

The initial dream presented by a client depicts the prognosis for the course of the counseling or psychotherapy. The dream is a useful instrument for opening dialogue with the inner dimensions of the psyche. It expresses psychological truths about the dreamer—often differently than the dreamer sees consciously. Maria's dream presents no definitive answer about whether she will get through her dilemmas.

The dream shows Maria swamped by unconscious contents that simultaneously call for a deepened relationship to them by understanding the images. Its recurrence demonstrates that the problem is not solved by her avoiding life or through self-denial. Maria's emotional upset after the dream shows the unconscious shaking her to attention. She associates the dream characters with anxiety and fear. Maria has a part of her personality which internally attacks; she feels powerless, disintegrating, and on the verge of giving up. As her ego position weakens, she is depleted and self-esteem decreases. Substituting the unhealed wounds with a persona adaptation does not work.

The dream portrays shadow aspects erupting from repression and in pursuit of Maria. The faceless figures represent unknown psychological parts. Their disturbing images confuse her in her attempts to find the way out. Having no exit denotes an existential crisis. Unrecognized shadow elements turn against the personality, become destructive, and negatively affect the urge for life. The shadow leads to transformation and renewal, but when obfuscated and laden with repressed guilt and shame, conflict results. The spirit darkens and the unconscious assumes a devouring nature, forcing attention inwards.

Maria is in the midst of a cultural and personal identity crisis demonstrated by her internal conflict. In the dream the warehouse represents a large, dark, and undefined space, like her psyche. What are the contents of the boxes and crates? Does she fear them as well as the large space? Her awaking with an unexpressed scream graphically shows the bottled-up fear about the encroaching unknown elements. She feels hopeless, threatened by destructive impulses, in turmoil, and without safety. Her tears represent sorrow, loss, cleansing, and purification. Maria might gain sustenance from remembering that water is a significant symbol in the Catholic Church for renewal through the baptismal ceremony and for receiving blessings.

The complex related to Maria's self-worth is activated and shows that the ego's networking capacity with other parts of the personality is torn apart from her mourning and losses. The current situation probably replicates earlier experiences. Depressive illnesses are often caused by painful losses inadequately mourned and summarily repressed. In mythology, death and dismemberment represent transitory stages to rebirth and new growth.

Maria stands between being an accomplished woman and being disabled by depression. The depression can be a force stopping her or initiating her toward individuation. It corresponds to the nigredo, the dark beginnings of the alchemical process, and progresses through various stages toward the treasure in the personality. These steps are integral to Maria's overcoming her psychic inertia and facing reality rather than being crushed by it.

The Jungian counselor or therapist sits with a client to cultivate the therapeutic alliance, develop rapport, and mutually explore messages from the dreams and her reactions. Every rent in a client's psychic life adds to her burdens and also can illuminate the path to be taken. The dream stimulates encountering these problems, yet Maria has not developed a means for internal communication. The affirmative feeling to her self is absent, and primary needs are unmet. The intensity of her suffering raises questions of timing and technical ability of the Jungian counselor or therapist—based on the careful observation and evaluation of her capacity to comprehend.

According to the *DSM-IV*, we can say the problem is a narcissistic disorder. Her wounding in love is masked by trying to please others rather than connecting to her Self. Inner emptiness, undifferentiated feelings, and the need to preserve the persona mask show internal estrangement. Maria's dark feelings gain access to the ego and disturb her ability to function. Discomfort in relationships and retreating to isolation signify a severe denial of her life.

What mixture of emotions does Maria feel about her family and the pressures she internalized from childhood? What psychological cost did she pay for her previous success? An authentic sense of self is rooted in a well-developed sexual identity based on identification with the parent of the same sex; hence the important influence in a daughter's early years of her mother's presence. There is discord between the inborn archetype of mother and Maria's behavior as a mother. She is distant and even rejecting of her children, who symbolize the future, potential, and new life. Denying her children indicates Maria's own psychological problems with love and intimacy. Because of her treatment from her former husband, Maria does not convey information about him in any positive light. Erasing him from her children's lives may be Maria's attempt to repress the pain, as well as a way of coping with his abuse. Therapy would explore what she experienced with her parents and their relation to her when she was the same age as her children are now.

Leaving home during college represents separation from the "participation mystique" binding Maria to her family and Hispanic background. This is a phrase Jung used to denote the interpersonal and unconscious melding between people. Whenever we are locked in and unable to escape the influence of another, we tend to be drawn back to the emotions of early life when escape was impossible. The child perceiving parents in a certain way tends to perceive herself, her partner, and her life in a similar pattern. The old therefore superimposes itself on the present. Tied to the parental complex, Maria cannot access her own position, and her frustration is now turned against herself through despair and lack of self-care. Although seemingly identified with her background, Maria radically broke from it by marrying outside its contained world to a man who denigrated it and her. If father or mother is insufficient emotionally, the psychological situation for healthy development is not fulfilled. A hole in the psyche of a daughter forms and fills with splits and confusions that destructively affect work, relationships, and self-regard.

Maria is not consciously aware of these archetypal energies symbolized in her name, a derivative of Mary. In the Catholic Church this name represents mother, virgin, and whore—encompassing many aspects of the feminine archetype. Maria's story can be likened to the Greek myth of Jason, who left his wife, Medea, for another woman. Medea, in despair and rage, killed her children. Maria is enacting a similar rage through the withdrawal of feelings and attention to her children, causing them harm. What did Maria introject concerning the masculine and feminine from her parents and the Hispanic culture? What psychological roots are causing this confusion, denial, and withdrawal into herself?

Why did she choose an abusive white male to marry? Most likely his behavior reflects her animus, or inner masculine side, her perception of women, and the attacks within herself. In another myth, that of Psyche and Eros, the heroine, Psyche, is given tasks to accomplish alone and before she returns to her lover, Eros. Psyche must learn care for herself rather than attending to the needs of others. Maria also must learn this lesson, or else she is in danger of losing her courage, resolution, and Eros, or feelings of relatedness.

The development of Maria's feeling side arises from an innate need for balance to her intellect. Maria prefers to be alone and shuns the passions of life. Even her children are held at a distance. These factors evidence the characteristics of an introverted thinking sensation type. Adaptation to the environment fails with an overdeveloped superior function, in this case thinking. Blocked libido causes the inferior feeling function to be activated. Jung states: "Over against the polymorphism of the . . . instinctual nature there stands the regulating principle of individuation. . . . Together they form a pair of opposites . . . often spoken of as nature and spirit. . . . This opposition is the expression and perhaps also the basis of the tension from which psychic energy flows" (1960, p. 58).

The immaturity of the psyche makes itself apparent in crisis situations. As the problem becomes acute, the lack of internal solidity is increasingly perceptible. The opposite sides of Maria's nature are embattled and unable to be contained within herself. Maria is on an edge of accessing the fundamental inner structures she needs to hold the anxiety and foster psychological growth. Jung referred to the **"canalization of libido,"** the energy transformation of psychic intensities or values from one psychological aspect to another. The psychological process of progression and regression creates internal adaptation so the personality flow recommences.

As stated earlier, Jungian treatment includes using the transference and countertransference. For Maria it may be affected by the conflict she exhibits with men and with herself as a woman—and the difficulties with trust and intimacy. As with dreams, the Jungian counselor or therapist does not direct, but listens to the way Maria's psyche leads them both. The psychological work is also affected by the conscious and unconscious impressions, input, and reactions of the counselor or therapist.

No captivity is more terrible and difficult to break than the one an individual imposes on him- or herself. As Maria's dream warns, the captivity by the shadow is threatening to break out. Natural parts turn negative when rejected, assume control, and then shut out life. The situation may be released through developing a conscious and responsible attitude to the shadow, making the contents knowable, and turning the energy. We are left not knowing what Maria will do.

The situation of distress, blackness of feeling, and the wishes and motives from the unconscious signal the reconciliation of warring elements for conscious differentiation of the psyche. Jung says, "No one can overlook either the dynamism or the imagery of the instincts without the gravest injury to himself. Violation or neglect of instinct has painful consequences of a physiological and psychological nature for whose treatment medical help is required" (1959, p. 57).

Collective answers cannot satisfy the individual, as each person has a unique psychological complexity. The path involves turning to the unconscious and gleaning its resources for creativity and knowledge in a process of differentiating and integrating unconscious contents. A relationship with oneself and others rests on the dynamism of the psychological quest for individual identity. Emergence of the personality is fraught with the struggle to separate from the chaos beginning any psychological endeavor. By going through the suffering, we discover the meaning of personal destiny and gain feeling for life. This entails taking the total self seriously.

References

Jung, C. G. (1953a). *Collected works: Two essays on analytical psychology.* New York: Pantheon.

Jung, C. G. (1953b). *Collected works 12: Psychology and alchemy.* New York: Pantheon.

Jung, C. G. (1954). *Collected works 16: The practice of psychotherapy.* New York: Pantheon.

Jung, C. G. (1959). *Collected works 9: The archetypes and the collective unconscious.* New York: Pantheon.

Jung, C. G. (1960). *Collected works 8: The structure and dynamics of the psyche.* New York: Pantheon.

Jung, C. G. (1963). *Memories, dreams, reflections.* New York: Pantheon.

Jung, C. G. (1964). *Man and his symbols.* Garden City, NY: Doubleday.

Jung, C. G. (1966). *Collected works 16: The practice of psychotherapy.* New York: Pantheon.

Jung, C. G. (1967). *Collected works 13: Alchemical studies.* New York: Pantheon.

Jung, C. G. (1968). *Collected works 18: Symbolic life.* New York: Pantheon.

Adlerian Theory

Thomas J. Sweeney
Professor Emeritus
Ohio University

Alfred Adler created not only a psychology of human behavior, but also a social movement to correct the methods of child rearing and human interaction that foster conflicts and individual discouragement. Born in Vienna in 1870, Adler was the middle child in a Jewish merchant family. He was subject to sickness and injury as a child, and these experiences likely influenced his pursuit of medicine as a vocation. Energetic and fun-loving, he was known to enjoy parties, singing, the theater, and time with friends and colleagues. He fled Nazi Germany in 1935, and lived in the United States long enough to help establish what is now the North American Society of Adlerian Psychology. He died in 1937 while on a lecture tour in Scotland. While Adler is probably best remembered for his work here and in Europe with families and children, his theory and work have been extended to include every dimension of counseling and therapy: individuals, couples, families, groups, and organizations.

Adler's theory is based on a phenomenological understanding of individual motivation and behavior. He rooted his interventions in the values and philosophy of social democracy. **Rudolf Dreikurs** was an articulate spokesman, a consummate teacher, and a clinician of Adlerian thought and practice. His books on parenting, marriage, and classroom management have become classics translated into several languages. Even a casual reading of Adler's and Dreikurs's works will reveal the depth of their insights into both individual behavior and societal needs. The practical applications of their insights, however, have given their work its greatest impact. While followers have added new dimensions to Adler's theory and new techniques to his methods, the foundation in philosophy and values remains essentially the same, and research across disciplines continues to corroborate the soundness of his ideas.

Background

Adler's theory is based on a phenomenological understanding of individual motivation and behavior. He rooted his interventions in the values and philosophy of social democracy. Called **individual psychology,** his approach was born in Vienna at the turn of the twentieth century. Adler has been historically overshadowed by his contemporary, Sigmund Freud, although these two pioneers of psychological theory and practice were collegial in their initial relationship. That relationship changed, however, as their ideological differences became more evident. In fact, the differences between them were so significant that the two eventually became antagonists.

Adler's interest in why people respond differently to similar life events is reflected in his early attention to the study of **organ inferiority** (1907). His later lectures, books, and articles illustrated even more clearly his conviction that individuals create their own evaluations and choices of how to respond to life events. In 1935, when the Nazis began their oppression of Europe, Adler had to flee to the United States with his radical and politically unacceptable ideas about a society of equals. Although he taught and lectured extensively in the United States before his death in 1937, there was great resistance to his ideas from people who had adopted the tenets of Freudian psychoanalysis. In addition, the United States was far from practicing the egalitarian principles upon which individual psychology is based.

Adler's most prolific advocate, Rudolf Dreikurs, published a number of books, monographs, and articles that are still widely read today. Dreikurs's book on marriage (1946) forecast the social revolution between men and women that we have experienced since World War II. His books *Children: The Challenge* (Dreikurs & Soltz, 1964) and *Maintaining Sanity in the Classroom* (Dreikurs, Grunwald, & Pepper, 1971) are classics in this country and abroad. Ridiculed and rejected by many of his peers in medicine and psychiatry, Dreikurs lived long enough to see his books become best-sellers among laypersons and professionals alike, and his work continues through his students and colleagues.

Human Nature: A Developmental Perspective

Early Development

Adler and Dreikurs are probably best-known for their work with children and the adults in their lives. Adler never considered the child totally dependent at birth. He believed that infants begin training adults far better than many adults train their children. Research has demonstrated that infants are far more responsive and capable of modifying adult behavior than was previously believed.

Adler firmly believed that love and parental interest are important ingredients to healthy personality development. Unfortunately, too much of what some parents consider to be love results in pampering or overprotecting. Pampered children may perceive that they are not able, that others must take care of them, or that terrible things may happen when their parents are away. If corrective training is not instituted during a child's early years, such notions may become a part of what Adler referred to as one's unique, private logic. **Private logic** is his term for an individual's unique pattern of thoughts, feelings, and attitudes that guides understanding, predicting, and managing life experiences and behavior.

In most instances, children begin developing a sense of their strengths and weaknesses while attempting mastery over those aspects of life that seem within their reach. They also begin to make observations about their place in events around them. As they grow in size and ability, others' expectations for them change. Then they must decide if and how they will respond. If they are convinced of their security in the family and assess their capabilities as adequate, they will require less attention, service, and outward encouragement from those around them.

On the other hand, many children make inaccurate assessments about being loved, appreciated, and secure within their family. These children likewise behave according to their assessments. Adler noted that children usually are excellent observers of others, but they often are poor evaluators and interpreters of their experiences. As a consequence, he believed that **feelings of inferiority** are common because of children's initial experiences as dependent, small, and socially inferior persons. Feelings of inferiority are not inherently good or bad. For example, individuals often move toward mastery and competence to compensate for these feelings. Through social interaction, they become persons whom Adler (1938) described as high in social interest and empathy. Children's responses to early experiences within the family unit, then, have importance for how they approach their basic life tasks, such as school, friendships, and family participation. Later in this chapter, the practical usefulness of understanding the goals of misbehavior in reorienting thoughts and feelings of discouragement will be illustrated.

Family Constellation

Adler placed considerable importance upon the **family constellation,** which Shulman and Nikelly (1971) define as follows:

> Family constellation is a term used to describe the socio-psychological configuration of a family group. The personality characteristics and emotional distance of each person, age differences, order of birth, the dominance or submission of each member, the siblings, and the size of the family are all factors in the family constellation and affect the development of the personality. . . . [C]ertain behavior types can be characterized by examining the individual's place in the constellation. Thus, the first born, the second born, and the only child have certain characteristics which render their personality predictable in terms of attitudes, personality traits and subsequent behavior. (p. 35)

Individuals' perceptions of their family position have special significance for understanding their outlook on life. While much is said about **birth order** or **ordinal position** in relation to the family constellation, Adlerians are aware that it is the individual's **psychological position** that must be studied. For example, two children born six or more years apart each may perceive themselves as only children—that is, not as one who is the older and another who is second or younger, but simply as not being in a sibling relationship.

Adlerians typically list five ordinal positions: **oldest, second, middle, youngest, and only child.** Each position is associated with certain common characteristics, but these characteristics are nomothetic impressions that should be quickly set aside when idiographic data about a given individual refute the validity of the classical characteristics. The general principle is that each child makes a unique place for him- or herself. The characteristics that distinguish a child from the other children in the family are singularly embraced as the child's very own. However, Adlerians also use these nomothetic characteristics as a way of uncovering an individual's uniqueness—for example, how he or she is different from other oldest or youngest children.

The **oldest child** is literally the first child of the family, most often the cause of glad tidings and happily the center of attention. Then one day a new child appears in the family. Considering the proximity in months or years, parental attitudes, sex, and other such variables, oldest children evaluate the threat to their position in the family. On the average, the oldest child learns to take the younger newcomer in stride, especially if the parents provide encouragement for the oldest child to recognize his or her place as secure within the family. Oldest children generally are able to relate well to adults, subscribe more readily to adult expectations and values, help with the younger children, assume social responsibility, and develop socially acceptable ways of coping with life's tasks. A tendency of oldest children is to strive for perfection as a goal, which can have negative consequences. When they assert their independence from parental dominance, they tend to do so covertly; that is, they do not "hear" instructions, or they "forget" things.

The **second child** arrives to find someone already ahead of him or her. Second children born within six years of the older child (again depending upon age and similar variables) typically will be less responsible, more independent, and more interested in whatever the oldest does not pursue or master. Second children often strive to be first in something. Sibling rivalry can be quite intense in families that encourage comparisons between children.

The **middle child** must compete with both an older and a younger sibling. Middle children often feel squeezed in their position. They perceive themselves as singularly disadvantaged. They believe that they have few, if any, of the privileges of the oldest youngster, nor any of the advantages of the youngest. What's more, oldest children often help take care of the youngest, thereby establishing for themselves an ally and leaving the middle children to fend for themselves. In this way, too, oldest children acquire a reputation among the other children as being "bossy."

Middle children will most likely establish their uniqueness in directions opposite to their older sibling. They may be more independent, rebellious, and sensitive, and they may overtly seek assurances of their place with their parents. As is true with each position in the family, children can transcend these early perceptions through compensatory behavior that eventually works to their benefit. Each child, however, often perceives his or her position as the most burdensome to bear.

Youngest children enjoy a position that they perceive as the center of attention. They have both parents and older siblings to entertain them and provide them service. While youngest children might be troublesome at times, they also have protectors to care for them. In fact, as youngest children get a little older, it is even fun to start something with the middle child and watch the older ally and the parents run to save the "baby." A youngest child is often described as cute, a charmer, and the family's baby, no matter how old he or she becomes. She may choose to use her manipulative ways to just get by and enjoy life's many pleasures. On the other hand, if both parents value academic achievement, the youngest might be the hardest runner and greatest achiever of them all if he perceives that approach as a way to make his unique place.

Only children may have the perceptions of the oldest child, but with one important exception. They are never dethroned and are less likely to feel the pressure of a close competitor. Only children may be perceived as precocious for their age, comfortable with adults, responsible, and cooperative. Unlike other youngsters, they may have little or no intimate give-and-take with other children. This can make early school experiences more difficult as these children begin coping with new life situations involving a peer group.

Major Constructs

Socio-Teleo-Analytic

Adler perceived humans as social beings with a natural inclination toward other people. Developmentally, human beings are among the most dependent of all creatures at birth. They must be cared for if they are to survive. As a consequence, they can be understood best through their early interactions with others, since through their early impressions they develop rules about life that they use throughout their lives to understand, predict, and manage their unique perceptions of themselves, others, and the world. They develop a private logic that becomes a part of their unconscious guiding principles for daily living. They live life as if their unique perceptions were fact or irrefutable reality. Through selective perceptions, these fictive notions tend to go unchallenged and often are self-fulfilling prophecies that only serve to reinforce themselves.

Socio.   Adler believed that human beings have a basic inclination toward *Gemeinschaftsgefühl,* that is, a striving to feel belongingness, a willingness to serve the greater good for the betterment of humankind. The closest interpretation of this German word in English is "social interest." An expression of this inclination is observed in each person's striving to make a place for him- or herself and to feel belongingness. Understanding individuals' striving becomes a significant factor in helping them to overcome self-defeating behaviors.

Adler was a phenomenologist who believed that human motivation was understood through the eyes of the beholder. He referred to the basic notions that guide us through life as our style of life or, as it is more commonly referred to now, **life-style.** He characterized life-style as "unity in each individual in his thinking, feeling, acting; in his so called conscious and unconscious, in every expression of his personality. This (self-consistent) unity we call the style of life of the individual" (Ansbacher & Ansbacher, 1967, p. 175).

Life-style is not determined by heredity or environment, but both are important antecedents. Individuals decide how they think, value, and feel about their gender, family position, or ethnicity. Each life-style is unique. Each is developed by an individual according to its usefulness in coping with other people and the world. Through an understanding of these unique perceptions, individuals also come to understand the consistency in their behavior.

Obviously, a psychology of personality that revealed no general or nomothetic rules of behavior upon which to base practice would be of little use. As I will show in subsequent sections, Adlerian principles do indeed provide many useful guidelines. Adler believed that individuals can be understood best within the social context of their transactions with others; and through this insight, a person's family constellation, early role models, and early recollections take on significance.

Teleo. *Teleo* denotes the goal-oriented nature of human beings. Behavior is purposive, even though this fact may be obscure to the observer. Individuals choose to act or not act because it is useful to them. They are not victims of instincts, heredity, environment, or experience. As Ansbacher (1969) writes, "The science of Individual Psychology developed out of the effort to understand that mysterious creative power of life—that power which expresses itself in the desire to develop, to strive and to achieve—and even to compensate for defeats in one direction by striving for success in another. This power is teleological—it expresses itself in the striving after a goal" (p. 1).

This teleological orientation has an optimistic and encouraging nature. As Rudolf Dreikurs (personal communication, June 1970) once said, "Tell a person what they are, schizophrenic, so what? Tell a person how they feel, sad or bad, so what? But, tell a person what they intend! Now that is something they can change!"

Because goals of behavior can be understood and anticipated, they can be changed. Individuals may choose to change the valuing of their goals or the behavior they use in their striving. Individuals, therefore, are not victims of circumstances beyond their control in any absolute way.

Analytic.   Individuals frequently report that they do not understand their behavior or motives. Closer inspection reveals that individuals often understand more than they willingly admit. The analytic aspect of individual psychology is derived from the observation that most behavior is based upon what is unconscious or not understood (Mosak & Dreikurs, 1973). In a helping relationship, however, individuals more readily accept direct disclosures about the purposes of their behavior, including purposes of which they were not consciously aware.

Adler was influenced by Vaihinger's *The Philosophy of "As If"* (1965). He concurred with Vaihinger that individuals behave "as if" circumstances were absolutely true: for example, life is threatening, I am inadequate, or others are more able than I. While some notions of individuals are stated clearly and believed beyond reproach, other notions are more subtle yet powerful in their influence upon behavior. Adler referred to both of these as **fictive notions.**

So long as individuals function fairly well in their daily lives, their fictive notions remain unexamined. When their notions are challenged or proved ineffective at maintaining feelings of belonging or adequacy, an emotional crisis develops. At these times, clients are most open to seeking counseling or psychotherapy. Individuals learn new or different behavior due to varying circumstances, including age, cultural milieu, and similar factors. One's life-style is not believed to change, however, except through psychotherapy, personally powerful life experiences, or other extraordinary causes such as brain injury, diseases, and drugs.

Holism

The **indivisibility** of a person is a fundamental belief of individual psychology. At a time when holistic approaches to medicine, mental health, and rehabilitation are coming into the forefront, a practitioner will find the usefulness of this view apparent.

Adlerians recognize the interaction between physical and psychological well-being. Biofeedback research and its application in stress management, for example, have helped to corroborate Adler's assumption that what one thinks can produce physiological symptoms similar to those that stem from a more physical origin. Infection, disease, and other injuries to the body have the potential to modify one's moods. Likewise, moods affect the physiological responses of the body. Fatigue, particularly due to distress, is symptomatic of the interaction of mind and body. In short, even personal experience suggests the validity of such a position. Adlerian practitioners also are aware that samples of an individual's behavior can help them understand a more global life plan and direction of movement. Such behaviors, however, are only an approximation of the total and must be kept in mind as such.

Holism, therefore, is a point of view from which to understand others as dynamic and self-directed. It also presents the concept of an interrelated mind and body moving through life with a unique plan for having significance in relation to others. Helping clients change how they think and feel in their relationships with others, for example, can result in better physical health, greater satisfaction with their work, and increased joy and interest in other aspects of their lives.

Function of Emotions and Feelings

Adler perceived emotions as tools necessary to the execution of behavior. Emotions are not considered entities unto themselves; love, joy, anger, sadness, guilt, and fear do not come to us out of a vacuum. We must perceive, value, feel, and then act.

Much of our valuing in regard to life, ourselves, and others is a blueprint already stored in our unconscious thought processes. Therefore, much of what is attributed to instant love, fear, or anger can be traced back to one's life-style data bank. This is the stuff of which self-talk is made.

Many clients wish to discredit this concept of emotions because it places responsibility on them for their present decisions and actions. Adlerians are very much interested in emotions, but more as signposts to the understanding of an individual's mistaken notions and intentions. As Dreikurs (1967) explained, the messages we send ourselves build the energy we use to act. We do not fall in love because we were struck by Cupid's arrow. Rather, we experience, value, and then emotionally commit to action to achieve our desired relationship.

Observers of the Adlerian counselor or therapist might conclude that he or she is insensitive to the anger, complaining, blaming, tears, or affection expressed in a counseling or therapy session. If the emotions are tools used by clients to distract or otherwise manipulate the counselor from the goals for counseling and psychotherapy, the practitioner may indeed seem unimpressed by their presence. It is the less visible feelings and attitudes that the Adlerian counselor or therapist will pursue—for example, isolation, lack of confidence, and insecurity. This deeper level of human empathy must be touched if genuine change and positive growth are to be realized.

Applications

Overview

This section is devoted to the goals of counseling, the process of change, and intervention strategies. From an Adlerian perspective, theory must be relevant to life, useful in practice, and contribute to positive outcomes for those who embrace its philosophy of social equality and human relations. This may be best expressed through an understanding of what Adler referred to as the "ironclad logic of social living," namely, that all persons, regardless of social station in life, are subject to the influence of natural and logical consequences and all must address the major life tasks of work, friendship, and love.

Naturally, there are great variations in the personal capabilities, family and social environment, education, and related factors which affect the development of individuals, couples, and families. Therefore, the goals of counseling and psychotherapy, as with education in general, are to facilitate human development by whatever methods and techniques are effective in achieving optimum wellness for all persons (Sweeney & Witmer, 1991; Witmer & Sweeney, 1992, 1998).

Personal change is primarily a result of individuals' choices and, under normal circumstances, is both their opportunity and responsibility to address as they move through life. Changes in thinking, feeling, and behaving come about by choices as a result of conscious or unconscious expectations for how one may meet life's tasks. Encouragement for meeting life's tasks, therefore, is the underlying strategy for helping to bring about change. Helping others to identify and understand the significance of their expectations through positive challenging of self, other, and life convictions is accomplished, for example, through life-style analysis, as in the case study of Maria later in this chapter.

Goals of Counseling and Psychotherapy

Adler believed that everyone is confronted by at least three major life tasks: **work, friendship,** and **love** (Dreikurs, 1953). In addition, Mosak and Dreikurs (1967) have identified two tasks only alluded to by Adler. The fourth task is one's dealing with the spiritual self in relation to the universe, God, and similar concepts. The fifth task concerns the individual's success in coping with the self as subject (I) and as object (me). The goals of counseling relate to helping others meet these tasks in meaningful, satisfying ways.

Figure 6.1 presents a model of wellness related to research across disciplines on longevity and quality of life. This model incorporates both Adler's concepts and those of Mosak and Dreikurs. In the figure, the five life tasks interact dynamically with one another and the life forces (shown in the outer band). Spirituality and self-direction are central to all other dimensions in relation to personality and human development. Self-direction incorporates twelve components: sense of worth, sense of control, realistic beliefs, emotional awareness and coping, problem solving and creativity, sense of humor, nutrition, exercise, self-care, stress management, gender identity, and cultural identity. Each of these components has importance in promoting or inhibiting good health and wellness, and each can be incorporated into a comprehensive counseling treatment plan (Myers, Witmer, & Sweeney, 1997). Likewise, spirituality as a life task has been found to be central to both quality of life and longevity. Optimism, hope, transcendence, and purposiveness as well as spiritual practices, religious affiliations, and altruistic benevolence are common

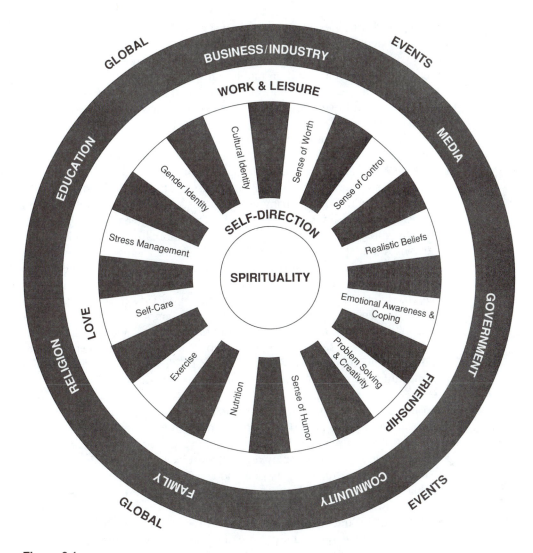

Figure 6.1
Model of Wellness
(Copyright 1996 by J. Melvin Witmer, Thomas J. Sweeney, & Jane E. Myers.)

characteristics of persons high in spirituality. Later in this chapter, the case of Maria will illustrate how both self-direction and spirituality can be incorporated into the goals of counseling. The major life tasks identified by Adler are discussed in the following sections.

Work.   Equipped with their unique rules or guidelines about life, themselves, and others, individuals move from childhood to preadolescence, adolescence, and adulthood with a societal expectation that they will become more responsible, cooperative, and able to creatively cope with life situations. Lack of success in the work task characterizes the most discouraged people in society. Although this task does not require gainful employment, persons who have difficulty sustaining employment are in all probability individuals who lack confidence in their worth and ability. In fact, individuals who have been successful earlier in life often experience doubts when faced with demotion, forced retirement, or loss of employment even when such circumstances have nothing to do with their work performance per se.

In the school situation, failure and dropping out are tantamount to demotion and unemployment—that is, loss of confidence and a sense of worth. Dreikurs (1968) believed that children who failed were not bad or lazy but instead discouraged. To face and fulfill one's life tasks requires the courage to be imperfect, to make mistakes, to fail occasionally but to try again. For too many children, school becomes a confirmation of their private assessment: they are not adequate. In later life, many of these individuals will be consistently unemployed, welfare recipients, or institutionalized. Although it appears difficult for persons to change in later life, Adler believed that we always have that capability.

Our goals in all such cases of discouragement are to build on the assets of the individual, challenge the prejudices, and instill greater confidence and faith in self through information, skill development, and emotional support (Savickas, 1998). Both in work settings and in schools, productivity and improved morale go hand in hand. Adlerian counselors working as consultants in business and school settings have much to offer in helping to promote a sense of belonging, cooperation, cohesiveness, and creative problem solving that enhances self-worth and team productivity. Work team groups and classroom meetings are methods used to achieve such outcomes.

Friendship and Love.   Dreikurs (1953) indicated that discouragement generally was not limited to one life task area. For example, most individuals can cope with the daily requirements of work whether by gainful employment or through services to others; and doubts, reservations, and fears may reveal themselves only at certain times. Friendship and intimate love relationships tend to demand cooperation, give-and-take, and respect. If an individual has persistent difficulties in either or both of these life tasks, discouragement is present that probably can be noted in the other areas as well. Obviously, not all life task difficulties can be traced to psychosocial origin. However, Dreikurs (1946) stated that whenever individuals persistently complain, blame, make excuses, report fears, or reveal disabilities, they are disclosing discouragement.

Of the life tasks, love relationships require the greatest courage and faith in self and the other party. Individual weaknesses, concerns, and peculiarities come under closer scrutiny here than in most other life situations. Adlerians have noted that the very characteristics that attract individuals to one another also contribute to their friction in marriage. Changing attitudes about the roles of men and women notwithstanding, the private logic of partners in their selection of a mate means getting more of those specific qualities than you like! A man may select a woman because, among other attributes, she is intelligent, interested in many areas, and admired by others for her competence. She may have liked him because of his fun-loving nature, his laid-back, "smell the roses" enjoyment of life, and his appreciation of her positive qualities. As their relationship unfolds, friction can develop if there is not a balance in these qualities: he needs to be sufficiently serious, competent, and successful; and she needs to appreciate his attributes, be able to slow down, and initiate some of the fun in their relationship.

Adler demonstrated that once individuals understand their own movement through life, they can decide to change their attitudes and behavior with renewed respect for themselves and one another. For example, through marriage enrichment groups as well as counseling, couples can learn to appreciate one another's private logic and to develop mutual respect on the basis of a deeper, more intimate knowledge of one another.

The Process of Change

Adlerians believe that the life-style of the individual is a unique, unconscious, cognitive "map" that facilitates one's movement through life (Mosak & Dreikurs, 1973). Life-style is a unifying set of convictions that permits individuals to evaluate, manage, and predict events within their experiences. Adlerian counseling and psychotherapy involve uncovering and using our understanding of these combinations of beliefs to reorient thoughts and goals related to self, others, and the world upon which individuals' expectations are based. These self-determined notions become the source of direction and movement through which an individual establishes his or her place in the world. By consciously examining these notions, change is possible.

In many instances, behavior change can take place with little more than an insight into how one's goals can be met more effectively by a modest change. For example, parents and children learn quickly that the use of natural and logical consequences—that is, negative results from children's poor choices in behavior—can win cooperation and peace for the family within as little as one counseling session. One illustration of this technique is letting a child who persistently forgets to take lunch to school experience hunger as a consequence. Without any punitive reaction of the parent, this child can learn more responsible behavior.

Also, within each individual's life-style is latitude for behavioral choice—that is, one's convictions may result in a variety of behaviors. For example, the belief that "life is a test that only the strong survive" may result in a person's choosing the vocation of special-forces commando or martial arts black belt. If that belief is combined with "I am a fragile person," the conviction may result in someone who is a submissive individual. The potential for pursuing socially useful or useless life activities, therefore, lies within the same life-style convictions.

Adlerians make a distinction between counseling and psychotherapy processes. In the case of counseling, behavior change within the existing life-style is the goal, whereas in psychotherapy, a change in life-style is the desired outcome. Adlerian success in psychotherapy requires **motivation modification.** Dreikurs (1963) stated: "We do not attempt primarily to change behavior patterns or remove symptoms. If a patient improves his behavior because he finds it profitable at the time, without changing his basic premises, then we do not consider that as a therapeutic success. We are trying to change goals, concepts, and notions" (p. 1046).

I have experienced instances in which this distinction with behavior modification was clearly justified. An illustration can be found in the life-styles of some individuals in professions related to counseling. For some people, the motivation for being a helper was intimately intertwined with their concept of self-worth. When unsuccessful as a helper, some individuals developed feelings of discouragement and disappointment. A change in behavior was not necessary, but they benefited from an examination of why they wished to help, which allowed them to determine how such notions were self-defeating. By reframing their motivations for helping, their behavior as a helper changed little, but their attitudes and feelings about their capacity as a helper changed in such a way as to be liberating personally and more effective professionally.

Many youngsters strive daily to please their parents, teachers, and others. They are rewarded for being "good" children. Although a change in behavior may not be necessary, the motivation for doing well deserves serious examination. The child striving for perfection is a discouraged person whose goal can never be attained. Providing encouragement for simply participating in life, including acceptance of their mistakes, can be one objective for helping such youngsters.

On the other hand, changes in behavior can open new alternatives to behavior and attitude change. For example, the counselor's knowledge of Dreikurs's **four goals of children's disruptive behavior**—that is, (1) excessive attention seeking, (2) personal power, (3) revenge, and (4) inadequacy—can help to suggest alternative behaviors to the youngsters without conducting a life-style analysis. The use of these goals is illustrated later in this chapter. Similarly, Dreikurs's (1971) **four steps for problem solving**—that is, (1) establishing mutual respect through effective, empathic communication, (2) pinpointing and neutralizing issues of contention such as who is "right," loss of respect, and power, (3) establishing *what* is needed and desired to ameliorate or improve a relationship, and (4) reaching agreement on a plan to achieve the desired goals—can be implemented in establishing a new agreement between marriage partners without changing basic life goals.

Therefore, for the purposes of this chapter, Adlerian counseling includes those methods and techniques used within the helping relationship that encourage situational, attitude, or behavior changes. This counseling frees individuals to function more fully as self-determining, creative, and responsible equals within their environment. By contrast, Adlerian psychotherapy results in fundamental changes in motivation as evidenced by changes in early recollections and the guiding themes of one's life-style. While psychotherapy is more dramatic in its holistic impact, it is truly only an extension of the encouragement process and methods designed to assist clients in becoming full participants in the human endeavor.

Intervention Strategies

The number and types of interventions used by Adlerians are those common to most professional counselors and psychotherapists today. In fact, to be Adlerian is to be eclectic with regard to methods and techniques. It is the understanding and importance of personal motivation, as well as the philosophy and values of individual psychology, which tend to set us apart from other approaches, not our methods or techniques per se. What follows, however, are interventions that have uniquely Adlerian aspects or are central to Adlerian intervention.

Adler, Dreikurs, and those who followed them have been in the forefront of community mental health in this country and abroad. In fact, Dreikurs was criticized by Americans early in his career for his radical practices of group work, family counseling, and individual therapy demonstrations. Because this work is no longer seen as radical, neophytes could miss the significance of his contributions. Among others are methods of encouragement, parent and teacher education, and life-style assessment with individuals and couples, including the significance of early recollections.

Encouragement.   **Methods of encouragement** prompt the recipient to act with responsibility, deliberation, and conviction. Courageous actions involve acting responsibly despite uncertainties or fears for the outcome. Equally important, they free one to live fully as an active participant each moment of each day. The essential element in the concept of encouragement is courage. As Gandhi said, "Courage is the one true foundation of character. Without courage there can be no truth, no love or religion. For one subject to fear can pursue neither truth nor love" (Nehru, 1958, p. i).

Actions that tend to encourage include:

1. Bringing attention to *what* someone is doing more so than *how* he or she is doing—that is, evaluating performance

   Example: That's a beautiful shine on the floor. What did you do to get it that way? (invites more explanation)

   Versus: I'll bet you take better care of your house than anyone else in town. (compares)

2. Focusing on present behavior more than the past or the future

   Example: It's really obvious that you're enjoying this project. I can tell by the effort and enthusiasm you have for it.

   Versus: I sure wish you'd work this hard all the time!

3. Acknowledging the deed rather than praising the person

   Example: I really appreciate your help. Thanks!

   Versus: You're such a good kid. You always do the right thing!

4. Emphasizing the effort rather than the product or outcome

   Example: That was fun! As I learn to be more patient and not rush the ball, I should be able to give you a better match! (emphasis on progress, what to do, and the enjoyment of increased competence)

   Versus: I ordered a new racket that's going to give me the advantage I need to beat that guy! (it's winning that counts)

5. Promoting intrinsic motivation (i.e., satisfaction, enjoyment, challenge) as preferable to extrinsic motivation

   Example: No matter how long it takes, nothing gives me more pleasure than capturing a moment in time that reflects the beauty in life.

   Versus: What do I get for doing it? What's in it for me?

6. Bringing attention to what is being learned rather than what is not being learned

   Example: You've just about mastered nouns and pronouns. That will be very helpful to you in learning to construct sentences. Now let's look at a couple of problems that gave you difficulty and help you master them.

   Versus: You need to get help at home or the rest of this term is going to be hard for you.

7. Attending more to what is being done correctly rather than to what is not being done correctly

   Example: You got 84 out of 100 correct. With just a little more effort, I know you'll be able to go on to the next lessons too.
   Versus: You missed 16 out of 100.

In short, a major emphasis of encouragement is helping individuals establish goals, attitudes, and competencies needed to cope with life as they experience it.

Effective verbal communication is also an important part of encouragement. It involves the following considerations:

1. Reflective listening, which reveals an awareness of the kinds and intensity of feelings expressed

2. Nonjudgmental attitudes, which show respect for the individual even though the counselor may not like what the person has done

3. Accepting responsibility for feelings and avoiding blaming, complaining, and nagging

4. Understanding the purpose of behavior and how it may be self-defeating to the other person or ourselves as we try to find solutions to life circumstances

However, limiting one's attention to verbal methods of encouragement is not sufficient. For example, Adlerians stress the significance of action, not words, when coping with discipline problems. The same principle can be espoused for encouragement. All of us look for evidence that what others say is revealed also in their behaviors. Nonverbal encouragement can be as simple as smiling or as involved as coordinating a surprise birthday party specifically designed to reflect love, respect, and genuine caring for another person. At such times, the recipients may not remember exactly what was said or what was given to them, but they will remember the manner in which it was given.

Acts of encouragement may include the following (Sweeney, 1998):

1. Help someone do a job that he or she might otherwise do alone.

2. Listen to someone describe a hobby, a vacation, or an event that he or she wanted to share.

3. Keep busy and remain patient while someone else completes a task that he or she found difficult.

4. Complete or do another's task in order to let that person have more leisure time.

5. Share a book or a recording that has value to you.

6. Offer to do a favor without being asked.

7. Send letters of appreciation, thanks, or remembrance, especially when such a gesture might easily be overlooked.

8. Intervene on another's behalf to help others appreciate his or her capabilities or contributions.

Encouragement is multifaceted. It is an essential part of helping others cope, change, and meet life's challenges. Mastering the art of encouragement is a continuing process that Adlerians incorporate into everything they do.

Parent and Teacher Education.   The following list summarizes Adlerian thought as it concerns adults who guide children:

1. Free yourself of the mistaken notion that you should control a child's behavior.
2. Accept responsibility for changing your own behavior first.
3. Respect the child or adolescent for making the best choices, as he or she perceives them, under the circumstances.
4. Realize that children are attempting to make a place for themselves by whatever means seem available, that is, by employing socially useful or useless behavior.
5. Understand that when children misbehave, their misbehavior is an outward sign of their internal discouragement as participating members of the class or family.
6. Commit yourself to helping children learn self-discipline and cooperation by friendly participation in the daily tasks that everyone must fulfill.

As a consultant to adults who are working and living with young people, you may find the following four steps helpful in summarizing what is required of you (Sweeney, 1998). You can remember these steps easily by using the acronym **CARE.**

1. **C**atch yourself; don't act impulsively.
2. **A**ssess goals. What goals are served by the behavior?
3. **R**espond with consequences and encouragement.
4. **E**xecute with consistency, friendliness, and respect.

Dreikurs believed that before an adult can begin doing something correctly, he or she must stop doing what is incorrect. Parents and teachers alike tend to behave toward their children and students the way their own parents and teachers behaved toward them. These old methods are not appropriate today because they were based on an authoritarian system. As a consequence, the following recommendations are offered.

Catch Yourself.   Behavioral research on conditioning affirms the Adlerian conviction that what most adults do impulsively when they respond to misbehavior is incorrect. Stopping what the adult has been doing opens the possibility for change by both the child and adult.

A comment on talking too much deserves special note. Adults tend to talk when annoyed by misbehavior, even though the children rarely listen. In fact, we have nonverbal agreements with the children about when they should listen. Counseling and consultation with parents, teachers, and children reveal that such factors as the number of times instructions are repeated, pitch of voice, and vocal inflection convey more to children than what is said. In such situations, silence becomes an adult's ally.

New rules can be established: for example, the adult gives instructions once, and after that they are repeated only under exceptional circumstances or when it is convenient. Action, not words, becomes the principal means of conveying intentions.

Assess Goals. Adlerians have been teaching adults about the goals of children's misbehavior as a means of redirecting the motivation and behavior of such children toward more cooperative, responsible self-discipline. Being aware of the goals can help adults understand children better and avoid inadvertently reinforcing the misbehaviors they wish to correct. The goals of children's misbehavior before the age of 12 (the age is approximate) are excessively seeking attention, pursuing personal power, seeking revenge, and withdrawing through inadequacy. To identify the goals and begin anticipating corrective action, the counselor should ask the adults four questions:

1. What did the youngster do?
2. What did you do?
3. How did the child respond to your action?
4. How did you feel?

An example will help to illustrate. The following excerpt is from a discussion between a teacher and a counselor.

TEACHER: Samantha is constantly passing notes, talking to other children, raising her hand at inappropriate times, or just blurting out her thoughts. She's really driving me crazy!

COUNSELOR: In your most recent encounter, what did she do? Then what did you do?

TEACHER: Well, just this morning I gave instructions for everyone to remain quiet while one of the children read from a book he had brought from home. Not two minutes later, Samantha was giggling and pointing at the boy across from her and passing a note to her friend behind her. When I told her to stop, she did; but a short time later she was doing something else.

COUNSELOR: In this case, would you say you were more annoyed than angry?

TEACHER: Well, yes. Most of the time she gets right back to work, but I just wish she'd stop bugging me.

In this case, we see a child who is seeking attention. We understand this goal because of two pieces of information. First, when the teacher corrects Samantha, *she stops what she was doing.* Second, the *teacher feels more annoyed* by Samantha's behavior than anything else. This feeling is significant because children seeking power usually will not stop their behavior until they have clearly challenged the adult and provoked anger to some degree. Children seeking revenge will do what is necessary to elicit hurt, disappointment, or similar feelings. Children wishing to withdraw through inadequacy will have succeeded when the adult finally says, "I give up. I can't do anything with her!" The feeling most often expressed by the adult is one of defeat.

Of the four goals of children's misbehavior, more than one goal may be in evidence. Correctly assessing the primary goal reveals both the level of discouragement and the mistaken notions underlying them. Assuming that a mistaken conviction or notion about how they can make their place motivates children's behavior, Adlerians have noted that children with a goal of misbehavior usually believe the following (approximately), in the order of relative discouragement (least to most):

- *Attention.* I only really count when others notice or serve me.
- *Power.* I only really count when others know I can do what I want to do.
- *Revenge.* I can't be liked, but I can hurt others and then they'll know I count, too.
- *Inadequacy.* I'm stupid, inadequate, really hopeless, so why try? Don't expect anything from me. Trying will only prove it to everyone.

Children generally are not aware of the purposes of their actions. Many will stop their disruptive behavior when made aware of its purpose by a counselor. Teachers and parents, however, are cautioned to refrain from confronting children with observations about goals to avoid the appearance of labeling. Still, understanding the purposiveness of the children's behavior frees adults to redirect the child's behavior toward more positive goals through the use of consequences and encouragement.

Respond With Consequences and Encouragement.   Responding with consequences and encouragement often involves the use of natural and logical consequences. A **natural consequence** is the result of an ill-advised action that brings about a negative result to the actor—for example, locking keys in the house or car, or damaging necessary items by using them carelessly. In a classroom example, children who persistently forget their pencils may not participate in certain writing activities for the day.

Logical consequences, however, result in negative social consequences to the actor—for example, others withhold service, cooperation, or invitation to participate in activities. Pupils who miss the teacher's instructions may be expected to wait until everyone else has started their lessons before having the instructions repeated. The concept behind the effectiveness of natural and logical consequences is the logical order and pressure of reality. There are literally hundreds of examples of these methods that have been found effective in homes and classrooms (Dreikurs & Grey, 1968). Methods for creating new consequences are also available (Sweeney, 1998).

The rationale and methods for responding with encouragement were discussed in the previous section of this chapter. In addition, for those who may be interested, a positive intervention plan form for use with case studies, treatment planning, and conceptualizing the process of intervention is illustrated in Sweeney (1998).

Execute With Consistency, Friendliness, and Respect.   Adults of all generations have tended to present rules and regulations without helping new generations understand or discover the logic of social living. Some rules are illogical and arbitrary, and children perceive this quickly. These rules are fair game for conflicts in a power struggle. Patience in helping children and adolescents learn to experience the natural and logical order of daily living, however, is one keystone of effective helping.

With social democracy as the basis for training methods, adults can extricate themselves from the arbitrary exercise of power. Consequences that work effectively seem to be associated with the following general guidelines (Sweeney, 1998):

1. Natural consequences are sought first, before an adult considers a logical consequence.

2. New class or family rules are generally presented or discussed before implementation.

3. New rules apply to everyone, including the adults, who are excused only when parental responsibilities logically supersede an agreement.

4. Alternatives are always open to the individual—for example, "You can stop crying, or go to your room and return when you have finished crying."

5. Consistency in implementing the rules or consequences is maintained with action, not words.

6. Logical consequences are avoided when power struggles are in process—that is, angry feelings, evidence of power's being exerted or challenged.

7. If consequences ensue from ill-advised acts of a family or class member, friendliness prevails before, during, and after; that is, "I told you so" comments do not precede or follow, either verbally or nonverbally.

8. Encouragement is highlighted for the many positive ways individuals share, participate, and cooperate. Everyone is made to feel and know that they have a place and belong, particularly when they reveal discouraged behavior.

9. Time for having fun together is an important part of the planning that takes place.

Through parent and teacher study groups, these methods can be learned in such a manner that new attitudes and behaviors can be mastered and shared with others. Counselors can not only establish and lead such groups, but they also can teach laypersons and other professionals to do the same. In fact, Adlerians strongly advocate the value of parent- or teacher-led study groups. With proper preparation, such study group leaders are at least as effective as other professionals. Guidelines and suggestions for such groups are beyond the scope of this chapter but are available elsewhere (Sweeney, 1998).

Life-style Assessment.   Adlerians have used both observation and interview techniques to derive insight into the motivation of their clients. A variety of techniques may be used to conduct what is referred to as a life-style analysis or assessment. Adler characterized life-style as the "unity in each individual in his thinking, feeling, acting; in his so called conscious and unconscious, in every expression of his personality. This (self-consistent) unity we call the style of life of the individual" (Ansbacher & Ansbacher, 1967, p. 175). Life-style assessment is an effort to make explicit the attitudes, beliefs, and convictions that one uses in approaching or avoiding life's tasks.

The Adlerian counselor is guided by a series of questions which help discover such information as the individual's ordinal position in the family, comparative characteristics with other members of the family, interaction patterns within the family, family values, and adjustment to physical and socioeconomic conditions. The following are from among the questions often asked in these interviews (Dreikurs, 1967, pp. 125–152):

A. *Ordinal Position.* List all the children in the family in their birth order and list their ages plus or minus years compared to the client's age, including siblings now dead and/or miscarriages which were known to the person as a child. For example:

Joshua   +2
Jacob   28 (client)
Sarah   −2
girl baby   −3 (stillborn)
Helen   −10

In the above example, Jacob is a middle child in a two-family constellation—that is, Helen is more likely to have the characteristics of an only child because she is more than 6 to 8 years younger than the next youngster.

B. *Description of Siblings*. Be specific in description as you remember them as a child:

   1. Who is most different from you? In what respect? (likely competitor) Only child: How different were you from other kids in general?
   2. Who is most like you? In what respect? (possible ally)
   3. What kind of kid were you?
   4. Describe the other siblings.

C. *Comparative Attributes*. Rate self and siblings on each of the attributes by indicating who you believed was highest or most, who was lowest or least, and if you were neither one, indicate to which sibling you were most similar (only child compared to other children). Often the counselor must ask the client to define or explain what it means to them to be the "most or least" of one of these attributes, for example, most spoiled in getting privileges versus getting objects like presents or attention from someone special to them.

1. Intelligence	5. Conforming	9. Sense of humor
2. Hardest worker	6. Rebellious	10. High standards
3. Best grades in school	7. Tried to please	11. Most spoiled
4. Helped at home	8. Got own way	12. Most punished

D. *Sibling Relationships*

   1. Who took care of whom?
   2. Who played with whom?
   3. Who was mother's favorite? Father's?
   4. Who got along best and who fought most?

E. *Parents*

   1. Parent ages
   2. What kind of person was each?
   3. Which child was most like father? Like mother? In what ways?
   4. What kind of relationship existed between father and mother?
   5. Who was more ambitious for the children? In what ways?
   6. Did any other persons live with or significantly influence you as a child?

Dreikurs (1967) and Shulman and Mosak (1988) discussed the significance of questions like these and others in much greater detail. The influence of early social experiences on one's biased apperceptions is the focus of attention. From the client's review of these early perceptions, the counselor can begin to develop a word portrait of the individual.

Early Recollections.   Typically, early recollections are recorded as a part of the interview process following the family constellation. Individuals frequently will begin sharing early recollections before the counselor even suggests that they do so. Adlerians note that what is remembered is done so selectively because it has significance to the individual in understanding, managing, and controlling life experiences. Specific early recollections are those recalled to approximately age 8 or 9.

The difference between a significant early recollection and a report must be noted. Many people recall family routines, frequent interactions, or general descriptions of early experiences. For example, one individual reported that every summer her family made ice cream as a pastime. Even with more detail, such a report is not to be confused with a recollection unless a specific episode is shared. A useful recollection brings attention to a particular incident. Often the early recollection will be so vivid that it takes on a "here and now" quality with an overt affective reaction as well.

We are especially interested in the feelings experienced at the time, who else was present (if anyone), what kind of behavioral activity was taking place, and by whom. An example of how life-style assessment techniques are used including early recollections will be found in the case study of Maria.

Evaluation

Overview

This section is devoted to research associated with the theory, concepts, and methods of Adlerian counseling, its limitations, and an overview of its major components. Much of the research is derived from studies not specifically designed to test the theory but which are clearly applicable to it. Likewise, many studies related, for example, to parent and teacher study groups' effect upon children's behavior are dated in the 1960s and 1970s and not reported here. Nevertheless, we continue to witness the proliferation of parenting and classroom management books based upon Adlerian concepts, methods, and techniques.

Supporting Research

Adlerian theory has been studied rather extensively, including concepts such as social interest, ordinal position, and early recollections. In fact, the number of studies increased between 1982 and 1990 over the previous 12-year period, 103 to 75, respectively (Watkins, 1992c). The number of studies in each area between 1982 and 1990 include: birth order, 25 studies; early recollections, 23; social interest, 21; life-style, 7; and other, 27. The greatest increase has been in the area of early recollections. Unfortunately, many of these studies are limited in scope and lacking in sound methodology.

The same author (Watkins, 1992a) noted the following regarding early memory (EM) research:

Adlerian-oriented EM research has increased substantially in the past ten years—seemingly more so comparatively than either Freudian, ego psychological, or cognitive-perceptual perspectives. This body of research as a whole provides some support for Adler's views about EM, but these studies are not without flaws (e.g., virtually no racial/cross-cultural subjects have been included, no pilot studies have been conducted). Currently, there is tentative support for Adler's views about EM's, but to draw any conclusions beyond that is inappropriate at this time. (p. 261)

In addition, birth order has been studied extensively over the years. Watkins's (1992b) review of birth-order research during the period 1981–91 resulted in the following conclusions:

Considering the limitations of these studies, the primary conclusions suggested by these data could be stated as:

1. firstborns often manifest characteristics consistent with the "firstborn profile" described in Adlerian literature, e.g., being more dominant, responsible . . . ;

2. achievement motivation patterns vary according to birth-order positions;

3. birth order when combined with the variable of sex (e.g., subjects' sex) relates to selected achievement variables and locus of control;

4. studies support the importance of "psychological position" in birth-order research; and some evidence suggests that birth-order effects vary as a result of ethnicity. (p. 365)

Cultural Relevance.   While addressing the need for more cross-cultural studies, I wish to draw attention to expert opinion regarding the relevance of the Adlerian philosophy, values, and methods. In an invited commentary on macrostrategies for delivery of mental health counseling services in the *Journal of Mental Health Counseling,* Corey (1991) offered the following:

The basic assumptions of all these authors [Herr, Ivey, Rigazio-DiGilio, and Dinkmeyer] appear to rest on an Adlerian foundation that stresses prevention, policies that are growth producing, visions that inspire individuals to feel competent, the process of reaching out to others, and finding meaning and a sense of community in a social context. This context for understanding counseling practice makes far more sense to me than gearing practice toward a medical model that focuses largely on the internal dynamics of the individual and tends to ignore the impact of the individual's external environment. . . . From my vantage point, Adler's ideas are certainly compatible with many of the macrostrategies for future delivery of services to a culturally diverse population. (pp. 53–54)

The authors of Chapter 17 in this book share a similar point of view when assessing the various common approaches to counseling. The success of Dreikurs's reprinted works in several other languages may suggest that there is relevance across cultures as well.

Life-style Studies.   Shulman and Mosak (1988) report on studies of reliability, validity, and construct validity related to life-style assessment. For example, early recollections have been found to be more consistent than Thematic Apperception Test (TAT) protocols, which can be influenced by situational variables to a far greater extent. There also are studies which demonstrate that changes in recollections reflect changes in outlook and mental status of clinical populations. Shulman and Mosak note: "Though far from exhaustive, the research is encouraging and almost universally supportive of Adlerian lifestyle conceptions. Continued research and empirical investigations will be required, however, to explore and clarify various issues and to delineate fine distinctions and differences" (1988, p. 259).

Wheeler, Kern, and Curlette (1993) reported on over 10 years of developmental work on the Life-Style Personality Inventory (LSPI), which was designed as an objective-format measure of social interest and Adlerian life-style themes. The authors provide what they consider a strong case for the idea that life-style can be measured in a reliable and valid manner. More recently, Curlette, Kern, and Wheeler (1996) and Wheeler (1996) report on their Basic Adlerian Scales for Interpersonal Success—Adult Form (BASIS-A) (Wheeler et al., 1993), which grew out of the earlier work. They provide both technical (Curlette, Wheeler, & Kern, 1993) and interpretative (Kern, Wheeler, & Curlette, 1993) manuals for critical analysis of their work. The BASIS-A appears to hold much promise for further research into this important area of investigation.

Cross-Disciplinary Research.   In the past, Adlerian theory and practice were validated primarily by use and incorporation into several other systems or approaches to counseling and psychotherapy. While some authors have credited Adler with holding ideas similar to their own or have considered him to be a foundation for certain of their practices, others seem unaware of his works or at least do not acknowledge them (Ellenberger, 1970). More recently, research in other disciplines has served to validate many of Adler's constructs (Witmer, 1985).

The literature on self-esteem tends to blend or combine sense of self-worth and sense of control (Branden, 1994). Accepting oneself as a person of worth and having a sense of competence or control corresponds to Adler's emphasis upon striving for significance. Maslow's research (1970) suggests that persons with a strong acceptance of themselves and their own nature are those who are most healthy. Likewise, a study by Campbell (1981) on satisfaction with life found that those who scored highest on satisfaction with self had extraordinarily high positive feelings of well-being. In addition, the satisfaction with self seemed to have little to do with objective circumstances such as education, income, or place of residence. Persons with positive self-esteem also have been found to cope better with stress (Witmer, Rich, Barcikowski, & Mague, 1983). In fact, poor copers have lower self-esteem and a greater amount of anxiety and physical symptoms.

Control is sometimes described in the literature as competence, locus of control, or self-efficacy. Adler (1954) identified the goal of superiority with power—that is, overcoming inferiority in a compensatory manner. There is much evidence accumulating to support the potency of perceived personal power with attributes of wellness. Beliefs about personal control have to do with feelings of mastery and confidence. Studies have confirmed that persons who perceive themselves as having a high degree of control over their lives are more likely to feel good about themselves mentally and physically, report fewer ailments, and manage stress more effectively (California Department of Mental Health, 1979; Witmer et al., 1983).

Supporting the concepts of holism and mind-body interaction, behavioral medicine, psychosomatic medicine, and psychoneuroimmunology have established a relationship between thoughts, feelings, and illness (Witmer, 1985). When negative emotions become chronic or are suppressed, they can be destructive to our well-being. Orstein and Sobel (1987), for example, found that hostility appears to be the most likely characteristic that contributes to high blood pressure, coronary artery disease, and death among competitive, hard-driving personalities. There are also findings that suggest that anxiety, loneliness, and depression are associated with suppressing the immune system, thus increasing the chances for illness (Locke et al., 1984). By contrast, relaxation and positive emotional states appear to enhance immune function (Dillon, Minchoff, & Baker, 1985; Kiecolt-Glaser et al., 1984; McClelland, Ross, & Patel, 1985). Indeed, responses to daily events influence internal bodily functions. Of special interest to Adlerians are findings showing that a negative mood results in lower antibody response and that a positive mood is associated with a higher antibody response (Stone, Cox, Valdimarsdottir, Jandorf, & Neale, 1987).

Private logic is the Adlerian conceptualization of personal beliefs that guide the feelings and behavior of individuals. It is *a biased apperception* about self, life, and others. Because it is a uniquely subjective view of reality, it is very much open to error with respect to objective reality. The greater the discrepancy between one's private logic and reality, the greater the probability for inappropriate behavior in response to life events.

Research and clinical evidence have documented that negative thoughts causing emotional turmoil nearly always contain gross distortions or unrealistic expectations (Beck, 1976, 1984; Ellis, 1962). In addition, research by Witmer et al. (1983) indicated that those persons with more positive outlooks and who scored lowest on five of Ellis's irrational beliefs were less anxious and had fewer physical symptoms. Kobasa's (1979) findings also suggest that executives who perceive change as a challenge rather than a threat are more hardy and half as likely to experience illness. In the latter case, losing a job is stressful for most people. The healthier individuals, however, tend to perceive changes as a challenge rather than a threat. Persons with unrealistic beliefs tend to expect stability or constancy; change is the enemy to be dreaded. In the case study of Maria later in this chapter, all of these components of the model—work, friendship, love, self-direction, and spirituality—are seen to be important, not only for assessment, but for positive intervention as well.

Krumboltz (1988) made the following observation after a review of related literature concerning internal and external locus of control characteristics among young people:

> So what have we learned? We know that internals achieve more and have fewer discipline problems than externals. We know that persons with good self-concepts tend to exhibit a strange inconsistency: They are responsible for their successes but not failures. We know that external beliefs can be changed to internal beliefs by persuasion, exhortation, goal setting exercises, cognitive restructuring, and telling the children, "you're good at this." We cannot be sure that changing beliefs changes academic achievement. (p. 41)

While research has not yet demonstrated that achievement will be affected by deliberate intervention to restructure the thinking of young people, this seems to be a likely by-product of such a change, from an Adlerian/cognitive point of view.

Adlerians base many of their recommendations upon the merits of cooperation in all human relationships. Likewise, they promote cooperative activities through which all youngsters can learn not only about academics but also about life. There are data to support such a position in the schools. Johnson (1981) reported a meta-analysis based on 122 studies dealing with the influence of cooperative, competitive, and individualistic goal structures on achievement:

> Cooperation promotes higher achievement than does interpersonal competition. These results hold true for all subject areas (language arts, reading, math, science, social studies, psychology, and physical education), for all age groups (although the results are stronger for pre-college students), and for tasks involving concept attainment, verbal problem solving, categorizing, spatial problem solving, retention and memory, motor performance, and guessing-judging-predicting. (pp. 56–57)

In addition, Johnson noted that cooperation promotes higher achievement and productivity than individualistic efforts. While these results are less conclusive, due to the number and types of studies conducted, there is some indication that cooperation without intergroup competition promotes higher achievement and productivity than cooperation used in conjunction with intergroup competition (as in team sports). In conclusion, Johnson recommends, "Given the general dissatisfaction with the level of competence achieved by students in the public school system, educators may wish to considerably increase the use of cooperative learning procedures to promote higher student achievement" (p. 58).

Slavin (1980) found that in 14 of 17 studies, student achievement was highest under a team learning approach as compared to an individualistic control group. In the remaining three studies, there were no significant differences between groups on achievement. In a study involving over 400 fourth- and fifth-grade students and 17 teachers, Slavin and Karweit (1981) found that students who spent most of the day in a cooperative classroom environment liked school more than the control-group students did, named more friends in school, and significantly increased their self-esteem. They also achieved significantly more on three academic tests of reading vocabulary, language mechanics, and language expression. There were no differences on four other tests of academic achievement. In short, the gains for the cooperative groups took place in both academic and social-personal variables.

In the light of the findings related to internally versus externally oriented students, Nowicki (1982) sought to determine if a cooperative learning environment favored one type of student over another. He found that both internals and externals achieved their best under the cooperative learning condition. However, when individuals were competing against themselves or other individuals, internals tended to improve more than externals.

When addressing the topic of encouraging teachers to experiment with forming cooperative classroom teams, Krumboltz (1988) went so far as to say: "If we were to take these [research] findings seriously, we would drastically alter the way in which American education is conducted. Each student would be assigned to a team in every class, members would be expected to help each other, and the performance of the whole team would determine the grade of each individual member" (p. 55).

In addition, a number of studies related to effective elementary and secondary school applications of Adlerian methods have been reported, as well as those related to birth order, early recollections, life-style assessment, and teacher and parenting programs (Burnett, 1988; Kern, Matheny, & Patterson, 1978; Sweeney, 1989). For example, based on a review of the literature that documents the usefulness of parent study-consultation groups, Burnett (1988) concluded, "The research studies . . . strongly support the effectiveness of Adlerian parenting programs. Changes in a positive direction were noted on measures of children's behavior, children's self-concept, parental behavior, and parental attitude. The studies were, on the whole, methodologically sound" (p. 74).

In addition, the evaluation of multimedia approaches has been added to the more traditional study-group methods (Kerney, 1980; Kibler, Rush, & Sweeney, 1985). One of the promising aspects of these study-group methods is the capability of assisting parents or others in child care without the requirement that adults must read in order to understand the methods. Films, audiotapes, and poster illustrations supplement the leader's materials.

There is still a need for much more research to explore new areas of Adlerian psychology. Crandall (1975) has sought to develop an instrument to measure social interest and reports some success in this validation. As with any approach to understanding human behavior, there are always more questions than answers, no matter how much data are collected. For the clinician, however, validity is seen in its application to real clients. In this respect, Adlerian practitioners agree with others who have used Adler's methods and philosophy of human relationships in any number of settings. This is a pragmatic, commonsense approach that grows in both depth and breadth over time.

Adlerians measure success in such a case in a variety of ways. Clearly, some of those ways are clients' and others' reports of more satisfying family relations, greater ease and satisfaction with work, and evidence of greater spiritual centeredness. Clinically, another useful index is change in life-style convictions, as revealed through new or significantly revised early recollections. Some or all of the recollections that Maria (in the case study) reported may be "forgotten" as though they never existed. In such a case, she will have recollections that reflect a reorientation to life in keeping with a goal of engaging life, meeting adversity, and celebrating its joys. In short, she will emerge healthier and more able to cope with and enjoy her participation in life without inhibiting fears.

Limitations

Adlerian theory and practice are criticized by others on a number of grounds. Depending upon the theoretical persuasion of the authors, some have argued that Adlerian theory lacks depth, that it is a "one size fits all" approach, or that "social interest" is no less than subjugating the individual to the tyranny of society. With respect to research, there is insufficient methodologically sound data to support its efficacy or to measure concepts such as "social interest."

Some say that Adlerian theory and practice are principally for middle-class, motivated clients whose difficulties are more situational, adjustment-related, or transitory in nature. There is also the element of a "movement" involved that is made up of true believers who require no proofs but their own life experiences to validate its usefulness. To be an Adlerian requires no degree or credentials per se. Thousands of parents and teachers who have studied Adlerian parenting and classroom guidance philosophy, methods, and techniques enthusiastically declare that they are "Adlerians." This is something of a heresy in a culture where degrees, credentials, and scope of practice are jealously guarded. On the other hand, to become truly competent in methods such as life-style assessment and its uses in therapy requires education and supervised experience not readily available to most practitioners. Adlerians may feel hope, however, as others discover and acknowledge its relevance and contribute to its comprehensiveness and validity, as noted in the prior sections.

Summary Chart—Adlerian Theory

Human Nature
Love and parental interest are important ingredients to healthy personality development. Private logic, individual perception of strengths and weakness, and family constellation each play a major role in the development of personality.

Major Constructs
Socio (striving to feel belongingness, a willingness to serve the greater good for the betterment of humankind); teleo (striving to achieve a goal); and analytic (striving to understand behavior that is based on what is not conscious) are three important aspects of individual psychology. Holism offers a point of view emphasizing the concept of an interrelated mind and body moving through life with a unique plan for having significance in relation to others. Emotions and feelings are perceived as tools necessary to the execution of behavior.

Goals
The major life tasks of work, friendship, love, dealing with the spiritual self in relation to the universe, and success in coping with self as subject (I) and object (me) can all be the goals of counseling and psychotherapy as clients seek to meet their goals in satisfying, meaningful ways.

Change Process
Adlerians believe that the life-style of the individual is a unique, unconscious, cognitive "map" that facilitates one's movement through life. Life-style is a unifying set of convictions that permits individuals to evaluate, manage, and predict events within their experiences. Adlerian counseling and psychotherapy involve uncovering and using our understanding of these combinations of beliefs to reorient thoughts and goals related to self, others, and the world upon which individuals' expectations are based.

Interventions
Adlerians are eclectic with respect to methods and techniques. Interventions include encouragement, parent and teacher education, and life-style assessment with individuals and couples.

Limitations
In spite of institutes in Adler's name and advocates of his approach, Adlerians have failed broadly to convince others of the efficacy of Adlerian methods, the comprehensiveness of the theory, and the relevance of this approach to the types of problems facing persons in the world today. There are some signs, however, that Adlerian theory and practices are being discovered and validated by individuals other than Adlerians as well.

The Case of Maria: An Adlerian Approach

Process Considerations

Adlerian counseling and psychotherapy include the following stages: (1) establishment of rapport, (2) psychological investigation, (3) interpretation, and (4) reorientation. These are dynamic in nature, as opposed to lockstep; that is, relationship issues are essential throughout the process. For example, while collecting the life-style data, there are many opportunities for reflecting, empathizing, and otherwise building a positive relationship. Likewise, interpretation and practical use of life-style insights may take place throughout the process. Very often, reference to metaphors within early recollections can be a shorthand technique for reminding clients of self-defeating attitudes or goals which tend to interfere with present functioning.

Establishing Rapport

An important source of validation available to the counselor is the **recognition reflex.** Simply put, when we hear something said about us that we know is accurate, we smile, laugh, or otherwise behaviorally acknowledge the accuracy of the observation. In fact, if I don't get a recognition reflex when I share insights about the private logic as stated in "I am" types of statements or disclosure of the hidden reasons for one's behavior, I seek to engage the client in correcting the statements to make them accurate or simply set them aside as not useful.

In *Problems of Neurosis* (1929), Adler noted that many ways are available to detect indications of another's life-style. Among his early observations were those revealed through organic problems. Some recent stress research suggests that individuals tend to respond to similar stressful circumstances with particular physiological reactions unique to their coping skills. When an individual says, "I can't stomach this situation," he literally means it! In Maria's case, she is affected both physically and psychologically by her inability to find a way out of her predicament with her family and, equally important, her relationship with her God. To ascertain the accuracy of such a hypothesis, we ask the client early in the identification of the presenting problem, "How would life be different if this were not a problem for you?"

The counselor with insight about the purposiveness of human behavior will be listening for the clients' responses as a story that reveals either organic (such as injury or infection) or social origin (an excuse to avoid meeting responsibilities), or a combination of both. In the case of suspected organic origin, a referral for medical diagnosis would be in order as well.

Psychological Investigation

Maria has been under medical treatment and was referred for counseling. While there are instances when physicians err in their diagnosis and organic problems are the culprit for socio-psychological problems, Maria's case leaves little doubt of her need for counseling. Her condition seems related to her inability to cope with home and work responsibilities, as well as familial and social relationships. From an immediate, practical point, I would expect to have a psychiatric consultation for purposes of helping Maria to begin getting the rest and relief she needs from the stress of her emotional state through a psychotropic prescription.

Maria's responses to the question of how life would be different include: "I would experience greater harmony with my family, satisfaction with my ability to parent my children, renewed enjoyment with teaching, an ability to initiate and sustain appropriate relationships with men including dating, and a greater spiritual sense of peace." At the present time, she perceives her problems as being beyond her control. As in her recurring dream, she perceives no way out. Worse yet, there are "shadowy figures" pursuing and closing in on her. These represent core psychosocial issues which medication alone will never address successfully.

Following a format similar to that developed by Dreikurs (1967), the counselor collects information helpful in uncovering the private logic and motivation of the client (Sweeney, 1998). This information is based upon perceptions of early childhood, usually before the age of 8. It includes summarizing data from the family constellation (psychological position in the family); comparisons on personal attributes (such as intelligence, sense of humor, sensitivity, pleasing others); perception of relationships with siblings or peers; perceptions of mother and father (e.g., characteristics, their relationship, problem or conflict resolution techniques); family and cultural values; and early recollections (such as memories of specific events and the feelings associated with them before the client was 6 to 8 years of age).

The following narrative summary follows a format developed by the author for such purposes. The life-style data from Maria are summarized below:

Individual Characteristics: Family Constellation and Personal Attributes.   Maria is the oldest of five children, including three younger brothers (Carlos, 18 months younger; Juan, 3 years younger; Pedro, 4 years younger; and a sister, Isabel, the "Princess" of the family, 6 years younger). Until her marriage and later divorce, she was the second "mother" in the family and was looked up to by her siblings. This was especially true for her younger sister, Isabel, until Maria's divorce.

When reflecting back on her first eight years with her siblings, she considered herself: the most intelligent, hardest worker, most responsible, most conforming (although inclined to covertly ignore her elders on occasion), trying hardest to please, most considerate, highest standards academically as well as in behavior and morals, strongest, and the most idealistic.

She reported that she was the least likely to be critical of others, to be selfish, to throw a temper tantrum, and was lowest in sense of humor ("it's hard to be responsible and have fun, too") and lowest in materialism.

She considered herself second most likely to rebel, but never in a mean or spiteful way. She also thought of her sister as "prettiest," but she, too, was pretty. She welcomed her menarche as a sign of her womanhood with which she felt much pride.

Adult and Gender Models.   Mother and father were away a lot taking care of their business. Their relationship tended to be loving, if not stormy, too. Father tended to be dominant and was quick to anger, while mother was the peacemaker. Most of their arguments were related to their business; although mother wanted more time with the children, she acquiesced to father's demands for her help. She remembers once father pushed her mother in anger but they made up later and she can't recall another instance of it. Otherwise, they loved each other and the children, and made sacrifices to ensure that the children got an education, attended church, and were "good" children.

When asked to describe her mother in a few words when she thought of her as a youngster, Maria said her mother was "caring, spiritual, tired a lot, quiet, and wise." Father was "strong, determined, passionate, and a hard worker." Together, they were "absent a lot." They tended to agree on discipline, although mother was less quick to anger and never struck the children. Father did both but infrequently because mother intervened or was more responsible for caring for the children.

Family and Cultural Values.   Mexican-American pride in heritage runs through the entire family. Unlike many Mexican families of today who flee poverty in Mexico for the promised land of the northern neighbor, Maria's father chose to come north to create his own business rather than stay in the family business in Mexico. While not wealthy by U.S. standards, her paternal grandfather was a successful businessman and his youngest son was determined to prove that he, too, could make it on his own. He also was intent on encouraging his children to get a good education and make it in the world on their own. In fact, it was a surprise to Maria when her father objected to her accepting a scholarship to a university 200 miles away from home. Unlike her mother, however, she would not acquiesce to father's demands.

While proud to be a legal citizen of the United States, both mother and father always spoke highly of the history and struggles of the Mexican people. They are a nation of many people, many noble people, not always poor or brought down by corrupt politicians. They are a people who, in spite of bad government, survive and dream of a better day. Their language, music, art, and rich heritage are second only to the warmth, energy, and passion of the people.

While not overly religious, father and particularly mother are devote Roman Catholics. Church was the social and educational center for all of Maria's formative years. Her attitudes and beliefs learned in school about right and wrong were firmly reinforced at home. These included expectations for appropriate sex, marriage, divorce, having children, and responsibility to others. Her own devotion to the Virgin Mary had been laid aside in her college years, and she now feels unworthy of that relationship.

Early Recollections.   These are specific events recalled before 8 years of age. We view them as metaphors that reveal expectations, interpretations, and attitudes about life, self, and others. They are what each of us calls upon when we perceive new or different situations that challenge us to respond. The counselor especially will note the meaning and intensity revealed through the feelings expressed. Much can be learned as well by the physical movement suggested in the actions taken, who else is involved, sounds, smells, colors, and initiative or passivity, for example. Maria recalled the following:

E.R. #1: 4 years old
I had just helped my brother learn to walk and my parents applauded! Everyone was laughing and excited, *me, too! I felt loved and special because I had helped my brother take his first steps. It was a happy time.*

Convictions:
Helping others learn gives me great pleasure.
Happy times are found through teaching others.
Teaching is a source of great pleasure to everyone involved.
Sharing good times with those you love is wonderful.

E.R. #2: 4 years old

My mother had bought me a new dress. It was beautiful! It had *many bright colors and a lovely pattern* with a *long flowing skirt* to it. *She put it on me and had me twirl around* and the skirt rose up and down as I turned. *I felt so proud, so feminine, and light as a feather, almost as if I could fly.*

Convictions:
To be feminine is to be lovely, feeling light, and fully alive!
Women can help me feel great pleasure.
I love pretty colors in everything around me.

E.R. #3: 5 or 6 years old

My two older brothers were playing while my mother was doing the wash. *I decided* to go outside because *I was curious* about the noise other kids were making. *I knew that I wasn't supposed* to go but I did anyway. Mother never found out because *I got back before she noticed. I felt naughty but excited by the idea that I could do what I wanted.*

Convictions:
Not everyone needs to know what you're doing, especially if you shouldn't be doing it!
I should be able to do what I want, but I don't want any bad consequences as a result.

E.R. #4: 7 years old

I was dressed in my white first communion dress. We were marched down the center aisle of the church with *everyone watching. I felt so holy and special* to be up in the front of the church to receive my first communion. Everything was so lovely.

Convictions:
I like the special feeling of being right with my God, my family, my community.
When I feel holy inside, I feel good before my family, my community, and my God.

E.R. #5: 7 years old

It was May and about the time of my first communion. We always had a devotion to Mary, the Mother of Jesus. I remember being in church *after confession and feeling very clean inside and out* (mother made us take a bath before going!) and I prayed to Mary for her help. I felt a special presence . . . a feeling like I was really being heard, *and I promised to be good and to continue praying* for guidance as the sisters had taught us. For a long time, I did. It really felt good.

Convictions:
I like feeling special in a holy way.
I feel loved and special when I think I have kept my promises.

Interpretation

Approach to Life Tasks.   Maria faces five life tasks: work, friendship and love, self, and spirituality. These will be discussed in the following sections.

Work.   Maria has many positive attributes as a colleague and partner. She says about herself in relation to work tasks: "I am responsible, cooperative, hard working, and hold high standards for performance, especially for myself. I feel best about myself when I am experiencing success in helping others achieve and celebrate their success."

Friendship and Love.   Maria has deep attachment to fundamental values that guide her in relationships. She says, "I am committed to being trustworthy, honest, loyal, trying to please, willing to give more than I receive from others, considerate of others, and devoted to duty. I long, however, for companionship, respect, and caring from others." And when asked by the counselor, she acknowledges a need to have friends who help her have fun.

Self.   Much of Maria's discouragement stems from the conviction that she is not living up to her own high standards, and this is confirmed in her mind through others' rejection of her decisions and behaviors as daughter, sister, mother, and daughter-in-law. The lack of congruence between her self-expectations (and capacity for positively meeting her life tasks) and her current performance are the abyss into which her emotions have fallen. In her words, "I have nothing to live for. No one cares for me. I have ruined my life and the life of two families and I am currently hurting my children." She might add, therefore, "I am a bad person," which leads us to the next task. It is important to note here that Maria's external locus of control focus is masking her many positive attributes, but with successful reframing of her predicament these can again be called upon as a part of the counseling reorientation process.

Spirituality.   "To be at peace with oneself, others, and God is the highest state of joy, satisfaction, and goodness" (or words to this effect) is what is closest to Maria's heart and soul. Central to this conviction is a belief that "I must keep my promises in order to be worthy of the love and respect I desire." Her responsibilities to her children, her students, her parents, her siblings, and God all are outward signs of her promise to be the best person she is capable of being. A promise made to no less than the mother of her Lord and God!

Comfort Zone: When Expectations Are Met versus Unmet.   Clearly, we see in Maria's case that to be at peace (in Adlerian terms, comfortable within her biased apperceptions) she would be functioning as a caring, competent person and professional, meeting her responsibilities with satisfaction to herself and others. She has the intelligence, education, and basic values needed to be successful. However, also imbedded within her life convictions is the source of her discouragement. An oldest child with high expectations for herself reinforced by "success" at home and school in meeting them throughout her early years, she finds that she is cut off from all that helped her to be what she is today. Worse yet, she feels no peace within her spiritual self from which to draw strength, and even feels unworthy of seeking it. It is not possible here to fully develop a treatment plan and illustrate specific techniques in the process. However, I will use some of the wellness model (see Figure 12.1) components to reflect the Adlerian perspective that regardless of one's current level of functioning developmentally, through deliberate encouragement we can enhance another's capacity to meet their life tasks and increase their enjoyment in doing so.

Reorientation

Self-Direction.   I would begin by attending to Maria's sense of worth, control, and emotional responsiveness. I would want to demonstrate the "push button" technique for relaxation by having her relax, imagine herself in control, safe, and at peace in whatever environment she chose. Likewise, I would invite her to experience the change of pushing the button metaphorically and seeing, for example, her children "talking back" to their mother (or another image if I judge that such an image is too emotionally stressful). The objective is to have her practice taking charge of her own images and, consequently, emotions. I also would work with her to redirect the outcome of her recurring dream by creating the outcome that she desired. Then, for her to use just before fully falling asleep, giving her subconscious a directive to implement the new outcome to her dream.

On other components of self-direction, I would attend to Maria's immediate needs with respect to exercise, nutrition, and related self-care. In addition to any medical care noted above, Maria will benefit from stress relief, sleep better, experience less depression, and have more energy through attention to her own physical needs. She apparently needs permission to do this and instructions on where and how to begin.

The life-style assessment and interpretative stages of the counseling process lay a foundation for challenging the fictive notions (unrealistic beliefs) within Maria's private logic. Empathy in this case has to do more with Maria's purposes and goals than with her feelings per se. I would begin early in the process with reaffirming her as a responsible, hard-working, loving individual. Likewise, I would challenge her mistaken ideas with respect to being unworthy of forgiveness, love, and respect. I would help her to understand that contrary to her current assessment of herself, she is more true to being like her mother and father than any of them realize.

In fact, it is this paradox which causes her such pain. She cares so deeply about her responsibilities that to not meet them in the slightest way causes her distress. Like her mother, she strives to be a caring parent. Like her father, she has worked diligently and independently to take care of not only herself but her children as well. I would ask her at an appropriate moment, "Tell me Maria, what is more important to you, to learn from your experiences and regain the feeling of respect you desire as the responsible, loving person that you are, or to feel unworthy of forgiveness and avoid getting on with doing the things that make you feel better?" (Dreikurs demonstrated this technique as a way of disclosing the "hidden reason" for one's disability or discouraged behavior, i.e., to avoid responsibility for meeting life's tasks.) In this case, I call upon Maria's greatest asset, her loving, responsible self, to redirect her attention to what she can do, what she has as assets, and what she has done that reveals the real person inside (i.e., toward more realistic beliefs in self-direction). Obviously, such a question must be within the context of a trusting, caring relationship where empathy has been demonstrated to Maria's satisfaction. Likewise, I often find that appropriate humor can help such a client regain a more positive attitude which facilitates using this technique.

Because the process of life-style assessment permits the counselor to acquire the metaphors and language appropriate to the self-talk of the client, humor is often an outgrowth of the predicament which the client readily acknowledges is self-created by unrealistic expectations or exaggerating negative consequences. In Maria's case, she has a "Mary Poppins" persona, a desire to be "almost perfect in every way!" When asked, "Could it be that you want to be like Mary Poppins—almost perfect in every way?" Maria smiles and says, "I never thought of it that way before, but, yes, I want to be able to do everything well . . ." And the counselor adds, ". . . and to have the love, respect, and support of all who are important to me." Maria agrees, still smiling. Naturally, discussion regarding the stress that follows from such high expectations helps Maria begin to understand that it is she who is creating these high expectations. Equally important, the counselor and Maria have a new method of communicating in a shorthand way when Maria reverts to her Mary Poppins way of thinking and behaving.

Work.   I would ask Maria if, with some rest, she thought she could imagine herself going back to teaching for up to a one-week trial. If this seemed too much, we would negotiate down to what she found comfortable. Naturally, her principal would need to understand that she was getting assistance and that this was a part of the plan. My expectation would be for her cooperation with this modest goal and through it the beginnings of recovery and empowerment. I would teach Maria to think about doing things "as if" she had all the confidence and support that she required. She would be asked to practice thinking this way outside of the counseling sessions and reporting how it felt to do so. As a responsible, oldest child in her family, she will be a willing learner. In fact, one of my admonitions will be to moderate her tendency to please and to do what is asked "perfectly!"

I would help her identify colleagues at school with whom she could spend time during lunch, recess, and after school to help re-create a professional network of friends from whom she can get support. We would rehearse when and how she would act on some specific behavioral goals to achieve these contacts.

Friendship.   Maria has friends, but she has been so dispirited that she has been unavailable to them. I would invite her to rediscover the joy and satisfaction she feels in being with others who respect and care for her, especially those who help her laugh. We would make a short list of individuals whose company she enjoys. She would be asked to pick one or two to invite to dinner, a movie, to play cards, or a similar activity for some specific time(s). We may talk about what she wishes to share with those she trusts the most and what she might reasonably expect from them in the way of support as caring friends.

We would address male companionship, dating, and courting in due course. Maria's "tool box" for relationship skills is based upon what she observed between her parents—and in this case, more of what she did *not* observe, that is, what went on between her parents which she did not see or could not understand as a child. Helping her to realistically assess her assets and needs for further development will be a part of the process. We always build upon assets, however, and as a consequence it is an encouraging process.

Love.   I would expect the children to be counseled with the purpose of winning their co-operation in reestablishing a happy home environment for all of them. I would invite Maria to observe an Adlerian family counseling session and, eventually, to participate in a par-ent study group. Through these experiences, she will learn how the challenges with her children are shared by other families. Equally important, the children will be given sup-port for the fact that they are not "bad" children and will be encouraged to feel loved and empowered as positive contributors to the household.

Naturally, the extended family is an important if not crucial component of Maria's present crisis. It would be my hope to invite the entire family to join us for family therapy once I determined that Maria was sufficiently strong to participate without undue risk. As-suming that some, if not all, family members were willing to participate, I would expect to have a female—preferably Mexican-American—co-counselor help to lead the sessions. Because a full explanation of the family process goes beyond the scope of this chapter, the major understanding I wish to convey is the appreciation for a systemic approach to understanding and intervening with such a situation. Both the intrapsychic and interper-sonal perspectives have validity when engaged in such a case. We wish to understand and empower Maria while acknowledging the powerful influence and potential of the family system to either facilitate or thwart her progress toward maturity and good health. Our goal would be to help all heal from the estrangement, to affirm Maria in her differentia-tion of self within the family, and to encourage all to share their love, support, and com-mon values once again, including celebration of grandchildren, spiritual practices and hol-idays, and open hearts.

Spirituality.   Maria has such a deep faith upon which to draw for strength and comfort that I would encourage her to focus upon it early in the counseling process. As a Catholic, she learned in her formative years that a contrite confession would absolve all "sins" and that even the worse sinner would be worthy of communion with her Lord once again. In addition, her relationship with the Virgin Mary as a source of comfort and support through intercession has a unique potential within her belief system to restore honor and right-eousness without further regret and shame. As a youngster, she was much admired by all who knew her as a responsible, even pious, young woman. Her parish priest would be one resource for her to reestablish her spiritual bonds and spiritual practices. In addition, there will be a support and social group for divorced Catholics to which she can belong. Her pastor also may help the family appreciate that what the church teaches is an ideal, but it is also aware of the human condition and ministers to all as God's children as did Jesus. Maria is their child still and needs their support, love, and understanding.

Case of Maria: Caveat

Adler had an expression that "everything can be something else!"—or words to that effect. By touching on only a few illustrations of Adlerian techniques within these paragraphs, we run the risk of omitting someone's favorite Adlerian technique or not illustrating ade-quately those that are mentioned. Life-style assessment, for example, is also a part of the intervention that will be drawn upon throughout the counseling process in a variety of ways. Encouragement is as much relationship as it is methods and techniques. Therefore, attempting to provide a brief overview does an injustice to the depth and breadth of this approach in theory as well as practice.

In addition, I have deliberately touched upon components of the wellness model as we have integrated them into the Adlerian constructs of life tasks. As presented in the case of Maria, we see the use of the model to help Maria move from a deficit mode of functioning to what is considered more "normal." In fact, I would continue to work with Maria to take her to new levels of functioning in as many areas as she found desirable, including those mentioned and more. By her admission, her sense of humor, for example, could be enhanced to her great benefit. In short, Maria is a terrific candidate not only to "get better," but to live life more fully, joyfully, and with greater satisfaction and peace of mind and spirit.

References

Adler, A. (1907). *Study of organ inferiority and its contribution to clinical medicine* (S. E. Jelliffe, trans.). New York: Moffat-Yard.

Adler, A. (1929). *Problems of neurosis.* London: Kegan Paul, Trench, Truebner & Co.

Adler, A. (1938). *Social interest.* London: Faber & Faber.

Adler, A. (1954). *Understanding human nature* (W. B. Wolf, trans.). New York: Fawcett. (Original work published in 1927)

Ansbacher, H. L. (Ed.). (1969). *The science of living: Alfred Adler.* Garden City, NY: Doubleday.

Ansbacher, H. L., & Ansbacher, R. R. (Eds.). (1967). *The individual psychology of Alfred Adler.* New York: Harper & Row.

Beck, A. T. (1976). *Cognitive therapy and the emotional disorders.* New York: New American Library.

Beck, A. T. (1984). Cognitive approaches to stress. In R. L. Wollfolk & P. M. Lehrer (Eds.), *Principles and practice of stress management* (pp. 255–305). New York: Guilford.

Branden, N. (1994). *The six pillars of self-esteem.* New York: Bantam.

Burnett, P. C. (1988). Evaluation of Adlerian parenting programs. *Individual Psychology, 44,* 63–76.

California Department of Mental Health, Office of Prevention. (1979). *In pursuit of wellness.* San Francisco: Author.

Campbell, A. (1981). *The sense of well-being in America: Recent patterns and trends.* New York: McGraw-Hill.

Corey, G. (1991). Invited commentary on macrostrategies for delivery of mental health counseling services. *Journal of Mental Health Counseling, 13,* 51–57.

Crandall, J. E. (1975). A scale for social interest. *Individual Psychology, 31,* 187–195.

Curlette, W. L., Kern, R. M., & Wheeler, M. S. (1996). Uses and interpretations of scores on the BASIS-A Inventory. *Individual Psychology, 52,* 95–103.

Curlette, W. L., Wheeler, M. S., & Kern, R. M. (1993). *BASIS-A Inventory technical manual.* Highlands, NC: TRT Associates.

Dillon, K. M., Minchoff, B., & Baker, K. H. (1985). Positive emotional states and enhancement of the immune system. *International Journal of Psychiatry in Medicine, 15*(1), 13–18.

Dreikurs, R. (1946). *The challenge of marriage.* New York: Hawthorne.

Dreikurs, R. (1953). *Fundamentals of Adlerian psychology.* Chicago: Alfred Adler Institute.

Dreikurs, R. (1963). Psychodynamic diagnosis in psychiatry. *American Journal of Psychiatry, 119,* 1045–1048.

Dreikurs, R. (1967). *Psychodynamics, psychotherapy, and counseling.* Chicago: Alfred Adler Institute.

Dreikurs, R. (1968). *Psychology in the classroom* (2nd ed.). New York: Harper & Row.

Dreikurs, R. (1971). *Social equality: The challenge of today*. Chicago: Regnery.

Dreikurs, R., & Grey, L. (1968). *Logical consequences*. New York: Hawthorne.

Dreikurs, R., Grunwald, B. B., & Pepper, H. C. (1971). *Maintaining sanity in the classroom*. New York: Harper & Row.

Dreikurs, R., & Soltz, V. (1964). *Children: The challenge*. New York: Hawthorne.

Ellenberger, H. (1970). *The discovery of the unconscious*. New York: Basic Books.

Ellis, A. (1962). *Reason and emotion in psychotherapy*. New York: Lyle Stuart.

Johnson, D. W. (1981). Effects of cooperative, competitive, and individualistic goal structures on achievement: A meta-analysis. *Psychological Bulletin, 89,* 47–62.

Kern, R., Matheny, K., & Patterson, D. (1978). *A case for Adlerian counseling: Theory, techniques, and research evidence*. Chicago: Alfred Adler Institute.

Kern, R. M., Wheeler, M. S., & Curlette, W. L. (1993). *BASIS-A Inventory interpretative manual*. Highlands, NC: TRT Associates.

Kerney, E. J. (1980). *The efficacy of an Adlerian child guidance study group on changing teachers' attitudes toward students' behavior*. Unpublished doctoral dissertation, Ohio University, Athens.

Kibler, V. E., Rush, B. L., & Sweeney, T. J. (1985). The relationship between Adlerian course participation and stability of attitude change. *Individual Psychology, 41,* 354–362.

Kiecolt-Glaser, J. K., Garner, W., Speicher, C., Penn, G. M., Holliday, J., & Glaser, R. (1984). *Psychosomatic Medicine, 46,* 7–14.

Kobasa, S. C. (1979). Stressful life events, personality, and health: An inquiry into hardiness. *Journal of Personality and Social Psychology, 37,* 1–11.

Krumboltz, J. (1988). The key to achievement: Learning to love learning. In G. R. Walz (Ed.), *Proceedings on building sound school counseling programs* (pp. 1–39). Alexandria, VA: American Association for Counseling and Development Press.

Locke, S. E., Kraus, L., Leserman, J., Hurst, M. W., Heisel, J. S., & Williams, R. M. (1984). Life changes, stress, psychiatric symptoms, and natural killer cell activity. *Psychosomatic Medicine, 46,* 441–453.

Maslow, A. H. (1970). *Motivation and personality* (2nd ed.). New York: Harper & Row.

McClelland, D. C., Ross, G., & Patel, V. (1985). The effect of an academic examination on the salivary norepinephrine and immuninoglobulin levels. *Journal of Human Stress, 11,* 52–59.

Mosak, H. H., & Dreikurs, R. (1967). The life task III, the fifth life task. *Individual Psychologist, 5*(1), 1622.

Mosak, H. H., & Dreikurs, R. (1973). Adlerian psychotherapy. In R. Corsini (Ed.), *Current psychotherapies*. Itasca, IL: Peacock.

Myers, J. E., Witmer, J. M., & Sweeney, T. J. (1997) *WEL Workbook*. Greensboro, NC: Authors.

Nehru, J. (1958). *Toward freedom*. Boston: Beacon.

Nowicki, S., Jr. (1982). Competition-cooperation as a mediator of locus of control and achievement. *Journal of Research in Personality, 16,* 157–164.

Orstein, R., & Sobel, D. (1987). *The healing brain*. New York: Simon & Schuster.

Savickas, M. (1998). Career-style assessment and counseling. In T. J. Sweeney, *Adlerian counseling: A practitioner's approach* (4th ed.). Muncie, IN: Accelerated Development.

Shulman, B. H., & Mosak, H. (1988). *Manual for lifestyle assessment*. Muncie, IN: Accelerated Development.

Shulman, B. H., & Nikelly, A. G. (1971). Family constellation. In A. G. Nikelly (Ed.), *Techniques for behavior change* (pp. 35–40). Springfield, IL: Charles C Thomas.

Slavin, R. E. (1980). Cooperative learning. *Review of Educational Research, 50,* 315–342.

Slavin, R. E., & Karweit, N. L. (1981). Cognitive and affective outcomes of an intensive student team learning experience. *Journal of Experimental Education, 50,* 29–35.

Stone, A. A., Cox, D. S., Valdimarsdottir, H., Jandorf, L., & Neale, J. M. (1987). Evidence that lg A antibody is associated with daily mood. *Journal of Personality and Social Psychology, 52,* 988–993.

Sweeney, T. J. (1989). *Adlerian counseling* (3rd ed.). Muncie, IN: Accelerated Development.

Sweeney, T. J. (1998). *Adlerian counseling: A practitioner's approach* (4th ed.). Muncie, IN: Accelerated Development.

Sweeney, T. J., & Witmer, J. M. (1991). Beyond social interest: Striving toward optimum health and wellness. *Individual Psychology, 47*(4), 527–540.

Vaihinger, H. (1965). *The philosophy of "as if."* London: Routledge & Kegan Paul.

Watkins, C. E. (1992a). Adlerian-oriented early memory research: What does it tell us? *Journal of Personality Assessment, 59,* 248–263.

Watkins, C. E. (1992b). Birth-order research and Adler's theory: A critical review. *Individual Psychology, 48,* 357–368.

Watkins, C. E. (1992c). Research activity with Adler's theory. *Individual Psychology, 48,* 107–108.

Wheeler, M. S. (1996). Using the BASIS-A Inventory: Examples from a clinical setting. *Individual Psychology: Journal of Adlerian Theory, Research, and Practice, 52,* 104–118.

Wheeler, M. S., Kern, R. M., & Curlette, W. L. (1993). *BASIS-A Inventory.* Highlands, NC: TRT Associates.

Witmer, J. M. (1985). *Pathways to personal growth.* Muncie, IN: Accelerated Development.

Witmer, J. M., Rich, C., Barcikowski, R. S., & Mague, J. C. (1983). Psychosocial characteristics mediating the stress response: An exploratory study. *Personnel and Guidance Journal, 62,* 73–77.

Witmer, J. M., & Sweeney, T. J. (1992). A holistic model for wellness and prevention over the life span. *Journal of Counseling and Development, 71*(2), 140–148.

Witmer, J. M., & Sweeney, T. J. (1998). Toward wellness: The goal of counseling. In Sweeney, T. J. (Ed.), *Adlerian counseling: A practitioner's approach* (4th ed.). Muncie, IN: Accelerated Development.

Existential Theory

Mary Lou Bryant Frank
North Georgia College and State University

The primary confrontation with death and being was addressed by the existential philosophers and has found life and significance in the existential therapies. **Existentialism** embodies the understanding of the individual in the culture and time as well as the nature, meaning, and feelings of that existence (Funder, 1997). While deriving from the term *ex-sistere,* meaning "to stand out" or "to emerge" (May, 1969a), *existence* also means "to become" (Feist, 1994) and as such implies a process. Similarly, existential theory is an emergent, vital part of the third force of psychology, attempting to look at the experiences, transitions, and meanings of our lives in the context of development, culture, and time.

Existential counseling and psychotherapy address issues of **death, freedom, responsibility, anxiety, phenomenology, isolation,** and **meaninglessness** (Abroms, 1993; Gould, 1993; Loy, 1996; May, 1953: Yalom, 1980). Despite the universal nature of these core struggles of life, existentialism is not a prevailing force in psychology, with only 5% of counselors adopting a predominately existential approach (Prochaska & Norcross, 1994). The emphasis on the rational, objective, and scientific techniques of behavioral, cognitive, and cognitive-behavioral counseling have relegated existentialism to a complementary function. Existentialists were the "homeless waifs who were not permitted into the better academic neighborhoods" (Yalom, 1980, p. 21). However, contemporary thought is leading many to an awakened need for existential answers. Current trends reflect an emphasis on health and wellness (Evans, 1997; Lightsey, 1996; Thauberger, Thauberger, & Cleland, 1983; Travis, 1981), loss and death (Kubler-Ross, 1975; Leifer, 1996; Nuland, 1996; Vaughan & Kinnier, 1996; Viorst, 1986), contextual and family of origin concerns (Krueger & Hanna, 1997; Mills & Sprenkle, 1995), religiosity or spirituality (McCullough, Worthington, Maxey, & Rachal, 1997; Westgate, 1996; Wilber, 1986), culture (Fine, Weis, Powell, & Wong, 1997; Ibrahim, 1985), gender (Good, Robertson, Fitzgerald, Stevens, & Bartels, 1996; Hall & Greene, 1996; Liddle, 1996; McCarn & Fassinger, 1996), and process issues in counseling (Bugental, 1978; Duncan, 1993; Milton, 1993). Each area is directly addressed by an existential perspective.

Psychological theories are an intimate reflection of the values and biases of the real people creating the theories, and existential theory is no exception. A behavioral approach reflects a theorist to whom science and logic are the organizing factors for existence. An existentialist is a theorist to whom science is complementary to **meaning,** for whom relationships are as important as the scientific advancement of a theory, for whom the **subjective** individual experience is as important as the objective factual report, and who is involved as much in the **process** as in the product (May, 1983; Willis, 1994). For an existentialist, the journey is as important as the destination (Bugental, 1978; Weisman, 1993); and the existential journey is not superficial:

> To explore deeply from an existential perspective does not mean that one explores the past; rather it means that one brushes away everyday concerns and thinks deeply about one's existential situation. It means to think outside of time, to think about the relationship between one's feet and the ground beneath one, between one's consciousness and the space around one; it means to think not about the way one came to be the way one is, but that one is. . . . The future-becoming-present is the primary tense of existential therapy. (Yalom, 1980, p. 11)

Unlike traditional psychoanalytic and psychodynamic counselors and therapists, existentialists are not deficiency-focused. Instead, they concentrate on potentialities. Existentialists hope to aid individuals in developing schemata to understand and cope with their lives.

Likewise, existentialists represent a diverse population. In as many ways that meaning can be gleaned from life, there are as many avenues to describe the process of finding meaning. Just as some existentialists are more psychodynamic in their orientation (Abroms, 1993; Yalom, 1980), others are more humanistic (Bugental, 1978; Maslow, 1968; Owen, 1994). Another circle of existentialists seems to be a part of the newest wave in psychology, transpersonal theory (Wilber, 1997).

For some individuals, meaning emerges from the struggle with life and death, destiny and freedom, isolation and connection. Anticipated by Maslow (1971), transpersonal psychology offers a haven for those individuals finding meaning in the spiritual realm. The existential philosophers **Buber** (1970) and **Tillich** (1987), as well as the psychological theorists Maslow (1968) and Wilber (1997), were explicit that from an existential quest, a spiritual awakening could unfold. For some people, hope emerges from despair. However, not all existentialists find meaning through spirituality. Some find that the quest for meaning is always filled with the anxiety of ultimate death (Cannon, 1991; Yalom, 1980). However, transpersonal psychology is a framework for examining the process of spiritual development that may surface after scratching the existential veneer.

The purpose of this chapter is to outline the background of existentialism, explore the developmental nature of the quest for meaning, examine the major constructs of existential thought, describe applications of the theory, summarize the evaluation of the theory, and explore the theory's limitations. The final analysis is a case discussion. In the process of understanding a theory about existence, it is my hope that the reader will gain a deeper sense of self, simpler appreciation of being in life, and a heightened respect for human struggle.

Background

Arising from the philosophic roots of **Kierkegaard, Nietzsche,** and **Sartre,** existentialism gained an audience within the post–World War II European community where it found form and voice. Emerging from the atrocities of war, vanquished idealism, and fragmented family life, the philosophers of this period developed a perspective reflecting the realities of their harsh existence. In the midst of the destruction, the ultimate loss was suggested: God must also be dead (Nietzsche, 1889). People saw death as the core experience permeating their existence. These experiences reflected a new perspective, which, though not always optimistic, was full of realism.

Kierkegaard was a primary influence on other existentialists such as Heidegger, Buber, and Nietzsche. Kierkegaard (1944) pursued scientific truth from the landscape of our humanness. Our greater problems were not due to lack of knowledge or technology, he believed, but lack of passion and commitment (May, 1983). Kierkegaard was convinced that the goal of pure objectivity was not only unattainable, but was also undesirable and immoral; these beliefs foreshadow recent findings in physics (Bohm, 1973; Evans, 1996; Miller, 1997) and gender studies (Belenky, Clinchy, Goldberger, & Tarule, 1997). Kierkegaard was clear that unless examined in a relational context, science alone does not produce truth (Bretall, 1951). The objective, detached examination is an illusion because a subject can never be truly separated from the object. It is no small wonder that Kierkegaard was not favored among the more objective, cognitive, and behavioral theorists who were influenced by Descartes.

According to Descartes an objective, rational examination was crucial to the development of empirical science. Consistent with Descartes was the prevailing thought of Copernicus who provided the scientific model of a detached observer that we see embodied in current scientific research methodology. From Descartes emerged a mechanistic theory of mind and body only causally interacting. In the midst of a Cartesian mindset, Heidegger (1949) developed an alternate paradigm.

Building on Kierkegaard, Heidegger continued to develop existential thought. Heidegger's concept was antimechanistic and antitheoretic in a Cartesian sense. To Heidegger (1962), theories and humans were imperfect, and an objective reality is not reality at all. Existence is only understood in terms of being in the world through subjective participation. Heidegger noted that in striving for exactness, the Cartesian system was missing reality.

Heidegger's (1962) notions of choice also influenced the existential psychologists. Heidegger reasoned that each choice one makes represents the loss of an alternative. The past becomes important in terms of lost opportunities. Future choices are limited due to past choices and the time remaining to fulfill them. We have the freedom to choose but must balance this with the responsibility for our choices. By encountering these limitations, we may experience nothingness, guilt, and anxiety. These core concerns reverberated among authors around the world. The field of literature was ripe for existential development (e.g., Dostoyevsky, Tolstoy, Kafka, Sartre, Camus, Hemingway, Eliot, Fitzgerald, Stein, Ellison, Faulkner, Wolfe, Pound, Blake, Angelou, Rand, and Frost). Both in the United States and Europe, the best literary minds echoed the existential rumblings.

North American psychologists initially reflected the focus on universal concerns through humanism. The third force arose as an answer to the limitations of the Freudian and behaviorist approaches. The positive aspects of humanness (e.g., love, freedom with responsibility, self-actualization, potential, transcendence, uniqueness, choice, creativity) were missing from Freudian and behavioral theories. The development of the Association for Humanistic Psychology spawned a positive arena for collaboration. The humanistic element focused on human capacities and potentialities (Craig, 1995; Milton, 1993). Demonstrating the natural evolution from humanistic to existential, many humanistic theorists (e.g., Maslow, Bugental, Buber, and May) moved into an existential position. Although humanism was the initial paradigm, existentialism built on the respect for the individual and added the dimensions of ontology, experiential awareness, and responsibility.

Existentialism also has roots in contemporary religious thought. Religion's differing perspectives kindle a conflict. The disagreement is one between essence (representing scientific, objectivity, and facts) and existence (representing what is real for each individual). In Western culture, essence has triumphed over existence (May, 1983). However, this battle takes place on holy ground, as indicated by Tillich: "The story of Genesis, chapters 1–3, if taken as myth, can guide our description of the transition from essential to existential being. It is the profoundest and richest expression of man's awareness of his existential estrangement and provides the scheme in which the transition from essence to existence can be treated" (1987, p. 190). The quest for knowledge and understanding is what eventually separates humanity from the safety of objectivity. Descartes may have won the battle, but Tillich would contend that the war is not resolved.

Existential questions themselves have a religious flavor. Some existentialists would say that religion is a superficial defense against the ultimate reality of death (Yalom, 1980), since it has nothing to do with the worldly questions of meaninglessness, anxiety, and existence (Tillich, 1987). However, the dichotomy may be more one of semantics than substance. As Tillich wrote:

> Whenever existentialists give answers, they do so in terms of religious or quasi-religious traditions which are not derived from their existential analysis. . . . [but] from hidden religious sources. They are matters of ultimate concern or faith, although garbed in a secular gown. . . . Existentialism is an analysis of the human predicament. And the answers to the questions implied in man's predicament are religious, whether open or hidden. (1987, pp. 187–188)

Tillich contends that the existential dilemmas are religious questions in secular terms.

Buber (1970) similarly emphasizes the religious lineage within existential ancestry through the reverence implicit in some relationships. When "a man addresses with his whole being the You of his life that cannot be restricted by any other, he addresses God" (p. 124). When an individual no longer relates to another as an object, as an extension of him- or herself or as a means to an end, he or she enters a relationship expressed by "I to

Thou" (p. 124). The essence of the ideal existential encounter embodies respect, honor, and divinity.

The religiosity that develops from the existential quest is developmental. From an individual's struggle with consciousness and responsibility, and from unconscious existential choices, the third stage of development emerges as a "spiritual unconscious" (Frankl, 1975). Unconscious religiosity is intrinsic to our ability to transcend our situation and transform our perspective and emotional reaction. Whether the spiritual dimension is labeled, inherently perceived, or ignored, it is an element of an existential development.

Beginning from a philosophical approach to the world, existentialism has evolved to an approach to helping people cope with the uncertainty and complex pressures of their lives. Recognizing the individual nature of experience in the context of an objective, scientifically oriented society, existential counselors and therapists validate the anxiety people experience. The importance of choice and responsibility in coping with these pressures has led existentialists today to honor the individual's experience and realize the religiosity embedded in existential questions. Central to the development of this approach and working through the existential concerns is the importance of the human encounter. Following the path of early existential theorists, existentialism is grounded in realism, attempting to acknowledge the authentically human experience, the importance of meaning, and the reality of change.

Human Nature: A Developmental Perspective

The universality of existential concerns is evident in children as well as adults. Pramling and Johansson (1995) and Yalom (1980) have examined the development of existential concerns with death. Their findings indicate that such concerns, first expressed as death anxiety, are found in preschool children. The anxiety produced by awareness of nonexistence is overwhelming, even to a young child. From ages 9 to 12, most children cope with death by denying it. Denial is fostered by parents and adults in the first phase of life by avoidance and hesitant confrontation. By the time of adolescence, however, denial becomes ineffective, and the initiation into adulthood reintroduces the reality of death and isolation and necessitates a search for new meaning.

Despite the contemporary focus on commercial fulfillment, many people still search for existential meaning. In a survey of mental health workers in Hong Kong (Yiu-kee & Tang, 1995), existential variables (e.g., death, freedom, responsibility, anxiety, isolation, meaninglessness) were found to be correlates of burnout, emotional exhaustion, and depersonalization. A public opinion poll in France indicated that 89% of people felt that a purpose was needed to give meaning to life (Frankl, 1984). In a group from a leading hospital training facility, 78% of students surveyed indicated that "finding a meaning in life" was their first life goal (Frankl, 1984, p. 122).

The existential treatment perspective, directly addressing the meaning found in relationships, is a central focus of group counselors (Brabender & Fallon, 1993). Yalom's (1995) survey of group clients also suggests that existential factors are very important to client growth. One question emerged as central to individual development in a group context. One of the top five curative factors of group counseling is clients' becoming responsible for their own behavior (Yalom, 1995).

Gaining understanding about the meaning of life and taking responsibility for one's life serve to influence and inspire our development. The process of development, whether spiritual or secular, is characterized by anxiety, for which death is the primary cause (Bolen, 1996; Frankl, 1984; Loy, 1996; May, 1979, 1992; Yalom, 1980). Existential concerns permeate human existence. Though beginning in childhood, most existential concerns become salient in adulthood (Bugental, 1978; Cannon, 1991; Wilber, 1993; Yalom, 1980). The developmental necessity of examining the issues of death may be coming to terms with nonbeing (Heidegger, 1949); ontological anxiety (Tillich, 1987); loss of the world (Bretall, 1951; Nietzsche, 1967); or realizing the fear of loss of self (Hillman, 1989). "To venture causes anxiety, but not to venture is to lose one's self" (May, 1979, p. 55). Facing death is critical in coming to terms with life (Howe, 1997; Leifer, 1996). Kubler-Ross (1975) indicates that "it is the denial of death that is partially responsible for people living empty, purposeless lives" (p. 164). Hillman (1996) also indicates that it is our denial and fear of death that leads us to devise theories focusing on development, parents, social conditions, genetic predispositions, and other concerns arising out of our perceptions. As Krueger and Hanna (1997) write, "Death has a paradoxical quality in that the fear of it is paralyzing to the individual who avoids it, while at the same time acceptance of its inevitability can free the individual from the trivial life that results from that avoidance" (p. 197). Whether one transcends (Willis, 1994), develops heightened awareness (Loy, 1996), or is shaken by the struggle (May, 1983), individuals are forever changed by their confrontation with or denial of death.

Psychopathology

Psychopathology is always a potential consequence of feeling alone in an isolating culture and context, living without meaning, suffering with loss and death, confronting anxiety, and struggling with responsibility and freedom. Whatever the reason, pathology represents the loss of individuals' potential. In the confrontation with life and death, many people develop a desperate sense of isolation (Cannon, 1991; Krueger & Hanna, 1997). Within a culture that is increasingly electronically distancing, it is a normal reaction for people to feel alone and disconnected. Isolation can also suggest the separation of self from individuals' inner experience. This too creates detached, unaffected people who often cover up problems by living cognitively and intellectualizing the human experience. Instead of being in the world, individuals feel alienated and forsaken. Until they have come to terms with their struggle, these individuals have literally lost their world and their community. Similarly, problems arise when people experience world changes and then have to readjust and find new meaning for their lives. Equally difficult is the loss of relationships, jobs, and potential. In every case, individuals can experience hopelessness and despair.

Existentialists have varying approaches to **angst,** or existential anxiety, but they all would concur with Tillich (1980) that "The basic anxiety, the anxiety of a finite being about the threat of nonbeing, cannot be eliminated. It belongs to existence itself" (p. 38). Anxiety is a universal experience of being "thrown" into existence (Heidegger, 1962), of being alive in a threatening time and being aware of the predicament. However, anxiety needs to be acknowledged and accepted. Without recognition and understanding, it may serve as the focus of existence and create other, more serious psychopathologies (e.g., depression, psychotic disorders, and somatic disorders). Resistance to addressing anxiety is natural and has been used to help facilitate understanding existential possibilities (Craig, 1995). Existentialists believe that anxiety can be transformed through counseling or psychotherapy to allow a person to live more authentically (Loy, 1996). Still, anguish and tension are always present in struggling to understand our purpose in life.

The existential crisis and confrontation also produces depression. Often, depression is a last attempt to hold on to the defenses against anxiety (Bugental, 1978) as well as being a natural reaction to a lack of meaning in life (May, 1992). **Anomic depression** (Frankl, 1984) is the term used to describe the affective reaction to meaninglessness. Lantz (1993) indicates that "feelings of emptiness and defeat, lowered self esteem, discouragement, and moral disorientation" (p. 60) characterize the anomic struggles which research has shown to be different from other forms of depression. Likewise, the more individuals are satisfied with life, the more at peace they are with death. Critically ill patients with meaningless lives (Yalom, 1980) were more anxious and subsequently more depressed than those whose lives were satisfying. Although depressed, the person really is not prepared for the emotional confrontation with death. The fear of approaching the universal questions is as strong as the fear of not approaching them. The individual is estranged in a chasm of existential depression.

In discussing the problems arising from inauthenticity, Heidegger (1962) described the genuine person as one who has a profound awareness of existence. The lack of *Dasein,* of "being there," implies that the person is unauthentic, avoiding presence, accessibility, responsibility, and expression. The individual adopting a "false self" is disconnected and wooden (Weisman, 1993). But, living an inauthentic existence does not happen in isolation. We all live in relationships, in a culture, and in a time period. Finding our authentic self is accomplished by "being there" and by "being with" others (Willis, 1994). By increasing our awareness, we become more authentic and more present, and we allow ourselves to learn to be comfortable with our world and ourselves. For instance, the counselor or therapist who views clients as individuals within a cultural system, not just as individuals defined solely by psychological diagnoses and treatment plans, is beginning to live authentically. Conversely, the inauthentic person pathologically resists being known. It is impossible to experience a veiled life. Everything that makes the person alive and allows the individual freedom remains imprisoned behind the mask of inauthenticity.

Maslow's (1954) seminal work with self-actualized people provided additional insight into the psyches of creative individuals who were unable to fulfill their true potential. Not everyone with capability becomes self-actualized. Maslow (1968) cites three reasons why people do not achieve their potential: lower instinctive pressure to self-actualize, cultural institutions that control or inhibit creativity, and tendencies toward fear and regression. Without these constraints, Maslow suggests, actualization is a natural process. But individuals who do not actualize experience shame, anxiety, and defeat. Remorse may be a guide back to actualization; but if the warning is not taken, individuals live knowing they did not reach their potential. In our culture, women and members of minority groups represent repressed individuals; these groups have often been discouraged to self-actualize and encouraged to self-doubt (Belenky et al., 1997; Bepko, 1989; Gerardi, 1990; Horner, 1972;

Parham & Helms, 1985; Sue, Ivey, & Pedersen, 1996). Although taking responsibility is ultimately the solution (Weisman, 1993; Yalom, 1992), often it is not deemed worthy of effort. Once self-actualization is aborted, individuals see their lives as meaningless.

Before the final stage of transcendence that seems to characterize most existential breakthroughs (Maslow, 1968; May, 1979; Tillich, 1987), some people get bogged down with existential guilt.

> Life is marked by ambiguity, and one of the ambiguities is that of greatness and tragedy. This raises the question of how the bearer of the New Being is involved in the tragic element of life. What is his relation to the ambiguity of tragic guilt? What is his relation to the tragic consequences of his being, including his actions and decisions, for those who are with him or who are against him and for those who are neither one nor the other? (Tillich, 1987, p. 228)

For one who is on the verge of understanding meaning in one's life, guilt may prove the ultimate undoing. Heidegger (1949) described the guilt flowing from heightened awareness and questioned the right of anyone to let him- or herself be killed for the truth. "He who does so," writes Tillich, "must know that he becomes tragically responsible for the guilt of those who kill him" (1987, p. 229). Existential guilt is not irrational, rather it is grounded in responsibility. Guilt is the "worm in the heart of the human condition, an inescapable consequence of self-consciousness" (Loy, 1996, p. 9). Still, it prohibits the individual from joining and participating in the awareness of reality. When unable to work through this existential crisis, the individual is left with the consequences of unremitting shame and responsibility.

Of all the pathologies discussed thus far, possibly the most unsettling is a loss of self in the world, or **existential isolation.** When individuals fail to develop inner strength, worth, and identity, they move beyond being isolated to feeling a profound sense of loneliness. Existential isolation occurs when an individual fails to develop an authentic sense of self in the world (Weisman, 1993). The person instead internalizes anxiety and searches for any available sanctuary. Willis (1994) and Yalom (1980) describe two basic means of escape for the existentially isolated individual: existing through others, and suffocating or fusing with them. For some people, safety lasts only as long as their existence is perceived. Being alone means being abandoned and forgotten. The other defense that individuals use to seek protection from existential isolation is fusion. By living through and for others, they lose their boundaries and, in essence, their personhood. Under the popular label of codependence, women have been stereotypically described as suffocating others to regain their symbiotic attachment (Hogg & Frank, 1992). Csikszentmihalyi's (1992) research indicates that the answer lies in becoming a part of life, in joining the "flow" and living "optimally." However, in the despair of existential isolation and loneliness, many individuals have lost hope of finding a place in the world.

A Worldview

Unique among theorists, existentialists have conceptualized their philosophy in context. They suggest that all theories have usefulness, but for different individuals and issues. As indicated by Bugental (1996), in a discipline that is at odds with itself, it is unique for any theory to see the utility of other approaches:

Psychology, or at least American psychology, is a second rate discipline. The main reason is that it does not stand in awe of its subject matter. Psychologists have too little respect for psychology. In the future, I hope that there would be more appreciation of the great range of human potential, and that attempts to be only objective or only subjective would seem as ludicrous as they really are. (p. 135)

As professionals, we seldom see value in approaches that do not fit personal or prevailing preferences. Bugental (1978) was the first to see the theories in perspective. According to Bugental, there are six levels of helping goals, extending from behavioral change to spiritual development. Corresponding to the six goals are six different types of helping, from behavioral to transpersonal.

Wilber (1986, 1993) also offers a broader viewpoint, incorporating other theoretical orientations into a developmental schema. Wilber's theoretical model is transpersonal and more reflective of Eastern religion than Tillich's (1987) focus on the Western perspective. For Wilber, an individual's pathology is seen as a matter of degree, beginning with psychotic symptoms and advancing to spiritual struggles. Like Bugental, Wilber sees each theory as subtly answering the questions raised at various levels of dysfunction. The physiological and biochemical interventions (psychiatry) are more effective for psychotic symptoms. Psychodynamic and existential therapies are the bridge to transpersonal techniques. Each theory is seen as having a contribution, but none has the answer for all people or all issues.

Besides viewing itself in the context of other counseling theories, existential theory also perceives the individual in an ever-changing environment. Within a family, a gender, a language, a culture, a time period, and a system, individuals struggle to find identity and meaning. Existentialism strives to help honor the pain that occurs at many levels of experience. As described by Van Kaam (1966), "Existential psychology sees man as living in a human world; therefore when my counselee enters my room, he is not alone, but rather brings with him a whole world . . . nothing exists for any human being that does not have a certain meaning for him" (p. 61). Unique among theories (Arciniega & Newlon, 1995), existentialism directly addresses the contextual elements shaping the individual's reality.

Major Constructs

Approaches to Existentialism

Existentialism embodies differing perspectives and approaches. It would be possible for an individual to see three forces within the existential perspective: **dynamic existentialism, humanistic existentialism,** and **transpersonal existentialism.** Common to all approaches is the nature and quality of the existential relationship. However, dynamic existentialists (Abroms, 1993; Cannon, 1991; Yalom, 1980), like their Freudian predecessors, focus attention on the resolution of inner conflict and anxiety. Humanistic existentialists emphasize unconditional acceptance, awareness of personal experience, and authenticity rather than resolving existential conflicts. The transpersonal existential approach perceives death as an opportunity for the individual to rise above the given circumstances. According to this approach, most people experience tragedy, but in equal proportion, they experience joy (Maslow, 1968). Health is the ability to transcend the environment, drawing from the joyful aspects of existence.

Death

Death is the ultimate truth. Both in myth and in reality, it is ever present. In *The Cry for Myth,* Rollo May tells us that "We are able to love passionately because we die" (1992, p. 294). How we have accepted this mortal condition—or found ways to ignore it—determines our psychological well-being. Death is encountered in all counseling experiences. Presenting concerns such as grief need to be addressed, but also most existential healing involves letting go of the unhealthy or dysfunctional parts of self, relationships, or ideals. Well-being involves becoming more honest and authentic. In working through resistance to authenticity, clients watch as part of themselves die. Suicidal and homicidal feelings are common during this period. Drawing from Horney's notion of idealized and despised images of self, Bugental (1978) asserts that both images are false and must die for the real person to emerge: "But there is a fearful wrenching involved in that relinquishment. The nakedness seems, and indeed is, so terribly vulnerable and so truly mortal. Usually the 'killing' of the old self occurs in some kind of break out experience" (p. 79). A confrontation with death signals the rebirth of a more aware and more authentic being.

Freedom

Freedom comes after our confrontation with our inaccurate representation of ourselves. It emerges only after we realize that the world is an arbitrary construction of our awareness. Hence, we can make each moment the way we wish, and make our future different from any moments in our past. Although we can choose each thought we have, there are costs and benefits for each decision. Bolen (1996) draws a parallel between the concentration camp situation described by Frankl (1984) and the situation facing individuals with AIDS and cancer. In both cases, we have the freedom to choose our reaction to these deplorable situations. Survivors of victimization have the power to choose their reaction to the injustice, just as those individuals hurt by society, others, or themselves can regain their dignity by honoring the pain and choosing not to be dominated by it (Walker, 1994). Kelly (1955) proposed that our choosing was ultimately a cognitive process built from our own constructions of reality. Individuals' emotional readiness for the decision and their choice of their reactions are key to the meaning to be gleaned from the encounter. Freedom is silhouetted by responsibility.

Isolation

Isolation is a separation from oneself as much as from others. The isolation from our true self keeps us from connecting and contributing to the larger social order in more productive ways. We are isolated and defended by our own false identities. Out of our own fears, we erect walls to prohibit the connections we most desire. As Bugental (1978) states, "When I begin to realize that my truest identity is as process and not as fixed substance, I am on the verge of a terrible emptiness and a miraculous freedom" (p. 133). However, our sense of self is mediated because our inner nature is not strong and overpowering and unmistakable like the instincts of animals. It is weak and delicate and can be easily overcome by habit, cultural pressure, and wrong attitudes

(Maslow, 1968). Even though our creativity never disappears, it may struggle to surface. Because of external pressures, we may not be totally free to actualize because of our own restraints.

Culture

Sartre defined culture as the "objective mind" (Cannon, 1991). It is the context of the world that concurrently shapes individuals as they construct it. Current work by existentialists has found differing roles for culture in our lives. Solomon, Greenberg, and Pyszcznski (1991) indicate that our culture gives our world meaning and protects us from anxiety regarding death. In several studies (Greenberg et al., 1990; Rosenblatt, Greenberg, Solomon, Pyszcznski, & Lyon, 1989), existentialists have shown that when individuals are asked to think about death or are faced with death anxiety, they tend to adhere more to their cultural values and biases. Culture can become a means of escape when one is faced with fear of demise.

Other existentialists believe that connecting with others individually and within our culture helps individuals to heal from their isolation (Maslow, 1954). However, the more we force a connection, the further we are pushed apart. The more we struggle to understand our feelings, the more they elude our realization. When we begin acknowledging and accepting who we are in our cultural context, we can start to connect with others and with ourselves.

Meaninglessness/Meaningfulness

Out of our will to love and live, we arrive at meaning in our lives (May, 1969b). In gaining a deeper awareness of ourselves, we also gain a deeper sense of others. Our efforts to gain understanding involve confronting aspects of ourselves before we develop a heightened sense of the world's meaning. The despair of the reality of meaninglessness in the world described by Yalom (1980) and the meaningfulness that Bugental (1978) believes we can attain once we become more open to life experience are echoed by Maslow (1971) with the notion that through awareness and actualization, people can transcend their present situation. We transcend—that is, find meaning in our world—by fully being aware of ourselves. Truly being oneself involves being more integrated within and without. Paradoxically, as people become more open to their true feelings, they are better able to join with others and be one with the world. The person is more able to love. Through transcendence, the person also becomes more capable. When people are most truly themselves they are also more creative, aware, and productive. Life is not as painful a struggle. People are more aware of the potentialities in their lives and within themselves. Meaning is implicit in discovering ourselves and in our awareness of others.

Authenticity and Vulnerability: Two Sides of the Existential Self

Becoming a more **authentic** person means that an individual lives grounded (Loy, 1996) with honesty, compassion (Dass & Bush, 1992), and awareness (Weisman, 1993). The **vulnerable** person, the authentic person's counterpart, is always in conflict, lacking self-honesty and honesty with others (Weisman, 1993). Bradshaw (1993) indicates that in our culture we may feel that a false, vulnerable self is needed to be loved. Needing courage and hope, the vulnerable individual passively lacks the confidence and support to sustain coping in an unpredictable and unsympathetic world. The virtue of authenticity is achieved with sustained effort, while vulnerability passively summons pain. Bound to autonomy, the authentic individual doesn't need people but is able to benefit from relationships, whereas through relationships the vulnerable false-self struggles to find comfort by escaping being genuinely known.

Existential Relationships

Outcome research indicates that the helping relationship is the most important aspect of the counseling or psychotherapy process (Mahoney, 1991). Across all of the applications of existential thought, the form and quality of the relationship are consistent. There is a sense of relational truth embedded in the encounter (May, 1983; Willis, 1994). Bugental (1978) describes the relationship as professional, dedicated to healing and growth, and sensitive. Reiter (1995) indicates that it is imperative that the counselor or therapist be emotionally authentic—otherwise the power imbalance is countertherapeutic as well as unresponsive to the emotional influence the client has on the counselor or therapist. Although skilled, the counselor or therapist is present with the client in a very real and immediate existence. But these only describe the functions, not the substance of the encounter.

The diversity and substance of relationships were probably best described by Buber (1970). According to Buber, relationships may be experienced at several levels or at a combination of different levels. Some individuals relate to the world and to others as "I to I." Because other people are not seen as objects or individuals, these relationships are characterized by indirectness. People speak at or about others, but seldom to them. These individuals take and never give.

"I to it" relationships depict an individual relating to another as an object. These relationships do not persist. The individual generally moves to another level of relating, whether it is more intimate or more detached.

Another level of relationship is among people who relate to others and the world as "it to it." For these individuals, *I* has little meaning, for they don't have much sense of self. People relating to others at the "it to it" level have no room for any "I"-ness.

The next relationship level is called "we to we." These people also have no sense of "I." This relationship is generally seen in young children. No one has any individuality or objectivity.

"Us to them" describes a relationship between the chosen few and the damned. Some people will triumph, and others will fail. The lesser individuals are not even heard by the chosen "us" because they represent "them." All the good attributes are wrapped up in "us;" all the negative ones are represented by "them."

The "I to you" relationship implies treating the other individual as a person. The encounter involves two rather than one to an object or one to a despised part. There are more possibilities for understanding within an "I to you" relationship.

The profound meeting, the core of the existential connection, is the "I to Thou" relationship. As discussed earlier, this relationship involves an encounter with God and a deeper respect for the individual. The notion of transcendence is a part of the connection at this level. The most potent form of help involves being present in a respectful, honoring encounter (Dass & Gorman, 1985). In the final analysis, "I to Thou" relationships provide hope for genuine understanding.

In the "I to Thou" relationship, the counselor or therapist is merely a guide on a journey (Bugental, 1978). Offering respect for the client, the counselor or therapist is also a traveler on the same road. In the "I to Thou" level, the whole person is considered and honored. "Existential healing occurs in this mode of existence and is accomplished by the action of the reality between a person and the other in dialogue" (Heard, 1996, p. 239). The counseling relationship may reflect several levels of encounter at a given time for the client and the counselor or therapist. Whatever the level, the counselor or therapist affects and is affected by the helping process.

Hazards on the Journey

The journey through the "dark night of the soul" can be difficult for counselors and therapists (Bugental, 1978, p. 77). They must protect themselves, their time, and their private lives. Making several such painful journeys with clients is bound to affect practitioners at a very personal level. Kopp writes: "Doing counseling is like remembering all the time that you are going to die. Because the counseling hour has a definite beginning and ending, we are kept aware of its being temporary. There is only me, and you, and here, and now. We know in advance that it will not last, and we agree to this" (1972, p. 42). Being an existential counselor or therapist means being open to continued learning and awareness because existential helping operates at an intense level of involvement.

If we are to listen to Freud's warning, truly being with clients may be harmful to the helping process. The counselor or therapist may be ineffective by engaging in an authentic encounter. Yalom (1980, 1992) argues that the helping relationship needs to achieve a balance, but the counselor or therapist should not be afraid of contact with another person or of being known. It requires a delicate harmony on a journey that is uncharted and unlike other counseling approaches.

Additionally, May (1979) suggests that there is a potential for losing the scientific focus when working with people at an existential level. In rebelling against the rationalistic tradition of contemporary psychology, existential counselors and therapists might be detached from philosophical or technical realities. The trend toward transpersonal theory only underscores the danger. Ignoring the need to delineate therapeutic interventions, the existential counselor or therapist may be professionally vulnerable.

Despite all the concerns and warnings, there is value in taking the risk to encounter another person at the existential level. For the field, existentialism is an alternative and the only viewpoint solidly grounded in theory (May, 1983) and philosophy (Engler, 1995). Most significantly, clients find this approach very helpful (Yalom, 1980).

Applications

Overview

Existential counseling and psychotherapy have found application among diverse settings, individuals, and groups. The field of family counseling (Charny, 1992; Goldenberg & Goldenberg, 1996; Lantz, 1993: Lantz & Alford, 1995) has embraced existentialism as providing a contextual approach based on choice, responsibility, and growth. Group counseling also has been an arena for applications of the existential model. The interpersonal relationships of a group are directly addressed by an existential approach (Brabender & Fallon, 1993; Meir, 1996; Yalom, 1995) because these struggles are easily addressed in the context of others. An existential model has also been applied to the following: individuals and families struggling with AIDS (Nord, 1996; Vaughan & Kinnier, 1996), children (Pramling & Johansson, 1995), developmental concerns (Chessick, 1996; Lantz & Gomia, 1995; Sheikh & Yalom, 1996; Steen, 1996), minorities (Corey, 1990; Lantz & Alford, 1995), those struggling with identity issues (Krueger & Hanna, 1997), individuals dealing with substance abuse (Ford, 1996), clients with serious pathology (Rosenbluth & Yalom, 1996; Warah, 1993), those with chronic illness (Leifer, 1996; Somerfield, Curbow, Wingard, & Baker, 1996), and individuals in supervision (Worthen & McNeill, 1996). Although existentialism is not the primary theory adopted by counselors and therapists, it is having a considerable impact.

Goals of Counseling and Psychotherapy

The existential goals of counseling and change are "tragically optimistic" (Frankl, 1984, p. 161). Existential counseling has the following core principles (Frankl, 1984): suffering is a human achievement and accomplishment, guilt provides the opportunity to change oneself for the better, vulnerability motivates us to become authentic, and life's unpredictability provides an individual incentive to take responsible action. Although steeped in philosophy, these principles hardly provide a working primer for the budding existential counselor or therapist. The goals for existential counseling and psychotherapy are simple. Existential change is a process whereby meaning is gleaned from common, worldly endeavors. Clients are transformed through courageous and subtle encounters with aspects of their humanness.

The Process of Change

Change evolves from a client's willingness to participate in the interpersonal encounter by confronting loneliness, experiencing individuality, encountering true connection, and developing the inner strength to transcend the life situation (Brabender & Fallon, 1993; May, 1953; Weisman, 1993). But the process of change begins much earlier. By reaching out to be with another person authentically, the client begins the process of transformation. Anxiety loses its power, and clients change as their fears melt into vital energy. Tillich (1980) indicates that courage to be oneself evolves out of personal anxiety.

The process of existential change involves coming to terms with anxiety through awareness of responsibility and choice. As Yalom writes in *When Nietzsche Wept* (1992), "Don't underestimate the value of friendship, of my knowing I'm capable of touching and being touched. . . . I realize I have a choice. I shall always remain alone, but what a difference, what a wonderful difference, to choose what I do—choose your fate, love your fate" (p. 301). Through increased awareness of self and experience of the world, combined with their awareness of choice and responsibility, clients can experience their potential. Instead of a veiled existence, they are living consciously and responsibly; they are connecting with others as well as with aspects of themselves. The actual process of change may move very rapidly: clients may bloom into creative, energized individuals able to self-actualize. The process may also unfold more gradually. Regardless, the catalyst for change is the relationship facilitating the development of awareness, acceptance, responsibility, vulnerability, and authenticity in the individual.

The change process discussed thus far has been in the context of individual counseling or psychotherapy. But as indicated by the numerous citations in a recent text for group counseling (Capuzzi & Gross, 1998), many people have found the existential model useful for understanding and implementing the group process. The multiple relationships provided by the group can promote a change toward greater awareness and genuineness through an awareness provided by the relationships. Additionally, existential counseling can facilitate change in counselors and therapists themselves. Dubin (1991) relates that "in all my years of graduate school, internship, and psychoanalytic training, I never had direct supervision on how to be with a patient" (p. 65). By receiving training in authenticity, counselors and therapists learn to be genuine. Supervisors promote change by not only "being" with their supervisees, but also by training the supervisee in the "I to Thou" encounter. The exact nature of the meeting may vary, but the helping relationship remains the most potent change agent available for the existential counselor or therapist (Bugental, 1978; May, 1983; Yalom, 1980).

Intervention Strategies

Although supported by a fully developed theory, existentialism offers no set of techniques (May, 1983). As you read about the interventions, you will notice that traditional techniques do not exist in this approach. In most theories, understanding follows technique, but the existential counselor or therapist allows the approach to flow from the clients rather than forcing a circumscribed intervention upon them. Existential theory is steeped in phenomenological awareness. Therefore, the following intervention strategies flow from a respectful understanding of clients.

Telling the Story: Finding the Meaning of Myth.   In his last work, May (1992) viewed myths as central to gaining existential meaning: "Each one of us is forced to do deliberately for oneself what in previous ages was done by family, custom, church, and state, namely, form the myths in terms of what we can make some sense of experience" (p. 29). In his book, he discussed the ways in which myths provide insight and meaning. In the counseling session, stories may be facilitative in helping clients understand events in their lives. The clients also create their story as they detail their past and future.

The intervention of canvassing a client's history is articulated by Binswanger and Boss (1983). The client's history is gathered but is not explained or categorized. Instead, the existential intervention "understands this life history as modifications of the total structure of the patient's being in the world" (p. 284). The practitioner is viewing the client's history through the client's being and awareness rather than focusing on pathological development. As the story unfolds, the client can see the patterns from a larger perspective. "Healing through narration and opening up involve an existential act of self-transcendence of an embodied person who organizes his or her experience in time" (Mishara, 1995, p. 180). Life myths literally order and focus the world, giving life meaning and value.

Sharing Existence in the Moment.   The existential relationship is the primary therapeutic intervention, and the client is an existential partner. Viewed with compassion, the client is not met with pity or sympathy (Dass & Bush, 1992; Dass & Gorman, 1985). The counselor or therapist must be genuinely present on the "sharp edge of existence in the world"

(Binswanger & Boss, 1983, p. 285). As Bugental (1978) asserts, "Presence is the quality of being in a situation in which one intends to be as aware and as participative as one is able to be at that time and in those circumstances. Presence is carried into effect through mobilization of one's inner (toward subjective experience) and outer (toward the situation and any other person in it) sensitivities. . . . Presence is being there in the body, in emotions, in relating, in thoughts in every way" (pp. 36–37). Emerging from the intervention is a deep sense of relatedness, which Heuscher (1987) calls love.

Included in the relatedness, and therapeutically significant, the counselor or therapist must be able to use him- or herself as an indicator of what is occurring within the client. "It is not possible to have a feeling without the other having it to some degree also. . . . The use of one's self as an instrument requires a tremendous self-discipline on the part of the therapist" (May, 1979, p. 122). Being not only implies presence but also restrains the counselor's or therapist's own distortions, thoughts, and feelings as he or she participates in the client's world.

Centered Awareness of Being.   The existential counselor or therapist helps the client become more centered, more aware. The key is becoming honest (Willis, 1994), clear, and responsive. "Analysis and confrontation of one's various inauthentic modes . . . particularly extrinsically oriented, non-autonomous, or death denying . . . seems to be the key therapeutic technique on this level" (Wilber, 1986, p. 137). By eliminating the extrinsically focused aspects of themselves, clients become more aware of themselves in the environment. The subjectivity gained in centering (Bugental, 1978) can lead to other levels of understanding or transcendence (Kopp, 1972; Maslow, 1968; Wilber, 1993). Only by looking inward does the client develop insight and a keener awareness of personal problems (May, 1983). The most important first step is becoming more conscious of reality and authentically examining the various aspects called self.

Self-Responsibility.   Taking responsibility for growth is important, but taking responsibility for self-destructive actions is not easy. This intervention involves helping clients take ownership of their lives. First, they must be accountable for their choices. Equally important is letting go of the responsibility that others own in the process of relating (Gould, 1993; Wilber, 1986). Being responsible acknowledges that obligation can be assumed, shared, and owned by others.

Dream Work.   Counselors and therapists working in a variety of approaches have seen dreams as the window to the unconscious. In existential counseling and therapy, dreams have an additional usefulness. The focus is on the client's "dynamic, immediately real and present" (May, 1983, p. 152) existence viewed through the dream rather than the set of dynamic mechanisms at work. "In the dream we see the whole man, the entirety of his problems, in a different existential modality than in waking, but against the background and with the structure of the a priori articulation of existence, and therefore the dream is also of paramount therapeutic importance for the existential analyst" (Binswanger & Boss, 1983, p. 285).

Through dream work, the counselor or therapist is better able to help the client see the pattern of being in the world and know the possibilities of existence through the dream (Binswanger & Boss, 1983). Though unsettling, the existential experience of dreams moves the individual closer to authenticity. Existential dreams "deepen self-perception" (Kuiken, 1995, p. 129). Dreams are like insight. They provide a reflection of inner vision, and the dreamer is compelled to discover their meaning.

Disclosing and Working Through Resistances. Addressing resistances to awareness requires a sensitive intervention, and the counselor or therapist is most effective when addressing issues supportively. This intervention creates both anxiety and joy for the client (May, 1983). Bugental (1978) suggests that counselors and therapists use comments such as "You can feel how much that way of being has cost you all of your life" and "You have wanted so much to be loved that you have often forgotten to take care of your own needs" (p. 90). The client owns the responsibility and the power to address the issues blocking awareness and authenticity. The counselor or therapist serves as the midwife in the birth of a more authentic being.

Confronting Existential Anxiety. Probably the most important intervention is being aware of the client's existential issues. The complex societal and individual reaction to death stirs complex emotions in most individuals (Kubler-Ross, 1975). It takes courage to discuss the forbidden subject of death. As Yalom (1980) says, "If we are to alter therapeutic practice, to harness the clinical leverage that the concept of death provides, it will be necessary to demonstrate the role of death in the genesis of anxiety" (p. 59). Sometimes this may be accomplished by a review of one's life (Vaughan & Kinnier, 1996). In such interventions, individuals are encouraged to examine and resolve issues by focusing on their life stories. By confronting the ultimate losses (e.g., relationships, life, and self) and by being present through the resultant anxiety, counselors and therapists have a powerful tool to help individuals work through fear.

Sustaining Changes in Being. When clients relinquish their old selves by stepping into the unknown, they place an inordinate amount of faith in their counselor or therapist guide. The guide needs to answer with faith in the client. Bugental (1978), who offers guidance to the counselor or therapist for this most critical period, suggests that the practitioner provide support by transferring power back to the client. Counselors may constantly be attuned to unresolved issues in therapy. As part of supporting the new ways of being, they must also address the paradigm shift from the objective to the subjective and then to the integrated reality. Life is not experienced by total detachment through immersion but rather by a combination of those perspectives. By mourning the disillusionment and years of unnecessary struggle, the client maintains growth.

Closure. Facing the end of the helping relationship is the final confrontation with reality. It is expected that additional issues will arise to delay the inevitable ending. The intervention of termination requires continued authenticity and willingness to be present. The counselor or therapist and the client may never meet again. Paralleling every other loss in the lives of both the client and the counselor or therapist, termination represents a very real death to both people. It is critical that the practitioner help the client by processing the ending of counseling or therapy, by creating a good parting. The difficulty with this intervention is that it exposes the reality of ending that is present in all relationships.

Evaluation

Overview

Most of the existential research falls into two categories: research that further develops existential concepts, and research that applies existentialism to specific populations. Unfortunately, existentialists tend to be congruent. The theory that focuses on existence over essence is more centered on theory, counseling, and people than on generating testable hypotheses, research design, and advancing the theory through scientific analysis (Binswanger & Boss, 1983; Funder, 1997; May, 1969a).

Supporting Research

The first section of research sets out to develop an understanding of existential behaviors. Yalom (1980) synthesized the research in existential theory before 1980 as demonstrating that a meaningful existence is associated with less pathology, strong religious beliefs, self-transcendent values, and interpersonal connectedness and purpose in life. Additionally, understanding the meaning of life changes over the periods of development. Unfortunately, Yalom indicates that all of the statistical relationships are associational and not causal. More studies are necessary.

Several other studies add to the investigation of existential theory. Bereavement, health and social behavior, religiosity, and emotional behavior have been explored in relationship to existential concerns. Yalom and Lieberman (1991) discovered that grief over the death of a spouse offered important information in studying existential reactions. In one study, Blyski and Westman (1991) found that existential anxieties were separate from religious concerns. Burris, Jackson, Tarpley, and Smith (1996) found that "quest is born out of existential struggle with tragedy and conflict and quest reflects an autonomous, self-directing approach to religion that may be inimical to established religious traditions" (p. 1068). However, other studies (Adams, 1996; Baldwin & Wesley, 1996; Nielsen, 1995) found existentialism to be linked to expressions of spirituality. Health and social behavior were studied by Thauberger et al. (1983), who discovered that people confronting death and those avoiding it experience advantages and disadvantages associated with their coping style.

Two studies examined levels of emotional development within existential concern. Existential development was "correlated directly with religious interest and emotional development" (Hazell, 1984a, p. 967). In a similar study of males, Hazell (1989) found that emotional development and consciousness about emptiness were positively correlated.

An interesting confound of a study (Addis & Jacobson, 1996) looking at cognitive and behavioral counseling found existential concerns to be a mediating variable. When examining depressed clients treated with cognitive versus behavioral counseling, researchers found that clients with existentially motivated depression were more amenable to a cognitive approach to treatment. The specific focus of the depression seemed to require counseling be directed at thoughts rather than behaviors. Again, the existential variable had specific differentiating value.

Efforts to apply existentialism to specific populations have been significant, but the lack of research is equally frustrating. Ibrahim (1985) made an excellent case for the importance of culture in existential theory. Jagers and Smith (1996) examined spirituality from an "Afrocultural" perspective with respect to several variables, including existential well-being. Attinasi (1992) proposed a rationale for examining outcome assessment for cross-cultural students that includes phenomenological interviews. In another study (Greenberg et al., 1990), it was found that confronting existential issues elicits more tenacious cultural values. A study by Baldwin and Wesley (1996) examined the impact of existential anxiety on students who were given scenarios measuring cultural polarization. In that study, even those individuals with higher self-esteem when exposed to existential anxiety showed more cultural bias. Existential variables continue to influence many different arenas. Still, more research is needed.

Single or group case studies have proved helpful in examining existential concerns. A schizophrenic was studied and found to have core existential concerns (Schmolling, 1984). Lantz and Pegram (1989) studied several clients and cited the importance of the "will to meaning" across all cases. All studies indicate the need for further investigation. Among the studies surveyed, some lack the ability to be generalized (Hazell, 1989), and others address association only (Blyski & Westman, 1991; Hazell, 1984b). Much work needs to be done to fully understand and apply existential theory.

Using Testing to Measure Existential Conflict.   Several tests have been constructed that can also be used as interventions in counseling or psychotherapy. The use of these instruments depends on the needs of the counselor or therapist and that person's comfort with assessment in an existential relationship. Each test offers additional information that may be helpful for the counselor or therapist and the client. Additionally, the assessment information might be useful in the continued efforts toward understanding, building, and substantiating existential theory.

The "Existential/Dialectical Marital Questionnaire" (EDMQ) was validated among couples in Israel (Charny & Asineli, 1996). It was compared with other instruments and found to be valid, useful, and meaningful. The EDMQ provides an existential tool for clinicians working with couples. The "Purpose of Life" test, which measures meaninglessness, was developed by Crumbaugh and Maholic (Yalom, 1980). This instrument measures existential concerns; however, it lacks the validity that would make it more applicable.

Two other scales were developed to measure avoidance of the ontological confrontation of death (the AOC scale) and avoidance of existential confrontation (the AEC scale). They are used to look at differences between those who avoid and those who confront the existential dilemmas. The reliability of both instruments has been high, but subsequent studies indicate that there are advantages and disadvantages associated with different strategies of gaining awareness (Thauberger et al., 1983).

The LRI ("life regard" index), developed by Battista and Almond, examines meaning in life (Yalom, 1980). Although theoretically sophisticated, it has not been used (Yalom, 1980). The LRI is another effort of little consequence.

The "Experienced Levels of Emptiness and Existential Concern" questionnaire developed by Hazell (1984a, 1984b) and the "Existential Anxiety Scale" (Frank, 1996) are two other existential instruments. Both examine the issues of meaninglessness and existential fear and anxiety. Like other tests, these scales would benefit from further study.

All of the instruments would benefit from increased validity, sensitivity to cultural differences, and awareness of societal gender pressures. One recent study points to the deficit. When Yalom and Lieberman (1991) were examining awareness and bereavement, they resorted to interviews because of the "poor construction" (p. 336) of existing instruments.

While new instruments for therapeutic intervention are needed, currently developed measures require further study. Ibrahim (1985) suggests that effective cross-cultural counseling requires an examination of existential concerns, and gender would also benefit from further existential study. Although many studies and applications of existential theory have been made in the last five years, existentialism would benefit from an instrument that addresses the worldview that existential theory advances.

Limitations

Existentialism is not for everyone. It proposes a worldview in which each theoretical approach has a place with optimal effectiveness. Systemic concerns by their nature deserve a family approach. Likewise, individuals with serious ego deficits will benefit from the psychoanalytic model. Each theoretical model reflects different levels of goals and needs of the client. Although existentialism may be used with a wide spectrum of concerns, it requires that individuals be ready to look at their fears, anxieties, and responsibilities. An existential approach also focuses on the interpersonal nature of counseling and psychotherapy. Not giving clients answers or direction may be unsettling to clients who want a more prescriptive, objective approach.

Existentialism faces the world acknowledging the subjective experience. Because subjectivity runs counter to much of today's thought, it is understandable that existentialism may not answer the client's perceived needs. For example, upon encountering existentialism, Szasz (1987) was struck by the fantasy of this relative world. Understandably, some clients may also be skeptical because of the lack of clearly defined steps involved in treatment. Existentialism is not for the client who wants to avoid pain or experience immediate relief from struggle. Whether or not counseling or psychotherapy is brief, the existential search tends to go beyond four or five sessions.

Existential counseling or psychotherapy relies heavily on the verbal encounter. The underlying assumption of healing for existentialists is rooted in the helping relationship. Individuals who avoid contact with others will find this approach intrusive. Silence has its uses in existentialist counseling or psychotherapy (Dass & Gorman, 1985), but most existential counselors and therapists rely on the verbal exchange.

Because existential counseling is based on existential theory, the criticism that existentialism lacks a guiding theory (Sue, Sue, & Sue, 1997) seems unfounded. A closer examination provides insight into the reason. By definition and historical development, existentialism is not based on the Cartesian, objectively oriented theory. As such, it lacks the common theoretical premise guiding the cognitive, behavioral, and psychoanalytic approaches. Although not sharing the theoretical assumptions of some predominant theories, it is not without a theoretical basis.

Probably the most evident challenge for existentialism is the lack of scientific exploration. While cognitive behaviorists are generating research to validate their theory, a lack of research permeates every aspect of the existential domain. Existentialists are left defenseless in a battle of science. Not only is the lack of validation of the theory problematic, but also individuals without a solid sense of integrity are attracted to a model lacking a sequence of techniques and guidelines. Encounter groups are only one example of an early experiential existential model lacking the scrutiny of validation. Until existentialists address this issue (which is not consistent with their subjective approach), existentialism will be a haven for unusual and fanciful approaches with no substance.

Because most strengths also embody weaknesses, the underlying faith in a client's potential for growth may appear shallow and unprofound. Met at a concrete level, the question of "Who am I?" appears inconsequential. Existentialism's strength in honoring the person may be comprehended as a cursory gesture.

Summary Chart—Existential Theory

Human Nature
Existential theory is realistically optimistic about human nature. People exist in a culture and context, and all struggle with the universal concerns of death, freedom, isolation, and meaninglessness. They have the capacity to utilize their anxiety to be in the world, and they also can stay stuck in existential anxiety and despair.

Major Constructs
Existentialism addresses the following constructs: confronting universal fears of death, understanding our ultimate isolation, finding purpose in a predominantly meaningless existence, coming to terms with anxiety, accepting the burden of freedom of choice, realizing the responsibility we have for our lives, and living authentically.

Goals
The goal of existential counseling and psychotherapy is to confront anxieties about the givens of existence. Existentialism involves learning to live more authentically and gaining meaning from the common, everyday endeavors and pain. Clients transform through courageous and subtle encounters with aspects of their humanness and through the interpersonal relationship with the counselor or therapist.

Change Process
Change evolves from a client's willingness to participate in the interpersonal encounter by confronting loneliness, experiencing individuality, encountering true connection, and developing the inner strength to transcend the life situation.

Interventions
Interventions in existential counseling and psychotherapy include understanding the client's world, sharing existence in the moment, fostering a centered awareness of being, encouraging self-responsibility, working with dreams, confronting existential anxiety, and learning to put closure on a relationship.

Limitations
Existential theory utilizes a subjective approach to understand a world that is currently most popularly understood within an objective system. Existentialism relies on verbal exchange and authenticity. The theory does not rely on scientific testing to validate the

theory. Because most strengths also embody weaknesses, the underlying faith in a client's potential for growth may appear shallow and unprofound.

The Case of Maria: An Existential Approach

Maria's presenting concerns reflect an existential struggle with death, isolation, freedom, and meaninglessness. The death of her relationships with her family was devastating. Adding to that, the "ideal" marriage never answered her search for self. She was forced to survive abuse, isolation, and shame. No one validated her pain or acknowledged her loss of self in the world. Maria has challenged the cultural traditions for Hispanics and for females on many levels and for many years. From her early separation at college to the present situation as a single parent, she has been isolated from her culture and family. Even more of an insult, the more she sought refuge in them, the more she was shamed even by those with whom she sought refuge. Confronting a loss of identity, Maria experiences existential isolation. To find meaning or to escape from finding it, she has become depressed, developed problems at work, lost the ability to adequately feed herself, and withdrawn from her relationships with others. Other than her children, the focus of her reason for existence, Maria has lost her identity and sense of self in the world. Even the freedom to date and get back into "circulation" provides memories of the trauma from her marriage and the responsibility for the choices she has made. The life Maria has constructed is fragile.

The potential loss of her role as a parent seems to have intensified the nightmares, as well as her declining ability to maintain herself, her relationships, and her children. Maria has coped in the past by creating meaning in and through others (a "new" family, teaching, her children). However, her choices have brought her pain and abuse and now have left her alone with responsibilities she feels unable to manage. She now lives through her children. Her brittle existence is crumbling with the threat of losing her independence. Maria's cultural ties, the core of her identity, have diminished as her family of origin has turned away from her. The religious foundation of her life also might be seen as abandoning her because her priest sent her to a physician due to her severe depression and helplessness. In facing her life without culture and with increased pressures to create a new meaning out of her broken past, Maria, as in her dream, has no way to turn to escape. She is left alone and afraid.

Treatment/Intervention Plan

Maria's desire to work on these issues is paramount. Her current depression and hopelessness could be paralyzing. A medication consult may be necessary if her depression does not abate and/or her suicidal ideation is increasing. Because her current defense of withdrawal is not working, she entered counseling expressing appreciation for an appointment. She seems to be motivated to change.

The goal of counseling will be to help gain an understanding of Maria's current condition (in this process, Maria also gains perspective on her situation). First, it will be important to discuss her cultural background and any feelings she has about the counseling experience as well as any cultural differences or similarities that may exist between Maria and the counselor. Also, it will be important to discuss the gender of the counselor with Maria. If she has any concerns about this, a referral will need to be made immediately. Next it will be important to hear her story. In telling of her pain, Maria will need to be validated. She will be facing her fears while she focuses on the issues prompting the depression: the separation from her family, the painful relationship with her husband, the relationships with her children, and her identity as a teacher. In all areas, Maria has experienced loss and meaninglessness (hopelessness). Ultimately, she will gain freedom by acknowledging her struggle and being heard and respected by the counselor. She will also find comfort in confronting her anxiety about having to choose a direction from this point in her life. Maria has moved counter to her parents, family, and culture. In seeking to establish herself in the world, Maria has found others in her life to be like arrows pointing her in different directions.

Her withdrawal has occurred over several years and has been in reaction to external pressures threatening her relationship with her children and her own integrity. Maria has developed a pattern of relating through others, which was enforced by her culture. It became the only sanctuary in a world without meaning or direction.

Case Analysis

The first phase of treatment will be developing a therapeutic relationship. Because Maria has been victimized by her culture and the majority culture, developing trust and groundwork for the "I to Thou" relationship is important. A concurrent component is helping her to reframe the paradigm for a cure. In the past she has sought to find herself through others, but now Maria will become instrumental in helping herself gain power in her life situation.

The dream seems to be a sign of positive prognosis for Maria. Understanding that the ideal and final interpretation will be made by Maria, the following discussion emerges from an existential interpretation. At a deep level, her real self is confronting her isolation from others ("shadowy figures") in a foreboding culture ("large warehouse-type structure"). The shadowy figures may very well be aspects of herself that she is facing (possibly aspects of her despised and idealized selves, manifest in her victimization and isolation) for the first time. She can't figure out how to escape from her situation and is afraid. This shows that Maria is focused and motivated to confront these aspects of herself and her world. Escape no longer is providing solace. She is ready to change.

The counselor will need to help Maria confront the anxiety of death. By meeting her fears of loss and engulfment and encountering the aspects of herself that are frightening, she will sense all that she has encountered and survived. Maria will also develop a stronger sense of herself and her responsibility for making her own choices. She can find a place in the world that is not bound by the figures that press in on her. By continuing to flee or withdraw from anxiety-provoking situations, Maria avoids being and living. She is trapped in her fears by her depression and isolation.

Counseling will involve helping Maria on her journey as she encounters the fears embodied by the shadowy figures and the many differing ways she may feel compelled to turn. It will be important for the counselor not to fall into the easy pattern of offering her advice (providing yet another box with another arrow). Instead, it will be important for Maria to gain her own voice and sense of self. This will occur through the process of validating her pain, hearing her story, and helping her to find meaning in herself and her existence. Unfortunately, the rational, mathematical lens through which Maria has viewed the world has not provided adequate perspective or appreciation of her subjective pain.

The counselor is providing a context of relating to others that will help Maria to learn that her sanctuary (escaping through depression, living through others, and looking to others for her answers) only perpetuates her anxiety. By facing her insecurities, Maria will gain a sense of inner strength, awareness, and individuality. By taking responsibility, she can realize the freedom she has to be herself. Once she has recognized her power and responsibility to choose, she can be herself in relation to others.

Group counseling might be helpful when Maria has developed a sense of her true self and feels better able to relate to others. The group would allow Maria to connect with others with similar struggles, to validate her pain and her abilities to survive, and to develop healthier ways of relating to others and herself. An interpersonal, process-focused group for survivors of abuse would be most helpful for Maria.

References

Abroms, E. M. (1993). *The freedom of the self: The bio-existential treatment of character problems*. New York: Plenum.

Adams, W. (1996). Discovering the sacred in everyday life: An empirical phenomenological study. *Humanistic Psychologist, 24,* 28–54.

Addis, M. E., & Jacobson, N. S. (1996). Reasons for depression and the process and outcome of cognitive-behavioral psychotherapies. *Journal of Consulting and Clinical Psychology, 64,* 1417–1424.

Arciniega, G. M., & Newlon, B. J. (1995). Counseling and psychotherapy: Multicultural considerations. In D. Capuzzi & D. Gross (Eds.), *Counseling and psychotherapy: Theories and interventions* (pp. 557–587). Upper Saddle River, NJ: Merrill/Prentice Hall.

Attinasi, L. (1992). Rethinking the study of the outcomes of college attendance. *Journal of College Student Development, 33,* 61–69.

Baldwin, M., & Wesley, R. (1996). Effects of existential anxiety and self-esteem on the perceptions of others. *Basic and Applied Social Psychology, 18,* 75–95.

Belenky, M. F., Clinchy, B. M., Goldberger, N. R., & Tarule, J. M. (1997). *Women's ways of knowing: The development of self, voice, and mind* (10th ed.). New York: Basic Books.

Bepko, C. (1989). Disorders of power. In M. McGoldnick, C. Anderson, & F. Walsh (Eds.), *Women in families* (pp. 406–426). New York: Norton.

Binswanger, L., & Boss, M. (1983). Existential analysis and Daseinsanalysis. In T. Millon (Ed.), *Theories of personality and psychopathology* (3rd ed.) (pp. 283–289). New York: Holt, Rinehart, & Winston.

Blyski, N., & Westman, A. (1991). Relationships among defense style, existential anxiety, and religiosity. *Psychological Reports, 68,* 1389–1390.

Bohm, D. (1973). Quantum theory as an indication of a new order in physics. Part B: Implicate and explicate order in physical law. *Foundations of Physics, 2,* 139–168.

Bolen, J. S. (1996). *Close to the bone: Life-threatening illness and the search for meaning*. New York: Scribner.

Brabender, V., & Fallon, A. (1993). *Models of inpatient group psychotherapy*. Washington, DC: American Psychological Association.

Bradshaw, J. (1993). Never knowing who we are. *Lear's, 5,* 42.

Bretall, R. (Ed.). (1951). *A Kierkegaard anthology.* Princeton, NJ: Princeton University Press.

Buber, M. (1970). *I and thou.* New York: Scribner.

Bugental, J. (1978). *Psychotherapy and process: The fundamentals of an existential humanistic approach.* Reading, MA: Addison-Wesley.

Bugental, J. (1996). 1943–1996: Highly personal reflections. *American Journal of Psychotherapy, 50,* 133–135.

Burris, C., Jackson, L., Tarpley, W., & Smith, G. (1996). Religion as quest: The self-directed pursuit of meaning. *Personality and Social Psychology Bulletin, 22,* 1068–1672.

Cannon, B. (1991). *Sartre and psychoanalysis: An existentialist challenge to clinical metatheory.* Lawrence: University Press of Kansas.

Capuzzi, D., & Gross, D. (Eds.). (1998). *Introduction to group counseling* (2nd ed.). Denver: Love.

Charny, I. (1992). *Existential/dialectical marital therapy: Breaking the secret code of marriage.* New York: Brunner/Mazel.

Charny, I., & Asineli, S. (1996). A validity study of Existential/Dialectical Marital Questionnaire (EDMQ): A psychometric questionnaire for assessing marital interaction, *Contemporary Family Therapy: An International Journal, 18,* 41–59.

Chessick, R. D. (1996). Heidegger's "authenticity" in the psychotherapy of adolescents. *American Journal of Psychotherapy, 50,* 208–216.

Corey, G. (1990). *Theory and practice of group counseling* (3rd ed.). Pacific Grove, CA: Brooks/Cole.

Craig, P. E. (1995). Being contrary, being human: The pregnant, paradoxical openness of resistance. *Humanistic Psychologist, 23,* 161–186.

Csikszentmihalyi, M. (1992). *Validity and reliability of the experience sampling method.* Cambridge: Cambridge University Press.

Dass, R., & Bush, M. (1992). *Compassion in action: Setting out on the path of service.* New York: Bell Tower.

Dass, R., & Gorman, P. (1985). *How can I help?* New York: Knopf.

Dubin, W. (1991). The use of meditative techniques in psychotherapy supervision. *Journal of Transpersonal Psychology, 23,* 65–80.

Duncan, L. (1993). A contextual theory of counseling. *TCA Journal, 21,* 55–68.

Engler, B. (1995). *Personality theories: An introduction* (4th ed.). Boston: Houghton Mifflin.

Evans, K. G. (1996). Chaos as opportunity: Grounding a positive vision of management and society in the new physics. *Public Administration Review, 56,* 491–494.

Evans, K. M. (1997). Wellness and coping activities of African American counselors. *Journal of Black Psychology, 23,* 24–35.

Feist, J. (1994). *Theories of personality* (3rd ed.). New York: Harcourt Brace.

Fine, M., Weis, L., Powell, L. C., & Wong, L. M. (1997). *Off-white: Readings on race, power, and society.* New York: Routledge.

Ford, G. G. (1996). An existential model for promoting life change. *Journal of Substance Abuse Treatment, 13,* 151–158.

Frank, M. L. (1996). The Existential Anxiety Scale: Initial validation of a multidimensional concept. Poster presented at the Southeastern Psychological Association, Norfolk, VA.

Frankl, V. (1975). *The unconscious god.* New York: Simon & Schuster.

Frankl, V. (1984). *Man's search for meaning.* New York: Washington Square Press.

Funder, D. C. (1997). *The personality puzzle.* New York: Norton.

Gerardi, S. (1990). Academic self-concept as a predictor of academic success among minority and low-socioeconomic status students. *Journal of College Student Development, 31,* 401–407.

Goldenberg, I., & Goldenberg, H. (1996). *Family therapy: An overview* (4th ed.). Pacific Grove, CA: Brooks/Cole.

Good, G. E., Robertson, J. M., Fitzgerald, L. F., Stevens, M., & Bartels, K. M. (1996). The relation between masculine role conflicts and psychological distress in male university counseling center clients. *Journal of Counseling and Development, 75,* 44–49.

Gould, W. B. (1993). *Victor E. Frankl: Life with meaning.* Pacific Grove, CA: Brooks/Cole.

Greenberg, J., Pyszcznski, T., Solomon, S., Rosenblatt, A., Veeder, M., Kirkland, S., & Lyon, D. (1990). Evidence for terror management theory II: The effects of mortality salience on reactions to those who threaten or bolster the cultural worldview. *Journal of Personality and Social Psychology, 58,* 308–318.

Hall, R. L., & Greene, B. (1996). Sins of omission and commission: Women, psychotherapy and the psychological literature. *Women and Therapy, 18,* 5–31.

Hazell, C. (1984a). Experienced levels of emptiness and existential concern with different levels of emotional development and profile of values. *Psychological Reports, 55,* 967–976.

Hazell, C. (1984b). Scale for measuring experienced levels of emptiness and existential concern. *Journal of Psychology, 117,* 177–182.

Hazell, C. (1989). Levels of emotional development with experienced levels of emptiness and existential concern. *Psychological Reports, 64,* 835–838.

Heard, W. G. (1996). The unconscious function of the I-it and I-thou realms. *Humanistic Psychologist, 23,* 239–258.

Heidegger, M. (1949). *Existence and being.* South Bend, IN: Regnery.

Heidegger, M. (1962). *Being and time.* New York: Harper & Row.

Heuscher, J. (1987). Love and authenticity. *American Journal of Psychoanalysis, 47,* 21–34.

Hillman, J. (1989). *A blue fire: Selected writings by James Hillman.* New York: Harper & Row.

Hillman, J. (1996). *The soul's code: In search of character and calling.* New York: Random House.

Hogg, A., & Frank, M. L. (1992). Toward an interpersonal model of codependence and contradependence. *Journal of Counseling and Development, 70,* 371–375.

Horner, M. (1972). Toward an understanding of achievement related conflicts in women. *Journal of Social Issues, 28,* 157–175.

Howe, J. M. (1997). A crisis of meaning. *Choice, 35,* 1373.

Ibrahim, F. (1985). Effective cross-cultural counseling and psychotherapy: A framework. *Counseling Psychologist, 13,* 625–637.

Jagers, R. J., & Smith, P. (1996). Further examination of the Spirituality Scale. *Journal of Black Psychology, 22,* 429–442.

Kelly, G. A. (1955). *The psychology of personal constructs.* New York: Norton.

Kierkegaard, S. (1944). *The concept of dread* (W. Lowrie, Trans.). Princeton, NJ: Princeton University Press.

Kopp, S. (1972). *If you meet the Buddha on the road, kill him.* New York: Bantam.

Krueger, M. J., & Hanna, F. J. (1997). Why adoptees search: An existential treatment perspective. *Journal of Counseling and Development, 75,* 195–202.

Kubler-Ross, E. (1975). *Death: The final stage of growth.* New York: Simon & Schuster.

Kuiken, D. (1995). Dreams and feeling realization. *Dreaming: Journal of the Association for the Study of Dreams, 5,* 129–157.

Lantz, J. (1993). *Existential family therapy.* Northvale, NJ: Jason Aronson.

Lantz, J., & Alford, K. (1995). Existential family treatment with an urban-Appalachian adolescent. *Journal of Family Psychotherapy, 6,* 15–27.

Lantz, J., & Gomia, L. (1995). Activities and stages in existential psychotherapy with older adults. *Clinical Gerontologist, 16,* 31–40.

Lantz, J., & Pegram, M. (1989). Casework and the restoration of meaning. *Journal of Contemporary Social Work, 70,* 549–555.

Leifer, R. (1996). Psychological and spiritual factors in chronic illness. *American Behavioral Scientist, 39,* 752–766.

Liddle, B. J. (1996). Therapist sexual orientation, gender, and counseling practices as they relate to ratings of helpfulness by gay and lesbian clients. *Journal of Counseling Psychology, 43,* 394–401.

Lightsey, O. R. (1996). What leads to wellness? The role of psychological resources in well-being. *Counseling Psychologist, 24,* 589–735.

Loy, D. (1996). *Lack and transcendence: The problem of death and life in psychotherapy, existentialism, and Buddhism.* Atlantic Highlands, NJ: Humanities Press.

Mahoney, M. J. (1991). *Human change processes.* New York: Basic Books.

Maslow, A. (1954). *Motivation and personality.* New York: Harper & Row.

Maslow, A. (1968). *Toward a psychology of being* (2nd ed.). New York: Van Nostrand.

Maslow, A. (1971). *The further reaches of human nature.* New York: Viking.

May, R. (1953). *Man's search for himself.* New York: Dell Publishing.

May, R. (1969a). *Existential psychology.* New York: Random House.

May, R. (1969b). *Love and will.* New York: Norton.

May, R. (1979). *Psychology and the human dilemma.* New York: Norton.

May, R. (1983). *The discovery of being.* New York: Norton.

May, R. (1992). *The cry for myth.* New York: Delta.

McCarn, S. R., & Fassinger, R. E. (1996). Revisioning sexual minority identity formation: A new model of lesbian identity and its implications for counseling and research. *Counseling Psychologist, 24,* 508–534.

McCullough, J. E., Worthington, E. L., Maxey, J., & Rachal, K. C. (1997). Gender in the context of supportive and challenging religious counseling interventions. *Journal of Counseling Psychology, 44,* 80–88.

Meir, E. (1996). The contributions of modern thought to a psychoanalytic phenomenology of groups. *Psychoanalysis and Contemporary Thought, 19,* 563–578.

Miller, D. (1997). New physics at last? *Nature, 385,* 768–769.

Mills, S. D., & Sprenkle, D. H. (1995). Family therapy in the postmodern era. *Family Relations, 44,* 368–376.

Milton, M. J. (1993). Existential thought and client centered therapy. *Counseling Psychology Quarterly, 6,* 239–248.

Mishara, A. L. (1995). Narrative and psychotherapy: The phenomenology of healing. *American Journal of Psychotherapy, 49,* 180–195.

Nielsen, M. (1995). Operationalizing religious orientation: Iron rods and compasses. *Journal of Psychology, 129,* 485–494.

Nietzsche, F. (1889). *Twilight of the idols* (W. Kaufmann, Trans.). New York: Viking.

Nietzsche, F. (1967). *The will to power* (W. Kaufmann & R. Hollingdale, Trans.). New York: Random House.

Nord, D. (1996). The impact of multiple AIDS-related loss on families of origin and families of choice. *American Journal of Family Therapy, 24,* 129–144.

Nuland, S. B. (1996). *How we die: Reflections on life's final chapter.* New York: Knopf.

Owen, I. R. (1994). Introducing an existential-phenomenological approach: Basic phenomenological theory and research: I. *Counseling Psychology Quarterly, 7,* 261–273.

Parham, T., & Helms, J. (1985). Relation of racial identity attitudes to self actualization and affective states of black students. *Journal of Counseling Psychology, 32,* 431–440.

Pramling, I., & Johansson, E. (1995). Existential questions in early childhood programs in Sweden: Teacher's conceptions and children's experience. *Child and Youth Care Forum, 24,* 125–146.

Prochaska, J. O., & Norcross, J. C. (1994). *Systems of psychotherapy: A transtheoretical analysis* (3rd ed.). Pacific Grove, CA: Brooks/Cole.

Reiter, L. (1995). The client's affective impact on the therapist: Implications for therapist responsiveness. *Clinical Social Work Journal, 23,* 21–35.

Rosenblatt, A., Greenberg, J., Solomon, S., Pyszcznski, T., & Lyon, D. (1989). Evidence for terror management theory: I. The effects of mortality salience on reactions to those who violate or uphold cultural values. *Journal of Personality and Social Psychology, 57,* 681–690.

Rosenbluth, M., & Yalom I. (1996). *Treating difficult personality disorders.* San Francisco, CA: Jossey-Bass.

Schmolling, P. (1984). Schizophrenia and the deletion of certainty: An existential case study. *Psychological Reports, 54,* 139–148.

Sheikh, J. I., & Yalom, I. (1996). *Treating the elderly.* San Francisco: Jossey-Bass.

Solomon, S., Greenberg, J., & Pyszczynski, T. (1991). A terror management theory of social behavior: The psychological functions of self esteem and world views. In L. Berkowitz (Ed.), *Advances in Experimental Social Psychology, 24,* 93–159.

Somerfield, M., Curbow, B., Wingard, J., & Baker, F. (1996). Coping with the physical and psychosocial sequelae of bone marrow transplantation among long-term survivors. *Journal of Behavioral Medicine, 19,* 163–184.

Steen, M. (1996). Essential structure and meaning of recovery from clinical depression for middle-adult women: A phenomenological study. *Issues in Mental Health Nursing, 17,* 73–92.

Sue, D. W., Ivey, A. E., & Pedersen, P. B. (1996). *A theory of multicultural counseling and psychotherapy.* Pacific Grove, CA: Brooks Cole.

Sue, D., Sue, D., & Sue, S. (1997). *Understanding abnormal behavior* (5th ed.). New York: Houghton Mifflin.

Szasz, T. (1987). Discussion by Thomas Szasz. In J. Zeig (Ed.), *The evolution of psychotherapy* (pp. 210–211). New York: Brunner/Mazel.

Thauberger, P., Thauberger, E., & Cleland, J. (1983). Some indices of health and social behavior associated with the avoidance of the ontological confrontation. *Omega, 14,* 279–289.

Tillich, P. (1980). *The courage to be.* New Haven: Yale University Press.

Tillich, P. (1987). *Paul Tillich: Theologian of the boundaries* (M. Taylor, Ed.) San Francisco: Collins.

Travis, J. (1981). *Wellness workbook* (2nd ed.). Berkeley, CA: Ten Speed Press.

Van Kaam, A. (1966). *The art of existential counseling: A new perspective in psychotherapy.* Denville, NJ: Dimension Books.

Vaughan, S. M., & Kinnier, R. T. (1996). Psychological effects of a life review intervention for persons with HIV disease. *Journal of Counseling and Development, 75,* 115–123.

Viorst, J. (1986). *Necessary losses.* New York: Fawcett.

Walker, L. (1994). *Abused women and survivor therapy: A practical guide for the psychotherapist.* Washington, DC: American Psychological Association.

Warah, A. (1993). Overactivity and boundary setting in anorexia nervosa: An existential perspective. *Journal of Adolescence, 16,* 93–100.

Weisman, A. D. (1993). *The vulnerable self: Confronting the ultimate questions.* New York: Plenum.

Westgate, C. E. (1996). Spiritual wellness and depression. *Journal of Counseling and Development, 75,* 26–35.

Wilber, K. (1986). The spectrum of psychopathology. In K. Wilber, J. Engler, & D. Brown (Eds.), *Transformations of consciousness* (pp. 65–159). Boston: New Science Library.

Wilber, K. (1993). *The spectrum of consciousness* (2nd ed.). Wheaton, IL: Theosophical Publishing House.

Wilber, K. (1997). *In the eye of spirit: An integral vision for a world gone slightly mad.* Boston: Shambhala.

Willis, R. J. (1994). *Transcendence in relationship: Existentialism and psychotherapy.* Norwood, NJ: Ablex.

Worthen, V., & McNeill, B. W. (1996). A phenomenological investigation of "good" supervision events. *Journal of Counseling Psychology, 42,* 25–34.

Yalom, I. (1980). *Existential psychotherapy.* New York: Basic Books.

Yalom, I. (1992). *When Nietzsche wept.* New York: Basic Books.

Yalom, I. (1995). *The theory and practice of group psychotherapy.* New York: Basic Books.

Yalom, I., & Lieberman, M. (1991). Bereavement and heightened existential awareness. *Psychiatry, 54,* 334–345.

Yiu-kee, C., & Tang, C. S. (1995). Existential correlates of burnout among mental health professionals in Hong Kong. *Journal of Mental Health Counseling, 17,* 220–229.

Person-Centered Theory

Richard J. Hazler
Ohio University

The person-centered theory of **Carl R. Rogers** is one of the most popular in the fields of psychology, counseling, and education. Rogers's perceptions of people and of how a supportive environment can assist in their development have had an immense impact on a wide variety of professions and on parenting. This approach to people was a major deviation from the psychoanalytic and behavioral models for working with people that were predominant in the early part of the 20th century.

Person-centered theory offered a new way to look at individuals and their development, as well as how people can be helped to change. From this frame of reference, people were viewed as fully in charge of their lives and inherently motivated to improve themselves. The responsibility for personal behaviors and the ability to choose to change them was also seen as belonging fully to the individual. Here was a way to view and deal with human beings that did not rely on other people (counselors, psychologists, parents, teachers, etc.) as the primary directors of change. People could now control their own change if the right conditions were offered.

Rogers saw all individuals as having inherent qualities that made nurturing possible; attempting to change basic personality characteristics or behaviors was not necessary. He believed people saw the world from their own unique perspective, which is referred to as a **phenomenological** perspective. No matter what that phenomenological view of the world was, it was further assumed that all people are continually attempting to actualize their best and most productive selves. This positive and optimistic view of human beings is often challenged by those who call attention to the unlimited opportunities for observing people as they think and act in ways that are harmful to themselves and others. But Rogers believed these thoughts and actions were primarily reflections of a distorted view of oneself and the world, distortions caused by trying to meet the expectations of others rather than trying to actualize one's own self.

The origins of Rogers's beliefs, their development into a major helping process, and an examination of the essential ingredients of that process will serve as a foundation for this chapter's discussion. Information on the counselor's or therapist's role in providing interventions and the methods used to carry out that role will then provide the practical base for beginning to implement the process.

Background

Carl R. Rogers

Person-centered theory began to make an impact on psychology in the 1940s. Carl R. Rogers was the individual behind the theory, and his influence was so great that it is commonly referred to as Rogerian theory. The major concepts of the autonomous self, reliance on one's own unique experiences, the desire and ability to make positive personal changes, and movement toward the actualization of potentials are all observable in Rogers's personal development.

Rogers was born in 1902 into a morally and religiously conservative family that was strictly religious, devoted to its children, and committed to the concept of hard work. Dancing, watching movies, smoking, drinking, and anything that vaguely suggested sexual interest were clearly forbidden, although little was said about them. The family was able to convey its directions in subtle ways that were generally unspoken but nevertheless very clear to everyone.

The family was largely self-contained, and the young Rogers had few friends. He became a loner of sorts, spending most of his time working, thinking, and reading. His early life-style caused him to pay close attention to his personalized experience of the world. In later years, this concept would become better known as a phenomenological approach to counseling or psychotherapy.

Rogers's family moved to a farm thirty miles west of Chicago when he was 12. It was here that his work ethic was reemphasized; he also developed an interest in science and experimentation. He spent much of his time studying the variety of insects and animals that were now available to him. A scientific approach to all issues was further emphasized by his father, who insisted that all farming should be as scientific and modern as possible. These concepts of hard work, scientific study, experimentation, and evaluation would later set Rogers apart from other theorists: he was the first to intentionally and creatively subject experientially recognized human development and therapeutic processes to rigorous scientific study. This aspect of his work is often overlooked by those interested in his theories, but it is a major contribution to the development of professionalism in counseling and psychotherapy.

Rogers left home to study agriculture in college but later turned to religious studies and eventually to clinical psychology as he became more interested in people, beliefs, and values. His religious beliefs, like those of his parents, were strong. However, the more he studied and discussed the issues, the more his views diverged from his parents'. A six-month trip to China as part of the World Student Christian Federation Conference encouraged his change to a more liberal viewpoint.

Explaining these changes to his parents was extremely difficult and often disappointing for all concerned. However, Rogers reported great growth in his intellectual and emotional independence from these open confrontations. The experience left him much more confident in himself, his beliefs, and his ability to deal with difficult situations. This idea that individuals can and must rely on themselves for direction and strength was to become another major emphasis in his theory, as well as in his own life.

Rogers graduated from the University of Wisconsin, married, and in 1924 began to study for the ministry at Union Theological Seminary in New York City. His focus of attention changed during his two years at Union as he became more and more interested in psychology and education. Consequently, he transferred to Columbia University to study psychology, and eventually earned his Ph.D. there in 1931.

Following graduation from Columbia, Rogers worked with children in Rochester, New York, for 12 years; later he was on the faculty at Ohio State University, the University of Chicago, and the University of Wisconsin. His final stop was at the Center for Studies of the Person at La Jolla, California, beginning in 1963. This period of time until his death in 1987 was extremely productive. It included work in education and in individual and group counseling and psychotherapy. The last years of his life were spent traveling in the most troubled places in the world, using his person-centered approach to promote peace among warring groups.

Theory Background

The field of counseling or psychotherapy in the 1920s and 1930s relied on techniques that were highly diagnostic, probing, and analytic as well as unsupported by scientific research. Rogers's first major work, *Counseling and Psychotherapy* (1942), was a clear reaction to this situation and to his work with children. "So vast is our ignorance on this whole subject [counseling and psychotherapy]," he wrote, "that it is evident that we are by no means professionally ready to develop a definitive or final account of any aspect of psychotherapy" (p. 16). He presented **nondirective** counseling and psychotherapy in this work along with a clear call for a more scientific approach to research on both his nondirective and other, more directive techniques.

Client-Centered Therapy (1951) was a culmination of a decade of practice and research in which Rogers expanded his concepts and renamed his approach. This new emphasis changed the role of the counselor or therapist from an individual who only reflected the content of client statements to one who identified the client's underlying emotions in client words and through the helping relationship. The effect of this new work was to expand the dimensions of accurate empathy with the client and to force the counselor or therapist to go beyond simple reflection of client words.

In 1957 Rogers moved to the University of Wisconsin, where his efforts at research on his theory increased and broadened. Here he tested his ideas on hospitalized schizophrenics rather than on the primarily normal population he had been working with at the University of Chicago. His research confirmed the view that the conditions present in the helping relationship did have a significant effect on both the progress of counseling or psychotherapy and the outcomes for clients (Rogers, 1967). Rogers's work with client populations ranging from normal to extremely disturbed encouraged him to broaden the use of his ideas to include all people.

Person-centered is the current term used to emphasize the personal nature of counseling or psychotherapy and other relationships in education, business, and government agencies. The therapeutic or helping relationship is now envisioned as one of person to person rather than healthy counselor to unhealthy client.

Person-centered theory developed out of a close examination of individual helping relationships, but during the 1970s and 1980s Rogers began focusing more on groups than on individuals. He was a major promoter of personal-growth groups, where individuals worked together for the purpose of self-actualizing growth rather than toward a more limited goal of overcoming psychological illnesses (Rogers, 1970). Another group adaptation saw Rogers using person-centered concepts in a group-process format to deal with critical world conflicts. He traveled to areas with major social conflicts, such as Central America (Thayer, 1987), South Africa (Rogers & Sanford, 1987), Northern Ireland (Rogers, 1987b), and even the Soviet Union (Rogers, 1987a), to run growth groups with leaders and nonleaders who had fought but never tried to understand each other. His accounts of these encounters make it clear that a person-centered orientation can be promoted in groups as well as in individual relationships.

Human Nature: A Developmental Perspective

The person-centered approach to counseling or psychotherapy implies great confidence in each client. This confidence arises out of a belief that all people have innate motivation to grow in positive ways and the ability to carry out such a growth process. This highly positive view of human nature varies widely from other theories that view human nature as evil, negative, or a nonissue. Such a positive view of human nature is essential for the person-centered practitioner because of the major responsibilities clients are given in the direction, style, and content of the helping relationship. The person-centered perception of people is based on four key beliefs: (1) people are **trustworthy,** (2) people innately move toward **self-actualization** and health, (3) people have the **inner resources** to move themselves in positive directions, and (4) people respond to their **uniquely perceived world** (phenomenological world). The interaction of these characteristics with a person's external environment brings about the most desirable aspects of development.

People Are Trustworthy

Person-centered counselors or therapists must treat their clients as trustworthy, or there will be no reason to allow them to take a leadership role in the helping relationship. From this point of view, words such as *good, constructive,* and *trustworthy* describe natural characteristics of human beings, although people also appear to take actions that demonstrate the opposite. These inappropriate actions are taken when the individual's ideal view of self does not match the real **self.** Individuals use defensive thoughts and actions to protect themselves from having to observe that they are not living the lives they believe they should. Such actions are not deceitful so much as they are direct actions based on conflicting perceptions of a person's world. All individuals are trying to improve and to act in the world as they see it in as honorable a manner as possible.

Consider the teenage boy who skips school and has been arrested for the fourth time for robbery. Many in society will judge this individual to be a bad person or one who cannot be trusted, and the boy knows this. The person-centered counselor must believe that the boy will be trustworthy in their relationship if and when he is convinced that he has a meaningful relationship with a genuine counselor. A major part of that relationship will be the counselor's conveying trust through words and actions. Anything less than this trusting relationship will serve to convince the boy that this is just another person who will not trust him. The result is that there will be little reason for the individual to work on his potential for trustworthiness.

Movement Toward Actualization

Human beings are viewed by the person-centered theorist as always striving to obtain the maximum amount from themselves. They seek any means to develop all their abilities "in ways that maintain or enhance the organism" (Rogers, 1959, p. 196). This is the driving force in the positive development of the individual. It clearly moves the individual away from control by others and toward **autonomy** and self-control. The movement toward actualization provides individuals rather than outside persons (parents, counselors, therapists, teachers, etc.) with the primary motivational strength behind development. This energy source is also seen as potentially more influential than environmental factors such as socioeconomic status, hunger, or danger, even though these often affect how the individual perceives or seeks self-actualization.

The problem teenage boy discussed previously would likely be seen by many to have inadequate self-control and little desire to overcome his problems. The result is that individuals and society as a whole will probably seek to control him and force him to grow in ways deemed appropriate by others. The person-centered view, however, emphasizes the concept that the boy is actually working toward making the most out of himself and that he will continue to do so regardless of what others do. What others can do is provide a safe environment where the boy can lower his defenses and antisocial behaviors without fear of failure and nonacceptance. When this occurs, he can be expected to continue to pursue self-actualization, but now in ways that are more appropriate and socially acceptable.

Inner Resources

The actualizing tendency provides the motive for positive development in people. But do individuals have the capacity to carry out this motivation? Person-centered theory presumes that individuals have that capacity (Rogers, 1961).

Having the belief that people have the motivation to grow in positive directions does not mean you will also have confidence in their ability to follow through on that motivation. The person-centered approach emphasizes a belief that this ability to grow in positive directions is available to them. Certainly some of the most heartwarming stories told throughout the ages have demonstrated how people can overcome tremendous odds to become successful. These same stories also cause people to question why it happens for some and not others. Person-centered theory emphasizes that these potential differences in degree of ability to overcome are not as important as persons' beliefs that they can accomplish what they set out to do. In many ways, it presumes a fairly well accepted principle of human dynamics, which states that people always have much more potential than they use most of the time. Person-centered counselors and therapists must believe in this principle if they are to help clients recognize and accept their own abilities.

The person-centered counselor must have the confidence that the troubled boy we have been discussing has the inner resources as well as the motivation to grow. Without this recognition the boy might very well feel that the ideals are reasonable but that he is doomed to failure due to his lack of ability. The counselor must recognize that this doubting attitude in the boy will most likely cause him to give up his efforts far short of his potential.

Individually Perceived World

The person-centered view recognizes that events will be perceived differently by different people (Rogers, 1961). Two armies fight, two adults argue, and relationships often break down because each side perceives what is "right" to be different from the other side's perceptions. The person-centered view of these examples is that individuals or groups relate to the world and their own actions from a unique context or phenomenological perspective. Therefore, words, behaviors, feelings, and beliefs are selected to match the specialized view of the world held by each individual.

The idea that no two people perceive the world in exactly the same way explains much of the variation we see in the previous three concepts. Our troubled boy surely does not perceive the world as the safe and kind place that another boy who is successful in school and has a comfortable family life does. Neither will he perceive it as the rational world that the counselor is likely to see. It is quite possible that the boy is stealing, in part, because of a different perception of the world. He sees this behavior as the only one available for him to help feed himself, his mother, and his infant sister. Person-centered counselors and therapists must recognize these differently perceived worlds, work hard to understand them, and seek to help clients grow through their personally perceived world rather than through the world as it is perceived by the counselor, therapist, or some other individual.

Interaction With External Factors

A person-centered view of human development gives attention to external factors that affect psychological development in addition to critical internal forces. Even as infants, people make choices that induce growth and actualize potential. They reject experiences that are perceived as contrary to their well-being. However, these naturalistic ways of making choices become confused as the developing person recognizes that other individuals may provide or withhold love based on how well the child assimilates values and behaviors set by others. This recognition can move individuals away from using their own best judgment to make personal choices and can provide a second method that requires taking actions based on the presumed desires of others. The two theoretical concepts used to explain this aspect of development are unconditional positive regard and conditions of worth (Rogers, 1959).

Individuals who are given **unconditional positive regard** by significant people in their lives receive recognition of their positive nature, including their motivation and ability to become increasingly effective human beings. The worth and value of the individual are never questioned in this case, although specific behaviors or beliefs can be rejected as inappropriate. Individuals who are given and can recognize unconditional positive regard that is provided to them feel permitted to continue trusting themselves as positive human beings. The belief is conveyed that they will make errors of judgment and behavior, but that as positive individuals they will also strive to examine themselves continually and be able to take actions for their own improvement. Being provided with unconditional positive regard helps individuals to continue seeking their own development with the confidence that they will become increasingly effective human beings.

Many times the regard and love offered by others have strings attached. For example, children might come to believe that they are only good, loved, cared for, fed, or valued if they do just as their parents say. These **conditions of worth** pressure developing persons to devalue their inherent potential for choice making and growth. They begin looking for directions and decisions to originate from external sources instead of trusting their more natural internal ones. This process moves developing individuals away from confidence in their ability to run their own lives and pushes them to seek validation based on the lives of other people who appear to be more positive than they are.

Major Constructs

The core of person-centered theory is a set of beliefs about people and relationships rather than a set of techniques to be used for behavioral counseling. Counselors and therapists interested in implementing this theory must look first to themselves and their perceptions of others rather than to what specific behaviors ought to be performed. This is a challenging task, particularly for new practitioners who are seeking to find out what they should "do" and to what extent they "do things well." The following constructs are essential beliefs involved in person-centered theory. Practitioners must have a clear perception of them before they can implement a person-centered approach effectively.

No Two People See the World Exactly Alike

According to the phenomenological approach, no two people can be expected to see things as happening in exactly the same way. Practitioners must recognize that whatever they personally believe reality to be will be different from the client's perspective and that each client will have a unique perspective. Therefore, asking the client to believe or act in a way that "everyone knows is right" becomes the counselor's or therapist's opinion, based on his or her own phenomenological view rather than some ultimate "fact." Because helping someone from a person-centered approach emphasizes the concept, it is imperative to understand the client's perspective as thoroughly as possible.

Empathic Understanding

Empathic understanding is critically important to the person-centered approach. It reflects the belief that individuals respond to a phenomenologically perceived world. **Empathy** refers to the understanding of the client's world from the client's point of view. This is no easy task because it is hard for counselors and therapists to set aside their own biased view of the world in an attempt to see things through the client's eyes. All other actions they take will be inappropriate without empathy because these actions will be based upon inaccurate perceptions of the client. This construct allows practitioners to respond effectively and assures clients that their confidence in the counselor or therapist is justified.

Empathic understanding has two equally essential dimensions that practitioners must accomplish to make it a useful construct: understanding, and accurately conveying that understanding. The most obvious of these is that counselors must set aside their own beliefs and enter the client's world so that they can understand. However, understanding by itself will not be effective. The client must also be aware of the degree to which the practitioner understands. This second dimension is crucial in order for empathic understanding to be useful. Empathic understanding only improves the helping relationship when the client clearly recognizes what it is the counselor or therapist understands.

People Make Simple Mistakes in Judgment

People make simple mistakes in judgment. They also make choices that appear to be right to them, but which are ineffective because they are made to match the perceived world of others' rather than an individual's own best judgment. People are attempting to act as they believe others would have them act (conditions of worth) rather than trusting their own positive, growth-oriented nature, their **tendency to actualize.** Counselors and therapists who demonstrate faith in the whole person rather than denigrating clients for mistakes of behavior allow their clients the freedom to explore their inner world without fear of rejection. Lacking such unconditional positive regard, clients may try to do what they believe the counselor or therapist wants in order to achieve a better life. Unfortunately, these actions will only increase clients' belief that they cannot personally make effective choices. They may find some more socially acceptable ways of behaving, but they will not have gained confidence in their own ability to seek more changes as the need arises.

Confidence in the Client

In comparison to other theories, person-centered theory places tremendous confidence in the client. This confidence is based on the belief that people are innately good and continually seeking a fully functioning experience in the world. People's tendency to actualize personal potential in positive ways is the force that the person-centered practitioner recognizes and seeks to free from self-induced constraints. Clients are treated as effective human beings who will succeed regardless of the nature of their difficulties. This contrasts with other views of the individual that do not allow the practitioner to trust clients because client difficulties are seen as weaknesses or deficiencies that will stand in the way of personal progress unless the counselor or therapist corrects them.

Perceived World of the Client May Not Approximate the World Sought

Individuals come to counseling or psychotherapy for help because of difficulties evolving from the fact that the world they perceive is not in close proximity to the world they naturally seek. The natural, growth-oriented, self-trusting nature of these people has been pushed into conflict with their chosen world, where they continually look outside their true selves for decisions. They act based on perceptions of what others think is right, and the results of their actions are not personally fulfilling or effective. This conflict is termed **incongruence.**

Congruent Individuals Trust Their Worldview

Congruent persons are the individuals who trust their view of the world and their ability to act on their basic positive nature. They feel confident about reacting in the present moment because of a belief in their organism's ability to discriminate between appropriate and inappropriate behaviors. This self-trust is then generally verified by those around them because their actions tend to be beneficial both personally and socially. Where human fallibility causes errors in reactions, congruent individuals also have a view of the world that allows the reactions of others to be evaluated and appropriate adaptive responses taken for the immediate and distant future. Congruent people are not infallible, but they do have the ability to recognize and use mistakes to grow without devaluing themselves.

The congruence versus incongruence construct helps explain the concept of anxiety in person-centered theory. Low personal anxiety occurs when the perceived self is in line with actual experiences (congruence). Alternatively, the degree to which individuals' perceptions of themselves do not match the way they actually are (incongruence) is directly related to higher levels of anxiety. It is significant for the practitioner to recognize that in person-centered theory, efforts are made to increase congruence in the client rather than directly reduce anxiety.

Applications

Overview

The person-centered concept of a growth-oriented and competent individual in need of counseling or psychotherapy presumes a scenario analogous to the growth of a simple garden bean. The bean seed has all the potential to grow but must be provided with the proper climate in order for it to achieve its full potential. It will develop as expected if placed in fertile ground where adequate warmth, sun, and water are available. Human hands do not need to touch it under the ground, nor should those hands help pull it out of properly prepared ground. In fact, such human attempts to directly manipulate will almost surely threaten the bean's development! The effective gardener knows that arranging correct conditions and leaving the actual plant alone as much as possible is the best way to allow it to reach its greatest potential.

Fostering the natural growth of the bean is analogous to how one applies person-centered theory to counseling and psychotherapy. The client has all the necessary but as yet unfulfilled potential for attaining greater **self-understanding, self-acceptance, self-growth, self-satisfaction,** and **self-actualization.** The practitioner's task is to provide the essential growth conditions of a **genuine** human relationship where acceptance, caring, and a deep understanding of the client are developed and communicated effectively to the client. The application of these conditions involves the intervention strategies that allow the person to make changes in the direction of their greatest potential.

Goals of Counseling and Psychotherapy

Movement from incongruence to congruence identifies the cornerstone person-centered goal for people who are having psychological or sociological difficulties. They are attempting to perceive more accurately their own positive nature and learn to use it more effectively in their everyday lives. As this occurs, they will better accept both their strengths and their weaknesses as legitimate and evolving parts of their positive nature. This acceptance reduces distortions in their view of the world and leads to greater accuracy in the match between how they see themselves and their interactions with people, ideas, and things.

Reduced distortions and a greater trust in one's evolving positive nature lead to other specific outcomes that practitioners often identify as goals of counseling or psychotherapy. People finding success in counseling or psychotherapy generally become more flexible and creative in their thoughts and actions as they free themselves from stereotypes and inappropriately imposed conditions of worth. They begin to see a wider range of feelings in themselves, gain more confidence in the expression of those feelings, and feel enthusiasm about the new aspects of their lives that are opened up by these experiences. These newfound levels of freedom to trust the accuracy of one's feelings and thoughts allows them to take the action necessary to overcome feelings of helplessness, powerlessness, and the inability to make decisions about the present and future. This new level of self-empowerment is perhaps the most noticeable outcome for everyone around an individual who has benefited from person-centered counseling or psychotherapy.

The Process of Change

The process of change through the helping relationship is guided by the presence of three basic conditions: genuineness, acceptance and caring, and empathic understanding. As Rogers writes, "Studies with a variety of clients show that when these three conditions occur in the therapist, and when they are to some degree perceived by the client, therapeutic movement ensues, the client finds himself painfully but definitely learning and growing, and both he and his counselor regard the outcome as successful." He continues, "It seems from our studies that it is attitudes such as these rather than the therapist's technical knowledge and skill, which are primarily responsible for therapeutic change" (1961, p. 63). Over the past 40 years this perspective on the significance of the helping relationship to the process of change has been integrated within virtually all schools of counseling and psychotherapy (Farber, Brink, & Raskin, 1996).

The first of these three conditions is the **genuineness** of the counselor or therapist. Clients must perceive that this individual is a real person who has feelings, thoughts, and beliefs that are not hidden behind facades. This genuine nature allows clients to trust that whatever specifics of the relationship emerge, they can be recognized as both personal and honest. It also allows the client to see that being open and genuine, which includes revealing one's fallibility, is not a condition from which competent human beings must shrink. Most of our daily relationships are not highly genuine but are instead controlled by facades and roles that cause us to doubt the information we receive from people.

The second condition is **acceptance and caring** provided by the counselor or therapist, which allows clients to be less anxious about their perceived weaknesses and the prospect of taking risks. The weaknesses we perceive in ourselves generally become those things we least want others to see, so we try to hide our weaknesses whenever possible. Limitations often result in some degree of embarrassment, with an accompanying tendency to work even harder at hiding them. Persons needing assistance are working hard to hide their perceived weaknesses both from others and from themselves. Often they will even identify a less threatening weakness as the problem in order to avoid examining a more personally threatening one. Acceptance and caring, if consistently felt by the client as **unconditional positive regard,** offer the opportunity to reduce the degree of stress caused by these fears in the relationship. This in turn will increase the chance that the client can recognize, discuss, and work on these problem areas rather than hiding from them.

The third condition for change is the practitioner's **empathic understanding** of the client. This deep recognition of the client's internal frame of reference must be successfully communicated to the client in order to be effective. Neither the practitioner nor the client can ever fully understand the client. However, the degree to which they effectively explore the client's world together to arrive at a common understanding will improve the client's abilities to understand and, therefore, take action in his or her life.

These three basic conditions provide the necessary environment that allows individuals to implement their **actualizing** tendencies. They arrive in counseling or psychotherapy questioning their abilities and ideas, afraid of the weaknesses they recognize, and even more afraid of those which they expect are unknown to them. They have been seeking answers from other people, whom clients believe "must clearly have better answers." All of these conditions make them fearful of letting their true selves be seen by others or even themselves, so they wear a variety of masks to present a "better" picture than what they believe is there. Providing the basic therapeutic conditions allows clients to explore themselves and their fears, and to experiment with new ways of thinking and behaving within a safe and growth-oriented environment.

Receiving attention and support from a genuine individual who can be trusted allows clients to explore themselves in areas and ways they cannot in less therapeutic situations. Having another person closely and consistently listen helps clients begin observing and listening to themselves better: "You're right, I am angry. And now that I say it out loud, I realize I've been angry for a long time." They begin to drop masks as they recognize aspects of themselves to be not quite as bad as they thought: "I do have the right to be angry even when someone else doesn't want me to be that way. I'm not comfortable with that idea, but it is there for now." Self-recognition and self-acceptance are key first steps in the growth process.

As individuals become open to their true experiences and more trusting of their own **organism,** they begin to see the blocks to growth that have burdened them. They also gain the confidence needed to both recognize and deal with their problems on their own. These new levels of self-confidence allow for the dropping of protective masks and for accepting strengths and weaknesses as aspects that are both real and changeable over time. An internal **locus of control** develops as clients take control of their lives rather than following the direction of others who have been running their lives.

A major part of the development process in clients is a recognition that they are fallible human beings who are always in a growth process. This is very different from the belief that one must be perfect in order to be good or loved. Acceptance of this position allows people to view themselves as continuing to learn and grow throughout their lives and to see success as regular improvement rather than perfection.

Clients' confidence in their own ability to evaluate themselves, decide how to change, actually change, and accept their errors reduces anxiety and the dependence on others for directing their lives. An accurate perception of the real world and their part in it will continue to give importance to the reactions and beliefs of others, but this information will now be seen as more equal in significance to their own views. Consequently, clients will take more responsibility for their own existence and need less external intervention.

Intervention Strategies

The counselor or therapist looking for a specific list of things to say, actions to take, or diagnoses to make will not find them in this theory. Person-centered theory is much more related to who counselors or therapists are rather than what they do. A practitioner's actions are focused around providing the conditions of genuineness, unconditional positive regard, and empathy in the relationship. No book can say how all individuals should be genuine, because each of us is different. Likewise, how a practitioner genuinely shows unconditional positive regard or empathy is also dictated to some degree by the type of person one is. This section suggests two general concepts regarding therapeutic intervention techniques: some thoughts on how to be genuine, and some specific behaviors that have consistently been identified with communication of the core conditions.

Being Genuine.   To be genuine, counselors and therapists need to look closely at themselves before deciding how to be or what to do. Obviously, one cannot be genuine by thinking, saying, or doing what someone else does. Knowing oneself, then, becomes critical: it allows actions and words to be congruent with the way one really is while at the same time helping the practitioner match the client's needs. Person-centered counselors and therapists need to be knowledgeable about themselves and reasonably comfortable with this information. They must be more congruent than their clients, or the likelihood is that more will be taken from the client than is given. One clear way to deal with these issues is for practitioners to seek quality helpful relationships, including counseling or psychotherapy, for themselves and to work as hard on their own continued growth as they ask their clients to work.

Being genuine does not mean sharing every thought or feeling with the client. Such a tactic would simply take the focus off the client and put it on the practitioner, which is not a part of person-centered helping or any other type of helping. What is appropriate is being a helpful, attentive, caring person who is truly interested in the client and able to demonstrate that interest. Everyone has experienced the type of situation in which an acquaintance says, "I know how you feel," and you know very well the words coming from this near stranger are nothing more than words. Not only do you reject the words, but also you lose faith in the person's honesty. The same person might have said, "I hardly know you, but if it's anything like my own loss it must hurt a great deal." The second statement recognizes the reality of the two people rather than trying to indicate more understanding than is reasonable to believe. There are as many genuine statements or nonstatements as there are people and situations. The right one matches the person you are with the unique situation you have with the client at a given time.

Active Listening.   The first technique emphasized in person-centered theory is **active listening** and its reflection of content and feelings. Demonstrating empathy for the client requires highly attentive and interactive listening skills. Counselors or therapists must first show that they are paying attention. The physical steps most common to this are facing the clients, leaning toward them, and making good eye contact. This position and the use of facial and body expressions that relate to the clients' comments will at least initially put practitioners and clients in physical contact. After putting themselves in the best possible position to listen, practitioners must then hear and see what is communicated. Both the words and the actions of the client are used to develop an understanding of the content and feelings being presented.

Taking in information is only the first part of active listening. Practitioners must then reflect the content and feelings of clients back to them for it to have value. "I hear you saying . . ."; "So you are feeling . . ."; and "You seem to be feeling . . . because of . . ." are samples of the ways counselors and therapists explore with the client how accurate their empathy truly is.

It is to be expected that the genuine counselor or therapist will not always have a full understanding of the client's world and will make varied degrees of mistakes trying to reflect it. The process of active listening helps both parties clarify the content and feelings of a situation and is a learning process for each participant. Practitioners who can treat their own mistakes and growth during this learning process in a genuine manner as a natural part of life also help clients accept their uncertainties and weaknesses.

Reflection of Content and Feelings.   The first steps in the empathy exploration process tend to be the recognition and reflection of the actual words stated and the feelings that are most obvious. As client and counselor or therapist get to know each other better, an effective practitioner becomes better able to see behind these surface interactions and begins to see and convey feelings clients do not even recognize they are expressing. For example, a client may be distracted or become more quiet periodically during the session. Initially, these reactions may appear related to the specific topic at hand. However, over time, the counselor or therapist may be able to tie those reactions to some general concept that pulls the different discussion topics together. Describing to the client what has been recognized can be very valuable when it is as little as extended listening, observing, and reflecting of the person's world. At its most powerful, reflection can also bring together complex elements of the client's world that draw a much more accurate picture of the client as a whole than the individual elements provide separately.

Appropriate Self-Disclosure.   A truly genuine relationship lets the client see relevant parts of the counselor or therapist's phenomenological world as well as the client's world. Appropriate **self-disclosure** allows clients to compare their views of the world with the view of another individual whom they have come to trust and value as a significant human being. Under nonthreatening circumstances, these comparisons give clients the chance to review and revise their views based on information they might otherwise not have had available or which has been too threatening to accept. The supportive relationship allows the client to go forward to try out new thoughts and behaviors based on the comparative information. Much like the growth of the bean mentioned earlier, clients are allowed to use the supportive atmosphere and comparative information to develop at the rate and in a manner most appropriate for them.

Immediacy.   Many of the most powerful interactions are those in which the content and feelings involved relate directly to the immediate situation between the client and the counselor or therapist; in other words, they depend on **immediacy.** Recognition, understanding, and use of feelings are seen as a major problem for clients from the person-centered perspective. Immediacy provides a here-and-now approach to the relationship in general and to feelings in particular. The relationship between client and practitioner is seen as the most important therapeutic factor in part because it is available for immediate examination. Therefore, the feelings that both client and counselor or therapist are currently experiencing are often the most therapeutic ones available. Statements that receive primary emphasis are ones like "How are you feeling now?" and "Your statements make me feel . . ." On the other hand, statements seen as less therapeutically useful might be, "Why did you feel that way?" "What did the other person think?" or "What did you believe then?"

A major reason for person-centered theory's emphasis on the here and now is that reactions between client and counselor or therapist can be verified, checked, and explored immediately by both participants. Statements or feelings from the past make use of only the client's perspective, thus giving the practitioner a reduced opportunity to be a vibrant part of the client's experience.

Personalized Counselor Actions.   One of the great misconceptions among new practitioners is that listening and reflecting is all the person-centered counselor or therapist does. This rigid reaction to his concept of an evolving and personalized theory was a major frustration to Rogers throughout his professional life. After one demonstration counseling session, Rogers was confronted by a workshop participant who said, "I noticed that you asked questions of the client. But just last night a lecturer told us that we must never do that." Rogers responded, "Well I'm in the fortunate position of not having to be a Rogerian" (Farber et al., 1996, p. 11). Rogers used his own thoughts and personality in many creative ways, just as all quality person-centered counselors and therapists do. These are the aspects of therapy that appear as metaphor, humor, confrontation, and at times even interpretation or directiveness.

Many counselors and therapists now use Rogers's relationship development model as the foundation on which to build other cognitive, behavioral, or emotional approaches. Boy and Pine (1990), for example, see additional stages in which person-centered counselors use their own creative methods to help clients recognize and deal with problems after the essential relationship elements have been established. They also argue that because each client is different, person-centered counselors and therapists must adjust their methods as much as possible to fit the specific preferred mode of the client. Their view is that a true person-centered approach will have a consistent foundation, but that the full range of the relationship must build upon the unique aspects of the counselor, the client, and their personalized relationship together.

Much of Rogers's work has been so well integrated into other theories and practices that the person-centered labels have been dropped. However, there are others who give more attention to the person-centered element of their work. They reflect a wide variety of diverse approaches, just a sample of which would include person-centered expressive therapy, person-centered family therapy, multimedia approaches to person-centered counseling, client-centered psychodrama (Brazier, 1993) and even psychological testing (Watkins, 1993). Person-centered theory may not get the name recognition that it did 30 years ago, but the impact of its core concepts can be seen throughout the field.

Non-Client-Centered Interventions.   It is important to note the kind of techniques that will *not* be used as true parts of person-centered counseling. One key example is diagnosis and detailed treatment planning, which have become significant parts of the mental health field today. Increasingly, insurance companies and government agencies require clear-cut statements of the client's so-called illness, its severity, and the estimated length of time it will take to be corrected. Since person-centered counselors and therapists do not view clients in an ill-versus-well context, they can have a great deal of trouble working with these issues. Person-centered theory is much better suited to helping people progress than it is for getting them over some designated condition. Person-centered practitioners who find themselves in situations where they need to design extensive diagnosis and treatment models must give close attention to how and to what degree they can integrate these relatively divergent processes.

Many new counselors and therapists identify with a person-centered approach because it fits what they want to do and what has helped them grow in other positive relationships. However, when they attempt to use this approach, they often get caught up in many non-person-centered techniques, mostly for their own comfort. For example, there is little need for extensive **questioning** in the person-centered approach, for the task is to follow the client rather than to continually suggest what issues need to be explored. New practitioners in particular tend to question clients more than necessary. They are likely to begin seeking extensive information in clients' pasts rather than talking about current interactions. Finally, they tend to find themselves overanalyzing client comments and reactions in order to develop elaborate rationales for why clients do what they do. These reactions may come in part from the fact that student trainees have completed many years of education where such tactics are highly effective methods for succeeding in academia. Now they are faced with doubts about their own ability to use the skills they have been taught with real clients who can be hurt. This lack of confidence and experience often causes them to fall back on the questioning and directing tactics of the traditional academic community rather than the responding and following tactics of the person-centered approach. Just as clients need time and proper conditions to learn to trust in their organism, it also takes time for new person-centered counselors to trust in their developing counselor organisms.

Evaluation

Overview

The person-centered movement brought about innovations in research and training as well as a new approach to counseling and psychotherapy. Emphasizing objectivity in examination of client/practitioner relationships moved the profession forward in the evaluation of specific interaction variables in the process of counseling. This solid research background has not erased all problems from this approach, however, as it still has limitations. These include being considered a simplistic theory when it is actually quite complex; requiring greater trust in the client than people often are able to offer; and having few of the specific tactics for new counselors or therapists to fall back on that other theories provide. An overview of these factors and others critical to understanding person-centered theory are summarized at the end of this section.

Supporting Research

Carl Rogers's perception of people, counseling, and psychotherapy as highly personal and individualized often gives newcomers to the field a sense that he and his theory deemphasize research over personal interaction. This perception could not be further from the truth. Rogers was a major innovator in the development of research techniques for counseling, psychotherapy, and person-centered theory. He recognized that for any theory or technique to remain credible and become more effective, solid research is essential (Rogers, 1986).

Rogers pioneered the use of taped transcripts (Cain, 1987) and other clinical measures of interacting to broaden the scope of psychological research (Hjelle & Ziegler, 1992). These techniques, along with the use of the Q-sort method, helped bring the more subjective aspects of people, counseling, and psychotherapy into respectability. Among his earliest significant publications were books on extensive research studies with standard mental health center populations (Rogers & Dymond, 1954) and more cases of people with schizophrenia (Rogers, 1967). All this work demonstrated his commitment to research on his theory and established his basic concepts as valid and reliable sources of client progress.

Rogers's research and teaching tool that gets the most use today is the tape recording and transcribing of sessions with clients. Note taking from memory was not satisfactory. He wanted to hear and see as much of the interaction as possible to judge both the client's reactions and his own work. This taping and evaluating of sessions has become common practice today, and many of Rogers's tapes and transcripts of counseling sessions continue to be reviewed and analyzed in detail (Farber, Brink, & Raskin, 1996).

The **Q-sort** method of data collection became a major influence in the acceptance of Rogers's theory. Developed by William Stephenson (1953), a colleague of Rogers's at the University of Chicago, the Q-sort method employs many different formats for people to sort attributes of themselves into various categories and levels. Generally, when the method is used in person-centered research, subjects are asked to perform the task once for self-description and another time for ideal self-description. These two sortings are then compared to see how well their perceived and real selves match. The theory suggests that the closer the match of the real and perceived selves in a person, the more congruent the person is. Because congruence is theorized to improve during effective person-centered interaction, researchers can look for increasingly closer matches between these two measures as counseling or psychotherapy continues. This procedure enabled Rogers to validate many of his theoretical constructs and procedures.

Most research on the person-centered approach has continued the focus on necessary and sufficient conditions for successful counseling or psychotherapy (Cain, 1987). It motivated many studies in its early years, but recently the momentum for such research has declined significantly (Combs, 1988). This may be due in part to the general acceptance of Rogers's basic concepts and the extensive research done on them in the 1950s and 1960s. This acceptance is so widespread throughout the thinking and practice of the profession that we no longer consider many of his concepts "Rogerian" (Goodyear, 1987). They are more often now referred to as basic essentials to the helping relationship.

Potential weaknesses in person-centered research have not been ignored by the profession. The methodological aspects of some studies have been questioned by some researchers. Concerns about sophistication and rigor have been raised (Prochaska, 1984), and similar comments have led others to ask whether these problems raise doubts about the validity of the theory (Watson, 1984). These concerns may deserve particular attention when considered alongside the fact that less person-centered research is now being conducted at the same time that the core conditions are widely accepted.

Person-centered theory has remained relatively unchanged over the last 30 years, according to some authorities (Cain, 1986). Combs (1988) suggested that this lack of development of the basic theory is the reason for a lessening of research in the area. Whether or not a lack of theory development has brought about less research in this area, it is clear that for the theory to grow, both new ideas and additional research will be necessary in the future.

Limitations

Person-centered theory may suffer most from the fact that it appears so simple to learn. The concepts are relatively few, there is not a long list of details to remember, and one does not need to recall a specific tactic for each diagnostic problem a client might have. The counselor or therapist can be lulled into a feeling of security by this apparent simplicity. For example, simple listening and reflecting of words and surface feelings are usually beneficial at the very beginning of a session. However, continued surface-level interactions that do not attend to the many dimensions of both the client and practitioner quickly become seen as repetitive, nondirectional, and trite.

The reality is that the few basic concepts in person-centered theory have a virtually unlimited complexity because counselors and therapists must be fully aware of both their clients' and their own changing phenomenological worlds. They must respond to the interactions between these worlds in ways that best fit the genuine natures of the client and the practitioner. This is a difficult task that requires an excellent understanding and continuing awareness of oneself and the client. New counselors and therapists in particular have a difficult time with this complexity. Persons who are working hard and feeling under pressure to remember and do a "new thing" or a "right thing" will naturally find it very difficult to be genuine and aware of all that is happening around and within themselves and others. Acting on what they recognize adds yet another level of difficulty to the task at hand.

The supportive nature of person-centered theory is often misinterpreted to mean that one should not be confrontational with clients. Counselors and therapists often need to do more than listen and reflect. Effectively functioning people confront themselves all the time, and counselors and therapists must recognize that appropriate confrontation is a natural part of an effective helping relationship. Person-centered theory makes room for such confrontation, but it gives few specific guidelines as to where, when, and how it should occur.

A great deal of trust in the positive motivation and abilities of oneself and one's clients is required of the person-centered counselor or therapist. Without this trust, many of the other person-centered concepts lose their true value, and a therapeutic interaction can become little more than polite conversation. Such trust in people and a process is not easy to provide in all circumstances. Human beings have difficulty suspending their mistrust because fears, previous experiences, and preconceived notions are a natural part of the human condition that affects everyone. The more extreme one's negative experiences and reactions are, the more difficult it is to act fully on the person-centered belief system. The result is that most practitioners can place confidence in a bright, college-educated, law-abiding, depressed client, but have more difficulty maintaining a similar confidence in a depressed rapist or murderer.

Person-centered practice requires a great deal of personal knowledge, understanding, and awareness, as well as a willingness to act on this information. There are few techniques or activities to fall back on if the counselor or therapist does not have or cannot act on this information about the helping relationship. Many other theories provide more activities or tactics that allow the practitioner to give the process a boost when the relationship is not all it could be.

Summary Chart—Person-Centered Theory

Human Nature
This theory emphasizes a highly positive view of human nature in which people can be trusted to be continually seeking productive directions toward maximum self-actualization. Perceiving unconditional positive regard from their environment supports this development, while conditions of worth inhibit it and produce non-self-actualizing thoughts and behaviors.

Major Constructs
Clients have psychological and sociological difficulties to the degree that their phenomenological worlds do not match their true positive nature (incongruent) and its use in their everyday lives. Empathic understanding of the client's world is essential in helping clients find a more congruent match between their phenomenological world and their actions, feelings, thoughts, and responses from others.

Goals
Counselors and therapists provide a safe, caring environment where clients get in closer touch with essential positive elements of themselves that have been hidden or distorted. Less distortion and more congruence lead to greater trust that their organisms can be relied on for effective reactions to people and situations. This added trust results in reduced feelings of helplessness and powerlessness, fewer behaviors driven by stereotypes, and more productive, creative, and flexible decision making.

Change Process
The change process is stimulated when counselors or therapists provide the core conditions of genuineness, acceptance and caring, and empathic understanding. Change takes place as clients perceive these conditions and begin exploring and testing new thoughts

and behaviors that are more in line with their positive, growth-oriented nature. This exploration, testing, and learning leads to increasing trust in their organisms' ability to think and act in a wider variety of circumstances.

Interventions

This theory is marked by a minimum of specific intervention techniques, as counselors and therapists are asked "to be genuine in a relationship" rather than to perform a rigid set of actions. Interacting in the immediacy of the situation and then evaluating the results with the use of active listening, reflection of content and feelings, appropriate self-disclosure, and other personally, professionally, and situationally responsive interactions are essential.

Limitations

Success is dependent on counselors and therapists maintaining high trust in the feelings and actions of the client and themselves. Lack of trust often causes practitioners to fall back on safe passive reflection responses. These are necessary early on, but become increasingly inadequate as the need for a more comprehensive therapeutic relationship develops, one that includes directness that comes with additional culturally, situationally, and personally relevant feelings and interactions.

The Case of Maria: A Person-Centered Approach

The use of a client case study to view person-centered theory raises several problems. To begin with, the standard case study concept suggests that a collection of historical factors will be used to describe and diagnose an illness. However, person-centered theory places more emphasis on clients' perceptions of and feelings about their world as opposed to the facts as seen by others. It disdains looking at work with clients as illness-focused. Additionally, the relationship with the counselor or therapist is much more critical to the success of therapy than the client's specific historical case development. Many person-centered practitioners might, therefore, choose to ignore the concept of a clinical case history.

The problem with this approach here is that it may convey the idea that person-centered counselors do not seek understanding of clients' perceived experiences or expect to observe specific progress outside the therapeutic relationship. The fact is that the reason person-centered practitioners attend so closely is precisely because they want to understand the clients' perceived experiences as well as possible. They then use that understanding within a therapeutic relationship that is unique to the particular phenomenological worlds of the client and the counselor. Finally, like all good counselors and therapists, person-centered practitioners also must evaluate the progress of clients both inside the therapeutic relationship and in the outside world. The modified case study that follows attempts to take each of these factors into account by examining potential phenomenological aspects of the client's situation as though the information had been acquired within the therapeutic relationship. Assumptions will be added that might reflect other information the counselor acquires about feelings and emotions not included in the more content-oriented case description. It will further emphasize Maria's relationship with the counselor, and suggest potential directions that Maria's growth might take due to a positive therapeutic relationship.

Maria's Phenomenological World

As would be expected with clients entering counseling, Maria has a phenomenological view of the world that is incongruent with her true feelings, abilities, and potential. She has incorporated unattainable conditions of worth that come from a mixture of culture, religion, family, and personal relationships. In her currently perceived world, she will never be able to be a good enough daughter, mother, Catholic, teacher, or partner to satisfy those whose approval she desires. The harder she tries to please, the further she gets away from personal feelings of self-worth. She has lost trust in her own organism's ability to feel, think, decide, and act in productive ways, and consequently she is trying to act in a world as others see it—a strategy that will not bring her feelings of success.

The fact that Maria's phenomenological world is frequently out of line with the world that actually affects her causes Maria great anxiety. She looks outside herself for ways to act, only to find that what others point to as the "right" way does not satisfy anyone—least of all herself. She knows that who she is and what she does are not working, but she cannot identify other ways to view the situation.

Actualizing Tendencies

It is clear that Maria has never fully given in to the conditions of worth that direct her in non-actualizing ways. She keeps experimenting and succeeding at new challenges even as significant others disapprove of her actions. Decisions to attend the college of her choice rather than the one her parents selected, to marry outside the religion, and eventually to get a divorce may or may not have been good decisions, but they do demonstrate an actualizing tendency that keeps Maria moving forward even in the face of disapproval and rejection. The fact that she has come for counseling is further confirmation that she wants more out of herself and will take the necessary actions to make that happen.

Maria is working hard to actualize her most appropriate self and has clearly demonstrated that she has the tools to succeed. This is a person who took responsibilities as a teenager that should have been handled by adults, achieved academically, proved herself as a teacher, made it through an abusive marriage, and managed to care for two children on her own. Her actualizing abilities should be clear even as her success is frustrated due to distorted views and the absence of caring relationships where she could be accepted for who she truly is and wants to be. This situation stops her from recognizing other alternative views of herself that could potentially lead to much greater self-actualization. The growth Maria seeks demands that she take exploratory risks into uncharted waters that are frightening and not easily undertaken.

The Counselor's Role

A counselor valuable to Maria will empathically work with her situation, see her inner strength, trust in her willingness and ability to move in positive directions, and provide the core therapeutic conditions that will allow her actualizing tendencies to flower. These conditions will help Maria both clarify the intricacies of her own feelings and see the value in sharing her views accurately with another person. Maria also needs a close relationship with a counselor who is not burdened by false fronts so that she can trust the legitimacy of the human interaction (genuineness).

Providing unconditional positive regard for Maria can be conveyed in part by showing confidence in her as a competent person who can think and act effectively. The counselor will not lead Maria to specific topics, suggest ways for her to act, identify her problems for her, or direct, reward, or punish her. Showing both attention and active listening without placing judgments on the information will help demonstrate this condition.

The counselor will listen and observe closely in order to grasp all of Maria's verbal and emotional aspects. To achieve this, the counselor will convey back to Maria what he or she sees, hears, and feels, and together they will check on the accuracy of their communications. Mistakes, underestimations, and overestimations are common in this process of developing accurate empathic understanding. It should be viewed as a learning process for both parties involved rather than a set of correct statements made by the counselor. The client presents ideas, the counselor tries to reflect them and possibly tie them into other previously recognized concepts, and both parties negotiate to reach mutual understandings. It is only from such struggle that accurate understanding arises.

Unconditional positive regard and accurate empathic understanding begin to look false and misleading to the client unless genuineness is also conveyed. Maria needs to see herself in a relationship that is open and honest. It must be made clear that what the counselor thinks, does, and says are consistent and that taking on the role of counselor does not mean one cannot be a real person at the same time. Such consistency will allow Maria to trust the relationship, as well as the ideas, skills, and behaviors that develop from it. She will learn to use the counselor as a model for the idea that she, too, can develop such congruence. As progress continues, Maria will recognize that because this is a real human relationship with a genuine person, the ideas and actions can be transferred to her life outside counseling. The relationship, therefore, will be viewed as an immediate, natural, real, and dependable experience that can be duplicated in many respects outside the helping relationship.

The person-centered practitioner is often considered to be caring and kindly, but it must also be recognized that the core conditions offer a great deal of challenge to the client. Maria will not always want to hear how the counselor is reacting to her, as this may require that she confronts aspects of herself she may find difficult to accept. Only the truly empathic counselor, who is also genuine, can successfully overcome such difficult issues. The many challenging times and confrontations in a person-centered approach are those that would be expected in any genuine human relationship.

Expectations for Progress

The person-centered counselor who adequately and consistently provides the necessary therapeutic conditions can expect Maria to progress in some general ways. It should be made clear, however, that Maria may not change in the ways that others deem to be best. Maria is seeking herself. Although that self is affected by certain other people, progress in counseling will likely reduce the control these others have over Maria. Such control will be replaced by increasing trust in her organism so that Maria will begin to see her personal ability to control her own life while still considering the needs of others.

As Maria starts to trust her relationship with the counselor, she becomes more free to talk of difficult issues and recognizes that this person will still think well of her, no matter how inappropriate certain aspects of her feelings, thoughts, and actions appear to her to be. These issues begin appearing in a different light that is different from what Maria had envisioned previously. Generally, the new view offers problems in a manageable form that is not nearly as terrible or insurmountable as Maria had believed. Excitement about finding new ways to see the world will likely be followed by struggles to understand her new world and how she will need to relate to it differently.

Maria will soon find a need to explore her new ways of viewing, feeling, and acting in the world outside of counseling. She will want to know how her children, family, boss, and dates would respond if she chose to act differently. Such issues will be explored in the therapeutic relationship before trying them out. Maria will want to understand both the good and bad results after they have been tried in real life. The new ideas, observations, and attempted behaviors in each new situation will expand Maria's view of the world and likely bring her back to the counselor for help in integrating the newfound information.

There will be pleasures, fears, successes, and disappointments in Maria's development, just as in everyone's. But she will come to recognize that she can learn from each experience and that each time she learns she increases the confidence in her own ability to direct herself and correct for mistakes. Eventually, she may learn to have enough confidence in her own immediate reactions to use a productive combination of her own ideas and those of others to develop positive outcomes. She will also recognize that even when things do not work out as planned, she is effective enough as a human being to overcome mistakes.

References

Boy, A., & Pine, G. (1990). *A person-centered foundation for counseling and psychotherapy*. Springfield, IL: Charles C Thomas.

Brazier, D. (Ed.). (1993). *Beyond Carl Rogers: Toward a psychotherapy for the 21st century*. London: Constable and Company Limited.

Cain, D. J. (1986). Editorial: A call for the "write stuff." *Person-Centered Review, 1*(2), 117–124.

Cain, D. J. (1987). Carl R. Rogers: The man, his vision, his impact. *Person-Centered Review, 2*(3), 283–288.

Combs, A. W. (1988). Some current issues for person-centered therapy. *Person-Centered Review, 3*(3), 263–276.

Farber, B. A., Brink, D. C., & Raskin, P. M. (Eds.). (1996). *The psychotherapy of Carl Rogers: Cases and commentary*. New York: Guilford.

Goodyear, R. (1987). In memory of Carl Ransom Rogers. *Journal of Counseling and Development, 65*, 523–524.

Hjelle, L. A., & Ziegler, D. J. (1992). *Personality theories*. New York: McGraw-Hill.

Prochaska, J. O. (1984). *Systems of psychotherapy: A transtheoretical analysis* (2nd ed.). Pacific Grove, CA: Brooks/Cole.

Rogers, C. (1942). *Counseling and psychotherapy*. Boston: Houghton Mifflin.

Rogers, C. (1951). *Client-centered therapy.* Boston: Houghton Mifflin.

Rogers, C. (1959). A theory of therapy, personality, and interpersonal relationships, as developed in the client-centered framework. In S. Koch (Ed.), *Psychology: A study of a science* (Vol. 3) (pp. 184–256). New York: McGraw-Hill.

Rogers, C. (1961). *On becoming a person: A therapist's view of psychotherapy.* Boston: Houghton Mifflin.

Rogers, C. (Ed.). (1967). *The therapeutic relationship and its impact: A study of psychotherapy with schizophrenics.* Madison: University of Wisconsin Press.

Rogers, C. (1970). *Carl Rogers on encounter groups.* New York: Harper & Row.

Rogers, C. (1986). Carl Rogers on the development of the person-centered approach. *Person-Centered Review, 1*(3), 257–259.

Rogers, C. (1987a). Inside the world of the Soviet professional. *Counseling and Values, 32*(1), 47–66.

Rogers, C. (1987b). Steps toward peace, 1948–1986: Tension reduction in theory and practice. *Counseling and Values, 32*(1), 12–16.

Rogers, C., & Dymond, R. (1954). *Psychotherapy and personality change.* Chicago: University of Chicago Press.

Rogers, C., & Sanford, R. (1987). Reflections on our South African experience. *Counseling and Values, 32*(1), 17–20.

Stephenson, W. (1953). *The study of behavior: Q-technique and its methodology.* Chicago: University of Chicago Press.

Thayer, L. (1987). An interview with Carl R. Rogers: Toward peaceful solutions to human conflict. Part I. *Michigan Journal of Counseling and Development, 18*(1), 58–63.

Watkins, C. E. (1993). Person-centered theory and the contemporary practice of psychological testing. *Counseling Psychology Quarterly, 6*(1), 59–67.

Watson, N. (1984). The empirical status of Rogers' hypotheses of the necessary and sufficient conditions for effective psychotherapy. In R. F. Levant & J. M. Shlien (Eds.), *Client-centered therapy and the person-centered approach: New directions in theory, research, and practice* (pp. 17–40). New York: Praeger.

Feminist Theory

Jacqueline M. Elliott
Portland State University

Feminist therapy theory has evolved as a result of and response to the feminist movement of the last 30 years. Like the feminist movement from which it was born, it has been championed and criticized by counselors, therapists, and laypeople alike. Before reviewing the concepts, it is important to dispel some misconceptions about feminist therapy (Russell, 1984). The term "feminist" holds greatly varied connotations for different people. Those unfamiliar with feminism often view it negatively, whereas those knowledgeable of its goals view it in a more positive light.

The negative perceptions regarding feminism stem from an erroneous assumption that because feminism is pro-female, it is, by default, anti-male. Feminist counseling and psychotherapy do not strive to replace male domination over women by female domination of men. This misconception arises from feminism's acknowledged goal of regaining female power. Because feminist counseling and psychotherapy seek to remedy the inequality that exists, and which has existed between the sexes, feminism calls for a reformation and equalization of the power relationships between men and women; in other words, men's power and responsibility will be shared equally with women. This clearly will have an impact on men, but the impact is not necessarily negative. Focusing the stress of power and responsibility on a single person within the relationship creates a heavier burden for men and can make relationships between men and women competitive and adversarial. Redistributing power equally in a relationship allows both men and women more life choices and can increase their sense of partnership with each other, thus building stronger relationships. The ultimate goal of feminist therapy is the realization of fairness and equality for all, an obvious benefit for everyone.

Feminist counseling and psychotherapy, because they must integrate women's history into therapy, require a pro-female stance; to take any other stance would be a denial of the history of inequality from which many women's mental health issues arise. Only a therapy that reevaluates and recognizes the contribution and assets of women and provides an increased opportunity for female development can fully meet the needs of women.

Feminist counseling and psychotherapy do not strive to exclude men or to isolate women from men; indeed, the opposite is true. The evaluation and definition of male/female relationships, where men and women clarify what they want and need from their relationships with each other, as opposed to what they have been socialized to expect, are important elements in feminist counseling and psychotherapy. The participation of men in the reconstruction of relationships is welcomed and encouraged by feminist therapists.

A final misconception about feminist counseling and psychotherapy is that it encourages the devaluation of home and family by encouraging all women to work outside the home. This is not accurate: the goal of feminist therapy is to increase women's choice of lifestyles, recognizing that homemaking is but one of many choices they might make. Feminist therapy hopes to empower women to make life choices based on personal skills and interests, rather than on stereotypical gender roles promoted by society (Russell, 1984).

Background

The Evolution of Feminist Therapy Theory

Feminist theory has evolved gradually over time as a response to women's rejection of traditional psychotherapies, which many felt "served to keep women oppressed and in their place" (Walker, 1990, p. 78). Feminist therapy evolved as a result of and response to the women's movements of the 1960s. These movements, in turn, can be traced back to the general climate of unrest and reform that characterized the 1960s. Young women joined the many social reform movements of the era to speak out against the hypocrisy of a democratic nation which upheld humanitarian beliefs while actively supporting racism and military aggression. Men assumed the leadership in each of these movements, and women were expected to assume the role of followers. However, women, having become more confident and politically savvy through participation in these movements, rejected these male-dominated structures of power. They began to reevaluate their secondary roles in the leftist movement and found that their new movement had become as corrupt as the establishment they were rejecting (Easton, 1994).

Groups of women began to splinter from the mainstream left-wing political movement. One notable group held that change for women could come about mainly through reforming traditional social structures, such as politics, education, and media. This group formed the National Organization for Women (NOW) in 1966. Other women began informally meeting in consciousness-raising groups to discuss their concerns over their lack of collective voice in the various movements (Kirsh, 1987). Women compared their experiences and discussed their feelings of anger and powerlessness, and from these discussions, commonalities of experience were uncovered. These groups helped to put women's personal experiences into a larger perspective, and women began to rely on each other for support. Thus, the development of feminist therapy theory arose from these consciousness-raising groups, and the women's movement "brought the psychology of women into direct focus and provided the theoretical starting point for the development of a psychotherapy for women with a feminist perspective" (Eichenbaum & Orbach, 1982, p. 12).

Dutton-Douglas and Walker (1988) chart the development of feminist therapy theory from its origins and suggest that there have been three distinct phases of feminist therapy theory development since the 1960s. Phase one began in the early 1970s and lasted about 10 years. This phase was characterized by activism: feminists actively explored the philosophies of feminism, named the issues faced by women, and applied conventional therapies to these issues. Through an experimental process, early feminist counselors and therapists borrowed techniques from other therapies that fit within feminist philosophy. For example, a feminist counselor or therapist could use the **reframing** technique applied by Albert Ellis in his rational-emotive behavior therapy to resolve a feminist issue. With this technique, the counselor or therapist redefines a negative situation by presenting it more positively. When it is adapted, it can, for example, help to reframe a woman's negative self-image by examining society's unrealistic expectations of what a woman's body should look like. Her perception of her appearance would then be redefined in a more positive manner.

Phase two is what Dutton-Douglas and Walker call "the mainstreaming of feminism" into other therapy theories. This mainstreaming involves injecting feminist philosophies into traditional therapies and eliminating **androcentric bias.** For example, feminist counselors and psychotherapists during this era applied a political gender analysis to traditional psychotherapies to try to eliminate the parts of the theory that promote a dichotomous view of men and women. Traditional psychotherapies are based, for the most part, on the assumption that male traits are preferable to female traits in a client. The focus on the factors within the individual makes it seem as if the issue is caused by the individual, whereas feminist therapy recognizes the fact that the issue may be caused by external forces, perhaps societal or family factors. These other theories fail to account for the context of an individual's life experiences and to acknowledge the impact of the many external, situational factors that also greatly affect the development of one's personality, such as gender, class, race, and educational status, as well as racial, ethnic, and cultural minority-group membership (L. S. Brown & Root, 1990).

The third and continuing phase of the development of feminist therapy theory is built on the acknowledgment of feminine potential and the idea that many of the issues faced by women are a result of society's failure to allow them to exercise their free will. According to Walker (1990), "The third phase is ongoing and consists of the development of a complete theory with developmental explanations for the common experiences of women who grow up in societies that do not value them for their full range of individual capabilities" (p. 80). Feminist theory takes the stand that situational factors of living in a patriarchal society where women are devalued, coupled with the individual factors of each woman's personal background experiences, have a profound impact on women's mental health. Feminist therapists today utilize either phase two or phase three theory in their practice.

Many of the modified theories and techniques used in phase two are integrated within the third phase of feminist theory. In reviewing phase two literature, many problems have been discovered with the traditional therapies. In the following sections, specific problems within a few of the traditional psychotherapies will be examined, as well as some of the problems with traditional models in general.

Psychoanalytic Theory

According to feminists, a problem with psychoanalysis is that it focuses primarily, almost exclusively, on **intrapsychic conflicts** rather than on the social factors that are responsible for those conflicts (Lerner, 1988). This approach tends to pathologize women rather than acknowledge that their symptoms may result from trying to survive in a patriarchal society in which they are undervalued. Marmor (1973) "criticized the emphasis on the female biological function and concepts such as penis envy, anatomy as fate, and masochism and passivity" (Lazerson, 1992, pp. 528–529), realizing that those ideas ignore the cultural context from which they were derived, and do not account for the changing roles of women in our society. Psychoanalysis also takes an androcentric position that men and women are dichotomous and that a woman embodies all that a man does not. For example, traditional roles dictate that men be breadwinners and women be homemakers. This dichotomy became apparent in two studies done in the 1970s which exposed the flaws in this line of thinking (Laidlaw, Malmo, et al., 1990).

Object Relations Theory

According to the **object relations** approach, the mother-child relationship is both necessary and inevitable, and mothering has the most influence on a child's development. This account of child development pathologizes women who choose careers over child rearing because they reject their "natural role." For this reason and others described in object relations theory, mothers are blamed for their babies' ego splits and later pathology. Object relations contributes to the perpetuation of the cultural devaluation of women, mother-blaming, and restricting women to stereotypical roles by assisting in the maintenance of a patriarchal society. This theory does not take into consideration the sociocultural factors that can affect the mother-infant relationship, such as the changing roles and positions of women. Also, object relations theory does not take into account how women's inequality shapes their psychology, as well as the psychology of men (Okun, 1992).

Jungian Theory

Jungian theory has also received its share of criticism from feminists. According to Romaniello (1992), "Jungian assumptions about women's nature, role, and appropriate function are sexist, and they have essentially gone unchallenged. The very construction of Jungian theory, through, for example, its primarily intrapsychic focus, fragmented definition of the personality, historical determinism of archetypes, dichotomous constructs, and gender-related evaluations of personality characteristics, creates a system that is counterposed to a feminist understanding of reality" (p. 66). Romaniello's understanding of reality for women involves a much broader construction of human personality than Jung's dichotomous splitting of the personality into the anima and the animus.

Cognitive-Behavioral Theory

In cognitive-behavioral theory, the counselor or therapist's goal is to help the individual to *adjust to* his or her environment rather than attempt to change it. Again, the client's "maladaptive" behavior is assumed to arise from an internal rather than external source; very little attention is given to the powerful effects that class, race, gender, ethnicity, or other factors can have on an individual (Kantrowitz & Ballou, 1992). There is little recognition in the theory and its applications that these experiences influence peoples' cognition, behavior, and emotion in diverse ways.

Family Systems Theory

In *The Invisible Web: Gender Patterns in Family Relationships,* Walters, Carter, Papp, and Silverstein (1988) review family therapy's main concepts and how their misuse can put women at a disadvantage in a family therapy setting. The first concept they address is **fusion,** the attempt to join two individuals into a united couple. Fusion is a problem within relationships caused when one partner, usually the woman, attempts to pursue or "merge" with the other. Fusion moves the relationship beyond intimacy and causes the "distant" partner, usually the male, to move away from the "overcloseness" of the other. This "merging and reactive distancing that occurs in couples and throughout family relationships" (Walters et al., p. 20) inappropriately labels the problem as being one of "closeness" rather than one of distance, thereby placing the blame for dysfunctional relationships on the woman. Such techniques also disrespect men, since they suggest that men are incapable of expressing any emotions within a relationship.

Another concept in family therapy that can be misused is **reciprocity.** According to this concept, everyone involved in a problem plays a part in the maintenance of that problem by reinforcing the behavior of the other (Walters et al., 1988). However, this concept overlooks the fact that the partners do not share an equal power base within the relationship; most often, the male partner has more power in the relationship. For example, it can be argued that if a woman is abused by her husband, she played a part in the abuse by provoking him. However, because the relationship is based on an inequality in the power relationship between the husband and wife, the woman has less power to change the abuse patterns. The part the woman plays and the part of the abuser are not equal in force; therefore it is the man, not the woman, who is in the position to stop the abuse.

Complementarity is another concept that is used in the systems theory of family therapy (Walters et al., 1988). Complementarity refers to the dynamic equilibrium that is necessary for any system to work. In the case of a relationship, the woman and man "complement" each other by fulfilling specific roles to balance their concerns of home and work. Problems arise with this concept because, by seeking balance for the family system as a unit, the theory brings sexist or stereotypical notions to the assignment of these roles and tends to maintain the patriarchal system. Family practitioners place a high value on the unified home without exploring the full range of options for both women and men. Men tend to get first choice at the tasks, while women tend to get the jobs that are left over. Men generally work outside the home and fulfill tasks that bring money and prestige to the family, while women are assigned roles that men choose not to do, like child rearing and homemaking. Women's tasks are viewed as being less valuable because of the corresponding lack of status, power, and money associated with those roles.

Dichotomous Sex Roles and Women's Pathology

Two classic studies further emphasize the flaws in traditional psychotherapy models. In her study of women's mental health, Chesler (1972) claimed that the institution of psychotherapy was second only to marriage in its control and suppression of women. She observed that women were often pathologized if they refused to conform to society's expected dichotomous sex-role standards. For example, women were often diagnosed with mental illness and subjugated to involuntary hospitalization as punishment for not conforming.

In a study by Broverman, Broverman, Clarkson, Rosencrantz, and Vogel (1970), psychotherapists were found to hold different standards of mental health for men and women. The study found that all of the characteristics used by the psychotherapists to describe a "normal" person, such as "aggressive," "rational," and "intellectual," were the same characteristics with which they described a "normal" male. Women, on the other hand, were described as being more "passive," "nurturing," and "emotional," characteristics that did not fit the description of a "normal" person. Therefore, women who had the characteristics of a "normal" person were not considered to be mentally healthy (Walker, 1990).

A problem inherent in all of the therapies listed above, and one that feminist therapy seeks to dispel, is the acceptance of the male/female dichotomy model. This model polarizes women and men into socially prescribed gender roles and behaviors. Feminist theory hopes to incorporate flexibility into roles rather than maintain outdated, dichotomous roles.

Counselors and therapists who work within feminist therapy theory's phase two level believe that removing the sexist aspects of traditional psychotherapies is adequate to achieve the feminist goal of empowering women to actualize their potential. However, feminists of the third phase are more radical and divergent in their approach; they feel that salvaging those theories, particularly psychoanalysis, is impossible. Instead of changing and reworking traditional therapies to fit feminist needs, they concentrate on developing a new theory altogether (L. S. Brown & Root, 1990).

Human Nature: A Developmental Perspective

Many of today's medical theories and treatments are based on male developmental models that are applied, sometimes inappropriately, to women. For example, studies of the treatment of cancer and heart disease, in the recent past, were conducted using only male test subjects. The findings of this research were then applied to women, despite their different physiological structures. Counseling and psychotherapy theories are based on the same assumption that men and women are alike. Feminism aims to rectify this error by asserting the differences between men's and women's development.

Inherent in feminist therapy theory is the need to redefine women's development in a positive way, a way that reflects their value and seeks to understand women in their own right, rather than defining them as the weaker half of the male/female dichotomy model. There is a need for traditional therapies to reevaluate their approach to the treatment of women in what Weiner and Boss (1985) call "conceptual affirmative action—a rethinking of gender-role issues based on research and theory development about women over the life cycle" (p. 15). To this end, some feminists are offering different explanations of female development throughout the life cycle—explanations that are currently being researched—that better account for the different experiences of women. Carol Gilligan, Deborah Tolman, Mary Pipher, Nancy Chodorow, and Jean Baker Miller are some of the pioneering feminist theorists whose work will be discussed in the following sections.

Reframing Resistance

In redefining women's psychological development, feminist therapists and counselors look first to the development of girls and adolescents. **Carol Gilligan** (1991) cites many research studies that describe a change in girls as they leave childhood and enter adolescence, during which they begin to adopt more stereotypical gender roles and lose a part of their "authentic selves" in the process. One example is Peterson's (1988) review of the literature on adolescence, which discusses numerous findings of evidence that girls experience psychological problems during this transition.

Gilligan explains that preadolescent girls are able to tell people how they feel and point out what they see as violations in relationships, whereas when they become adolescents they begin to cover up feelings in order to maintain relationships. Adolescent girls learn from the culture to dissociate themselves from their bodies, feelings, relationships, and from reality. This dissociation is called **resistance;** they resist being genuine or authentic. They must do so in order to take on the images of goodness and perfection that society demands of women (L. M. Brown & Gilligan, 1990; Gilligan, 1990a, 1990b, 1991).

Gilligan (1991) notes that feminist therapists and counselors hope to stop girls from undergoing this change, to not become resistant to or disconnected from their authentic selves. She suggests that young girls are naturally unyielding to disconnection, and if they can be caught at the moment of their revision—before they begin to dissociate themselves from what they know to be true and become inauthentic versions of their former selves—much psychological suffering could be avoided. Thus, research of girls has emerged as an important aspect of women's psychological development (L. M. Brown, 1989; Gilligan, Brown, & Rogers, 1990).

Feminist therapists and counselors must deal with those women who build up resistance to their authentic selves. Gilligan explains that "resistance in clinical practice has meant obscuring or burying psychological truths or avoiding key memories and feelings, and thus has been seen as an impediment to the creation of a working therapeutic relationship" (1991, p. 1). Feminists prefer to reframe the definition of resistance so that it is seen as a psychological strength or an act of courage in which girls and women resist inauthentic or false relationships. Reframing resistance is turning resistance upon itself, that is, resisting the aspects that originally cause the girl to dissociate from her authentic self.

The Authentic Self versus the Inauthentic Self

Mary Pipher (1994) expands on this idea in *Reviving Ophelia: Saving the Selves of Adolescent Girls*. She says adolescent girls develop into inauthentic selves as they try to fill the narrow, stereotypical roles allotted to them by our male-oriented culture. Three things that particularly take their toll on the self-esteem of adolescent girls and force them to develop inauthentic selves are what Pipher refers to as lookism, capitalism, and sexuality.

Lookism permeates our everyday lives; it is common knowledge that women are often judged more by their looks than by any other single feature. This leads to problems with body image such as anorexia, bulimia, and excessive dieting as adolescent girls and women struggle to attain society's ever-changing ideal of feminine beauty.

Capitalism is how Pipher describes the pressure put upon adolescent girls to adopt the "junk values" of our culture. She cites examples of capitalism as the pressure to consume chemicals such as alcohol and nicotine to appear sophisticated; read teen magazines which pressure girls to consume products for hair, makeup, clothing, and dieting; and purchase the right things—that life will be better if one buys into the materialistic world of fashion.

Sexuality is a problem for adolescent girls, also, because of the ambivalent cultural models for ideal female sexuality. Pipher describes the difficulty that adolescent girls face in the development of their sexual identity. She discusses how difficult it is for them to define a sexual self, make sexual choices, and learn to enjoy sex. Our culture gives its young women mixed messages: it expects them to be sexy, with their bodies always on display, yet it also expects them to abstain from having sex until marriage. There is also a lack of female role models for adolescent girls who express healthy sexual desire and satisfaction. Other feminists note similar findings. Tolman (1991) describes a "missing discourse of desire" in our society, in which any discussion of adolescent female sexual desire is absent or discouraged. Fine (1988), a psychologist, observed that a discussion of female desire is missing from schools' sex education curriculum, except to discourage girls' exploration of sexuality by warning against pregnancy, sexually transmitted diseases and AIDS, and sexual victimization.

The Sexual Division of Labor

Nancy Chodorow (1978) examined the social construction of the psychological processes of mothering that contributes to how women develop in their relationships. Chodorow believes that stereotypical gender roles result from the economic system of Western capitalism, which requires an adult to work outside the home. Because this system makes it easier and more financially rewarding for men to work outside the home, we find women relegated to work within the home. She calls this the "sexual division of labor." Because women fulfill the role of primary caregiver, society is built on the belief that a woman's place is in the home. The fact that women are responsible for raising the children leads Chodorow to surmise that the way the children relate to their mother is reflected in their socialization; girls tend to realize that they are like their mothers and stay within the home, while boys tend to realize they are different than their mothers and pursue activities outside the home. Chodorow concludes that these roles are so ingrained in our society that the processes that socialize our children will not change until men begin to participate equally in the raising of children and the care of the home.

The Quality of Connectedness

Another feminist theorist who challenged traditional assumptions regarding women's behavior and psychosocial development was **Jean Baker Miller.** Her book *Toward a New Psychology of Women* (1976) provides a model of female development that accentuates the feminine quality of **connectedness,** "of valuing, enlarging, and deepening human relationships" (Avis, 1988, p. 31). Earlier theories, such as the concept of fusion in systems theory, faulted feminine connectedness as being counterproductive to the development of strong relationships. Miller's model challenges this concept. Her belief that women's traditional capacities for nurturing and relationship building are authentic expressions of a healthy female gives value to these feminine qualities; she suggests that these capacities are essential to the human community and that they should form the foundation of a values system shared by everyone, men as well as women (Avis, 1988).

Separation versus Connection

Gilligan's *In a Different Voice* (1982) also supports the idea of connectedness as a way of conceptualizing female development. In this book, she recognizes and explores women's natural tendency to bond with others. Gilligan celebrates this behavior as characteristic of women, and it forms the basis of her disagreement with Lawrence Kohlberg's theory of moral development. She was disturbed by the fact that Kohlberg's stages of moral development were based solely on interviews with men; the information derived from these interviews was then generalized to women as well, on the assumption that men and women were the same. However, Gilligan noted that there was a distinct difference in the way men and women responded to moral dilemmas. While men generally responded with a masculine "morality of justice," in which they responded in a very legalistic way that emphasized individual rights, women tended to approach moral dilemmas with a feminine "morality of responsibility," in which they made decisions that took into account the welfare of others. Gilligan proposes that men more typically construct their relationships in terms of separation and women in terms of connection. She does not view these differences as biologically determined but rather as derived from social constructs (Cotroneo, 1988).

The Self-in-Relation

Supporting Miller's and Gilligan's work is Jordan and Surrey's **self-in-relation theory** (1986). Their theory challenges traditional psychoanalytic theory, which is based on Freud's perspective that the individual's psychological development can be understood apart from the larger social context in which the development takes place. Jordan and Surrey's work shows that human development is not free from society's influence, but rather is intimately connected to it. Thus, their theory is based on the central premise that the "self" is developed through "relation" with others, that "women organize their sense of identity, find existential meaning, achieve a sense of coherence and continuity, and are motivated in the context of a relationship" (p. 102). Their theory differs from traditional views that normal human development and maturity are tied to the attainment of autonomy and separation from others. Object relations theory often pathologizes a mother's close relationship with her children, particularly with the daughter, whereas Jordan and Surrey's self-in-relation theory treats the interdependence in the mother-daughter dyad as normal behavior (H. G. Lerner, 1988).

Listening to Women's Stories at Midlife

Mary Gergen (1991) has added to feminist theory by studying women at midlife. She felt that the psychological research focused too strongly on women's biological function of childbearing, often neglecting other important aspects of their psychological, social, and personal development, and often ignoring older women because they could no longer produce children. Gergen took an interest in women's individual life stories during middle age. These stories revealed richly diverse paths of development that women undergo after their childbearing years and showed that women's development should not be tied solely to their biological functions. Theories about male development, she noted, do not focus purely on procreative biology, and neither should theories about female development (Levinson, Darrow, Klein, Levinson, & McKee, 1978). Gergen suggests that a feminist approach in studying women at midlife should celebrate the diversity of human development at this stage of life and "emphasize political, economic, moral, and aesthetic" development (Lazerson, 1992, p. 480).

Major Constructs

Feminist counselors and therapists practice feminist therapy in various ways, depending on their choice of approach; according to Taylor and Whittier (1993), "Feminist ideology today continues to be a mix of several orientations that differ in the scope of change sought, the extent to which gender inequality is linked to other systems of domination, especially class, race/ethnicity, and sexuality, and the significance attributed to gender differences" (p. 534). Despite the variety among feminist therapies, there are seven common principles that apply to most models (Valentich, 1996):

1. Establishment of an egalitarian relationship
2. Acknowledgment that only women's unique experiences can provide the foundation of knowledge for thinking about women
3. The belief that women's psychological development is pluralistic in nature
4. Promotion of independence and assertiveness in women
5. Focusing on women's strengths rather than their flaws
6. Careful use of self-disclosure to enhance the therapeutic relationship
7. The belief that "the personal is political"

In many traditional therapies, the counselor or therapist takes a position of expert authority in the therapeutic relationship, directing all the interactions that take place. This is not so in feminist therapy. One of the most important components of feminist therapy is the establishment of an **egalitarian relationship** between the counselor or therapist and the client. Each person contributes equally to the relationship: the counselor or therapist contributes by applying her skills and knowledge of therapeutic interventions; the client contributes by taking personal responsibility for knowing herself and what she wants (Walker, 1990; Espin & Gawelek, 1992).

As part of the egalitarian principle, there are **ethical issues** that can affect the power balance in the helping relationship. The first issue involves maintenance of a nonexploitative therapeutic relationship. According to L. S. Brown, the American Psychological Association Task Force (1975) and the Feminist Therapy Institute (1987) clarified the issue as follows:

> Feminist therapists were among the first psychotherapists to call for more clearly defined ethical standards in the traditional helping professions, particularly regarding sexual exploitation of psychotherapy patients and the harassment and exploitation of others in less powerful positions. Feminist therapists added to the definition of ethics the concept that sexist, racist, homophobic, or other discriminatory attitudes on the part of the therapist could be evidence of unethical behavior. (L. S. Brown, 1991, p. 324)

The second ethical issue involves the maintenance of appropriate political, social, and personal **boundaries** within therapeutic relationships (Brown, 1991, 1994a; Lerman, 1994; Parvin & Biaggio, 1991). Some counselors and therapists are concerned with the issue of "women therapists engaging in sexual and other dual or multiple overlapping relationships with their women clients" (Lerman, p. 86). Sexual relationships between a client and her counselor or therapist would be inappropriate for obvious reasons. But in the small social circles within which, for example, lesbian clients and their lesbian therapists or counselors circulate, there are situations where appropriate boundaries will be clouded. There are questions as to the appropriateness of client and therapist being affiliated with the same political organizations, having mutual friends within a social circle, attending the same parties, and so forth (Brown, 1991). Generally, if the feminist therapist or counselor and her client have overlapping political, social, or personal relationships, the therapist or counselor needs to be sensitive of the influence she has over her clients and should know when a violation of the relationship could exist and avoid any possibility of exploitation.

A second feminist principle states that only women's unique experiences can provide the foundation of knowledge for thinking about women. This principle supports several conclusions. First, viewing women through the existing androcentric literature denies the development of models of mental health based on women's experiences. Second, development of feminist models will prevent women from being pathologized because they do not follow the male model of mental health. Third, it supports feminism's attempt to know all women and means that comprehension of women's stories is necessary to complete the base of knowledge upon which women may then be reconceptualized (Ballou, 1990; Lerman, 1986). Ballou states: "The principle of valuing women's experience has come to mean separating the internal from the external and validating the female experience. Women's experience as felt, lived, and processed is a valid method of knowing" (p. 36). Ballou's term "external" speaks to the societal oppression that affects women negatively. Oppression plays a role in women's development; women's experiences are a response to that influence, and stories of this oppression are a valid way of coming to know themselves and the world around them. Women must use the experiences of other women to evaluate their own experiences in understanding themselves and the effects that society has on them, which are revealed through defense mechanisms and other negative behaviors.

A third feminist principle is the belief that women's psychological development is **pluralistic** in nature. Pluralism celebrates the sociocultural differences among women, as well as differences between women and men, and these differences deserve to be valued equally. This takes a different stance from that of our culture, which defines reality according to the dominant male perspective and continues to keep men in positions of power and relegate women to secondary roles. Pluralism, however, would value the diversity of all perspectives of knowing (Ballou, 1990; Espin & Gawelek, 1992).

A fourth feminist principle involves promoting independence and assertiveness in women. Feminist counselors and therapists believe that women need to develop these skills in order to function effectively in both work and social settings. Independence is gained by realizing the scope of one's rights within social or working relationships and being assertive in order to achieve and maintain those rights. Women can develop these skills if they are taught how (Walker, 1990).

A fifth principle of feminist therapy involves positively focusing on and valuing women's unique strengths rather than negatively focusing on and correcting their "flaws." The counselor or therapist can reframe feelings of inadequacy within the female client by pointing out that the "inadequacy" can be a strength rather than a flaw. For example, a close relationship to one's child could be viewed by a counselor or therapist as being enmeshed or "overprotective," while another counselor or therapist might view it as reasonable nurturance. In this way, many women can reevaluate themselves in a more positive light (Walker, 1990).

A sixth principle of feminist therapy involves the careful use of **self-disclosure** to enhance the relationship between the client and the counselor or therapist (Brown & Walker, 1990). Self-disclosure helps to form a bond that replaces the teacher/student relationship found in many traditional approaches. The client may feel validation by realizing that the counselor or therapist has dealt with many of the same issues herself, thus reducing feelings of isolation and permitting "more empathic connections around issues brought up in therapy" (Walker, 1990, p. 82). However, self-disclosure should be used with caution and only to help the client; the ethical code of the Feminist Therapy Institute (1987) states, "A feminist therapist is responsible for using self-disclosure with purpose and discretion in the interests of the client" (p. 17).

A final feminist principle is understanding that "the personal is political." Feminists believe that gender (the personal) and power (the political) are intertwined and cannot be separated. Thus, the feminist counselor or therapist views the client through a critical lens through which power and gender influences are noted and incorporated into understanding the client's presenting problem (Lazerson, 1992).

Applications

Overview

The goal of feminist therapy involves a process of positive change in which the client gains control of her life through social and political empowerment. In order to create positive change within the client, there are four steps, described by Sturdivant (1980), that one must undergo to achieve empowerment. Finally, this section explores seven issues pertinent to feminism and some intervention strategies that address those issues.

Goals of Counseling and Psychotherapy

Because women have been historically oppressed, feminism strives to add value and meaning to women's existence by taking as its main goal the **empowerment** of women (Hartman, 1993). Empowerment is increasingly becoming a main focus of many feminist therapies. A working definition of *empowerment* involves the process of change and development of a powerless entity (person or group) to become socially and politically aware and active. Becoming aware involves discovering the influences that guide or control one's life, and becoming active involves developing skills to gain control over these influences while supporting and respecting the boundaries of others (McWhirter, 1991).

The Process of Change

In *Therapy With Women: A Feminist Philosophy of Treatment,* Sturdivant (1980) describes four ways through which feminist therapy fosters the process of change:

> (1) removal of socially conditioned, internalized barriers to optimal functioning through cognitive restructuring of the way in which a woman perceives herself, women as a group, and the political and economic structure of society; (2) identification and resolution of individual, soluble problems, with the support of other women . . . [particularly in all-female therapy groups]; (3) facilitation of self-actualization through the resocialization process, which provides positive role models, affords opportunities for experiential learning and practice of new behaviors, and gives validation of feelings and perceptions by other women; and (4) support and encouragement for participation in action to change the societal causes of women's distress. (p. 148)

In feminist therapy, change must be more than the awareness of oppression; it must involve activity to end the oppression. In Russell's (1984) opinion, the client's recognition of the source of oppression is not enough for therapy to be considered successful. The therapist or counselor must also perceive change in the client's behavior, such as the client's proactively, rather than passively, interacting with others.

Intervention Strategies

Feminist therapy is still evolving, but as mentioned previously, two groups of therapists and counselors have emerged. The first group uses intervention strategies borrowed from traditional psychotherapies, whereas the second group is developing new strategies. Whatever intervention strategies they may use, all feminist therapists filter the client's presenting problem through a feminist analysis. The emerging diagnosis and treatment plan is influenced by the counselor's or therapist's training and knowledge of feminism. A number of intervention strategies emerge in the literature.

In contrast to the literature of unified theories, which names a list of generic intervention strategies and applies them across a broad range of problems, the literature of feminist theory tends to first focus on a problem and then identify the strategies used to address it. The latter format will be maintained here.

Due to the large number and variety of therapeutic strategies, scholars are faced with special challenges in enumerating the intervention strategies that are associated with feminist therapy. No attempt will be made here to compile an exhaustive list; however, a representative sample will be given.

Body Image.   In their article "Feminist Cognitive-Behavioral Therapy for Negative Body Image," Srebnik and Saltzberg (1994) discuss the problems women have dealing with society's unrealistic expectation of female body weight and offer intervention strategies based on a model that integrates both feminist and cognitive-behavioral therapy. Negative feelings about body image result when women attempt to emulate the cultural standard of the ideal female body, an unrealistic standard that changes with the fashion. The plump Rubens beauty, the narrow-waisted Victorian figure, the waif-like flapper of the 1920s, the full-figured Marilyn Monroe of the 1950s, the super-thin Twiggy look in the 1970s, and more recently the thin, muscular, athletic look have shown the variation in "ideal" body size over time (Fallon, 1990; Greenspan, 1983). This look, coupled with the increasing use of breast implants, liposuction, and plastic surgery, makes the image of the ideal body increasingly difficult for women to attain naturally. Women who do attain these looks of fashion do so at great expense to their self-esteem and health.

The pressure society places on women to conform to the style of body images can result in **negative body image.** Feeling that one's body doesn't measure up to the cultural standard can also lead to poor self-esteem (R. Lerner & Karabenick, 1974; Noles, Cash, & Winstead, 1985). According to Srebnik and Saltzberg (1994), women develop coping behaviors such as "avoidance of body exposure, exercise, social situations, and certain clothes and foods" (p. 119) in order to assuage feelings of inferiority.

In their article, Srebnik and Saltzberg offer scores of intervention strategies that help women establish more positive body images. This article reflects the rich diversity of effective interventions that are available in feminist therapy. They treat the issue with effective techniques from a variety of approaches, using psychoeducational, behavioral, and cognitive restructuring approaches, within a feminist framework, to combat negative body image.

One effective strategy using the psychoeducational approach is a homework assignment that assists the woman in learning to recognize the immense impact that societal factors have on her body image. The client would be assigned a project at the end of one counseling session that would be used for discussion during the next session, such as designing a media presentation that depicts the latest body "ideal" (Srebnik & Saltzberg, 1994).

An effective strategy using a behavioral intervention is to confront **avoidance behaviors** in women who have negative body images. Clients can participate in exposure exercises (Laidlaw et al., 1990), such as wearing in public a bathing suit or other tight clothing they would not normally wear, in order to reduce their fear and anxiety surrounding such activities (Butters & Cash, 1987). Clients can discuss ahead of time how they think they will be perceived, then wear the clothing, and finally discuss the actual outcome to see if their assumptions were correct (Rosen, Saltzberg, & Srebnik, 1989).

A third effective strategy, this time from a cognitive restructuring approach, begins with identifying the negative beliefs a client has about her body. Once this is done, the cognitions can be described as errors in terms such as black-and-white thinking, catastrophizing, "musts," or overgeneralizations (Beck, Rush, Shaw, & Emery, 1979) and then reframed in a more positive way.

Another strategy involves identifying, through introspection and discussion, family messages about body image, and family models of body size and shape. Treatment involves looking back at stages of life when the client's body underwent changes (i.e., puberty) and asking her to reflect on her emotional state regarding body image. She may also be asked how she formed her opinions of body image and identify those who played a part in her development of these beliefs (Brouwers, 1990). Once emotions are identified by the client, she needs to deal with them through a process of **disidentification** in which the client clarifies her emotions toward those family members who presented her with unrealistic expectations of body size and image (Hutchinson, 1985).

Treatment of Depression in Women's Groups.   According to the *DSM-IV* (1994), women suffer from depression at twice the rate of men. Counselors and therapists have postulated various reasons for this difference. Feminists realize there are many causes of depression, such as endocrinological and genetic factors (Haussman & Halseth, 1987), but they discount traditional medical models where biology and intrapsychic forces are blamed. These traditional models tend to blame women for their depression, rather than realizing that the external context of female socialization must also be taken into account.

A combination of external variables tends to make women more vulnerable to depression than men. The gender socialization process for most women encourages interdependence and passivity, thus dissuading autonomy and assertiveness. Our culture engenders submissiveness in women by promoting financial and psychological dependence on men (Arieti, 1979). This is seen in "traditional" marriages, where the woman is expected to complement rather than compete with the man. Also, occupational choices for women are more restricted, tend to pay less, and frequently offer little or no opportunity for advancement (Rothblum, 1982). Women behave submissively because they have been conditioned by society to do so; however, more assertive behaviors can be learned to replace the maladaptive ones.

Intervention strategies that are often used in feminist group therapy can facilitate the learning of assertive and self-reliant behavior through sex-role analysis. In consciousness-raising groups, women can share common experiences that help them see beyond their personal problems (Kravetz, 1987). Women can then play an important role in reinforcing other women's alternative life-style choices by supporting those choices through their words and actions (Kirsh, 1974). Women can also begin to see the limitations that are placed on them by society and can recognize their depression as caused by their inability to be authentic. **Assertiveness training** can be used to build self-esteem, establish personal rights, and create authenticity—attitudes that can then be reinforced through role-play within the group (Butler, 1976). As women develop a greater sense of their authentic selves, they are then empowered to recognize and act to defeat the societal biases that are the source of their depression (Beck & Greenberg, 1974).

Lesbians: The Process of Coming Out.   Feminist counselors and therapists were among the first mental health professionals to normalize, not pathologize, homosexuality. They realize that lesbians, because of their marginal status in society, face problems not encountered by other groups of women. Homosexual behavior is viewed as abnormal by much of society, so many lesbians hide their sexual orientation from family, business associates, and friends (Morgan & Eliason, 1992). They may fear the judgment or abandonment of loved ones, who may disagree with their life-style choices. Because lesbians must often hide their sexual orientation, they frequently lack the support of family or friends during periods of romantic upheaval, such as a breakup with a partner. Lesbians may find themselves in a difficult situation: they fear "coming out" because of the rejection they will encounter, yet they despise the deception their secret life-style demands (Roth, 1985). The issue of "coming out" is an important one for lesbian couples.

Some lesbians deny their homosexuality, refuse to acknowledge their attraction to other women, and view themselves as "straight." Others realize they are "different" and take the first step of coming out, which is self-acknowledgment of a homosexual orientation. After realizing they are homosexual, the next step involves self-acceptance. "Closeted" lesbians have to confront their internalization of the social stigma associated with homosexuality. They need to shed any homophobic, negative images they have and find value in their own sexuality. After self-acknowledgment of their sexual orientation, lesbians have to determine and weigh the risks involved in revealing their secret to others. Lesbians may or may not want others to know. A feminist counselor or therapist may work with the lesbian at any or all of the stages of coming out.

L. S. Brown (1988) and others suggest some useful strategies to help clients deal with this issue. First, a therapist or counselor can ease the coming-out process for a lesbian by helping her realize that human sexual behavior exists along a continuum and that homosexuality is but a point on the range of normal expressions of sexuality (Kinsey, Pomeroy, & Martin, 1948). She may do this by having the client define her sexual orientation and describe how she, in all her varied roles, fits into the continuum. The client needs to evaluate the history of her social development and any sexist or homophobic stereotypes she may harbor. She must discover which stage of the coming-out process she is at and define any positive and negative feelings or experiences she is facing. For example, she may enjoy the support of friends who are privy to her secret, but fear the rejection she may face from others for her sexual preference. According to Brown, "A feminist approach can be of enormous help, both in sorting out the differences between gender role and sexual orientation, as well as in creating an opportunity to examine and question the validity of sexist and homophobic stereotypes" (p. 215). Before a lesbian takes the final step of coming out into the community, a counselor or therapist can help weigh the benefits and risks to determine whether this action is appropriate. She can help the lesbian explore imagined scenarios concerning the act of coming out and determine if the client is realistic in her expectations.

Single-Parent Mothers and Stress.   The number of single-parent mothers has greatly increased since 1980. Divorced, abandoned, widowed, or unmarried mothers face many mental health issues, among them stress. An increase in divorce rates and the resulting loss of family income has left many families in poverty. Many single mothers lack the skills needed to get jobs that pay adequately, and many rely on welfare. This commonly occurs when the mother marries young, before she has a chance to develop job skills. She enters into the marriage contract and fulfills the complementary child-rearing role in exchange for financial support. When the support is withdrawn, she finds she has few marketable job skills. Those who do work face difficulties with living expenses, child care, and health insurance. Society may unfairly judge single mothers as being unfit and stigmatize their children. Financial problems put much stress on women and can lead to "lowered self-esteem, anxiety and guilt" (Richard, 1982, p. 17).

These women can be helped through counseling or psychotherapy. After identifying the type of client and her family situation, Richard (1982) then adapts a six-phase model to each case:

A. The establishment of trust and communication

B. The recognition of losses

C. The acknowledgment of single-parenthood

D. The identification of related stress factors

E. The development of skills and resources

F. The ability to separate and deal with unrelated issues. (p. 22)

By winning the client's trust and assisting her in recognizing the external stress factors and her internal responses to them, the counselor or therapist can then aim to uncover the client's strengths.

Feminist Therapy With Men.   Women obviously benefit from the empowering philosophy of feminist therapy, but can a feminist counselor or therapist meet the needs of men? Walker (1990) explored men's issues using feminist therapy and discovered that men respond favorably to feminist treatment. Culture plays a pivotal role in the socialization of women, but men, too, are negatively affected by being forced into stereotypical masculine roles. For example, cultural expectations restrict the range of emotions that are acceptable for men to display. Men are socialized to mask any "weak" emotions (e.g., pain or sadness) with anger or to internalize them. This explains why some men lose their temper and respond with violence when they are under emotional stress (Ganley, 1988; Walker, 1990). To deal with the inappropriate display of anger, the client's feminist counselor or therapist would help him explore his anger through self-examination and learn to identify and appropriately express a full range of emotions.

Another sex-role stereotype that affects men is the belief that they should wield power over women, and that they have the natural right to do so. This dominion over women causes marital and family problems. Using cognitive restructuring, a client who has adopted a traditional sex role can begin to see ways in which such a use of power can be detrimental, as well as beneficial. For example, a man who is socialized to be the head of his household will see that being solely responsible for controlling the household finances, business, and social activities of the family (perceived as beneficial) can take its toll on his mental and physical health (perceived as detrimental). The client then realizes that his attitudes are responsible for conflict, and perhaps abuse, within his marriage and family and that too much effort is required to maintain control over others. He can then be taught to relinquish control in favor of a more egalitarian relationship with his wife and to discard his competitive attitude in favor of a more collaborative one. This restructured response to wielding power will lessen tensions in the marriage (Ganley, 1988; Walker, 1990).

The women's movement allowed women to reform their social context, to redefine and expand their life roles. As women's experiences began to broaden, men, too, began to question their social context. They realized life could offer more choices than the forty-hour work week; for example, a man could choose to raise the children while his wife worked. Alternative life-styles are seeming more attractive to men as they begin to reevaluate the stressful, competitive nature of our society. They are beginning to share power with women and give up their competitive attitudes in order to seek greater meaning and self-fulfillment in their lives. However, many more men will need to make significant changes in their cultural attitudes before society can make any effective changes (Slive, 1986).

Issues for African-American Women.   McNair (1992) discusses important cultural issues that counselors and therapists must understand for their therapeutic work with African-American women to be successful, and suggests guidelines for combining **Afrocentric** and feminist models. Non-African-American counselors and therapists must avoid pathologizing African-American women by interpreting them through stereotypes that are commonly held to be true about this group of women (McNair, 1992). According to McNair,

African-American women are often depicted as "strong, dominant, and aggressive." Another stereotype is that of the **black matriarchy** (Staples, 1977), which pathologizes the large number of African-American female-headed households. These two stereotypes lead to the incorrect conclusion that African-American women are pushy, authoritative, and contentious. The imposing of stereotypes such as these upon African-American women can lead them to feel that they must fit these roles, particularly by playing the role of the emotional "rock," the one that everyone can depend upon in times of crisis. While this may seem complimentary at times, it also has the tendency to cause women to suppress their own emotions, lest they appear "weak," and hinders them from being permitted their own emotional support network. This may then lead to difficulty in self-disclosure in the therapeutic environment. Rather than pathologizing this behavior, McNair suggests exploring the "discrepancy between socially- and self-generated expectations of self as they may contribute to the client's ability to self-disclose emotions" (p. 14).

Another way in which African-American women are often misunderstood is the failure of counselors and therapists to recognize the importance of family and community to the African-American woman's self-concept. From the Afrocentric perspective, connectedness to these resources, especially in decision making, is emphasized over independence. The non-African-American counselor or therapist must be careful not to impose an autonomous perspective upon the client.

McNair (1992) offers the following therapeutic framework for working with African-American women. First, the counselor or therapist must understand Afrocentric and feminist perspectives and realize that pathology is the direct consequence of experiencing racism and sexism. The therapist must be careful not to impose his or her own cultural or gender perspectives or racist beliefs on the client. It is also important to discount internal or biological explanations for pathology. The counselor needs to take the view that external factors, such as oppression, racism, lack of political power, and economic disadvantages, affect the mental health of African Americans.

In the course of treatment, the counselor or therapist needs to recognize that behaviors that may be considered pathological in traditional therapies may be normal displays of **culturally reinforced behavior,** and the therapist should take pains to find the positive aspects of all behaviors before finding them pathological. Whenever possible, solutions should incorporate the family, neighborhood, or church of the client. According to McNair (1992), this "reinforces the Afrocentric notion of community-oriented as opposed to individualistic solutions" (p. 16). The counselor needs to avoid promoting changes in the client's behavior that lead to conformity to or blind acceptance of the social conditions that caused the pathology. Finally, the counselor needs to help the client realize the value of her sense of self and guide her into taking positive actions toward goal setting.

Working With Battered Women.   In *The Battered Woman Syndrome,* Walker (1984) explains that counselors and therapists who work with battered women face special challenges that must be overcome in order to address these women's needs adequately. Battered women develop certain defense mechanisms over time as protective devices, and some of these mechanisms can interfere with the counselor's or therapist's interventions if not addressed.

One issue that Walker describes is a battered woman's need to constantly control her surroundings in order to reduce the occurrence of stressors that might trigger a battering incident. This leads to symptoms of high anxiety, such as **hypervigilance,** and the inevitable anxiety that accompanies it. Hypervigilance is a result of constantly needing to survey one's environment in order to detect danger and try to avoid harm. One way in which the client can be assisted in establishing more control in her life is through **deep muscle relaxation techniques** (Walker, 1984, 1994), in which the client learns to contract and release various muscle groups in order to relax when feelings of hypervigilance begin to take hold.

In situations where the woman will not or cannot leave the batterer, Walker (1984) notes that **hypnosis** can be helpful in controlling the ever-present anxiety that accompanies hypervigilance. She describes how many battered women are able to induce self-hypnosis to deal with the trauma of being physically abused. Once the client has learned these self-hypnotic techniques, she can then use this protective skill to dissociate during an attack.

Walker also recommends teaching the client new behaviors, such as using **guided imagery,** to visually reenact the battering scenarios and change the endings, in which the woman has more control, including the ability to remain safe. This helps the woman realize that she can control the negative thoughts that enter her mind, making those thoughts less intrusive and disturbing. By learning this new way of responding, she will begin to feel more in control overall, and less hypervigilant and anxious.

An obvious psychological result of enduring physical abuse over an extended period of time is low self-esteem. The counselor or therapist can help a battered woman increase her self-esteem by using the feminist technique of emphasizing strengths rather than weaknesses. Focusing on the fact that the battered woman was able to survive past incidents of physical abuse, combined with exploring other situations in which she has tapped into her "core of strength," can help the woman see a new image of herself as one of worth (Walker, 1984).

Finally, the battered woman needs to establish feelings of empowerment, first in the counseling setting, and then in her relationships with others. Walker (1984) explains that empowerment can be achieved either through individual counseling or through group work with other battered women: "Listening to other women's descriptions of both the violent and the loving parts of their relationship helps put it all in perspective. A second stage group for women to learn new ways of relating to men and women is a powerful adjunct or alternative to individual therapy" (p. 128). Once a woman achieves feelings of empowerment in her life, she can then begin to put the past behind her and begin a new life.

Evaluation

Overview

Much research is currently being conducted in order to more fully develop a unified feminist therapy theory in the following areas: integrating multiculturalism and diversity with feminist therapy, working with impoverished women, and establishing a theory of women's personality development. However, the practice and further development of feminist therapy is hindered by the fact that feminist therapy theory is rarely included in the formal training of graduate students, and when it is, those classes are generally offered as electives.

Supporting Research

Feminist therapy theory is not static; it is constantly evolving and growing as further research is done. There are many directions in which research continues to expand and redefine feminist therapy. Some scholars have begun examining the ways in which a multicultural and diverse perspective of feminist therapy addresses the oppression of minority women rather than viewing oppression solely from a white, middle-class perspective (Brown & Root, 1990; Mays & Comas-Diaz, 1988). The topic of oppression was also addressed by Faunce (1990) regarding therapy with impoverished women. Her belief is that the current boundaries and rules used in therapy serve to further oppress these women.

An integrated feminist theory of personality development is another area that requires further study. Feminist Mary Ballou (1990) contends that this theoretical framework must not only include feminist tenets to shape the construction of reality, but also must use pluralistic methods rather than a single method of knowing. Another feminist doing current research in this area is Ellyn Kaschak (1992), who seeks to redefine men's and women's gender roles. There is still a long road ahead for those feminists who seek to accurately define women's psychological development without further oppressing them by adopting a restrictive feminist theory of women's development. As L. S. Brown (1994b) states, "It is difficult to promulgate 'the' theory of human development when one's basic operating assumptions have to do with the diverse and complex parameters of human experiences" (p. 231). However, in order for feminist therapy to succeed, this attempt must be made.

Limitations

Feminist therapy theory is constantly growing and changing as feminist counselors and therapists continue to challenge assumptions and develop new insights into their work with women. Therefore, it is difficult to pinpoint a particular limitation within the theory. Rather, the real limitation of feminist therapy is that feminist counselors and therapists lack access to adequate training programs in which they might study feminist therapy. According to L. S. Brown (1994b), "Some training programs in the mental health disciplines welcome feminist theory as an elective focus for students, but others continue to be actively hostile to inclusion of feminist epistemologies and scholarship in the mental health curriculum" (p. 229). Brown describes an example of this hostility by relating an incident about a pro-feminist male educator who was fired from his position at an "alternative" graduate school because he wanted to teach feminist personality theories. In addition, a book that Brown edited was banned from the classroom at the time he was fired.

Until such barriers are overcome, feminist therapy will have to be pursued through independent study, with little formal supervision and training, by most graduate students who are interested in practicing it. However, the fact that a chapter devoted to feminist therapy has been included in this book along with the more traditional counseling and psychotherapy approaches may indicate that feminist therapy's time has finally arrived.

Summary Chart—Feminist Theory

Human Nature
Many models of human psychological development address male development while ignoring female development. By inappropriately applying these models to women, counselors and therapists may pathologize women.

Major Constructs
Although there is much variance in the practice of feminist therapy, there are seven common feminist tenets that are used by most counselors and therapists: (1) establishment of an egalitarian relationship; (2) acknowledgment that only women's unique experiences can provide the foundation of knowledge for thinking about women; (3) the belief that women's psychological development is pluralistic in nature; (4) promotion of independence and assertiveness in women; (5) focusing on women's strengths rather than their "flaws"; (6) the careful use of self-disclosure to join with the client; and (7) the personal is political.

Goals
The main goal of feminist therapy involves a process of positive change in which the client experiences self-actualization as she gains control of her life through social and political empowerment.

Change Process
Sturdivant (1980) describes four ways through which change occurs in feminist counseling or psychotherapy: (1) the use of cognitive restructuring to remove the negative, internalized messages through which a woman perceives herself; (2) identification and resolution of individual problems with the support of other women; (3) resocialization of the client in order to promote self-actualization and validate her feelings and perceptions; and (4) support for and encouragement of the client's participation in action to change the societal causes of women's distress.

Interventions
Feminist counselors and therapists filter a client's presenting problem through a feminist analysis that examines the external factors that negatively affect the client. Depending on their approach, feminist counselors and therapists may either borrow intervention techniques from traditional psychotherapies or they may apply strategies that are unique to feminist therapy. Rather than provide a generic list of strategies and apply them across a broad range of problems, the literature of feminist theory first focuses on a problem (e.g., negative body image, depression) and then identifies strategies that appropriately address it.

Limitations
The main limitations of feminist therapy are the hurdles which developing counselors face in trying to access formal training and supervision in feminist therapy theory and in trying to overcome the hostility directed toward feminism in general.

The Case of Maria: A Feminist Approach

Diagnosis

Maria's presenting problems include suicidal ideation, depression, the stressors of being divorced and raising two children alone, and low self-esteem combined with a distrust of men as a result of her husband's abuse. In addition, Maria has very few reliable support systems in place to help her cope with these difficulties.

Treatment Plan

First, the counselor or therapist would set the stage for therapeutic treatment by explaining her feminist philosophies to Maria and emphasizing the need for an egalitarian relationship between them. Then, in order to treat Maria's main presenting problem of depression, the counselor or therapist would need to determine Maria's emotional state and ensure her safety, if necessary. This could be achieved by discussing her suicidal ideation to determine whether Maria has any intention of acting on her suicidal thoughts. Based on the information given, it is assumed that Maria has no real intention of doing so, but in her state of depression she has become very discouraged. The counselor or therapist and Maria will then develop a mutual goal-attainment plan, based on the information she has presented thus far. These goals would be reevaluated and adapted, if necessary, during future sessions.

It would be important to begin with a cognitive approach to alleviate Maria's symptoms of depression. At this point, the counselor or therapist would focus on Maria's strengths, rather than her "flaws." It is apparent from the case study information that Maria has several strengths—her academic successes in both high school and college, her ability to raise two children as a single parent, her bilingual skills, and her skills as a teacher—that could be brought out during counseling.

The next step would be to find out what Maria has learned from her unique family and life experiences that affect her current functioning, and to determine what negative messages she has internalized throughout the course of her psychological development. One negative message Maria received was that a woman can be "too" independent. For example, she was expected to be independent and self-sufficient enough to care for her younger siblings and the household while her parents worked. However, when she graduated from high school and received scholarships for two different universities, her family (except for her sister) disapproved when she chose to leave the close-knit family unit and the rest of the Hispanic community where she "belonged" in order to attend college two hundred miles away. In other words, it was OK to be independent, but not too independent.

Another negative message she internalized was that it was wrong to marry someone from a different racial background. Both Maria and Mark had to deal with the issue of racism from their families. Maria was made to feel that she was being disloyal to her family and her Hispanic heritage by marrying a non-Hispanic. When they eventually divorced, her family's message that Maria had made a mistake by not marrying "her own kind" was further reinforced.

A third negative message, that of Maria's worthlessness, was internalized after Mark's repeated physical assaults and his degrading remarks about her as a Hispanic woman. A further blow came to Maria's sense of self-worth when no one believed her stories of Mark's abuse or offered emotional support. Feeling trapped, Maria divorced Mark and then gained further negative criticism from her family for divorcing ("Catholics don't get divorced") and for not caring properly for her children. Alone and with only her priest as a source of emotional support, Maria internalized further feelings of low self-worth.

The next step in the therapeutic process would be to use cognitive restructuring to remove these negative, internalized thoughts through which Maria perceives herself. The counselor or therapist would take each negative message and reframe it in such a way that Maria would perceive herself in a more positive light. For example, Maria had begun to view her Hispanic heritage negatively after Mark's verbal criticism of her appearance, cultural customs, and strong religious beliefs. Maria would learn to value her cultural differences by studying her Hispanic roots. Some ways she could do this would be by creating a family genogram, tracing the roots of family customs, and sharing Hispanic traditions and recipes with friends over the course of several homework assignments. She could benefit from her close association with her church by becoming involved in a church social group for adults. This would not only increase her sense of self-esteem, but also it would help establish a new emotional support network outside her immediate family.

After identifying her problems and reframing the socially conditioned, negative messages she had internalized, Maria and her therapist could then apply a gender and political analysis to her situation to help her understand the external forces that have contributed to her feelings of depression, stress, and low self-esteem. The gender socialization process in Maria's family created conflicting feelings within her. She struggled for independence, which conflicted with her parents' stereotypical sex-role expectations for Hispanic women, and their need for family relatedness clashed with her desire for autonomy.

Maria's feelings of being trapped and overwhelmed by the responsibility of caring for two young children as a single mother, as well as the feeling of not being able to live up to the expectations of others, contributed to feelings of stress and depression. Another cause of her depression was the lack of power in her relationship with Mark. His physical abuse, which met with indifference from her family and denial from his family, caused Maria to internalize her anger, which only increased her depression and self-blame.

Maria's next step would be to join a therapy group for abused women, where she could work on some of these issues and receive support from other women during the process. Maria's group would explore the coping strategies that they have adopted, and the counselor or therapist would help the women build on these in new ways, putting their survival skills to better use. Maria would then be resocialized by practicing new behaviors and coping skills to replace those that no longer work well for her. For example, Maria could use behavioral rehearsal to practice feeling anger, which she had learned to internalize for fear of physical assault. She could also engage in assertiveness-training exercises. Most importantly, Maria would have other women to provide her with positive female role models, which she did not have available to her previously. Resolution of therapy would occur when Maria feels empowered; resolves many of her individual problems;

puts the role of feedback from her family and friends into perspective; learns new ways of relating to both men and women; makes competent, informed choices about her life roles; and finally, takes participation in action to change the societal distresses of other women, perhaps by volunteering for a crisis hotline or working more directly with other Hispanic women who have been abused.

References

American Psychiatric Association. (1994). *Diagnostic and statistical manual of mental disorders* (4th ed., rev.). Washington, DC: Author.

American Psychological Association Task Force. (1975). Report of the task force on sex bias and sex-role stereotyping in psychotherapeutic practice. *American Psychologist, 30,* 1169–1175.

Arieti, S. (1979). The roots of depression: The power of the dominant other. *Psychology Today, 54,* 57–58, 92–93.

Avis, J. M. (1988). Deepening awareness: A private study guide to feminism and family therapy. In L. Braverman (Ed.), *Women, feminism, and family therapy* (pp. 15–46). New York: Haworth.

Ballou, M. B. (1990). Approaching a feminist-principled paradigm in the construction of personality theory. In L. S. Brown & M. P. P. Root (Eds.), *Diversity and complexity in feminist theory* (pp. 23–40). New York: Haworth.

Beck, A. T., & Greenberg, R. L. (1974). Cognitive therapy with depressed women. In V. Franks & V. Burtle (Eds.), *Women in therapy: New psychotherapies for a changing society* (pp. 113–131). New York: Brunner/Mazel.

Beck, A., Rush, A. J., Shaw, B., & Emery, G. (1979). *Cognitive therapy of depression.* New York: Guilford.

Brouwers, M. (1990). Treatment of body image dissatisfaction among women with bulimia nervosa. *Journal of Counseling and Development, 69,* 144–147.

Broverman, I. K., Broverman, D. M., Clarkson, R., Rosencrantz, P., & Vogel, S. (1970). Sex role stereotypes and clinical judgments of mental health. *Journal of Consulting and Clinical Psychology, 34*(1), 1–7.

Brown, L. M. (1989). *Narratives of relationship: The development of a caring voice in girls ages 7 to 16.* Unpublished doctoral dissertation, Harvard University Graduate School of Education, Cambridge, MA.

Brown, L. M., & Gilligan, C. (1990). Meeting at the crossroads: Women's psychology and girls' development. *Feminism and Psychology, 3,* 11–36.

Brown, L. S. (1988). Feminist therapy with lesbians and gay men. In M. A. Dutton-Douglas & L. E. Walker (Eds.), *Feminist psychotherapies: Integration of therapeutic and feminist systems* (pp. 206–227). Norwood, NJ: Ablex.

Brown, L. S. (1991). Ethical issues in feminist therapy: Selected topics. *Psychology of Women Quarterly, 15,* 323–336.

Brown, L. S. (1994a). Boundaries in feminist therapy: A conceptual formulation. In N. K. Gartrell (Ed.), *Bringing ethics alive: Feminist ethics in psychotherapy practice* (pp. 29–38). New York: Haworth.

Brown, L. S. (1994b). *Subversive dialogues: Theory in feminist therapy.* New York: Basic Books.

Brown, L. S., & Root, M. P. P. (Eds.). (1990). *Diversity and complexity in feminist therapy.* New York: Haworth.

Brown, L. S., & Walker, L. E. A. (1990). Feminist perspectives on self-disclosure. In G. Striker & M. Fisher (Eds.), *Self-disclosure in the therapeutic relationship* (pp. 135–154). New York: Plenum.

Butler, P. A. (1976). *Self-assertion for women: A guide to becoming androgynous.* San Francisco: Harper & Row.

Butters, J., & Cash, T. (1987). Cognitive-behavioral treatment of women's body-image disturbance. *Journal of Consulting and Clinical Psychology, 55*(6), 889–897.

Chesler, P. (1972). *Women and madness.* Garden City, NY: Doubleday.

Chodorow, N. (1978). *The reproduction of mothering.* Berkeley: University of California Press.

Cotroneo, M. (1988). Women and abuse in the context of the family. In L. Braverman (Ed.), *Women, feminism, and family therapy* (pp. 81–96). New York: Haworth.

Dutton-Douglas, M. A., & Walker, L. E. A. (Eds.). (1988). *Feminist psychotherapies: Integration of therapeutic and feminist systems*. Norwood, NJ: Ablex.

Easton, B. (1994). Feminist struggles for sex equality. In N. F. Cott (Ed.), *History of women in the United States: Historical articles on women's lives and activities* (pp. 442–467). Munich: K. G. Saur.

Eichenbaum, L., & Orbach, S. (1982). *Outside in, inside out: Women's psychology: A feminist psychoanalytic approach*. New York: Penguin.

Espin, O. M., & Gawelek, M. A. (1992). Women's diversity: Ethnicity, race, class, and gender in theories of feminist psychology. In L. S. Brown & M. Ballou (Eds.), *Personality and psychopathology: Feminist reappraisals* (pp. 88–107). New York: Guilford.

Fallon, A. (1990). Culture in the mirror: Sociocultural determinants of body image. In T. Cash & T. Pruzinsky (Eds.), *Body images: Development, deviance, and change* (pp. 80–109). New York: Guilford.

Faunce, P. S. (1990). Women in poverty: Ethical dimensions in therapy. In H. Lerman and N. Porter (Eds.), *Feminist ethics in psychotherapy* (pp. 185–194). New York: Springer.

Feminist Therapy Institute. (1987). *Feminist therapy ethical code*. Denver: Author.

Fine, M. (1988). Sexuality, schooling and adolescent females: The missing discourse of desire. *Harvard Educational Review, 58*(1), 29–53.

Ganley, A. (1988). Feminist therapy with male clients. In M. A. Dutton-Douglas & L. E. A. Walker (Eds.), *Feminist psychotherapies: Integration of therapeutic and feminist systems* (pp. 186–205). Norwood, NJ: Ablex.

Gergen, M. M. (1991). Finished at 40: Women's development within the patriarchy. *Psychology of Women Quarterly, 14,* 471–494.

Gilligan, C. (1982). *In a different voice*. Cambridge: Harvard University Press.

Gilligan, C. (1990a). Joining the resistance: Psychology, politics, girls, and women. *Michigan Quarterly Review, 29*(4), 501–536.

Gilligan, C. (1990b). Teaching Shakespeare's sister: Notes from the underground of female adolescence. In C. Gilligan, N. Lyons, & T. Hanmer (Eds.), *Making connections: The relational worlds of adolescent girls at Emma Willard School* (pp. 6–29). Cambridge: Harvard University Press.

Gilligan, C. (1991). Women's psychological development: Implications for psychotherapy. In C. Gilligan, A. G. Rogers, & D. L. Tolman (Eds.), *Women, girls, and psychotherapy: Reframing resistance* (pp. 5–32). New York: Haworth.

Gilligan, C., Brown, L. M., & Rogers, A. (1990). Psyche embedded: A place for body, relationships, and culture in personality theory. In A. Rabin et al. (Eds.), *Studying persons and lives* (pp. 86–147). New York: Springer.

Greenspan, M. (1983). *A new approach to women and therapy*. New York: McGraw-Hill.

Hartman, A. (1993). The professional is political. *Social Work, 38*(4), 365–366, 504.

Haussman, M. J., & Halseth, J. H. (1987). Reexamining women's roles: A feminist approach to decreasing depression in women. In V. Franks (Series Ed.) & C. M. Brody (Vol. Ed.), *Springer series: Focus on women: Volume 10: Women's therapy groups: Paradigms of feminist treatment* (pp. 217–226). New York: Springer.

Hutchinson, M. (1985). *Transforming body image*. Trumansburg, NY: Crossing Press.

Jordan, J. V., & Surrey, J. L. (1986). The self-in-relation: Empathy and the mother-daughter relationship. In T. Bernay & D. W. Cantor (Eds.), *The psychology of today's woman: New psychoanalytic visions* (pp. 81–104). Hillsdale, NJ: Analytic Press.

Kantrowitz, R. E., & Ballou, M. (1992). A feminist critique of cognitive-behavioral therapy. In L. S. Brown & M. Ballou (Eds.), *Personality and psychopathology* (pp. 70–87). New York: Guilford.

Kaschak, E. (1992). *Engendered lives: A new psychology of women's experience*. New York: Basic Books.

Kinsey, A., Pomeroy, W., & Martin, C. (1948). *Sexual behavior in the human male*. Philadelphia: Saunders.

Kirsh, B. (1974). Consciousness-raising groups as therapy for women. In V. Franks & V. Burtle (Eds.), *Women in therapy: New psychotherapies for a changing society* (pp. 326–354). New York: Brunner/Mazel.

Kirsh, B. (1987). Evolution of consciousness-raising groups. In V. Franks (Series Ed.) & C. M. Brody (Vol. Ed.), *Springer series: Focus on women: Volume 10: Women's therapy groups: Paradigms of feminist treatment* (pp. 43–54). New York: Springer.

Kravetz, D. (1987). Benefits of consciousness-raising groups for women. In V. Franks (Series Ed.) & C. M. Brody (Vol. Ed.), *Springer series: Focus on women: Volume 10: Women's therapy groups: Paradigms of feminist treatment* (pp. 55–66). New York: Springer.

Laidlaw, T. A., Malmo, C., et al. (1990). *Healing voices: Feminist approaches to therapy with women*. San Francisco: Jossey-Bass.

Lazerson, J. (1992). Feminism and group psychotherapy: An ethical responsibility. *International Journal of Group Psychotherapy, 42*(4), 523–546.

Lerman, H. (1986). *A mote in Freud's eye: From psychoanalysis to the psychology of women*. New York: Springer.

Lerman, H. (1994). The practice of ethics within feminist therapy. In N. K. Gartrell (Ed.), *Bringing ethics alive: Feminist ethics in psychotherapy* (pp. 85–92). New York: Haworth.

Lerner, H. G. (1988). *Women in therapy*. New York: Harper & Row.

Lerner, R., & Karabenick, S. (1974). Physical attractiveness, body attitudes, and self-concept in late adolescence. *Journal of Youth and Adolescence, 3,* 308–316.

Levinson, D. J., Darrow, C. N., Klein, E. D., Levinson, M. H., & McKee, B. (1978). *The seasons of a man's life*. New York: Knopf.

Marmor, J. (1973). Changing patterns in femininity: Psychoanalytic implications. In J. B. Miller (Ed.), *Psychoanalysis and women*. Baltimore: Penguin.

Mays, V. M., & Comas-Diaz, L. (1988). Feminist therapy with ethnic minority populations: A closer look at blacks and Hispanics. In M. A. Dutton-Douglas & L. E. A. Walker (Eds.), *Feminist psychotherapies: Integration of therapeutic and feminist systems* (pp. 228–251). Norwood, NJ: Ablex.

McNair, L. D. (1992). African American women in therapy: An Afrocentric and feminist synthesis. *Women and Therapy, 12*(1/2), 5–19.

McWhirter, E. H. (1991). Empowerment in counseling. *Journal of Counseling and Development, 69*(3), 222–227.

Miller, J. B. (1976). *Toward a new psychology of women*. Boston: Beacon.

Morgan, K. S., & Eliason, M. J. (1992). The role of psychotherapy in Caucasian lesbians' lives. *Women and Therapy, 13*(4), 27–52.

Noles, S., Cash, T., & Winstead, B. (1985). Body image, physical attractiveness, and depression. *Journal of Consulting and Clinical Psychology, 53,* 88–94.

Okun, B. F. (1992). Object relations and self psychology: Overview and feminist perspective. In L. S. Brown & M. Ballou (Eds.), *Personality and psychopathology: Feminist reappraisals* (pp. 20–45). New York: Guilford.

Parvin, R. A., & Biaggio, M. K. (1991). Paradoxes in the practice of feminist therapy. *Women and Therapy, 11*(2), 3–12.

Peterson, A. (1988). Adolescent development. *Annual Review of Psychology, 39,* 583–607.

Pipher, M. (1994). *Reviving Ophelia: Saving the selves of adolescent girls*. New York: Ballantine Books.

Richard, J. V. (1982). Addressing stress factors in single-parent women-headed households. In the New England Association for Women in Psychology (Eds.), *Current feminist issues in psychotherapy* (pp. 15–28). New York: Haworth.

Romaniello, J. (1992). Beyond archetypes: A feminist perspective on Jungian theory. In L. S. Brown & M. Ballou (Eds.), *Personality and psychopathology: Feminist reappraisals* (pp. 46–69). New York: Guilford.

Rosen, J., Saltzberg, E., & Srebnik, D. (1989). Cognitive behavior therapy for negative body image. *Behavior Therapy, 20,* 393–404.

Roth, S. (1985). Psychotherapy with lesbian couples: Individual issues, female socialization, and the social context. *Journal of Marital and Family Therapy, 11*(2), 273–286.

Rothblum, E. D. (1982). Women's socialization and the prevalence of depression: The feminine mistake. In the New England Association for Women in Psychology (Eds.), *Current feminist issues in psychotherapy* (pp. 5–13). New York: Haworth.

Russell, M. N. (1984). *Skills in counseling women: The feminist approach*. Springfield, IL: Charles C Thomas.

Slive, Z. S. (1986). The feminist therapist and the male client. *Women and Therapy, 5*(2/3), 81–87.

Srebnik, D. S., & Saltzberg, E. A. (1994). Feminist cognitive-behavioral therapy for negative body image. *Women and Therapy, 15*(2), 117–133.

Staples, R. (1977). The myth of the black matriarchy. In D. Wilkinson & R. Taylor (Eds.), *The black male in America* (pp. 174–187). Chicago: Nelson Hall.

Sturdivant, S. (1980). *Therapy with women: A feminist philosophy of treatment.* New York: Springer.

Taylor, V., & Whittier, N. (1993). The new feminist movement. In L. Richardson & V. Taylor (Eds.), *Feminist frontiers III* (pp. 533–548). New York: McGraw-Hill.

Tolman, D. L. (1991). Adolescent girls, women, and sexuality: Discerning dilemmas of desire. In C. Gilligan, A. G. Rogers, & D. L. Tolman, (Eds.), *Women, girls, and psychotherapy: Reframing resistance* (pp. 55–70). New York: Haworth.

Valentich, M. (1996). Feminist theory and social work practice. In F. J. Turner (Ed.), *Social work treatment: Interlocking theoretical approaches* (4th ed.) (pp. 282–318). New York: Free Press.

Walker, L. E. A. (1984). *The battered woman syndrome.* Vol. 6 in V. Franks (Series Ed.), *Springer series: Focus on women.* New York: Springer.

Walker, L. E. A. (1990). A feminist therapist views the case. In D. W. Cantor (Ed.), *Women as therapists: A multitheoretical casebook* (pp. 78–95). New York: Springer.

Walker, L. E. A. (1994). *Abused women and survivor therapy: A practical guide for the psychotherapist.* Washington, DC: American Psychological Association.

Walters, M., Carter, B., Papp, P., & Silverstein, O. (1988). *The invisible web: Gender patterns in family relationships.* New York: Guilford.

Weiner, J. P., & Boss, P. (1985). Exploring gender bias against women: Ethics for marriage and family therapy. *Counseling and Values, 30,* 9–23.

Gestalt Theory

Mary Finn Maples
University of Nevada, Reno

Conrad Sieber
Portland State University

Background

Although Fritz Perls is credited with being the foremost practitioner of Gestalt counseling and psychotherapy, his counseling method was influenced by the Gestalt psychologists who preceded him. Max Wertheimer, Wolfgang Köhler, and Kurt Koffka of the "Berlin school" initiated the Gestalt movement in the United States when they fled the rise of Nazism in Germany (Rock & Palmer, 1990). Perls's biographer, Martin Shepherd (1975), wrote that "the traditional Gestalt psychologists claim [Perls]" (p. 198), but Perls stated that "the academic Gestaltists, of course, never accepted me. . . . I certainly was not a pure Gestaltist" (1969a, p. 62). The Austrian philosopher Christian von Ehrenfels may be credited with the initial use of the term *gestalt,* which appeared in his essay "On Gestalt Qualities" in 1890. This publication ignited a current of thought which created a strong position in both philosophy and psychology during the first half of the 20th century. Yet it was the psychologists of the Berlin school who laid the psychological groundwork for Perls's application of Gestaltism in counseling and psychotherapy.

Perls himself first used the term **Gestalt therapy** in his 1947 text *Ego, Hunger, and Aggression.* Readers of this early work had mixed reactions. Yontef (1981) stated that while the roots for Gestalt therapy were established in Gestalt psychology, there were doubts as to whether "the Gestalt therapy system has much to do with Gestalt psychology" (p. 1). Henle (1978) concluded that "the two approaches, Gestalt psychology and Gestalt therapy," have "nothing in common" (p. 26), and Cadwallader (1984) stated that Gestalt therapy has "rather little to do with Gestalt psychology" (p. 192). Yet Emerson and Smith

(1974) wrote that "no one can understand Gestalt therapy well without an adequate background in Gestalt psychology" (p. 8).

Emerson and Smith (1974), Kogan (1976), and Yontef (1981) believe that Perls moved from psychoanalysis to Gestalt therapy in 1947, and Perls confirmed this in *Ego, Hunger, and Aggression*. The modern Gestalt counselor or therapist who learns theory, research, and practice from the writings and demonstrations of Fritz Perls will understand his ideas more thoroughly and better appreciate his works after learning more about his predecessors.

Max Wertheimer

Max Wertheimer (1880–1943) was one of the "Berlin Three" (with Koffka and Köhler) who influenced Perls's works. In a sense, Wertheimer was a second-generation Gestaltist, having attended many lectures given by Christian von Ehrenfels when the latter was a professor at the German University in Prague (Smith, 1988). It was in Prague and from Ehrenfels that Wertheimer developed the doctrine he later called "cerebral integration," which gave rise to the Berlin School. Also of interest is the fact that Lore (later Laura) Perls had studied with Wertheimer. Her husband actually learned much about Wertheimer's work from her (Latner, 1992).

Wertheimer's writings on motivation and perception were particularly influential. They contributed to one of Perls's most important constructs, that of **client awareness.** Wertheimer's *Perception of Apparent Movement* (1912) gave rise to his reputation as the founder of Gestalt psychology (Hartmann, 1935). It was at this time that Wertheimer gathered around him a group of brilliant young disciples, including Kurt Koffka and Wolfgang Köhler, who were active human subjects in several of his experiments (Smith, 1976).

Kurt Koffka

Kurt Koffka (1886–1941) was concerned with the definition of *gestalt*. He asserted: "The term gestalt is a short name for a category of thought comparable to other categories like substance, causality, and function. But gestalt may be considered more than simply an addition to pre-existing conceptual principles; its generality is so great that one may ask whether causality itself or even substance does not fall legitimately under it" (1935, p. 16). Koffka and other Gestaltists who studied perception described Gestalt as "a pattern or shape"; but in psychology, and particularly in counseling and psychotherapy from Perls's perspective, the word means "configuration" (Rock & Palmer, 1990). Perls used the word *gestalt* to mean a specific type of patterning (configuration) where parts can be integrated into perceptual wholes. This wholeness concept is used extensively in counseling and psychotherapy, education, and social psychology (Passons, 1975).

Koffka was passionate in his belief in Gestaltism. He said, "I wanted to present a system of psychology that was not a dead or finished system but a system in the making, a system in a state of growth" (1935, p. ix). Perls continued to nurture that growth by extending Gestalt psychology to counseling and psychotherapy.

Wolfgang Köhler

The writings of **Wolfgang Köhler** (1887–1967), like those of Koffka and Wertheimer, contributed much "humanness" to Perls's work. Of the three precursors to Perls's work in

Gestalt counseling and psychotherapy, Köhler was probably the most humane. His friends and colleagues described him as an affective and sensitive person, "one who could see beyond what others could" (Henle, 1971, p. 89) and was able to "show us what a man is capable of being" (Hormann, 1967, p. 202).

Henle (1971) felt that Köhler's sensitivity was reflected in his life and his writings. Those writings, however, also emerged as a result of disintegration, disenchantment, and even disbelief in the favored psychological theories of the 1920s and 1930s: structuralism and behaviorism. One of the more readable and enjoyable of his writings is the second chapter in his 1929 work *Gestalt Psychology,* entitled "Psychology as a Young Science," in which Köhler compares the young science of psychology with the "old" and proven science of physics. He warns of the subjectivity of psychology as being incompatible with the scientific "proof" testing necessary in physics because psychology is the study of the ever changing human mind while physics lends itself to a variety of proven tests (Köhler, 1929).

Frederick (Fritz) Perls

Frederick (Fritz) Saloman Perls was born in 1893, the middle child and only son of middle-class Jewish parents in Berlin. His childhood experiences were much like those of most American children who became adults in the middle of the 20th century. He recalled that his childhood was fairly happy, although he related more positively to his younger sister than his older. He did well in primary school, but by the seventh grade his spirit of rebellion began to assert itself. Nevertheless, he persevered and tolerated the mediocrity of those years, receiving a medical degree in 1920 after a brief stint as a medical corpsman during World War I—an experience that he found to be of both practical and personal importance.

His early training in psychoanalysis took place in Austria and Germany, and he became associated with neurologist Kurt Goldstein. While working as Goldstein's assistant at Frankfurt am Main's Institute for Brain Injured Soldiers in 1926, Perls became interested in the transforming of Gestalt psychology into Gestalt therapy (Perls, 1969b). Goldstein's work significantly affected Perls's later counseling and psychotherapy interventions (Wheeler, 1991). However, Perls's early works reveal that he had disagreements with principles of psychoanalytic, behavioral, and structural theories.

Perls's ability to think for himself and create his own theories may have been rooted in his nature: he was always a free spirit (Perls, 1969b). Henle (1978) believes that Perls viewed most of his differences with Gestalt psychology as insurmountable because he regarded himself as an organismic psychologist, or a viewer of humankind in its holistic sense. According to Henle (1978), "Gestalt psychology deals primarily with perception and cognition, while Gestalt therapy (counseling) is concerned with personality, psychopathology, and psychotherapy" (p. 29). Perls particularly admired the work of Kurt Lewin because of his holistic approach to human nature (Perls, 1969b).

When Hitler came to power, Perls and his new wife, Lore, relocated to Johannesburg, South Africa, and he shed the Freudian psychoanalytic influence. They were, in fact, the first psychologists in South Africa (Segal, 1997). In 1946 he immigrated to the United States, where he published *Gestalt Therapy: Excitement and Growth in the Human Personality* in 1951. Following the favorable reception of this text, he established several

Gestalt Institutes throughout the country, the first in New York in 1952. His work at the Esalen Institute in California established him as a prominent practitioner of Gestalt counseling and psychotherapy.

It is important to consider the historical period in which a particular theorist lived and worked in order to better understand and appreciate that person's theory or model of psychotherapy. The language of the time and the way people lived and loved, worked and played, are crucial to understanding counseling theorists and practitioners decades later. Consider Perls's 1969 statement in *Gestalt Therapy Verbatim* (1969a): "It took us a long time to debunk the whole Freudian crap. We are entering the phase of the quacks and the con-men who think if you get some breakthrough, you are cured" (1969a, p. 1). In fact, Perls had a negative experience with Freud in 1936 when the two engaged in a brief conversation at a convention in Vienna. Perls felt humiliated by Freud, which may have triggered a sensitivity to the humiliating experiences he had with his father during childhood. Thus, this interchange may have contributed to Perls's desire to prove Freud's theories obsolete (Perls, 1969a).

Having been influenced by the works of Wertheimer, Koffka, and Köhler, Perls made his most memorable representations, translations, extensions, and practice during a time of unrest, questioning authority, the rejection of traditional customs, and the opening of the free spirit during the decade of the 1960s. Perls felt that those years when he was still strengthening his theory helped him make this discovery: "The meaning of life is that it is to be lived; and it is not to be traded and conceptualized and squeezed into a pattern of systems. We realize that manipulation and control are not the ultimate joy of life" (1969a, p. 3). But we are left to ponder whether he was merely *reflecting* the growing freedom of the human spirit at that time, or *advancing* it.

Gestalt counseling and psychotherapy is now in the third generation of a holistic approach to facilitating growth and health. The first generation began with the philosophical underpinnings of Ehrenfels (1890). That generation then opened the door to the psychological works of Wertheimer, Koffka, and Köhler (from 1912 through 1960), each of whom dealt with the mental aspects of the human being: cognition (thinking), perceiving, and motivation. In the third generation, Perls extended the research into the physical and emotional aspects of the human being to include the medical model of psychotherapy (Gilliland, James, & Bowman, 1994; Polster & Polster, 1973a; Zinker, 1978). Gestalt counseling and psychotherapy is intended to bring more meaning to the counseling process with individuals, families, and groups who are in relatively good health, psychologically and physically, but who are experiencing roadblocks or difficulty adjusting to an increasingly complex, diverse, and problematic world.

Laura Perls

Fritz Perls's work was carried on after his death in 1970 by his wife, Laura Perls. It has become increasingly clear since her own death in 1990 that Lore (Laura) Posner Perls (b. 1905) contributed significantly to Gestalt counseling and psychotherapy, having studied with Max Wertheimer and gaining recognition as a Gestalt psychologist in her own right (Rosenblatt, 1991). She continued her work long after her husband's death, becoming an influential force in Gestalt therapy and the training of Gestalt therapists until her own death.

The Gestalt Journal, initiated in 1977, has published two interviews with Laura Perls. The first interview was conducted by Edward Rosenfeld on May 23, 1977, and published in 1978 and again in 1982 (Rosenfeld, 1978/1982); the second was published posthumously in 1991 (Rosenblatt, 1991). In the 1977 interview, Laura stated that she had written two chapters in *Ego, Hunger, and Aggression:* "the chapter on the dummy complex and the one on insomnia" (Rosenfeld, 1978/1982, p. 13). She also stated that she and Fritz originally wanted to call their approach "existential therapy," but at the time "existentialism was so much associated with Sartre, with the nihilistic approach, that we looked for another name" (p. 13).

Phenomenology, Existentialism, Field Theory, and Gestalt Therapy

Gestalt therapy was not influenced by Gestalt psychology only. Phenomenology, existentialism, and field theory also contributed to form the underpinnings of Gestalt therapy. In this perspective, the focus is on improving clients' awareness of their subjective experience, facilitating their ability to become authentic and make choices that lead to a meaningful life, and setting in motion the natural process of growth that moves toward integration within self, and between self and the environment.

Phenomenology.   **Phenomenology** is the study of human experience through attending to the subjective observations of individuals. Inquiry into experience, or observing one's own experience, is inherently a subjective undertaking. The focus of inquiry may be internal, on the self, or external, on the environment, but the observations of the individual are considered to be relevant and meaningful. Phenomenology suggests a conscious awareness of the subject's own experience through self-observation. This contrasts with the empirical objectivist perspective, which views individual subjective experience with suspicion and assumes that it obscures rather than reveals "reality." A phenomenologist might point out that empirical study of human experience is itself a process in which the observer/researcher helps shape what is observed. Empiricists bring their own personal history and subjective experience to the undertaking, which help define what they do and do not attend to and how they interpret results to draw conclusions. An example of this process in action is the concept of **demand characteristics** from research design methodology. Demand characteristics are those unconscious biases that occur in research which tend to lead researchers to find results that seem to confirm their preconceived assumptions about what their data will show. Thus, subjectivity and objectivity may not be so easily deconstructed, since in these instances there is some form of interaction between the subjectivity of researchers and their attempts at objectivity through the use of empiricism. In Gestalt therapy, what is subjectively experienced by the client in the present is seen as relevant and important information for improving accurate awareness. Thus insight is developed through focused awareness and experimentation (Yontef & Simkin, 1989).

Existentialism.   **Existentialism** is concerned with human existence as directly experienced. People seek to find meaning in their experience. They often discover in this process that they live in a context, within a society, that molds and shapes experience based on shared assumptions about "reality"—what is, how the world is, what people should be and do. These constructions of reality may distort one's understanding and experience of self, others, and the larger world. Yontef and Simkin (1989) note that the basis for inauthenticity is self-deception, which is often based on an uncritical acceptance of societal values and norms that construct reality. When one becomes a false self, living in ways that do not have their basis in truth, one feels dread, guilt, and anxiety. Gestalt therapy helps clients become authentic by increasing self-awareness, thereby enabling them to make choices about how they organize their experience to be more truly genuine and meaningful.

Field Theory.   The Gestalt therapy perspective relies heavily on **field theory,** which is explored at more length later in this chapter (Yontef & Simkin, 1989). In contrast to a reductionistic, unilinear, cause-and-effect model, field theory focuses on the whole, in which all the elements found within the field are in relationship to and influence one another. Thus no individual part operates in isolation from any of the other parts in the field. For example, individuals have a body and a mind which interact to create the whole person. They do not exist in isolation from one another. This approach is descriptive rather than interpretive. The emphasis taken by Gestalt therapy from field theory is in observing, describing, and defining the structure of the field.

Human Nature: A Developmental Perspective

Perhaps one of the most attractive features of Gestalt theory is its attention to the holistic nature of humankind. As in existentialism and phenomenology, genuine knowledge is the expected outcome of what is apparent and evident in the experience of the perceiver. While the traditional Gestalt psychologists remained focused on cognition, perception, and motivation, Gestalt counselors and therapists engage the whole organism (person) and operate from the perspective that human beings have the capacity and strength to grow, to develop, and to become the person they are meant to be. A basic assumption is that individuals can cope with their life problems, especially if fully aware of what is happening in and around them.

Kurt Lewin had a significant impact on Perls's view of human nature (Perls, 1969a). In his chapter "Education and Reality" in *A Dynamic Theory of Personality* (1935), Lewin discussed a holistic view of education as exemplified in a Montessori setting. This holism can be found in Lewin's classic equation $B = f(P \times E)$. Behavior is a function of the interaction between the person and his or her environment. The Montessori educational system was developed by Maria Montessori as an alternative to educating children by parts—that is, breaking education down into arithmetic, spelling, language, and the like. She believed in the education of the whole child, much in the manner that John Dewey proposed in the United States. Discussing Montessori's method, Lewin wrote that the "extension of psychological life space and time and the demand for a life in the present is realized to an extreme degree in the young child" (1935, p. 172). He said that the child has "levels of reality and unreality from kindergarten and perhaps even before" (p. 174) and that even "in the infant the forces of psychological environment are determined essentially by his own needs" (p. 175). Lewin's influence on Perls's view of human nature is particularly valuable because the holistic approach in Gestalt counseling and psychotherapy can be applied effectively to children in a school or in a family counseling and psychotherapy setting. Other theories or systems are often ineffective because their application is limited to adults (family systems theory) or children (play therapy) and cannot address both.

Smith (1976) suggests that Gestalt counseling and psychotherapy has also been expanded and honed by the influence of Jung in at least three ways: first, the Jungian belief in facilitating growth through self-realization; second, the Jungian principle of personality development through wholeness; and third, the Jungian illumination of the transpersonal realm in counseling. These influences contributed to Perls's belief in the wholeness and completeness of life. Centered in the present (Kempler, 1973), the person in Gestalt counseling or psychotherapy is always in the process of being what he or she *is* in the here and now, in the process of becoming the person that he or she *can* be. Further, Perls believed in the ability of persons to change and to be responsible for both their behavior and, inevitably, the directions they take in their lives. A valuable aspect of the Gestaltist's view of human nature is that persons gain more from experiences and involvement in activities than from talk. That is, sharing direct experience of feelings, thoughts, or sensations is more valuable than talking about these experiences.

Perls was seen by his contemporaries as a consummate actor (Shepherd, 1975). That is, they viewed him as successful in eliciting behaviors from clients that traditional psychoanalysts, behaviorists, and structuralists may not have been able to elicit. Perls, Hefferline, and Goodman (1951) commented on the psychoanalytic belief that the ego confines itself to perceiving and is otherwise inactive. In contrast, in Gestalt counseling and psychotherapy, they suggest, the client is active, dynamic, and involved in the counseling and psychotherapy process, not just a passive observer (p. 71). Furthermore, Perls (1969a) described his view of human nature by noting that the person or organism always works as a whole: "We *have* not a liver or a heart. We *are* liver and heart and brain and yet, even this is wrong—we are *not* a summation of parts but a *coordination* of the whole. We do not have a body, we *are* a body, we *are* somebody" (p. 6).

Perls valued the Gestalt approach to counseling and psychotherapy because "we see the whole being of a person right in front of us. Gestalt counseling is being in touch with the obvious, the human being, the wholeness of his/her frailties, strengths, weaknesses, joys, and sorrows" (Perls, 1969a, p. 14). An example of a client's coming to believe in her wholeness, simplicity, and individual responsibility for her own behavior as a worthwhile human being was demonstrated by Swanson (1984) in a videotaped session with a woman client. The client had come for help because she was unable to express herself in an honest manner. She felt that she always had to "hide [her] true feelings so as not to make others angry at [her]" (Swanson, 1984). In a series of six sessions, Swanson facilitated her "response-ability" and her emerging worth as a person (Perls, 1969a, p. 29). He did not reduce her to the sum of her parts but instead worked with her as a whole person (Swanson, 1984).

Major Constructs

Field Theory: Organism and Environment

The scientific paradigm forming the basis of the Gestalt therapy perspective is **field theory** (Yontef & Simkin, 1989). In contrast to a reductionistic, unilinear, cause-and-effect model, field theory focuses on the whole, in which all the elements found within the field are in relationship to and influence one another. Field theory is based on the principle of interdependence. The metaphor of a baseball game helps illuminate this construct. In a baseball game there is a field defined by boundary lines demarcating the field of play from that which is outside the field of play. All the elements central to play are on the field: players, bats, ball, and bases. All these elements interact to create the game. Just as a pitcher and batter must interact for the game to occur, there must also be a first baseman, shortstop, and outfielders. Even the bases themselves are needed. All are necessary for the whole called a baseball game. For instance, a ball without a bat is meaningless when it comes to having a game. Thus no individual part operates in isolation from any of the other parts in the field.

Phenomenological Field.   The phenomenological field is one kind of field, the one which is the focus of Gestalt therapy. This field changes according to the individual's focused awareness. At one moment the focus may be entirely internal, attending to self and its interrelated parts. During the next moment, the phenomenological field may shift to a focus on the person in relationship to his or her external environment, which is made up of its own constituent and interacting parts. When the focus is internal, the field is represented by parts of the self, which may be broadly defined as mind and body. This includes thoughts, feelings, senses, and actions, all of which are inseparable, just as the person's relationship to the external environment forms a set of interacting elements. For instance, one's family or school/workplace environment involves many other people with whom one relates and whom one influences. Thus, interacting parts of self such as thought, feeling, and sensing influence one another and cannot be understood in isolation, just as the person is influenced by and influences his or her environment.

The phenomenological field—that is, the subjective focused experience of the person—is defined by individuals, as they are observers of their own experience both internally and/or externally. For instance, an internal focus on the phenomenological field of the individual reveals the interrelated parts of self—mind, body, thoughts, feelings, and senses. They are interdependent. If the phenomenological field is external—focused, for example, on the person in relationship to the family environment, each family member is recognized as a part of a larger whole. In this field, family members are a part of the whole that is family, and for the family to exist each part or family member has a relationship to all other family members. It is the interdependence and reciprocal influences of family members on one another that creates the whole family. The family cannot be known by focusing only on one member; the interrelationship of family members to one another must be explored while allowing for the fact that individuals within the family also have differences from one another. Knowing isolated parts of a whole independent from their influence on one another does not fully describe the dynamic nature of that whole, whether that is the whole person or the family. These examples help illustrate another key concept of Gestalt therapy—**holism.** Gestalt therapy is holistic rather than reductionistic, it is concerned with the differentiation of and interrelationship of the parts that make up the whole, rather than focusing on parts in isolation from one another. As the old saying goes, "The whole is greater than the sum of its parts."

Differentiation and Contact.   In Gestalt therapy, a healthy individual is one who can differentiate self while also making contact with others. In fact, life is described as a constant process of contact and separation between the person and those one is in relationship to, such as family members and loved ones, colleagues, and employers. Contact and differentiation, connection and separation define a goal of Gestalt therapy: to help clients become more integrated within themselves and in relationship to others—in other words, helping to create **differentiated unity.** Differentiated unity for the client as a whole person means awareness of thoughts, feelings, and senses (i.e., taste, smell, hearing, touch, sight)—an integration of mind and body; in the organism/environment field, this means integration of the person into his/her environment. Thus, concepts of mind-body integration are not new to Gestalt therapy, which through its foundation in field theory critiques the prevailing medical model paradigm that dichotomizes mind and body as separate entities.

Boundaries.   For survival, the organism—that is, the individual—must make contact with the environment. The function of the individual's boundaries is to simultaneously be firm enough to differentiate self from others, yet open or permeable enough to make contact with others. In this process, the individual assimilates nourishment from the environment and rejects or keeps out that which is not nourishing. For instance, within a family a teenager may have boundaries firm enough to understand that he is unique in certain ways from an admired older brother and therefore accept pursuing his own interests, yet flexible enough to accept his brother's love and support. Thus, differentiated contact naturally leads to health and development (Yontef & Simkin, 1989).

Boundary disturbances occur when boundaries between self and others are overly rigid, creating isolation, or overly permeable, creating a merger in which differentiation of self is lost to confluence with the other. An example of a boundary disturbance is **retroflection,** an internal split within the self in which elements of the self are rejected as not-self. In this situation, the individual does to self what is normally done to the environment (Yontef & Simkin, 1989)—that is, differentiating between nourishing and toxic elements in the environment, assimilating the former and rejecting the latter. The individual in this case disowns parts of self. This undermines health and functioning. **Introjection** occurs when material from the environment is taken in without discrimination concerning its nourishing or toxic qualities. For instance, children usually introject parental and societal values, not having the maturity to differentiate between beliefs that are and are not congruent with their growth and health. It is often in young adulthood that people begin to recognize the difference between values congruent with their well being and those introjected from parents and society that create difficulties.

Projection involves taking parts of self and directing them outwards onto others. Some people are unaware of disowned parts of themselves and routinely project them onto others. This interferes with self-awareness, coming to terms with these disowned elements of the person, and accepting them. **Deflection** is the avoidance of contact through diversion. That is, instead of being direct and genuine in a relationship the individual may present a disingenuous, false image of him- or herself to others as a way of avoiding contact. On the other hand, deflection also occurs when the individual fails to receive from, attend to, or be aware of information coming from the environment. An example would be a situation where an individual pretends to listen to a colleague while his or her thoughts are actually elsewhere. The information from other to self is deflected (Yontef & Simkin, 1989).

Dichotomies and Polarities.   In field theory, there is a distinction made between dichotomies and polarities. **Dichotomies** are unnatural splits in which a field is made up of separate, competing, either/or parts instead of integrated elements in relationship to one another that form a whole. For instance, dichotomizing the self into good and bad parts and then attempting to ignore or repress the bad parts is detrimental to growth and health. On the other hand, **polarities** are a natural part of fields. Fields are differentiated into polarities—opposite parts that work in tandem or contrast one another to help clarify meaning. Here we are describing a process based on electrical fields, that is, their complementary differentiation into positive and negative poles (Yontef & Simkin, 1989). Health and energy are found through integration, not dichotomization of polarities.

Another way to think of this is to consider the difference between continua and categories. A continuum represents a domain that is connected along a line where differences reside at opposite ends or poles, yet the poles are connected along the continuum. Categories split a domain—for example, separating caring for self and caring for others into dichotomous categories with no connection to one another. The individual develops integration by, for instance, discovering both easily accepted and disowned parts of self. The caring, kind, and nurturing mother comes to recognize and also identify with the more aggressive, assertive side of herself which seeks to get her own needs met. Meeting her own needs can complement her capacity to nurture. Here, caring for others and caring for self lie at two ends of a continuum, with each pole representing the greatest distinction between the two.

When integration fails, splits occur. The parts of the person, those elements of mind and body that make him or her what they are, are experienced as separate, not integrated. Thus a mother may dichotomize her capacity to be a caretaker from her ability to care for herself. Yet health is found in integration where difference is accepted and various parts of the self work together. Thus the process of healing dichotomies requires increased awareness of the way the client dichotomizes experience, whether the focus of awareness is internal or external dichotomies. Yontef and Simkin (1989) describe this process of healing as integrating into a whole that which is differentiated into natural polarities that complement and/or help define one another.

Foreground and Background.   Another principle of Gestalt therapy is that of the **foreground** and **background** in a phenomenological field. The goal, if it can be called this, is a well-formed figure standing in contrast to a broader, less well defined background. The figure is in the forefront of the individual's awareness of the phenomenological field at any one time. Thus, for example, the phenomenological field could be defined as the family as background, and the specific relationship between two family members, such as mother and daughter, in the foreground. Problems occur when foreground and background are not well formed and clearly distinct from one another. Continuing the foregoing example, with the mother-daughter relationship in an ambiguous foreground, it is difficult to distinguish that relationship from the background of the family as a whole. In this instance, it is easy to see that attempts to become more aware of and work with this relationship are obscured by the lack of clarity between foreground (the mother-daughter relationship) and the background of the family.

For instance, some families have members so enmeshed with one another that it is difficult to distinguish between each in terms of their thoughts, feelings, beliefs, attitudes, or the nature of member-to-member relationships. The members appear like carbon copies of one another even in terms of maintaining the same feelings and attitudes, and exist in an undifferentiated enmeshed family relationship where, for instance, the marital relationship is difficult to distinguish from parent-child relationships. However, health is found when foreground is clear enough to be differentiated from background so that the most important current needs and concerns within the field can be properly attended to. Thus, in a healthy person or person-environment field, the figure changes as needed to meet new and ever changing circumstances. The most important needs/concerns come into the foreground and are distinguishable from the background. For instance, in the preceding family example, once the mother-daughter relationship has been in the foreground and is appropriately defined and tended to, it can recede into background as another element of the family comes to foreground, possibly the relationship between the parents themselves. Or, if the phenomenological field is the individual client, awareness of feelings in the present may be in the foreground at one moment, while awareness of current thoughts about betrayal by a loved one may move to the foreground in the next. Here, ill-defined foreground and background would lead to thoughts and feelings that are amorphous and cannot be differentiated from one another. Clients with this difficulty often need the therapist's help in distinguishing between thoughts and feelings so that each may be better understood and the relationship between thought and feeling can be clarified—in other words, how one affects the other.

Yontef and Simkin (1989) state that health defines a situation where awareness accurately represents and brings to the foreground the dominant need of the whole field. Gestalt therapy also abides by the law of **homeostasis**—that is, the organism's tendency to seek balance within itself and between itself and its environment. Thus, if the person needs food for energy he or she becomes hungry, the need for food comes to the foreground, and the person eats. This returns the body to a state of homeostasis where there is enough food to provide the energy needed for proper functioning.

The Gestalt psychology principle of **pragnanz** is instructive in concluding the examination of the foreground-background dynamic. It states that the field will form itself into the best Gestalt that global conditions will allow. That is, interacting elements in a field, and their structure in relationship to one another, tend to form themselves, creating foreground and background in the best possible way. Thus, there is an innate drive toward health and growth found in nature, of which humans are a part.

Awareness

Awareness is the key to Gestalt therapy. In fact, the only goal of Gestalt therapy is awareness itself. Through awareness, the organism/person naturally proceeds toward growth, integration, and differentiated unity, in which the parts of the field are separate from and in contact with one another. Awareness is consciousness of what is, whether that is being in touch with the various parts of self—mind, body, thoughts, feelings, and senses—or consciousness of self in relationship to other elements in the environment, both those that are potentially nourishing as well as those that are toxic. The premise is that the person has the capacity to be aware of his or her own needs and priorities. Persons can accurately know themselves and the environments of which they are a part and make decisions that are congruent with their growth. Awareness, knowing the environment, and being in touch with one's self means that the individual is responsible for self-knowledge, self-acceptance, the ability to make contact, and ultimately to make choices.

Yontef and Simkin (1989) note that some people don't know their own behavior, others live in the present as if there were no past, and "most" live in the future as if it were now. They are commenting on the lack of awareness and consciousness of many people for what is, right now, in the present moment. Awareness sounds like a simple thing, but in Western societies, with all their rush and distraction, awareness can be rare. Awareness requires individuals to make "vigilant" contact with the most important aspects of the organism/environment field using the full support of their sensorimotor, emotional, cognitive, and energy processes (Yontef & Simkin, 1989).

In Gestalt therapy, clients are directed to move from talking about experience to directly experiencing what they are focusing on at any given moment in therapy. For instance, experiencing and expressing feelings is different as a process from talking about those very same feelings. Thus, Perls differentiated between intellectualizing and/or a tendency of people to talk about their feelings and experiences versus the direct experience and thus increased awareness of thoughts, feelings, and senses. Yontef and Simkin (1989) state that aware persons know what they do, how they do it, that alternatives exist, and that they choose to be as they are. This does not mean that the environment, or genetics, or previous learning don't create some constraints on the individual. However, it highlights the importance of differentiating between what is chosen and what is given (Yontef & Simkin, 1989). Often people have more choices and/or are unconsciously making choices that constrict their lives and growth potential. For instance, children do not choose the family they are born into, but once they begin to mature, they do have choices about familial values they do or do not accept as congruent with their emerging sense of self. Similarly, parents don't choose the specific child they give birth to, but they do choose how to parent.

Gestalt therapists focus in the here and now. Thus, the process of becoming aware is taking place here and now. The process of awareness—owning, choice, responsibility, and contact—leads to natural and spontaneous change. Therefore, clients do not need to be manipulated by the therapist to make growth-enhancing changes. Instead, the therapist engages the client in a process of increasing awareness of self, others, and the environment. Through therapy, clients come to master their own process of awareness, setting in motion their natural tendency to heal and grow (Yontef & Simkin, 1989).

Clearly, if the natural process of growth were going well, a client would be unlikely to come to therapy. Thus it is helpful to understand the meaning of impasse. Typically, clients reach an impasse—that is, become stuck—when they doubt their ability to be self-supporting and have relied too heavily on external support which is no longer available. According to Yontef and Simkin (1989), clients become stuck when they replace the normal need for internal self-support with overdependence on external support. That is, they get their needs met, not through healthy self-support, but by manipulating others to do what needs to be done for themselves. Clients usually bring this dynamic to the therapy process. They enter therapy with the wish that the therapist do their work for them. In Gestalt therapy, the therapist facilitates client awareness, while declining to do the client's work. For instance, Gestalt therapists eschew therapist interpretation of client material—a replacement of client awareness with therapist awareness—in favor of facilitating clients' coming to their own understanding through a process focused in the here and now on the "what and how" of the clients and their concerns. That is, what the client is doing and how the client does it is the focus. In Gestalt therapy why clients do what they do is not important. In fact, focusing on why tends to lead to client rationalizations and defensiveness that distract from, rather than contribute to, the process of growth.

Responsibility

Clients are seen as responsible or response-able. While it can be important to distinguish between true limitations and real alternatives, ultimately the client has the responsibility to choose and value, to create a healthy balance between self and surroundings. On a personal level, the choice is often between organismic and arbitrary regulation—that is, self-determination through awareness and acceptance of one's own values and beliefs versus an arbitrary regulation created by the introjection of another's—often one's parents' and society's—worldview. Thus, clients need to sort out which values and beliefs are theirs and which have been imposed by others, and whether or not these imposed values are consistent with their own health and growth. For instance, in a society that views women as less capable than men, a female client will need to identify these introjected societal values and choose her own. Her values will hopefully reflect a healthier view of the competence of the members of her gender.

In this process of taking responsibility, the aim of the therapist is to help the client become more self-regulating instead of acquiescing to arbitrary regulation, and to become more appropriately self-supporting instead of being overly dependent on external support. To accomplish this the client must address **unfinished business**—those important needs, concerns, and issues that require the client's attention. Through increased conscious awareness, clients also discover disowned parts of self. These disowned parts of self are raised into awareness, considered, and assimilated if congruent with the core of the client's true self, or rejected if alien to the client's deepest sense of self. This process of re-owning and taking responsibility facilitates integration. In this therapy model both client and therapist are self-responsible. Therapists are responsible for the nature of their presence with the client, having both self-knowledge and knowledge of the client. They maintain nondefensiveness, while keeping their awareness and contact processes clear and in tune with the client (Yontef & Simkin, 1989).

Shoulds

Arbitrary regulation creates shoulds that can control the client's thoughts, feelings, actions, and relationships. Regulation of human behavior and experience is to a greater or lesser degree organismic, coming from within individuals themselves, or it is "shouldistic," based on arbitrary imposition of what some controlling agent believes should be (Yontef & Simkin, 1989). Any therapist who has worked with clients has often seen the strong pull between clients' sense of what they should think, feel, or do and the emerging awareness of what they, in actuality, do think, feel, and/or want to do. It is apparent that Gestalt therapy places a high value on autonomy and self-determination. Although Gestalt therapy maintains a "no should" ethic, there is one exception. The exception is the situation. Perls believed that when clients understand the situation they find themselves in and allow it to shape their actions, then they have begun to learn how to cope with life (Yontef & Simkin, 1989).

I-Thou, What and How, Here and Now

A shorthand of sorts for Gestalt therapy is reflected in the phrase "I-thou, what and how, here and now" (Yontef & Simkin, 1989). The therapist and client form an alliance based on self-responsibility and an agreement to strive to be present with one another during their time together. Furthermore, the focus of therapy is the what and how of a client's experience in the present, in the moments that therapist and client are together. Client and therapist explore together through **experiments** that reveal what the client does and how it is done. In this light, why is viewed as a diversion, not as illuminating. A here-and-now focus on the what and how of the client's internal and external processes increases awareness, a necessity for growth.

Furthermore, the therapist is aware of the centrality of the client-therapist relationship and tends to it by being present, respectful of the client's capacity to heal and grow, and willing to be an authentic person in the therapeutic relationship. The client-therapist relationship is viewed as horizontal, not vertical. Thus the two parties seek equality in relation to one another. In this process, the therapist may choose, when appropriate, to share his or her own experience in the moment as it helps to facilitate the client's awareness. Yontef and Simkin (1989) state that therapist and client speak the same language of present-centeredness, emphasizing the direct experience of both participants, which helps therapist and client to show their full presence to one another. In this process, the therapist may share observations of the client that for whatever reason are not directly accessible to the client's awareness. Thus the client shares awareness of what is experienced internally while this process is observed externally by the therapist.

Direct experience is the tool used to expand awareness, while the focus on the client's present experience is made deeper and broader as therapy unfolds. Awareness is viewed as occurring now; it takes place now, although prior events can be the object of present awareness. While the event took place in the past, the focus is on the awareness of it that is taking place in the now, in this moment. Thus the present is understood as an ever-moving transition between past and future (Yontef & Simkin, 1989).

Applications

In recent years, the application of Gestalt counseling and psychotherapy has extended beyond the realm of individual and group therapy into the field of business—specifically, organizational development and team building. In the following section, several applications from business consulting will be highlighted in addition to the practice of Gestalt psychotherapy.

Overview

This section will be concerned with the goals of counseling and psychotherapy, the desired outcomes of Gestalt counseling; the process of change that leads to client growth; and the specific strategies used in the change process.

Goals of Counseling and Psychotherapy

According to Tillett (1991), "As creativity and spontaneity are central to Gestalt, and as there is intrinsic antipathy towards the concept of therapy as technique, it can be difficult to reach an acceptable definition of Gestalt therapy" (p. 290). This view is shared by many respected practitioners (Clarkson & Mackeron, 1993; Dryden, 1984; Yontef, 1981). However, practice may be illuminated by examining the goals of Gestalt therapy. According to Tillett (1991), they include the following:

- Development and expansion of both physical and emotional awareness. Intellectual insight and interpretation are limited.
- Relationship between client and therapist is existential and is central to the counseling process.
- Conversations between client and counselor are useful only to the extent that they support enactment and experimentation.
- Change should occur as the result of heightened awareness of the interactional process between client and counselor or by the activity and experimentation within the counseling process. (p. 291)

Yontef (1995) suggests that Gestaltists are not concerned with a "preset end goal" (p. 273). However, they do recommend, as most Gestalt therapists would, the particular goal of *phenomenological exploration,* rather than reconditioning of behavior or interpretation of the unconscious. This goal is valuable in that it places "ownership and responsibility" (Segal, 1997, p. 332) directly on the client and facilitates the client's engaging in an inherently natural process of growth.

Creative and spontaneous intervention is the method of the experienced counselor or therapist. The major goal of Gestalt counseling toward which interventions aim is autonomy and growth of the client through increased awareness. According to Yontef (1995), this can be "microawareness"—awareness of a particular content area and "awareness of the awareness process" (p. 275). Through heightened awareness, clients can know what they are choosing to do and can ultimately accept responsibility for these actions, as well as discover available choices and alternatives they may not have recognized due to limited self-awareness. How the counselor or therapist intervenes with the client to bring about this awareness is discussed in the next section.

To help facilitate client awareness and growth, the practitioner:

- Identifies themes or presenting problems that are central to the client's self-organization.
- Conceptualizes the issues and concerns of the client that will guide the sequence, timing, and methods of the counseling process.
- Establishes and maintains a safe and professional environment.
- Provides an atmosphere that invites contact between client and therapist and encourages interaction.

The Process of Change

> Reality is nothing but
>
> The sum of all awareness
>
> As you experience here and now. (Perls, 1969a, p. 30)

While this statement may appear overly simplistic, it is Perls's dismissal of the mind-body dichotomy in favor of holism, and it presents a challenge to the student of Gestalt counseling and psychotherapy (1969a). Understanding the process of change from a Gestalt perspective calls for an appreciation of Perls's goal for the process: "The Gestalt approach attempts to understand the existence of any event through the way it comes about, which is to understand becoming by the *how* and not the *why;* through the all-pervasive gestalt formation; through the tension of the unfinished situation (business)" (Perls, 1966, p. 361).

One of the major differences between the process of change in Gestalt therapy and Freudian psychoanalysis, for example, is that instead of being reductionistic and deterministic, as the Freudians were, the Gestalt therapist views the client as a whole person in the context of family, school, and work relationships, and as having an innate capacity for growth. The methods of recognition, consideration, and working within are unique to Gestalt practitioners. Thus, "there are specific skills, techniques and knowledge that should not be overlooked by the Gestalt counselor" (Shepherd, 1975, p. 196). Another aspect of the process of change in the Gestalt approach is the excitement that is generated when the client contacts something new, leading to the creation of a new Gestalt or a new experience. The Swanson tape noted earlier demonstrated the client's excitement: "It's all so simple—all I have to do is to say what I really am feeling, be honest about it, and be willing to be responsible for the results" (Swanson, 1984).

Specifically, the process of change in Gestalt counseling and psychotherapy consists of the identification and working through of a variety of blocks or interferences that prevent the client from achieving a balance (Wallen, 1970). Perls (1969a) described clients who block:

1. Those who cannot maintain eye contact, who are unaware of their own movements.

2. Those who cannot openly express their needs.

3. Those who use repression, examples of which are insomnia and boredom. (p. 72)

According to Levitsky and Perls (1970), the process of change, which is aimed at helping clients become more aware of themselves in the here and now, involves several precepts, including the following:

1. *A continuum of awareness.* Clients focus constantly on the how, what, and where in the body, in contrast to the why.

2. *Statements rather than questions.* Many theorists and practitioners have found the establishment of response-ability to be more helpful and respectful than expecting answers to questions (Gazda, 1986).

3. *Use of the first-person pronoun "I" rather than "it" or "they."* If a client says that people feel "thus and so," the therapist asks the client to restate this sentence using "I." Then the client owns his or her feelings instead of distancing himself or herself from them by saying "I feel thus and so."

4. *The contact issue of addressing someone directly.* Clients are helped to express themselves, their feelings, thoughts, needs, and concerns, as they occur in the moment directly to the therapist. Talking about and/or "beating around the bush" are discouraged.

The process of change in Gestalt counseling and psychotherapy involves experience and activity. Yontef (1981) believes that all Gestalt techniques are a means of experimentation. He further states that experimentation in the change process can be used to study any phenomenon that the client has experienced. Perls (1969a) postulated that as clients change and grow, they move through five layers of neurosis:

1. *The cliché layer:* one of noncontact with others; the "Hello, how are you?" "Fine, how are you?" routine.

2. *The phony layer:* the role-playing layer; the boss, the victim, the good boy/bad girl layers; the superficial and pretend layers; Perls believed that people devote much of their active lives to this game-playing layer.

3. *The impasse layer:* the place between dependence on outside support (parents, for example) and the ability to be self-supportive; an avoidance of autonomy.

4. *The implosive layer:* all the previous roles in the process are exposed, stripped, and seen for what they are—roles; this layer involves "pulling oneself together, contracting, compressing, and imploding" (Perls, 1969a, p. 60).

5. *The exploding layer:* tremendous energy is released at this stage. The "death layer comes to life and this explosion is the link-up with the authentic person who is capable of experiencing and expressing his emotions" (Dye & Hackney, 1975, p. 89).

This complete process, particularly from impasse to explosion, is often difficult for the client to comprehend. Yet most people have at one time or another reached that soul-searching depth that leads to getting in touch with values and self-perceptions that form the core of existence. The process, according to Dye and Hackney (1975), is best understood "only after it has been experienced" (p. 40).

Finally, the process of change in Gestalt counseling and psychotherapy contains a crucial feature that is both a valuable asset and a critical handicap: its **open-endedness.** Gestalt counselors and therapists rarely use techniques or tools that can be quantified from a "proof of theory" perspective. However, this open-endedness is the very quality that encourages creativity, inventiveness, response-ability, and spontaneous change and growth by the client.

Intervention Strategies

Specific interventions are the concrete behaviors of experimentation that emerge from the cooperation that exists between the client and the practitioner. They are labeled **experiments** because they are procedures aimed at discovery, rather than exercises (in the traditional sense). They are not designed to control or initiate behavior change. Instead, experiments are conducted through therapist recommendations or suggestions for focusing awareness that clients can use to heighten intensity, power, flexibility, and creativity.

Yontef (1995) provides the following examples of experiments:

- To clarify and sharpen what the client is already aware of and to make new linkages between elements already in awareness

- To bring into focal awareness that which was previously known only peripherally

- To bring into awareness that which is needed but systematically kept out of awareness

- To bring into awareness the system of control, especially the mechanism of preventing thoughts or feelings from coming into focal awareness (p. 280)

Miriam Polster (1987a) sees experiments as a way of bringing out internal conflicts by making the struggle an actual process. She aims at facilitating a client's ability to work through the stuck points in his or her life. The strategies of experimentation can take many forms, according to Polster, such as imagining a threatening encounter; setting up dialogue with a significant other; dramatizing the memory of a painful event; and reliving a particularly profound past experience in the present through role-playing, exaggerated gestures, posture, body language, or other signs of internal expression.

Most theories value the personhood of the counselor or psychotherapist. In Gestalt counseling and psychotherapy, however, practitioners are particularly important as persons because of the active nature of the helping relationship. The following views about counseling and psychotherapy are particularly appropriate for Gestalt practitioners. "The most important element in counseling is the personhood of the counselor. The most powerful impact on the client may be that of observing what the counselor is and does" (Gilliland et al., 1994, p. 7). Zinker (1978) focuses on the importance of the counselor or therapist as a creative agent of change who must be both caring and compassionate as a human being. Polster and Polster (1973a) see the "therapist as his own instrument" (p. 19). Further, Yontef and Simkin (1989) stress that *who* the counselor or therapist is as a person is more important than *what* he or she is doing to or with the client.

Perls believed that counseling and psychotherapy was a means of enriching life (Dye & Hackney, 1975). From his perspective, it is clear that "well people can get better" (Bates, Johnson, & Blaker, 1982). Intervention strategies suggested in this section are for clients who are fundamentally well but who need assistance in "making it" in a complex world (Maples, 1996). The main purpose, then, of intervention with persons who are seeking counseling or psychotherapy is to "simply sit down and start living" (Enright, 1970, p. 112). According to Dye and Hackney (1975), the aim of Gestalt counseling and psychotherapy is to take advantage of all dimensions of humanness by "achieving an integration of the thinking, feeling and sensing processes. The goal is to enable *full experiencing* rather than merely a cognitive understanding of certain elements" (p. 44).

Given the goals of completeness, wholeness, integration, and fulfillment of the essentially healthy but needy individual (in the sense of an incomplete Gestalt), the following intervention strategies may be used.

Locating Feelings.   Instead of asking the client, "What are you feeling?" the Gestaltist encourages him or her through statements such as "Show me where you are feeling this anxiety, apprehension, nervousness" (Swanson, 1984). The idea is to encourage the client to directly experience sensations in the body that are connected to his or her current feelings.

Confrontation and Enactment.   Because the client must be involved in the change process, acquiring new behaviors requires confronting old behaviors and acting out new ones. Confronting the self is a very important strategy in which the client must face disowned aspects of themselves. The **confrontation** of self and then the **enactment** of disowned thoughts, feelings, sensations, or actions allow the client to discover and then re-own neglected parts of self (Polster & Polster, 1973b). An example of this is demonstrated in the following session between a counselor or therapist and a female client who is, but does not want to be, pregnant (Maples, 1992):

Counselor/Therapist: Show me where you are feeling this anger at being pregnant.

Client: In my heart. (points to heart)

Counselor/Therapist: In your heart, rather than where you're carrying the child.

Client: I think it means that I'm sorry that I don't want to be pregnant, but I know that I should feel wonderful.

Counselor/Therapist: Should.

Client: My husband and my family. They think it's great that we're having a baby.

Counselor/Therapist: And you don't.

Client: Oh, no, I really do. I just don't think I'm ready.

Counselor/Therapist: But you want to be ready.

Client: My goodness! I really do—but I've been living with this "putting off pregnancy" for so long that I guess if I wasn't pregnant now, I could put it off forever.

By enacting her feelings, the client begins to see that things aren't as bad as she had thought. Some counselors may reject Gestalt therapy because of the perception that the theory is direct and confrontational. Yontef (1993), in describing Perlsian therapy as a "boom-boom-boom approach," claimed that it was characterized by theatrics, abrasiveness, and intense catharsis (p. 201). In recent years, however, with a more intellectual base, the confrontational aspect takes on different dimensions. The therapist suggests challenging experiments that invite clients to face some of their deeper fears. Both counselor and client need to be willing to be active and challenging. One of the more challenging intervention strategies to both counselor and client is the empty-chair experience.

Empty-Chair or Two-Chair Strategy.   An extension of enactment and confrontation, the **empty-chair** (Perls, 1966) or **two-chair** (Clarke & Greenberg, 1986; Greenberg, 1980) strategy allows clients a clearer view of how their behavior may be affecting the behavior of other people. Using this strategy, the practitioner asks the client to play one or more roles in addition to his or her own real self. This is accomplished by providing the necessary number of chairs. The client is then asked to speak the part of each person connected with the problem by moving back and forth from chair to chair. For example, in the case of the reluctantly pregnant young woman, she is asked by the counselor or therapist to respond from the perspective of people who may be part of the presenting problem—her husband, a parent, or a friend—by physically moving to the designated chair. This contributes to the client's awareness that she is not isolated, that others are or may be there for her and may see the situation from a different perspective.

Greenberg (1980), who experimented with and researched the empty-chair or two-chair technique, has turned it into an art form used to resolve decisional conflict. Here clients can play out both sides of their conflict. Greenberg's results appear to reinforce Perls's (1966) premise that this technique results in an awareness of the disparate aspects of experience and contact among these polarities, and leads to integration and conflict resolution. Greenberg and Webster (1982) contend that the two-chair intervention is more effective than traditional problem-solving techniques in counseling and psychotherapy. They use the two-chair technique effectively in resolving decisional conflict as it relates process to outcome.

Dream Work.   Instead of using the Freudian concept of dream interpretation, the Gestaltist uses dreams to help the client in the present, to understand what may be going on in the here and now. Perls believed that dreams are projections of the person, that parts of a person's dream reveal certain aspects of the person (Staemmler, 1994). For instance, dreaming that a friend dies may represent an awareness that some valued part of self is dying or being lost. Thus, the client is asked to reenact the dream in the present and to play out the parts of the dream as if it were happening now. This allows the counselor or therapist to help the client come into contact with, own, and accept responsibility for parts of the self that may not be well known or accepted. Specifically, according to Cushway and Sewell (1992), there are eight steps to follow:

1. Counselor encourages dreamer to recount dream from the start, in the present tense and first person.

2. Counselor helps dreamer to speak the main elements of the dream.

3. Counselor helps dreamer to develop a dialogue between characters and elements in the dream.

4. Counselor supports the dreamer to make the "underdog" stand up to the "top dog."

5. Dreamer continues the method of dialoguing ("hot seat") in order to explore issues.

6. Counselor helps the dreamer consider what the dream tells him or her about the way he or she lives now.

7. Counselor gives feedback and suggests personal work for the dreamer.

8. Counselor and client must focus on what is noticed or felt in the dream work session—asking too many questions is discouraged. This allows the dreamer to take responsibility for his or her statements.

Additional Strategies.   Levitsky and Perls (1970) describe several additional intervention strategies, including the dialogue exercise, making the rounds, unfinished business, playing the projection, rehearsal, and exaggeration. These are worth exploring and should be adapted to the skill of the practitioner and the needs of the client.

Evaluation

Overview

There are several unique contributions made by the Gestalt counseling and psychotherapy model:

- The emphasis on the client's inherent wholeness and capacity for self-awareness. The work of the therapist is to help clients use focused awareness of their own to free up energy for health and growth.

- The application of dialogue in the counseling relationship. The counseling dialogue provides contact between the client and the counselor. Dialogue is used to engage clients, not to manipulate or control them. The goal of the Gestalt therapist is to embody authenticity and responsibility in conversations with the client (Yontef & Simkin, 1989).

- The emphasis on the therapy process rather than reliance solely on techniques. Beginning practitioners often tend to depend on techniques more than process to help their client. In the application of Gestalt therapy this creates difficulties because the process of counseling must be a flexible one according to the personalities and experiences of the counselor and client. This often makes it difficult for the novice therapist to pinpoint an appropriate technique to apply to a particular problem. In Gestalt therapy, any activity that contributes to clients' awareness of self, others, and their experience of the larger world is seen as useful.

- The confrontation with "unfinished business" through dream work or other interventions allows the practitioner to challenge the client's past in a lively and provocative manner. The purpose of engaging the past is for the client to become aware of and work with concerns, even those from the past, that are a part of present experience and therefore undermine the client's current functioning.

- The use of dream work in Gestalt counseling is often confused with the technique of dream interpretation as practiced by counselors using other psychotherapy models, such as psychodynamic approaches in which dream content is interpreted by the therapist. Dream work in Gestalt counseling is action oriented. Clients are encouraged to bring specific parts of the dream to life and experience their meaning directly. They participate actively in understanding the dream's meaning while sharing significant aspects of the dream with the counselor. The aim is to increase awareness of the important themes in their lives.

- Finally, in this age of requirements for accountability to those who pay for services, such as third-party payers, the Gestalt approach lends itself well to treating certain diagnoses. According to Seligman (1986), Gestalt therapy is appropriate for treating certain affective disorders, including anxiety, somatoform, and adjustment disorders as well as occupational and interpersonal problems.

Supporting Research

Yontef and Simkin (1989) point out that Gestalt therapies focus on phenomenology, and the subjective experience of the client does not lend itself well to nomothetic psychotherapy outcome studies. However, evaluation of client outcomes in Gestalt therapy is idiographic—that is, assumed to be based on individual experiences unique to the subject of evaluation. Thus, outcome research on Gestalt therapy is sparse. Although individuals can be questioned about their unique experience of growth in Gestalt therapy, these reports do not lend themselves well to empirical research and the summation of findings via statistical analyses of group data.

Much has been done to extend Perls's individual approach to group work (Frew, 1984; Gladding, 1995; Staemmler, 1994; Yontef & Simkin, 1989). Applying Gestalt principles to families, Nevis and Harris (1988) highlight and reinforce the three constructs of *awareness, contact,* and *withdrawal*. For example, in one videotape, the counselor or therapist demonstrates the pattern she has in mind: how the family arranges itself physically, how they talk to each other, and what theme emerges in the counseling process. In this case, the theme involves the family members' abilities to provide clean, clear, positive messages of support for each other.

Applications of Gestalt therapy are cited in works by Alexander and Harman (1988) and Enns (1987). Alexander and Harman used Gestalt therapy as a means of dealing with the surviving classmates of a student who committed suicide. Through the task process of enhancing students' awareness of their feelings, of the choices for how they would respond both to the student's death and their own feelings, and of the experiences that would keep them in the present and not the past, the authors contended that the students experienced a more long-lasting and effective healing process. The authors believe, however, that this contention cannot be easily measured beyond self-report. They further caution that using a Gestalt approach with traumatic events such as suicide should be done only with "support of comparable theory, knowledge and skill" (1988, p. 283).

Enns presented a proposal for integrating the Gestalt goals of self-responsibility with a feminist perspective that values the web of relationships in women's lives and focuses attention on the "environmental constraints and socialization that affect women's lives" (1987, p. 93). Her use of Gestalt therapy included the empty-chair technique and the exploration of polarities or fantasy journeys.

Yontef and Simkin (1989) note that Perls provided no research to support his model of psychotherapy. Although traditional research on groups of clients is viewed by Gestalt therapists as having limited value in guiding the practice of Gestalt therapy with specific individual clients, they conclude that Gestalt therapy is not opposed to outcome research per se. Gestalt therapists are skeptical of the value of outcome research for informing practice because it fails to account well for therapy process variables. The interested student of Gestalt therapy practice may want to review the contributions many recent researchers (e.g., Ciorni, 1994; Freidman, 1993; Yontef, 1993, 1995) have presented in the *Gestalt Journal*. These add significantly to the work of earlier theorists, including the German psychologists.

Limitations

One of the limitations related to Gestalt counseling and psychotherapy has little to do with the theory itself, but with Perls. The reliance on the workshop format developed during the 1960s seemed to lead to a reliance on Perls himself as a sort of guru who could answer any problem by demonstrating Gestaltism in a workshop, almost like an actor with an adoring audience. According to Miriam Polster (1987a), "We, as Gestalt therapists, often became identified with burlesques of our principles with no possibilities of clarification [other] than [what] is available in any spread of rumor" (p. 34).

Ciorni (1994) suggests the difficulty in applying Gestalt theory across cultures. She indicates that Perls's emphasis (and that of most white American therapists) on "I-ness" may prove a challenge to clients of other cultures (p. 14). However, she makes some suggestions for adapting Gestalt to the Hispanic/Latino culture. Perhaps the crucial factor in applying any Euro-American theory, including Gestalt, is that the counselor or therapist be familiar with and perhaps experienced in working with clients of various cultures before selecting an appropriate theory (Torres-Rivera, Maples, & Thorn, in press).

The temptation for novice counselors is to employ such Gestalt "techniques" (i.e., processes) as empty chair, top dog/underdog, figure-ground, and locating feelings without sufficient practitioner training. However, these processes alone can be of little value in helping the client. For example, the empty-chair or two-chair process was developed by Perls (1969a) to deal with the five layers of neurosis mentioned earlier in this chapter. However, if the practitioner lacks knowledge and understanding of those layers, the client may be misled.

Other limitations of Gestalt counseling and psychotherapy:

- How does a counselor or therapist *prove* that the client has achieved "understanding," "meaning," or "organization" in the helping relationship? While this question is difficult to answer with most theoretical counseling approaches, it is a particular challenge for Gestaltists.

- Perls's work is sometimes seen as a potpourri of various theories—a little Freud, a little Jung, and a lot of the Berlin school—yet Perls seldom credits them for their contributions.

- According to Yontef (1993), some practitioners believe the client's cognitive process is important in counseling work, yet many Gestaltists tend to deemphasize cognition, focusing more on feeling.

- The holistic nature of Gestalt counseling and psychotherapy and its allowances for therapist creativity in developing treatments flies in the face of today's trend toward specialization in the medical field (i.e., medical specialists such as cardiovascular surgeons who treat very specific diseases such as heart disease). However, holism fits the human condition better so there is something to be said for bucking this medical trend.

- Perls's here-and-now orientation could limit the freedom that a counselor or therapist might like to use in exploring the history of an issue, problem, or concern fully.

Despite the limitations that may exist in Gestalt counseling and psychotherapy, its holistic nature is one of its most appealing features. Contrasted with more empirical scientific approaches, it offers a wide variety of opportunities to facilitate the client's journey toward greater health and development.

Summary Chart—Gestalt Theory

Human Nature
Rooted in existentialism and phenomenology, Gestalt counseling and psychotherapy focuses attention on the holistic nature of humankind. Gestalt counselors and psychotherapists strive to encompass the whole organism and operate from the perspective that human beings have the capacity and strength to grow, to develop, and to become the person they want to be. A basic assumption is that individuals can deal with their life problems if they are fully aware of what is happening in and around them.

Major Constructs
There are a number of major constructs connected with Gestalt counseling and psychotherapy: *holism,* the concept of unifying wholes, which includes mind and body, past and present, and individual and environment; *field theory,* the idea that the individual in his or her environment produces a psychological field in which self-regulation

can take place; *figure-ground,* the idea that the client's unfinished business becomes "figure" or foreground during the therapeutic process and everything else temporarily recedes to "ground" or background; *here-and-now orientation,* emphasis on the present rather than on the past or the future for the purpose of promoting the growth process; *boundaries and polarities,* the client's "definition" in relation to the environment and traits existing on the opposite ends of the same continuum.

Goals
1. Identifying themes that are central to the client's self-organization.
2. Conceptualizing the issues and concerns of the client that will guide the sequence, timing, and methods used.
3. Establishing and maintaining a safe professional environment.
4. Providing an atmosphere that invites contact between client and counselor or therapist.

Change Process
Change results from the identification and working through of a variety of blocks or interferences that prevent the client from achieving a holistic integration of all aspects of self and the capacity to achieve responsibility for self. Clients work through the cliché, phony, impasse, implosive, and exploding layers of neurosis during this process.

Interventions
Usually labeled as "experiments" because they are procedures aimed at discovery and not exercises (in the traditional sense) that are designed to control or initiate behavior change. Gestalt interventions may include locating feelings, enactment and confrontation, empty-chair, dream work, dialogue, making the rounds, unfinished business, playing the projection, rehearsal, and exaggeration.

Limitations
1. Deemphasizes the cognitive components of the counseling and psychotherapy process.
2. Often seen as a potpourri of theories and philosophies.
3. Holistic approaches are incompatible with today's emphasis on time-limited, brief approaches.
4. Too much emphasis on the here and now.

The Case of Maria: A Gestalt Approach

According to Torres-Rivera et al. (in press), for any counselor, no matter the theoretical orientation, there are prerequisites to working with a client of a different ethnic or cultural orientation. It is important that the practitioner possess knowledge that is culture-specific to the client, an awareness of self (the counselor's), and skills to help the client that are consonant with the client's culture.

Awareness and wholeness are key constructs for Gestalt counselors to seek to facilitate in clients. Perls's (1948) view seems appropriate as a goal for Maria: "A treatment is finished when the patient achieves the basic requirements: a change in outlook, a technique of adequate self-expression and assimilation, and the ability to extend awareness to the verbal level. He has then reached that state of integration which facilitates its own development and he can safely be left to himself" (p. 585).

Although it may be tempting to the counselor to revert to Maria's past history as the cause of her present problems, one of the values of using Gestalt with Maria is its emphasis on the here and now. Naranjo (1970) suggests nine guidelines that might provide direction for the counselor to use in helping Maria (p. 285):

- Live now.
- Live here.
- Stop imagining.
- Stop unnecessary thinking.
- Express rather than manipulate, justify, or judge.
- Give in to pleasure as well as pain or unpleasantness.
- Accept no should or ought other than your own.
- Take full responsibility for your actions.
- Surrender to being who you are.

Several of these guidelines seem customized for Maria:

Live now. The counselor will help Maria to understand that her past, family, and friends are no longer her support system. She needs to focus on the present and the limits that prevent or assist her in taking control of her life.

Live here. The most significant move she made in her life was to college 200 miles away, and it resulted in the "disaster" of Mark. The counselor can help Maria to understand that the here and now can be her "tools" rather than her "burdens."

Stop imagining and unnecessary thinking. The counselor has a significant advantage here and can assist Maria through dream work, by helping her to use the dream (not interpret it), and by focusing on the boxes and exit signs to help her avoid imagining what she cannot prove. By placing herself in the dream and working through the physical manifestations, Maria can reach the calm she is seeking.

Express rather than manipulate. Maria can be encouraged to take responsibility for her situation. Using bodywork, she can be helped to focus on where she feels abandoned by Mark and knows something is causing estrangement from her children. By focusing on the part of her body that is responding to these issues, the counselor might ease Maria's physical and mental anxiety. Part of a session might follow this pattern:

COUNSELOR: Maria, you described your nightmares as exhausting you because you don't know why you're having them. Perhaps we can relive one of them now by going into the one about the boxes and the shadowy figures.

MARIA: Yes, those figures, I believe they're expecting me to do something, but I'm frightened and I don't know where to turn.

COUNSELOR: Frightened? Where do you feel your fright?

MARIA: My heart! It's pounding and I know I should get out of here.

> COUNSELOR: Should? Is that why your heart is pounding?
> MARIA: Yes, I can't breathe, because I don't know what I should do.
> COUNSELOR: "Should" again.
> MARIA: My parents! My sisters! My priest!
> COUNSELOR: And what about Maria? What does she think *she* should do?

Maria takes a deep breath at this point and says: "I never considered that."

Confrontation and Enactment

Often when counselors remain facilitative and accommodating, as some theories suggest, they can delay the healing process for a client. According to Bates and Johnson (1988) and Maples (1991), confrontation in Gestalt counseling is necessary and can be gracious. When considering Perls's confrontational nature, the counselor often confuses the strategy with the strategist. In Maria's case, confrontation and enactment are necessary to achieve awareness and self-regulation. Passons (1975) states that if the counselor is skilled in the use of confrontation, the client may not realize that he or she has been confronted. Consider the following example:

> COUNSELOR: Maria, in your dedication and commitment to your students, you seem to be using much of the energy that might be focused on your own children. Might that behavior be similar to the treatment you received from your own parents?
> MARIA: That's not true! There's no connection! (fists clenched, tears starting, frowning)
> COUNSELOR: I notice the strong emotion in that statement. Where are you feeling this anger? Why the clenched fists?
> MARIA: You sound just like my mother and my sister. My stomach is churning just like when they say that I'm selfish and neglecting my children.

Empty Chair

According to Freidman (1993), the first stage of chairwork is to enable polarity (between the two sides) to come into awareness and for the client to take responsibility for both sides. Perls saw the two sides as top dog and underdog (1969b). The second stage is to encourage the top dog (in this case, Maria's mother) and the underdog (Maria) to confront one another and to intensify the conflict. The last stage begins when the top dog lets go of the oppositional role and tries to "listen" to the underdog—or as Greenberg (1984) says, "softens." Goodman (in Stoehr, 1994) suggests that the conflict must be joined and suffered through rather than "removed," as in the following example:

> MARIA: My mother never liked anything I did. She just wanted me around to take care of the other kids.
> COUNSELOR: And what does that feel like?
> MARIA: It felt rotten then and it feels rotten now.

COUNSELOR: Tell your mother that now.

MARIA: (addressing empty chair) Mama, you're always criticizing me. I need help now and you're not giving it!

COUNSELOR: (checking to see that Maria is "with" what she's saying) Switch over.

MARIA: (as Mama) Well, you know, Maria, that I only want what's best for you and I'm afraid you'll make another mistake—like Mark.

COUNSELOR: Switch back.

MARIA: That's insane! If you love me so much, why don't you help me? I'm so depressed all the time.

MARIA: (as Mama) Well, if you hadn't married Mark, you'd be happy now and have no reason for all of your nightmares and depression.

COUNSELOR: As Mama, what do you feel now?

MARIA: (as Mama) That she's messed up her life!

Maria and the empty chair (Mama) continue to lash out at each other back and forth until the counselor says to "Mama":

COUNSELOR: What do you need from Maria?

MARIA: (as Mama) To make me feel that I'm not responsible.

COUNSELOR: How?

MARIA: (as Mama) By living her life the way she was brought up.

COUNSELOR: To make up for your *own* failure?

MARIA: (as Mama) Dear God, am I really responsible!

The process continues with some emphasis on unfinished business until Maria sees and appreciates the impact that her family has had on her self-esteem, her dreams, and her role as a mother.

Maria reaches awareness and takes the first steps toward self-regulation, following eight additional sessions with the counselor.

References

Alexander, J., & Harman, R. (1988). One counselor's intervention in the aftermath of a middle school student's suicide: A case study. *Journal of Counseling and Development, 66,* 283–285.

Bates, M., & Johnson, C. (1988). *Group leadership: A manual for leaders* (2nd ed.). Denver: Love.

Bates, M., Johnson, C., & Blaker, J. (1982). *Group leadership.* Denver: Love.

Cadwallader, E. (1984). Values in Fritz Perls' Gestalt therapy: On the dangers of half-truths. *Counseling and Values, 4,* 192–201.

Ciorni, S. (1994). The importance of background in Gestalt therapy. *Gestalt Journal, 18*(2), 7–34.

Clarke, K., & Greenberg, L. (1986). Differential effects of the Gestalt two-chair intervention and problem-solving in resolving decisional conflict. *Journal of Counseling Psychology, 33*(1), 11–15.

Clarkson, P., & Mackeron, J. (1993). *Fritz Perls.* Newbury Park, CA: Sage.

Cushway, D., & Sewell, R. (1992). *Counseling with dreams and nightmares.* London: Sage.

Dryden, W. (Ed.). (1984). *Individual therapies: A comparative analysis in individual therapy in Britain.* London: Open University Press.

Dye, A., & Hackney, H. (1975). *Gestalt approaches to counseling.* Boston: Houghton Mifflin.

Ehrenfels, C. (1890). Vierteljahrsschrift fur wissenschaftliche Philosophie. Richard Avenarius (Ed.) in *Journal of Scientific Philosophy* as quoted in Smith, B. (1988). *Foundations of Gestalt theory.* Berlin: Philosophic Verlag Munchen Wien.

Emerson, P., & Smith, E. (1974). Contributions of Gestalt psychology to Gestalt therapy. *Counseling Psychologist, 4,* 8–13.

Enns, C. (1987). Gestalt therapy and feminist therapy: A proposed integration. *Journal of Counseling and Development, 66,* 93–95.

Enright, J. (1970). An introduction to Gestalt techniques. In J. Fagan & I. Shepherd (Eds.), *Gestalt therapy now: Theory, techniques, and applications.* Palo Alto: Science & Behavior Books.

Freidman, N. (1993). Fritz Perls's "layers" and the empty chair: A reconsideration. *Gestalt Journal, 16*(2), 94–113.

Frew, J. (1984). Enlarging what is not figured in the Gestalt group. *Journal for Specialists in Group Work, 8,* 175–181.

Gazda, G. (1986). *Human relations development: A manual for educators.* Boston: Allyn & Bacon.

Gilliland, B., James, R., & Bowman, J. (1994). *Theories and strategies in counseling and psychotherapy.* Upper Saddle River, NJ: Prentice Hall.

Gladding, S. (1995). *Groups: A counseling specialty* (2nd ed.). Upper Saddle River, NJ: Merrill/Prentice Hall.

Greenberg, L. (1980). An intensive analysis of recurring events from the practice of Gestalt therapy. *Psychotherapy: Therapy, Research and Practice, 17,* 143–152.

Greenberg, L. (1984). A task analysis of interpersonal conflict resolution. In L. N. Rice & L. S. Greenberg (Eds.) *Patterns of change: Intensive analysis of psychotherapy process.* New York: Guilford.

Greenberg, L., & Webster, M. (1982). Resolving decisional conflict by Gestalt two-chair dialogue relating process to outcome. *Journal of Counseling Psychology, 29*(5), 468–477.

Hartmann, G. (1935). *Gestalt psychology: A survey of facts and principles.* New York: Ronald Press.

Henle, M. (Ed.). (1971). *The selected papers of Wolfgang Köhler.* New York: Liveright.

Henle, M. (1978). Gestalt psychology and Gestalt therapy. *Journal of the History of Behavioral Sciences, 14,* 23–32.

Hormann, H. (1967). Wolfgang Köhler zum gedenken. *Psychologische Forschung, 31,* xvii.

Kempler, W. (1973). Gestalt therapy. In R. Corsini (Ed.), *Current psychotherapies* (pp. 251–286). Itasca, IL: Peacock.

Koffka, K. (1935). *Principles of Gestalt psychology.* New York: Harcourt, Brace, & World.

Kogan, G. (1976). The genesis of Gestalt therapy. In C. Hatcher & P. Hililstein (Eds.), *The handbook of Gestalt therapy* (pp. 255–257). New York: Aronson.

Köhler, W. (1929). *Gestalt psychology.* New York: Horace Liveright.

Latner, J. (1992). Origin and development of Gestalt therapy. In E. C. Nevis (Ed.), *Gestalt therapy: Perspectives and applications.* Cleveland: Gestalt Institute of Cleveland Press.

Levitsky, A., & Perls, F. S. (1970). The rules and games of Gestalt therapy. In J. Fagan & I. Shepherd (Eds.), *Gestalt therapy now: Theory, techniques, and applications* (pp. 140–149). Palo Alto: Science & Behavior Books.

Lewin, K. (1935). *A dynamic theory of personality.* New York: McGraw-Hill.

Maples, M. (1992). *Gestalt counseling session with pregnant female client* [Videotape]. Reno: University of Nevada, Instructional Media Center.

Maples, M. (1996). Conerstones of a civilized society: Law, morality, faith and spirituality. *Juvenile and Family Court Journal, 47*(3), 41–60.

Naranjo, C. (1970). Present-centeredness: Techniques, prescriptions, and ideals. In C. Hatcher & P. Hililstein (Eds.), *The handbook of Gestalt therapy* (pp. 320–321). New York: Aronson.

Nevis, S., & Harris, V. (1988). *A session of Gestalt therapy with families* [Videotape]. Cleveland: Gestalt Institute of Cleveland.

Passons, W. (1975). *Gestalt approaches in counseling.* New York: Holt, Rinehart, & Winston.

Perls, F. (1947). *Ego, hunger, and aggression: The beginning of Gestalt therapy.* New York: Random House.

Perls, F. (1948). Theory and technique of personality integration. *American Journal of Psychotherapy, 2,* 563–585.

Perls, F. (1951). *Gestalt therapy: Excitement and growth in the human personality.* New York: Julian Press.

Perls, F. (1966). *The meaning of Gestalt therapy*. Workshop presented in Atlanta, GA (cited in Fagan & Shepherd, 1970, pp. 360–362).

Perls, F. (1969a). *Gestalt therapy verbatim*. Lafayette, CA: Real Person Press.

Perls, F. (1969b). *In and out of the garbage pail*. Lafayette, CA: Real Person Press.

Perls, F. (1972). *The Gestalt approach*. Ben Lomand, CA: Science & Behavior Books.

Perls, F. (1973). *The Gestalt approach and eyewitness to therapy*. New York: Bantam.

Perls, F., Hefferline, N., & Goodman, P. (1951). *Gestalt therapy*. New York: Dell.

Perls, L. (1982). A workshop with Laura Perls. In E. W. L. Smith (Ed.), *Gestalt voices*. Norwood, NJ: Ablex.

Polster, E., & Polster, M. (1973a). *Gestalt therapy integrated*. New York: Vintage.

Polster, E., & Polster, M. (1973b). *Gestalt therapy integrated: Contours of theory and practice*. New York: Brunner/Mazel.

Polster, M. (1987a). *Every person's life is a novel*. New York: Norton.

Polster, M. (1987b). Gestalt therapy: Evolution and application. In J. K. Zeig (Ed.), *The evolution of psychotherapy*. New York: Brunner/Mazel.

Rock, I., & Palmer, S. (1990). *The legacy of Gestalt psychology*. Springfield, IL: Charles C Thomas.

Rosenblatt, G. (1991). Interview with Laura Perls. *Gestalt Journal, 12*(2), 16–27.

Rosenfeld, E. (1978/1982). An oral history of Gestalt therapy part one: A conversation with Laura Perls. *The Gestalt Journal*. Highland, New York.

Segal, M. (1997). *Points of influence: A guide to using personality theory at work*. San Francisco: Jossey-Bass.

Seligman, L. (1986). *Diagnosis and treatment planning and counseling*. New York: Human Sciences Press.

Shepherd, M. (1975). *Fritz*. New York: Saturday Review Press.

Simkin, J. (1975). An introduction to Gestalt therapy. In F. Stephenson (Ed.), *Gestalt therapy primer* (pp. 9–10). Springfield, IL: Charles C Thomas.

Smith, B. (Ed.). (1988). *Foundations of Gestalt psychology*. Munich: Philosophia Verlag.

Smith, E. (1976). *The growing edge of Gestalt therapy*. New York: Brunner/Mazel.

Staemmler, F. (1994). On layers and phases: A message from overseas. *Gestalt Journal, 17*(1), 5–31.

Stoehr, T. (1994). *Here, now, next: Paul Goodman and the origins of Gestalt therapy*. San Francisco: Jossey-Bass.

Swanson, J. (1984). *Gestalt counseling with an adult client* [Videotape]. Corvallis: Oregon State University, Communications Media Productions.

Tillett, R. (1991). Active and non-verbal therapeutic approaches. In J. Holmes (Ed.), *Textbook of psychotherapy in psychiatric practice*. Edinburgh: Churchill Livingstone.

Torres-Rivera, E., Maples, M., & Thorn, A. (in press). Who is teaching multicultural counseling in CACREP accredited institutions? *Counselor Education and Supervision*.

Wallen, G. (1970). Gestalt therapy and Gestalt psychology. In J. Fagan & I. Shepherd (Eds.), *Gestalt therapy now: Theory, techniques, and applications* (pp. 116–117). Palo Alto: Science & Behavior Books.

Wertheimer, M. (1912). *Perception of apparent movement*. New York: Harper.

Wheeler, G. (1991). *Gestalt reconsidered: A new approach to contact and resistance*. New York: Gardner.

Wysong, J., & Rosenfeld, E. (1982). *An oral history of Gestalt therapy*. Highland, NY: The Gestalt Journal Press.

Yontef, G. (1981). *Gestalt therapy: Past, present, and future*. Paper presented at the International Council of Psychologists conference, London.

Yontef, G. (1993). *Awareness, dialogue, and process: Essays on Gestalt therapy*. Highland, NY: The Gestalt Journal Press.

Yontef, G. (1995). Gestalt therapy. In A. Gurman & S. Messer (Eds.) *Essential psychotherapies: Theories and practice*. New York: Guilford Press.

Yontef, G., & Simkin, J. (1989). Gestalt therapy. In R. Corsini & D. Wedding (Eds.), *Current psychotherapies* (4th ed.) (pp. 323–361). Itasca, IL: Peacock.

Zinker, J. (1978). *Creative process in Gestalt therapy*. New York: Vintage.

Cognitive-Behavioral Theories

Cynthia R. Kalodner
West Virginia University

Cognitive-behavioral theories are best conceptualized as a general category of theories, or a set of related theories, which have evolved from the theoretical writings, clinical experiences, and empirical studies of behavioral and cognitively oriented psychologists and other mental health workers. The hyphenated term **cognitive-behavioral** reflects the importance of both behavioral and cognitive approaches to understanding and helping human beings. The hyphen brings together behavioral and cognitive theoretical views, each with its own theoretical assumptions and intervention strategies. The amalgamation of cognitive and behavioral theory is described as "a purposeful attempt to preserve the demonstrated efficiencies of behavior modification within a less doctrinaire context and to incorporate the cognitive activities of the client in the efforts to produce therapeutic change" (Kendall & Hollon, 1979, p. 1).

Throughout this chapter, the blending of aspects of behavioral and cognitive approaches into cognitive-behavioral counseling and psychotherapy can be seen. There is no single definition of cognitive-behavioral theory since there are so many different cognitive-behavioral theories. At present there are over twenty different forms of theoretical approaches that fit into a cognitive-behavioral conceptualization (Craighead, Craighead, Kazdin, & Mahoney, 1994). Many current theories fit into the category of cognitive-behavioral, including (but not limited to) Beck's **cognitive therapy** (Beck, 1976; Beck, Rush, Shaw, & Emery, 1979), Ellis's **rational-emotive behavior therapy** (1962, 1993), and Meichenbaum's **stress inoculation training** (1985) and **self-instruction training** (1977). Although there are differences among the approaches, all of these theorists value the role cognitions play in the development and maintenance of psychological problems (Hollon & Beck, 1994). This chapter provides an overview of the highlights of these cognitive-behavioral approaches to helping people.

Background

To understand cognitive-behavioral theories, it is necessary to study the history of the development of behavioral theory, various cognitive models, and the union of these approaches into cognitive-behavioral theories.

Watson and the Beginnings of Behavior Theory

Early behaviorism was based on learning theory, the development of clearly defined techniques, and systematic, well-designed research (Hayes & Hayes, 1992). The behavioral history of cognitive-behavioral theory began with the behavioral approaches developed by **John B. Watson,** who is usually recognized as the most influential person in the development of behaviorism (Craighead, Craighead, & Ilardi, 1995). **Behaviorism** was formed as a reaction against the Freudian emphasis on the unconscious as the subject matter of psychology and introspection as the method of its investigation. Watson (1930) claimed that behavior should be the sole subject matter of psychology, and that it should be studied through observation. Furthermore, according to Watson, conscious processes (e.g., thinking) were determined to be outside the realm of scientific inquiry.

Using **Pavlov's** principles of classical conditioning, in which unconditioned stimuli (loud bell) paired with conditioned stimuli (white rat) lead to a conditioned response (startle), Watson trained Little Albert to fear a white rat, white cotton, and even Watson's white hair! This demonstration is important because it indicates that human emotions can be learned and modified using learning principles. There are several other well-known conditioning model behaviorists, including Eysenck, Rachman, and Wolpe, who developed treatments such as systematic desensitization and flooding, based on classical conditioning and counterconditioning (Kazdin & Wilson, 1978). The relationship between stimulus and response is essential to these classical behavioral paradigms.

A critical contribution Watson brought to psychology is the methodology for conducting research. Methodological behaviorism is concerned with procedures for scientific inquiry and data collection. It has the following characteristics: an assumption of determinism; an emphasis on observation of behavior and environmental stimuli; the use of specific operational definitions of independent and dependent variables such that measurement is reliable; the necessity to be able to falsify the hypotheses through research; use of controlled experimentation; replication of research findings allows generalization to other subjects or situations. Methodological behaviorism continues to have a strong influence on cognitive-behavioral research.

Skinner and Operant Conditioning

The work of **B. F. Skinner** on the principles of reinforcement and operant conditioning further developed the school of behaviorism. Skinner is the best-known and most controversial figure in the field of behaviorism (Craighead et al., 1995). Despite the fact that until his death, in 1991, Skinner maintained an adamant denial of the importance of cognitions and affect in understanding of human behavior, his work has been tremendously influential in the field of counseling and psychotherapy. Skinner developed applied behavioral analysis, which is based on **operant conditioning.** In operant conditioning, reinforcers shape behavior by being contingent on the response (Kazdin & Wilson, 1978; Miller, 1980). Skinner's schedules of reinforcement (1969) define how different amounts of reinforcement can be delivered to continue to support behavioral changes. Key interventions in applied behavior analysis include reinforcement, punishment, extinction, and stimulus control, each of which involves a search for environmental variables that will lead to changes in behavior.

In operant conditioning, reinforcement is used to increase behavior. Examples of positive reinforcement include praise or money. Negative reinforcement, which also increases behavior, involves the removal of a negative stimulus, such as electric shock or a ringing bell. An example of negative reinforcement is turning off a loud bell after a rat presses a bar. Punishment and extinction decrease behavior by the addition of an aversive stimulus or the removal of a positive reinforcer, respectively. An example of punishment involves following cigarette smoking with electric shock. In extinction, a behavior to be decreased is ignored; a person who has the habit of interrupting conversation is ignored by friends when he or she interrupts, but friends listen when the comment is made in conversation without interrupting. These and many other applied behavior analysis techniques are included in Miller's (1980) text, which is a programmed learning manual designed to demonstrate the role of behavioral techniques in everyday situations.

Wolpe and Systematic Desensitization

Joseph Wolpe is another major contributor in the development of behavior therapy. **Systematic desensitization,** a behavioral procedure used to treat phobias, is the most thoroughly investigated behavioral procedure to treat simple phobias (Emmelkamp, 1994). According to the theory of reciprocal inhibition which underlies systematic desensitization, when a response incompatible with anxiety (i.e., relaxation) is paired with an anxiety-evoking stimuli (whatever the client reports is anxiety-producing), then the association between the anxiety-producing stimulus and anxiety will be lessened (Wolpe, 1958). Through the use of systematic desensitization, clients are "desensitized" to their fears. First, clients are taught to use progressive relaxation to become completely relaxed. Using a hierarchy of stimuli arranged with the least-anxiety-provoking first and the most-anxiety-provoking last, the counselor asks the client to imagine each stimulus while remaining relaxed. Kalodner (1998) provides details on the technique of systematic desensitization.

A Brief History of Cognitive Therapy

The cognitive revolution brought forth by Beck and Ellis and others began as clinicians found that the available systems of therapy were not satisfactory. **Albert Ellis** is usually credited with formulating the first comprehensive model of cognitive intervention (Craighead et al., 1995). As Ellis (1962) pointed out, "Human beings . . . are not the same as Pavlovian dogs or other lower animals; and their emotional disturbances are quite different from the experimental neuroses and other emotional upsets we produce in the laboratory" (p. 14). He found that the language aspects of neurosis were missing in other theoretical systems and believed that individuals have psychological difficulties owing to their ability to communicate with others and with themselves in a manner that is different from what is available to animals. The basis of Ellis's rational-emotive behavior therapy is that human beings generate psychological disturbances by faulty or **irrational thinking.** Through the Institute for Rational Living, Ellis and his colleagues have been very influential in developing this therapeutic approach, which will be described in greater detail later in this chapter.

Aaron Beck (1976) also responded with dissatisfaction to psychoanalysis and behavior therapy. Though trained as a psychoanalyst, Beck objected to the unconscious aspects of Freud's theory, asserting that people can be aware of factors that are responsible for emotional upsets and blurred thinking. Beck indicated that his work with depressed individuals did not substantiate the psychoanalytic theory (Weinrach, 1988). At the same time, he found the radical behavioral explanation for human emotional disturbance to be too limited to adequately explain human emotional difficulties. For Beck, psychological disturbances may be the result of "faulty learning, making incorrect inferences on the basis of inadequate or incorrect information, and not distinguishing adequately between imagination and reality" (1976, pp. 19–20). Beck's work in cognitive therapy has been extremely influential in the treatment of depression and has been expanded to other psychological problems. The basics of his theory will be presented later in this chapter.

Human Nature: A Developmental Perspective

One wonders what "development" is for behaviorists and cognitive-behaviorists. Early behavioral theory, with its emphasis on learning, seems somewhat antithetical to developmentalism. Early behaviorists' view of the development of human nature was limited to the learning concepts of operant and classical conditioning. Individuals, born with a **tabula rosa** (blank slate), learn to associate stimuli and responses; development can be seen as the sum total of these associations.

Cognitive-behavioral theories are not developmental in the same sense that stage theories are. There is a stated assumption that behavior is learned (Kazdin & Wilson, 1978; Mueser & Liberman, 1995); this applies equally to the explanation of how problem behaviors and adaptive behaviors are developed. Behavior is assumed to be developed and maintained by external events or cues, by external reinforcers, or by internal processes such as cognition. Development is based on each individual's different learning history, the unique experiences provided by the environment, and the individual's cognitive understanding of the world.

The use of the here-and-now, ahistorical perspective in cognitive-behavioral therapy highlights the emphasis on the present in understanding the presenting problems of a client. Childhood learning experiences are not usually the variables that are functionally related to current behavior, and the functional relationship is critical to assessment and treatment. Except as they may relate to present problems, past problems are not attended to in the same way as they might be within other counseling and psychotherapy systems (Beck et al., 1979). Since current problems are influenced by individual social learning history, past problems are not ignored, though it is clear that there is a relative lack of importance of early childhood experiences.

Major Constructs

Since cognitive-behavioral theories are an amalgamation of behavioral and cognitive approaches, the cognitive-behavioral theoretical constructs contain aspects of both behavioral and cognitive theory. Considering the separate behavioral and cognitive roots may illustrate the key constructs in cognitive-behavioral theories. Kendall and Hollon (1979) consider the treatment target, treatment approach and treatment evaluation for behavioral, cognitive, and cognitive-behavioral theories (see Table 11.1). For behavioral interventions, purely behavioral terms such as *behavioral excesses or deficits, learning theory,* and *observed changes in behavior* are used. Likewise, the cognitive interventions are based on purely cognitive terms such as *cognitive excesses or deficits, semantic interventions* (cognitive), and *changes in cognitions.*

   Cognitive-behavioral interventions are considered to encompass a range of approaches limited by the purer behavioral and cognitive interventions (Kendall & Hollon, 1979). Treatment targets range from behavioral excesses and deficits to cognitive excesses and deficits, and cognitive-behavioral interventions target both cognitive and behavioral excesses and deficits. The treatment interventions also range from an emphasis on behavioral interventions, to an emphasis on cognitive interventions with some behavioral strategies included, to a full integration of cognitive and behavioral strategies. The evaluation strategy associated with cognitive-behavioral counseling and psychotherapy interventions includes an emphasis on behavior changes, to an emphasis on cognitive changes, and in the middle are observed changes in behavior and cognition with methodological rigor. What cognitive-behavioral theories provide, given this amalgamation model, is

Table 11.1
General Characteristics of Cognitive-Behavioral Interventions

	Treatment Target	Treatment Approach	Treatment Evaluation
Behavioral	Behavioral excesses or deficits	Behavioral "learning theory" interventions. Environmental manipulations (e.g., token economies, contingency management)	Observed changes in behavior with rigorous evaluation
Cognitive-Behavioral	Behavioral excesses or deficits	Behavioral interventions. Skills training, information provision (e.g., modeling, role playing)	Observed changes in behavior with rigorous evaluation
	Behavioral and cognitive excesses or deficits	Broadly conceived behavioral and cognitive methods	Observed changes in behavior and cognition with methodological rigor
	Cognitive excesses or deficits	Cognitive interventions with adjunctive behavioral procedures	Examination of cognitive and, to a lesser extent, of behavioral changes
Cognitive	Cognitive excesses or deficits	Semantic interventions	Changes in cognitions, "integrative changes," often, but not always, nonempirically evaluated

Source: From Hollon, S. D., & Kendall, P. C. (1979). Cognitive-behavioral interventions: Theory and procedure. In P. C. Kendall & S. D. Hollon (Eds.), *Cognitive-behavioral interventions: Theory, research, and procedures* (pp. 445–454). New York: Academic Press. Copyright 1979 by Academic Press. Reprinted by permission.

greater flexibility in treatment targets and interventions, with an emphasis on rigorous standards in measurement of change and research evaluation (Kendall & Hollon, 1979).

The Importance of Cognitions

The unifying characteristic of cognitive-behavioral counseling and psychotherapy approaches is the fundamental emphasis on the importance of cognitive workings and private events as mediators of behavior change (Craighead et al., 1995; Hollon & Beck, 1994). All cognitive interventions attempt to produce change by influencing thinking, which is assumed to play a causal role in the development and maintenance of psychological problems (Hollon & Beck, 1994). The relationship between thoughts and behavior is a major aspect of cognitive-behavioral theory and counseling and psychotherapy. The cognitive-behavioral approaches assume that cognitive processes mediate behavior and experience, that these processes can be studied and altered, and that desired behavior change can be achieved through cognitive change (Dobson & Block, 1988).

The Importance of Learning

The cognitive-behavioral model of psychological disturbance asserts that abnormal behavior is learned and developed the same way that normal behavior is learned and that cognitive-behavioral principles can be applied to change the behavior (Mueser & Liberman, 1995). The importance of this statement lies in the focus on learning as the way behavior is acquired, rather than underlying intrapsychic conflicts. It rejects the psychodynamic and quasi-disease models of development, which assume that underlying intrapsychic conflicts cause maladaptive behavior.

The Importance of Operational Definitions and Functional Analysis

In cognitive-behavioral approaches, problems are viewed operationally. The definition of the presenting problem must be concrete and specific, and observable whenever possible. It is assumed that problems are functionally related to internal and external **antecedents** and **consequences.** This assumption means that in order to understand behavior, it is necessary to know the events that precede (antecedents) and follow (consequences) the behavior. These events may be external and observable behaviors or internal thoughts and feelings. The functional relationship conceptualization of problems necessitates a clear understanding of the internal and external antecedents that contribute to a problematic behavior, as well as the internal and external consequences that maintain behavior. This also means that the causes and treatments of problems should be multidimensional. Causes might include behaviors, environmental circumstances, thoughts, beliefs, or attitudes. Treatments are addressed in the intervention section of this chapter. Since there is rarely a single cause for a problem, treatments are comprehensive and designed to address the multiple issues.

Although it is beyond the scope of this chapter to provide details on Lazarus's multimodal approach, the concept of the BASIC ID provides an excellent example of the importance of operational definitions and functional analysis. **BASIC ID** is an acronym for behavior, affect, sensation, imagery, cognition, interpersonal relationships, and biological factors (the D represents drugs, but is intended to include the broader base of biological factors) (Lazarus, 1985). The multimodal approach is used to assess the presenting problems and to develop interventions based on responses to the information in each of the BASIC ID categories. Interested readers are encouraged to pursue additional information about multimodal therapy in Lazarus's work (1985, 1990).

The Importance of Therapeutic Empathy

Often when cognitive-behavioral counseling is described, the techniques and theory are emphasized while the importance of the relationship between the client and the counselor or therapist is underemphasized. This inaccuracy is unfortunate (in most cases, although there is a prominent exception which is described below). Although cognitive-behavioral treatment manuals focus on the specific treatment techniques, the helping relationship is also addressed. Both Beck and Meichenbaum describe the importance of the relationship and include strategies for developing a therapeutic relationship in their manuals.

Burns and Auerbach (1996) highlight the necessity for a warm, empathic therapeutic relationship in cognitive therapy. They provide an empathy scale that patients can use to rate how warm, genuine, and empathic their therapists were during a recent session. The necessary and sufficient conditions for personality change developed by Carl Rogers are included in Beck's cognitive therapy as "necessary, but not sufficient." In other words, these factors form the basis for the relationship, but the techniques of cognitive therapy are viewed as necessary to produce therapeutic change. The efficacy of the intervention is dependent on a relationship that is characterized by therapist warmth, accurate empathy, and genuineness (Beck et al., 1993).

Ellis takes a different view of the helping relationship. In his 1962 text on rational-emotive therapy, Ellis downplayed its importance. More recently, he has indicated that therapeutic empathy may not even be desirable (Ellis, personal communication to D. Burns, 1993, cited in Burns & Auerbach, 1996), since empathy may help a client to feel better, but the temporary mood elevation may prevent the client from doing the necessary work to actually get better.

Applications

Overview

There is great variability in the interventions practiced in cognitive-behavioral counseling and psychotherapy. Cognitive-behavioral interventions include various combinations of cognitive and behavioral techniques and are aimed at changing either cognitions, behavior, or both (Kendall & Hollon, 1979; see Table 11.1). Cognitive-behavioral interventions are directive, structured, goal-directed, and time-limited treatment, and most types involve the client in a collaborative relationship with the counselor or therapist. The use of homework assignments and skills practice is common, along with a focus on problem-solving ability.

Goals of Counseling and Psychotherapy: Beginning With Assessment

Before selecting a goal for counseling or conducting any intervention with a client, the counselor or therapist must be able to answer the following four questions (Mueser & Liberman, 1995): First, what are the problems and goals for therapy? This includes the presenting problem understood in terms of the full range of behavior, affective, cognitive, and social aspects. Second, how can progress in counseling be measured and monitored? Since behaviorally oriented counselors are often focused on measuring outcome, it is important to know how the changes will be noted. For example, perhaps the counselor or therapist will ask the client to keep a diary of maladaptive thoughts, or a count of binge eating episodes. Third, what are the environmental contingencies maintaining the behavior? This refers to the relationship between the problems and the antecedents and consequences. For example, a client's depressed feelings may follow negative evaluations of schoolwork or job performance. And fourth, which interventions are more likely to be effective? Interventions that have been empirically supported (i.e., research has demonstrated that these treatments work for this type of problem with this type of client) are preferred.

Counselors or therapists using a cognitive-behavioral theoretical orientation begin work with clients by using a behavioral assessment framework to collect information (Nelson & Barlow, 1981). Behavioral assessment, perhaps now better titled "cognitive-behavioral assessment," has evolved from its early emphasis on purely observable behavior to include cognition and cognitive processes. A comprehensive behavioral assessment attends not only to overt behavior, but also to emotional and cognitive behaviors (Galassi & Perot, 1992; Nelson & Barlow, 1981). As a result of the cognitive revolution, assessment strategies have been developed to collect information from clients about their imagery, attributions, beliefs, expectations, and self-statements (Galassi & Perot, 1992).

The **triple response mode** (Nelson & Barlow, 1981) provides a conceptual framework for counselors or therapists conducting assessment. This term refers to attention to overt behavior, emotional-physiological, and cognitive-verbal areas. It is critical that the counselor or therapist ask questions with the intention of collecting data in these three modes to obtain a complete functional analysis of behavior. The overt behavior response might be assessed by asking, "If I were watching you, what would I see you do?" Emotional-physiological data could be obtained by asking, "How does your body react?" And the cognitive-verbal area could be questioned with "What statements run through your mind?" (Nelson & Barlow, 1981).

The purposes of behavioral interviewing are to identify the target behavior and the controlling variables and to plan an appropriate intervention (Nelson & Barlow, 1981). Behavioral assessment focuses on the current determinants of behavior, since these are viewed as more important than past behavior in selecting an appropriate intervention (Mueser & Liberman, 1995). Behavioral assessment is concerned with what the client does, feels, and thinks in particular situations. The counselor or therapist works to define the presenting problem concretely and to understand the antecedents and consequences of the problem.

The counselor or therapist begins the assessment by asking the client to describe the problem. However, clients do not always describe the most important problem in initial sessions. Sometimes they may not be ready to reveal the true problem until they have developed trust and confidence in the practitioner (Nelson & Barlow, 1981). It is for this reason that a global assessment is recommended. There are several structured interviews that assess employment, sleep, stress, and relationships (e.g., Lazarus, 1990). The counselor or therapist can then use information derived from the structured interview along with the initial description of the presenting problem to develop an accurate picture of the problem.

Behavioral assessment may include the use of questionnaires, role playing to assess certain skills (interpersonal, phobias), and interviews with significant others (Nelson & Barlow, 1981). An often-used assessment tool is self-monitoring, in which clients are asked to record their thoughts, feelings, and behaviors as they happen. For example, an individual in treatment for social anxiety might be asked to keep records of attempts to talk to strangers. These records might include the thoughts before trying to say something, pre-approach feelings rated on an intensity scale of 1 to 10, the comment actually made, and affective reaction to the situation. Open-ended comments may also be helpful in planning interventions.

Behavioral assessment is idiographic (concerned with the individual) in that it attempts to understand the antecedents and consequences of behavior for the individual client (Galassi & Perot, 1992). This is important because it is this specificity that is necessary to develop individualized treatment plans. One of the contributions of the behavioral approaches is the close relationship between assessment and treatment (Galassi & Perot, 1992).

The Process of Change

The process of change is concerned with understanding how the theory explains the mechanisms for therapeutic change. This is particularly important in the cognitive-behavioral arena since there are many different theories and many different interventions.

Self-Efficacy.   The **self-efficacy theory** of **Albert Bandura** (1977, 1986) has been used to provide a cognitive-behavioral theoretical explanation for how people change. It has been proposed as a common pathway to explain how people change despite using different therapeutic techniques. Self-efficacy theory asserts that individuals develop expectations for their success in performing specific behaviors and that these expectations influence their decision to try new behaviors and maintain behavioral changes (Bandura, 1977, 1986). Self-efficacy may be thought of as a sense of personal competence or feelings of mastery. The degree to which a person feels efficacious influences the amount of effort that he or she will apply in given situations. Thus, cognitive-behavioral therapy may work through increasing self-efficacy of clients.

Bandura (1986) described four mechanisms through which self-efficacy can be developed: **enactive attainments, vicarious experience, verbal persuasion,** and **recognition of physiological state.** Enactive attainments, the most powerful contributors to self-efficacy development, refer to an individual's own experience with achieving a goal. Vicarious experiences refer to observing others as they succeed or fail. Through the process of observing, individuals are provided with a basis for making comparisons to their own competence to perform the task. Verbal persuasion is a less powerful way to influence self-efficacy. The final source of self-efficacy, physiological states, refers to the emotional arousal or degree of apprehension one feels. Feelings of fear may lead to a decreased performance, whereas a moderate amount of anxiety may be helpful when performing a new task.

Examples of how clients learn assertive behavior can be used to apply these sources of self-efficacy. When clients are taught assertiveness skills, they practice making appropriate assertive comments. Enactive attainments are the experience of success which leads clients to feel able to repeat the assertive behavior. In assertiveness training groups, clients watch each other perform new behaviors; this is an example of vicarious experiences. Verbal persuasion is the source of self-efficacy based on telling clients "You can do it"; like encouragement, it might increase self-efficacy, but other sources are more powerful. The physiological states mechanism can be used in assertiveness training to inform clients that a moderate amount of anxiety may be helpful as they attempt to make changes in their behavior.

It is important to recognize that when applying the self-efficacy model to how cognitive therapy and other cognitive-behavioral interventions work, all four of the sources of self-efficacy are involved. In the process of learning that cognitions contribute to behavior and affective difficulties, enactive attainments, vicarious experiences, verbal persuasion, and physiological states play major roles.

Does Changing Beliefs Lead to Change in Behavior?   Addressing the question of how people change, Beck (1976) asserts that behavioral and affective change are hypothesized to occur through the change in cognitions. The assumption is clearly that changing beliefs is the key to helping people. Research has demonstrated that cognitive therapy does indeed change thoughts and that there are reductions in psychological disturbances. However, it has not been clearly demonstrated that changes in cognitions cause changes in behavior or affect. In fact, changes in cognition occur in behavioral programs not designed to change thoughts (DeLucia & Kalodner, 1990) and in pharmacological treatment (see Hollon & Beck, 1994).

Intervention Strategies

Since cognitive-behavioral interventions include aspects of both behavioral and cognitive interventions, this section will provide a few examples of some commonly used intervention strategies. The separation of behavioral, cognitive, and cognitive-behavioral techniques is rather artificial, since most cognitive procedures include behavioral components and some behavioral interventions also contain cognitive elements (Emmelkamp, 1994). However, in spite of this, a sample of some techniques most often associated with behavioral approaches follows. In addition, cognitive interventions are described briefly. The greatest attention is devoted to providing detail of several cognitive-behavioral theories of counseling and psychotherapy.

Behavioral Interventions.   Behavioral interventions focus primarily on changing specific behaviors. Examples of purely behavioral interventions include reinforcement, extinction, shaping, stimulus control, and aversive control (Miller, 1980).

Reinforcement is a well-known behavioral strategy. **Positive reinforcement** is a procedure in which some behavior is increased by following it with something rewarding; for example, children who clean their room are given praise and attention, a gold star, or a new toy. Most important about reinforcement is that the receiver views the reinforcer as positive. **Negative reinforcement** is the removal of something aversive to increase behavior. The buzz most cars make when the key is put in the ignition is a negative reinforcer designed to increase seat belt use. Both positive and negative reinforcement increase behavior and can be applied when clients want to increase a behavior.

Extinction is a behavioral intervention designed to decrease a problematic behavior. In this case, a reinforcer that has followed the behavior in the past is removed, and the problem behavior decreases. By way of an example, think about the child who repeatedly gets out of his or her seat in a classroom. When the teacher notices and asks the child to sit down, the child may return to the seat. However, the attention of the teacher is reinforcing and the problem of out-of-seat behavior usually continues. Extinction is the procedure in which the teacher ignores the behavior until it stops. Extinction is characterized by response burst, which is a phenomenon in which the child may get out of the seat and wander around and continue to engage in negative behavior in an increasing manner, still trying to get the attention of the teacher. If the teacher gives in and attends to the behavior now, negative behavior is actually being reinforced! Response burst is to be expected, and usually subsides when the individual learns that no amount of negative behavior will get the attention that has been reinforcing.

Shaping is a behavioral intervention used to gradually increase the quality of a behavior. Often used to teach a new skill, shaping works by reinforcing the behavior as it gets closer to the final goal. Shaping is used when there is a clearly identified behavior to be changed and when differential reinforcement (reinforcing the behavior that gets closer and closer to the target, while ignoring the other behavior) can be applied to successive approximations of the behavior.

In **stimulus control,** some event in the environment is used to cue behavior. When a stimulus leads to behavior that is desirable and will be reinforced, the cue is called a discriminative stimulus. For example, seeing exercise shoes in the living room may act as a cue to use an exercise tape to do aerobics. The exercise shoes are a discriminative stimulus for exercise.

One example of **aversive control** is punishment, which is defined as the addition of an unpleasant event following a negative behavior to decrease the occurrence of that behavior. Punishment is not used often by behaviorists, but it has been used to eliminate dangerous behavior such as head banging or other self-mutilative behaviors in severely emotionally disturbed children.

Cognitive Interventions.   Cognitive interventions focus on the role of cognitions in the life of clients. Different types of **cognitive distortions** are identified and changed through the process of cognitive therapy. Some types of cognitive distortions include all-or-nothing thinking, disqualifying the positive, and catastrophizing (Burns, 1980). **All-or-nothing thinking** is characterized by assuming that things are either 100% perfect or absolutely terrible; there is no grey area. Since few things are perfect, all-or-nothing thinking usually leads to depression since everything is viewed as terrible. **Disqualifying the positive** is defined as the rejection of any positive experiences (i.e., compliments) and assuming that these positive events don't really count for some reason. The person using this type of distortion may say "I only received an A because the test was so easy" or "She is only complementing me because she wants a ride in my new car." **Catastrophizing** is the exaggeration of a negative event so that it has much more impact that it deserves. Making a mistake at work or receiving a B on a quiz may be catastrophized into losing the job or failing the course.

Cognitive therapy works through using many kinds of procedures, including thought stopping and positive self-statements, to change these negative or maladaptive kinds of thoughts. **Thought stopping** is a procedure designed to interfere with thoughts that run through the mind of the client and make it difficult to change behavior. In this procedure, the client imagines the troublesome thought running through his or her mind and the counselor or therapist shouts "Stop!" While the client may be a bit surprised, the shout does usually stop the thought. The client can then replace the thought with a more adaptive one, like "I can handle this situation." Clients can learn to do this procedure on their own, and can stop their own thoughts and substitute more useful ones.

The use of **positive self-statements** can go along with thought stopping. Statements such as "My opinion is important" or "I am an assertive person" can be practiced over and over. It is normal that these thoughts may not feel quite right at first. The important point is that what clients tell themselves influences their feelings and behavior. The counselor or therapist may use the self-statements as a way to cue assertive behavior by saying, "If it were true that your opinion was important, how might you behave?" The client might be encouraged to try acting as if the statements were true.

Cognitive-Behavioral Interventions.   The essence of cognitive-behavioral therapies is the union of behavioral and cognitive strategies to help people. Often cognitive-behavioral strategies include the use of treatment manuals, or guidelines for the implementation of interventions, which counseling and psychotherapy strategies to be operationalized and evaluated. Other advantages of treatment manuals include facilitation of counselor or therapist training and an increased ability to replicate research (Dobson & Shaw, 1988). Beck's cognitive therapy, Ellis's rational-emotive behavior therapy, and Meichenbaum's self-instructional training and stress inoculation training have well-developed treatment manuals available for practitioners to use.

Beck's Cognitive Therapy.   The primary principle underlying **cognitive theory (CT)** is that affect and behavior are determined by the way individuals cognitively structure the world. In an interview with Weinrach (1988), Beck described CT as "based on the view of psychopathology that stipulates that people's excessive affect and dysfunctional behavior are due to excessive or inappropriate ways of interpreting their experiences" (p. 160). First developed to treat depression, CT was later extended as a treatment for anxiety and is now being used to treat other psychological problems such as panic disorder and agoraphobia, drug abuse, and eating disorders. Interested readers are referred to full descriptions of CT in *Cognitive Therapy of Depression* (Beck et al., 1979), *Anxiety Disorders and Phobias* (Beck & Emery with Greenberg, 1985), *Cognitive Therapy of Personality Disorders* (Beck, Freeman, & Associates, 1990), and *Cognitive Therapy of Substance Abuse* (Beck, Wright, Newman, & Liese, 1993).

Beck and Emery (1985) identified the following 10 principles of CT:

1. It is based on the cognitive model of emotional disorders.

2. It is brief and time-limited.

3. It is based on a sound therapeutic relationship, which is a necessary condition.

4. It is a collaborative effort between the client and the counselor or therapist.

5. It uses primarily the Socratic method.

6. It is structured and directive.

7. It is problem-oriented.

8. It is based on an educational model.

9. Its theory and techniques rely on the inductive model.

10. It uses homework as a central feature.

The cognitive model of disturbance asserts that cognitions play a central role in human emotional problems. In CT there is an emphasis on internal thoughts, feelings, and attitudes rather than on behavior, although behavioral techniques are used in conjunction with cognitive therapy to help clients test their maladaptive cognitions and assumptions. Cognitive restructuring is used to identify automatic thoughts, evaluate their content, test the hypothesis that is generated, and identify underlying assumptions.

Unlike some dynamic therapies, CT is time-limited; treatment of anxiety disorders may take from five to twenty sessions (Beck & Emery, 1985), and treatment for moderate to severe depression may take twenty sessions over fifteen weeks (Beck et al., 1979). The pace of intervention is rapid, and longer-term therapy is viewed as unnecessary to facilitate change. Some guidelines useful for keeping the counseling and psychotherapy process brief include keeping treatment specific and concrete, stressing homework, and developing the expectation that intervention will be brief for both the client and the counselor or therapist (Beck & Emery, 1985).

The therapeutic relationship is highly valued in CT. In order for the cognitive methods to work well, the counselor or therapist must work to establish good rapport with the client. Accurate empathy and warmth are necessary to enable the client to engage in a relationship with the practitioner such that cognitive techniques can be implemented. Using CT requires a collaboration between the counselor or therapist and the client. It is the practitioner's role to provide structure and expertise in solving the problems presented by the client, but this process involves teamwork. CT has been described as using collaborative empiricism, which is a continual process used by the counselor or therapist and the client to identify, reality-test, and correct cognitive distortions. Clients are encouraged to be active in the process of learning how maladaptive thoughts interfere with desirable behavior change.

The Socratic (or inductive) method is one in which the counselor or therapist leads the client through a series of questions in order to become aware of thoughts, identify the distortions in thinking, and find and implement more adaptive replacements for the distortion. Beck et al. (1979) provide the following interaction which illustrates the use of questions to assist the client in disputing irrational thoughts.

PATIENT: I think anyone who isn't concerned with what others think would be socially retarded and functioning at a pretty low level.

THERAPIST: Who are the two people you admire most? (The therapist knew the answer from previous discussion.)

P: My best friend and my boss.

T: Are these two overconcerned with others' opinions?

P: No, I don't think that either one cares at all what others think.

T: Are they socially retarded and ineffective?
P: I see your point. Both have good social skills and function at high levels.
                (pp. 265–66)

This example shows how the counselor or therapist can use examples and questions to guide the client to the conclusion that the initial statement was inaccurate.

CT is a structured and directive approach to counseling and psychotherapy. Treatment manuals have been developed which are used to structure the counseling and psychotherapy process. Treatment plans are developed for each individual, and each session has an agenda to organize the discussion of specific problems. It is clear that CT is problem-oriented, which means that the focus is on solving present problems. CT is based on an educational model; since it assumes that people learn inappropriate ways of coping with life, the process of change involves learning new ways of learning and thinking.

The inductive method is essential to CT because it involves a scientific way of thinking about problems (Hollon & Beck, 1994). This means that clients are taught to think of their beliefs as hypotheses that require testing and verification. Counselors or therapists are trained to help the clients disconfirm maladaptive beliefs by confronting them with evidence contrary to those beliefs. Hypotheses often require behavioral assignments to test assumptions outside of the counseling or psychotherapy session, and clients report on their experiences. In addition, CT requires the client to do regular homework assignments. This involves applying the techniques learned in the counseling or psychotherapy office in the client's world and reporting the results to the counselor or therapist. Homework is used to reinforce the learning and to give the client a place to try out new behaviors.

Ellis's Rational-Emotive Behavior Therapy.   In 1993, Ellis changed the name of rational-emotive therapy (RET) to **rational-emotive behavior therapy (REBT).** This name change was necessary because the name RET was misleading since it omitted the behavioral aspect of this approach (Ellis, 1993). Ellis indicated that RET has always been one of the most behaviorally oriented of the cognitive-behavioral therapies and therefore the title of the approach should include the term "behavior." REBT will be used to refer to all of Ellis's work.

REBT uses cognitive, emotive, and behavioral methods to facilitate change in clients. Cognitive methods include disputing irrational beliefs and may also involve the use of other cognitive methods such as thought stopping, reframing, and problem solving. The emotive methods associated with REBT are role playing, modeling, the use of humor, and shame-attacking exercises. Some examples of the behavioral component of REBT include the use of homework assignments, risk-taking exercises, systematic desensitization, and bibliotherapy.

The goals of REBT are to help clients to think more rationally (scientifically, clearly, flexibly), to feel more appropriately, and to act more functionally (efficiently, undefeatingly) in order to achieve their goals of living longer and more happily (Ellis & Bernard, 1986). REBT relies heavily on the **ABCDE model** for understanding how thoughts and behaviors are related (Ellis & Bernard). In this model, A stands for activating events, which are related to B, a belief. Beliefs may be rational or irrational, and they influence the outcome of the activating event. C is the consequence of the belief. The consequence may be an emotional disturbance. Ellis later added D, to represent the process of disputing the belief, and E, which stands for effective philosophy.

Using this model, consider the problem a client might describe. A women with an eating disorder indicates that she ate two pieces of pizza at 9:30 P.M. while studying with friends and then felt guilty and depressed. Using the REBT model, A is eating pizza. The irrational belief, B, is that she ruined her whole day because she had promised herself that she would restrict all snacks and that she is a terrible person since she can't control her eating. C is that she feels depressed and angry at herself for losing control. In REBT, the task is to dispute the thoughts ("I ruined my whole day," "I'm a terrible person"), since they are irrational and lead to negative emotional consequences.

REBT is a highly directive, structured, and confrontational approach to working with clients (Ellis & Grieger, 1986). The process of REBT counseling is to identify the problem using the model and then identify goals for change. It is important that the practitioner explain the process of REBT to the client. Clients are taught the ABCDE model. It is especially helpful for the client and the counselor or therapist to analyze the client's presenting concerns using the model. Next, the counselor works to show the client that it is irrational to hold the beliefs that are related to negative outcomes. The client is taught that the emotional problems are the direct result of irrational thinking, thus the irrational thoughts must be attacked and disputed. This is the major focus of REBT. The client is taught to think more rationally and logically about the specific issue brought to counseling. In addition, the therapist may discuss more general irrational beliefs that are held by society.

Ellis is well known for describing irrational beliefs which are seen as the cause of emotional disturbances (Ellis, 1962). These irrational beliefs are the major ideas present in society which cause neurosis. Eleven such irrational beliefs (described fully in Chapter 3 of Ellis's 1962 text) are

1. The idea that it is a dire necessity for an adult human being to be loved or approved of by virtually every significant other person in his community.

2. The idea that one should be thoroughly competent, adequate, and achieving in all possible respects if one is to consider oneself worthwhile.

3. The idea that certain persons are bad, wicked, or villainous, and they should be severely blamed and punished for their villainy.

4. The idea that it is awful and catastrophic when things are not the way one would very much like them to be.

5. The idea that human unhappiness is externally caused and that people have little or no ability to control their sorrows and disturbances.

6. The idea that if something is or may be dangerous or fearsome one should be terribly concerned about it and should keep dwelling on the possibility of its occurring.

7. The idea that it is easier to avoid than to face certain life difficulties and self-responsibilities.

8. The idea that one should be dependent on others and needs someone stronger than oneself on whom to rely.

9. The idea that one's past history is an all-important determiner of one's present behavior and that because something once strongly affected one's life, it should indefinitely have a similar effect.

10. The idea that one should become quite upset over other people's problems and disturbances.

11. The idea that there is invariably a right, precise, and perfect solution to human problems, and it is catastrophic if this perfect solution is not found.

To provide an example of the manner in which Ellis disputes irrational beliefs, consider the first irrational belief, which concerns the need for love and approval. Ellis (1962) argues that demanding that you are approved by all whose approval is important sets a perfectionistic standard that is not attainable, because there will always be someone who does not love or accept you. Next, Ellis states that even if it were possible to have everyone love and approve of you, if you need this kind of acceptance, you will be so consumed with worry about maintaining it that anxiety will develop associated with the need to be loved. Further, Ellis believes that it is not possible for you to always be lovable and that no matter how hard you try, some people who you wish would approve of you will either dislike or be indifferent to you. He goes on to say that even if you could have everyone love and approve of you, you would have to spend so much energy doing this that you couldn't do anything else. He also indicates that in the pursuit of this love and approval you may become so ingratiating that you lose your own self-direction, and that you may behave so insecurely that others will become annoyed and actually respect you less. His final argument is that real loving is inhibited by the dire need to be loved.

REBT has become part of the practice of a wide variety of therapists and counselors. It can be used in individual counseling as well as in group or family settings, and has been used to treat a wide variety of problems (Ellis & Grieger, 1986). Ellis is the most frequently cited contributor to major counseling psychology journals (Heesaker, Heppner, & Rogers, 1982). It seems likely that REBT will continue to be influential in the helping professions.

Meichenbaum's Self-Instructional Training and Stress Inoculation Training. Meichenbaum's work has been described as the prototype of cognitive-behavioral work because it is a full integration of cognitive and behavioral elements (Hollon & Beck, 1994). Meichenbaum began his work on self-talk by studying schizophrenia (1969). He found that when individuals with schizophrenia were trained to use "healthy" self-talk (self-statements) such as "Be relevant," they were able to repeat these phrases and behave more appropriately. He continued to consider the role of self-statements in his work with impulsive children (Meichenbaum & Goodman, 1969) and developed the procedures for self-instructional training, which he published in a treatment manual in 1977.

Self-instructional training (Meichenbaum, 1977) is a technique in which the clients learn to keep track of self-statements and to substitute more adaptive statements. Clients learn to make these adaptive statements through homework assignment and practice in nonstressful situations. It is important that the statements be phrased in the words of the client to be personally meaningful. Later, the adaptive statements are practiced in increasingly stressful situations to deal with anxiety or phobia. Self-instructional training has been used alone and within the stress inoculation treatment package.

Stress inoculation training (SIT) is a cognitive-behavioral intervention package that combines "didactic teaching, Socratic discussion, cognitive restructuring, problem-solving and relaxation training, behavioral and imaginal rehearsal, self-monitoring, self-instruction and self-reinforcement, and efforts at environmental change" (Meichenbaum, 1985, p. 21). Its title highlights the emphasis on *stress* as the problem, *inoculation* as an analogy to the medical concept of inoculation against biological disease as a way to develop the "psychological immunities" to cope with stress, and *training* as part of the clinical technique.

SIT consists of three phases: conceptualization, skills acquisition and rehearsal, and application and follow-through (Meichenbaum, 1985). The **conceptualization** phase has as its primary focus the development of a therapeutic relationship between the client and the counselor or therapist, and provides the client with the background to understand stress and its effects on human life. The second phase, **skills acquisition and rehearsal,** consists of learning a variety of coping skills and practicing these skills in session and in vivo. In cases in which clients have coping skills they are not using, the practitioner might assist the client to understand the intra- and interpersonal issues raised by using the skills and help the client to remove inhibitors to using appropriate coping skills. The final phase, **application and follow-through,** is included to bring attention to the importance of a booster session, follow-up activities, and relapse prevention.

The specific goals and objectives for each phase of SIT are clearly outlined in Meichenbaum's *Stress Inoculation Training* (1985) and in Meichenbaum and Deffenbacher (1988). The conceptualization phase of SIT is structured to tie assessment of the problematic situation to the development of the helping relationship. This phase is educational and conceptual (Meichenbaum & Deffenbacher). The therapeutic relationship is critical to mediate the behavioral changes, since SIT, like CT, is a collaborative intervention. Meichenbaum highlights the need for warmth, accurate understanding, and acceptance in developing a trusting relationship. Assessment consists of a semi-structured interview in which the client is asked to describe the problem and provide concrete examples of stressful events. A cognitive-behavioral analysis of stressful reactions is obtained by asking about specific antecedents (What was going on the last time the problem occurred?) and consequences (What happened afterward?). Assessment may include imagery-based recall, a procedure in which clients are guided through an imaginal reexperiencing of a stressful event. This is done to collect information about the thoughts, feelings, and behaviors associated with stress. Self-monitoring and open-ended diaries or stress logs can be used to bring valuable information back to the sessions. Other sources of information include in vivo behavioral assessments and psychological testing. It should be clear that the conceptualization phase is important because it provides the background necessary for the implementation of coping strategies and helps the practitioner choose the types of coping skills to be introduced in the next phase.

The second phase of SIT—skills acquisition and rehearsal—is designed to ensure that the client learns and can implement various coping skills (Meichenbaum & Deffenbacher, 1988). Clients should complete this phase with a repertoire of strategies to cope with stressful situations. Relaxation training is a very commonly used technique. Meichenbaum does not present a single type of relaxation technique; instead, he highlights the need to work with individual clients to ensure that the relaxation training procedure will be practiced regularly and used in anticipation of stressful situations. Cognitive restructuring strategies such as Beck's CT may be used to make clients aware of the role that thoughts and feelings have in maintaining stress. Problem-solving training is another intervention that may be implemented. Self-instructional training (Meichenbaum, 1977) is often used to help clients learn to make and use adaptive self-statements.

The major objective of the third phase of SIT—application and follow-through—is to facilitate the use of the coping strategies learned in the skills acquisition phase. Clients practice more than one strategy and learn to identify the circumstances under which a particular strategy is likely to work well. Imagery rehearsal is an important part of this phase of SIT. Imagery is used to practice the coping strategies in stressful situations. Clients might imagine themselves becoming stressed and having stressful thoughts and feelings, and then use the coping skills they have learned to handle the stress. Behavioral rehearsal, role playing, and modeling can also be used in sessions to practice the coping skills and to evaluate the effectiveness of the coping skills for specific situations. Greater generalization to clients' real-life experiences may be facilitated through the use of homework assignments in which the clients try out the new strategies and report on the outcomes.

Marlatt and Gordon (1984), who have developed strategies for relapse prevention, assert that clients are likely to have slips in their ability to practice new skills. To counter the negative effects of relapse, clients are told that it is very likely that they will make mistakes and want to give up trying the coping skills they have learned. This is viewed as a normal part of the process of change, and strategies are planned to deal with these events. Since stress is a part of life, clients should expect to continue to face stress, but through the use of the coping skills, they have learned to manage the effects. Follow-through is included as a reminder that treatment effects may deteriorate after formal treatment ends. Booster sessions may be helpful to provide a refresher of the skills and the principles of SIT.

SIT is a flexible system for working with clients who have anxiety disorders. Meichenbaum and Deffenbacher (1988) indicate that it may be used along with medication or other interventions to help individuals with various anxiety disorders to cope with stress-related problems.

Evaluation

Overview

There is a tremendous amount of research literature on the effectiveness of various cognitive-behavioral interventions for different types of disorders. Hollon and Beck's (1994) chapter entitled "Cognitive and Cognitive-Behavioral Therapies" and Emmelkamp's (1994) chapter entitled "Behavior Therapy With Adults" provide comprehensive reviews to date. Ellis's work from 1977 to 1982 is reviewed in McGovern and Silverman (1986). The following review will be limited to research on the work of Beck and Meichenbaum. Other reviews can be found in the *Annual Review of Behavior Therapy* and *Progress in Behavior Modification*.

Overall, research based on the use of cognitive-behavioral interventions demonstrates that these interventions are helpful in treating a wide range of problems, including depression and panic and anxiety disorders as well as a large number of other problems faced by clients. Hollon and Beck (1994) indicate that cognitive-behavioral approaches are also efficacious for the treatment of bulimia. Since research on cognitive-behavioral treatment is ongoing, readers may find interesting articles published in journals such as *Behavior Therapy, Cognitive and Behavioral Practice, Cognitive Therapy and Research,* and *Addictive Behaviors.*

Supporting Research

Beck's Cognitive Therapy for Depression.   The treatment of depression has received a great deal of attention from cognitive-behavioral researchers. Beck's CT, developed for the treatment of depression, has been the subject of numerous treatment outcome studies. It has been compared to waiting list controls, nondirective therapy, behavior therapy, and various antidepressant medications with favorable findings.

In an older but often-cited study, Shaw (1977) compared Beck's CT to behavior therapy treatment for depression developed to restore an adequate schedule of positive reinforcement (included activity scheduling, verbal contracts, and communication and social skill development), nondirective therapy, and a waiting list control. Those treated by CT had the best outcomes on self-report measures of depression. In addition, ratings by clinicians unaware of the type of therapy received by individual clients also were more favorable for the CT treatment group.

A meta-analysis of treatment studies comparing CT to no-treatment controls yielded the finding that CT clients had lower final depression scores than 99% of the no-treatment control subjects (Dobson & Shaw, 1988). It is clear that CT is better than no treatment.

The next test involved a comparison of the effects of CT with antidepressant medication. In a landmark comparative outcome study, Rush, Beck, Kovacs, and Hollon (1977) compared the use of CT to pharmacotherapy based on the tricyclic antidepressant imipramine. The clients were moderately to severely depressed individuals seeking treatment for depression. Clients were randomly assigned to CT or drug treatment. CT consisted of no more than 20 sessions in 12 weeks, and the imipramine treatment consisted of 12 weekly sessions. Weekly self-report depression ratings were obtained. In addition, an independent (though not unaware of the treatment being received) clinician interviewed the subjects to provide a clinical rating of depression. Although both interventions led to a reduction in depression, the results indicated that CT outperformed medication in client self-report ratings and in clinician evaluations. Over 78% of the clients treated with CT showed marked reductions in depression, whereas only 22% of those treated with medication experienced similar reductions in depression. In addition, there was a greater drop-out rate associated with the medication treatment. These results are particularly astounding in the light of the fact that many of the therapists were psychoanalytically oriented and were relatively inexperienced in conducting CT (however, the therapists did follow a specified CT treatment manual and received weekly supervision). It seems that CT is an effective intervention for depression.

Another study which also used medication and CT to treat depression found that the use of drugs and CT was no better than CT alone (Beck, Hollon, Young, Bedrosian, & Budenz, 1985). CT and drug treatment were better than drug treatment alone, leading Beck to conclude that if a client needs antidepressant medication, the individual should get CT with the medication. Hollon and Beck (1994) conclude from these and many other studies that CT is about as effective as pharmacotherapy regardless of the severity of the depression.

Meichenbaum's Self-Instructional Training and Stress Inoculation Training for Anxiety Disorders.   Meichenbaum's intervention approaches were developed primarily for the treatment of disorders related to anxiety. The original research conducted using these interventions were treatments for test, speech, and social anxiety and simple phobias and agoraphobia. However, Meichenbaum and Deffenbacher (1988) list a host of studies that have supported the use of SIT with problems ranging from anxiety-related disorders (test anxiety, performance anxiety, social phobias, generalized anxiety disorder) to anxiety-related medical problems (dental phobias, Type A behavior, tension headaches, low back pain). SIT has also been studied as a treatment for high-stress occupational groups such as teachers, police officers, and nurses. A small sample of the research follows.

In a study that compared the effects of self-instructional training and systematic desensitization on test anxiety, Meichenbaum (1972) found that self-instructional training was more effective in reducing test anxiety and increasing grade point averages. Deffenbacher and Hahnloser (1981) used the separate components of SIT and the entire package to treat test anxiety in college students. Single components were more effective than wait list controls, and the entire package was more effective than single components.

In a study of social anxiety, Glass, Gottman, and Shmurak (1976) found that male college student volunteers treated with self-instructional training performed better in role-played vignettes than did those exposed to a behavioral skills training. Follow-up data revealed that those exposed to self-instructional training also were able to initiate more telephone calls to females through a six-month follow-up assessment.

A study with interesting results was a comparison of the behavioral in vivo exposure, RET, and self-instructional training with socially anxious outpatients (Emmelkamp, Mersch, Vissia, & Van der Helm, 1985). All of the therapies reduced social anxiety, but each was most successful in changing the dependent variable associated with the treatment. In other words, RET changed irrational beliefs, but not pulse rate. Exposure changed pulse rate, but not irrational beliefs. The importance of this study is that it demonstrated construct validity for the interventions; the specific effects of particular interventions may be seen in measures tied theoretically to that intervention, but not in measures not related to the intervention.

Limitations

The union of cognitive and behavioral counseling and therapy into "cognitive-behavioral" has been able to overcome many of the limitations of either type of therapy alone. However, those individuals who are more inclined toward psychodynamic interpretations continue to object to the lack of attention to unconscious factors in determining behavior and to concepts such as ego strength and insight, which are not included in this approach. In addition, experiential counselors and therapists indicate that cognitive-behavioral strategies do not pay enough attention to feelings. Insight and an emphasis on the past are features of other types of counseling and therapy that do not fit within the purview of cognitive-behavioral theory.

The behavior therapy roots of current cognitive-behavioral theory may be criticized as lacking attention to the role of thoughts and feelings, ignoring the historical context of the present problems, and allowing the counselor or therapist too much power to manipulate the client. Since the origins of behavioral theory emphasized operationally defined behaviors and functional analysis, these are features that define the approach. These are the things that make behavioral counseling behavioral! The idea that behavioral counselors and therapists are manipulative comes from the use of external reinforcers and stimulus control types of treatments. It seems that this notion is maintained by token economy systems. In individual practice, behavioral counselors or therapists use informed consent to make changes in the contingencies of behavior.

The cognitive therapy roots may be described as too difficult to study empirically and as paying too much attention to cognitive factors while minimizing affective ones. Cognitive therapies focus to a large extent on internal events (thoughts), which cannot be directly observed. Although the radical behaviorists object to this, most other types of counseling or psychotherapy would also fit this criticism. Cognitive therapy researchers have continued to develop thought-listing and monitoring strategies to alleviate this criticism. In addition, the cognitive strategies have been challenged for the lack of sufficient attention to affective factors. It seems that the emphasis on cognitions may lead to an intellectual understanding of the problem, but may not help change the feelings associated with the thoughts. This limitation is related to the fact that the mechanism for understanding how behavior, thoughts, and feelings change is still not understood.

Summary Chart—Cognitive-Behavioral Theory

Human Nature
Cognitive-behavioral theories are not developmental in the same sense that stage theories are. There is a stated assumption that behavior is learned which applies equally to the explanation of how problem behaviors and adaptive behaviors are developed. Behavior is assumed to be developed and maintained by external events or cues, by external reinforcers, or by internal processes such as cognition. Development is based on each individual's different learning history, experiences, and cognitive understanding of the world.

Major Constructs
The major constructs of cognitive-behavioral theories are an amalgamation of behavioral and cognitive approaches and include emphasis on behavioral and cognitive excesses or deficits, learning theory, observed changes in behavior, semantic interventions, and changes in cognitions. Operational definitions, functional analysis, and therapeutic empathy also serve as major constructs.

Goals
The goals of cognitive-behavioral theories are best viewed in terms of understanding the nature of the presenting problem from a behavioral, affective, cognitive, and social perspective; how progress in counseling can be measured and monitored; the environmental contingencies maintaining the behavior; and which interventions are more likely to be effective.

Change Process

Because many different theories and interventions comprise the cognitive-behavioral arena, the process of change is best understood in terms of how the theory explains the mechanisms for change. For example, Bandura's self-efficacy theory asserts that individuals develop expectations for their success in performing specific behaviors and that these expectations influence their decisions to try new behaviors and maintain behavioral changes, whereas Beck asserts that behavioral and affective change occur through the change in cognitions.

Interventions

The interventions used in cognitive-behavioral theories are best viewed in terms of behavioral interventions (reinforcement, positive reinforcement, negative reinforcement, extinction, shaping, and stimulus control) and cognitive interventions (identifying cognitive distortions, thought stopping, the use of positive self-statements, cognitive restructuring, use of the empathic therapeutic relationship, the Socratic method, disputing, reframing, role playing, modeling, humor, homework, risk-taking exercises, systematic desensitization, bibliotherapy, shame-attacking exercises, self-instructional training, stress inoculation training, and relapse prevention).

Limitations

Based upon the views of the critics of cognitive-behavioral theories, the theories are limited due to their lack of attention to unconscious factors in determining behavior and to concepts such as ego strength and insight, which are not included in the approach. Experiential counselors and therapists indicate that cognitive-behavioral strategies do not pay enough attention to feelings. Insight and an emphasis on the past—often seen as important in other theories—do not fit within the purview of cognitive-behavioral theory.

The Case of Maria: A Cognitive-Behavioral Approach

A cognitive-behavioral counselor or therapist would begin with a thorough assessment of Maria and then implement one of the cognitive-behavioral intervention strategies. As indicated earlier, Mueser and Liberman (1995) state that the practitioner must be able to answer four questions before selecting a treatment. First, what are the problems and goals for therapy? This includes the presenting problem understood in terms of the full range of behavior, affective, cognitive, and social aspects. Second, how can progress in counseling be measured and monitored? Third, what are the environmental contingencies maintaining the behavior? And fourth, which interventions are more likely to be effective?

The case study provides bits and pieces of the kind of information necessary to obtain a complete analysis. The first question focuses on the presenting problem and goals for counseling. Maria's presenting problem revolves around depression, which is evidenced by difficulty sleeping, crying, weight loss, and suicidal ideation. She also seems to have some difficulties in interpersonal relationships, especially those involving her children and other family members. Her job situation is a part of the presenting problem since she indicates that she has difficulty concentrating and has been absent more than is acceptable to the principal. Asking Maria to describe her problem would help the counselor identify the primary presenting problem and provide the basis for deciding on goals for counseling. The goals can be expressed in cognitive, behavioral, or affective statements. For example, Maria might indicate that she wants to stop thinking about suicide, to attend work daily, and to feel less depressed.

How can progress in counseling be measured and monitored? The counselor might select cognitions, behaviors, or feelings to monitor. Maria could complete thought diaries or record the kinds of maladaptive thoughts she has during the day. She might be asked to keep track of how often she cries, what she eats, or some other target behavior. She could record a rating of her feelings, which would provide useful information about how her behaviors and thoughts contribute to her depressed affect. The counselor could also use a variety of self-report measures such as the Beck Depression Inventory to provide a record of depression.

What are the environmental contingencies maintaining the behavior? In this arena, it is important to study Maria's depression in the particular contexts of her daily life. What happens at work that contributes to her negative thoughts and feelings? It could be that she is telling herself that she is an awful teacher since she finds her mind wandering more often than she likes. Likewise, what are her thoughts about her children? It might be that she believes that if her children do not follow every direction she provides, she is a bad parent and will never gain control of her children.

Which interventions are likely to be effective? It seems that the cognitive-behavioral interventions described in this chapter would be valuable for working with Maria. I have selected Beck's cognitive therapy to demonstrate how a particular approach would be used. Establishing rapport is a critical part of Beck's approach. The counselor will have to take special steps to establish good rapport with Maria. It is noted in the case study that Maria originally sought help from her priest and later from a physician. This may indicate that Maria has difficulty with the notion of counseling. This is consistent with her cultural background and indicates that the counselor will have to be especially attentive to relationship issues. Maria may also express skepticism about the value of cognitive-behavioral interventions, and this may be an ongoing issue in the therapeutic relationship. Accurate empathy and warmth conveyed throughout the assessment and intervention are necessary to engage Maria in collaborative efforts to test some of the thoughts she identifies and to try new strategies in her work setting and personal relationships. A strong therapeutic relationship is necessary to allow therapeutic effects to be maximized.

A cognitive-behavioral counselor would establish a plan to work with Maria that focused on developing an understanding of the role her thinking is having in his current situation. Maria would be challenged to identify the thoughts that go through her mind at work and at home, especially thoughts that are tied to depression. Patterns of thoughts might be classified into general categories of cognitive distortions, such as all-or-nothing thinking, overgeneralization, or disqualifying the positive. As Maria learns how to identify thoughts, she may also begin to talk about some feelings and see that the thoughts and feelings are related to depression. It is the primary task of the counselor to demonstrate that the thoughts, feelings, and behaviors are interrelated and that the counseling will work through changing the maladaptive thoughts.

Once there is an understanding of some of the thoughts that Maria may be having, the counselor begins the process of changing the thoughts. Questions like "What's the evidence?" "What's another way of looking at the situation?" and "So what if it happens?" (Beck & Emery, 1985, p. 201) are useful. Hypothesis testing, generating alternative interpretations, and decatastrophizing are some cognitive strategies that might be used. Self-monitoring thoughts might be used as a homework assignment to help Maria focus on thoughts and how they affect her behavior and feelings.

We also know that one of the ways Maria copes with depression is to withdraw from interaction with people. Although this withdrawal behavior is a consequence of the depression, it ultimately increases the depressed feeling she has since it isolates her from others who may be able to help her. Withdrawal from others is acting as an antecedent to additional depression. It seems that Maria has created a situation in which the depression she feels actually maintains her problems since the strategies she has chosen to cope with the depression create more depression.

There are certainly other features of Maria's case study that a counselor would address, including her risk of suicide and her parental and family relationships. I have focused primarily on the depression since it seems that it is the primary problem, and one for which there is great motivation to seek solutions. As Maria learns the strategies in cognitive therapy, she may be better equipped to address the other problem areas in her life.

References

Bandura, A. (1977). Self-efficacy: Toward a unifying theory of behavior change. *Psychological Review, 84,* 191–215.

Bandura, A. (1986). *Social foundations of thought and action.* Upper Saddle River, NJ: Prentice Hall.

Beck, A. T. (1976). *Cognitive therapy and emotional disorders.* New York: International Universities Press.

Beck, A. T., & Emery, G. (1985). *Anxiety disorders and phobias.* New York: Basic Books.

Beck, A. T., Freeman, A., & Associates. (1990). *Cognitive therapy of personality disorders.* New York: Guilford.

Beck, A. T., Hollon, S. D., Young, J. E., Bedrosian, R. C., & Budenz, D. (1985). Treatment of depression with cognitive therapy and amitriptyline. *Archives of General Psychiatry, 42,* 142–148.

Beck, A. T., Rush, A. J., Shaw, B. F., & Emery, G. (1979). *Cognitive therapy of depression.* New York: Guilford.

Beck, A. T., Wright, F. D., Newman, C. F., & Liese, B. S. (1993). *Cognitive therapy of substance abuse.* New York: Guilford.

Burns, D. D. (1980). *Feeling good: The new mood therapy.* New York: Signet Press.

Burns, D. D., & Auerbach, A. (1996). Therapeutic empathy in cognitive-behavioral therapy. In P. M. Salkovskis (Ed.), *Frontiers of cognitive therapy* (pp. 135–164). New York: Guilford.

Craighead, L. W., Craighead, W. E., Kazdin, A. E., & Mahoney, M. J. (1994). *Cognitive and behavioral interventions: An empirical approach to mental health problems.* Boston: Allyn & Bacon.

Craighead, W. E., Craighead, L. W., & Ilardi, S. S. (1995). Behavior therapies in historical perspective. In B. Bongar & L. E. Beutler (Eds.), *Comprehensive textbook of psychotherapy: Theory and practice* (pp. 64–83). New York: Oxford University Press.

Deffenbacher, J., & Hahnloser, R. (1981). Cognitive and relaxation coping skills in stress inoculation. *Cognitive Therapy and Research, 5,* 211–215.

DeLucia, J. L., & Kalodner, C. R. (1990). An individualized cognitive intervention: Does it increase the efficacy of behavioral interventions for obesity? *Addictive Behaviors, 15,* 473–479.

Dobson, K. S., & Block, L. (1988). Historical and philosophical bases of the cognitive-behavioral therapies. In K. S. Dobson (Ed.), *Handbook of cognitive-behavioral therapies* (pp. 3–38). New York: Guilford.

Dobson, K. S., & Shaw, B. F. (1988). The use of treatment manuals in cognitive therapy: Experience and issues. *Journal of Consulting and Clinical Psychology, 56,* 673–680.

Ellis, A. (1962). *Reason and emotion in psychotherapy.* New York: Lyle Stuart Press.

Ellis, A. (1993). Changing rational-emotive therapy to rational-emotive behavior therapy. *Behavior Therapist, 16*(10), 257–258.

Ellis, A., & Bernard, M. E. (1986). What is rational-emotive therapy (RET)? In A. Ellis & R. Grieger (Eds), *Handbook of rational-emotive therapy* (Vol. 2) (pp. 3–30) New York: Springer.

Ellis, A., & Grieger, R. (1986). *Handbook of rational-emotive therapy* (Vol. 2). New York: Springer.

Emmelkamp, P. M. (1994). Behavior therapy with adults. In S. L. Garfield & A. E. Bergin (Eds.), *Handbook of psychotherapy and behavior change* (4th ed.) (pp. 379–427). New York: Wiley.

Emmelkamp, P. M. G., Mersch, P. P., Vissia, E., & Van der Helm, M. (1985). Social phobia: A comparison of cognitive and behavioral interventions. *Behaviour Research and Therapy, 23,* 365–369.

Galassi, J. P., & Perot, A. R. (1992). What you should know about behavioral assessment. *Journal of Counseling and Development, 70,* 624–631.

Glass, C., Gottman, J., & Shmurak, S. (1976). Response acquisition and cognitive self-statement modification approaches to dating skills training. *Journal of Counseling Psychology, 23,* 520–526.

Hayes, S. C., & Hayes, L. J. (1992). Some clinical implications of contextual behaviorism: The examples of cognition. *Behavior Therapy, 23,* 225–249.

Heesaker, M., Heppner, P. P., & Rogers, M. E. (1982). Classics and emerging classics and counseling psychology. *Journal of Counseling Psychology, 29,* 400–405.

Hollon, S. D., & Beck, A. T. (1994). Cognitive and cognitive-behavioral therapies. In S. L. Garfield & A. E. Bergin (Eds)., *Handbook of psychotherapy and behavior change* (4th ed.) (pp. 428–466). New York: Wiley.

Kalodner, C. R. (1998). Systematic desensitization. In S. Cormier & B. Cormier (Eds.), *Interviewing strategies for helpers* (4th ed.) (pp. 497–529). Pacific Grove, CA: Brooks/Cole.

Kazdin, A. E., & Wilson, G. T. (1978). *Evaluation of behavior therapy: Issues, evidence, and research strategies.* Lincoln: University of Nebraska Press.

Kendall, P. C., & Hollon, S. D. (1979). Cognitive-behavioral interventions: Overview and current status. In P. C. Kendall & S. D. Hollon (Eds.), *Cognitive-behavioral interventions: Theory, research, and procedures* (pp. 1–9). New York: Academic Press.

Lazarus, A. A. (1985). *Casebook of multimodal therapy.* New York: Guilford.

Lazarus, A. A. (1990). *The practice of multimodal therapy.* Baltimore: Johns Hopkins University Press.

Marlatt, A., & Gordon, J. (1984). *Relapse preventions: A self-control strategy for the maintenance of behavior change.* New York: Guilford.

McGovern, T. E., & Silverman, M. (1986). A review of outcome studies of rational-emotive therapy from 1977–1982. In A. Ellis & R. Grieger (Eds.), *Handbook of rational-emotive therapy* (Vol. 2) (pp. 81–102). New York: Springer.

Meichenbaum, D. (1969). The effects of instructions and reinforcement on thinking and language behaviors of schizophrenics. *Behaviour Research and Therapy, 7,* 101–114.

Meichenbaum, D. (1972). Cognitive modification of test anxious college students. *Journal of Consulting and Clinical Psychology, 39,* 370–380.

Meichenbaum, D. (1977). *Cognitive behavior modification: An integrative approach.* New York: Plenum.

Meichenbaum, D. (1985). *Stress inoculation training.* New York: Pergamon Press.

Meichenbaum, D. H., & Deffenbacher, J. L. (1988). Stress inoculation training. *Counseling Psychologist, 16,* 69–90.

Meichenbaum, D., & Goodman, J. (1969). Training impulsive children to talk to themselves: A means of developing self-control. *Journal of Abnormal Psychology, 77,* 115–126.

Miller, L. K. (1980). *Principles of everyday behavior analysis* (2nd ed.). Monterey, CA: Brooks/Cole.

Mueser, K. T., & Liberman, R. P. (1995). Behavior therapy in practice. In B. Bongar & L. E. Beutler (Eds.), *Comprehensive textbook of psychotherapy: Theory and practice* (pp. 84–110). New York: Oxford University Press.

Nelson, R. O., & Barlow, D. H. (1981). Behavioral assessment: Basic strategies and initial procedures. In D. H. Barlow (Ed.), *Behavioral assessment of adult disorders* (pp. 13–43). New York: Guilford.

Rush, A. J., Beck, A. T., Kovacs, M., & Hollon, S. (1977). Comparative efficacy of cognitive therapy and pharmacotherapy in the treatment of depressed outpatients. *Cognitive Therapy and Research, 4,* 17–37.

Shaw, B. F. (1977). Comparison of cognitive therapy and behavior therapy in the treatment of depression. *Journal of Consulting and Clinical Psychology, 45,* 543–551.

Skinner, B. F. (1969). *Contingencies of reinforcement: A theoretical analysis.* New York: Appleton Century-Crofts.

Watson, J. B. (1930). *Behaviorism* (2nd ed). Chicago: University of Chicago Press.

Weinrach, S. G. (1988). Cognitive therapist: A dialogue with Aaron Beck. *Journal of Counseling and Development, 67,* 159–164.

Wolpe, J. (1958). *Psychotherapy by reciprocal inhibition.* Stanford: Stanford University Press.

12

Reality Therapy Theory

Robert E. Wubbolding
Xavier University, Cincinnati

Background

William Glasser, M.D., the originator of reality therapy, first began to develop this approach to counseling and psychotherapy while working in a correctional institution and a psychiatric hospital. A board-certified psychiatrist, Glasser had been trained in the traditional methods of psychiatry. He was taught to help clients gain insight so that after transference was worked through, they could achieve a higher degree of sanity. However, his experience had shown that even if these goals of the analytic approach were achieved, clients did not necessarily change their behavior, and many continued to have difficulty making productive decisions. With support and input from a sympathetic professor named G. L. Harrington, Glasser formulated the early principles of his new treatment modality.

The watershed year for reality therapy came in 1965, when Glasser published *Reality Therapy: A New Approach to Psychiatry*. In this then-controversial book, Glasser emphasized that people are responsible for their own behavior and that they cannot blame the past or outside forces and at the same time achieve a high degree of mental health. He asserted that behavior involves choices and that there are always options open to most people. Consequently, the objective of counseling and psychotherapy should be measurable behavioral change, not merely insight into and understanding of past events or current unconscious drives.

Though not greeted enthusiastically by the medical profession, Glasser's theory was well received by many, including corrections personnel, youth workers, counselors, therapists, and educators. He was asked to consult in schools to help students take more responsibility for their behaviors and to blame others less, and out of this work came his book *Schools Without Failure* (1968). In this work he discussed how reality therapy can be used in large groups—what he called "class meetings." While not the same as group counseling or psychotherapy, the meetings have some of the same goals, such as increased self-esteem, feelings of success, and group members' involvement with and respect for each other.

At that time, reality therapy was seen by many professionals as a method rather than a theory. Then Glasser (1972), in *The Identity Society,* formulated what might be called the theory's sociological underpinnings. He explained that three forces had contributed to the radical changes in Western civilization in the 1950s and 1960s: the passage of laws that guaranteed human rights, increased affluence that satisfied the basic need of survival for the majority of people, and the advent of instant communication via electronic media. These three gradual but important changes facilitated the arrival of the "identity society"— a world in which persons are more focused on their identity needs than on their survival needs. Most people want an opportunity to move beyond economic and political serfdom. Therefore, reality therapy found acceptance because it is a theory that facilitates personal empowerment by means of self-evaluation and positive planning for the future.

Still, this pragmatic and culturally based method needed solid theoretical grounding. Such a foundation was provided by a relatively unknown theory of brain functioning. Powers (1973) described the brain as an input control system similar to a thermostat that controls the temperature of a room. Glasser (1984) extended Powers's **control theory** (or control system theory) by incorporating a system of needs to explain human motivation, and then molded the theory to the clinical setting and the practice of counseling and psychotherapy. With the addition of these and many other ideas, it was no longer appropriate to call Glasser's theory "control theory," and consequently the recognized name is now **choice theory.** The delivery system is reality therapy.

Human Nature: A Developmental Perspective

Reality therapy provides a comprehensive explanation of human behavior as well as a methodology for addressing the vicissitudes of the human condition. Choice theory explains why and how human beings function; and the **WDEP system** (Wubbolding, 1989, 1991), explained briefly in the following paragraph and in greater depth later in the chapter, provides a delivery system for helping oneself and others to remediate deficiencies, make better choices, and become more fully self-actualized.

W implies that the counselor or therapist helps clients explore their *wants. D* means that clients *describe* the direction of their lives as well as what they are currently doing or how they spend their time. *E* indicates that the counselor or therapist helps in the client's self-*evaluation* by asking such questions as "Are your current actions effective?" Clients are then helped to make simple and attainable action *plans,* as implied by *P.* Thus, reality therapy is not a theory of developmental psychology per se. Still, as discussed in detail later, it contains ideas that harmonize with various stages of development.

Fundamental to reality therapy is the principle that human needs are the sources of all human behavior. So an infant as well as a senior adult seeks to control or mold the world around him- or herself in order to fulfill his or her inner drives. But here the commonality among persons at various stages ends. For as persons grow, they develop specific wants unique to themselves. An infant, child, adolescent, young adult, middle-aged person, or senior adult has formulated a wide range of wants that are unique to that person, yet similar to needs experienced by others of the same age and culture.

Similarly, though the behavior of all human beings is designed to fulfill inner needs, it differs according to age and culture. Human behavior has an impact on the external world and, in a sense, shapes it, as a sculptor molds clay. As a result, the input or perception that one gets from the world—a person's worldview (perception)—is dynamic, always changing, and unique to each person depending on age and culture.

A developmental implication of the principles of choice theory is that the perceptual system or worldview is a storehouse of memories. Because human problems at many levels of development are rooted in relationships, Ford (1979) and Wubbolding (1988) emphasize the necessity of interpersonal **quality time** as a facilitative component of healthy development. When parent and child, friend and friend, spouse and spouse, or colleague and colleague spend quality time together, they build a storehouse of pleasant and healthy perceptions of each other. In order for quality time to serve as a solid support for effective growth and development, it must be characterized by the following traits:

- *Effortful.* The activity requires effort. Watching television and eating together can help, but they are less effective than other activities because they require little or no energy.

- *Awareness.* The persons are aware of each other. Playing a game or engaging in a hobby is very useful in facilitating the relationship and individual development. Again, watching television without talking to each other qualifies only minimally.

- *Repetition.* The activity is not an isolated event but is performed on a regular basis. Consistent walking with a friend deepens the relationship and enhances the growth of both.

- *Free of criticism and complaining.* While the activity is being carried out, there should be no criticism of the other person. For instance, child development is enhanced if a parent creates an accepting atmosphere and encourages positive conversation.

- *Need-fulfilling for all persons.* The activity is geared to the interest and ability of all concerned. Attending a rock concert with an adolescent might be so painful for the parent that the relationship—and, therefore, the development of both—fails to improve.

- *Performed for a limited time.* Persons of various age levels require various amounts of time to ensure appropriate development. A child obviously requires more quality time than an adult.

Quality time is a crucial component of human growth and development. Moreover, the application to various individuals of activities labeled *quality time* is determined by the persons' interests and levels of intellectual functioning as well as their ages and degree of mental health.

Development of Mental Health

Besides looking at development from a chronological point of view, Glasser (1996) and Wubbolding (1988) have described mental health in terms of both regressive and positive stages.

Regressive Stages.   The stages in which mental health is seen as regressive are not viewed in terms of pathology. Rather, in reality therapy the stages are seen as ineffective ways to fulfill needs. They are sometimes called failure-directed or irresponsible, but the most useful way to describe them is as a person's best but quite ineffective effort to fulfill human needs.

Stage 1: "I give up."   This person has attempted to fulfill human needs effectively but has not been able to do so. The only alternative that appears reasonable is to cease trying. The person is characterized by behaviors such as listlessness, withdrawal, and apathy. This stage is quite temporary and is followed by the symptoms of the more identifiable second stage.

Stage 2: Negative Symptoms.   The following behaviors, like all choices, are seen by clients as their best efforts to fulfill their wants and needs. However, they lead to more frustration. The following behaviors are descriptive of these symptoms:

- *Actions.* Someone exhibiting this negative symptom chooses destructive actions harmful to self or others. These range from mildly acting out to severe antisocial behavior such as murder, rape, or suicide.
- *Thinking.* Cognitive disturbances are also attempts to fulfill needs. Such efforts often succeed in controlling others; nevertheless, they are self-destructive or harmful to others. The word *disturbance* is used in a wide sense to include negative cognition, ranging from the chronically pessimistic and negativistic thinker to a person with severe psychotic conditions.
- *Feelings.* Negative emotions include a spectrum ranging from mild to severe depression, from chronic aggravation to habitual anger or rage, and from the "worried well" (Talmon, 1990) to phobic disorders.
- *Physiology.* Other ineffective attempts to fulfill needs, used when other choices do not appear to be available to a person, include physical ailments. Many such maladies are best treated not only with good medical care but also through counseling or psychotherapy designed to help the client make better choices— that is, to choose positive symptoms.

Stage 3: Negative Addictions.   Negative addictions to, for example, drugs, alcohol, gambling, and work represent another regressive stage of ineffective behaviors that attempt to fulfill needs.

These three stages of regressively ineffective behaviors are not seen as rigid and exclusive of one another. On the contrary, they provide a way to conceptualize ineffective human behavior related to need-fulfillment. They also represent the reverse of effective behaviors.

Positive Stages.   The positive stages of mental health are seen as effective ways to fulfill human needs. They serve to balance the negative stages and can be presented to clients as goals for the counseling or therapy process.

Stage 1: "I'll do it"; "I want to improve"; "I am committed to change."   Such explicit or implicit statements made by clients represent the first stage of effective choices. This stage, like its negative mirror image, is quite temporary.

Stage 2: Positive Symptoms.   The following behavioral choices are effectively need-fulfilling and lead to less frustration:

- *Actions.* Effective choices aimed at fulfilling human needs include both assertive and altruistic behaviors. Healthy individuals know how to get what they want, yet they contribute to society through family life, employment, and so on.
- *Thinking.* The mirror image of cognitive disturbance is rational thinking. Among the many rational thinking patterns implicit in reality therapy are a realistic understanding of what one can and cannot control, acceptance of what is unchangeable, and knowledge that one is responsible for one's own behavior. Therefore, the perception that all early childhood traumas must of their nature continue to victimize a person's adulthood is rejected.
- *Feelings.* Patience, tolerance, sociability, acceptance, enthusiasm, trust, and hope are among the emotions that are positive behaviors and useful goals in the practice of reality therapy.
- *Physiology.* Another symptom of an effective lifestyle is the effort to attend to one's physical needs. Care of one's body, proper diet, and reasonable exercise are symbols of effective need-fulfillment.

Stage 3: Positive Addictions.   Glasser (1976) has identified activities that he calls **positive addictions** which enhance mental health and are intensely need-satisfying. Included are running and meditation. Such behaviors, as well as others that approach positive addiction, are the opposite of negative addictions. Rather than being self-destructive, positive addictions add to psychological development and increase feelings of self-worth and accomplishment. Such addictions are the result of habitually but noncompulsively choosing the behavior for 12 to 18 months, for a limited time such as 45 minutes per day (or at least on a regular basis), and in a noncompetitive way.

Like the negative stages, the stages of growth are not absolutely discrete categories. Human beings exhibit many characteristics and can float back and forth from the negative to the positive. No one lives entirely in a world of ineffective or effective choices. Even the most disturbed person occasionally chooses effective behaviors, just as even the most well-adjusted person makes unhealthy or ineffective choices at times.

In summary, the principles of reality therapy allow for applications to any stage of a person's chronological and psychological development. The use of quality time, for instance, can be adapted to persons of any age at any stage of development. Furthermore, development is seen as a series of choices leading to stages of regression or the stages of effective need-satisfaction.

Major Constructs

The underlying theory that justifies the methodology of reality therapy is called **choice theory.** While choice theory is separate and existed before reality therapy was developed, the terms *choice theory* and *reality therapy* are now sometimes used interchangeably. Norbert

Wiener, a Harvard University mathematician, formulated many of the principles that have been subsumed under the name **control theory** (Wubbolding, 1994). Wiener described the importance of feedback to both engineering and biological systems (1948), as well as the sociological implications for human beings (1950). However, Wubbolding (1993) has emphasized that the more proximate basis for the clinical applications was formulated by Powers (1973). Powers rejected the mechanism of behaviorism by emphasizing the internal origins of the human control system.

Most significant in the development of choice theory, however, is the work of Glasser (1980b, 1984, 1986, 1996, 1998), who expanded Powers's work and adapted it to the clinical setting. Human beings, Glasser states, act on the world around them for a purpose: to satisfy their needs and wants. He speaks of **total behavior,** which is comprised of action, thinking, feelings, and physiology. All behaviors contain these four elements, although one element or another is more obvious at a given moment. Such behaviors, negative or positive, are the output generated from *within* a person in order to gain a sense of control or satisfy needs.

Wubbolding (1988) has provided a summary of Glasser's choice theory as it applies to counseling and psychotherapy:

1. *Human beings are born with five needs.* These needs are belonging; power (competence, achievement, recognition, self-esteem, etc.); fun or enjoyment; freedom or independence (autonomy); and survival. These needs are general and universal. Along with wants, which are specific and unique for each person, they serve as the motivators or sources of all behavior.

2. *The difference between what a person wants and what one perceives one is getting (input) is the immediate source of specific behaviors at any given moment.* Thus, reality therapy rests on the principle that human behavior springs from internal motivation, which drives the behavior from moment to moment (Glasser, 1998; Wubbolding, 1985a). Another consequence of this principle is that human behavior is not an attempt to resolve unconscious early-childhood conflicts. The sources of effective behaviors ("I'll do it," positive symptoms, and positive addictions) as well as ineffective behaviors ("I give up," negative symptoms, and negative addictions) are current, internal, and conscious.

3. *All human behaviors are composed of doing (acting), thinking, feeling, and physiology.* Behaviors are identified by the most obvious aspect of this total behavior. Thus, someone counseled for poor grades in school is seen as presenting an action problem. People are labeled "psychotic" because the primary and most obvious aspect of their total behavior is dysfunctional thinking. Depression, anger, resentment, and fear are most obvious in other persons, so their behavior is called a feeling behavior. For others the most obvious component of behavior is the physiological element, such as heart disease, high blood pressure, or other ailments.

Because behavior is total—that is, made up of four components—and because it is generated from within, it is useful to see behavior not as static but as ongoing. Therefore, total behavior is often expressed in "-ing" words. Feelings, for example, are described as "depressing," "guilting," "anxiety-ing," and so on. Another implication of this principle is that all behavior has a purpose. Human choices are not aimless or random. They are all teleological; in other words, they serve a purpose: to close the gap between the perception of what a person is getting and what he or she wants at a given moment.

4. *Because behavior originates from within, human beings are responsible for their behavior.* In other words, we are all capable of change. This change is brought about by choosing more effective behaviors. The aspect of human behavior over which we have the most direct control is that of acting, and secondarily, that of thinking. Therefore, in counseling and psychotherapy the focus is on changing total behavior by discussing current actions along with the evaluation of their effectiveness in fulfilling needs, by discussing current wants and the evaluation of their realistic attainability, and by discussing current perceptions or viewpoints along with their helpfulness to the individual.

5. *Human beings see the world through a perceptual system that functions as a set of lenses.* At a low level of perception, the person simply recognizes the world, giving names to objects and events, but does not make judgments about them. At a high level of perception, the person puts a positive or negative value on the perception. Exploring the various levels of perception and their helpfulness is part of the counseling or psychotherapy process.

In summary, choice theory is a psychology built on principles that emphasize current motivation for human choices. It stands in opposition to both psychological determinism and what Glasser (1998) calls **external control psychology.** Human beings are free to make choices; thus, although the past has propelled us to the present, it need not determine our future. Similarly, our external world limits our choices but does not remove them.

Applications

Overview

Reality therapy is a practical method based on theory and research. It aims at helping people take better charge of their lives. In order to help clients make such changes, the counselor or therapist focuses on realistic choices, especially those touching on human relationships. It is first necessary to establish a safe therapeutic environment similar to that espoused in most theories, although choice theory offers some unique ways to accomplish this. The **WDEP system** details the specific reality therapy procedures used to help accomplish these goals.

Goals of Counseling and Psychotherapy

The goal of reality therapy is to help clients fulfill their needs. Consequently, the counselor or therapist helps clients explore current behaviors and choices related to belonging, power, fun, and freedom. More specifically, the precise wants related to each need are examined so as to help clients fulfill their specific objectives or their **quality world** wants. Therefore, assisting clients to make more effective and responsible choices related to their wants and needs is the aim of the counselor or therapist. These choices are seen as motivated by current needs and wants, not by past traumas, unresolved conflicts, peer pressure, or previous training.

The Process of Change

To understand how change can occur in the life of a client, it is necessary to understand the following principles in the theory and practice of reality therapy.

Present Orientation.   Choice theory, the theoretical basis for reality therapy, rests on the principle that the human brain functions like a control system—for example, like a thermostat—seeking to regulate its own behavior in order to shape its environment so that the environment matches what it wants. Therefore, human behavior springs from current inner motivation and is not an attempt to resolve past conflicts or a mere response to an external stimulus. In other words, human beings are not controlled by past history or victimized by the world around them; rather, they have control over current and future behavior—to varying degrees, to be sure, but they have control nevertheless.

Emphasis on Choice.   One of the goals of counseling and psychotherapy for the practitioner of reality therapy is to help clients make positive choices. Therefore, it is useful to see behavior as a result of one's choices, to treat it as such, and to talk to clients as if they have choices. While no human being has total freedom to make better choices easily, it can still be helpful to see even severe emotional disturbance as a person's best choice for a given period of time. The work of the counselor or therapist is to reveal more choices to clients, to help clients see that better choices are possible. Of course, the word *choice* is not used with the same meaning for every behavior. Choosing to keep an appointment is quite precise and specific and is more within one's control than becoming free of drugs or more assertive. Even though it is empowering to the client to see the latter options as choices, they can also be called goals comprised of many short-range objectives (wants) and more specific steps (choices).

Control of Action.   In bringing about change, it is useful to recognize that the component of one's total behavior over which a human being has the most control and, therefore, choice is the action element. Although some persons have an amazing amount of direct control over their physiology (some can stop bleeding when they are cut), people seen in counseling and psychotherapy can rarely change their blood pressure, their ulcer condition, or their headaches by an act of will. Also, they can rarely change their feelings of depression, guilt, anxiety, or worry merely by choosing to do so. And though they have some control over their thoughts, it is still not easy for them just to begin thinking differently from the way they have in the past.

Because people have the most control over the action element, helping them change their actions is more efficacious than helping them think differently or helping them feel better. It is more productive to help spouses choose to talk politely to each other than to help them feel better about each other. Increasing self-esteem is possible if a client chooses to act in ways that are different from ways in which he or she has acted previously. The reason for this is that all four elements of behavior are connected. Total behavior is like a suitcase containing four levels of behavior. The handle of the suitcase is attached to the action. Beneath it are thinking, feeling, and physiology. When the suitcase is moved, it is seized by the handle, the part most easily grabbed. Yet when this occurs, the entire suitcase changes location. So, too, when we help a client change actions, there is a change of all behaviors.

Importance of Relationship.   The specific procedures of the WDEP system are based on the establishment of an empathic relationship. As is abundantly clear from research, the relationship between the client and the counselor or therapist is critical in effecting change. Reality therapy offers specific interventions aimed at helping clients make more effective choices, and these are most effective when there is a genuine relationship established. Counselors and therapists who use reality therapy effectively employ many of the same skills and possess the same qualities as other counselors and therapists: empathy, congruence, and positive regard. Reality therapy offers specific ways, some unique to reality therapy and some incorporated from general practice, for establishing and maintaining a therapeutic relationship.

Metacommunication.   The procedures of reality therapy are straightforward and direct. Yet when these procedures are used repeatedly, clients seem to gain more than the surface meaning allowed for by the questioning. The art of helping clients define what they want for themselves, examine what they are doing to get it, and make plans is based on an underlying belief that is often heard and incorporated by clients—namely, that they have the ability inside of themselves to make changes, to feel better, to take better charge of their own lives. They gain self-confidence and a sense of hope, messages that extend beyond the mere asking of questions (specific questioning procedures are discussed in the following section). Yet it is best for the practitioner to refrain from trying to send a metamessage to clients. Rather, client attitudinal changes will often occur if the WDEP system is skillfully used.

Reality therapy developed out of a desire to see change happen in clients rather than have clients merely gain insight and awareness. Contributing to the efficacy of reality therapy is its emphasis on present orientation, choice, action, the relationship, and the underlying message that is communicated through skillful questioning.

Intervention Strategies

The methodology employed in reality therapy consists of establishing an appropriate environment or psychological atmosphere and then applying the procedures that lead to change: the WDEP system. Together these constitute the "cycle of counseling" (see Figure 12.1). This cycle illustrates that the specific interventions summarized as WDEP are built upon a trustful relationship. Trust-destroying and trust-building ideas (see "Do" and "Don't") are listed. The process is described as a cycle because there is no single place to start when it is applied to clients. Counselors need to use their creativity to match the system to each client.

Environment.   An atmosphere that provides for the possibility of change is characterized by specific guidelines and suggestions about what to do and what to avoid. These are designed for use by counselors, therapists, and case managers as well as supervisors and managers in the workplace. They can also be taught to clients, parents, teachers, and others for use in improving their interactions with clients, students, employees, and children. The specific applications vary slightly, but the principles are quite consistent.

Among the behaviors to be avoided is arguing. The counselor or therapist is quite active when applying the procedures; thus there is danger that in helping clients evaluate their behavior, the practitioner will overstep the proper use of reality therapy by arguing about the best choice for the client. This mistake results only in resistance. Also, bossing,

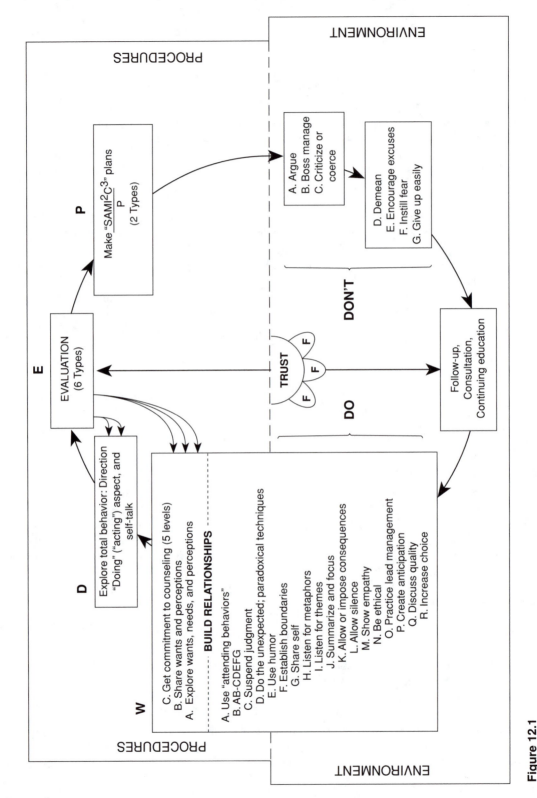

Figure 12.1
Cycle of Counseling

Adapted by **Robert E. Wubbolding, EdD,** from *Basic Concepts of Reality Therapy,* Institute for Control Theory, Reality Therapy and Quality Management, Los Angeles, 1986 & 1996. Copyright 1986 Robert E. Wubbolding, EdD. 9th Revision 1996.

criticizing, demeaning, or finding fault with clients only creates resistance and poisons the atmosphere. In fact, even "constructive criticism" is best avoided in relationships with clients.

One of the most important counselor and therapist behaviors to avoid is that of accepting excuses. Too much empathy or sympathy reinforces the perceived helplessness and powerlessness of clients. For instance, clients often describe how they did something harmful to themselves or someone else, not because they made a choice but because of an outside force. For example, the teacher gave an unfair test. Someone rejected me. Another person got me into trouble. They are depressed because of some unfavorable outside event. The alternative to the quicksand of excuses is the effective use of the WDEP system. Asking about wants or goals gets quickly beyond the discussion of a perceived external locus of control.

In the early stages of the development of the reality therapy delivery system, the advice was to never give up. A more realistic formulation is to stay with the person as a helper past the time he or she expects to be abandoned. In other words, don't give up easily.

Similarly, the counselor or therapist might be tempted to give up on the WDEP system if it fails to render the desired results immediately. Wubbolding (1996b) emphasizes that this is because the principles *appear* to be easy to practice, in view of the fact that the vocabulary is uncomplicated. Yet to be proficient in the practice of the skills, repeated practice and preferably supervision are required.

A positive environment that serves as the basis for the WDEP system is built not only on avoiding the uncongenial behaviors of arguing, criticizing, or giving up, but also on the global admonition to "be friends." Such efforts to establish an agreeable and harmonious atmosphere are sustained and nourished by the use of the following intervention strategies.

Use Attending Behaviors.   **Attending behaviors (ABs)** described by Ivey (1980) are especially useful in the practice of reality therapy. Eye contact and facial expression include looking at the client without staring and displaying a genuine interest. Physical posture includes sitting in an open, receptive position. Verbal following includes tracking the client's comments and reflecting in a manner that communicates that you are listening. Nonverbal behavior includes attending to the client's manner of expression, such as tone of voice. Paraphrasing means restating the client's comments occasionally. These skills serve as an effective foundation for an enhanced relationship between the client and the counselor or therapist. The abbreviation **AB-CDEFG** stands for the following interventions:

- *Always be **courteous.*** Being courteous is a behavior that counseling theory rarely mentions, perhaps because it is assumed to exist in the helping relationship. Authority figures are well served by treating the client with respect while refraining from venting anger.
- *Always be **determined.*** The determination of the counselor or therapist is perceived as an explicit and implicit belief or attitude. The metamessage, relayed to the client by the verbal and nonverbal behavior of the practitioner, is simply that no matter what the circumstances of the client's life, no matter how dreadful the past history, a better life is possible.

- *Always be **enthusiastic.*** In this context, enthusiasm is not cheerleading. Nor is it a naive belief about longstanding disturbances and the difficulty in dealing with them. Rather, it is the continuous effort to look at the bright side; to emphasize what the client *can* do; to discuss possibilities, not merely problems; and to take a problem-solving approach. The session thus need not degenerate into an empty ventilation of negative feelings. Thomas Edison, a man who dealt with towering obstacles, once remarked that if we leave our children nothing but enthusiasm, we leave them a legacy of incalculable value.

- *Always be **firm.*** In establishing an empathic environment, the counselor or therapist remains firm. There is no contradiction between seeing the client's point of view and taking a stand for honesty and sobriety while disclosing opposition to dishonesty, drunkenness, or abusive behaviors. Moreover, disclosure that the counselor or therapist supports the policies of the practitioner's employer and applies them unapologetically does not damage the relationship. Rather, it facilitates the establishment of boundaries. On the other hand, firmness is not intended to serve as an excuse for the authoritarian personality to impose his or her whims on clients.

- *Always be **genuine.*** Personal authenticity and congruence are seen as necessary prerequisites in reality therapy as well as in other helping methods. Those personal qualities are summarized in Glasser's often-repeated statement, "The counselor must be healthier than the client."

The above attending behaviors are intended to serve as guidelines that can be adapted not only by professionally qualified counselors and therapists, but also by anyone who wishes to use the principles of reality therapy. It is important to remember that they constitute an ideal that few people can attain 100% of the time. They can be among the personal, internal goals of the counselor or therapist.

Suspend Judgment.   As stated earlier, all behavior is a person's best effort at a given time to fulfill his or her needs. Consequently, a counselor or therapist who keeps this principle in mind can more easily see quite harmful choices from a low level of perception, without approval or disapproval. Balancing such suspension of judgment with "always be firm" is a tightrope on which every counselor or therapist walks daily.

Do the Unexpected.   Unpredictability is a quality that facilitates a helpful counseling or psychotherapy environment. Focusing on a strength, a success, or a time when the client felt good often generates the type of discussion that clients do not expect. Nevertheless, clients who are characterized by negative symptoms also choose positive symptoms (Wubbolding, 1981). Therefore, it is good to discuss in detail the circumstances when clients chose effectively, felt good, and remained in effective control of their lives. Wubbolding has described other ways for doing the unexpected and has incorporated paradoxical techniques such as reframing, redefining, and relabeling into reality therapy (1984, 1988). However, in order to be effective using these and other paradoxical techniques, it is necessary to invert one's thinking. Causes are seen as effects; the objectionable is now a strength (Dowd & Milne, 1986; Fay, 1978; Seltzer, 1986; Weeks & L'Abate, 1982). Wubbolding (1993) states:

A depressed child is seen as pensive, gentle, and thoughtful. An angry child is outgoing and has deep conviction. The bully is a leader and has ambition, while a submissive child is kind and cooperative. This paradoxical technique is, therefore, a technique that is useful to establish a relationship and can even serve as a procedure leading to change. However, it is not to be used indiscriminately and manipulatively. Rather, it is a psychological condiment, to be used sparingly. And like the other "guidelines" it is primarily a way to establish a safe counseling environment. (p. 293)

Use Humor.   A healthy and democratic sense of humor is a curative factor for the mental health specialist. Victor Borge once remarked that laughter is the shortest distance between two people. Peter (1982) states that laughter is helpful in dealing with anxiety, depression, and loss. Children learn by having fun. One of Aristotle's definitions of human beings is that we are risible; that is, we can laugh. Consequently, to function fully as a human being, as a person in effective control who is characterized by positive symptoms, it is advantageous to have a sense of humor. Indeed, an effective counselor using the principles of reality therapy can enhance the counseling or psychotherapy environment by laughing *with* the client.

Be Yourself.   Though it is to be expected that students learning counseling and psychotherapy skills will adopt the style of their teachers or that of the leaders in each theory, they also need to adapt the skills that fit their own personality. Whether they are assertive, placid, exuberant, dispassionate, expressive, restrained, confrontational, or laid back, they can practice the method effectively. It is a matter of practicing and assimilating the skills and thereby adapting them to a personal style.

Share Yourself.   The creation and maintenance of a trusting relationship is facilitated by appropriate self-disclosure. According to a Swedish proverb, "A joy shared is twice a joy. A sorrow shared is half a sorrow." While self-disclosure by a counselor or therapist can be helpful, caution is necessary. Cormier and Cormier (1985) warn that there can be a danger of accelerating self-disclosure to the point where the client and the counselor or therapist spend time swapping stories about themselves. As with all the techniques for building a trusting relationship, self-disclosure is best used moderately.

Listen for Metaphors.   Metaphors in this context are figures of speech, analogies, similes, and anecdotes that serve to quantify problems and thereby make them manageable. Barker (1985) states that if properly constructed, stories and other metaphors offer choices to clients. He observes that they are often helpful because "psychotherapy is essentially a process of providing people with more choice in the matter of how they behave, or respond emotionally, in various situations" (p. 17). Also, stories and anecdotes can be humorous and thus help clients perceive their problems and decisions in a different light. Metaphors used by clients are often overlooked by counselors and therapists, or they are paraphrased. It is better, however, to use the metaphor, to extend it, and to return to it in subsequent sessions. The following metaphors might be stated by clients or initiated by counselors and therapists:

"I feel like a floor mat."

"Cleaning my desk is like climbing Mount Everest."

"You sound like you've been on a merry-go-round."

"It sounds like warfare in your house."

"I don't know if I'm going up or down."

"I feel like I'm winning."

"Our relationship has gone sour."

"You seem to be back on track, heading in an upward direction."

Using these metaphors, the counselor or therapist can offer clients specific choices, such as "Would you like to get off the floor?" "Do you want to get off the merry-go-round?" and "What would you be doing today if you were on solid ground, away from the merry-go-round?" As with all such techniques used to enhance the counseling and psychotherapy environment, metaphors do not constitute the essence of reality therapy. They do serve, however, to build trust between the client and the counselor or therapist.

Listen for Themes.   Tying together the ideas, feelings, and actions of clients helps them to gain a sense of direction and control. The practitioner using reality therapy listens carefully for themes such as previous attempts to solve problems, wants that are fulfilled, and what has helped and not helped the client. This technique is not exclusive to the practice of reality therapy, but in using it the counselor or therapist listens for themes that are linked to the WDEP interventions (see "Procedures: The WDEP System").

Summarize and Focus.   Similar to the identification of themes, this technique helps the counselor or therapist listen carefully and communicate to clients that they are being heard. Unlike summaries used in other theories, this one concentrates on components of the WDEP system. A counselor or therapist might summarize a client's statements by responding, "You've stated that you've tried to get a promotion at work and been unsuccessful, that you've approached your boss and described what you want, that you've put in extra hours. Nothing so far has gotten you what you want." The counselor or therapist has summarized what the client has done that has not worked and has omitted many other details.

Focusing means to center the conversation on the client rather than on outside forces over which neither involved party has control. Very little can be done to cause changes in other people. Nothing can be done to change the past. Thus, it is most helpful if the counselor or therapist gently and positively assists clients to discuss their own here-and-now wants, total behaviors, plans, hopes, frustrations, and perceptions.

Allow or Impose Consequences.   Professional counselors and therapists have fewer opportunities to use this element of the environment than those who wish to integrate reality therapy into their work. Probation and parole officers, halfway-house workers, and others often function in a supervisory role and are required to impose consequences. It is assumed that the consequence is reasonable and not punitive, and also that it is imposed to help rather than merely control the client.

Even counselors and therapists occasionally impose consequences when life-threatening or evidently dangerous situations are described by the client. The code of ethics of the American Counseling Association states: "The general requirement that counselors keep information confidential does not apply when disclosure is required to prevent clear and imminent danger to the client or others or when legal requirements demand that confidential information be revealed. Counselors consult with other professionals when in doubt as to the validity of an exception" (Herlihy & Corey, 1996, p. 34).

Allow Silence.   The use of silence in reality therapy, if timed properly, allows the client to conduct inner self-evaluation, reassess wants, think about what is controllable and, therefore, uncontrollable, and in general take responsibility for the direction of the session. Trainees learning reality therapy tend to ask questions nervously in rapid-fire order. They are well advised to slow down and allow a few incisive questions to reverberate inside the client.

Be Ethical.   The ethical principle concerning clear or imminent danger is one of many that the practitioner of reality therapy practices. A trusting relationship and a professional atmosphere conducive to helping are built around solid ethical principles. Anyone using reality therapy properly knows, understands, and practices the ethical standards of various professional organizations. Professional disclosure is often required, as in Ohio (State of Ohio, 1984). Thus counselors, therapists, and social workers must provide clients with a written description of their professional qualifications. Wubbolding (1986) emphasizes that counselors and therapists should provide clients with information about the nature of reality therapy. These details help clarify the boundaries of the relationship as well as the advantages and limitations of the assistance that the practitioner can offer. He also emphasized the importance of knowing how to assess suicidal threats and how this assessment is used in the practice of reality therapy (1990). Informed consent, dual relationships, confidentiality, and proper record keeping are among the many ethical issues impinging on the relationship between counselor or therapist and client.

Be Redundant or Repetitious.   Often the same questions are asked in various ways. When a client is defensive and offering excuses in the form of denial, the counselor or therapist sometimes repeats the same question in a different way. It becomes a theme aimed at helping clients evaluate their own behavior. "When you made that choice, did it help?" "Did it work for you?" "What impact did that action have on you and on others?" "Did it help you enough?" "Was the action the best you were capable of?" Such questions asked at various times become a haunting theme that gradually and supportively lessens denial and facilitates the clients' assumption of responsibility. Yet like the overall art of counseling or therapy, the skill of being redundant is developed through practice and self-evaluation.

Create Suspense and Anticipation.   In a counselor or therapist's effective use of reality therapy there can be an element of drama. A counseling or psychotherapy session should be a significant event in the lives of clients. An authentic buoyancy on the part of the counselor or therapist and a desire to reassure can elicit a feeling of curiosity and a sense of impending success. The ability to communicate a sense of optimism is an advanced skill and is developed with practice and training.

Establish Boundaries.   There are limits within which a counselor or therapist operates, and these should be clarified. The ethical principle of dual relationships, discussed earlier, is clearly part of boundary classification. Further, the client might wish to shield certain areas from discussion. A useful question for counselors or therapists to ask is, "Is there any topic you do not want me to ask about?" Such questioning empowers clients to choose what they want to work on. If clients have numerous topics that are forbidden territory (which is rarely the case), the counselor or therapist can ask them if it is helpful for them to conceal or mask potential topics. In any event, the wishes of the client are paramount and are respected.

The above guidelines are designed to help the counselor or therapist using reality therapy to establish rapport, mutual trust, and a safe atmosphere by being aware of obstacles and barriers to involvement. They also consist of positive interventions that facilitate the client's expectation that the experience is worthwhile and significant. Moreover, a truly skilled practitioner of reality therapy engages in an ongoing self-evaluation process by means of follow-up with past clients, consultation with peers, and continuing education. These environmental building blocks aimed at establishing and deepening the relationship provide a fundamental prerequisite for what is essentially the practice of reality therapy: the WDEP system.

Procedures: The WDEP System.   The specific interventions that are the essence of reality therapy are based on the trusting relationship described as environment. The procedures or determinations (Wubbolding, 1985b) are most appropriately formulated as the WDEP system (see Figure 12.1) (Wubbolding, 1989, 1991). They should not be seen as steps to be used sequentially or mechanically; and although they are described in simple, jargon-free language, they can be difficult to implement. For instance, a counselor or therapist working with a student referred for a school discipline problem would probably not begin with a lengthy discussion of W (wants) but with an exploration of D (doing): in other words, what happened to bring about the referral?

Thus, in conceptualizing the entire process, it is useful to see it as a cycle that can be entered at any point.

W: Discussing Wants, Needs, and Perceptions.   Because human beings are motivated to fulfill their wants and needs, it is important for the counselor or therapist to take the time to explore the specific wants of the client. The questions might include "What do you want from your spouse? From your school? Your job? Your career? From your friends? Your parents? Your children? Your supervisor? From yourself? What do you want from me? From your church?" Thus, there are at least 11 generic questions that can be asked. These are multiplied threefold if the counselor or therapist asks more precisely about each category: (1) "What do you want that you are getting?" (2) "What do you want that you are *not* getting?" (3) "What are you getting that you don't want?"

The areas for exploration and clarification become almost endless when the counselor or therapist adds, "How much do you want it?" "What would you need to give up to get what you want?" "What will you settle for?"

All wants are related to the five needs: belonging, power or achievement, fun or enjoyment, freedom or independence, and survival. Therefore, it is useful to help clients link their wants explicitly to their needs by asking, "If you had what you wanted, what would you have?" or "If your wants were met, what would that satisfy inside?" Such questioning of a parent often elicits the following: "I want my child to keep the curfew, get good grades, stay away from drugs, do the house chores, and be pleasant to the rest of the family. If I had that I would have peace of mind. I would know that I am a good parent." The parent has specific wants and has identified the underlying need: achievement or power.

Discussing perceptions is also an important part of W. Questions about clients' perceptions are slightly different from those specifically relating to wants. A parent might be asked, "What do you see when you look at your child?" The answer might be, "I see a child who is rebellious at times and cooperative when she wants something from me." Asking about perceptions is especially useful in groups and in family counseling and psychotherapy because arguments can be prevented. A counselor or therapist can intervene by reminding all present that they are discussing their viewpoints—what they see, not what "is."

W: Sharing Wants and Perceptions.   Counselors and therapists using reality therapy share their own wants and perceptions when such disclosure is helpful to clients. They share their wants regarding such issues as how many sessions are necessary and remind clients that the practitioner's role is to help clients make decisions but not to remove responsibility. On occasion the counselor or therapist might even make a specific suggestion about what kind of action would be helpful. In the case of a parent, the counselor or therapist might say, "When I look at your child, I see similar things, but I also see a person struggling to grow up, one who doesn't need lectures but quality time from parents."

Counselors and therapists who share wants and perceptions do not take responsibility for clients, nor do they lecture or admonish clients. They lead but do not coerce.

W: Getting a Commitment to Counseling.   Change and growth will occur only if the client is committed to making changes in his or her actions. Thus, it is imperative that the counselor or therapist discuss the client's **level of commitment** to the process and its outcomes. The question "How hard do you want to work at changing your situation?" gives the client an opportunity to look inward and reflect on the degree of responsibility he or she wishes to assume.

Wubbolding (1988) has identified five levels of commitment as described by clients:

1. *"I don't want to be here."* This statement clearly illustrates that the client is at best reluctant and resistant. It is even possible that he or she has been coerced into counseling or psychotherapy. In fact, this level of commitment is actually no commitment at all, but it is included because it seems to fit an increasing number of clients who are seen by practitioners.

2. *"I want the outcome but not the effort."* This level indicates that the client does want to change and is perhaps at stage 1 ("I'll do it") in gaining effective control and taking personal responsibility. It is a higher commitment than the first level, but it will still result in no change until a higher level is achieved.

3. *"I'll try; I might."* Trying to make a change for the better constitutes the middle level of commitment to change. Still, trying to get out of bed early is not the same as doing it.

4. *"I will do my best."* At this level a person goes beyond trying and commits to specific action. However, such a commitment still allows the possibility of failure.

5. *"I will do whatever it takes."* The highest level of commitment represents an outcome centered on a no-excuses level of commitment. It is the most desirable level from the view of the counselor or therapist.

The levels of commitment are developmental. The higher levels are more helpful than the lower ones. Yet for some clients, "I'll try" is a major improvement. They should not be pushed too vigorously or too quickly to move to a higher level. Rather, the skillful counselor or therapist helps clients to evaluate their level of commitment and gently leads them to the next level.

D: Discussing Behavioral Direction and Doing (Total Behavior).   The counselor or therapist helps the client review his or her overall direction by inquiries such as "Where do you think you're going if you continue on the same path?" A child might be asked, "If you continue to flunk in school, resist your parents' requests, and continue on the same pathway, where will you be in two or three or twelve months?"

The exploration of the overall direction is only the embarkation point for further questioning about current total behavior. More time and effort are needed to help clients examine their specific actions. The counselor or therapist helps the client verbalize exactly what he or she did for a specific amount of time. The client becomes a television camera, as it were, relating not typical events but what happened that was specific and unique.

Similarly, clients might describe their thoughts and feelings at the time of the actions as well as what they now think and feel about them. Likewise, they could even describe how their overall direction and specific actions are affecting the physiological component of their total behavior.

So important is the generic question "What are you doing?" that a book of reality therapy cases has that name (Glasser, 1980). Each word in the question serves as a signpost for the practitioner (Wubbolding, 1990, 1996a). "What" implies that the counselor or therapist asks for precise details. When clients take refuge in generalities, they should be encouraged to be more specific. "Are" emphasizes the importance of stressing the present rather than indulging in endless discussions of past behaviors that are beyond the client's control. "You" focuses on the client rather than on other people, excuses, and uncontrollable events. Finally, "doing" connotes total behavior: the exploration of direction, specific actions, thoughts, feelings, and physical symptoms accompanying the client's choices.

E: Helping Clients Conduct Evaluations.   In the cycle of counseling and in the WDEP system of procedures, the element of evaluation occupies the central position (see Figure 12.1). Like a keystone in an arch, its pivotal place supports the entire structure. If it is absent, the arch crumbles. The practice of reality therapy is firm and effective to the degree that the counselor or therapist assists clients in evaluating their own behavior, wants, perceptions, level of commitment, and plans.

Because of the prominent place of self-evaluation in the cycle of counseling, reality therapy is properly placed among the cognitive counseling theories. It is here, especially, at the cardinal point of self-evaluation, that cognitive restructuring takes place. Clients look inward and examine the effectiveness of their lifestyle and its specific aspects. Only now, when they have concluded that some part of their control system (wants, behaviors, perceptions) is not helping them or is not as beneficial as it could be, do clients see that a change is necessary.

More specifically, evaluation contains the following elements:

- *Evaluation of behavioral direction.* After helping the client describe the overall direction of his or her life, the counselor or therapist assists in evaluating the significance of this direction. Is it the best direction in the mind of the client? Is it helpful or harmful, and does the direction have what, for the client, is high quality?

- *Evaluation of specific actions.* The questions about specific actions are geared to the descriptions provided in the client's explanation of how a specific segment of his or her day was spent. Such questions as the following might be asked: "Did sleeping until 10:00 in the morning help or hurt your effort to find a job?" "What were the consequences of hitting your brother?" "When you shout at the kids, do you get what you want?" "Even if they obey for a while, does it help both in the short run and in the long run?" "Does it help to the degree you were hoping for?" "If you continue to eat a diet of ice cream, sweets, and starch, will you ever attain the weight you said you wanted?"

- *Evaluation of wants.* The client is assisted in making judgments about the appropriateness and the attainability of his or her wants: "Is what you want truly good for you?" "How realistic is it for you to get your parents totally off your back?" "How realistic is it for your adolescent child to become 100% cooperative or perfect in your own eyes?"

- *Evaluation of perceptions or viewpoints.* Perceptions are not easily changed. Rarely are they changed by a simple decision to view a person, a situation, or an event differently. Yet they can be changed by changing behavior (Glasser, 1980b, 1984; Powers, 1973). But because perceptions involve what people want, they occupy an important place in the evaluation process. So even though they are not directly changed, their desirability and appropriateness should be evaluated. More specifically, human beings seek the perception of being adequate, popular, skilled, in control, helpful to others, and comfortable. They also have more specific perceptions relative to each generic perception. Thus, the client is helped to evaluate general and specific perceptions or viewpoints. Evaluative questions for perceptions might include "Does it help if you see your son only as rebellious and lazy?" "What is accomplished if you see only the negative aspects of your parents' behavior?" "When you nurse a negative attitude toward your boss, does it help you to improve your situation at work?"

- *Evaluation of new direction.* As new possibilities unfold for clients, it is useful to help them determine whether those possibilities are need-satisfying. The rebellious student is asked, "How will cooperation at home benefit you and your family?" "If you were to make an effort to learn, do your homework, ask questions in class, and, in general, do what 'successful' students do, would you feel better?" "What impact would this approach have on your friends and family?"

- *Evaluation of plans.* After a new direction is defined, and often even before clients have committed to a change of direction, they can be encouraged to make plans. At first glance these plans might appear to be meager and insignificant, but they often represent the first steps toward more effective and positive need-satisfaction. In working with an adolescent, Wubbolding (1980) was able to help him make a modest plan of action. This high school student had shut himself in his room on the weekends with the curtains and drapes closed. Although resistant at first, he eventually made plans to open the blinds and let the light in. He subsequently developed a healthy social life by making rudimentary changes in his overall direction. Thus, the evaluation of plans is based not on whether they solve the basic problem but on whether they address the problem and aim toward the more effective fulfillment of belonging, power, fun, and freedom.

P: Planning.   According to one saying, "To fail to plan is to plan to fail." Glasser (1980a) states that plans vary; some are detailed, while others are quite simple, yet he emphasizes that "there must always be a plan. People who go through life without some sort of a long-term plan, usually divided into a series of small plans to reach larger goals, are like ships floundering without rudders" (p. 52).

The procedure of planning is often mistakenly viewed as the essence of the practice of reality therapy. And though it is important, it is effective only if based on a client's inner self-evaluation.

Plans that are truly efficacious, or at least more likely to be carried out by the client, have at least eight qualities, which can be summarized by the acronym **SAMI^{2}C^3** (Wubbolding, 1996a):

S   **Simple:** The plan is uncomplicated.

A   **Attainable:** If the plan is too difficult or too long range, the client will become discouraged and not follow through.

M   **Measurable:** The plan is precise and exact. The client is encouraged to define a clear answer to the question, "When will you do it?"

I   **Immediate:** The plan is carried out as soon as possible.

I   **Involved:** The helper is involved if such involvement is appropriate. The involvement is, of course, within the bounds of ethical standards and facilitates client independence rather than dependence.

C   **Controlled by the client:** An effective plan is not contingent on the actions of another person but is, as much as possible, within the control of the client.

C   **Committed to:** The counselor or therapist helps the client to pledge firmly to put the plan into action.

C   **Consistent:** The ideal plan is repetitious. A single plan can be a start, but the most effective plan is one that is repeated.

The common denominator to all planning is **persistence** on the part of the counselor. This coincides with the injunction "Don't give up."

Planning and follow-through are crucial elements in personal growth, enhanced mental health, decision making, and remediation of problems. Helpful plans aimed at achieving these ultimate goals are not forced on clients. Rather, clients are taught that the achievement of their goals will be the result of their own positive choices and plans. Clients are accordingly led to discover within themselves desirable plans aimed at their own need-satisfaction.

In summary, the cycle of counseling is a design for understanding reality therapy and an outline for knowing how to apply it. The environment consists of specific recommendations for building a firm but friendly atmosphere in which a client can feel safe and confident while realizing that the counselor or therapist actively seeks to be of help. The WDEP formulation is not a system that is intended to be followed in a mechanical manner, but rather a system from which the proper intervention is selected at a given time because of its apparent appropriateness.

Evaluation

Overview

While more research could be conducted to validate the use of reality therapy, the widespread interest in the theory indicates that many practitioners have confidence in its efficacy. In 1993 more than 400 persons worldwide completed the 18-month training program and were certified in reality therapy. Anecdotal evidence points toward the theory's usefulness with a wide variety of issues, such as eating disorders, child abuse, marriage, aging, elective mutism, career satisfaction, study habits, self-esteem, assertive behavior, and many others (Glasser, 1980, 1989).

Supporting Research

Practitioners of reality therapy represent virtually every helping profession: therapists, educators, managers, chemical dependency workers, corrections specialists, and many others. This overview of research represents a sampling of some such studies.

Glasser (1965) described the dramatic effect of a reality therapy program in a psychiatric hospital. The average stay in a ward of 210 men was 15 years. Within 2 years, 75 men had been released with only 3 returning. According to Shea (1973), the use of reality therapy produced significant results in increasing self-concept and lowering court referrals. Gang (1975) showed that the use of reality therapy resulted in more socially acceptable student behavior in the classroom. The teachers in the study also believed that the relationship skills resulting from the use of reality therapy were essential if change were to result.

German (1975) investigated the effects of reality therapy in group counseling or psychotherapy with institutionalized adolescents. In relation to a comparative group, the students displayed significantly fewer behaviors requiring disciplinary action. Poppen,

Thompson, Cates, and Gang (1976) found that after reality therapy was used with disruptive students, appropriate behavior increased 18 to 47%. In a study of juvenile offenders, Yarish (1986) found significant differences in the participants' perceived **locus of control.** They became aware that they made their own choices rather than being controlled by external forces.

Gorter-Cass (1988) studied the use of reality therapy in an alternative school and stated that the overall trend was toward "less severe behavior" and that there were significant changes in self-worth and self-concept among students. Elementary school students ages 9 to 11 were studied by Hart-Hester, Heuchert, and Whittier (1989). The students were counseled in groups, and action plans were formulated. The study showed a "pronounced increase in the percentage of time-on-task for each targeted student" (p. 16).

In a study of the effects of reality therapy in a rural elementary school, Bowers (1997) found improvements in relationships and self-concept, but little change in school attendance. The author noted that school attendance was not much of a problem at this school.

Studying the effects of reality therapy in a therapeutic community in Ireland, Honeyman (1990) found significant changes in the residents' self-esteem, awareness of their inability to control their drinking, and insight into living in a more inner-controlled manner. Positive effects have also been shown when reality therapy has been used with teachers (Parish, 1988, 1991; Parish, Martin, & Khramtsova, 1992), undergraduate students (Peterson & Truscott, 1988), graduate students (Peterson, Woodward, & Kissko, 1991; Peterson, Chang, & Collins, 1997), foster parents (Corwin, 1987), negatively addicted inmates (Chance et al., 1990), and student athletes (Martin & Thompson, 1995).

This brief selection of research studies illustrates the value of reality therapy as a reliable tool for counselors and therapists. However, many areas for possible study remain. Researchers could investigate further the effects of reality therapy on the areas already mentioned, as well as on other issues dealt with by counselors and therapists.

Limitations

Reality therapy should be seen as an open system that will grow and change. It is not a narrow theory that is rigidly applied. Yet as a free-standing theory and practice of counseling and therapy, it has limitations. Some of these are inherent in the theory, and some reside in the skill of the practitioner.

Many clients believe that in order to make changes in their lives or to feel better, they need to gain insight into their past, resolve early conflicts, describe the negative aspects of their lives, or tell how they arrived at their present state. Many of these clients could be successfully encouraged to emphasize their present behavior, but some believe that no change can result without dealing specifically with past pain, and for them reality therapy will appear to avoid the real issues.

Part of this limitation resides in the skill of the counselor or therapist rather than the theory, but in the minds of clients it is often difficult to separate the theory from the practitioner. For such clients, the practitioner needs to adjust the therapy rather than cling to the principle of discussing current behavior. Practitioners who have been trained to emphasize a discussion of feelings as the true test of effective counseling or therapy find the quick emphasis on clients' actions premature if not hasty. On the other hand, a skillful reality counselor or therapist is aware of all aspects of clients' behavior—actions, thinking, and feelings—and responds to them as a unit rather than as disconnected from one another. Still, if feelings such as anger are seen as the root cause of problems rather than as feelings caused by unmet needs, the counselor or therapist will probably be less effective when using the WDEP system of reality therapy.

The concrete language of reality therapy may be another limitation. It contains little jargon or technical terminology, and the theory and practice employ words like *belonging, power, fun, freedom, wants, plans, self-evaluation,* and *effective control*. Because the language of reality therapy is easily understood, its practice can appear to be easily implemented. Nevertheless, the effective use of reality therapy requires practice, supervision, and continuous learning.

Because reality therapy is straightforward and deals with present issues, its subtlety is often obscured. The discussion of current and future actions and plans is often the most obvious part of the counseling or therapy process, yet the most important components are the clarification of clients' wants and their self-evaluation. In learning reality therapy, practitioners who are in a hurry to see results frequently proceed too rapidly to action planning. Such efforts to help clients make decisions, solve problems, or take more effective control of their lives result in resistance due to the inappropriate use of reality therapy principles.

Summary Chart—Reality Therapy Theory

Human Nature
Human beings are motivated by current drives, not by past events, fixations, or external stimuli. They have choices related to their motivation. Often human beings make choices that are ineffective, even harmful to themselves. Through counseling and education they can learn to achieve inner harmony and happiness without infringing on the rights of others.

Major Constructs
Human needs are the basis for the practice of reality therapy. Inner motivation is rooted in the ever-present search for and effort to gain survival or self-preservation, love and belonging, power or achievement, fun or enjoyment, and freedom or independence. These motivators are made concrete and specific through wants or desires unique to each individual. People choose specific behaviors to fulfill these wants and needs. Thus the purpose of behavior is to gain the perception that we are getting what we want— that is, that needs are fulfilled.

Goals
The primary goal of reality therapy is to help clients make more effective choices to meet their needs more efficiently and effectively. Specific goals, formulated with clients, depend on their stage of development, their perception of what they want, and their ability to realistically fulfill their specific wants. When clients learn to make better choices, they can relinquish the prison of the past and the current pressures of their environment.

Change Process
Change occurs when clients decide to change. When counselors believe clients have the power to change, they communicate this to clients. They present realistic choices and

proceed on the assumption that a better life is possible. Developing a relationship based on this unshakable belief enables clients to make more effective choices and to gain a sense of inner control and need-satisfaction.

Interventions

Two generic kinds of interventions are used: first, establishing a firm but friendly environment that enables clients to spontaneously explore their control systems; and second, utilizing the WDEP procedures, which consist in helping clients explore their wants, discuss all aspects of their current behavior, evaluate the attainability of wants and the effectiveness of their choices, and finally formulate realistic and repetitive plans.

Limitations

For clients who believe that they need to gain insight into their past or resolve early conflicts in order to change or feel better, reality therapy will appear to avoid the real issues. In order to use the principles effectively, the counselor or therapist needs to genuinely believe in them and be trained in them; this poses a problem for practitioners who have an inadequate understanding of the principles or practice of reality therapy. Finally, the simple language of reality therapy can be a barrier to its effective implementation. The system is easy to understand but more difficult to practice.

The Case of Maria: A Reality Therapy Approach

It is evident that Maria, a bright, conscientious, sensitive woman with close ties to family and religion, is not fulfilling her needs effectively. Her belonging need is unmet in many ways. She feels like her life is out of control. Even the principal of the school, an authority figure, suggests that she take a leave of absence. She feels trapped and alone and cannot even feel free from this prison in her sleep. Fun and enjoyment seem to be totally lacking.

Her behavior is characterized by a total absorption in her problems. She sees virtually no way to escape. Her attempts to relate to men are ineffective and unsatisfying. In short, her overall behavior is characterized by giving up and by negative symptoms related to her actions, thinking, and feelings. Perhaps she has come to counseling before her health is seriously affected.

Establishing the Environment

As in any counseling, a warm, caring relationship is the foundation for change. It is important to listen carefully to Maria, allowing her to tell her story in her own words. Reflective listening and empathy are crucial at this stage. However, the user of reality therapy does not listen passively, but rather attempts to identify themes related to the procedures. For example, Maria's frustrations can be translated into wants. Because she is a verbal client, Maria will probably use metaphors to describe how she feels as well as other aspects of her current plight. Such metaphors might include "I feel like I'm in prison," "I'm really down," "I'm at the end of my rope," and "I feel like a floor mat." These can be used later in the counseling to help her gain a sense of inner control.

In establishing the environment, the reality therapist intervenes directively and empathically but does not encourage "ventilation of feelings" in such a way as to indirectly communicate that merely talking will solve a problem. Feelings are always connected to actions. Such questions as "What did you do yesterday when you felt so depressed?" are very useful.

After a friendly atmosphere has been established, the therapist uses the WDEP system more explicitly.

Using the Procedures

The use of the WDEP system is not a step-by-step process. In fact, there is no absolute delineation between environment and procedures (see Figure 12.1). At the beginning of the session, Maria was encouraged to talk about actions (*D*) when she described her sorrow, pain, guilt, loneliness, and depression. Still, there are many more explicit interventions that are built on the friendly, warm, helping relationship, and these interventions should not be used precipitously in the session.

Exploration of Wants and Locus of Control.   Maria would be asked to describe what she wants (*W*) from the counseling process. She would discuss how she thinks the counselor could help her. The counselor would disclose how he or she can be of assistance, what is realistic, and so forth. Maria would be asked what she wants from the men she dates. Perhaps she would clarify these wants for the first time, and in disclosing this to an empathic listener she would change some of her expectations. The counselor would inquire about her wants relative to her family, her job, her principal, and so forth. Most importantly, the counselor would ask her about what she wants from her church. She may feel guilt at marrying outside her church and then divorcing. The counselor would ask her if she feels guilty and if she wants to resolve this guilt. She would evaluate whether this is possible. The counselor would provide an abundance of assurance that more than likely she can be reconciled to her church, be in good standing again, and be free to marry if she chose to do so. Like any effective counselor, the practitioner of reality therapy recognizes the spiritual aspect of Maria's pain and attempts to deal with it within her cultural and spiritual framework. The counselor would refer her to a priest who would handle the case expeditiously and empathically. This part of her life would have a happy beginning. This discussion is clearly related to her power need.

Exploring Her Specific Actions and Self-Evaluation.   After this exploration of the overall direction of her life, Maria would be asked to describe specifically how she spends her time regarding the other three psychological needs. Belonging relates to family, men, colleagues, and so forth. She would describe specific scenarios related to each. She would then be asked to evaluate her own behavior. Did it work for her? Was it helpful and satisfying?

She would go into detail about the last time she was able to have fun. It would have been a long time since she did something enjoyable. Preoccupation with problems, depression, and fear would be the reasons she would offer for not scheduling fun. Self-evaluation (*E*) would be a major part of this dialogue. If she doesn't allow time for fun, is she helping or hurting herself? Does she think she deserves to get away from her problems for even brief periods of time? The counselor would interject appropriate humor into the session to help her laugh. When she reflects on her laughter and says she felt better for a few seconds, she will come to realize that she can feel better for longer periods of time if she chooses to insert some fun into her schedule.

She would also explore the feeling of being trapped and her lack of freedom. Again, her current actions would be the focus of the discussion. When was the last time she felt freedom or independence? What was she doing? If she doesn't do the same things that helped her feel some degree of freedom earlier in her life, how will anything change for her?

Planning.   The planning phase (*P*) is always dependent on the client's judgments. Thus it is assumed that the plans described below are what Maria wants to do. It is also assumed that she is committed to them and that she has made firm evaluations that her current direction and specific activities are not helping. She is, therefore, ready for a new series of choices. The planning is connected with her needs: belonging, power, freedom, and fun.

Belonging

1. She will continue to date men, but she will have the expectation of merely socializing. She is, therefore, not looking for an intensive relationship or a husband.

2. She will keep the conversation light and friendly with her family for a while. She will be with them spending time that fulfills the conditions for quality time.

3. She will spend quality time with her children each day following the guidelines of no arguing, no blaming, and no criticizing.

4. She will make an effort to "hang out" with the other teachers and have a good time with them.

Power

1. She will make every effort to keep her job and not take the leave of absence. She will go to work unless she is very sick.

2. She will talk to an appropriate priest about her marriage and divorce. This is the top priority to her because her religion is deeply rooted within her, in the family, and in her cultural background.

Freedom

1. She will think about the counselor's comments that nightmares are normal for her and that each time she experiences one, that means she will need to have one less after that. They are not a sign of sickness but are the way she releases tension. She might even be encouraged to try to have a nightmare when she goes to bed.

2. She will also take brisk walks every day and read about the benefits of walking.

Fun

1. She will schedule brief periods of enjoyable activities. At first these might not seem like fun, but eventually she will find them need-satisfying.

2. When she returns to counseling she must tell the counselor two jokes that she read in a book or magazine.

Summary

The goal of this process is helping Maria fulfill her needs more effectively, not merely to remediate problems. Thus the discussions emphasize possibilities rather than problems. The plans must be hers, not merely those of the counselor or therapist who suggests them. The plans are also developmental. Not all of them are formulated at the same time. Perhaps in the first session only one plan is selected.

Finally, using the WDEP system built on the proper atmosphere or relationship, Maria can make significant changes in her life in eight to ten sessions.

References

Barker, P. (1985). *Using metaphors in psychotherapy.* New York: Brunner/Mazel.

Bowers, E. (1997). The effects of CT/RT "Quality School" programming on attendance, academic performance, student self-concept, and relationships in a rural elementary school. *Journal of Reality Therapy, 16*(2), 21–30.

Chance, E., Bibens, R., Cowley, J., Prouretedal, M., Dolese, P., & Virtue, D. (1990). Lifeline: A drug/alcohol treatment program for negatively addicted inmates. *Journal of Reality Therapy, 9,* 33–38.

Cormier, W., & Cormier, L. (1985). *Interviewing strategies.* Monterey, CA: Brooks/Cole.

Corwin, N. (1987). Social agency practice based on reality therapy/control theory. *Journal of Reality Therapy, 7,* 26–35.

Dowd, E., & Milne, C. (1986). Paradoxical interventions in counseling psychology. *Counseling Psychologist, 14*(2), 237–282.

Fay, A. (1978). *Making things better by making them worse.* New York: Hawthorne.

Ford, E. (1979). *Permanent love.* Minneapolis: Winston.

Gang, M. (1975). Empirical validation of a reality therapy intervention program in an elementary school classroom. *Dissertation Abstracts International, 35*(8B), 4216.

German, M. (1975). The effects of group reality therapy on institutionalized adolescents and group leaders. *Dissertation Abstracts International, 36,* 1916.

Glasser, N. (Ed.). (1980). *What are you doing?* New York: Harper & Row.

Glasser, N. (Ed.). (1989). *Control theory in the practice of reality therapy.* New York: Harper & Row.

Glasser, W. (1965). *Reality therapy.* New York: Harper & Row.

Glasser, W. (1968). *Schools without failure.* New York: Harper & Row.

Glasser, W. (1972). *The identity society.* New York: Harper & Row.

Glasser, W. (1976). *Positive addiction.* New York: Harper & Row.

Glasser, W. (1980a). Reality therapy. In N. Glasser (Ed.), *What are you doing?* (pp. 48–60). New York: Harper & Row.

Glasser, W. (1980b). *Stations of the mind.* New York: Harper & Row.

Glasser, W. (1984). *Control theory.* New York: Harper & Row.

Glasser, W. (1986). *A diagram of the brain as a control system.* Los Angeles: Institute for Reality Therapy.

Glasser, W. (1996). *Programs, policies, and procedures of the William Glasser Institute.* Los Angeles: The William Glasser Institute.

Glasser, W. (1998). *Choice theory.* New York: HarperCollins.

Gorter-Cass, S. (1988). Program evaluation of an alternative school using William Glasser's reality therapy model for disruptive youth. *Dissertation Abstracts International, 49,* 1702A.

Hart-Hester, S., Heuchert, C., & Whittier, K. (1989). The effects of teaching reality therapy techniques to elementary students to help change behaviors. *Journal of Reality Therapy, 8*(2), 13–18.

Herlihy, B., Corey, G. (Eds.) (1996). *ACA ethical standards casebook.* Alexandria, VA: American Association for Counseling and Development.

Honeyman, A. (1990). Perceptual changes in addicts as a consequence of reality therapy based on group treatment. *Journal of Reality Therapy, 9*(2), 53–59.

Ivey, A. (1980). *Counseling and psychotherapy.* Upper Saddle River, NJ: Prentice Hall.

Martin, S., & Thompson, D. (1995). Reality therapy and goal attainment scaling: A program for freshmen student athletes. *Journal of Reality Therapy, 14*(2), 45–54.

Parish, T. (1988). Helping teachers take more effective control. *Journal of Reality Therapy, 8*(1), 41–43.

Parish, T. (1991). Helping students take control via an interactive voice communications system. *Journal of Reality Therapy, 11*(1), 38–40.

Parish T., Martin, P., & Khramtsova, I. (1992). Enhancing convergence between our real world and ideal selves. *Journal of Reality Therapy, 11*(2), 37–40.

Peter, L. (1982). *The laughter prescription.* New York: Ballantine.

Peterson, A., Chang, C., & Collins, P. (1997). The effects of reality therapy on locus of control among students in Asian universities. *Journal of Reality Therapy, 16*(2), 80–87.

Peterson, A., & Truscott, J. (1988). Pete's pathogram: Quantifying the genetic needs. *Journal of Reality Therapy, 8*(1), 22–32.

Peterson, A., Woodward, G., & Kissko, R. (1991). A comparison of basic week students and introduction to counseling graduate students on four basic need factors. *Journal of Reality Therapy, 9*(1), 31–37.

Poppen, W., Thompson, C., Cates, J., & Gang, M. (1976). Classroom discipline problems and reality therapy: Research support. *Elementary School Guidance and Counseling, 11*(2), 131–137.

Powers, W. (1973). *Behavior: The control of perception.* New York: Aldine.

Seltzer, L. (1986). *Paradoxical strategies in psychotherapy.* New York: Wiley.

Shea, G. (1973). The effects of reality therapy oriented group counseling with delinquent, behavior-disordered students. *Dissertation Abstracts International, 34,* 4889–4890.

State of Ohio. (1984). Counselor and Social Worker Law (chap. 4757, rev. code). Columbus, OH: Author.

Talmon, M. (1990). *Single-session therapy.* San Francisco: Jossey-Bass.

Weeks, G., & L'Abate, L. (1982). *Paradoxical psychotherapy.* New York: Brunner/Mazel.

Wiener, N. (1948). *Cybernetics.* New York: Wiley.

Wiener, N. (1950). *The human use of human beings: Cybernetics and society.* Boston: Houghton Mifflin.

Wubbolding, R. (1980). Teenage loneliness. In N. Glasser (Ed.), *What are you doing?* (pp. 120–129). New York: Harper & Row.

Wubbolding, R. (1981). Balancing the chart: Do it person and positive symptom person. *Journal of Reality Therapy, 1*(1), 4–7.

Wubbolding, R. (1984). Using paradox in reality therapy: Part I. *Journal of Reality Therapy, 4*(1), 3–9.

Wubbolding, R. (1985a). Characteristics of the inner picture album. *Journal of Reality Therapy, 5*(1), 28–30.

Wubbolding, R. (1985b). Counseling for results. *Not Out of Sight, 6,* 14–15.

Wubbolding, R. (1986). Professional ethics: Informed consent and professional disclosure in reality therapy. *Journal of Reality Therapy, 6*(1), 30–35.

Wubbolding, R. (1988). *Using reality therapy.* New York: Harper & Row.

Wubbolding, R. (1989). Radio station WDEP and other metaphors used in teaching reality therapy. *Journal of Reality Therapy, 8*(2), 74–79.

Wubbolding, R. (1990). Evaluation: The cornerstone in the practice of reality therapy. *Omar Psychological Series, 1*(2), 6–27.

Wubbolding, R. (1991). *Understanding reality therapy.* New York: HarperCollins.

Wubbolding, R. (1993). Reality therapy. In T. Kratochwill (Ed.), *Handbook of psychotherapy with children* (pp. 288–319). Boston: Allyn & Bacon.

Wubbolding, R. (1994). The early years of control theory: forerunners Marcus Aurelius and Norbert Wiener. *Journal of Reality Therapy, 13*(2), 51–54.

Wubbolding, R. (1996a). *Reality therapy training* (9th ed.). Cincinnati: Center for Reality Therapy.

Wubbolding, R. (1996b). Working with suicidal clients. In B. Herlihy & J. Corey (Eds.), *ACA ethical standards casebook.* Alexandria, VA: American Association for Counseling and Development.

Yarish, P. (1986). Reality therapy and locus of control of juvenile offenders. *Journal of Reality Therapy, 6*(1), 3–10.

Integrative Theoretical Applications

A textbook focused on the topic of counseling and psychotherapy would not be complete without the perspectives contained in Part III. Chapter 13, "Family Theory," provides the reader with ideas for working with families since it is important to understand that individual approaches do not adequately address the patterns of communicating and relating that connect individuals to each other in families. The purpose of the chapter is to help the reader find ways to add systems-level interventions to the individualistic approaches studied in previous chapters. We think readers will find this chapter both interesting and informative.

The field of counseling and psychotherapy has made a dramatic shift toward brief counseling and psychotherapy during the past decade. Chapter 14, "Brief Theories," provides the reader with information about brief solution-focused counseling and psychotherapy as well as systematic treatment selection for brief counseling and psychotherapy. We think readers will find this information pertinent to their future roles as practitioners.

Because all of the theoretical positions presented in Part II of this text have a foundation in Western culture, we feel it is important for our readers to be exposed to counseling and psychotherapeutic orientations stemming from Eastern philosophy and religion. It is our hope that such exposure will broaden the readers' perspective by presenting them with diverse viewpoints regarding human nature, theoretical constructs, and their application based upon a philosophical and religious perspective too often missing from current educational programs in counseling and psychotherapy. Chapter 15 provides not only an overview of Eastern theories but also specific information emphasizing Morita therapy and its application to individual counseling and psychotherapy.

Chapter 16, "Counseling and Psychotherapy With Children," provides the reader with information dealing with the child in today's world, developmental perspectives, legal and ethical issues, treatment setting issues, child treatment issues, models for counseling children, and counseling techniques for both younger and older children. We have included this chapter because the majority of the theories used by practitioners were designed to deal mainly with adults.

For the past three decades, writers, researchers, and professionals have been espousing the need for multicultural and cross-cultural strategies and approaches to counseling and psychotherapy. Traditional counseling and psychotherapies were developed for white middle- and upper-middle-class clients. These theories were developed by white practitioners who were enmeshed in Western cultural values; hence the applicability of these theories, without modification, to multicultural populations is questionable. We agonized over the issue of whether to ask each contributing author to include discussion of multicultural and cross-cultural variations or to include a chapter focused solely on this topic and written by individuals known for their expertise in this area. We decided on the latter approach in order to avoid repetition throughout the text and to ensure content of the highest quality. We think you will find Chapter 17, "Counseling and Psychotherapy: Multicultural Considerations," extremely pertinent to your work with racial, cultural, and ethnic minorities. We recommend that you reevaluate the strengths and weaknesses of each of the theories presented in this text after you finish reading Chapter 17.

The authors of Chapter 18, "Counseling and Psychotherapy: An Integrative Perspective," pose the possibility that the profession may be moving away from an idealistic adulation of a "grand master" or a "grand therapy" toward greater personal responsibility in creating clinicians who use an integrative approach in the process of counseling and psychotherapy. The authors discuss three models for integrative work with clients: atheoretical, which emphasizes commonalities or techniques to the exclusion of theory; technical, which emphasizes a single theory base but uses a wide variety of techniques from other orientations; and synthetic, which stresses a blending of two or more theories and a variety of techniques. A discussion of the strengths and weaknesses of an integrative approach, along with considerations for developing such an approach, gives readers some thought-provoking ways to begin assessing their own theoretical orientations. We think this chapter provides appropriate closure for the book and will help readers carefully think through their perspectives about individual work with clients.

Family Theory

Cass Dykeman
Eastern Washington University

Valerie E. Appleton
Eastern Washington University

Background

Why a Chapter on Family Theory?

Up to this point, the chapters in this textbook have focused on counseling and psychotherapy with individuals. Why care about the application of counseling to families? After all, the fathers and mothers of counseling did not seem to care about applying their ideas to whole families. In this chapter, we will present reasons why you should care about the familial applications of counseling and psychotherapy. In addition, we will define key terms, detail prominent theories, and discuss practical applications of these theories.

So why should you care about family therapy? The following questions suggest possible reasons: What would family therapy theories add to your clinical reasoning? What would family therapy techniques add to your clinical tool bag? At the end of this chapter we hope you can list many answers for both questions. Right now, let us start with the assertion that family therapy can enlarge the scope of your clinical reasoning and practice. Specifically, it can enlarge your scope from individuals to families and the larger sociocultural contexts that make up an individual's environment. Family therapy can help you look at the patterns of communication and relationship that connect people to each other and to their social and physical environments (and vice versa).

Definitions

In elementary school education, there is a principle that in grades 1 through 3 a child *learns to read,* and in grades 4 through 6 a child *reads to learn*. In other words, literacy must precede the acquisition of ideas and their applications. This principle is especially true when it comes to learning about family therapy. Family therapists have a maddening habit of both coining new terms and using common terms in unique ways. This habit can sometimes leave neophytes to family therapy in a daze. So, to enhance your understanding of the theoretical and applied discussions in this chapter, we present the following family therapy terms.

Family. This term applies to two or more people who consider themselves family. These persons generally share a common residence and assume the obligations, functions, and responsibilities generally essential to healthy family life, such as economic support (Barker, 1995).

Nuclear Family. The nuclear family is the kinship group that consists of a father, a mother, and their children (Barker, 1995).

Family Therapy. This is an umbrella term for therapeutic approaches where the whole family is the unit of treatment. This term is theoretically neutral, since one can conduct family therapy using a variety of frameworks (Reber, 1986).

Family Therapists. Family therapy is practiced either as a specialty within a profession (e.g., counseling, clinical psychology) or as a stand-alone profession (e.g., marriage and family therapy). Persons who practice family therapy usually possess at least a master's degree (Dykeman & Noble, 1997).

Family System. A family system is a social system built by the repeated interaction of family members. These interactions establish patterns of how, when, and to whom family members relate (Sauber, L'Abate, Weeks, & Buchanan, 1993).

Marital Dyad. This term denotes a relationship composed of a husband and wife (Sauber et al., 1993).

Cybernetics. This term refers to the study of the processes that regulate systems, especially the control of information (Barker, 1995).

Holon. Koestler (1967) coined this term to name whole units nested in larger whole units; for example, the marital dyad in a nuclear family.

Family Boundaries. This term denotes the explicit and implicit rules within a family system that govern how family members are expected to relate to one another and to non-family members (Barker, 1995).

Family Homeostasis. This term is used to describe a family system's tendency to maintain predictable interactional processes. When such processes are operating, the family system is said to be in equilibrium (Sauber et al., 1993).

Centripetal and Centrifugal. These terms were borrowed from physics to describe different relational styles in families. Centripetal families look inward to the family as the source of pleasure, joy, and satisfaction. As such, these families seek to maintain rigid boundaries and harmonious familial interaction. Centrifugal families look outside the family for pleasure, joy, and satisfaction. As such, familial boundaries and interactions are minimized (Beavers & Hampson, 1990).

Feedback Loop.   This term identifies the process by which a system gets the information required to correct itself. This self-correction is exerted either to maintain a steady state (i.e., homeostasis) or to move toward a goal (Nichols & Schwartz, 1995). A system that receives *negative* feedback attempts to maintain a steady state. *Positive* feedback increases deviation from the steady state, enabling the family to evolve to a new state (Kaslow & Celano, 1995).

Family Projection Process.   This term refers to the transmission of a problem in a marital dyad to one of the children. Such a process helps maintain the illusion of a harmonious marital relationship. However, this process occurs at the expense of transmitting the symptoms of the problem to one of the children. Typically, this child is presented at the beginning of family therapy as the "problem to be fixed" (Sauber et al., 1993). Among family therapists, this child is called the "identified patient" or "IP."

The goal of the above section was to add some new terms to your professional vocabulary. Now let us take a closer look at some major family theories and their clinical applications.

Human Nature: A Developmental Perspective

As with individual development, family systems can be seen as a developmental process that evolves over time. Developmental models of family life include the **family life cycle,** the **family life spiral,** and the **family genogram.**

The Family Life Cycle

Jay Haley (1993) offered the first detailed description of a **family life cycle.** He identified six developmental stages, stretching from courtship to old age. Haley was interested in understanding the strengths families have and the challenges they face as they move through the life cycle. He hypothesized that symptoms and dysfunctions appeared when there was a dislocation or disruption in the anticipated natural unfolding of the life cycle: "The symptom is a signal that a family has difficulty in getting past a stage in the life cycle" (p. 42).

Over time, tension inevitably emerges in families because of the developmental changes they encounter (Smith & Schwebel, 1995). Family stress is most intense at those points where family members must negotiate a transition to the next stage of the family life cycle (Carter & McGoldrick, 1988). On one level, this stress may be viewed as part of the family's response to the challenges and changes of life in their passage through time—for example, a couple may encounter tension while making the transition to parenthood with the birth of their first child. On another level, pressures may emerge from the family's multi-generational legacies that define the family's attitudes, taboos, expectations, labels, and loaded issues—for example, over several generations a rule that men cannot be trusted to handle the money may impose stress when the female is absent. When stress occurs on both levels, the whole family may experience acute crisis.

Family therapists can find it difficult to determine the exact sources of stress on a family. Papp and Imber-Black (1996) present an interesting vignette describing the power of illuminating a wide spectrum of stressors for a family. In this vignette, Papp and Imber-Black connect what was viewed as the developmental struggle between a mother and an adolescent son to a three-generation theme of "footsteps." In this case, the adolescent's grades had plummeted and he was both depressed and argumentative. Furthermore, he had engaged in some stealing activity. On the surface, these behaviors can be understood as either symptomatic of family life with an adolescent or symptomatic of life after creation of a blended family. However, by teasing out a specific theme, Papp and Imber-Black discovered that the family's fears emerged as a story about the son "following in the footsteps"—in particular, the footsteps of a drug-dealing father and a larcenous grandfather. The therapists skillfully challenged three generations of the family to tell the family myth about their men who chose the "wrong path." Sorting out the current stressors on the family through the lens of the family scripts encouraged the adolescent to leave behind the old stories to develop his own story. The process also helped his mother to realize how these historic scripts hid her son from her. This multigenerational storytelling intervention worked to free the young man from a catastrophic prophecy while bringing all members of the family into better communication.

The Family Life Spiral

Combrinck-Graham (1985) constructed a nonlinear model of family development called the **family life spiral.** The spiral includes the developmental tasks of three generations that simultaneously affect one another. Each person's developmental issues can be seen in relation to those of the other family members. For example, midlife crisis involves the reconsideration of status, occupation, and marital state for adults in the middle years of their lives. This crisis may coincide with their adolescent children's identity struggles and the parents' plans for retirement. Similarly, when a family's childbearing experience is viewed in terms of grandparenthood, the birth of a child "pushes" the older generations along the timeline, whether or not the grandparents are prepared for their new roles.

The family life spiral looks like an upside-down tornado. This spiral is compact at the top to illustrate the family's closeness during centripetal periods. Also, it is spread out at the bottom to represent centrifugal periods of greater distance between family members. Centripetal and centrifugal periods are further discussed in the following sections.

Centripetal Periods.   The close periods in family life are called "centripetal" to indicate the many forces in the family system that hold the family tightly together (Combrinck-Graham, 1985). **Centripetal periods (CPs)** are marked by an inner orientation requiring intense bonding and cohesion such as early childhood, child rearing, and grandparenting. Both the individual's and the family's life structure emphasize internal family life during these periods. Consequently, the boundaries between members are more diffuse so as to enhance teamwork among the members. In contrast to diffuse internal boundaries, external boundaries may become tightened as if to create a nest within which the family can attend to itself.

Centrifugal Periods.   By contrast, the distant or disengaged periods have been called "centrifugal" to indicate the predominance of forces that pull the family apart (Combrinck-Graham, 1985). **Centrifugal periods (CFs)** are marked by a family's outward orientation. Here the developmental focus is on tasks that emphasize personal identity and autonomy, such as adolescence, midlife, and retirement. As such, the external family boundary is loosened, old family structures are dismantled, and distance between family members typically increases.

The Family Merry-Go-Round.   The terms *centripetal* and *centrifugal* are derived from physics and indicate the push and pull of forces on and within things—in this case, families. These forces might also be compared to the process of riding a merry-go-round. On a merry-go-round, the centripetal force is the push you will need to keep you on your horse. You push against the spinning ride toward the center of the rotation. The centrifugal force is what tries to pull you off and out into the world away from the spinning direction. For example, if you let go of your horse's pole, this force will pull you away from the merry-go-round. In this case your seat belt will help!

It is important to recognize that families are also in a constant process of pushing and pulling in order to adapt to life's events. Families move between centripetal and centrifugal forces depending on the developmental tasks required of them at various stages of the family life cycle. A family will typically move through one cycle each 25 years. This period is the time required to produce a new generation. Within each family cycle, different members will experience:

1. One's own childhood (CP) and adolescence (CF).
2. The birth (CP) and adolescence (CF) of one's children.
3. The birth (CP) and development (CF) of one's grandchildren.

These developmental shifts have been called "oscillations" that provide opportunities for family members to practice intimacy and involvement in the centripetal periods and individuation and independence in the centrifugal periods (Combrinck-Graham, 1988).

Implications for Practice.   Neither direction—centripetal or centrifugal—defines a pathological condition. These directions describe the relationship styles of the family at particular stages of the family life spiral. Symptom formation often occurs when the family is confronted with an event that is out of phase with the anticipated development of the family life spiral. Such events include untimely death, birth of a disabled child, chronic illness, or war. For some families, stress will develop around typical developmental demands, such as children's needs for dependency as infants, or adolescents' demands for more autonomy. The intensity and duration of family anxiety will affect the family's ability to make the required transitions. The purpose of family therapy is to help the family past the transitional crisis so that they can continue toward the next stage of family life.

The Family Genogram

Genograms give family therapists another useful way to conceptualize family development. Typically genograms are used to chart the progression of a particular family through the life cycle over at least three generations. It is like a family tree that includes information about birth order, family members, their communications, and issues of relationships. The work of McGoldrick and Gerson (1985) provides an excellent resource for clinicians unfamiliar with the use of genograms. Genograms often provide the basis of clinical hypotheses in family work and offer a culturally sensitive method for understanding individual or family clients. For example, Magnuson, Norem, and Skinner (1995) recommend mapping the relationship dynamics in the families of gay or lesbian clients. They point out the importance of mapping the relationship markers of gay or lesbian couples that are not recognized by general society (e.g., marriage). A genogram is included as an organizing element in the case study presented later in this chapter.

Major Constructs

Theoretical Antecedents

The present family systems theories emerged out of the ideas and debates in the social and physical sciences after World War II. In the next two sections we will outline the specific ideas that led to the development of a systems approach to counseling and psychotherapy.

Bateson.   **Gregory Bateson** is acknowledged by many as the pioneer in applying cybernetic systems thinking to human interaction. He saw that cybernetics provided a powerful alternative language for explaining behavior—specifically, a language that did not resort to instinct or descriptions of the internal workings of the mind (Segal, 1991). Bateson began to use these ideas to understand social interaction (Bateson, 1951). For instance, he applied cybernetic principles to the study of families of schizophrenics (Haley, 1976). Bateson considered pattern, process, and communication as the fundamental elements of description and explanation. He believed that by observing human systems he could formulate the rules governing human interaction.

The Palo Alto Group.   In 1952, while based in Palo Alto, Bateson received a grant from the Rockefeller Foundation to investigate the general nature of communication. He was joined on this project by Jay Haley, John Weakland, William Fry, and Don D. Jackson. This research team defined the family as a cybernetic, **homeostatic** system whose parts (i.e., family members) co-vary with each other to maintain equilibrium by means of error-activated negative feedback loops (Jackson, 1957). For example, whenever deviation-amplifying information is introduced (e.g., an argument between two family members or the challenge of a new stage in the family life cycle), a designated family member initiates a counter-deviation action (e.g., a family member exhibits symptomatic behavior), such that the family's existing equilibrium is restored (i.e., threatened changes are defeated). The emphasis on homeostasis prevailed in family therapy theory into the 1980s.

The recognition of the **symptomatic double bind** as a homeostatic maneuver regulating family patterns of relationship is considered the definitive contribution of the Palo Alto Group. The symptomatic double bind most often cited is Bateson's classic example of the interaction between a mother and her son who had "fairly well recovered from an acute schizophrenic episode." Bateson described this interaction as follows:

[The son] was glad to see her and impulsively put his arm around her shoulders, where-upon she stiffened. He withdrew his arm and she asked, "Don't you love me any more?" He then blushed, and she said, "Dear, you must not be so easily embarrassed and afraid of your feelings." The patient was able to stay with her only a few minutes more, and follow-ing her departure, he assaulted an aide and was put in the tubs. (Bateson, Jackson, Haley, & Weakland, 1976, pp. 14–15)

The Palo Alto Group noted both the incongruence of the mother's message and the fact that the son could not clearly and directly comment on it. They concluded that the son's craziness was his commentary on his mother's contradictory behavior.

Bateson's work in the 1950s spawned the development of many family therapy mod-els, including the strategic model of Haley (1991) and Madanes (1991). An examination of this model will follow our discussion of the ideas of another Palo Altoan—Virginia Satir.

Conjoint Theory

Virginia Satir is among the best-loved of all theorists in the field of family therapy—and, arguably, beyond. After leaving a career as a schoolteacher, she first practiced as a psy-chiatric social worker, then engaged in private practice work with families. In 1959 she joined the Mental Research Institute in Palo Alto. Satir gained international recognition with the publication of her first book, *Conjoint Family Therapy,* in 1964.

Satir acknowledged the impact of a diverse group of theorists on her life's work (Satir & Bitter, 1991). These included Fritz Perls (Gestalt therapy), Eric Berne (transactional analysis), J. J. Moreno (psychodrama), Ida Rolf (life-posturing reintegration), Alex Lowen (bioenergetics), and Milton Erickson (hypnosis). Her family therapy model reflects a growth perspective rather than a medical model for assessing and working with families. In her frame, illness was seen as an appropriate communicative response to a dysfunc-tional system or family context. Health, therefore, is developed when the system is changed so as to permit healthy communication and responses.

Like other communication theorists, such as Bateson, Satir defined **congruence** as the use of words that accurately match personal feelings. In other words, congruence is where direct communication and the meta-communication are the same. When using con-gruent communication, the person is alert, balanced, and responsive to any question or topic without needing to hold back. In contrast, **incongruence** is seen as communication wherein the nonverbal and verbal components do not match. Examples of incongruent communication include double messages, assumptions, ambiguous messages, and in-complete communication. Satir saw self-esteem as the basis for family emotional health. Her perspective was that there is a correlation between self-esteem and communication. Low self-esteem is associated with poor communication because low self-esteem affects behavior and interactions among the members of the system. She also held that mal-adaptive communication can be both learned and unlearned.

To demonstrate concretely to a family how incongruence occurs and is a source of pain and poor self-esteem, Satir would ask them to join into a game. The communication game would typically be used to work with two members. She observed that when a per-son delivers an incongruent or mixed message there is little skin or eye contact. It is as though the sender is "out of touch" with the other person. In the communication game, Satir taught families to improve their communication through a series of interactions that concretely show people what happens when they do not look, touch, or speak congruently. Satir (1983) outlined these steps as follows:

1. Place two persons back to back and ask them to talk.
2. Turn them around and have them "eyeball" each other without touching or talking.
3. Then they "eyeball" and touch without talking.
4. Then they are asked to touch with eyes closed and without talking.
5. They "eyeball" each other without touching.
6. Finally the two talk and touch and "eyeball" and try to argue with each other.

By the last stage of the game the couple usually finds it impossible to argue with one another. The problem of delivering an incongruent message is clear to the family when one is touching, talking, and looking at the listener.

Besides the humor of this process, the provocative nature of this game encourages a deeper examination of the ways family members suffer and feel inadequate or devalued when engaged in incongruent communication patterns. These revelations are supported through steps toward increasing self-esteem and communication as the family moves from a "closed" to a more "open" system. Satir believed that a functional family is an **open system** wherein there is a clear exchange of information and resources both within the system and with the others outside the family. In contrast, a **closed system** is rigid and maladaptive.

Satir observed that family pain is symptomatic of dysfunction. She did not feel that the problems the family brought to her were the real difficulty. Rather she saw that methods of coping within the family and rules for behavior that were fixed, arbitrary, and inconsistent decreased the family's ability to cope over time. Her approach involves the following treatment stages:

1. Establish trust.
2. Develop awareness through experience.
3. Create new understanding of members and dynamics.
4. Have family express and apply their new understandings with each other.
5. Have the family use their new behaviors outside therapy.

As the family moves through this cycle of change, they feel less anxious and more fully valued and valuing of each other (Satir & Bitter, 1991). In this way, self-esteem, communication, and caring are raised and pain is decreased.

Strategic Theory

Jay Haley left Palo Alto in 1966 and joined **Salvador Minuchin** in Philadelphia to pursue his growing interest in family hierarchy, power, and structure. In 1974 he established the Washington Institute of Family Therapy, where he was joined by **Cloe Madanes.** Their family therapy model has three roots: the strategic therapy of Milton Erickson, the theories of the Palo Alto Group, and the structural therapy of Minuchin.

Haley (1991) and Madanes (1981) asserted that a family's current problematic relational patterns were at some point useful because they organized family members in a concerted way to solve an existing problem. These patterns persisted because they protected the family from the threat of disintegration. Haley held that therapeutic change occurs when a family's dysfunctional protective patterns are interrupted. He noted that the role of family therapists, through the use of directives, is to provoke such interruptions. Haley offered therapist provocations such as the following:

- A husband and wife with sexual problems may be required to have sexual relations only on the living room floor for a period of time. This task changes the context and so the struggle.

- A man who is afraid to apply for a job may be asked to go for a job interview at a place where he would not take the job if he got it, thereby practicing in a safe way.

For Haley, therapist directives served three purposes: to facilitate change and make things happen; to keep the therapist's influence alive during the week; and to stimulate family reactions that give the therapist more information about family structure, rules, and system. Haley held that the goal of therapy was not client insight—in fact, the actual mechanisms of change need not be understood by the family. Furthermore, the therapist should act without trying to convince the family that the set of hypotheses guiding the therapy is valid. Haley commented that "the goal is not to teach the family about their malfunctioning system but to change the family sequences so that the presenting problems are resolved" (p. 135).

Haley's ideas have direct consequences for the family therapist wishing to practice a strategic approach. First, a strategic family therapist attends to what is defined by the family members experiencing the problem as the "nature of the problem." Second, the therapist focuses on how the family is responding in attempting to resolve the problem. The assumption here is that it is often the very ways in which families are defining a problem and responding to it that may "keep it going" in a vicious problem-solution cycle.

Structural Theory

Structural family therapists do not "sit on the sidelines" during therapy. Rather, they become involved with family members, pushing and being pushed. Minuchin put a strong emphasis on action in his own work as a family therapist. His justification for this emphasis was his belief that "if both I and the family take risks within the constraints of the therapeutic system, we will find alternatives for change" (Minuchin & Fishman, 1981, p. 7). He commented that observers of his structural family therapy work would notice (a) his concern with bringing the family transactions into the room; (b) his alternation between participation and observation as a way of unbalancing the system by supporting one family member against another; and (c) his many types of response to family members' intrusion into each other's psychological space (Minuchin & Fishman).

Minuchin's therapeutic maneuvers were based on his theoretical schema about family structure and family transformation. He carried out his vision by being uniquely himself. He stated:

> In families that are too close, I artificially create boundaries between members by gestures, body postures, movement of chairs, or seating changes. My challenging maneuvers frequently include a supportive statement: a kick and a stroke are delivered simultaneously. My metaphors are concrete: "You are sometimes sixteen and sometimes four"; "Your father stole your voice"; "You have two left hands and ten thumbs." I ask a child and a parent to stand and see who is taller, or I compare the combined weight of the parents with the child's weight. I rarely remain in my chair for a whole session. I move closer when I want intimacy, kneel to reduce my size with children, or spring to my feet when I want to challenge or show indignation. These operations occur spontaneously; they represent my psychological fingerprint. (Minuchin & Fishman, 1981, p. 7)

For Minuchin, family therapy techniques are uniquely integrated in the person of the counselor or therapist who goes "beyond technique" to wisdom, specifically, wisdom concerning "knowledge of the larger interactive system—that system which, if disturbed, is likely to generate exponential curves of change" (Bateson, 1972, p. 439).

Transgenerational Theory

Murray Bowen's approach to family therapy, like Haley's, had many roots. Specifically, Bowen merged concepts such as Freud's unconscious id and Darwin's theory of evolution with his own observations of schizophrenics at the Menninger Clinic and the National Institute of Mental Health. His core idea was the concept of the **differentiation** of self. It was through this concept that Bowen addressed "how people differ from one another in terms of their sensitivity to one another and their varying abilities to preserve a degree of autonomy in the face of pressures for togetherness" (Papero, 1990, p. 45).

Bowen also posited that there were two different systems of human functioning: an emotional and reactive system which humans share with lower forms of life, and an intellectual and rational system that is a more recent evolutionary development. The degree to which these two systems are fused or undifferentiated is the degree to which the individual is vulnerable to the impulses of his or her emotional system and less attentive to his or her intellectual and rational system. For example, people are more likely to react emotionally rather than rationally when they are anxious. Bowen asserted that the extent to which persons have differentiated their thinking system from their emotional system will determine how able they are to maintain a sense of self in relationships with others, particularly members of their family.

Bowen believed that emotional illness was passed from one generation to another through the **family projection process (FPP).** FPP theory suggests that the ego differentiation achieved by children will generally approximate that of their parents. However, FPP often distributes the capacity for differentiation unevenly among family members. For example, one child may grow up with a high level of ego differentiation, while a sibling may grow up with a low level of differentiation. The hallmark of a high level is a well-defined sense of self and low emotional reactivity, whereas a low level is characterized by a poorly defined sense of self and high emotional reactivity.

Low levels of ego differentiation occur when parents "triangulate" a child into their conflicts in order to dissipate the stresses of their relationship. Bowen (1978) held that "triangles" were the natural consequence of two poorly differentiated people who are overwhelmed by anxiety and seek relief by involving a third party. Triangulation is how parents' low level of differentiation is passed on to the next generation. Bowen's work has influenced many of the present family therapy theorists. One of the best examples of the extension of Bowen's ideas is McGoldrick's (1985) work on genograms. This work was discussed earlier in the chapter.

Narrative Theory

Long before "constructivism" or "narrative" became common terms in counseling, family therapists used story-making. Papp and Imber-Black (1996) cite various names coined to identify the role of story in family work, including "family myth," "family paradigm," and, more recently, "landscape of consciousness."

The narrative therapy approach of family therapist **Michael White** (1992) was built on the writings of French philosopher and social historian Michel Foucault (1980), who described the process whereby knowledge is embedded in language and serves the values of the dominant culture. Narrative has become a popular method for therapy based on the notion that individuals, families, and entire cultures are given a different level of power as creators of their realities.

Concerning reality creation, White and Epston (1990) asserted that the social sciences classify and minimize people around a norm that becomes internalized. People take on these objective categorizations and see themselves as "a schizophrenic" or as "having a behavior disorder." Solutions to such internalized and normative problems are limited. To overcome this internalization, narrative family therapists work to help families "externalize" problems through storytelling. This **externalization** can give a family the ability to construct a story wherein the problem is subject to manipulation or change because it exists as a separate entity. Also, externalization can break the retelling of complaint-saturated stories and offer a sense of personal agency. A common question asked in narrative family therapy is "How has the problem affected your life?" Such a question works to separate the family from their problem.

Families have styles for telling their stories. Roberts (1995) defined six types of story styles: intertwined, separated, interrupted, secret, rigid, and evolving. For example, family members may offer intertwined stories so the events described at one time are used to make sense of other circumstances. Conversely, a rigid story is frozen and told over and over in the same way without interpretations. Everyone in the family knows these stories by heart because they have been told so often. Once the type and goals of the story style are determined, the counselor or therapist can work with the family to see what resources they have available and open possibilities for making new meaning out of personal histories. Roberts's work offers another method for assessing the types of stories told and their possible therapeutic uses.

The major constructs discussed in this section were developed by clinicians to understand how families function. As we have seen, family theorists conceptualized the communication patterns, structures, relationship dynamics, and story-making processes of their client families. The concepts they developed reflected their own therapeutic interventions. In this way family theory is a rich resource to students and family practitioners. Table 13.1 provides an overview and comparison of these major theoretical constructs.

Table 13.1
Major Family Therapy Theoretical Constructs

	Conjoint	Strategic	Structural	Trans-generational	Narrative
Major theorists	Satir	Haley, Madanes	Minuchin	Bowen, McGoldrick	White
What family members participate in therapy?	Flexible	Everyone involved in the problem	Whoever is involved and accessible	The most motivated family member(s)	Flexible
What is the theory of dysfunction?	Low self-esteem; poor communication	Confused hierarchy; rigid behavioral sequences	Enmeshed or disengaged boundaries; intrafamilial coalitions	Emotional fusion (symbiosis with family of origin); anxiety; triangulation	Disempowerment by the dominant cultural narrative
What are primary goals of therapy?	Improved communication; personal growth	Problem solving; restore hierarchy	Change the family structure; increase flexibility	Greater differentiation of self; reduced anxiety	Empowerment through reauthoring the family's life story
How is family functioning assessed?	Family life chronology	Structured initial interview; intervene and observe the reaction	Joining the family to experience its process; chart family structure	Genogram	Narration of family history and myths
What is the temporal focus of therapy?	Present	Present	Present	Past	Present and past
What are common intervention practices?	Modeling and coaching clear communication; family sculpting; guided interaction	Directives are used to change behavior; they may be straightforward, paradoxical, or ordeals	Reframing is used to change the perception of the problem; structure is changed by unbalancing and increasing stress	Reducing anxiety by providing rational, untriangulated third party; coaching to aid in differentiation from family of origin	Externalization of family problems through narration
What characterizes the therapist's approach to the family?	Active, directive, matter-of-fact, nonjudgmental; models open communication	Active, directive, but not self-revealing; planful, not spontaneous	Active, directive, personally involved; spontaneous; humorous	Interested but detached; reinforces calmness and rationality	Active partnership; encourages the telling of family history and myths

Applications

Overview

All counseling and psychotherapy approaches share a common goal of producing change in clients. In this section, we will differentiate family therapy applications from the applications of the individualistic approaches you have studied in the previous chapters. Our goal is to help you find ways to add systems-level interventions to both your clinical reasoning and your counseling tool bag.

Goals of Counseling and Psychotherapy

Family therapy represented a watershed in the history of counseling. Before family therapy, the focus of counselors and therapists had been solely on the individual. The goal of counseling was always to change some cognitive, affective, or behavioral component of an individual. In contrast, family therapists aim to change systems within which individuals reside. Becvar and Becvar (1993) compared how the worldview of individual psychotherapy differed from that of family systems psychotherapy. Table 13.2 details the major differences they mentioned.

The Process of Change

Family therapists use cybernetics to understand change—specifically, the cybernetic control processes involving information and feedback. Information in the form of feedback precipitates shifts that either amplify or counteract the direction of change. Family therapists differentiate between **first-order change** and **second-order change.** Lyddon (1990) succinctly defined these different types of change as follows: "First-order change is essentially 'change without change'—or any change within a system that does not produce a change in the structure of the system. In contrast, second-order change is 'change of change'—a type of change whose occurrence alters the fundamental structure of the

Table 13.2
Worldview Comparison

Individual Psychotherapy	Family Systems Psychotherapy
Asks, Why?	Asks, What?
Linear cause/effect	Reciprocal causality
Subject/object dualism	Holistic
Either/or dichotomies	Dialectic
Value-free science	Subjective/perceptual
Deterministic/reactive	Freedom of choice/proactive
Laws and lawlike external reality	Patterns
Historical focus	Here-and-now focus
Individualistic	Relational
Reductionistic	Contextual
Absolutistic	Relativistic

system" (p. 122). At any given moment, counselors and psychotherapists can only bring about one or the other type of change in their clients. Now let us look at these change types more closely.

First-Order Change.   First-order change occurs when a family modifies problem behaviors yet maintains its present structure. An example of a first-order change intervention is a family therapist's instructing parents when they can fight with their son over bedtime. By this intervention, the family therapist hopes to give the family relief from their problem behavior; radical change of present family system is not a goal. Family therapists call the process of bringing about this type of change "negative feedback."

Second-Order Change.   **In contrast to first-order change, **second-order change refers to transformations in either the structure or the internal order of a system. Family therapists often seek to generate or amplify change processes that will alter the basic structure of a family system (Nichols & Schwartz, 1995). This goal embodies second-order change. An example of a second-order change intervention is a family therapist's directing the more passive parent to take over bedtime compliance responsibility with the goal of changing the power dynamics in the marital dyad. Family therapists call the process of bringing about second-order change "positive feedback."

Intervention Strategies

The case study for this chapter will illustrate in detail one way to conduct family therapy. Besides the strategies presented in the case study, there are two additional points on family therapy applications to which we would like to draw your attention. The first is an understanding of the significance of nonspecific factors in family therapy outcomes. The second is how to structure the first session so that family therapy can get off to a good start.

Specific Versus Nonspecific Factors.   **A strong current trend in individual-focused counseling research is an examination of the specific and nonspecific factors involved in treatment outcomes. **Specific factors are those counseling activities that are specific to a particular counseling approach—for example, a strategic family therapist's use of a "proscribing the symptom" intervention. **Nonspecific factors** are those change-producing elements present in counseling regardless of theoretical orientation. Many nonspecific factors have been proposed, but few have withstood empirical testing. One exception is working alliance. In fact, working alliance scores are the best-known predictor of counseling outcomes (Horvath, 1994).

The modern transtheoretical definition of **working alliance** was promulgated by **Edward Bordin** (1994), who posited that there were three components of working alliance: task, goal, and bond. He conceptualized these three components as follows:

- **Task** refers to the in-therapy activities that form the substance of the therapeutic process. In a well-functioning relationship, both parties must perceive these tasks as relevant and effective. Furthermore, each must accept the responsibility to perform these acts.

- **Goal** refers to the counselor and the client mutually endorsing and valuing the aims (outcomes) that are the target of the intervention.

- **Bond** embraces the complex network of positive personal attachments between client and counselor, including issues such as mutual trust, acceptance, and confidence. (Adapted from Horvath, 1994)

Overall, Bordin's working alliance model emphasized "the role of the client's collaboration with the therapist against the common foe of the client's pain and self-defeating behavior" (Horvath, p. 110).

Family therapists have been slower to examine the nonspecific factors involved in positive treatment outcomes. One exception was **William Pinsof** of The Family Institute (Evanston, Illinois). In his research, Pinsof (1994) found a positive relationship between working alliance and family therapy outcomes. The few other studies conducted on working alliance in family therapy produced similar results to Pinsof's research (Friedlander, Wildman, Heatherington, & Skowron, 1994).

Given the effectiveness of working alliance concerning treatment outcomes, persons practicing family therapy would be wise to attend carefully to such alliances. However, such attention would run counter to the preeminence family therapists give to technique. Coady (1992) noted that the emphasis in family systems theory on homeostasis has led to family therapists' viewing family members as being dominated by the family system. Thus, family therapists "often expect families to exert an oppositional force against change efforts, and they feel compelled to manipulate the family into change" (p. 471). Unfortunately, such a perspective runs exactly counter to formation of strong working alliances. We want to be careful to note that a commitment to build strong working alliances with your client families does not mean you have to dismiss technique. Rather, it means acknowledging that techniques should not be separated from the interpersonal and cultural contexts in which they occur (Coady).

The Family Interview.   From the start, Haley (1991) advocated brevity and clarity in counseling work with families. He stated that "if therapy is to end properly, it must begin properly—by negotiating a solvable problem and discovering the social situation that makes the problem necessary" (p. 8). To help family therapists start on a good note, Haley outlined a structured family interview for use during an initial session. The five stages of this structured family interview are as follows:

1. *Social*—the interviewer greets the family and helps family members feel comfortable.

2. *Problem*—the interviewer invites each person present to define the problem.

3. *Interaction*—the interviewer directs all members present to talk together about the problem while the interviewer watches and listens.

4. *Goal setting*—family members are invited to speak about what changes everyone—including the "problem" person—wants from the therapy.

5. *Ending*—directives (if any) are given and the next appointment is scheduled.

The information gained from the first interview helps the family therapist form hypotheses about the function of the problem within its relational context. Moreover, this information can help the family therapist generate directives to influence change. For Haley, "the first obligation of a therapist is to change the presenting problem offered. If that is not accomplished, the therapy is a failure" (p. 135).

Evaluation

Overview

The emergence of managed care has radically altered the delivery of mental health services. Increasingly, those who pay for treatment are demanding proof of efficacy. This demand for efficacy has extended to those professionals practicing family therapy (Crespi, 1997). In this section we will review what is known about the efficacy of family therapy.

Supporting Research

Historically, empirical research has not been a strong component of family therapy (Gladding, 1998). Lebow and Gurman (1995) noted that "at one time, most research on couples and families was conducted with little or no connection to the outstanding clinical developments in the field. Alternative modes of investigation such as inductive reasoning, clinical observation, and deconstruction have dominated in the development of methods and treatment models. Some couple and family therapists have even been reluctant to acknowledge that empirical research has an important role" (p. 29). Fortunately, this reluctance was overcome and solid research evidence for the efficacy of family therapy now exists—evidence that professionals practicing family therapy can use to defend their work in the world of managed care.

The key review of family therapy efficacy research can be found in Lebow and Gurman (1995). The two reported finding support for family therapy as an efficacious intervention with a variety of mental health concerns, including adolescent drug abuse, depression, alcoholism, delinquency, parenting, schizophrenia, and agoraphobia. In another major review, Alexander and Barton (1995) noted research support for family therapy as an effective treatment for anxiety, pediatric psychopathy, and adolescent behavior problems.

Research on treatment outcome predictors is useful to family therapy practitioners. Unfortunately, little credible research has been conducted in the area. One notable exception is a recent study by Hampson and Beavers (1996), who studied family and therapist characteristics in relation to treatment success. Their subjects were 434 families treated at an actual family therapy clinic in Dallas. Hampson and Beavers reported the following predictors of successful treatment:

- Number of family therapy sessions attended.
- Third-party ratings of family competence.
- Self-ratings of family competence.
- Therapists' ratings of working alliance.

Hampson and Beavers's measure of family competence included items on family affect, parental coalitions, problem-solving abilities, autonomy and individuality, optimistic versus pessimistic views, and acceptance of family members. The two reported that the six-session mark was the breakpoint in increasing the probability of good results. However, a sizable subset of families did well with fewer than six sessions. What distinguished this subset of families was their strong self-ratings of competence. Hampson and Beavers were careful to note that family size, family income, family structure (e.g., blended), family ethnicity, and therapist gender did not predict outcome.

Limitations

One of the basic ethical principles in health care is the principle of non-maleficence—that is, "above all, do no harm." To carry out this ethical principal, you must make yourself aware of the limitations of each counseling approach contained in this textbook. To that end, we now present three limitations to family therapy approaches.

First, the early language chosen for describing family systems was "combative and bellicose, often suggesting willful opposition: double bind, identified patient, family scapegoat, binder, victim, and so on" (Nichols, 1987, pp. 18–19). The choice of language emphasized the destructive power of families and contributed to an assault on the family by several pioneers in family therapy (Cooper, 1970). This assault has continued to the present because many family therapy educators and practitioners have overread this language and adopted a directive, manipulative approach to treatment. This overreading led to unfortunate consequences. For instance, Green and Herget (1991) discovered that at their family therapy clinic many families found "paradoxical prescriptions as signs of therapist sarcasm or incompetence, that engender massive resistance, sometimes destroying all together the clients' faith and cooperative attitude in therapy" (p. 323). Also, Patterson and Forgatch (1985) uncovered in their study of families in treatment a direct relationship between client resistance and frequency of therapist directives.

Second, family is a culturally determined phenomenon. Kaslow, Celano, and Dreelin (1995) correctly noted that "the dominant American definition, reflecting white Anglo Saxon Protestant (WASP) values, focuses on the intact nuclear family unit. African Americans' definition of family refers to a wide network of kin and community. For many Italian Americans, family implies a strong, tightly knit three- or four-generation unit including godparents and old friends. The traditional Chinese definition of family includes ancestors and decedents" (p. 622). You will serve your clients well if you remember that the proper application of family therapy always involves a consideration of cross-cultural limitations.

Third, family therapists have ignored the different socialization processes operating for men and women. Thus, family therapists have not adequately considered how these socialization processes have disadvantaged women (Friedlander et al., 1994). Walters, Carter, Papp, and Silverstein (1988) called for family therapists to review all family therapy concepts through the lens of gender socialization in order to eliminate the dominance of male assumptions. Their hope was that such a review would promote the "recognition of the basic principle that no intervention is gender-free and that every intervention will have a different and special meaning for each sex" (p. 29).

Summary Chart—Family Theory

Human Nature
Like models used to explain individual development across the life span, the creation and maintenance of a family system can be viewed as a developmental process that evolves over time. Developmental models of family life include the family life cycle, the family life spiral, and the family genogram.

Major Constructs
There are a variety of constructs associated with family theory, and each theory contributes discrete concepts. Conjoint theory, strategic theory, structural theory, transgenerational theory, and narrative theory are overviewed in this chapter as points of departure for some of the major constructs connected with counseling and psychotherapy with couples and families.

Goals
The goals of individual counseling are usually aimed at changing cognitive, affective, or behavioral components of the individual. In contrast, family counselors and psychotherapists aim to change whole systems.

Change Process
Family counselors and psychotherapists use cybernetics to understand change. Specifically, the cybernetic control processes involve information and feedback. Information in the form of feedback precipitates shifts that either amplify or counteract the direction of change. Family counselors and therapists differentiate between first-order and second-order change.

Interventions
Strategies and interventions associated with systemic change in families are varied; many were first introduced in the context of a specific family theory. Since systemic change can be difficult to precipitate, family therapists must be well schooled and supervised in the application of interventions. In addition, practitioners must be able to set boundaries and limits with couples and families and be "powerful" and strategic in their choices and development of treatment plans.

Limitations
The choice of language connected with couples and family counseling and psychotherapy often emphasizes the destructive power of families and contributes to an "assault" on the family. At times, practitioners forget that the proper use of interventions always involves consideration of cross-cultural variations that may limit applicability. Often, practitioners have ignored the different socialization processes operating for men and women and how these processes have disadvantaged women.

The Case of Maria: A Family Theory Approach

Presenting Problem

Juanita Van Pelt (age 8) was suspended by Roosevelt Elementary School for stealing money from her classmates. Juanita was suspended along with two other classmates, both of whom had a long history of discipline problems despite their young age. This suspension was Juanita's first. After the suspension, Roosevelt's school counselor, Domingo Chavez, held a conference with Juanita's mother, Maria Van Pelt (age 32). He reported to Maria that Juanita has recently committed many disciplinary infractions—something they had not seen before in Juanita. Maria acknowledged that she was having problems at home with both Juanita and Norberto, Juanita's brother. Mr. Chavez noted that the kindergarten teacher was concerned that Norberto (age 6) always seemed sullen and uncooperative.

In talking with Maria, Mr. Chavez sensed that she was feeling overwhelmed with her children's problems. He asked if she had considered counseling to work on these problems. Maria said that she had, in fact, consulted her physician and that this doctor had given her a referral to a respected psychiatrist located downtown. However, Maria reported that she had not followed up on this referral due to the cost and travel involved. Also, she commented that her faith was very important to her and she was unsure if the psychiatrist would respect her faith. Mr. Chavez suggested to Maria that an alternative existed. He reminded her that since Maria was a school district employee, she could take advantage of the services offered by the school district's employee assistance program (EAP). Mr. Chavez said that currently the EAP allowed six counseling sessions per year at no cost. Also, he noted that Catholic Social Services was one of the contracted EAP providers. Maria went home and immediately called the Catholic Social Services office at her local parish, St. Gregory's. She scheduled an appointment for herself, Juanita, and Norberto for the next Tuesday.

Therapists

Mrs. Mesa and Sr. Benedict were the co-therapists assigned to work with Maria and her children. They are both staff therapists with the diocese's Catholic Social Services. Mrs. Mesa possesses a national certification in family therapy. Sr. Benedict holds a national certification as an art therapist and has worked extensively with families.

Family Demographics and History

Maria and her children live in a blue-collar neighborhood of Tucson, Arizona. Maria's former husband, Mark Van Pelt (age 33), is a civil engineer. He lives in Boston and has no direct contact with Maria or his two children. Maria works as a junior high math and science teacher. Also living in Tucson are Maria's parents—Jose Maria Flores (age 52) and Rosa Flores (age 51)—and Mark's parents—Joe (age 54) and Babs (age 50). Both sets of grandparents interact periodically with Maria and her children, but these relationships are very strained. Besides these grandparents, all of Maria's siblings live in Tucson. These include Juan (age 31), Enrique (age 30), Ernesto (age 29), and Bonita (age 28). Maria's relationships with her siblings are tension-filled. Especially painful to Maria is Bonita's refusal to talk to her. In contrast to the present, Maria and Bonita were close as children.

Maria's marriage outside her faith caused intense familial discord. This discord exposed subtle tensions and power alliances that existed in the Flores family. Only Ernesto attended Maria's wedding. Bonita blames all current interpersonal conflicts in the Flores family upon Maria and her "disloyalty" to the family. Following the lead of Maria's father, the Flores family maintains a strong covert adherence to a rule of not directly addressing personal problems such as family conflict (i.e., a "no talk" rule). The one exception to this rule is the sacrament of confession with the parish priest. Besides this exception, the Flores family views sharing personal problems as a sign of weakness. Maria's genogram appears in Figure 13.1.

Family Therapy Process

Intake Interview. Maria arrived 15 minutes early for her appointment and brought Juanita and Norberto as planned. Norberto sucked his thumb during the interview. Juanita was also quiet and appeared to believe she was being punished. In the intake interview, Maria spoke of her financial fears, frustrations with parenting, and sense of alienation from her parish and family.

Case Conceptualization and Treatment Planning. Mrs. Mesa and Sr. Benedict diagnosed Maria as suffering from late-onset Dysthmic Disorder (Axis I: 300.4). The therapists conceptualized this disorder as a post-traumatic symptom. The specific traumas in Maria's case were the psychological and physical battering from Mark, her family's rejection of her because of her out-of-faith marriage, and her perception that she could not fully participate in the sacramental life of her parish because she was divorced. Mrs. Mesa and Sr. Benedict decided that their family therapy work would need to occur on three levels: Maria's immediate family (i.e., Maria, Juanita, and Norberto), Maria's family of origin, and Maria's

Figure 13.1
Maria Van Pelt's Genogram

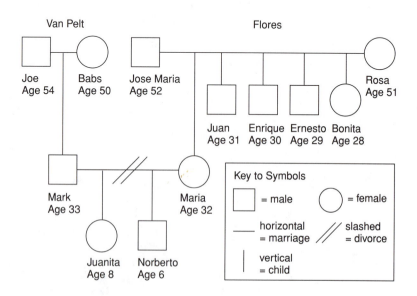

parish family. The therapists prioritized the addressing of Maria's traumas in the following order: (1) family-of-origin level, (2) parish family level, and (3) immediate family level. The therapists felt that Juanita's and Norberto's acting out was a symptom of the children's vicarious traumatization, a traumatization that took place and was maintained by living in a family system with a parent who was a trauma victim. Mrs. Mesa and Sr. Benedict believed that if they could adequately address Maria's traumas, they could remediate the family structures that maintained Juanita and Norberto's problematic behaviors.

To address Maria's alienation from her family of origin, the two therapists proposed that Maria bring her parents and siblings to the next session. Maria cried and stated that she doubted if they would all come, because "We don't talk about problems in the family." Sr. Benedict proposed that she call each family member and invite them to come to the next session. Maria thought that they might consider an invitation from Sr. Benedict, and she eagerly gave her permission. Sr. Benedict did call the family members, and after some persuading they all agreed to come. Mrs. Flores's sister agreed to baby-sit Juanita and Norberto during the sessions.

Trauma survivors such as Maria pose intense challenges for family therapists (Balcom, 1996). Unfortunately, most trauma treatment techniques are oriented toward individual or group work. However, art has been shown to be effective with both family dysfunctions (Sobol, 1982) and trauma resolution (Appleton, 1993). Haley (1990) held that metaphor was a basic means of family communication, and Sobol (1982) drew upon this idea in designing her family therapy interventions. She chose art because its inherent metaphorical qualities can facilitate productive family communication—specifically, by permitting family members to express and represent problems in a less destructive way than do words or action. Mrs. Mesa and Sr. Benedict decided that they would ask the members of the Flores family to participate in a series of drawing tasks and then use the information obtained through the art products to set goals and plan directives. They felt that art tasks could help "restructure" the Flores family system—specifically, by restructuring that system through reconnecting family members via culturally powerful symbols. As in narrative therapy approaches, the metaphor that would emerge from the Flores family's art processes helped family members to rediscover their deep interconnectedness to each other.

Session 1.   The first session involved building a working relationship with the members of the Flores family and engaging them in a series of art tasks to help them begin to express themselves.

Building Working Alliances.   Mrs. Mesa and Sr. Benedict have both worked extensively with Latino families. This experience influenced the selection and application of their interventions. For instance, they initiated *la platica* (i.e., small talk) with family members at the initial session. La platica is an essential part of creating a working relationship with Latino families.

Combining Strategic Family Therapy With Art.   Both Mrs. Mesa and Sr. Benedict were worried about the Flores family's covert "no talk" rule. They designed a series of four art tasks to help the family members begin to express themselves. The first drawing task eased the family into the art-making process by introducing the material with a warm-up process (individual free drawing). The second and third drawings focused specifically on the problems and resolutions identified by each family member. The final art process put the entire family together to create a family mural on one piece of paper. Through the art task sequence, the family was moved from a distant to a closer physical proximity. At the end of the family art process, the therapists reviewed all of the drawings with the family. The assignments given for each of the tasks were:

- "Make an individual free drawing of anything that comes to mind."
- "Make an individual drawing of why you think you are here."
- "Make an individual drawing on how you would like the 'problem' to change."
- "Now together, make a joint mural about your family."
- "At this time we will review the drawings you have made."

Sr. Benedict often used this series of tasks with families like Maria's that maintained structure by covert communication norms. The use of such tasks allows a family therapist to do the following:

- Elicit metaphorical information for planning future intervention.
- Provide drawing tasks that disrupt dysfunctional family communication patterns (e.g., a family's covert "no talk" rule).
- Help family members express themselves free of covert familial communication norms. (Adapted from Sobol, 1982)

Given the tension present in the family system, each member of the Flores family welcomed Sr. Benedict's initial suggestion that they start out by working on their own drawing. The therapists had a wide array of drawing materials available for the family members to use, including oil and chalk pastels and felt marker pens.

Free Drawing Art Task.   Maria's free drawing was a weeping, pregnant image of the Virgin. In high school, Maria and Bonita were members of their parish's Legion of Mary. They enjoyed belonging to this group because of a strong devotion to Our Lady rooted in Latino cultures (i.e., *Marianismo*).

After 20 minutes, Mrs. Mesa had the family members stop their drawings and share them with the whole family. Maria showed her drawing of the Virgin. The family was moved to tears by Maria's expressive representation of the Virgin. Without words, they surrounded Maria. Bonita even took Maria by the hand. Sr. Benedict read these nonverbal behaviors as a sign that the family had moved to some new level of communication, a new level that contained acknowledgment of, and empathy for, Maria's suffering. To concretize this new connection to Maria, Sr. Benedict directed the other family members to add to Maria's drawing through the production of a joint mural.

Family Mural Art Task.   After the mural was completed, Mrs. Mesa asked each family member to discuss the feelings the mural evoked about the family. At this point, Bonita asked Maria why her drawing of Our Lady was weeping. Maria hesitated, and then looked toward her mother. In a halting voice, Maria replied that the Virgin weeps for Maria because the Virgin understands the sorrow of pregnant, unmarried women. Then Maria walked over and knelt in front of her mother. Maria began to weep uncontrollably. Rosa looked at her and softly said, "This is why you married Mark and left the family." Maria nodded yes, and Rosa kissed her on the forehead in reconciliation.

Sessions 2-5.   The next four sessions involved rebuilding family connectedness and "trying on" new styles of communication. Again, Sr. Benedict used art tasks to facilitate culturally salient modes of communication. Despite this work, Maria's full reentry to her familial life remained blocked by her belief that as a divorced woman, she could not participate in the sacramental life of her parish. This left Maria feeling marginalized in the Flores family. Sr. Benedict corrected Maria's mistaken notion that divorced persons could not receive communion. She also set up an appointment for Maria with a member of her own community who does marriage tribunal work. This sister would help Maria to receive a marriage annulment so that she would become free to remarry in the Church.

During one of these middle sessions, the art tasks served as a potent stimulus for self-discovery. Maria's chalk pastel drawing recounted her strong devotion to the Blessed Sacrament during her high school years. Maria shared how this devotion had helped her weather the typical turmoils of adolescence. Mrs. Mesa helped Maria negotiate with her parents to baby-sit Juanita and Norberto three time a week so she could spend an hour meditating in the Perpetual Adoration Chapel at St. Gregory's. Later, Maria reported to Mrs. Mesa that these hours were meaningful to her and gave her a sense of peace she had not felt in a long time.

Session 6: Termination.   As Maria began to reenter full family and parish life, her dysthmia lifted and she began to have more energy for her work and her children. By the final session of family therapy, Maria reported that neither Juanita nor Norberto was having any disciplinary problems in school. Also, the renewed consistency in Maria's parenting had begun to help her build a productive relationship with Joe and Babs Van Pelt. Mrs. Mesa and Sr. Benedict worked with Maria to help her outline the boundaries she wanted to set in her relationship with the Van Pelts.

References

Alexander, J., & Barton, C. (1995). Family therapy research. In R. H. Mikesell, D. Lusterman, & S. H. McDaniel (Eds.), *Integrating family therapy* (pp. 91–112). Washington, DC: American Psychological Association.

Appleton, V. (1993). An art therapy protocol for the medical trauma setting. *Art Therapy Journal of the American Art Therapy Association, 10,* 71–77.

Balcom, D. (1996). Interpersonal dynamics and treatment of dual trauma couples. *Journal of Marital and Family Therapy, 22*(4), 431–442.

Barker, R. L. (1995). *The social work dictionary*. Washington, DC: National Association of Social Workers.

Bateson, G. (1951). The convergence of science and psychiatry. In J. Ruesch & G. Bateson (Eds.), *Com-*

munication: *The social matrix of psychiatry* (pp. 257–272). New York: Norton.

Bateson, G., Jackson, D. D., Haley, J., & Weakland, J. G. (1976). Toward a theory of schizophrenia. In C. E. Sluzki & D. C. Ransom (Eds.), *Double bind: The foundation of the communicational approach to the family* (pp. 3–22). New York: Grune & Stratton.

Bateson, M. C. (1972). *Our own metaphor.* New York: Knopf.

Beavers, W. R., & Hampson, R. B. (1990). *Successful families.* New York: Norton.

Becvar, D. S., & Becvar, R. J. (1993). *Family therapy: A systemic integration.* Boston: Allyn & Bacon.

Bordin, E. S. (1994). Theory and research on the therapeutic working alliance: New directions. In A. O. Horvath & L. S. Greenberg (Eds.), *The working alliance* (pp. 13–37). New York: Wiley.

Bowen, M. (1978). *Family therapy in clinical practice.* New York: Jason Aronson.

Carter, B., & McGoldrick, M. (1988). Overview: The changing family life cycle: A framework for family therapy. In B. Carter & M. McGoldrick (Eds.), *The changing family life cycle* (pp. 3–28). New York: Gardner Press.

Coady, N. F. (1992). Rationale and directions for the increased emphasis on the therapeutic relationship in family therapy. *Contemporary Family Therapy, 14,* 467–479.

Combrinck-Graham, L. (1985). A developmental model for family systems. *Family Process, 24,* 139–150.

Combrinck-Graham, L. (1988). Adolescent sexuality in the family life spiral. In C. J. Falicov (Ed.), *Family transitions* (pp. 107–131). New York: Guilford.

Cooper, D. (1970). *The death of the family.* New York: Pantheon.

Crespi, T. D. (1997). Managed mental health care and institutional downsizing: Status, directions, and considerations for the family therapist. *Family Therapy, 24,* 1–8.

Dykeman, C., & Noble, F. C. (1997). Counseling couples and families. In D. Capuzzi & D. R. Gross (Eds.), *Introduction to the counseling profession* (pp. 366–396). Boston: Allyn & Bacon.

Foucault, M. (1980). *Knowledge/power: Selected interviews and other writings.* New York: Pantheon.

Friedlander, M. L., Wildman, J., Heatherington, L., & Skowron, E. A. (1994). What we do and don't

know about the process of family therapy. *Journal of Family Therapy, 8,* 390–416.

Gladding, S. T. (1998). *Family therapy: History, theory, and practice* (2nd ed.). Upper Saddle River, NJ: Merrill/Prentice Hall.

Green, R., & Herget, M. (1991). Outcomes of systemic/strategic team consultation: III. The importance of therapist warmth and active structuring. *Family Process, 30,* 321–335.

Haley, J. (1976). Development of a theory: A history of a research project. In C. E. Sluski & D. C. Ransom (Eds.), *Double bind: The foundation of the communicational approach to the family* (pp. 59–104). New York: Grune & Stratton.

Haley, J. (1990). *Strategies of psychotherapy.* New York: Norton.

Haley, J. (1991). *Problem-solving therapy.* San Francisco: Jossey-Bass.

Haley, J. (1993). *Uncommon therapy.* New York: Norton.

Hampson, R. B., & Beavers, W. R. (1996). Measuring family therapy outcome in a clinical setting: Families that do better or do worse in therapy. *Family Therapy, 35,* 347–361.

Horvath, A. O. (1994). Empirical validation of Bordin's pantheoretical model of the alliance: The Working Alliance Inventory perspective. In A. O. Horvath & L. S. Greenberg (Eds.), *The working alliance* (pp. 109–130). New York: Wiley.

Jackson, D. D. (1957). The question of family homeostasis. *Psychiatric Quarterly Supplement, 31,* 79–90.

Kaslow, N. J., & Celano, M. P. (1995). The families therapies. In A. S. Gurman & S. B. Messer (Eds.), *Essential psychotherapies* (pp. 343–402). New York: Guilford.

Kaslow, N. J., Celano, M., & Dreelin, E. D. (1995). A cultural perspective on family theory and therapy. *Cultural Psychiatry, 18,* 621–633.

Koestler, A. (1967). *The ghost in the machine.* London: Hutchinson.

Lebow, J. L., & Gurman, A. S. (1995). Research assessing couple and family therapy. *Annual Review of Psychology, 46,* 25–57.

Lyddon, W. J. (1990). First- and second-order change: Implications for rationalist and constructivist cognitive therapies. *Journal of Counseling and Development, 69,* 122–127.

Madanes, C. (1981). *Strategic family therapy.* San Francisco: Jossey-Bass.

Madanes, C. (1991). Strategic family therapy. In A. S. Gurman & D. P. Kniskern (Eds.), *Handbook of family therapy* (Vol. 2) (pp. 396–416). New York: Brunner/Mazel.

Magnuson, S., Norem, K., & Skinner, C. H. (1995). Constructing genograms with lesbian clients. *The Family Journal: Counseling and Therapy for Couples and Families, 3,* 110–115.

McGoldrick, M., & Gerson, R. (1985). *Genograms in family assessment.* New York: Norton.

Minuchin, S., & Fishman, C. (1981). *Family therapy techniques.* Cambridge: Harvard University Press.

Nichols, M. P. (1987). *The self in the system: Expanding the limits of family therapy.* New York: Brunner/Mazel.

Nichols, M. P., & Schwartz, R. C. (1995). *Family therapies.* Boston: Allyn & Bacon.

Papero, D. V. (1990). *Bowen family systems theory.* Boston: Allyn & Bacon.

Papp, P., & Imber-Black, E. (1996). Family themes: Transmission and transformation. *Family Process, 35,* 5–20.

Patterson, G. R., & Forgatch, M. S. (1985). Therapist behavior as a determinant for client noncompliance: A paradox for the behavior modifier. *Journal of Consulting and Clinical Psychology, 53,* 846–851.

Pinsof, W. M. (1994). An integrative systems perspective on the therapeutic alliance: Theoretical, clinical, and research implications. In A. O. Horvath & L. S. Greenberg (Eds.), *The working alliance* (pp. 173–198). New York: Wiley.

Reber, A. S. (1986). *Dictionary of psychology.* New York: Penguin.

Roberts, J. (1995). Exploring story styles. *The Family Journal: Counseling and Therapy for Couples and Families, 3,* 158–163.

Satir, V. M. (1983). *Conjoint family therapy* (Rev. ed.). Palo Alto: Science & Behavior Books.

Satir, V. M., & Bitter, J. R. (1991). The therapist and family therapy: Process model. In A. M. Horne & J. L. Passmore (Eds.), *Family counseling and therapy* (pp. 13–45). Itasca, IL: F. E. Peacock.

Sauber, R. S., L'Abate, L., Weeks, G. R., & Buchanan, W. L. (1993). *The dictionary of family psychology and family therapy.* Newbury Park, CA: Sage.

Segal, L. (1991). Brief therapy: The MRI approach. In A. S. Gurman & D. P. Kniskern (Eds.), *Handbook of family therapy* (Vol. 2) (pp. 171–199). New York: Brunner/Mazel.

Smith, G. B., & Schwebel, A. I. (1995). Using a cognitive-behavioral family model in conjunction with systems and behavioral family therapy models. *American Journal of Family Therapy, 23,* 203–212.

Sobol, B. (1982). Art therapy and strategic family therapy. *American Journal of Art Therapy, 21,* 23–31.

Walters, M., Carter, B., Papp, P., & Silverstein, P. (1988). *The invisible web: Gender patterns in family relationships.* New York: Guilford.

White, M. (1992). Deconstruction and therapy. In D. Epston & M. White (Eds.), *Experience, contradiction, narrative, and imagination: Selected papers of David Epston and Michael White, 1989–1991* (pp. 105–151). Adelaide, Australia: Dulwich Centre Publications.

White, M., & Epston, D. (1990). *Narrative means to therapeutic ends.* New York: Norton.

Brief Theories

Conrad Sieber
Portland State University

Rolla E. Lewis
Portland State University

Background

Brief Counseling and Psychotherapy

How do the results of **brief therapy** compare with those of **long-term therapy?** This is the perspective from which brief counseling and psychotherapy have often been examined. This approach dichotomizes many issues that do not lend themselves well to such dualistic thinking. Defining the processes and outcomes of counseling and psychotherapy is rarely an either/or, cured/not cured kind of issue. In fact, when you read the case example at the end of this chapter you will review a case that might best be addressed by a combination of brief symptom-focused intervention and a more ongoing counseling process once the client is stabilized. Brief therapy, at least in part, has grown out of the context of limited resources for mental health care. That is neither bad or good—it just is. Given a wide spectrum of brief therapies, our intent here is to be integrationist because brief counseling is an expansive topic encompassing many divergent theories that cannot be examined all at once. Therefore, as you read, look for themes and contrasts and as best you can frame the question and promise of brief counseling and psychotherapy in a nondichotomous way.

To be sure, the field of counseling and psychotherapy has made a dramatic shift toward brief treatment in the past two decades, but this does not mean that these interventions are a panacea (Wells & Giannetti, 1990). Simply put, the bottom line we face as prac-

The authors wish to thank Alex Aginsky for his assistance in the development of this chapter.

titioners is first, efficacy, and second, efficiency (Posavac & Carey, 1996)—that is, does it work, and how much does it cost? Efficiency and resourcefulness go to the heart of limiting treatment length and creating brief therapy interventions. Thus, the move toward brief therapy indicates a change in orientation guiding a growing number of counselors. As O'Hanlon (1990) says, "The issue isn't whether therapy is brief or not, but whether it is effective. Brief therapy can teach us much about how to do effective therapy" (p. 88).

If effectiveness is an essential quality of brief therapy, then **outcome research** should help guide our study of this topic. In fact, outcome research indicates that the factors central to success in therapy are often not specific to the interventions themselves but are best described as client and therapist characteristics (Beutler & Clarkin, 1990). After reviewing the outcome research literature, Beutler (1994) concluded that 75% of client improvement is due to the context within which treatment occurs (i.e., setting, mode, format, frequency, duration), the amount of support an agency can provide, and the internal and external resources of the client. Only 10% of change is accounted for by type of intervention. Yet this is where most research—not to mention most teaching, training, and writing—focuses. In fact, given over 400 theories of psychotherapy, it is improbable that each represents independent and original interventions (Beitman, 1987; Beutler & Clarkin, 1990). Thus, exploring client characteristics, therapy relationship variables, and the strengths and limitations of various treatment settings is necessary as we evaluate brief counseling and psychotherapy.

Sometimes brief interventions have been trivialized by an excessive focus on the issue of treatment length. Focusing primarily on treatment duration to define an intervention is a very blunt instrument and the wrong focus (Beutler, 1994). At its extreme this means that client resources, therapist knowledge, assessment, and interventions are less important than the time itself. It is analogous to saying that the most important thing physicians offer patients is time, not what is done with that time. For example, would it make sense to allot six 30-minute office visits to all medical patients regardless of diagnosis? This very equation has been used in mental health treatment by mental health agencies and insurance providers that establish maximum session limits without enough regard for diagnosis, client problems, and resources. We hope the point is clear: who we and our clients are—including their resources and difficulties and how we work with them—are the important domains of focus. Assessment of these domains logically determines treatment length.

Another way to frame the discussion is to acknowledge the reality and challenge of practicing in a marketplace of limited and sometimes scarce resources. Brief therapy can guide the use of these limited resources. The pressure from **stakeholders** who pay for the bulk of treatment to move practice toward brief counseling has not only been driven by economics but has also been influenced by the difficulty or reticence of therapists to evaluate counseling outcomes, with the result that **third-party payers** cannot easily determine treatment efficacy, duration, or cost based on diagnosis or client problem type (Beutler, 1994). As a profession we need greater clarity, specificity, and evaluation of our work to truly be a discipline that remains meaningful for improving clients' lives. This is substantiated by studies showing that many clients may get better whether or not they see a professional (Strupp & Hadley, 1979).

Studies that report average length of treatment are another confusing issue in the debate over brief therapy. For instance, the mean number of sessions for most outpatient counseling is six with a mode of one (Beutler, 1994). These numbers are often bandied about to justify extensive use of brief counseling with widely divergent groups of clients. However, this fact alone may be misleading. We need to know about the client population and clinicians studied in order to better understand the meaning of this finding. For instance, one of us worked in an agency that reallocated resources to prevention and therefore instituted a six-session limit based on the aforementioned statistic. However, if a client fails to return after one session because he or she did not feel heard, how should we view this treatment outcome? And should all these one-session visits be included in calculating an average number of client sessions? In reviewing the literature on treatment duration, Beutler (1994) concluded that most **single-session clients** actually seek treatment from another provider! On the other hand, if a client sees a counselor or therapist weekly for three years with no improvement in functioning or symptoms, should we include this in our study on treatment duration? If taken out of context, studies on average length of treatment can be misleading. In fact, several agencies anecdotally report that average length of treatment increased when session limits were instituted, supposedly because many clients began to define their use of therapy by the maximum number of available sessions. Beutler (1994) substantiates this claim, noting that the average number of sessions for brief therapy is 15 possibly because treatment duration is determined at the outset.

Arbitrary session limits are also dangerous to some clients. For instance, one of us worked with a mother who had been severely battered by her former partner. This woman was struggling with post-traumatic stress disorder and depression. Her previous service provider had a session limit of ten. After ten sessions this client was terminated, although it should have been clear from the diagnosis and common sense alone that she needed additional assistance. For her the arbitrary session limit became a barrier to regaining her health and a subtle message that she was either too damaged or too needy to be helped. Two years passed before she was back in therapy and her needs could be addressed adequately and realistically. In the intervening period the system's failure, as well as the client's naïveté in seeking assistance or feeling worthy of help, led to disruption of her employment and the threatened loss of her parental rights. At a systems level, much money was being spent, albeit outside the realm of treatment. On the other hand, how much could have been saved had children's services, the employer, and the community mental health agency worked together to truly serve this client?

Beutler (1994) has described studies of treatment duration in a helpful way. He states that clients with more complex problems transition from what we think of as brief therapy to longer-term therapy at about sessions 8 through 12. That is, as treatment continues beyond 8 to 12 sessions, client and therapist appear to make a transition to a more ongoing, longer-term therapy process. In fact, he concludes that clients terminating between sessions 10 and 15 do worse after treatment than those who terminate earlier or later, possibly because they leave with much unfinished business or at an inappropriate time in the change process.

For advocates of brief counseling, the good news is that many clients with situational difficulties, and those with more serious mental disorders who are stable and can select a circumscribed focus, can be effectively helped in a relatively short time. For example, Beutler (1994) reports that over a 12-week period, 80% of clients with symptoms of 6 weeks' duration respond well to any form of treatment. In cases that present with more long-standing difficulties, treatment appears to take longer. For instance, 50% of clients with major depression and anxiety disorders are usually asymptomatic by the 25th session, while 80% of this group are improved by the 50th (Beutler, 1994). Thus, clients with more serious long-standing problems benefited from longer-term interventions lasting 6 to 12 months. On the other hand, it is distressing to note that the number one recommendation by therapists to clients who do not improve in therapy is more of the same therapy with the same therapist (Beutler, 1994)! This certainly affects treatment duration.

In the earlier example of the battered woman, a common dilemma was raised for the practitioner who could only offer brief counseling. That is, should a client with long-term treatment needs be served in a setting where there is a 10-session limit? If the answer is no, where will a low-income client find long-term help, and what if any responsibility does the brief counselor or therapist have for this client? For that matter, once treatment began, was there an ethical or moral responsibility to inform the client more thoroughly about the limitations of her current care and the need for more extensive work based on her diagnosis in order to advocate or refer her for the assistance she needed? Sometimes therapists doing brief therapy must use case management skills to help clients who need longer-term assistance seek out such help.

In this chapter, brief counseling will be examined through description of **brief solution-focused therapy (BSFT),** a mental health resource model, and **systematic treatment selection (STS),** an integrationist model. STS is informed by psychotherapy outcome research and guides counselors in choosing the appropriate treatment setting, intervention, duration, and focus for counseling (Beutler & Clarkin, 1990). The focus in this chapter is on using STS for brief counseling interventions. Metaphorically, BSFT can be thought of as a tree in the broader forest of therapy that STS attempts to capture in its fullness and complexity. The message here is that in reality the practice of counseling and psychotherapy is not easily fragmented and compartmentalized into separate units such as brief and long-term treatment.

Brief Solution-Focused Therapy

Cade and O'Hanlon (1993) identify BSFT as a cognitive-behavioral treatment influenced by strategic therapy. De Jong and Berg (1998) more accurately define BSFT as a strengths perspective model with a **social constructionist philosophy.** In a number of brief therapies we find a mental health resource model that emphasizes client strengths and innate capacity for mental health (De Jong & Berg, 1998; de Shazer, 1990; Durrant, 1995; Durrant & Kowalski, 1993; Hart, 1995; Mills, 1995, 1996; Mills, Dunham, & Alpert, 1988; Pransky, Mills, Sedgeman, & Blevens, 1997). Social constructionism is a well established perspective in the discipline of sociology (Sarbin & Kitsuse, 1994). It asserts that people make meaning of reality through their interactions with others. Given individual, family, and group relationships, individual and social meanings develop, evolve, and persist over time.

To understand the social constructionist perspective, it is important to note that any historical-personal-theoretical construct encompasses a "complex narrative" that lends itself to "multiple truths and alternative interpretations" (Sarbin, 1993; Sarbin & Kitsuse, 1994). That is, constructs such as "shy" or "introverted" come to have meanings that are influenced by the historical, personal, and theoretical context of both their creators and their consumers. Any story or **narrative** serves two functions: "(1) it provides forms for interpretation and (2) it provides guides for action" (Sarbin, 1993, p. 57). Thus, BSFT focuses on client strengths, and challenges our profession to move beyond what Gergen (1990) calls a "language of mental deficit" that leads to dependency on the helping professions and to progressive infirmity and self-enfeeblement. As a mental health resource model, BSFT is concerned with collaborating with clients to develop solutions for difficulties that are viewed as a natural part of life. "From a constructivist vantage point, psychotherapy can be defined as the variegated and subtle interchange and negotiation of (inter) personal meanings" (Neimeyer, 1995, p. 2). **Constructivism** is a concept used in theories of psychotherapy to focus on the centrality of meaning-making to human experience, as meaning is co-created by the individual in relationship with others. It explores similar territory as social constructionism. Therefore, the counseling process is not about counselors helping clients correct objectively defined problems; instead, therapy is a collaborative process that promotes the creation of meaning, personal responsibility, and agency (Cade & O'Hanlon, 1993; De Jong & Berg, 1998; de Shazer, 1994; Mahoney, 1995; Monk, Winslade, Crocket, & Epston, 1997; Neimeyer & Mahoney, 1995; Sarbin & Kitsuse, 1994). Understanding the value placed on utilizing client resources is critical to becoming competent as a solution-focused counselor or therapist.

De Shazer (1994) describes the historical roots of BSFT. In the 1950s, Don Jackson, Gregory Bateson, John Weakland, and Jay Haley worked in a research group that applied the scientific model of its time to psychotherapy. This model emphasized systems, homeostasis, redundancy, communication, relationships, and circular causes. This group consulted regularly with **Milton Erickson,** who had a profound influence on the development of brief therapy. "Erickson viewed clients as having within them or within their social systems the resources to make the changes they needed to make. . . . [He] didn't view people as fundamentally flawed or in need of fixing" (O'Hanlon & Weiner-Davis, 1989, p. 16). Erickson is one of the principal innovators in the therapeutic field because he challenged the medical model's dominant problem-classification system, with its problem-solving premises guided by a linear, cause-and-effect view of clinical practice. Erickson broke through the convergent reasoning that viewed client problems as medical puzzles with single answers. He used divergent thinking to see problems as having more than one correct solution and clients as having answers within themselves.

Another influence on the development of BSFT was the **Mental Research Institute (MRI),** founded by **Don Jackson** in 1958. Although Bateson and Erickson were not a part of this group, their ideas influenced its thinking about the role of systems in creating and sustaining problems (Cade & O'Hanlon, 1993; Cooper, 1995). In 1966, **Richard Fisch** initiated the **brief therapy project** at MRI. In essence, the MRI tactic was to resolve problems by narrowing the treatment focus and helping clients change specific behaviors that were connected to their difficulties (Fisch, 1990; Fisch, Weakland, & Segal, 1982).

Steve de Shazer co-founded the **Brief Family Therapy Center** with **Insoo Kim Berg** in Milwaukee, Wisconsin, and was influenced by the work at MRI. He moved beyond a focus on problem-sustaining factors to develop a model based on **focused solution development.** By asking clients questions and prescribing tasks to clarify their needs, goals, and personal resources for finding solutions, the therapeutic process focused on looking forward to changes and striving to promote positive growth. BSFT continues to grow and evolve, and the strengths perspective influences counseling practice worldwide (De Jong

& Berg, 1998; de Shazer, 1990; Durrant, 1995; Durrant & Kowalski, 1993; Hart, 1995; Mills, 1996). In Australia and New Zealand the concept of helping clients focus primarily on finding their own resources and solutions grew independently of de Shazer's work and developed into **narrative therapy.**

A fruitful and sometimes heated dialogue over the years has revealed common ground and differences between BSFT and narrative therapy (Hart, 1995). Influenced by Bateson's notion that all understanding requires acts of interpretation on the part of individuals, **Michael White** and **David Epston** (1990) created a narrative model that helped clients understand their inherent knowledge of solutions while taking authorship of their lives by **restorying** their self-limiting, problem-saturated life stories. Drawing on the work of French historian and philosopher **Michel Foucault,** White challenged the mental health profession to question its "move, deliberately or inadvertently, into the role of classifying, judging, and determining what is a desirable, appropriate, or acceptable way of life" (Monk, 1997, p. 8). By focusing on the unique outcomes (i.e., successes) that contradict clients' self-limiting, problem-saturated view of their lives, narrative therapists collaborate with clients to re-author alternative stories. In the process, clients are helped to recognize their **personal agency** and **power.** Solutions constructed in the narrative approach help people address issues of power, meaning, and narrative (Durrant & Kowalski, 1993; Hart, 1995; Monk et al., 1997; White & Epston, 1990). Narrative therapists' essential credo is that "the person is never the problem; the problem is the problem" (O'Hanlon, 1994, p. 23). Narrative therapy's constructs and practices have influenced the work of solution-focused counselors (Durrant, 1995; Durrant & Kowalski, 1993; Hart, 1995; Metcalf, 1995; Murphy, 1997; Selekman, 1993).

Systematic Treatment Selection for Brief Counseling

According to Beutler and Clarkin (1990), clinical wisdom has relied upon the belief that client and problem factors lead to the use of specific interventions. They conclude that the inability of research to demonstrate specific definable factors leading to choice of specific interventions is caused by "coarse-grained diagnostic systems" (p. 14) and the bias of researchers who focus on variables different from those valued by clinicians. If this is so, no wonder there is so much confusion about what does and doesn't work! Thus it is necessary to identify more sensitive and specific measures of predisposing client, technique, and counseling relationship factors to fully evaluate the hypothesis that these variables can lead to the selection of specific interventions.

Based on the above analysis, the STS model is designed to enhance treatment outcomes while making the counseling process amenable to evaluation. Outcome information can then be used to make changes in theory and practice that lead to improved treatment efficacy. The STS model is grounded in theories of eclectic treatment. **Technical eclecticism** seeks to develop empirical models for improving the effectiveness of prescribing counseling interventions. **Systematic eclectic psychotherapy** (Beutler, 1983) is a form of technical eclecticism (Lazarus, 1981) that creates decision-making guidelines for specifying treatment interventions irrespective of the theories that led to their development. Thus, systematic eclectic psychotherapy prefers pragmatism to theoretical dogma, a theme found in many brief counseling theories. **Common factors eclecticism,** another eclectic treatment theory, focuses on the role of **nonspecific treatment factors** found in the counseling relationship that affect treatment outcomes, such as caring, empathy, credibility, and supportiveness (Garfield, 1980; Parloff, 1986). These nonspecific treatment factors are common to many psychotherapies and are often described as (therapy) relationship factors. In the STS model, these common treatment factors are considered to be definable and controllable patterns of communication "characteristic of caring therapists" (Beutler & Clarkin, 1990). These variables are created by counselors who can have control over their development and can be trained to make effective use of this control.

In summary, systematic eclectic psychotherapy, a theory of technical eclecticism, focuses on prescribing discrete interventions based on client factors such as problem complexity and defenses, whereas common factors eclecticism, a theory of eclectic treatment, focuses on counseling relationship variables (Beutler & Clarkin, 1990). Creating a confluence of these approaches, STS is comprehensive and integrationist. It focuses on several interrelated dimensions across time which provide criteria for determining length and duration of treatment, its focus, short- and long-term treatment goals, and choice of intervention. Thus treatment efficacy is improved by providing the counselor or therapist with tools that guide increasingly specific treatment decisions as the phases of therapy unfold. STS rectifies the tendency among researchers and practitioners to focus on one class of variables (e.g., therapy relationship factors) to the exclusion of others (e.g., client problem factors). Although a more detailed discussion of the theoretical foundations of STS is beyond the scope of this chapter, the interested reader is referred to Beutler and Clarkin (1990) and Beutler, Consoli, and Williams (1995).

Human Nature

Brief Solution-Focused Therapy

Although BSFT does not offer a developmental perspective, it clearly states that people create the meaning in their lives. People construct reality with language, and many of their problems are maintained as the result of a **construction of reality** that discounts their natural competence and resources. The emphasis on creating meaning appears to be rooted in an understanding of how language works to help people perceive and define the world around them. Thus de Shazer (1994) draws upon **postmodern philosophy, linguistics,** and **epistemology** in developing his theory.

Solution-focused counselors believe that **objective reality** does not exist because the act of describing experience itself requires subjective interpretation. As such, this non-objectivist view challenges the belief that language describes reality, and points to a perspective where meaning and understanding of reality are negotiated: "Neither authors (or speakers) nor readers (or listeners) can be assured that they can get at what the other person meant with any certainty because they each bring to the encounter all their previous and unique experiences. Meaning is arrived at through negotiation within a specific context" (Berg & de Shazer, 1993, p. 7). In other words, reality is not out there to be grasped; rather, we continually negotiate meanings in our conversations with others. People are natural storytellers trying to make sense of and take action in the world.

BSFT's emphasis on **story making** to understand and define experience creates the current exchange of ideas with narrative therapists. Solution-focused counselors would agree with the storied nature of human existence. On the other hand, narrative counselors are very mindful of the larger social context within which their work is embedded and the inherent potential for counselors and therapists to reproduce, in the helping relationship, patterns of domination and oppression that exist in society. Narrative therapy's awareness that some human stories are oppressive helps identify issues of gender, race, culture, and power in the therapeutic relationship, whereas such issues are not deemed central by solution-focused therapists.

Solution-focused counselors hold the belief that people are experts on their own lives, are naturally competent and capable of change, and have self-correcting tendencies, personal responsibility, and personal agency. They can get unstuck and change (Durrant & Kowalski, 1993). This emphasis on competence rather than pathology, and on therapists collaborating with clients to help them draw upon their inherent resources, is not a new perspective on human nature (Avis, 1987; Cade & O'Hanlon, 1993; de Shazer, 1994; Mahoney, 1995; Mills, 1995; Monk et al., 1997; Neimeyer & Mahoney, 1995; Sarbin & Kitsuse, 1994). It is one that capitalizes on client strengths, expertise, and inherent mental health (Mills, 1995, 1996).

Systematic Treatment Selection for Brief Counseling

As an integrationist and eclectic theory, STS draws on many sources with divergent views of human nature. Its atheoretical, pragmatism-based foundation makes it difficult to categorize in terms of human nature. However, STS may be broadly described as an **ecological model** that views human behavior and experience as resulting from an interaction between the person and the **social and physical environment.** Thus, brief interventions may focus on changing client environments to facilitate and support change. Human behavior results from transactions in which people bring their genetic makeup into play in a social and physical environment full of possibilities and constraints. Individuals both influence and are influenced by these environments. Given STS's reliance on pragmatism and concrete evaluation of therapy outcomes, it can be presumed that people have a natural capacity to change and improve their lives given the appropriate challenges and support.

Major Constructs

Brief Solution-Focused Therapy

BSFT is not a cookbook of techniques. It is a constantly evolving theory and philosophy of counseling and psychotherapy. In essence, BSFT practice requires an optimistic orientation (Walter & Peller, 1992). Its main assumptions include the following:

1. People are always making sense of their experience. The beliefs they have guide their actions and how they view the world.

2. Problems are experienced as problems, and people want to make things better.

3. Problems do not equal pathology. Problems are part of life; generally, problem patterns include both "viewing" and "doing" in relation to the problem.

4. People try to solve their problems, but not all their attempts are successful. Not solving problems leads people to feel stuck and focused on problems rather than generating alternative solutions.

5. People have abundant resources that are both known and unknown.

6. The problem is the problem; the person is not the problem.

7. Change is constant and inevitable, and one small change can lead to another.

8. There are exceptions to any problem pattern. The problem does not always occur.

9. There are different ways to look at a problem.

10. If it works, don't fix it.

Counseling conversations deemphasize problems, pathology, and **objectification** of people and instead lead to a **collaborative dialogue** that creates positive alliances in which the counselor co-creates solutions with clients (Walter & Peller, 1992). The focus is on helping people in **social contexts** to enhance their sense of responsibility and power in their lives. Solution-focused counselors point out that the person is not the problem; the problem is the problem. For example, saying your client is a person with depression is different from describing the client as a depressed person. BSFT is concerned with competence and assumes that there are inherent resources to be found in the experiences and stories of clients. This approach depends on clients' competence to find solutions with the help of the counselor. Counseling begins by respecting **clients as experts** on their own lives, and noticing the times when a client's life is not affected by the problem. The therapist enters a collaborative dialogue by respecting the client's lived experience, incorporating what clients are saying into the therapeutic conversation, and identifying exceptions to the occurrence of the problem in the client's life (O'Hanlon, 1993).

BSFT contrasts with psychotherapies that require clients to enter the practitioner's experiential realm. For instance, clients are not asked to see their problems in terms of *DSM* diagnoses or to understand their coping behaviors as defenses and resistance to change. The collaborative nature of the counseling relationship helps solution-focused counselors make use of what is going right in clients' lives rather than trying to "fix" what is wrong. Instead of asking "What is the cause of the problem?" or even "What maintains it?," solution-focused counselors ask "How do we construct solutions?" The counseling stance or perspective helps the practitioner enable clients to use their resources instead of focusing on and defining the client's pathology. In fact, de Shazer (1990) sees no need during therapy to return to conversations about problems, and concentrates instead on behaviors and goals that will lead to and maintain solutions. Emphasizing strengths may prompt more rapid change than focusing on pathology and problems.

Systematic Treatment Selection for Brief Counseling

Four major constructs characterize STS and provide the framework within which brief counseling takes place. **Patient predisposing factors** are the characteristics of the client that best predict response to treatment. They include sociodemographic background, intelligence, personality characteristics, age, gender, family structure, learning history, and patterns of reactions to the environment. Other significant predictors of positive client response to therapy include problem type, current level of distress, degree of success in solving current dilemmas, and coping strategies (Beutler & Clarkin, 1990). These factors interact to create expectations about treatment, self, and others that are key to selecting counseling interventions because of their power to influence treatment outcome.

Environments and circumstances are aspects of the client's social and physical environment that influence treatment outcome. This domain also includes those situational variables such as loss of job, divorce, and strained family relationships which affect response to counseling interventions, potential for change, and change maintenance. Differentiation is made between transient and habitual life strains resulting from life roles (e.g., parent, employee, student) and stressors or life events seen as more intense due to their acute effect on one's health, finances, and relationships.

Relationship variables are those factors found in the helping relationship that either impede or facilitate treatment progress. Therapy-enabling variables found across treatments include caring, genuineness, empathy, and credibility, while those that can interfere include matching clients and counselors with widely divergent backgrounds and beliefs, such as pairing a low-income client with an upper-middle-class therapist who has little knowledge of class differences and how they shape expectations.

Strategies and interventions are based on pragmatism, not dogma. Thus, choosing an appropriate intervention involves matching the counseling strategy with the appropriate diagnosis, client problems, and other patient predisposing factors. For instance, an intelligent, introspective client with relationship problems due to internalized conflicts over assertiveness may benefit from a conflict-focused **brief psychodynamic** approach to therapy, while a low-income individual suffering from depression after a divorce may benefit from a more structured brief **cognitive-behavioral** intervention.

Applications

Overview

In the following sections, the use of brief solution-focused therapy and STS for brief counseling is examined with a focus on applying each theory to practice. The goals of counseling, the change process, and intervention strategies for both theories are discussed.

Brief Solution-Focused Therapy. Clients are viewed as partners in a collaborative relationship concerned with facilitating solutions to problems or restorying client lives (Cade & O'Hanlon, 1993; De Jong & Berg, 1998). A consolidation of the assumptions previously enumerated leads to three basic rules that guide application. First, "if it ain't broke, don't fix it." The problem is the problem, and the client is the expert with the resources to solve the problem. The therapist's job is to help clients explore the problems they have defined as problems. Second, once you know what works, do more of it. Identifying parts of the client's life that are not dominated by the problem, a process known as finding exceptions, is important in helping the client do more of the same. This means that the therapist does not need a great deal of information about the problem in order to help. It is important to recognize that small changes are all that is necessary to bring about larger change. Third, if it doesn't work, don't do it again; *do something different.* This means that practitioners help clients to stop doing what is not working. Take what is not working as information and avoid doing it. Counseling is about helping the client do something differently (De Jong & Berg, 1998; de Shazer, 1990).

Systematic Treatment Selection for Brief Counseling.   The issue of treatment frequency and duration goes to the heart of brief counseling interventions. One way to think about length of treatment is to use a medical analogy. **Dosage of therapy** can be considered a function of frequency and duration of counseling. How often and for how long does the therapist work with the client? In STS, indicators for the use of time-limited or brief counseling are enunciated, as are factors that suggest more or less frequent office visits. Logically, treatment ends when treatment goals have been accomplished; however, this proves to be an overly simplistic view of the dynamic process of therapy since therapist and client may have different implicit and explicit goals that evolve over time in therapy. Furthermore, certain clients may not respond as quickly as a counselor assumed they would at the outset (Beutler & Clarkin, 1990).

A clear formula for determining duration and frequency of treatment would require a model for clearly conceptualized, well-articulated treatment goals that are measurable and agreed upon by therapist and client. Such a model does not yet exist (Beutler & Clarkin, 1990). However, STS does propose an evaluation of several specific factors to help predict treatment frequency and duration. Many of these variables are illustrated by the following case example, in which a brief counseling intervention required the therapist to confront treatment frequency and duration issues. Several factors, including client, counseling relationship, and treatment context variables came into play. The client was an adult learner seen in a university counseling center with a 12-session limit. She was referred by her physician, who believed her physical problems were stress-related. During the first meeting, the client looked quite apprehensive and was confused over the referral to counseling. She acknowledged that she had an anxiety problem when speaking in class and in asking professors for assistance. At these times her anxiety could become incapacitating, and she either avoided such situations altogether or forced herself to speak or ask for help while enduring very intense distress. Her family history included allusions to physical abuse during her childhood.

Based on the client's fearful presentation, symptoms, and family history, it was hypothesized that she could be suffering from post-traumatic stress disorder (PTSD) and possibly depression as well. However, the client's clear discomfort with being in the therapist's office, stated confusion about her needs, and questioning the efficacy of counseling led the practitioner to be circumspect about treatment and to align with her in questioning the physician's referral. Although elaborate and long-term treatment goals were apparent to the therapist, the client's high interpersonal sensitivity and expectation of a brief course of counseling, if any, led to a much more modest agreement. The counselor and client agreed to explore whether or not the client had a condition that could be helped by counseling, and, if so, to identify the treatment options.

Over the next 6 months, the client was seen every 3 to 4 weeks. This titration of dosage evolved through the client's pattern of canceling appointments scheduled on a weekly basis but showing up faithfully at least once a month. Clients with PTSD who have been traumatized by significant others they should have been able to trust often experience excruciating anxiety at the outset of treatment. They need time to discover whether or not the therapist creates enough safety for them so they are not totally overwhelmed by the torrent of dissociated emotional pain and turmoil that can lead to extreme feelings of loss of control. They also must pace themselves, or they become vulnerable to being flooded by their traumatic memories. Changing the frequency of sessions also helps illustrate the flexibility therapists who do brief therapy must have in designing brief therapy interventions.

By the sixth session the client was sufficiently conscious of her symptoms and had developed sufficient trust in the counselor that she could tolerate a discussion of diagnosis without being overwhelmed and fleeing treatment. She was asked if she had ever considered the possibility that she had PTSD. The client spontaneously reported her interest in the description of PTSD in a psychology text and her identification with that description. She seemed relieved to have been given the diagnosis by a professional (i.e., "I'm not crazy after all. There is actually a diagnosis that describes what I experience"). She was then ready to see a psychiatrist to consider medication for her sleep disturbance and other symptoms of PTSD.

By the end of the school year, the client completed a brief course of therapy lasting 10 sessions spaced out over 6 months. She had begun to sleep better and feel more rested and alert. She also experienced less anxiety and depression as a result of taking medication and through her successful confrontation of anxiety-arousing situations. This case demonstrates that brief therapy can accomplish symptom reduction and improved functioning in the short term even with clients who could benefit from longer-term intervention, and it illustrates the factors that come into play and interact to create treatment frequency and duration. Treatment setting, therapeutic relationship, and patient predisposing variables, including interpersonal reactance level, all affected this brief counseling intervention.

Goals of Counseling and Psychotherapy

Brief Solution-Focused Therapy.   O'Hanlon (1990) describes two essential tasks for brief counseling: **changing the viewing** and **changing the doing.** BSFT highlights various ways to help clients recognize their own resources (De Jong & Berg, 1998; Hart, 1995). It is concerned with goals and behavior. In essence, the goal of counseling is to help clients develop a view of themselves as competent and capable of change. De Shazer's (1990) psychotherapy focuses on defining goals with the client in the present or future when the problem is not occurring.

Systematic Treatment Selection for Brief Counseling.   STS is pragmatic and holistic. Client and counselor work collaboratively to define client problems for which psychosocial interventions are effective. Clients and the therapy relationship itself pass through stages of change. Therefore, establishing the stage of change helps determine treatment goals. STS not only seeks change within the client but also attempts to help clients create changes in their environment that support their therapy goals. This is one way to make interventions briefer—that is, brief therapy advocates point out that there are many therapeutic experiences available in the client's life outside of professional counseling, and environmental changes may solve problems or aid in their resolution.

The Process of Change

Brief Solution-Focused Therapy.   The change process is directed toward enhancing client competence and developing a view of a successful future. The process begins by socializing and getting to know the client, then proceeds to **setting the agenda** and assessing the client's wishes and complaints. The goal is to explore what brought clients to therapy, where they think they are going, and what they think would be helpful for the counselor to know. During therapy, the counselor keeps in mind the client's desired changes. Practitioners may choose a series of future-oriented questions or explore exceptions and past successes. If the problem appears too large, the counselor helps a client to define the problem in a solvable manner by reframing or externalizing it. **Externalizing the problem,** a technique borrowed from narrative therapy, is used quite commonly by solution-focused counselors. In externalizing, problems are defined as residing outside the client. This helps clients discover exceptions to their problems and/or past successes. Clients are then invited to entertain ideas about their own agency and to build a new view of themselves based on their hypothetical solutions. These solutions lead clients to see themselves as doing things differently as they move toward a preferred reality with the problem solved. Then, future-oriented questions are used to keep the changes going.

For solution-focused counselors and therapists, there is no specific formula for change because the practitioner wants to avoid rigid and inflexible practice. The change process requires curiosity about the client rather than certainty. It promotes self-exploration and understanding by discovering clients' concerns and stories. The counseling process involves **deconstructing clients' stories** in such a way that hidden meanings, gaps, and evidence of conflicting information are found.

The change process leads to conversations that promote a separation between the person and the problem in order to help clients become active agents in their own lives. By focusing discourse on the problem rather than on the person, the client's resources are mobilized against the problem and toward contributing to solutions. This may be particularly helpful to clients who are ashamed of their difficulties or who blame themselves for struggling with their concerns. Therefore, the change process is fluid because people are not fixed entities in need of repair; instead, they are works in progress that can be revised as they go.

Systematic Treatment Selection for Brief Counseling.   Research indicates that of all the factors predicting change and benefit from psychotherapy, client characteristics are the strongest predictor of outcome, more powerful than variables such as therapy relationship and diagnosis (Beutler & Clarkin, 1990). However, developers of the STS model concluded that the "nature, breadth, and severity" of a client's problems must determine the treatment prescribed. When this is not done, clinicians often simply apply their favored intervention indiscriminately to all client problems. Historically, the method for problem identification and prescribing treatment is **diagnosis of the individual,** as developed by Western medicine. This same method has been applied to mental health with limited success (Beutler & Clarkin, 1990).

In practice, mental health workers offer very different interventions for clients with similar diagnoses. For instance, consider the fact that clients with major depression often report differing antecedents and consequences of their depressions. The specifics of triggers and consequences of a client's depression rarely affect the resulting choice of psychotropic medication. Thus, depressed clients with similar clusters of depressive symptoms are likely to be prescribed a similar if not identical antidepressant regardless of the causes and consequences of their depression. However, the psychosocial treatment of a depressed parent who has lost his or her child to Sudden Infant Death Syndrome is likely to be different from that for a depressed adolescent whose family is functioning poorly due to a parent's alcoholism. The antecedents of both depressions are quite different and lead to very different counseling interventions. Therefore, consulting the *DSM* is a necessary but not sufficient step toward problem classification that helps psychiatrists determine **pharmacotherapy,** while it offers limited utility to the counselor for guiding selection of specific counseling interventions (Beutler & Clarkin, 1990). Thus it is necessary to develop a means of classifying client problems that evaluates both the antecedent conditions that helped create the client's difficulties and the consequences of the difficulties themselves.

Therefore, effective treatment planning depends on defining the relationship between symptom descriptions and treatment interventions. Thus there are several organizing domains that need to be evaluated in planning treatment, such as client variables (diagnostic and nondiagnostic), therapy relationship variables, and available interventions (Beutler & Clarkin, 1990). STS also challenges the *DSM*'s focus on individual symptoms, which fails to adequately account for the fact that distressing or disturbing behaviors are created within **systems of relationships.** Thus the *DSM*'s focus restricts the clinician's ability to examine the relevant structure of the environment as it contributes to creating problems, and taking this factor into account when prescribing an intervention. STS attempts to deal with the complexity of behaviors generated by systems (e.g., families, the workplace) through a careful analysis of the role of these variables in a client's difficulties (Beutler & Clarkin). This dovetails with another theme of brief counseling—that is, using interventions that alter systems because they can be more powerful in producing change and therefore contribute to much briefer treatments than those focused solely on changing the individual.

Beutler and Clarkin (1990) note that "we all go through surprisingly similar sets of processes as we cope with internal discomfort and a world which often interferes with our sense of safety and predictability" (p. 65). STS is informed by Prochaska and DiClemente's work on **stages of change,** which identifies a four-step client change process: precontemplation, contemplation, action, and maintenance (Prochaska & DiClemente, 1982; Prochaska, 1984). Another model used by STS was developed by Beitman (1987) and defines the four **phases of treatment** as engagement; search for patterns of client thought, behavior, and feeling; change; and preparing for termination. Research support for these models is very good (Beutler & Clarkin). The latter model of treatment phases helps the clinician develop mediating or short-term goals that contribute to positive treatment outcomes. The practitioner can identify discrete short-term goals within each phase of treatment and direct the client toward achieving these sub-goals. Thus, during the engagement phase the goal may be rapport building, while during termination the goal may be helping the client consolidate the gains he or she has made in counseling. Beutler and Clarkin warn against the inclination to see treatment as a unidimensional A-to-B process. At the commencement of therapy the stage of problem change will obviously effect the amount of time necessary to achieve behavior change goals. For example, a client in the precontemplation stage will probably take more time in counseling than a client already in the action stage of problem change. Beutler and Clarkin note that therapy may be cut short by "ill-conceived terminations" when clients move from one phase of change to another. For instance, termination as the client moves from contemplation to action can disrupt the client's attempts to change. Instead, interventions should be adjusted to match the client's degree of progress.

Beutler and Clarkin (1990) point out that change in therapy is dependent on clients' tolerating life experiences beyond their control. They assert that therapy is by definition an experience that threatens an individual's sense of self-control. Thus clients seek treatment when their belief in their self-efficacy is weak. Given that counseling is interpersonal, it puts another person (i.e., the counselor or therapist) in a powerful position in relationship to the client. Paradoxically, counseling diminishes self-direction in the short term to help create greater autonomy in the long run (Beutler & Clarkin). Effective practitioners are aware of this paradox. The fact that some students, and even some professionals, express the belief that the therapeutic relationship can be power-free or egalitarian, without significant differences in power between counselor and client, is a concern. One needs to recognize that this belief is not only overly idealistic but describes a situation that is impossible to fully achieve. Another way to say this is that issues of power and authority are inherent in all relationships, and therapy relationships are no exception. If you doubt this, make an appointment with a therapist and see if you feel equal in relationship to this professional! Thus competent counselors recognize their power and influence and help clients establish external support, as well as reinforce decision making that leads to empowerment. Since counselors have power in relationship to the client, they are in a position to manage their influence and seek greater equality by their actions. Advocating more egalitarian therapy relationships clarifies that politics and power dynamics are an inherent part of counseling. As feminist therapists have pointed out, the "personal is political" (Rave & Larsen, 1995).

Intervention Strategies

Brief Solution-Focused Therapy.   Interventions are used in the context of the BSFT process and frequently draw on other interactive models such as narrative therapy (Durrant, 1995; Epston & White, 1995; Metcalf, 1995; Selekman, 1993; White & Epston, 1990). **Client selection criteria** for BSFT are not dealt with directly by the creators of this model, but it is generally accepted that client and counselor must be able to create a contract for change through early collaboration in the counseling process. It is acknowledged that some clients may enter into a **visitor relationship** with the counselor and not define a problem or goals that can be addressed (De Jong & Berg, 1998). In this case there is no basis for engagement in BSFT.

Solution-focused counselors use a variety of questioning strategies. **Exception-oriented questions** help the client find examples of situations where the problem is not occurring (De Jong & Berg, 1998; de Shazer, 1988, 1991; Walter & Peller, 1992). For instance, when the client has described an overwhelming experience, the therapist can respond, "That's incredible. There is so much going on for you. Just one of those problems would be enough to knock most people for a loop. How have you managed to do things as well as you have?" **Presuppositional questions** convey the inevitability of change (De Jong & Berg, 1998). For instance, "If you were to show me a movie about how things would look as soon as the problem is solved, what would we see?" and "What would you be doing differently?" **Miracle questions** help the client see the possibility of finding a solution to the problem and help to clarify their counseling goals (De Jong & Berg, 1998; de Shazer, 1988, 1991). De Shazer (1988) offers the classic question: "Suppose that one night, while you were asleep, there was a miracle and this problem was solved. How would you know? What would be different?" (p. 5).

Scaling questions help clients reflect on and discuss their own perspective regarding the problem, themselves, or others (De Jong & Berg, 1998; Berg & de Shazer, 1993), as in the following example: "Let's say that on a scale of 1 to 10 that 10 means being brave in social situations and 1 means acting timidly. If in a month from now you will be able to go to the dance and ask someone to dance, how brave would you be on that scale between 1 and 10?" **Difference questions** are used to invite clients to break out of restrictive beliefs or rules they have about themselves (Walter & Peller, 1992). Typical difference questions are "How did you get the problem to go away?" and "What is different about the times when the problem is not as intense?"

Solution-focused therapists provide specific tasks for clients to perform. **Formula first-session tasks** are designed to be used at the end of the first session to help clients with vague complaints (de Shazer, 1985). **Observation tasks** require clients to look, pay attention to, and observe, whereas **behavior tasks** (or "do something different" tasks) direct clients to take action (De Jong & Berg, 1998; de Shazer, 1988; O'Hanlon & Weiner-Davis, 1989). An observation task would be presented in the following manner: "Between now and the next time we meet, I would like you to observe, so that you can describe to me, what happens in your family that you want to continue to have happen" (de Shazer, 1985, p. 137). A behavior task might be: "I would like each of you to do something different, no matter how strange, weird, or off-the-wall what you do might seem" (de Shazer, 1985, p. 123). Goals that are clearly defined are critical and frequently must be broken down into smaller steps or sub-goals (De Jong & Berg, 1998; Cade & O'Hanlon, 1993). Important questions to ask are "What would be the first sign that things are getting back on track?" "What do you want?" and "What would you be doing differently?"

Some solution-focused counselors use interventions developed by narrative therapists. Like solution-focused counselors, narrative therapists see themselves as taking a position in relation to their clients that is based on a philosophy of human experience and meaning-making. They do not see themselves as technicians merely using a series of techniques to promote client change. They explore clients' problem-saturated stories to help them develop their own preferred alternative stories. Positions narrative therapists take include **externalizing the problem.** This means redefining the difficulty as an object outside of the client. For instance, rather than using language that internalizes problems within the individual by talking about the individual as a "depressed client," the therapist will ask "How long has depression been pushing you around?" (White & Epston, 1990). **Unique outcomes** are essentially exceptions used to describe when the problem has not dominated the client's actions (White & Epston, 1990). Clients are asked questions such as "How did you manage to take this important step?" "How did you turn that around?" and "What does this tell you about yourself?" (Selekman, 1993). Because the term *unique* implies that the outcome is not a normal, everyday event, Monk (1997) uses the term "sparkling moments" to emphasize the regularity of these occurrences.

Systematic Treatment Selection for Brief Counseling.   Few specific procedures are unique to any given theoretical system; therefore, strategies and techniques are assigned from an analysis of the dimensions that affect psychotherapy transactions and outcomes (Beutler & Clarkin, 1990). These dimensions are:

1. *Selecting focal targets of change.* A client's problems are defined and formulated to establish a consistent counseling focus over time. There are two groups of strategies: those most effective in changing symptoms (e.g., brief cognitive-behavioral interventions), and those focused on changing intrapsychic conflicts (e.g., brief psychodynamic interventions). Problem complexity also affects selection of interventions. Symptom- and conflict-focused interventions are more or less appropriate depending on the complexity of the client's problems. For instance, an acute situational difficulty may lend itself best to a symptom-focused intervention such as brief cognitive-behavioral therapy. In brief counseling, choosing a focal problem and maintaining this focus throughout treatment is essential.

2. *Identifying level and mediating goals of treatment.* Interventions are matched to the client's style of coping with threatening experience because treatment strategies affect different levels of client experience. For instance, a brief cognitive-behavioral focus on exposure to anxiety-arousing situations is focused at a different level or depth than a brief psychodynamic exploration of internalized conflicts connected to dependency in relationships. Specifying mediating goals that lead toward longer-term goals for counseling also affects choice of intervention. For instance, if an initial sub-goal of treatment is decreasing depressive symptoms, a brief cognitive-behavioral intervention may be used. On the other hand, a mediating goal of increasing awareness of internal conflicts that interfere with intimacy may lead to a brief psychodynamic intervention. The counselor focuses on exploring thoughts, feelings, and needs for intimacy and interpretation of the material presented by the client. Therefore counselor formulation of the problem must be consistent with the type of problem to be addressed (symptom- or conflict-focused), and interventions are altered as clients and circumstances change (Beutler & Clarkin, 1990).

3. *Conducting therapeutic work.* The most specific level of matching brief interventions to client needs occurs within the dynamic process of interactions between client and counselor. Many decisions are made by the practitioner on a moment-to-moment basis to direct the client's focus and facilitate progress toward treatment goals. Counselors determine the directiveness of interventions, whether to increase or decrease client arousal to facilitate motivation and learning, and whether to address issues within or outside the therapeutic relationship. Brief therapists are typically directive and keep the client's attention on the specific problem or theme for which treatment has been contracted.

Client Selection Criteria for Brief Counseling.   In STS for brief counseling, as in brief therapies in general, client selection is primary. STS differentiates between treating **symptom-focused problems** and **conflict-focused problems.** In applying STS to brief counseling for treating symptom-focused problems, cognitive-behavioral brief therapy criteria for client selection can be used, whereas psychodynamic client selection criteria can be used for short-term conflict-focused therapy. Cognitive-behavioral brief interventions are deemed appropriate for treating clients with anxiety disorders, agoraphobia, panic disorder, generalized anxiety, test anxiety, interpersonal anxiety, depression of mild to moderate severity, social skills deficits, sexual dysfunction, and compulsive rituals. Clients who have a concrete problem focus are best for brief cognitive-behavioral interventions (Beutler & Clarkin, 1990).

For working with intrapsychic conflict issues, the brief dynamic therapy client selection criteria include treating clients with intrapsychic conflicts involving separation, narcissistic injury, or stress-response syndromes where the goal is character change in one specific area. Client factors that facilitate brief dynamic therapy and therefore make clients good candidates for this treatment include clients who can relate quickly, flexibly, and openly to the counselor and who have had at least one significant relationship in early childhood. Clients who can focus on a central conflict (e.g., an internalized conflict concerning caring for others versus caring for oneself) in the first meeting are also preferred, as are those who are willing to examine feelings and behavior, including those in response to the counselor. Intelligent clients with relatively high ego strength who are motivated to understand themselves better and change their behavior are especially appropriate for these interventions (Beutler & Clarkin, 1990). Although most brief counseling theories establish stringent client selection criteria, the application of these criteria in practice has been at best inconsistent. Possibly this occurs because brief therapists encounter clients with many needs who do not have the resources to pay for or the desire to engage in longer-term treatment. This issue deserves greater systematic attention.

Selecting Treatments.   In choosing treatment strategies, Beutler and Clarkin (1990) focus on several factors, including patient predisposing variables, careful analysis of problem complexity and severity, environmental factors, and therapy relationship factors. Patient predisposing factors include expectations of social roles and treatment, personality factors including motivation, and **response-specific personality styles.**

Clients bring expectations to therapy that influence its course. Beutler and Clarkin (1990) identify treatment-relevant expectations in three areas: first, the congruence between client expectations of the therapist and therapy process and the client's experience in the current therapy; second, the congruence between social role expectations and treatment objectives (i.e., do treatment goals complement or conflict with clients' social role expectations?); and third, changes in expectations as those expectations brought to treatment by the client are confirmed or dispelled. Since too much incongruence undermines treatment and can lead to premature termination, savvy therapists examine the congruence between their own and their clients' expectations of therapy and its outcomes. Thus the client's expectations regarding treatment length and roles of therapist and client should be examined and worked with directly. For example, it is our experience that clients often enter counseling expecting the duration to be much shorter than their counselor does.

Many, if not most, clients expect and want brief counseling, and these expectations should be addressed.

Regarding social roles it is imperative to be aware of **sociodemographic-based expectations.** For instance, one of us worked with a Latin American client whose previous, well-meaning therapist took such a strong stand on women's autonomy from patriarchal families that the client was alienated and their work together was undermined. This young woman was unprepared for a message that was so discordant with her social role expectations and which she interpreted as meaning that she needed to choose between her own and her family's best interests. In particular, Beutler and Clarkin (1990) exhort clinicians to gather information on the nuclear family and its structure to ascertain likely social role expectations. In the last example, greater attention to these variables could have saved the therapeutic relationship and the therapy itself. It is noteworthy that client expectations created by sociodemographic background (e.g., lower-income versus upper-middle-income clients) contribute to treatment length, motivation to change, and effectiveness of therapy. However, sociodemographic background and treatment outcome do not correlate well with the efficacy of specific counseling interventions (Beutler & Clarkin). There is one exception. Clients of lower socioeconomic status seem to respond better to active-directive brief interventions than to open-ended or nondirective approaches. Practitioners would be wise to recognize that low-income clients often have expectations of therapy relationships and the process of therapy that are incongruent with the therapist's, so that they are rapidly discouraged and lose motivation (Beutler & Clarkin).

It also appears that counselor expectation of treatment duration and outcome, when it is responsive to client preferences, predicts change better than client expectations alone. Thus Beutler and Clarkin (1990) admonish therapists to modify their assumptions about treatment duration and format to be congruent with the expressed desires of the client. Essentially, as with most brief therapies, counselors need to be flexible. Recall the case of the anxious college student with PTSD. The counselor showed flexibility in creating a brief symptom-focused treatment for a client who could have benefited from long-term therapy but was unprepared to commit to this undertaking. She expected a brief intervention that reduced her painful symptoms and improved her functioning. Pressing long-term therapy probably would have led to premature termination and treatment failure. On the other hand, a positive experience in brief therapy may help encourage her to return to treatment in the future should she need assistance.

As patient predisposing variables, **response-specific personality style** refers to personal characteristics that research shows are most directly influenced by treatment, while the client functioning domain includes problem complexity and interpersonal reactance. Problem complexity can be broken into two categories: **habits and transient responses** maintained by lack of knowledge or reinforcement, and **complex problems,** which are repetitive self-defeating behaviors created by internalized conflicts from the client's past (sometimes called characterological issues or disturbances of personality). Complex problems develop from remnants of efforts to avoid punishment and/or a response to perceived threats that no longer exist—for instance, adult clients who withdraw from intimate relationships as a result of being physically abused as children by their parents. A clue to problem complexity is the clarity of the relationship between triggers and psychological symptoms. For example, clients with anxiety reactions having no clear origins or initial triggers have more complex problems than those who have clear triggers, such as an individual who becomes fearful of flying after a particularly rough flight. Clients with less complex problems that are more transient, acute, and situational are often good candidates for brief counseling (Beutler & Clarkin, 1990).

Clients with complex problems whose repetitive behaviors occur in the absence of being rewarded are usually candidates for therapy of longer duration. For instance, the college student with PTSD who avoided speaking up or asking questions in class and seeking the professor's assistance could identify no negative precipitating events that led to her classroom anxiety reactions. Instead, it became the counselor's hypothesis that these symptoms communicated a complex problem developed in childhood as a reaction to the unpredictable actions of the parent who abused her. That is, she had internalized the belief that environments like the family, where being vulnerable should be safe, were in fact unpredictable and dangerous places where she could be violated without warning. Although, in the present, the classroom was a reasonably safe place, she continued to respond out of her past experience.

Symptom severity is distinguished from problem complexity, and although it can affect frequency of sessions, it may have no relationship to treatment length. High symptom severity can lead to more frequent sessions in the early phases of treatment, but this does not mean that brief therapy is automatically contraindicated.

Interpersonal reactance or sensitivity, as a class of patient predisposing variables, refers to the degree to which a client fears loss of interpersonal control in interactions with others. Highly sensitive clients are easily threatened by therapist actions. Thus interpersonal reactance is an estimation of the force with which a client will resist external influence. In the foregoing example of the college student with PTSD, the counselor was neutral about the referring physician's attempt to influence the client regarding psychotherapy's ability to help her. Having had a chaotic and dangerous childhood, this client had learned to resist external influence in order to protect herself. Unfortunately, as with many traumatized clients, she feared what she needed the most—a caring, supportive, and informative therapeutic relationship. Less interpersonally reactive clients who can accept therapist support, guidance, and help are more likely to be successful in short-term counseling, while their more reactive peers are probably in need of longer-term, less directive assistance.

Evaluation of client environments and circumstances also influences selection of interventions. In theories of psychotherapy, environmental factors are seen as responsible to a greater or lesser degree for the development and maintenance of a problem. STS focuses, in part, on the environment's influence on creating and maintaining client problems. In an integrated brief approach to counseling it is necessary to identify the relationship between environmental circumstances, client problems, and treatment interventions. STS defines environments as both social and physical. They include family, social relationships, work, and school. Therapist awareness of a client's family ties, friendships, recreational resources, and reference groups is "imperative" to identifying treatment-enabling factors for support and maintenance of change (Beutler & Clarkin, 1990).

Environmental stressors are stressful events—including major life changes in health, finance, and relationships—that can be distinguished from **life strains,** which are the specific stresses created by everyday roles such as parent, partner, employee, and student. Research indicates that past and present stressful events are cumulative and have an important influence on psychopathology (Beutler & Clarkin, 1990). **Environmental resources** that facilitate treatment include sociocultural environments, social support systems (including family support), work, and school. Beutler and Clarkin note the misfortune created by a dearth of research on the influence of sociocultural variables and socioeconomic class, especially lower SES, on therapy. Few outcome studies have adequately focused on the relationship between client and therapist socioeconomic backgrounds (i.e., class differences). However, it has been found that client SES correlates negatively with obtaining and remaining in counseling, and the absence of stable social support networks among these clients interferes with adaptive change. Counseling students who do practica and internships in community counseling or social service agencies, as well as their supervisors, often work with low-income clients and need to be aware of this information. Successful programs for working with the disadvantaged focus in two areas: addressing practical and clearly defined difficulties while promoting nurturing supportive relationships. In fact, these goals are compatible with brief counseling interventions in general. Group and family therapies may also be helpful because they can mitigate economic class differences between therapist and client while attacking isolation directly.

Two areas of potential support and conflict deserve further comment. Competent brief therapists are aware of family factors that enable adaptive change, as well as those that help develop and/or maintain client difficulties. Work and school environments are also important. Beutler and Clarkin (1990) point out that the workplace has all too infrequently been a focus of mental health research. A similar critique may be made for the effect of the school environment on children. Awareness of environmental influences on client distress and change is essential. Helping clients to seek out healthy, constructive environments that support adaptation and diminished disturbance can yield positive results and possibly reduce client need for therapy, thus shortening its duration. When one is determining the likelihood of adaptive change, the interaction between social support and life stresses must be evaluated, as social support predicts change maintenance (Beutler & Clarkin).

Understanding and using therapy relationship variables to intervene with clients (Beutler & Clarkin, 1990) is also important because of the connection between therapeutic relationships and treatment outcome. Although therapy relationship factors and client-counselor compatibility are recognized by many theories as important, the degree to which they are perceived to be under counselor control is often unclear or ignored as an intangible. STS is based on the assumption that effective treatment involves systematic development and management of client expectations, perceptions, and evaluations of self and others through the influence of a collaborative treatment relationship. A positive relationship with the brief therapist provides the basis for faith, hope, and feelings necessary for commitment and change. This relationship is seen as both predictable and controllable, not random or mystical (Beutler & Clarkin). Well-matched and compatible clients and therapists would logically be assumed to facilitate briefer interventions. Using **role induction**—that is, preparing the client for therapy and clarifying client and therapist roles—also has a positive effect on treatment length and the speed with which counseling objectives are met. This illustrates another theme of brief counseling: the need for counselors to rapidly develop rapport with clients and to be explicit about treatment methods and expectations of counselor and client roles (Beutler & Clarkin).

Beutler and Clarkin (1990) state that "treatment settings tend to weave an average expectable treatment duration into their fabric" (p. 155). Anyone who has worked in an agency or hospital will concur! They distinguish between **setting** and **funding mechanisms,** which also strongly influence treatment length. For instance, HMOs almost exclusively support brief therapy and often seem to almost exclusively reject long-term treatment, whatever the diagnosis. STS acknowledges that when it comes to treatment settings and funding mechanisms, treatments are prescribed fairly independently of the client and are most affected by the institution employing the therapist. Beutler and Clarkin conclude that given this inattention to client needs and problems, creating effective treatment plans often requires combining treatment settings in a manner responsive to a client's difficulties and needs.

Evaluation

Overview

In the following sections, the research on brief therapy is examined, as well as outcome research on BSFT and STS. Limitations of both theories are also explored.

Supporting Research

From his reading of the research, Garfield (1994) makes two critical points regarding client attitudes toward brief therapy: first, most clients are not interested in insight or exploring their past; and second, they want to resolve their current problem. Thus he concludes that most clients are not interested in long-term therapy. After polling psychotherapy experts concerning the trends that are likely to influence the profession through the next decade, Norcross and Freedheim (1992) concluded that interventions used in practice will increasingly be present-oriented, structured, and directive. The popularity of brief therapy is expected to continue as the enthusiasm for long-term therapy continues to decline. Generally speaking, brief therapy has become the prevailing model of practice, and most professionals consider it to be effective (Budman & Gurman, 1988; Koss & Shiang, 1994).

However, blanket statements of efficacy with diverse populations notwithstanding, it is important to recognize the current state of affairs with regard to the factors influencing practice and the challenges of doing outcome research. For instance, O'Hanlon (1990), a brief solution-focused therapist, states, "You'd think I'd be happy that my side seems to be winning, but something about the newfound popularity of brief therapy worries me. After all, the real question is not how long therapy takes but how effective it is and whether it serves those who seek it. I believe effective therapy is usually brief, but not in every case. Although I see clients on the average of about five sessions, I occasionally do long-term work. Sometimes I see people for several years" (p. 48). In summarizing the research on the efficacy of brief therapy, Koss and Shiang (1994) acknowledge the difficulty of conducting outcome research. They note Garfield's (1990) conclusions that outcome research presents "extreme and varied challenges," including selecting therapies, therapists, and clients; training the therapists; selecting criteria to measure outcome; and finding control groups and resources to pay for the study. Thus it is appropriate to have a healthy level of skepticism in reviewing outcome studies and to be critical in evaluating their claims. On the other hand, outcome research, although imperfect, must help inform practice as the ability to evaluate counseling processes and outcomes improves.

One approach to evaluating outcome studies is to conduct a meta-analysis of several completed investigations. In their meta-analysis of brief therapies, Svartberg and Stiles (1991) found that brief dynamic therapy and cognitive-behavioral therapy were more effective than no treatment at all. An important finding was that both of these treatments were *differentially* effective depending on problem type. In a similar vein, Koss and Shiang (1994) note the prevalent belief that outcomes of different psychotherapies are equivalent but conclude that this may be an artifact of methodology limitations and lack of equivalence in the measurement of outcome criteria across therapies.

Bellack's (1985) explanation for the apparent equivalent efficacy of brief cognitive, behavioral, and interpersonal therapies for depression is an example of a common factors approach to exploring elements of therapy found across treatments. These brief therapy (common) factors were clear rationale, time-limited contracts, and a planned and focused theme. However, Beutler and Clarkin (1990) criticize the belief that all brief therapies are effective for all depressed clients, since the diagnostic category of depression encompasses a very heterogeneous group of clients with different kinds of problems. Rather than view these brief therapies as equivalent treatments for depression, Beutler and Clarkin reconceptualized them as multifaceted treatments for problems created by social skills deficits, cognitive distortions, and interpersonal conflicts, "all of which can result in the appearance of depressive symptoms" (p. 148). Thus these therapies are not so much driven by diagnosis, as Bellack assumed, but instead are models of conflict and symptom development that provide direction for selecting an appropriate intervention to change personal and psychosocial variables that helped produce symptoms of depression.

The National Institute of Mental Health conducted another study of short-term therapies for depression that compared four brief treatments (Elkin et al., 1989). These were all 16 weeks in duration and included (1) prescription of antidepressant medication with clinical case management, (2) interpersonal psychotherapy, (3) cognitive-behavioral therapy, and (4) placebo with clinical case management. Clients in all four groups showed significant improvement in symptoms, with antidepressant/case management being most effective, followed by cognitive-behavioral and interpersonal therapies, and finally placebo/case management. One might conclude that antidepressant treatment is best for depression, but Seligman (1992) points out that clients treated with cognitive-behavioral therapy usually maintain their gains (i.e., change maintenance) at a much higher rate and for longer than do those who use antidepressants alone. These few examples demonstrate the usefulness and pitfalls of outcome studies. Methodology and the interpretation of results makes a difference.

Concerning research on the practice of BSFT, de Shazer (1985, 1990, 1991, 1994) offers abundant case material, but there is little outcome research to examine. Since solution-focused therapy uses a non-normative model, clients are considered the best judges of their own success (de Shazer, 1991). De Shazer (1991) has summarized a Brief Family Therapy Center evaluation of clients' perceptions of treatment efficacy. Clients reported an 80.4% success rate initially and an 86% success rate 18 months later. De Jong and Berg (1998) studied clients receiving BSFT who were categorized by *DSM-III-R* diagnoses. Clients clustering into groups of five or more per diagnosis were identified. These included those with dysthymia, adjustment disorders of several kinds, oppositional defiant disorder, and attention deficit hyperactivity disorder. Overall outcome results indicated that 39% met treatment goals, 40% made some progress, and 21% made none. Clients with more serious disorders were absent from this study, and different treatment protocols for more serious problems were not discussed. Clearly, there is a need for additional outcome research to substantiate claims of efficacy for BSFT.

Beutler, Consoli, and Williams (1995) report that supporting research for systematic eclectic psychotherapy, a foundational theory for the development of STS, shows "promising, if not confirming results of the major constructs" (p. 276). Outcome research is a primary concern in the evolution of STS, which is based on selecting the most empirically sound indicators for assigning treatment interventions (Beutler, Zetzer, & Williams, 1996). This method has created an empirically valid model for treatment decision making which has three distinct advantages over other psychotherapy models: (1) dimensions selected for inclusion are based on empirical evidence of efficacy; (2) the model outlines a series of relationships between primary dimensions that lead to treatment selection which can be subjected to prospective study; and (3) these proposed relationships cover the range of treatment decisions therapists are likely to encounter. The four domains that encompass the STS model have received different levels of research attention over the three decades of its evolution (Beutler et al., 1996).

In the 1980s, therapy relationship factors as they affected treatment outcomes were the focus. A thorough analysis of research findings suggested that the quality of the therapy relationship was enhanced by counselor and client demographic similarity, although modest differences in attitudes and beliefs between counselor and client—especially in the area of attachment and intimacy—were most predictive of positive change. A compelling finding is that effective therapy is usually associated with a convergence of client beliefs and values in the direction of the therapist (Beutler et al., 1996). This supports Beutler's notion that psychotherapy is, at least in part, concerned with teaching a philosophy of life (Beutler, 1994). In the 1990s the focus of outcome research shifted to the relationship between client characteristics and the selection of treatment interventions.

Recent research has focused on five patient predisposing factors: functional problem severity, subjective distress, problem complexity, coping style, and interpersonal reactance or resistance potential. As predicted by STS, clients whose coping style was to internalize problems benefited more from a brief insight-oriented therapy, while those who externalized their difficulties benefited more from cognitive-behavioral therapy that focused on symptoms. Also, clients high in interpersonal reactance fare better with nondirective treatments, while those low in resistance potential responded best to directive interventions such as cognitive-behavioral therapy (Beutler et al., 1991). It should be noted that a one-year follow-up study showed that properly matched clients continued to improve, while those mismatched to therapy based on coping style and interpersonal reactance did not show such continued gains (Beutler, Machado, Engle, & Mohr, 1993). Currently, Beutler, Patterson, Jacob, Shoham, Yost, and Rohrbaugh (1993) are completing data collection for a study that uses STS to match treatments to couples being seen for alcohol-related problems. This study promises to add further evidence to support the efficacy of creating counseling decision-making criteria based on empirical research and an integrative view of psychotherapy.

So, what can we conclude about brief therapy in general? It has become the treatment model of choice and is used quite broadly for a diverse set of clients with divergent problems. Outcome research has supported the efficacy of brief therapy in treating everything from job-related stress and anxiety disorders to depression and interpersonal problems (Koss & Shiang, 1994). However, the methodological issues of conducting outcome research should lead us to be wary of accepting any generalized claim of efficacy without careful review of the studies involved. Beutler and Clarkin's (1990) critical analysis of brief treatments for depression is an example of a thoughtful reading of the outcome research in one specific area that can guide clinicians in practice. In general, brief therapy is often effective in helping clients with acceptable internal and external resources to achieve specific treatment goals, under appropriate circumstances. Appropriate application of brief and long-term therapies reveals treatment modalities that overlap but often provide qualitatively different therapeutic experiences. For instance, the depth and intensity of the counseling relationship is different in brief and long-term counseling; thus the opportunity to use and explore the meaning of transference reactions is more likely to arise in long-term work. On the other hand, brief therapies often focus more directly on specific symptoms and problems, and may in this way produce more rapid change in symptoms and functioning than many long-term treatments.

Limitations

Brief Solution-Focused Therapy.   Although De Jong and Berg (1998) offer outcome data regarding BSFT, the lack of additional and more comprehensive research continues to limit claims of efficacy. Overall, two client limitations that affect practice are generally cited by solution-focused counselors: clients not interested in changing the problem, and those lacking a clear goal (Walter & Peller, 1992). In other words, counseling will not work unless there is some agreement between the therapist and client about defining a problem to be changed.

Other limitations involve the manner in which counselors apply BSFT in practice. Those who use this treatment in a formulaic way without understanding the underlying philosophy and theory may strike clients as simplistic and/or lacking an understanding of their problems. A counselor who rigidly discourages a client's focusing on problems when the client is struggling with serious concerns could appear insensitive and tactless. Counselors should not use techniques advanced by this theory without fully understanding how and why they are being used as this is clearly counterproductive. Also, if the philosophy of not pathologizing clients by focusing on diagnoses is adhered to too rigidly, important information on treating specific disorders such as depression may be unavailable to the client and therapist. For instance, some depressed clients can benefit from referrals to psychiatrists for medication while also engaging in BSFT. The point is that practice of brief counseling demands flexibility, and rarely do therapists limit themselves to one way of doing things.

Systematic Treatment Selection for Brief Counseling.   The use of STS for choosing brief counseling interventions has many strengths that fit the practice of brief therapy in general. It is flexible and pragmatic, as well as outcome- and goal-oriented. It appreciates the powerful influence of factors such as client resources, therapist rapport-building skills, and the client's environment on treatment outcome. Its weaknesses are closely tied to its strengths. Given the comprehensiveness of STS and concern about avoiding theoretical dogma, it may trade expedience for coherence. Also, it may be so broad in its scope that practitioners have difficulty maintaining the integrity of the treatment philosophy. Furthermore, its breadth may make it vulnerable to critiques that have followed all eclectic therapies—that is, the perception that many counselors who say they have an eclectic treatment philosophy use this as a rationalization for not having a well-defined theory that guides their work. The trap becomes using techniques without a sound basis and rationale for their use. Also, the STS model's attempt to inform practice through outcome research may not be welcomed by practitioners who see evaluation and research as distinct from the art of therapy. This is unfortunate because the two need not be at odds or in competition. Trusting the subjective judgments of experienced clinicians need not invalidate the knowledge gained from outcome research that is empirically based, and vice versa (Beutler, Williams, Wakefield, & Entwistle, 1995). Finally, counselors who have difficulty seeing the big picture or taking a more systemic view of their work and their clients may not respond well to this model.

Summary Chart—Brief Theories

Human Nature

Brief Solution-Focused Therapy. Language and meaning-making define humanness. People are social beings that co-create meaning through their social interactions.

Systematic Treatment Selection for Brief Therapy. As an integrationist and pragmatic theory, STS is not aligned with any specific philosophy of human nature. However, it may be viewed as an ecological model given its focus on the interaction between individuals and their social and physical environments. People are seen as capable of change with appropriate challenge and support, while the influences of intelligence, learning experience, family, culture, and society and its institutions are recognized.

Major Constructs

Brief Solution-Focused Therapy. A consolidation of the major assumptions that guide application of BSFT leads to three principles:

1. If it ain't broke, don't fix it. The problem is the problem, and the client is the expert with the resources to solve it.
2. Once you know what works, do more of it. Finding exceptions where the problem does not dominate the client's life is important in helping the client "do more of the same."
3. If it doesn't work, don't do it again. Do something different.

Systematic Treatment Selection for Brief Therapy. The major constructs of STS are patient predisposing factors, environments and circumstances, relationship variables, strategies and interventions.

Goals
Brief Solution-Focused Therapy. Help clients change how they view their problem (interpretation) and what they do around the complaint. The latter means changing behavior, taking action that is new, different, and more effective in response to the problem.

Systematic Treatment Selection for Brief Therapy. Treatment goals are determined through assessment of client problems relevant to the selection of psychosocial interventions that have demonstrated empirical support for their efficacy.

Change Process
Brief Solution-Focused Therapy. Focusing on the problem is unnecessary; change involves collaborating with clients to define solutions. Counselors help clients stop focusing on problems and to shift their attention to creating solutions.

Systematic Treatment Selection for Brief Therapy. Counseling addresses symptom- or conflict-focused problems of greater or lesser complexity. Change occurs in definable stages. Stage of change, and client problem type and complexity determine mediating treatment goals and the interventions used to achieve longer-term goals. A client's personality, coping style, and interpersonal reactance (i.e., sensitivity) must be considered in choosing interventions that facilitate change. Taking into consideration the environment's affect on facilitating or interfering with client change and making use of this knowledge is important.

Interventions
Brief Solution-Focused Therapy. In BSFT, therapy interventions include exception-oriented questions, presuppositional questions, miracle questions, scaling questions, difference questions, formula first-session tasks, observation tasks, "do something different" tasks.

Systematic Treatment Selection for Brief Therapy. In STS a number of interventions are employed:

- Explicit selection criteria used for brief symptom- or conflict-focused counseling.
- Careful evaluation by using psychological tests and the clinical interview to assess patient predisposing factors, counseling relationship variables, and environmental influences that lead to selection of effective interventions.
- Directive counseling interventions for clients low on interpersonal reactance, and nondirective interventions for those high on this dimension (i.e., resistant).
- Clarification of client issue(s) as symptom- or conflict-focused leads to choice of affective, behavioral, or cognitive interventions.
- Strategic use of therapy relationship factors to create a collaborative relationship that can influence client attributions and facilitate change.
- Conceptualizing client problems as existing within systems of relationships and helping the client make systems-level changes.

- Helping the client make use of and/or find environmental resources (e.g., cultural, social, familial, work, and school) to aid in change and the maintenance of change.
- Awareness of the process of change to assist clients in setting short-term goals appropriate to their stage of change.

Limitations

Brief Solution-Focused Therapy. In general there is a lack of outcome research on the efficacy of BSFT. In part this is due to the theory's focus on the subjective experience of clients and eschewing rigidity on the part of counselors in helping clients construct their own solutions. Clients who are not interested in changing the problem and who cannot be helped to define clear goals may not find BSFT effective (Walter & Peller, 1992).

Systematic Treatment Selection for Brief Therapy. Integrative theories by definition are holistic and draw on many divergent theories. Therefore, they must strive to maintain coherence and central organizing themes lest they become unmanageable and difficult to understand. A focus on pragmatism may downplay the importance of theory in providing the purpose and meaning for using specific interventions.

The Case of Maria: A Brief Approach

A counselor using BSFT views Maria as a competent woman with the resources to create solutions to her problems. Therefore, instead of focusing on pathology-based diagnoses, the counselor works with her to define treatment goals and change her view of her situation, and assists Maria in taking actions that lead to meeting therapy goals. Although the literature on BSFT does not deal directly with the issue of client selection, there is a basic assumption that counselor and client must be able to develop treatment goals together. BSFT recognizes that not all clients are committed to change. Those who have an investment in maintaining their problems would be poor candidates for this approach. Thus we proceed with the case under the assumption that we can help Maria shift her attention from problems and self-blame to setting goals and exploring solutions.

From a viewing and doing perspective, the counselor starts by examining Maria's description of the events that are causing her distress. For instance, given a divorce from an abusive spouse, conflict with her family, and recent job difficulties, she may have become focused on self-blame and a highly negative interpretation of the events that lead her to see herself as a failure. This kind of viewing is inherent in her remark, "I've ruined my life and the lives of two families, and I'm currently hurting my children." We can work with Maria to find experiences that don't fit the view that she has "ruined everyone's life." One way to do this is to assign a formula first-session task that shifts focus to exceptions—times when things are going right and she is not dominated by her problems. This task can also help Maria take her broad, vague complaints such as "I've ruined everyone's life" and become more specific about those things she wants to work toward maintaining or enhancing. It helps her see that there is still some good even now when she is very distressed.

Another way to prompt Maria to develop goals for treatment is to use the miracle question: "If you went to sleep one night and woke up the next morning with your problems solved, what would your life look like? What would be different?" Here Maria is helped to begin to develop a more positive view of her life from which treatment goals can emerge. In general, she is likely to want relief from her disturbing symptoms of depression and to improve her functioning as a parent and teacher. The counselor works with Maria to be specific about her goals, stay focused on solutions, and increase her recognition of exceptions to the times when problems occur. If Maria says, "I want to be happier at work and less distressed," the counselor can explore concrete and modest goals to move her in the direction of improved satisfaction at work and diminished stress. Capitalizing on her internal resources, we can point out that she has been a successful teacher in the past and ask what she knows from this experience that could guide her toward greater satisfaction with teaching. We can collaborate with Maria to identify and access external resources such as friends or co-workers who can be supportive. Possibly a co-worker would be willing to take walks with Maria at lunch so she gets some exercise and can relax during the noon hour. Brief solution-focused therapists believe that small positive changes can lead to bigger successes. Maria may also say that she would like to feel closer to her children. We could wonder aloud when during the week, instead of feeling alienated from them, she had noticed a time they were getting along better (i.e., a difference question). Then we encourage her to do more of the same.

Clearly, Maria defines herself as the problem. Using a narrative therapy technique, we will work with her to externalize her depression. For instance, we might say, "How long have depression and trauma had the upper hand in your life?" or "Isn't that something how depression convinces you that you are powerless?" As long as Maria defines herself as the problem, it is unlikely that she will have the power to make substantive changes. As Maria separates herself from some of her problems, she may free herself from the tyranny of shame and guilt. This may relieve some of her feelings of helplessness and inadequacy, empowering her to make changes. Taking the stance that Maria is capable and has the resources to solve her problems affects our work with her, we may exhibit a quiet, calm confidence that she can find solutions to her problems. Hopefully, the implicit message to Maria in the early phases of treatment is: "You are not your problems. There are alternative interpretations of events in your life. The counselor is confident you have what it takes to succeed. Even now there are times of peace and exceptions to your difficulties."

Using another narrative therapy technique, the counselor can ask Maria to reinterpret her experience in a more constructive way by examining the stories she tells herself about the current situation. Many clients who have experienced trauma and major losses go through a period of self-blame and feelings of victimization. They are also vulnerable to secondary wounding experiences in which friends and family say or do things that give the message that those who have been traumatized are to blame for their own misfortune. An alternative story Maria may develop is that of a survivor. Shifting from a story of victimization to one of survivor, when it occurs at a deep level, can greatly diminish feelings of powerlessness and helplessness which are apparent themes in Maria's nightmares. Attention then can shift to problem solving and action. This process also helps clients find meaning in their suffering. For instance, clients often have a desire to use their experience to help others. Maria may become determined to reach out to those affected by domestic violence and divorce. This kind of effort can be empowering.

A source of support that has been disrupted is Maria's relationship with her parents and sister. The counselor can suggest observation tasks or difference questions to draw her attention to times when problems do not dominate these relationships. For instance, if Maria is locked in a negative cycle of blame and criticism with her sister, a "do something different" task can be assigned which helps her explore ways to spend time with her sister without engaging in problem behaviors. Possibly the two could take Maria's children on an outing for a picnic, swimming, or ice skating. The point is to stop doing what doesn't work and to do something different. Scaling questions can be used to help Maria evaluate the success of these outings, with 1 being a disaster and 10 being a smashing success. Scaling can help prevent all-or-nothing thinking. A 5 or 6 is different from judging the outing a failure if it's not a 10! Throughout, Maria is helped to become an observer rather than a victim of her circumstances.

Finally, this case is clearly affected by cultural issues. A counselor of any theoretical orientation would be advised to be aware of Maria's cultural background and the ways in which it helps shape who she is, her resources, and her difficulties. A counselor's credibility with this client may be compromised by ignoring cultural differences that exist between them. The case example states that Maria comes from a "culturally encapsulated Hispanic neighborhood" and is proud of her "Hispanic heritage." But the counselor must remember that there is diversity within the Hispanic culture. The case example does not specify whether Maria is Mexican American, Puerto Rican, Colombian, or of some other Hispanic cultural background. It is risky to assume cultural homogeneity between various related groups.

Finally, the nature of Maria's bicultural experience is an important consideration. The bicultural influence of being raised in a "traditional Hispanic family" while attending college and beginning her career in what appears to be a more white, middle-class cultural setting must be addressed. It is not uncommon for clients from bicultural backgrounds to have internalized cultural conflicts that can affect the course of their recovery from trauma and depression. Also, significant others with differing cultural backgrounds may pull the client in different directions based on their cultural values and beliefs. For instance, Maria's family may define success for their daughter in a way quite different from that of a more white middle-class perspective. This is suggested by their opposition to her attending a university far from home and in their being left out of her wedding to a Caucasian man because of Maria's fear of their disapproval. One way to approach this topic is for the counselor to educate him- or herself concerning the cultural background of this client, seek supervision from a supervisor knowledgeable about cultural issues, and be open to discussion of cultural issues in therapy. Maria may need assistance in making potentially unconscious cultural conflicts conscious. This can help her examine how she has been affected by cultural experiences and can facilitate making more conscious choices concerning her values and cultural identifications.

References

Avis, J. P. (1987). Collaborative counseling: A conceptual framework and approach for counselors and adults in life transitions. *Counselor Education and Supervision, 27,* 15–30.

Beitman, B. D. (1987). *The structure of individual psychotherapy.* New York: Guilford.

Bellack, A. (1985). Psychotherapy research in depression: An overview. In E. Beckham & W. Leber (Eds.), *Handbook of depression: Treatment, assessment, and research* (pp. 204–219). Homewood, IL: Dorsey Press.

Berg, I. K., & de Shazer, S. (1993). Making numbers talk: Language in therapy. In S. Friedman (Ed.), *The new language of change: Constructive collaboration in psychotherapy* (pp. 5–24). New York: Guilford.

Beutler, L. E. (1983). *Eclectic psychotherapy: A systematic approach.* New York: Pergamon.

Beutler, L. (1994). *What psychotherapy outcome research can teach us in the age of managed care.* Salishan, OR: Oregon Psychological Association Spring 1994 Workshop.

Beutler, L., & Clarkin, J. (1990). *Systematic treatment selection: Toward targeted therapeutic intervention.* New York: Brunner/Mazel.

Beutler, L. E., Consoli, A. J., & Williams, R. E. (1995). Integrative and eclectic therapies in practice. In B. Bongar & L. E. Beutler (Eds.), *Comprehensive textbook of psychotherapy: Theory and practice* (pp. 274–292). New York: Oxford University Press.

Beutler, L. E., Engle, D., Mohr, D., Daldrup, R. J., Bergan, J., Meredith, K., & Merry, W. (1991). Predictors of differential response to cognitive, experiential, and self-directed psychotherapeutic techniques. *Journal of Consulting and Clinical Psychology, 59,* 333–340.

Beutler, L. E., Machado, P. P. P., Engle, D. E., & Mohr, D. (1993). Differential patient treatment maintenance among cognitive, experiential, and self-directed psychotherapies. *Journal of Psychotherapy Integration, 3,* 15–31.

Beutler, L. E., Patterson, K. M., Jacob, T., Shoham, V., Yost, E., & Rohrbaugh, M. (1993). Matching treatment to alcoholism subtype. *Psychotherapy, 30,* 463–472.

Beutler, L. E., Williams, R. E., Wakefield, P. J., & Entwistle, S. R. (1995). Bridging scientist and practitioner perspectives in clinical psychology. *American Psychologist, 50,* 984–994.

Beutler, L. E., Zetzer, H. A., & Williams, R. E. (1996). Research application of prescriptive therapy. In W. Dryden (Ed.), *Research in counseling and psychotherapy* (pp. 25–48). Thousand Oaks, CA: Sage.

Budman, S. H., & Gurman, A. (1988). *Theory and practice of brief therapy.* New York: Guilford.

Cade, B., & O'Hanlon, W. H. (1993). *A brief guide to brief therapy.* New York: Norton.

Cooper, J. F. (1995). *A primer of brief psychotherapy.* New York: Norton.

De Jong, P., & Berg, I. K. (1998). *Interviewing for solutions.* Pacific Grove, CA: Brooks/Cole.

de Shazer, S. (1985). *Keys to solution in brief therapy.* New York: Norton.

de Shazer, S. (1988). *Clues: Investigating solutions in brief therapy.* New York: Norton.

de Shazer, S. (1990). What is it about brief therapy that works? In J. K. Zeig & S. G. Gilligan (Eds.), *Brief therapy: Myths, methods, and metaphors* (pp. 90–99). New York: Brunner/Mazel.

de Shazer, S. (1991). *Putting difference to work.* New York: Norton.

de Shazer, S. (1994). *Words were originally magic.* New York: Norton.

Durrant, M. (1995). *Creative strategies for school problems: Solutions for psychologists and teachers.* New York: Norton.

Durrant, M., & Kowalski, K. (1993). Enhancing views of competence. In S. Friedman (Ed.), *The new language of change: Constructive collaboration in psychotherapy* (pp. 107–137). New York: Guilford.

Elkin, I., Shea, M. T., Watkins, J. T., Imber, S. D., Sotsky, S. M., Collins, J. F., Glass, D. R., Pilkonis, P. A., Leber, W. R., Docherty, J. P., Fiesler, S. J., & Parloff, M. B. (1989). National Institute of Mental Health collaborative research study. *Archives of General Psychiatry, 46,* 971–982.

Epston, D., & White, M. (1995). Termination as a rite of passage: Questioning strategies for a therapy of inclusion. In R. A. Neimeyer & M. J. Mahoney (Eds.), *Constructivism in psychotherapy* (pp. 339–354).

Washington, DC: American Psychological Association.

Fisch, R. (1990). Problem-solving psychotherapy. In J. K. Zeig & W. M. Munion (Eds.), *What is psychotherapy? Contemporary perspectives* (pp. 269–273). San Francisco: Jossey-Bass.

Fisch, R., Weakland, J. H., & Segal, L. (1982). *Tactics of change: Doing therapy briefly.* San Francisco: Jossey-Bass.

Garfield, S. L. (1980). *Psychotherapy: An eclectic approach.* New York: Wiley.

Garfield, S. L. (1990). Issues and methods in psychotherapy process research. *Journal of Consulting and Clinical Psychology, 58,* 273–280.

Garfield, S. L. (1994). Research on client variables. In A. E. Bergin & S. L. Garfield (Eds.), *Handbook of psychotherapy and behavior change* (4th ed.) (pp. 190–228). New York: Wiley.

Gergen, K. J. (1990). Therapeutic professions and the diffusion of deficit. *Journal of Mind and Behavior, 11,* 353–368.

Hart, B. (1995). Re-authoring the stories we work by situating the narrative approach in the presence of the family of therapists. *Australian and New Zealand Journal of Family Therapy, 16,* 181–189.

Koss, M. P., & Shiang, J. (1994). Research on brief psychotherapy. In A. E. Bergin & S. L. Garfield (Eds.), *Handbook of psychotherapy and behavior change* (4th ed.) (pp. 664–700). New York: Wiley.

Lazarus, A. A. (1981). *The practice of multimodal therapy.* New York: McGraw-Hill.

Mahoney, M. J. (1995). Continuing evolution of the cognitive sciences and psychotherapy. In R. A. Neimeyer & M. J. Mahoney (Eds.), *Constructivism in psychotherapy* (pp. 39–68). Washington, DC: American Psychological Association.

Metcalf, L. (1995). *Counseling toward solutions: A practical solution-focused program for working with students, teachers, and parents.* West Nyack, NY: Center for Applied Research in Education.

Mills, R. C. (1995). *Realizing mental health: Toward a new psychology of resiliency.* New York: Sulburger & Graham.

Mills, R. C. (1996, August). *Empowering individuals and communities through health realization: Psychology of mind in prevention and community revitalization.* Paper presented at the meeting of the American Psychological Association, Toronto, Canada.

Mills, R. C., Dunham, R. G., & Alpert, G. P. (1988). Working with high-risk youth in prevention and early intervention programs: Toward a comprehensive wellness model. *Adolescence, 23,* 643–660.

Monk, G. (1997). How narrative therapy works. In G. Monk, J. Winslade, K. Crocket, & D. Epston (Eds.), *Narrative therapy in practice: The archaeology of hope* (pp. 3–31). San Francisco: Jossey-Bass.

Monk, G., Winslade, J., Crocket, K., & Epston, D. (Eds.). (1997). *Narrative therapy in practice: The archaeology of hope.* San Francisco: Jossey-Bass.

Murphy, J. J. (1997). *Solution-focused counseling in middle and high schools.* Alexandria, VA: American Counseling Association.

Neimeyer, R. A. (1995). An invitation to constructivist psychotherapies. In R. A. Neimeyer & M. J. Mahoney (Eds.), *Constructivism in psychotherapy* (pp. 1–10). Washington, DC: American Psychological Association.

Neimeyer, R. A., & Mahoney, M. J. (Eds.). (1995). *Constructivism in psychotherapy.* Washington, DC: American Psychological Association.

Norcross, J. C., & Freedheim, D. K. (1992). Into the future: Retrospect and prospect in psychotherapy. In D. K. Freedheim (Ed.), *History of psychotherapy: A century of change* (pp. 881–900). Washington, DC: American Psychological Association.

O'Hanlon, W. H. (1990). A grand unified theory for brief therapy: Putting problems in context. In J. K. Zeig & S. G. Gilligan (Eds.), *Brief therapy: Myths, methods, and metaphors* (pp. 78–89). New York: Brunner/Mazel.

O'Hanlon, W. H. (1993). Take two people and call them in the morning: Brief solution-oriented therapy with depression. In S. Friedman (Ed.), *The new language of change: Constructive collaboration in psychotherapy* (pp. 50–84). New York: Guilford.

O'Hanlon, W. H. (1994, November/December). The third wave. *Family Therapy Networker,* 19–29.

O'Hanlon, W. H., & Weiner-Davis, M. (1989). *In search of solutions: A new direction in psychotherapy.* New York: Norton.

Parloff, M. B. (1986). Frank's "common elements" in psychotherapy: Nonspecific factors and placebos. *American Journal of Orthopsychiatry, 56,* 521–530.

Posavac, E. J., & Carey, R. G. (1996). *Program evaluation: Methods and case studies.* Upper Saddle River, NJ: Prentice Hall.

Pransky, G. S., Mills, R. C., Sedgeman, J. A., & Blevens, J. K. (1997). An emerging paradigm for brief treatment. In L. Vandecreek, S. Knapp, & T. L. Jackson (Eds.), *Innovations in clinical practice: A source book* (Vol. 15) (pp. 401–420). Sarasota: Professional Resource Press.

Prochaska, J. O. (1984). *Systems of psychotherapy: A transtheoretical analysis.* Pacific Grove, CA: Brooks/Cole.

Prochaska, J. O., & DiClemente, C. (1982). Transtheoretical therapy: Toward a more integrative model of change. *Psychotherapy Research and Practice, 19,* 276–288.

Rave, E. J., & Larsen, C. C. (1995). *Ethical decision making in therapy: Feminist perspectives.* New York: Guilford.

Sarbin, T. R. (1993). The narrative as the root metaphor for contextualism. In S. C. Hayes, L. J. Hayes, H. W. Reese, & T. R. Sarbin (Eds.), *Varieties of scientific contextualism* (pp. 51–65). Reno: Context Press.

Sarbin, T. R., & Kitsuse, J. I. (Eds.). (1994). *Constructing the social.* Thousand Oaks, CA: Sage.

Selekman, M. D. (1993). Solution-oriented brief therapy with difficult adolescents. In S. Friedman (Ed.), *The new language of change: Constructive collaboration in psychotherapy* (pp. 138–157). New York: Guilford.

Seligman, M. E. P. (1992). *Learned optimism.* New York: Pocket Books.

Strupp, H. H., & Hadley, S. W. (1979). Specific versus nonspecific factors in psychotherapy: A controlled study of outcome. *Archives of General Psychiatry, 36,* 1125–1136.

Svartberg, M., & Stiles, T. C. (1991). Comparative effects of short-term psychodynamic psychotherapy: A meta-analysis. *Journal of Consulting and Clinical Psychology, 59,* 704–714.

Walter, J. L., & Peller, J. E. (1992). *Becoming solution-focused in brief therapy.* New York: Brunner/Mazel.

Wells, R. S., & Giannetti, V. J. (1990). *Handbook of brief psychotherapies.* New York: Plenum.

White, M., & Epston, D. (1990). *Narrative means to therapeutic ends.* New York: Norton.

Eastern Theories

Larry D. Burlew
University of Bridgeport

Catherine B. Roland
University of Arkansas, Fayetteville

Introduction

A recognition is growing within the discipline of Western mental health counseling and psychotherapy that counselors and counselors-in-training must consider theoretical approaches from diverse cultures and areas of the world. Understanding how different cultural groups comprehend and value life, as well as their worldviews, facilitates the practice of counseling within our society. The vast differences between clients and client groups availing themselves of mental health services today require that counselors and therapists cultivate a broadened understanding and acceptance of cross-cultural philosophical and psychological beliefs so that they may offer the best service to clients. Knowledge of Eastern thought concerning mental health counseling practices for the traditional Western-culture therapist expands traditional Eurocentric worldviews of counseling. This chapter explores the basic philosophies of Eastern psychological thought and mental health practice, with a focus on **Morita therapy** as a specific approach.

Eastern Psychological Thought

When we speak of Eastern therapies, we are referring to the three major cultural/religious traditions of Asia—Indian, Chinese, and Japanese—which focus mainly on the transpersonal and existential beliefs that are grounded in the philosophy of the East. Traditionally, Westerners have perceived a lack of analysis in contemporary Eastern psychotherapies regarding pathology (Murphy & Murphy, 1968). Westerners perceive the Eastern focus on mental health to be strictly religious or philosophical in nature, concentrating mainly on states of consciousness and stages of enlightenment that could not be practiced by unenlightened people.

The three Eastern systems of thought have their roots in religion. They approach the psychological tradition through the definition of various ethical and religious practices that embrace as goals the understanding of the mind, as well as the liberation of the mind from negativity, misery, and delusion (Murphy & Murphy, 1968). To acquire a working knowledge of Eastern mental health core values, one must delve into Eastern psychological thought as it relates to practice.

Therefore, it is impossible to discuss Eastern mental health practice and core values without looking toward Eastern religious and philosophical thought. The ancient and traditional philosophy of the East is fused with the basic principles of Eastern mental health practices. A basic concept of all Eastern ideas about psychological health is a focus on calm and contemplation in everyday life.

Meditation and yoga are the two traditional approaches one typically finds mentioned when researching the Asian quest for ideal psychological health, comprised of advanced enlightenment or liberation (Walsh, 1995). Although it is sometimes argued that meditation and yoga are not pure forms of psychological therapy due to their individual nature, the broad definitions of meditation as a means to cultivate awareness, concentration, love, and compassion, and of yoga as having similar goals (with the addition of ethical and intellectual capacities), indicate that both meditation and yoga are the mainstays or underpinnings of Asian therapies. Practiced for several thousands of years, and by tens of millions of people, meditation and yoga remain an integral part of almost all of the Eastern therapies utilized today (Kutz, Borysenko, & Benson, 1985; Walsh, 1995; West, 1987).

Eastern philosophy has influenced Eastern psychological therapies through such concepts as high regard for ethical thought and conduct, unselfishness and generosity to self and others, and an understanding of personal well-being. Within the Eastern tradition, **individual will** is often thought of as selfish, immature, and out of sync with the societal and familial loyalties and goals inherent in Eastern culture (De Vos, 1980). A close and necessary relationship exists between body and mind in Eastern thought. Japanese philosopher Eriken Kaibara (1630–1714) recognized and wrote of the traditional **_Ki_** concept, which represents psychological energy or mental force. For mental energy or _Ki_ to be fluid and consistent, the individual must rid him- or herself of things harmful to the body, such as desires and unhealthy conditions (e.g., consuming desire for food, sex, or sleep, and feelings of sorrow, joy, anger, or anxiety). Deep anger may induce the _Ki_ to go too high, and extreme or excess pleasure may induce it to lose strength (Murphy & Murphy, 1968). Several Eastern therapies utilize this concept in the acceptance of life _as is_ and support the practice of deep contemplation coupled with cleansing.

Eastern Mental Health Practice

Eastern mental health practice has as a broad goal the transformation of attitude concerning self. As observed in the meditative and yogic training, shifts in lifestyle, mirrored by changes of the mind, body awareness, relationships, and self-awareness, require commitment (Walsh, 1995). Just as the therapist is committed to the best ethical practice for the good of the client, so are clients committed to an ethical, honest assessment of their lives and to an openness to the avenues that might be taken to reach a self-fulfilled, calm state.

Therapeutically, the first shift is a basic tenet of ethical behavior (i.e., not engaging in lying, stealing, sexual misconduct, murder, or ingesting mind-altering drugs) (Walsh,

1995). The quest for **purification** is a vital step in the Eastern model of the mental health journey. Through the preliminary skill development of concentration and cultivation of calm, the mind-body focus goes on to incorporate **agape** (unconditional love) for the purpose of self-awareness and the therapeutic processes of introspection and evaluation.

Within the Asian tradition, positive mental health is most characterized by a mind that is peaceful. From that peace can subsequently flow the tranquillity and empathy of the continuum of human suffering and joy (Walsh, 1995). The controlled, homeostatic state of the mind, devoid of anger, is essential to the Eastern therapies and to Eastern philosophical thought. Contemplation and quiet isolation allow the individual's positive nature to emerge toward enlightenment and tranquillity. Once this occurs, individuals can participate in the fullness and positiveness of the natural being of self as connected to all others, unselfishly and securely.

De Vos (1980) presented the Buddhist perspective concerning therapy as including an emphasis on the sense of connectedness and obligation to family; self-discipline; and an inherent need to express gratitude. Eastern philosophical thought relative to mental health encourages strength of mind and body, a positive outlook that does not dwell upon personal sorrow, and a self-efficacious belief that the "illness" can be controlled through allowing natural and flowing pain and joy to permeate the mind. As De Vos writes, "In Buddhism the self is an illusion, and the sense of separateness so painfully a part of becoming human is transitory, in that it will not persist through all eternity. . . . One's ultimate duty, as well as one's ultimate psychological security, is to be found in family or group continuity, not in the continuity of the self" (p. 121).

An Introduction to Morita Therapy

Morita therapy, a Japanese example of an Eastern approach to counseling, has gained recognition in North America, Europe, and Asia. **David Reynolds** studied Morita therapy intensively and has been its principal proponent in the United States. He immersed himself in the therapy, actually going through the traditional "bed rest" version as a client. From his experiences and studies, he developed his own adaptation of Morita therapy in a book titled *Constructive Living* (1984a). As many as 80 certified Constructive Living instructors have been trained and are using the principles here and in other countries (Hedstrom, 1994). However, other practitioners (e.g., Bankart, 1997; Fujita, 1986; Ishiyama, 1990; Walsh, 1995) have also described and promulgated the concepts and practice of Morita therapy.

Readers may eventually use Morita concepts with Western clients, but we remind you that Morita therapy is not a Eurocentric approach to counseling. It was developed to address the needs and cultural beliefs of the Japanese people. Therefore, we urge you not to make comparisons between this Eastern approach to counseling and Western approaches such as existential, person-centered, or cognitive-behavioral theories. Although Hedstrom (1994) compared Western approaches to Morita therapy, we ask you to resist doing the same for several reasons. First, Morita therapy was developed for a unique worldview and needs to be viewed through that cultural lens to be fully appreciated. Second, you may (un)consciously negate aspects of Morita therapy by trying to make it (a separate reality) adapt to your perspective, a Western habit that Weisz, Rothbaum, and Blackburn (1984) called **primary control.** Studying Morita therapy without comparing it requires "aligning yourself with existing realities" (Weisz et al., p. 955), or **secondary control,** which is more of an Eastern habit. Finally, by not comparing, your study of Morita therapy begins with ***arugamama*** (i.e., accepting reality as it is) (Iwai & Reynolds, 1970; Kitanishi & Mori, 1995), the foundation of this approach. For our purpose, experiencing *arugamama* as you read means that Morita is a reality in and of itself; it stands alone and can be accepted, studied, and incorporated into your counseling approach if it feels right.

Background of Morita Therapy

Shoma Morita (1874–1938) was trained as a psychiatrist and taught at the Jikei University School of Medicine in Tokyo. He initially called his approach **experiential therapy, natural therapy,** or **awakening therapy** (Kitanishi & Mori, 1995). Only later did it become known as Morita therapy. He first wrote about this approach in 1917 for treating a condition he called ***shinkeishitsu,*** a form of anxiety and obsession disorder. However, he worked since the early 1900s (i.e., for at least 15 years) trying to find an effective treatment for "clients with a nervous predisposition" (Ishiyama, 1990, p. 566).

Morita's initial knowledge about *shinkeishitsu* stemmed from his own experience with this condition. Reynolds (1981a) writes that "as a young man Morita suffered from a variety of neurotic complaints, including inability to concentrate, death anxiety, palpitations, and gastrointestinal complaints" (p. 489). The methods he used for his self-cure helped him function as a productive member of society, and he most likely included them in his work with other neurotics. Fujita (1986) labeled "understanding" as the critical factor in the client-counselor relationship and claimed that "understanding comes from the therapist's personal experience of suffering from shinkeishitsu" (p. 224).

Despite his training, Morita's experiential therapy clearly deviated from traditional psychoanalysis. He initially tried three therapeutic interventions—Weir Mitchess's "rest therapy," Otto Binswanger's method of "life normalization," and Dubois's "persuasion method"—but without much success (Kitanishi & Mori, 1995, p. 245). However, Mitchess's and Binswanger's approaches are particularly evident in Morita therapy. Using these approaches convinced Morita to disregard the psychoanalytic tradition of examining childhood etiologies for neurotic symptoms. Morita therapists are not concerned with the cause of neurotic symptoms, but rather focus only on the present moment, accepting reality as it is, whether good or bad, and working in spite of one's neurotic symptoms (Ishiyama, 1990; Kora & Ohara, 1973; Reynolds, 1981a).

Interestingly, Morita first counseled clients in his own home with his family present. His family, particularly his wife, was crucial to the therapeutic process as assistant therapist (Kitanishi & Mori, 1995). In Japan the family is sacrosanct and a "haven of security and protection in times of trouble" (Reynolds & Kiefer, 1977, p. 398), so counseling clients within the day-to-day life of a real family made sense. Additionally, since the major symptom of *shinkeishitsu* is selfish preoccupation (i.e., ***toraware***), these clients avoid their intuitive social obligations (i.e., ***on***) to family and society (Bankart, 1997; Ishiyama, 1990; Reynolds, 1980, 1981a; Walsh, 1995). Rather than talk about *on* with clients and have them respond respectfully within their families, the *on* was stimulated experientially by incorporating clients into the life of Morita's own family. The in-home therapy began with complete bed rest and minimal contact with the family; eventually the client would assume work responsibilities within the family. Although it is no longer practiced, this in-home method was a rare form of experiential counseling whereby clients learned about *on* and work phenomenologically.

Morita's original method of in-home counseling with his family present would shock the mental health profession should a practitioner attempt it today—in fact, the practice would be reported as an ethical violation, particularly regarding dual relationships and boundary issues. Similarly, in Japan, Morita therapy moved from the counselor's home to inpatient work in a hospital or clinic, with absolute bed rest still required. The clinic's task, however, is to create a family-like environment, as much as that can occur with staff and other patients. A clinic does provide a social setting for the therapeutic process, and this setting is a critical phenomenological requirement for tapping into Japanese character (Kitanishi & Mori, 1995; Reynolds & Kiefer, 1977).

The traditional method of absolute bed rest is not much in practice today, and Reynolds reported "only about a dozen hospitals still practicing it in the mid-1980s" (cited in Hedstrom, 1994, p. 154). More frequently Morita therapy occurs on an outpatient basis, occurring in group counseling and group meetings as well. Additionally, innovative forms of the approach are in practice, including correspondence therapy, cassette tapes, and bibliotherapy (i.e., monthly magazines) (Hedstrom, 1994; Reynolds, 1981a).

Because Morita therapy is considered a philosophy of life, its principles are used for public education. A self-help organization called Seikatsu no Hakkenkai ("The Discovery of Life Organization") has about 5,000 members, many of them former clients, who meet and support living life according to Morita principles (Hedstrom, 1994; Reynolds, 1981b). Krech (1989) also uses Morita principles in consulting with organizations and businesses. He teaches the principles to individual employees, helps work groups operate as teams, and conducts workshops on conflict resolution. Morita principles extend beyond the traditional client-counselor setting because "Morita therapy is a system of therapeutic instruction through which the [client] is taught a lifeway which focuses on living fully in each moment" (Reynolds, 1981b, p. 201).

Human Nature

Morita therapy was developed to address a particular type of neurosis, *shinkeishitsu*. Understanding the nature of the Japanese character may help you understand what contributes to the occurrence of *shinkeishitsu* in a Japanese individual. Keep in mind, however, that a Morita therapist would not be concerned with causes. Neither the etiology nor causes are explored with clients, since such introspection would only cause clients to turn further inward and obsess more on themselves rather than focus on the outer world and what needs to be done (Reynolds, 1981a, 1984a, 1989). However, knowing the nature of the Japanese character that is admired, respected, and desired may help you appreciate the *shinkeishitsu* client's "urgent" desire to be cured. Yet you must also understand the nature of *shinkeishitsu* as an entity in and of itself within the Japanese character.

Aldous (1994) described *shinkeishitsu* clients as "nervous, anxious, hypochondriacal, behaviorally avoidant and procrastinating" (p. 239). If they cope by avoiding, then they can't be facing reality *arugamama*. Instead, they turn inward, obsessively creating ideals such as "If I only thought people liked me, I'd go to that party, but I know they won't so I'm not going." As long as they remain in this cycle of ideal, avoidance, and obsessing on self (i.e., *toraware*), they can never truly contribute to the good of all. They do not fulfill their *on* because their *toraware* controls their behavior. These clients seem unusually sensitive to the fact that their drives are not constructive and not contributing to society. Therefore, they are unusually anxious to be cured (Reynolds, 1976).

We have chosen three constructs—family and **amae,** collectivism, and naturalness—that we believe contribute to the healthy development of the respected Japanese character. However, our review is a generalization culled from the literature and viewed through the experience and perceptions of Westerners. We have, therefore, excluded many constructs due to lack of space and of greater familiarity. Additionally, differences also exist within the Japanese culture that we are most likely not even aware of. To completely describe the Japanese character, these differences would also need to be considered, but this is not our goal. Rather, the three concepts included should help you better understand the nature of *shinkeishitsu* neurosis, and the client's desire to be cured.

Family and *Amae*

The Japanese are raised to see the family as sacrosanct and that they "belong" to the family (Bankart, 1997; Reynolds & Kiefer, 1977). This belonging to the family is represented by the term **miuichi,** which means "being a member of the inner circle," as distinguished from **tanin,** who are "recognized outsiders" (Bankart). Weisz et al. (1984) referred to this as "skinship" because of child-rearing practices such as "prolonged body contact with family members" (p. 958) and actions such as locking children out of the house as discipline. The latter is symbolic for casting the child out of *miuichi,* and letting the child back into the house is symbolic of "realignment" with the family. Realignment is cherished and respected, so the misbehaving child desires to be "back in the house."

This reliance on family is hierarchical or vertical in nature, with a respect for and dependence upon senior or elder family members. However, the hierarchical nature is not a matter of some persons are "at the top" and others are "at the bottom." Rather, the family is a unit, its members merging with each other (called **ittaikan**) within the hierarchical structure to promote harmony of the whole (or **wa**) (Bankart, 1997; Pelzel, 1977; Weisz et al., 1984). Children learn that the family will protect them from "dangerous outsiders" and is thus a safe place (Pelzel, 1977). Being a productive working member of the family, or eventually of small primary groups, in order to promote *wa* is highly respected.

Within this safe *miuichi,* the child experiences *amae* (or learns to "use" *amae,* depending on how one is defining this term) with the family. Bankart (1997) defines *amae* as "passive love," which means that one doesn't actively seek love; it is provided no matter what. This, in turn, taps into a family member's *on* (i.e., intuitively experienced obligation) to all members of *miuichi,* which eventually yields **giri,** which is the "assurance of belonging to a group" (Bankart, 1997). Being alone, isolated, and separate, and thus without *giri,* is an insufferable condition that yields pity for those caught in such a situation.

On the other hand, Doi Takeo, a Japanese psychoanalyst (cited in Pelzel, 1977), criticized *amae* (literally meaning to seek goodwill of, presume upon, take advantage of) as an unhealthy dependence on the family. This explanation of *amae* indicates a tight, inseparable bond with the family. The dependence is so strong that the self is less important than the collective family because "the family is the very center of the web of their obligation" (Bankart, 1997, p. 452). The family shares in everything any individual of the *miuichi* does (called vicarious experiencing); similarly, any shame caused by an individual within the *miuichi* is felt by the family. According to Doi, the overwhelming *amae* causes a lack of ***jibun***, which Bankart defines as "a conscious awareness of self or ego" (p. 449). Yet the experience of *amae* is the desired and expected relationship with the family.

Collectivism

Because of the prevalence of childhood teachings promoting respect for and harmony with the family in Japanese society, Weisz et al. (1984) claimed that the Japanese character has an "orientation to persons and society [in general]" (p. 958). The Japanese tend to be very polite, try not to hurt or insult others, and keep hostile feelings to themselves (Abel, 1977). Bankart (1997) believes that "communal groups such as the family, coworkers, and the nation as a whole take precedence in everyday life over needs and desires of the individual" (p. 440). Therefore, dominant individualism or selfish egoism would be avoided because such behavior is not for the good of the whole. According to Reynolds and Kiefer (1977), "The resulting sense of self has two distinct facets: tatemae, or the social self, emphasizing role performance and dependence on others, and honne, or the stream of personal thoughts and feelings that makes up the private inner world. The ideal in Japan is to be sensitive to others' honne, and to try to adjust one's own honne so that it resonates in harmony with the tatemae" (pp. 408–409). The ***tatemae,*** then, promotes social harmony, and the Japanese are keenly aware of their social obligations. They have a sense of "contributing to the common good" (Bankart, p. 446). From childhood they are taught pro-empathy. The mother sometimes disciplines with statements like, "If you don't stop doing that, it is I who will suffer most. Try to put yourself in my place" (Weisz et al., 1984, p. 959).

The respected Japanese character, then, is group oriented and unusually socially sensitive. Social cues are important because "every act is defined in terms of its social consequences" (Hedstrom, 1994, p. 155). Generalizing from family interactions, the same principles of *on* and *giri* are also expected in the larger context of society. For example, if you do your job well and meet your obligations (i.e., *on*) at work, then you have accomplished for the whole company because you "belong" (i.e., *giri*) to that particular work group (Weisz et al., 1984). Individuals who cannot meet *on* and who do not experience *giri* are considered unfortunate and in need of help (perhaps reeducation).

Naturalism

This final construct is inherent in Zen Buddhism and relates to "an acceptance of the world as it is" (Pelzel, 1977, p. 306). Many writers (e.g., Aldous, 1994; Hedstrom, 1994; Iwai & Reynolds, 1970; Reynolds, 1976, 1980, 1981a, 1989) discuss **naturalism** as reality with connections to ***un*** (i.e., fate), and wise individuals align themselves to reality, whether good or bad (Weisz et al., 1984). Reynolds and Kiefer (1977) refer to this as "the interdependence of self and environment" (p. 409). You cannot control realities because they simply are, and you shouldn't waste time on ideals or "shoulds" because they aren't real. Weisz et al. claimed that "an ability to peacefully accept one's outcomes arugamama ('as they are') is considered a sign of great maturity and wisdom" (1984, p. 962). Therefore, individuals who act on ideals and who cannot accept reality *arugamama* must be immature and unwise, thus not growing and developing.

Morita's view of human nature was optimistic and naturalistic, most likely in consideration of the Japanese character. He believed that "most human beings have basically decent, constructive drives" (Kora & Ohara, 1973, p. 68). People desire to live, grow, and work despite the many obstacles they face in life (Hedstrom, 1994; Kondo, 1953; Walsh, 1995). They "seek self-preservation and self-actualization by the compatible forces of fears and desires" (Ishiyama, 1990, p. 568). They face reality *arugamama* and make adjustments to themselves as necessary. They express ***sei no yokubo*** (the desire to live) and have ***sei no chikara*** (the strength of life) (Fujita, 1986).

Major Constructs

Walsh (1995) claims that Asian psychotherapies do not focus much on pathology, but instead "contain detailed maps of states of consciousness, developmental labels, and stages of enlightenment" (p. 388). Morita therapy fits this description as a "natural therapy" that helps individuals become more conscious of the mind and body as natural phenomena over which we have no control (Fujita, 1986). Once clients accept the environment *arugamama,* they can do what needs to be done to create "a meaningful life for self and a usefulness to society" (Reynolds, 1981a, p. 500). Morita considered this stimulation of consciousness a reeducation process for clients, who might be called "students" (Reynolds, 1984b).

We have selected seven major constructs to help you better appreciate this "natural therapy": neurosis, misfocused mind, homophobia, *arugamama,* meaningful life, work, and cure.

Neurosis

Neurosis is not viewed from a pathology perspective in Morita therapy. Like other natural phenomena, it is a response to one's environment, only it is one that clients "have generated within themselves in the fruitless struggle to avoid inevitable and natural psychological and physiological reactions" (Bankart, 1997, p. 456). Neurotics respond more to the "what ifs" and "shoulds" (i.e., the ideal) than to what is (i.e., reality). Reynolds (1981a) referred to this as "mental overspinning" which results in too much thinking and not enough action. Neurotics act based on the ideal (e.g., "I'll take care of it when I feel happier") while the mental overspinning is focused on feelings and thoughts—things they have no control over. Their character becomes misfocused *toraware* and thus requires a form of "character education and the essence of the character is learning to accept the world as it is—not as you would like, hope, wish, or force it to be" (Bankart, p. 458).

As early as 1953, Asihisa Kondo listed seven characteristics of the neurotic personality: hypochondriasis; attempting to make the impossible possible; trying to avoid anxiety; not accepting facts and learning from them; thinking of oneself and one's experiences as different from others' and their experiences; wishing to have happiness without effort; and feelings of inferiority and incapacity (pp. 31–32). The umbrella term Kondo used for these terms was "egocentricity." Egocentricity, then, is a form of neurosis because the *tatemae* is deemphasized, which disrupts the potential for *wa*. Morita developed his approach to help *shinkeishitsu* clients who were deep in the throes of egocentricity.

Shinkeishitsu.   *Shinkeishitsu* neurosis generally includes three clinical groups: neurasthenia, anxiety neurosis, and obsessional fears. These clients are introverted, pessimistic, socially inhibited, perfectionistic, oversensitive, critical of self, have somatic and psychologic complaints, and feel inferior (Aldous, 1994; Chang, 1980; Hedstrom, 1994; Kitanishi & Mori, 1995; Kondo, 1953; Kora & Ohara, 1973; Reynolds, 1981a; Walsh, 1995). They can experience anthropophobia, a form of debilitating shyness (Reynolds & Kiefer, 1977), and they experience anxieties with a strong social focus, often with concomitant social phobias (Hedstrom, 1994; Reynolds, 1981a). In Japan, this condition centers around *toraware,* which has been defined as a selfish preoccupation, fixation of attention, and prepossession (Bankart, 1997; Kitanishi & Mori, 1995; Kora & Ohara, 1973). *Toraware* is conceptualized as a flight from reality to an obsessive turning inward of attention (Reynolds & Kiefer) that inhibits the performance of *on* to family and society.

On the other hand, *shinkeishitsu* clients are described as demonstrating the Japanese concept of *sei no yokubo* (i.e., the desire to live fully) (Fujita, 1986). They tend to be brighter than normal, ambitious, high achievers, intellectually oriented, and anxious to be rid of their symptoms (Fujita, 1986; Kora & Ohara, 1973; Reynolds, 1981a). Morita believed that the *shinkeishitsu* symptoms indicate just how strongly they have *sei no yokubo*. These individuals have *sei no chikara* (i.e., the strength of life) (Fujita) that obsessively drives them to seek a "cure" (i.e., to be rid of their symptoms). *Sei no chikara* probably makes them good clients if the "strength" can be "refocused" appropriately on *sei no yokubo*.

Morita conceptualized the *shinkeishitsu* condition as a vicious cycle that will intensify without intervention (see Figure 15.1). The *shinkeishitsu* temperament might be genetically predisposed (i.e., "Disposition" in the figure). Such persons emotionally respond to experiences (i.e., "Opportunity" in the figure) like other people, but their responses are "a negative reaction to [their] own survival and adaptation and [focus their] attention on this reaction" (Kitanishi & Mori, 1995, p. 246). The emotional reaction is felt more intensely and for longer periods of time, and the client fixates attention on the anxious feelings (i.e., "Psychic Interaction" in the figure). Morita (cited in Kitanishi & Mori, 1995) referred to this as "the conflict between the ideal [e.g., dreading having to go to school because others might ridicule you] and real [i.e., school is an experience and you can go despite your dread]" (p. 246).

What then happens in the cycle? *Shinkeishitsu* clients' hypochondriacal/neurotic symptoms become exaggerated, and they begin to dread the next opportunity that might occur and try to avoid it, thus being controlled by their anxious feelings, the psychic interaction (Kitanishi & Mori, 1995).

Misfocused Mind

Writing about Zen, Bankart (1997) has described its central idea as "focusing the misfocused mind away from preoccupation with self and toward the accomplishment of what needs to be done" (p. 458). The "curing" process in Morita therapy embodies this Zen belief as a central concept. *Shinkeishitsu* clients suffer with *toraware,* or selfish preoccupation

Figure 15.1

The *Shinkeishitsu* Condition

Adapted from Kitanishi & Mori, 1995, p. 246.

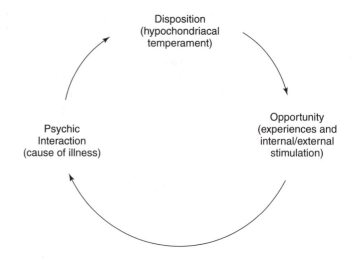

Disposition
(hypochondriacal
temperament)

Opportunity
(experiences and
internal/external
stimulation)

Psychic
Interaction
(cause of illness)

(Bankart, 1997; Ishiyama, 1990; Kitanishi & Mori, 1995; Reynolds, 1976). This condition causes a misfocus of attention, and "clients become less aware of the situation at hand and suffer from the lack of appropriate action and reduced effectiveness in living" (Ishiyama, p. 567). The misfocused attention is on all the anxieties and concerns about self, "an internal subjective world" (Reynolds, 1981b, p. 201), rather than on reality and the outer world.

Toraware causes the client to become "individualistic, alienated, and selfish" (Bankart, 1997, p. 442), and part of the "cure" in Morita therapy is for "the ego to lose power" (Kitanishi & Mori, 1995, p. 251). To accomplish this, clients' attention must be focused away from excessive self-absorption. The refocusing is not just an intellectual exercise of telling oneself, "Now quit thinking about me and my problems. What's going on today?" Rather, the refocusing is experienced as the counselor guides, instructs, and encourages clients to interact with the outer world while accomplishing *on*. Fujita (1986) writes: "Mental shifts take place within an onozu-kara-naru (natural or spontaneous) mentality in response to whatever conditions we confront, and this phenomenon cannot be manipulated intentionally, irrespective of our wishes" (p. 222). Most importantly, the refocusing helps clients learn to focus on reality *arugamama* (Bankart, 1997; Ishiyama, 1990; Kora & Ohara, 1973; Pelzel, 1977; Reynolds, 1981a, 1989; Reynolds & Kiefer, 1977; Weisz et al., 1984).

Control.   A major part of *shinkeishitsu* clients' focus is on what they can't control: feelings and thoughts (Bankart, 1997; Fujita, 1986; Hedstrom, 1994; Ishiyama, 1990; Krech, 1989; Reynolds, 1976, 1980, 1981a, 1984a, 1984b, 1989). Krech writes, "If we could control our moods why would we ever choose to be anxious, or depressed, or angry or unhappy?" (pp. 109–110). Rather, feelings are reality, come and go regularly, and should be experienced *arugamama*. Because we have no control over our feelings, the Morita therapist gives clients "permission" to feel or think whatever they are feeling or thinking. Therefore, one is not responsible for one's feelings (Hedstrom, 1994). These are good reasons for why "Morita explicitly questions the importance of emphasizing feelings in therapy" (Hedstrom, 1994, p. 157).

However, "one is morally, socially, and personally responsible for what one does" (Reynolds, 1981a, p. 492) because we have complete control over our behavior and actions. Krech (1989) explains that "since we can't control our feelings and thoughts we should simply accept them and get on with doing what needs to be done. This brings us to what is controllable—Doing" (p. 110). While feelings are not focused on in counseling sessions, neither are they avoided. Clients are reeducated to consider them a natural reaction of the mind and body to stimulation (Kitanishi & Mori, 1995). More importantly, clients experientially learn that doing and accomplishments equal life satisfaction (Fujita, 1986; Reynolds, 1980), in spite of how one feels.

For example, one of our clients once said, "I get so worked up and anxious about my boss after work that I just sit in the garage and smoke pot, even though I know my wife gets mad because I don't do anything around the house. I don't even take out the garbage." Imagine the power this client assigned to the feelings of "worked up and anxious." My response at the time was, "What's getting you so worked up and anxious?" This response kept the client "ruminating" on a feeling state, thus reinforcing his "bad habits of thinking and not acting" (Reynolds, 1984b, p. 13). From a Morita therapy perspective, a more instructive response might have been, "It is natural to feel worked up and anxious because you and your boss aren't getting along. Now what is it that needs doing around the house?"

Homophobia

Bankart (1997) used the term **homophobia** to describe the common social focus of the *shinkeishitsu* anxieties. Unlike the American use of the term, in Japan it refers to "undue or irrational anxiety, fear, and discomfort in or in prospect of interaction with fellow human beings" (Bankart, p. 455). In his research in Japan exploring psychopathology, Bankart found that "three-fourths of all mental health treatment in Japan are oriented toward removing homophobic reactions" (p. 455). Although we did not find this use of the term in other sources, we feel it amply describes (as defined by the Japanese culture) an important construct in Morita therapy.

Shinkeishitsu clients are generally overly sensitive, have problems relating to people, and are self-conscious in public (Ishiyama, 1990; Reynolds, 1981a, 1981b; Reynolds & Kiefer, 1977). They can be anthropophobic. Reynolds (1980) claimed they bombard themselves with questions such as "What do people think of me?; Does everyone see my weaknesses?; Why don't I accomplish more?" (p. 6). Their response to this, of course, tends to be avoidance of social situations, when possible, and more of a flight inward. They fail to meet their *on* because they have become "spoiled, pampered, self-indulgent, isolated, egotistical, uncooperative burdens on the rest of society" (Bankart, 1997, p. 456). Therapy, therefore, is conducted in a social setting which eventually restimulates the *tatemae* to help *shinkeishitsu* clients once again become productive members of society.

Arugamama

Arugamama is a pivotal construct in Morita therapy. The term technically means "accepting reality as it is" or "accepting things as they are" (Bankart, 1997; Pelzel, 1977; Reynolds, 1976; Weisz et al., 1984). For Morita therapy, *arugamama* becomes a means to a more constructive lifeway. Kora and Ohara (1973) define *arugamama* as "accepting one's symptoms as they are and accepting one's life as it is" (p. 68). In order to do this, clients learn to overcome "attitudinal blocks" preventing them "from implementing desirable actions" (Ishiyama, 1990, p. 566). Thus we are back to the basic principle of working despite debilitating thoughts and feelings.

Learning to live with both good and bad feelings and thoughts *arugamama* means that one doesn't use them as an excuse for avoiding *on* and constructive activity. For example, a teacher might say to herself, "I'm feeling so good today because my principal praised me and it's the first sunny day in weeks. How can I think about grading these papers?" A Morita response might be, "You're right, don't think about grading the papers, just grade them." The praise, sunny weather, and good feelings can be acknowledged *arugamama;* they are a natural occurrence in the environment. The teacher really has no control over them. However, she does have control over her behavior. She should accept the good feelings *arugamama* and grade the papers (a form of *on* to students) in spite of the good feelings.

Meaningful Life

Morita considered the *shinkeishitsu* condition to involve two sides of the same coin (Aldous, 1994). Although *shinkeishitsu* clients are filled with excessive worries and anxieties, this excessiveness may actually be an indicator of desires to grow and develop or for *sei no yokubo* (Fujita, 1986; Weisz et al., 1984). Part of the character reeducation, then, is helping clients move away from *toraware* enough to experientially align themselves with the other side of the coin, *sei no yokubo*.

What, then, is this other side of the coin directed toward? Perhaps "having a purpose in the physical world that holds one's attention" (Reynolds & Keifer, 1977, p. 406). Notice that "attention" is directed toward the outer world, which certainly includes *on* to family and society. Therefore, a meaningful life provides service to others and a "usefulness to society" (Reynolds, 1981a, p. 500). As clients experientially learn that they can become more sociocentric, then healthy qualities emerge such as mindfulness, love, compassion, concentration, and calm (Walsh, 1995).

Work

Work is a vital construct in Morita therapy, only not work as the Western reader might be thinking. Kitanishi and Mori (1995) describe work as "an assertion to be active, to pay attention to the outside" (p. 250). In the traditional Morita therapy, clients experienced a week of bed rest, after which various levels of work were prescribed and/or allowed. The initial level of "light work" was the beginning of refocusing; that is, "attention is directed away from the self to the task" (Hedstrom, 1994, p. 155). At first the client might be instructed to sweep a patio or weed a garden. After a week of bed rest and no activity, clients oftentimes report a feeling of exhilaration, even though that feeling too passes. They were also instructed to look around them; the environment would hold the answers to what needed to be done. "Work [then] allows the self-centered person to 'lose [him- or herself],' that is, to transcend [him- or herself]" (Reynolds, 1976, p. 32).

Work is a therapeutic technique used to (1) focus attention on something other than self; (2) become aware of the outer world; (3) acknowledge experiences moment-by-moment; (4) take control over behavior and become involved in life activities; and (5) eventually realize that one can work in spite of one's feelings (Aldous, 1994; Hedstrom, 1994; Ishiyama, 1990; Reynolds, 1976, 1980, 1981a, 1984b). A Morita therapist could just tell a client, "Look. Why don't you do what needs to be done in your life? Take responsibility for yourself, and you won't get in so much trouble with people." Trying to "talk" clients into this insight may actually be counterproductive. Besides forcing the client to now "ruminate" about a "new thought," insight alone is, as Reynolds (1984b) says, "a way of avoiding making the effortful, sometimes painful, changes in behavior" (p. 17).

The experiential learning of "work" actively helps clients move toward a major goal: "[to] achieve satisfactory control over what they do in life, regardless of their feeling state" (Hedstrom, 1994, p. 157). Additionally, by actually doing something and accomplishing, "we learn our true capabilities, our true limitations, and, invariably, what needs to be done next" (Reynolds, 1984b, p. 36).

Cure

Shinkeishitsu clients come to therapy to be "cured" of their symptoms. However, what clients mean by "cured" is being anxiety free, not fearful, able to be social without extreme self-consciousness, and self-confident (i.e., free of their symptoms). The cure through Morita therapy is exactly the opposite. Weisz et al. (1984) cited Reynolds's idea that "a [client] is considered cured when [he or she] has stopped groping for means to relieve [his or her] symptoms" (p. 964). Bankart (1997) used Reynolds's earlier concepts in writing, "The heart of the 'cure' in Morita therapy is in arugamama, which means 'accepting one's self, one's symptoms, and reality as they are'; lit., 'as it is'" (p. 458).

Cured clients, then, realize that their attention has been obsessively internal and self-focused, thus prohibiting them from doing what needs to be done. Morita therapy leads them through experiential learning so they can (1) transcend their symptoms; (2) accept self, feelings, and thoughts *arugamama;* (3) direct attention outward, seeing what needs to be done (work); and (4) take responsibility and actively work (i.e., accomplish). Cured, then, "does not mean removing symptoms but living productively in spite of them" (Reynolds, 1980, p. 7). Living productively means accomplishing. However, accomplishment is not viewed from a Western perspective (i.e., meaning we accomplished in terms of "doing well or great"). On the other hand, accomplishment is just that . . . you did what you set out to do. When clients learn to "work, socialize and behave normally in spite of [their symptoms]" (Weisz et al., 1984, p. 964), they are "cured" and discharged or terminated.

Applications

Overview

We consider Morita therapy to be a phenomenological approach to counseling and psychotherapy. Some researchers (e.g., Hedstrom, 1994) noted the behavioral aspects of Morita therapy, giving Morita credit for introducing Eastern behavioral therapy before Western behavioral therapy came to Japan. However, we caution the reader not to parallel Morita therapy too closely with the Western idea of behavioral counseling and psychotherapy.

While Morita therapy does concentrate on taking action, the "action" is not conditioning any particular behavior (e.g., asking people out on dates). The action is part of the natural experience of living that *shinkeishitsu* clients tend to overlook, and thus avoid, because of their intense self-absorption. There would be no rhyme or reason to what activity occurs in a given day because phenomenologically each day unfolds as a new flower with new responsibilities. One day I might scrub my kitchen floor, buy a new coffeemaker, and guest lecture in a friend's class. The next day I might fly to Washington, DC, and visit the Department of Education about a grant, visit with long-lost friends, and eat at my favorite bagel shop in Dupont Circle. No systematic conditioning of a particular behavior deficiency occurs; instead, the whole experience of the individual is considered as each day unfolds.

Researchers (e.g., Kitanishi & Mori, 1995) have addressed the deconditioning of *toraware*. From our perspective, this deconditioning may take place by a technique called "disregarding method" (Kitanishi & Mori, 1995) in which the counselor doesn't respond, thus doesn't reinforce, discussions about symptoms, the past, or etiology of clients' neuroses. However, Morita therapists would not think of it this way (from our perspective). *Toraware* is a form of awareness gone astray (Reynolds, 1976) because in the *shinkeishitsu* condition one is egotistically self-absorbed. As counseling progresses and clients become experientially involved in activities in the outer world, they discover that they lose themselves in work, in the moment, and forget about their symptoms (Hedstrom, 1994). Rather than undergo any type of systematic deconditioning, clients learn through their experiencing to shift their attention to the outer world and accomplish things in spite of symptoms (Ishiyama, 1990; Reynolds, 1976, 1980). The shift seems to be toward accepting symptoms *arugamama* and doing what needs to be done.

Goals of Counseling and Psychotherapy

As we mentioned earlier, the overall goal of Morita therapy is reflected in the Zen concept of "focusing the misfocused mind away from the preoccupation with self and toward the accomplishment of what needs to be done" (Bankart, 1997, p. 458). Clients strive to become aware of the outer world to determine what needs to be done and to act in spite of feelings such as hopelessness, depression, anger, and frustration (Abel, 1977; Hedstrom, 1994; Kitanishi & Mori, 1995; Kondo, 1953; Kora & Ohara, 1973; Reynolds, 1976, 1980, 1981a, 1984b; Reynolds & Kiefer, 1977). The following example may make this goal clearer.

Jorge had a rotten day at work because he didn't complete a major report, had to work through lunch, and found out he wasn't getting the promotion he thought he deserved. Therefore, he came home feeling angry, tense, and disappointed with the way his life was going.

Before counseling, Jorge might have walked into his urban condo, grabbed a container of ice cream from the freezer, flopped on the sofa, eaten the ice cream, and sulked. He'd ruminate on the day with thoughts like: "I'm never going to succeed like everyone else; maybe they're never going to be as fair with Latinos as they are with Anglos; it's not right that I get the long, complex reports to write; I'm too timid to ask my supervisor to lessen my workload—I start to stutter and sound stupid; I dread going back to work." As you can see, the "mental overspinning" leads to (1) complete self-absorption; (2) failure to act in any meaningful way; (3) increased anxiety; and (4) dread of the situation yet to come.

Jorge represents a typical *shinkeishitsu* client. As his Morita therapy progresses, he might react differently to the above scenario. He'd come home accepting the anger, disappointment, and depression. He might even acknowledge that he has no control over these feelings and that they make sense based on his work day. Then he might examine his environment (both physical and mental) and actively engage in "work" (i.e., see what needs to be done and do it). The hallway closet needs to be reorganized. He calls Mom to see how she's doing and to ask if there's anything he can help her with. He might plan a quiet time to talk with his supervisor about workload despite his fear and stuttering. Then he'd practice what he wants to say.

As you can see, Jorge's outer-world focus and physical/mental work lead to (1) accepting symptoms and feelings *arugamama;* (2) living in the present moment; (3) becoming aware of the outer environment to see what needs to be done; and (4) working (i.e., doing) alongside the feelings and symptoms. As he focuses on tasks at hand and works on them, his symptoms fade into the background.

Obviously, to achieve the broader goal of "focusing the misfocused mind," other goals must also be met. These goals are not separate or even sub-goals, but rather form the *wa.* This harmony of the whole allows clients to eventually work productively. The other goals are:

1. Accept self and the world *arugamama* (Aldous, 1994; Bankart, 1997; Hedstrom, 1994; Ishiyama, 1990). When you achieve this goal, you stop asking for symptom elimination because you realize how foolish this is. You have no control over your feelings and thoughts, but must learn to live and work in spite of them.

2. Learn that you have complete control over your behavior and be socially and morally responsible by doing what needs to be done (Hedstrom, 1994; Pelzel, 1977; Reynolds, 1976, 1980, 1981a, 1981b). Kora and Ohara (1973) believed that "purposive, goal-directed behavior must be reestablished in order to reorient the life pattern" (p. 68). This goal cannot be accomplished without a change in awareness from internal to external, from the ideal to reality, and from subjective introspection to doing (Kitanishi & Mori, 1995).

3. Learn to live in reality experientially. Kitanishi and Mori (1995) claimed that "the experience [of behavior and practice] . . . modifies the self-centered ego called the experience of helplessness and giving up" (p. 251). Reality is moment-by-moment as you experience your environment and world (both internal and external). Only by living in reality can you live fully (for each moment brings new challenges), experience constructive living patterns (Hedstrom, 1994; Reynolds, 1984a, 1984b), and build a history of success with life (Reynolds, 1981a).

4. Reynolds (1981a) believed that a goal of Morita therapy is to "recognize [one's] purpose" (p. 500). Purpose comes from living life fully, and you accomplish this by developing more effective work habits, leading to a more organized life (Hedstrom, 1994). The idea of a purpose relates directly back to the Japanese character. Hedstrom writes that the "emphasis [is] upon fulfilling one's social obligations (giri) and accepting the hierarchical structures of society . . . [the client is] encouraged to fit in and make a positive contribution to society" (1994, p. 157).

The Process of Change

The counseling process in Morita therapy is based on phenomenological and experiential concepts. Clients don't "talk" about their symptoms in an effort to gain insight into "why" they are the way they are hoping not to be. Rather, the "chief treatment process in Morita therapy is centered on the actual life activities of a [client]; the therapist-[client] relationship is secondary and serves only as a setting in which the [client's] activities may be stimulated" (Fujita, 1986, p. 223). Clients learn how to refocus attention and accomplish life activities mostly through experiential learning. The actual therapeutic intervention with the client is considered short-term, lasting anywhere from 40 to 60 days (Iwai & Reynolds, 1970; Kitanishi & Mori, 1995; Kondo, 1953; Kora & Ohara, 1973; Reynolds & Kiefer, 1977). However, Morita therapy is a lifeway or life path, and clients live by Morita principles after termination. Guidance can continue via self-help groups, follow-up visits to the counselor, and reading materials sent from the counselor or clinic.

Traditionally, four phases occurred in the counseling process: absolute and complete bed rest; light work therapy; heavier mental and physical work therapy; and life activities training therapy (Fujita, 1986). Each phase is briefly described below. We also describe a pre-counseling phase that others include as part of Phase 1. However, we believe that it is critical enough in establishing the client-counselor roles to include as a separate phase.

To fully understand the richness of Morita therapy and the phases it progresses through, we urge the reader to seek such resources as David Reynolds's (1976) original and first English-language text on this topic, titled *Morita Psychotherapy;* Takehisa Kora and Kenshiro Ohara's (1973) original article in *Psychology Today,* titled "Morita Therapy"; or more current overviews of the phases, such as L. James Hedstrom's (1994) article in *Psychotherapy* titled "Morita and Naikan Therapies: American Applications."

Pre-Therapy Phase.   Once an individual is diagnosed as appropriate for Morita therapy, the counseling process begins. The counselor meets with the client and describes the process therapy will take. Reynolds (1980) explains that "with absolute confidence, the [counselor] tells [the client] that if he follows directions and applies himself, he will be cured" (p. 7). If Morita therapy is a form of character education (Bankart, 1997), then the counselor is a type of teacher or guide who has "surmounted [his or her] own self-imposed limitations through this method" (Reynolds, 1981a, p. 493).

The counselor-client relationship is beginning to conform to the Japanese hierarchical structure familiar to the Japanese client. Although the counselor exhibits understanding, empathy, and an accepting attitude, the relationship itself is only secondary to the process (Fujita, 1986). Reynolds (1981a) believed that "[the counselor] goes on with instruction in the Moritist lifeway whatever the relationship. The [counselor], like the [client], must know [his or her] behavioral purpose and cling to it" (p. 493). While a positive relationship is the goal, it is not a necessary condition for therapy to continue and be successful. However, trust seems to be a necessary factor—trust that the counselor is knowledgeable and experienced enough to help "stimulate" life activities (Fujita).

During this phase, the counselor, like a helpful and concerned guide, explains the following:

1. The *shinkeishitsu* condition as a psychological problem, and the client's experience with this condition up to this point

2. The phases that therapy progresses through

3. The client's feelings and reactions to various phases (e.g., the counselor predicts that ultimate experience of bed rest will not be pleasurable) (Reynolds, 1980)

4. What the client can or cannot do during each phase (e.g., if therapy is inpatient, outside visitors cannot come until Phase 4) (Fujita, 1986)

5. The role of the counselor, such that "the [client] must entrust the [counselor] to apply effective therapy" (Fujita, p. 200)

6. The role of the client to "begin life activities in this new direction and to cooperate in the therapeutic procedure" (Fujita, p. 200)

Because so much of what the counselor describes is actually experienced, "the [client] eventually accepts and learns that the [counselor] really does understand and is able to predict the course of [his or her] recovery with some degree of accuracy" (Reynolds, p. 7).

Phase 1: Absolute, Isolated Bed Rest.   In the traditional form of Morita therapy, the inpatient counseling process started with isolated bed rest that lasted anywhere from four to seven days (Fujita, 1986; Hedstrom, 1994; Kitanishi & Mori, 1995; Kondo, 1953; Kora & Ohara, 1973; Reynolds, 1976, 1980, 1981a; Reynolds & Kiefer, 1977). Fujita described this process: "The [client] must be completely isolated, with visitors, conversation, reading and smoking prohibited and with bed rest imposed at all times except for use of the lavatory, washing the face or eating at mealtimes" (p. 201). Clients are left alone and given little opportunity for external stimuli, distractions, or diversions (Hedstrom, 1994; Reynolds, 1976). They are instructed to focus on any and all thoughts and feelings as they occur. The counselor checks on their progress daily (Hedstrom, p. 155). As the counselor has predicted, this experience is at first restful for the client, then moves to boring and tedious, and eventually leads to feelings of suffering and anguish, becoming unendurable. Clients are instructed to endure and accept any feelings and symptoms as they occur (Fujita, 1986; Hedstrom, 1994; Kora & Ohara, 1973; Reynolds, 1976).

This form of absolute bed rest is the ultimate experiential learning of how "unnatural" complete self-absorption is. The process makes concrete what is occurring (i.e., isolation from outer world) with *toraware*. Rather than "talking" about withdrawing internally and discussing what that does to one's life and *on,* clients learn about the consequences of withdrawal via an experiential process. Many researchers (e.g., Fujita, 1986; Hedstrom, 1994; Reynolds, 1980) describe this period of bed rest as helping clients learn the following:

1. They have no control over their thoughts and feelings. Feelings and thoughts come and go, pleasant and unpleasant, so they may as well experience them *arugamama.*

2. They will endure and continue living regardless of the feelings and symptoms. Surprisingly, even the feelings and symptoms go away after a period of time, just as they can return without notice.

3. The outer world exists, and isolating oneself isn't so pleasant or natural after all.

4. The counselor is an effective guide because he or she predicted that the bed rest would become boring, unendurable, and unpleasant.

Phase 2: Light Work Therapy.   Phase 2 lasts approximately three to seven days (Reynolds, 1980; Reynolds & Kiefer, 1977). During this phase of inpatient therapy, clients are introduced to the facility and assigned light tasks such as weeding a garden, sweeping a floor, or washing clothes (Hedstrom, 1994). Walking outside is allowed, as is reading serious material, but no daytime napping is permitted (Aldous, 1994).

Clients keep a diary from now on, write about a page a night, and focus on what they "saw and did during the day," but they are instructed "not to write about [their] symptoms or [their] subjective feelings" (Reynolds, 1976, p. 36). The diary is collected each morning, and the counselor comments in red ink, providing "guidance and encouragement." Reynolds and Kiefer (1977) describe the theme of the counselor's comments as "life must be lived constructively regardless of one's feelings" (p. 399).

While clients may not yet socialize or converse with other clients, each week they are required to attend an educational, philosophical lecture called a **kowa.** The lecture is conducted by a counselor and focuses on the Japanese character and ideas related to Morita therapy (Reynolds, 1976).

The second phase is designed for clients to experience taking "attention away from himself or herself and toward the task at hand. Activity is required to be purposeful and careful" (Aldous, 1994, p. 242). Directing clients' attention toward simple tasks is a form of redirecting their awareness to the outer world and "[substituting] constructive living patterns" (Hedstrom, 1994, p. 155). Yet clients must ultimately develop attentiveness (i.e., **ki-kubari**) spontaneously, choosing work that interests them (Fujita, 1986). Naturally, after a week of bed rest, clients are initially happy to be involved in activities of any kind. They may even feel joy and excitement at simply walking around and observing nature, giving it special qualities because they have overlooked it for so long. However, clients' symptoms eventually return because these symptoms are an inherent part of who they are. By this time, though, clients are feeling somewhat satisfied with working, are more aware of the outer world, and are accomplishing, thus learning that they can work despite the symptoms.

Phase 3: Heavier Mental and Physical Work Therapy.   The third phase lasts anywhere from three to seven days or longer (Reynolds, 1980). Clients become involved in more strenuous work, such as chopping wood or building something, with more of an emphasis on "what needs to be done" (Hedstrom, 1994). Hedstrom suggests that clients may work with others at this time, while Fujita (1986) suggests that the work is still done alone. In either case, clients cannot be involved in "idle" social interaction. Interaction that occurs is likely to be around some work activity. Clients can read anything now and take care of personal business (e.g., going to the store to purchase toiletries) outside the facility (Fujita). They still attend the *kowa,* which presents "work as intrinsically good, and an aid to the growth of the individual and society" (Hedstrom, p. 155). The diary is still maintained, but now with a stricter focus on daily activities and what was done (Reynolds).

The experience of heavy work and of work that clients may usually not do (e.g., building something) gives clients a sense of "confidence and joy in accomplishment" (Aldous, 1994, p. 242). Don't confuse this type of accomplishment with the Western idea that to accomplish means to "do something well or that other people perceive as worthy of praise." The Morita idea of accomplishment is simply that "one completed what needed doing" (Reynolds, 1976). As a matter of fact, concentrating on how well you did something might lead you back to *toraware;* the important fact is that you did something which contributed to the good of all.

Clients learn experientially that arduous activity causes one's attention to shift, leaving symptoms in the background. When one is actively involved, the symptoms are no longer a problem. As Reynolds (1984) states, "A neurotic symptom is only a problem when we are noticing it" (p. 13). The important shift from *toraware* is occurring as clients experience "doing what needs to be done and putting things in order" (Hedstrom, 1994, p. 155) and focus on the outer world. They are beginning to live a more organized, constructive life. Clients no longer wait for suggestions about what to do but spontaneously "see" what needs to be done and do it.

Phase 4: Life Activities Training Therapy.   The last phase in inpatient Morita therapy prepares clients to reenter their environments, deal with the social realities, and continue to work productively. Hedstrom (1994) writes: "At the time of discharge, there may still be symptoms, including fears and unhappiness, but the [client] should be ready to carry out the tasks of life irrespective of [his or her] symptoms" (p. 155). All restrictions on activities are removed. Therapy now involves working clients into the social environment of the clinic and having them learn to interact with other clients regardless of one's symptoms. Clients continue the heavy work, but may work directly with other patients on projects. They become involved in group excursions and sports and recreational activities with other clients. They can be sent on errands within the community (Kora & Ohara, 1973; Reynolds, 1976, 1980).

Clients continue to see their counselors on a daily basis, along with the guidance provided by comments in the diary. Fujita (1986) believes that the "chief objective is to get a [client] to participate in everything spontaneously as the need arises and, further, to make the [client] feel, in this manner, that he or she can do whatever he or she wants to do" (p. 207). When clients leave the clinic, they have experientially learned about "purposeful, goal-directed behavior" and can apply that to their own lives outside the clinical setting (Kora & Ohara, 1973). They also have learned that their "cure" doesn't mean that they no longer have *shinkeishitsu* symptoms; rather, their "cure" means they are no longer demanding to be rid of them. They accept them *arugamama* and get on with their lives.

Morita therapy is a "lifeway," so upon discharge, clients can attend ex-patient meetings which may be in the form of the self-help organizations called Seikatsu no Hakkenkai ("The Discovery of Life Organization"). Additionally, they receive the clinic's magazine, which contains articles about Morita life principles as well as comments about treatment. They have their diary, can always refer back to the counselor's comments, and will continue to keep the diary for as long as it is useful. Finally, they might correspond with the counselor, share their diary again, or set up follow-up appointments (Reynolds, 1980). The experiential treatment becomes the stepping stone for a change in life pattern that is more constructive, outwardly focused, and of benefit to self and society.

Intervention Strategies

Most researchers (e.g., Aldous, 1994; Hedstrom, 1994) describe the inpatient Morita therapy process but have little comment on the outpatient process. Through his own adaptation of Morita therapy in the text *Constructive Living,* Reynolds (1984a) shared his own techniques and practice with clients outside a clinical setting. A separate section on outpatient Morita therapy is not necessary because the goals are the same regardless of the setting in which they are applied. The therapy is also still based on experiential learning, not traditional talk therapy.

Experiential learning is critical to the practice of Morita therapy. Clients experience absolute bed rest rather than talk with the counselor about the experience of *toraware*. Clients learn that they have no control over feelings and thoughts so they may as well accept them arugamama. Talking clients into insight is not as powerful as having them "live" the principles.

Therefore, every strategy must be considered experiential. Similarly, every strategy, in some ways, has clients refocusing the misfocused mind from self to what ought to be done (Bankart, 1997). Finally, each strategy still occurs in a **social setting**—that is, clients move toward accomplishing *on* and becoming productive to self and others (Hestrom, 1994). The social settings in which clients function are part of their environments, so strategies are geared to have them accomplish *on,* thus "reorienting the life pattern" (Kora & Ohara, 1973, p. 68) to *giri* (in this case, a sense of belonging to the world).

From our perspective, the difference between outpatient and inpatient Morita therapy is how one views the phases. In outpatient counseling, the phases are not as discrete as they are in inpatient work. Whereas the counselor has physical control (to some extent) over clients' movements in a clinic, visits with them daily, and provides daily guidance and instruction, such is not the case in outpatient work. For outpatient counseling, what should be accomplished in each phase should be viewed as guidelines for experientially reaching the goals of Morita therapy. When strategies or techniques occur and what phase they are attributed to are not as easily and discretely identified in outpatient counseling (nor perhaps as important). Therefore, as we describe the strategies below, we comment on both inpatient and outpatient use if applicable.

Bed Rest.   Absolute, complete bed rest is an important strategy in the traditional form of Morita therapy. What is the purpose of isolating the client from external stimuli? As we mentioned earlier, we view it as the ultimate experiential learning of how "unnatural" complete self-absorption is. It teaches the client to accept feelings and thoughts *arugamama,* as well as to be able to endure and continue living. At the end, it gives the client an appreciation and urgency to reconnect with the outer world, thus a flight away from *toraware*.

While bed rest is an inpatient strategy, the experiential learning that occurs through this strategy must also be accomplished in outpatient therapy. Reynolds (1984b) suggests exercises and activities, both in and out of sessions, that allow clients to experience the moment and refocus on the outer world. For example, during a first session clients may converse for forty minutes on their symptoms. When clients finish, Reynolds (1984b) asks them to close their eyes and describe what is in his office. This exercise starts the important teaching process typical for Phase 1: (1) symptoms will be neither ignored nor reinforced in session; (2) your attention is directed toward *toraware;* and (3) when attention is directed toward *toraware,* you aren't attending to the many things going on in the outer world, moment-by-moment.

Refocusing clients' attention starts immediately with various guided activities. Meditation (explained in a later section) is also used in lieu of bed rest. Homework is frequently used to help clients focus on the outer world. Reynolds (1984b) asked a client to drive home the same way but focus on every detail of the environment. She was asked to journal about this. Clients soon learn via experience that *toraware* isolates them from the outer world, and a sense of urgency develops to act on this awareness.

Personal Counseling: Guidance and Instruction.   Reynolds (1981a) described Morita therapists as "explicitly directive. They are teachers, experienced guides who, for the most part, have surmounted their own self-imposed limitations through this method" (p. 493). During inpatient work, guidance and instruction begin during the pre-therapy phase when the counselor explains and predicts what will happen if clients cooperate with the counseling. Clients are checked on daily during bed rest for progress reports only, and as counseling progresses, "informal" (Abel, 1977) sessions occur during which guidance is provided for daily activities, instruction is provided about living via Morita principles, and encouragement is given to help clients continue living constructively.

A unique type of counseling relationship is then formed between the counselor and client. This relationship is hierarchical in nature, with the counselor becoming the guide/master to his or her clients, the students. The counselor-guide must, through his or her own experience, help the client-student refocus *toraware* to a more meaningful, outer-world focus. Like any guide, the counselor is directive, keeping the client's attention away from symptoms and on daily activities. This is partly accomplished through a "human relationship situation" called *fumon* (Fujita, 1986).

Fujita defined *fumon* as "an attitude of completely 'cutting off' the therapist as a listener to the [client's] complaints" (1986, p. 226). If a client presents complaints around "uncontrollable" feelings and thoughts, the counselor cuts off the discussion by *ma* (i.e., "pause"). *Ma* creates a "proper distance" initiated by the counselor so that clients can gain "control" of themselves. Most likely the "control" gained is to dialogue on what clients have control over (i.e., behavior and life activities), not on what they don't have control over (i.e., feelings and thoughts). In other words, the counselor at times completely ignores dialogue about symptoms (Fujita, 1986). Kitanishi and Mori (1995) called this the "disregard method." The counselor "disregards [by] not exploring the pathology" (i.e., either etiology or symptoms), but instead discusses "the importance of clarifying the patient's toraware" (p. 251). Overall, *fumon* "is an opportunity to open up the self and to grow by means of a momentary silence in the mutual relationships that take place between human beings" (Fujita, p. 225).

In outpatient work, clients are seen on a weekly basis. However, the personal counseling is similar to inpatient work. The counselor explains and reinforces the principles of Morita therapy. Reynolds (1981a) believes that "therapy sessions focus on the application of these understandings [i.e., Morita principles] and suggestions for living to the patient's daily life" (p. 494).

In one session, a counselor might:

1. Use *ma* as the client complains that he or she still can't get a supervisor to lighten the workload.

2. Give the client permission to feel hopeless about the situation, since he or she is not responsible for that feeling.

3. Congratulate the client for having such a strong *sei no yokubo* related to concern about the supervisor because that will surely motivate him or her to act assertively in the workplace.

4. Instruct the client through use of a Zen Koan, which is "sort of a puzzle with a solution that must be arrived at by more than rational thought" (Reynolds, 1984b, p. 23).

5. Evaluate "immediate daily life [which] does not focus on subjective content such as pain, uncertainty, distrust and difficulty felt during the process of activity, but, rather, is limited to activities that are goal-directed" (Fujita, 1986, p. 226). For example, the counselor might say: "You talked to your boss two different times this week despite the fact that you're frustrated with your work. Keep up the good effort and maybe try a new strategy. Say to your boss, 'Thank you for giving me wonderful opportunities. What is most important on my list that I can do for you in return?'"

6. Encourage the client to continue living life constructively. For example, the counselor might say: "You have made much progress in your cure. You have a better idea of what you can control and what you can't control."

7. Assign a specific activity, such as: "Think about ways your supervisor has helped you. Write them in your diary. Then buy her a gift and thank her." This assignment is a modified version of one by Krech (1989). The assignment helps the client realize that he or she is narrowly focusing on one aspect of the relationship (i.e., his or her feeling overworked) and overlooking the whole (i.e., all the other times the supervisor has been involved in his or her work).

Work.   In both inpatient and outpatient Morita therapy, work, physical activity, and acting/doing are at the heart of treatment (Aldous, 1994; Hedstrom, 1994; Fujita, 1986; Kitanishi & Mori, 1995; Reynolds, 1976, 1980, 1981a, 1984b). Along with explicit instructions about behavior being the only thing we control, therapy is built around experiencing how symptoms can fade into the background when one is involved in some activity (i.e., life). Kitanishi and Mori describe the significance of work as follows: "1) the exertion of the desire to be active which is part of human nature (the exertion of the desire to live fully); 2) experiencing a situation in which one finds that it is possible to work despite the existence of symptoms; and 3) paying attention to the outside (change from self-serving attitude to matter-oriented attitude)" (p. 250).

Even in outpatient work, the activities should at first be simplistic and somewhat meaningless, leading to more complex, important, and meaningful physical and mental work (Reynolds, 1976, 1981a, 1984a, 1984b). Work stimulates a focus away from *toraware* to what needs to be done. Reynolds (1984b) suggests using "physical activity to accomplish tasks when we feel overwhelmed by feelings" (p. 51).

Although initially the counselor can recommend or suggest activities, particularly during inpatient work, ultimately clients must develop *ki-kubari* (attentiveness) as Fujita (1986) described, thus choosing activities of personal interest. Early activities might simply be looking around the kitchen and seeing what items need to be cleaned. Or one might simply go outside and watch the sunset every night while observing everything that is in the environment. The initial activities help focus clients on the outer world more, helping them see and observe what they've been missing. Eventually, activities can be more meaningful, such as visiting one's child more regularly, going to an art museum, taking the class on photography you've been wanting to take, dealing with a tension-producing situation at work, or sitting down and writing this book chapter. Once clients start actively doing things, they do learn that they can work in spite of feelings, and they learn that an organized life is a productive life.

Diary. The diary is an important therapeutic tool for both the counselor and clients. Clients monitor their experiences, begin to realize what is and is not controllable, organize themselves better by more carefully detailing the diary, and learning from the comments provided by the counselor. The counselor uses the diary as an instructional method via comments made in the diary, as a progress check, and, particularly for outpatient work, as a form of therapy continuation (i.e., work extends beyond the counseling session) (Fujita, 1986; Hedstrom, 1994; Krech, 1989; Reynolds, 1976; Reynolds & Kiefer, 1977).

Reynolds (1980) describes how clients might organize their diaries. Divide a sheet of paper in half. On the left side, write what you felt like doing at any given moment, including your feelings, moods, and fancies. On the other side, write what you actually did at the moment. For example, I (Larry Burlew) finished writing my diary for the day. On the left side, I wrote: "I dreaded getting up because I knew I had to finish this book chapter (feeling). I wished I could have just stayed in bed and forgotten about finishing it (fancy)." On the right side, I wrote: "I got up, did my morning exercises, sat at the table and wrote for four hours. I did forget my dread feeling after all" (this last sentence should have been on the left side because I have no control over the dread feeling). Reynolds claimed that from the diary we "can learn that much of daily life is carried out regardless of one's felt needs at a given moment, and even in spite of them" (p. 17).

Clients maintain the diary daily, normally about one page per day (Fujita, 1986). Abel (1977) says that "a [client] writes about his thoughts and his feelings, but emphasizes mainly what work he has accomplished" (p. 556). Fujita described the diary as a tool for clients to communicate with the counselor "without feeling much resistance as compared to the resistance that arises in direct conversation" (p. 216). According to Fujita, clients use the following guidelines for the diary:

1. As a rule, no restriction is placed on content. The patient can write anything, but it must be centered chiefly on the experiences gained by the patient's activities each day.

2. The time spent on writing entries must be 30 minutes or less per day.

3. The entries should be limited to one page of a 179–252mm notebook per day.

4. The writing must be legible enough to be read easily. (p. 216)

The counselor collects the diary at the beginning of each day or at the end of the counseling session in outpatient work. Reynolds (1984b) suggests that clients read the diary in session as well (outpatient), so that discussion occurs around what clients accomplished during the week. The counselor makes comments in red ink, and underlines critical text. These comments are for instruction, guidance, and encouragement (particularly toward cure). According to Reynolds and Kiefer (1977), the theme of the comments is that life must be lived productively in spite of one's feelings.

Because the counselor's comments are often didactic and direct, aimed at helping clients lead more disciplined, organized lives, some readers may see the comments as brusque (Kora & Ohara, 1973). Included below are samples of diary entries from various sources with sample comments from their counselors. (Counselor comments are in parentheses. Underlined text was what the counselor considered "critical.")

1. After washing my face, I came face to face with two female patients. <u>Greet them with my eyes averted. Became agitated,</u> probably because it is the first time I have met other people after being released from complete isolation. (It felt good to greet them even if your eyes were averted and you became agitated. Do this again in the future.) (Fujita, 1986, p. 216)

2. After supper, two or three people were talking in the living room. <u>As I thought I would try to participate, I introduced myself while trying to form a suitable facial expression by desperate efforts.</u> (You introduced yourself because you wished to participate. Doing this in itself is sufficient. Avoid any artifice.) (Fujita, 1986, p. 216)

3. Ate lunch. Still shy eating in front of others and being so slow about it. Talked quite a bit with most of the patients. Sometimes it was fun, sometimes I felt frightened that I was strange. (Either feeling is all right. Now just put out effort to do the best work you can.) (Reynolds, 1989, p. 98)

4. The work of trying to get rid of cobwebs is dull. (We do not work to enjoy ourselves.) (Reynolds, 1980, p. 23)

5. All the anxieties and agonies disappeared shortly after I rested for awhile, sitting on the bench in the bank. With all these experiences, I still firmly believe that the agonies I experienced in the train or while walking will never leave me for good. (You are right in your assumption here. Anxieties occur when they occur; they disappear when they disappear. You should absolutely refrain from trying to make them disappear yourself. In our life, worries and reassuring feelings exist side by side. This is life.) (Reynolds, 1980, p. 26)

Meditation.   Meditation is probably not used in inpatient Morita therapy. This may even be contraindicated for a therapy milieu aimed at having clients focus on the outer world and become reinvolved in a social setting. However, Reynolds (1984b) suggests its use in outpatient counseling "to still the mind in order to allow subsequent attention to moving about in ordinary life" (p. 23). He is not interested in the "enlightenment" aspect of meditation. He also uses it to teach clients to focus on one thing over a period of time. Focusing is important because clients must learn to choose an activity and then do it, which requires an outer-world focus. Eventually, one must also be observant enough of the world, and of one's life, to see what needs to be done. Additionally, as clients meditate, Reynolds (1984b) asks them to think of (1) knowing their purpose, (2) accepting their feelings, and (3) doing what needs to be done.

In some ways, meditation may help clients during the week to realize that they can focus their attention enough to complete tasks. It can also help them review their purpose in the physical world. Meditation may not be necessary for inpatient work because the counselors, staff, and other patients are daily reminders of focus, attention, purpose, and activity.

Readings.   Bibliotherapy is a strategy used in both inpatient and outpatient Morita therapy. Assigned readings take the form of education, both about Morita principles and about life pathways/morals. During most of inpatient therapy, readings chosen by clients must be "serious" books on topics related to "history, natural sciences and biography" (Fujita, 1986, p. 205). However, clients are instructed not to read so intensely that they're distracted by trying to find meaning in the words. Rather, they only do a "light scanning" and are told not to worry about the meaning (Fujita). For *shinkeishitsu* clients this lessens their perfectionistic anxiety to know what everything means and allows them the luxury of accomplishing reading as an act in itself.

Hospital magazines are provided to ex-clients for outpatient follow-up. Reynolds (1976) described them as "professional-looking journals which appear at least twice a year. The forty pages or so in a typical issue contain articles about Morita therapy by therapists and patients, excerpts from diaries, kowa notes, records of symposia, testimonies, advice, poetry, slogans, news of meetings and trips, and human-interest stories about inpatients and therapists" (p. 38). The magazines serve as a reminder about Morita principles, thus reinforcing clients' following a constructive lifeway.

For outpatient work, the counselor might assign articles about Morita therapy to educate clients about the process and principles of a Morita lifeway. Clients could be instructed not to read fantasy or fictional material of any sort during therapy. Such reading material could easily precipitate a flight inward, an escape to another form of *toraware*. Again, whatever they read, they must be instructed not to worry about the meaning, just to accomplish the reading. Readings can be discussed in session if appropriate.

Homework and Guided Activities.   Both of these strategies are geared to clients' experientially learning about *arugamama, toraware,* refocusing, and doing/behavior. An example of a guided activity in an outpatient session is the one Reynolds (1984b) uses when asking clients to close their eyes and describe his office. This activity forces clients to experience the moment, thus turning their focus away from *toraware* and all the isolation it brings. Rather than telling clients, "I bet you don't realize you're not experiencing your moment-by-moment reality," the counselor helps clients realize this fact via experiential learning, a powerful therapeutic strategy.

Homework assignments can be anything that helps clients experience life rather than ruminate on feelings and thoughts (i.e., symptoms). An early assignment might be to do a very simple task like picking up newspapers you've allowed to pile up or forcing yourself to be sad all day (paradoxical intention). As clients learn that they can't control their feelings and thoughts but can work in spite of them, less homework is needed because they develop *ki-kubari* and act on the world *arugamama* and figure out what needs to be done.

Kowa.   This strategy is used during inpatient therapy. Clients attend a lecture once a week, even though outpatients may come back for the lectures. Abel (1977) describes the *kowa* as having "sort of [a] philosophical, perhaps, semi-religious, moral, and esthetic tone which may make a deep impression on patients" (p. 557). This method fits well with Morita therapy because the counselors usually give the *kowa,* and they are "honored" teachers after all (Reynolds & Kiefer, 1977).

In *Morita Psychotherapy,* Reynolds (1976) described the following as sample topics for the *kowa:*

1. You can't control your likes. You can't make yourself like snakes. But you can control your behavior. That's important.
2. If you can't gaman ("stick it out") you can't be cured.
3. Don't focus so much on the past. Turn your attention to what you will do from now on.
4. If you're always talking about yourself you can't listen.
5. We all feel afraid of cancer. It's sensible to fear cancer. People die from cancer, and we don't want to die. But we can work anyway. (p. 88)

As you can see, a *kowa* is built around Morita principles. It reinforces what clients are experiencing in therapy. Such lectures could also occur during outpatient work, perhaps on a more informal basis—even during a session itself. However, haven't we all assigned clients homework to attend community lectures on procrastination and parenting skills, or provocative lectures by political scientists, poets, and philosophers? If a counselor is in tune with the community, particularly with any postsecondary institutions, there may be valuable lectures available that reinforce Morita principles. And certainly the counselor could eventually offer a *kowa* for the community and clients.

Goal Setting.   This strategy is not to be confused with plans of action. In fact, Morita "[discouraged] the constructing of elaborate plans for recovery" (Reynolds & Kiefer, 1977, p. 410). Too rigid a plan of action is unnatural in some ways and disregards the "interdependence of self and environment" (Reynolds & Kiefer, p. 409). Each day is different and may bring new challenges to act on, thus a new purpose. This purpose is what produces daily goals, and for both inpatient and outpatient work, clients find a purpose each day with *ki-kubari* (Fujita, 1986). Ultimately, "purposive, goal-directed behavior must be reestablished in order to reorient the life pattern" (Kora & Ohara, 1973, p. 68).

For example, yesterday I (Larry Burlew) noticed my purpose was in fulfilling my *on* as a journal editor. Relying on my interdependence with my environment, this activity lay waiting for me to complete. Therefore, my goal was to mail letters to authors and mail manuscripts to reviewers. Completing this goal related to my *on* as journal editor doesn't relieve me from *on;* this *on* will always exist as long as I am the editor. Once I complete this mailing task, then I have accomplished that goal. However, I cannot escape activities related to this *on,* but I also do not know what those activities are yet. As they arise, another goal emerges and brings my purpose for the day back to the *on* of journal editor. An interdependence exists between me and this part of my environment, and I will fulfill my *on* as the need arises. In fact, today my purpose is fulfilling my *on* as the chair of a search committee, and my goal is mailing letters to applicants for a vacancy we have.

Evaluation

Overview

Morita therapy was developed in Japan by Shoma Morita. Since he first wrote about his approach in 1917, the therapy has consistently been practiced in Japan (Hedstrom, 1994; Kitanishi & Mori, 1995). While Morita therapy has gained recognition in Western cultures, its use is not as common. Therefore, most of the research and evaluation on effectiveness is published in Japanese. The available reports on the effectiveness of the approach are mostly small parts of articles summarizing the results of Japanese reports. However, the summaries are sufficient to suggest the continued use of Morita therapy.

Supporting Research

As Morita therapy is recognized and more frequently practiced in Western cultures, more research on its effectiveness will occur and be reported in the English language. Hedstrom (1994) claims that "familiarity with Morita therapy in the Western world is increasing as English language accounts of the therapy grow" (p. 154). Until then we will have to accept Morita therapy *arugamama* and believe in its worth if for no other reason than the fact that it is still a reality after 70 years.

Research is available in Japan on the effectiveness of Morita therapy and is summarized in English-language publications. The reported rate of "cured" and "improved" clients ranges from 60% to 90% (Kondo, 1953; Kora & Ohara, 1973; Reynolds, 1980). The higher effectiveness rates seem to occur "when selecting the treatment population" (Kitanishi & Mori, 1995, p. 247). Two important facts must be considered about higher effectiveness rates. First, "cured" or "improved" means that clients have "stopped groping for a means to relieve symptoms" (Weisz et al., 1984, p. 964) and have learned to work in spite of them (Aldous, 1994; Reynolds, 1976, 1980, 1981a, 1984a, 1984b). Second, Morita developed his theory for *shinkeishitsu,* not for all types of neurosis (Aldous, 1994; Reynolds, 1976). Clients with the requisite diagnosis, then, were originally included in treatment and apparently were successfully treated through Morita therapy.

As the use of Morita therapy became more common, however, effectiveness rates changed, revealing important information about the types of clients who are best helped. Kitanishi and Mori (1995) included their own summary of "cured" and "improved" rates through the years: 1919–29, 93.3%; 1929–37, 92.9%; 1963–74, 92.7%; 1972–91, 77.6% (p. 247). They attribute the lower 1972–91 effectiveness rate "to the fact that [they] have been actively attempting to treat atypical cases [i.e., not diagnosed with *shinkeishitsu*]" (p. 247). They conclude that Morita therapy works best with young males who (1) exhibit typical *shinkeishitsu* symptoms; (2) allow an appropriate amount of time to be treated; and (3) voluntarily want to be treated with this approach. Clients who seem not to benefit as much from Morita therapy include delusional, obsessive-compulsive behavior, borderline personality, and some schizophrenia.

Suzuki and Suzuki (1981) examined the long-term effects of Morita therapy. They surveyed 1,287 ex-clients who had been discharged for at least 2 years, with 6.3 years as the average length of discharge. A majority ($n = 1,044$; 81.1%) of these clients were diagnosed with *shinkeishitsu*. They received a 71.1% usable survey return rate (914 surveys). Their results shed interesting light on Morita therapy, particularly in support of its being a lifeway or life path. Upon discharge, approximately 78.6% of the clients felt that they were fairly or highly improved in terms of being able to "live either an active daily life or a relatively normal life" (Suzuki & Suzuki, p. 207). However, 96.1% of the clients reported being able to live an active life, as compared to only 3.7% reporting being unable to do so, as their current status (i.e., 2 or more years after discharge). The greatest change between immediate discharge and long-term reports occurred in the top two categories related to a highly improved condition. Immediately upon discharge, only 12.1% put themselves in these categories; by 2 or more years after discharge, 59.4% included themselves in these categories. Clearly, the initial 40- to 60-day active counselor intervention is only the beginning for putting Morita principles into practice and experience to produce change.

The Suzuki and Suzuki (1981) study again had unique qualities with regard to the sample of clients. The clients' mean age was 26 years with a range of 16–30 years involving 76.2% of the whole sample. A majority (75.9%) were male and unmarried (78%). Overall, those clients with hypochondriasis and anxiety neurosis improved over time more than those with obsessive and depressive neurosis. Suzuki and Suzuki again reinforce that the "willingness to do what needs to be done in spite of one's symptoms is an important criterion for discharge" (p. 211).

The results available in the English language support the use of Morita therapy, particularly with *shinkeishitsu* clients. Therefore, careful diagnosis may be required if one intends to use this approach with clients. Kora and Ohara (1973) state only two reasons why Morita therapy might not help clients change: injudicious selection of patients and lack of client motivation to follow the regime. They conclude that "only a very few show no progress at all" (p. 66).

Limitations

Based on research findings and written reports describing Morita therapy, practitioners need to be cautious in using it with all clients. The approach was developed for *shinkeishitsu* and seems to be most effective with this population of clients. Therefore, a careful diagnosis of any client's condition should occur to determine if the client falls under this rubric or some aspect of *shinkeishitsu*. The approach doesn't seem as effective and may even be contraindicated for children, addicts, mentally challenged individuals, sociopaths, depressives, psychotics, borderlines, compulsives, and schizophrenics (Kitanishi & Mori, 1995; Reynolds, 1980; Suzuki & Suzuki, 1981). With appropriate medication, however, some of the above neuroses (e.g., depressives) might benefit from Morita therapy.

More research and practice need to occur with populations other than young males. Although Reynolds (1980, 1984) is working with a much more variable client population, caution must be used when using Morita therapy with women of all ages and midlife and older adults. The caution is not because it won't be useful; rather, it relates to the lack of reports from practitioners or researchers about Morita therapy's effectiveness with these populations. Additionally, clients who have difficulty sticking to a regimen or who are unmotivated may not do well with this approach (Kora & Ohara, 1973). Finally, more practitioner reports need to occur with specific populations like people of color, low-income groups, gay men and lesbians, and special populations like prison inmates to determine the full potential of this counseling approach. Until then, nobody can with complete confidence say that it crosses racial, ethnic, geographic, and socioeconomic boundaries.

Summary Chart—Morita Therapy

Human Nature

Morita therapy suggests that humans are optimistic, naturalistic, and basically decent, with constructive drives. They face reality *arugamama* and make adjustments as necessary. They express *sei no yokubo* and have *sei no chikara*.

Major Constructs

Morita therapy is a natural, experiential therapy. Its major constructs include neurosis and egocentricity; *shinkeishitsu* (a form of anxiety and obsession disorder); misfocused mind; *toraware* (selfish preoccupation); *giri* (assurance of belonging to a group); *aruga-mama* (accepting reality as it is); *onozu-kara-naru* (natural or spontaneous); control; homophobia (irrational anxiety, fear, and discomfort in or in prospect of interaction with fellow human beings); *amae* (passive love or take advantage of); *on* (intuitively experienced obligation); meaningful life; work; and cure (stop groping for means to relieve symptoms and live productively in spite of them).

Goals

1. Focus the misfocused mind away from preoccupation with self.
2. Accept self and world *arugamama*.
3. Be socially and morally responsible for behavior.
4. Live a full and constructive life.
5. Recognize one's purpose.

Change Process

The change process involves reeducation of character; experiential learning; phases; pre-counseling; complete bed rest; light work therapy; heavier mental and physical work therapy; life activities training therapy; follow-up contact; and lifeway and life path constructive living.

Interventions

Interventions in Morita therapy include bed rest; guidance and instruction; work; diary; meditation; readings; homework and guided activities; *kowa;* and a family-like environment in a social setting.

Limitations

Morita therapy is most useful with *shinkeishitsu* clients. It is not normally used with children, addicts, or the mentally challenged, and is not as effective with sociopaths, depressives, psychotics, borderlines, and schizophrenics. More practitioner reports are needed on its use with women, midlife and older adults, people of color, and members of low-income groups.

The Case of Maria: A Morita Therapy Approach

Overview

Maria's case fits the profile of clients successfully treated with Morita therapy: she is young, displays typical *shinkeishitsu* symptoms, and is voluntarily seeking treatment (Kitanishi & Mori, 1995). However, as part of the diagnosis process, Maria's suicide potential and level of depression must be assessed. If she is not actively suicidal, then counseling could proceed. If she has severe depression, then psychopharmacological intervention is recommended along with Morita therapy. Maria should have a physical examination, since she hasn't been eating and has lost weight.

Morita therapy might work well with Maria because her symptoms resemble those of *shinkeishitsu* neurosis. She is nervous, anxious, and pessimistic, and has been a high achiever who "urgently" (i.e., "could not have waited much longer") wants help (i.e., to be "cured"). Her attention is misfocused *toraware,* as ultimately expressed by "keeping away from work and people . . . spending more time alone." She is avoiding her *on* to work, children, and family of origin. Additionally, she seems fearful of men and dating, which is a form of social inhibition. Ultimately, she has lost her purpose (i.e., "I have nothing to live for") because of *toraware.* Her *tatemae* is minimally operating (e.g., "she finds herself buying fast food for the children so that she won't have to cook"), causing a major disruption of *wa* (disruption in family of origin relations and cannot control children).

Counseling Process

Maria's children are with her, and since Morita therapy occurs within a social and family-like setting, I see no problem with their attending later sessions. The ultimate decision about that, though, rests with Maria. In any case, after Maria "tells her story," I instruct and explain (i.e., as "teacher") about the Morita process and principles. I comfort her by saying that her condition is psychological in nature and that it is natural to feel depressed considering her current situation. I explain the basic principles of her neurosis (e.g., *toraware,* avoidance, *on,* constructive living, work, purpose). Additionally, I congratulate her on her strong desire to live life fully (i.e., *sei no yokubo*), evident in her not wanting to wait any longer for help. Finally, I'll give her hope of "cure" with the condition that she cooperates fully with my guidance, counseling, and instruction, despite questions and doubts she may have about Morita therapy. At this time, I give her an article to read (i.e., scan lightly) about Morita therapy.

Goals of Counseling

1. Maria will become aware that she is selfishly preoccupied (i.e., *toraware*), which is causing the psychic interaction shown earlier in Figure 15.1. She will realize that *toraware* causes her to isolate herself even more from the outer world (i.e., "opportunities" such as healthier interactions with her family of origin). She will become focused on the outer world so that she can live her life fully, moment-by-moment instead of "giving up" and living life as an "emotional cripple."

2. Maria is not accepting feelings and thoughts *arugamama.* Instead, she is living life as if the feelings are reality and is allowing them to run her life. She will learn to accept that she cannot control her feelings or be happy all of the time. Feelings of depression, unhappiness, and guilt are a part of living; they come and go based on life situations. She will find that she can live a constructive life of benefit to self and society in spite of those feelings.

3. Maria will get back on track and be responsible for her behavior. She has responsibilities and obligations (i.e., *on*) to her children, family, and work. As she focuses more on the outer world, she will begin to see what those responsibilities are and "work" at them (e.g., make dinner for the children; address the family issues). Additionally, she

has a responsibility to herself and will begin to take care of herself physically, as well as act on her heterosexual impulses and date when attracted to a man.

4. As she lives life constructively, she will begin to find purpose in living again because each day brings purpose. Each day brings new goals and activities that must be accomplished. She might even make longer-range goals eventually.

Interventions

How will Maria accomplish her goals? I have included four examples of the counseling process below, each example corresponding to the goals above. They provide the reader with ideas of how I might tap into each of Maria's goals. Separating them in this manner, of course, is artificial and would not occur in practice. Rather, an intervention for each goal could occur in the same session. I would guide Maria from the simple to the complex as counseling progresses and as she is ready for more complex responsibilities.

1. Maria is so preoccupied (i.e., *toraware*) with herself that she doesn't recognize her social responsibilities to her children, her family of origin, and her work (*on*). She has become selfish and egotistical and just wants to "give up." I must immediately help her recognize this as *toraware* and force the misfocused mind away from preoccupation with self. Having Maria meditate may help teach her to focus, but it may also help calm her down so that she can sleep better.

At the end of the first session, I ask Maria to close her eyes and describe exactly how her children look at this minute (whether they're in session with her or in the waiting room). I want her to give as much detail as possible (e.g., color of hair and eyes, height, clothes they're wearing, condition of clothes, hair, fingernails, skin). This guided activity experientially allows Maria to see that her all-encompassing internal focus keeps her from experiencing her outer world moment-by-moment. How can she accomplish her *on* if she isn't fully in touch with her environment, thus distanced from this natural interdependence?

As homework Maria goes to her favorite room in the house and examines every detail of the room (down to the dust balls). Most likely she'll notice things (like the way the light enters the room) that she never paid much attention to before. She might begin to think, "What else have I been missing in my environment?" She journals about this experience and comes prepared to tell me what she discovered about the room. As her counseling progresses, the guided activities and homework become more complex. For example, she might have to describe step-by-step what her children did when they got home from school; or she might have to describe students in her class and what they did; or the actions and behaviors of family members when they were around. She begins to expect that I'm going to ask her about her environment and what is occurring around her—not a sketchy description, but for detail. Maria might say, "My mother was ignoring me," and I might respond with, "What was your mother wearing? What did she have in her hands? What did her hair look like when she was standing in the light versus when she was in the shade?"

2. Maria is not accepting feelings and thoughts *arugamama*. Instead, she is living life as if the feelings (particularly the negative ones) are the only reality and allowing them to

run her life. In some ways, she is acting out her "depressing" and "giving up" feelings—she is "spending more time alone" and says, "I have nothing to live for." To help her accept her feelings and thoughts *arugamama,* I explain the principle first and tell her that she is not responsible for her feelings and thoughts; they just are. I ask her to try and feel extremely happy right now, in the session. When she can't, I explain that "just like you can't make yourself happy, you can't control when you're sad or depressed. Otherwise, I assume you'd not let yourself be sad or depressed." I explain that since she can't control her feelings, the best she can hope for is to live her life constructively in spite of them.

Maria begins to keep a diary immediately. On the left half of the page she writes her feelings and thoughts, and on the right side she writes what she accomplished. As she reads the diary in session, we discuss what she learned (e.g., that she does live despite negative feelings; that these feelings are not always or consistently present; that she's letting her internal focus and selfish preoccupation with feelings guide her behavior). From the diary, she learns that feelings come and go during the week, and that she does accomplish things (e.g., taking kids out for fast food) despite those feelings. I review the diary each week and make instructive comments related to Morita principles.

The diary is also a means to organize Maria's life. Therefore, she writes for no more than 30 minutes at the end of each day and uses no more than one sheet of paper. Initially, she writes anything that she wants. Eventually, I ask her to focus more on what she learned from "working" and "doing," as well as what she accomplished, and less on the feelings.

Additionally, I conduct my counseling from a *fumon* framework. As Maria presents complaints in session, I use *ma* (the disregarding method) at times until she gains control of herself and discusses what she has control over—her work and behavior. I might also instruct. If Maria says, "My sister was absolutely horrible to me yesterday. I just went home and cried." I might say, "You gave up too easily on your social obligation [*on*] to your sister. Family is very important to you, and you want to reestablish a sisterly relationship. Think of everything your sister has done for you throughout your life, rather than this one instance in time. Go to her home and talk with her about how much you appreciate everything—with specific examples—that she has done for and with you. Then, give her a gift."

3. Maria has given up and totally immersed herself in *toraware.* Thus she doesn't "see" the reality around her and what needs to be done, both for herself and for her social groups (i.e., *on*). Therefore, I'm initially directive about getting Maria actively involved in reality until she develops *ki-kubari* (i.e., attentiveness) and spontaneously chooses activities (i.e., work) that interest her (Fujita, 1986).

I begin with simple tasks but remain focused on Maria's living a more organized life and fulfilling *on.* I ask her to get up 30 minutes earlier than usual and read one page aloud from Reynolds's (1984a) text, *Constructive Living.* She is not to do anything but read the page aloud, then put it away. She does not have to make sense out of the words, even though we discuss the principles in session. She must do the same right before she goes to bed. Once finished reading, she is to look around her room and take care of one thing (e.g., dust a dresser). Pretty quickly, I also advise her to cook a nice dinner for her children each evening and, as she cooks, to really get into the experience because I will ask her about each experience. I ask her to sit and eat with the children at every meal, being sure to sample all of the different dishes she prepares. Her loss of weight should slow down somewhat. She should include the children in the cooking experience as well.

These early homework assignments are directed toward having her work, begin to organize her life again, live in reality, assume responsibility for her behavior, and begin to actively meet her *on* (i.e., initially to children). This work will be discussed in detail in session, particularly focusing on the fact that she can work in spite of her feelings or thoughts. Additionally, she learns that as she works and fully invests herself in life activities (i.e., work), her symptoms disappear.

Another activity that helps Maria realize that she can work in spite of her feelings is the assignment that she go to work every day regardless of how she's feeling (physically or emotionally). Eventually, Maria develops *ki-kubari* and chooses her own activities, but it is important to start slow and help her learn to focus on one accomplishment at a time. I will also teach her that "accomplish" doesn't mean "to excel or do well"; rather, it simply means finishing what you started. As she gains more confidence and feels successful, she can tackle more complex mental and physical actions. The following activities seem important to Maria:

- Keeping her job so that she can support her lifestyle and children. She will find a balance between giving to the students and giving to her own children.

- Meeting her *on* to her own children. As she gets more of an outer-world focus, she will realize the needs of her children and meet them, thus also gaining "control" over the children once again.

- Meeting her *on* to her family of origin. Maria's Hispanic culture highly values family. Similarly, in Japan, losing *giri* by losing connection to one's family would be an insufferable human condition. However, the past is past, and Maria's activities with the family must center on the present and establishing a satisfying working relationship with them. She will determine what activities might work toward this goal.

- Finally, Maria will develop goals and activities around a more organized, constructive life for herself. This will involve eating appropriately, resting, and dating as desired. This goal in itself requires special attention. For example, Maria was physically abused by her ex-husband, so she might take a class on self-defense prior to dating again to take some responsibility for her physical safety.

4. Maria uses her diary each and every day to record activities that give her life meaning. Remember that each day she awakens, she will examine her outer world and see what goals must be accomplished. In session, we initially discuss how these goals give her purpose in meeting *on* and lead toward constructive living of benefit to self and others. She may eventually develop longer-term interests for herself (e.g., learning to mountain climb) or for others (e.g., helping one of her children become an ice skater). She'll choose projects and activities because they have meaning to her. If they extend into days and weeks, that will be her decision.

When Maria can "work, socialize and behave normally in spite of [her symptoms]" (Weisz et al., 1984, p. 964), then she is "cured" and therapy is terminated.

References

Abel, T. M. (1977). Review: David Reynolds' *Morita Therapy*. *Journal of Personality Assessment, 41,* 556–558.

Aldous, J. (1994). Cross-cultural counselling and cross-cultural meanings: An exploration of Morita psychotherapy. *Canadian Journal of Counselling, 28,* 238–249.

Bankart, C. P. (1997). Contemporary Japanese psychotherapies: Morita and Naikan. In C. P. Bankart, *Talking cures: A history of Western and Eastern psychotherapies* (pp. 440–462). Pacific Grove, CA: Brooks/Cole.

Chang, S. C. (1980). Morita therapy. In R. Herink (Ed.), *The psychotherapy handbook* (pp. 391–393). New York: Meridian.

De Vos, G. (1980). Afterward. In D. K. Reynolds, *The quiet therapies: Japanese pathways to personal growth.* Honolulu: University Press of Hawaii.

Fujita, C. (1986). *Morita therapy: A psychotherapeutic system for neurosis.* Tokyo: Igaku-shoin.

Hedstrom, L. J. (1994). Morita and Naikan therapies: American applications. *Psychotherapy, 31,* 154–160.

Ishiyama, F. I. (1990). A Japanese perspective on client inaction: Removing attitudinal blocks through Morita therapy. *Journal of Counseling and Development, 68,* 566–570.

Iwai, H., & Reynolds, D. K. (1970). Morita psychotherapy: The views from the West. *American Journal of Psychiatry, 126,* 1031–1036.

Kitanishi, K., & Mori, A. (1995). Morita therapy: 1919 to 1995. *Psychiatry and Clinical Neurosciences, 49,* 245–254.

Kondo, A. (1953). Morita therapy: A Japanese therapy for neurosis. *American Journal of Psychoanalysis, 13,* 31–37.

Kora, T., & Ohara, K. (March, 1973). Morita therapy. *Psychology Today, 6*(10), 63–68.

Krech, G. (1989). Kyoryoku: The application of Morita and Naikan principles to the work setting. In D. K. Reynolds, *Flowing bridges, quiet waters,* (pp. 108–122). Albany: State University of New York Press.

Kutz, I., Borysenko, J., & Benson, H. (1985). Meditation and psychology. *American Journal of Psychiatry, 142,* 1–8.

Murphy, G., & Murphy, L. (1968). *Asian psychology.* New York: Basic Books.

Pelzel, J. C. (1977). Japanese personality-in-culture: From the psychiatric aerie. *Culture, Medicine, and Psychiatry, 1*(3), 299–315.

Reynolds, D. K. (1976). *Morita psychotherapy.* Berkeley: University of California Press.

Reynolds, D. K. (1980). *The quiet therapies: Japanese pathways to personal growth.* Honolulu: University Press of Hawaii.

Reynolds, D. K. (1981a). Morita Psychotherapy. In R. J. Corsini (Ed.), *Handbook of innovative psychotherapies* (pp. 489–501). New York: Wiley.

Reynolds, D. K. (1981b). Preface. *Psychiatric Quarterly, 53,* 201–202.

Reynolds, D. K. (1984a). *Constructive living.* Honolulu: University of Hawaii Press.

Reynolds, D. K. (1984b). *Playing ball on running water.* New York: Quill.

Reynolds, D. K. (1989). *Flowing bridges, quiet waters: Japanese psychotherapies, Morita and Naikan.* Albany: State University of New York Press.

Reynolds, D. K., & Kiefer, C. W. (1977). Cultural adaptability as an attribute of therapies: The case of Morita psychotherapy. *Culture, Medicine, and Psychiatry, 1*(4), 395–412.

Suzuki, T., & Suzuki, R. (1981). The effectiveness of in-patient Morita therapy. *Psychiatric Quarterly, 53,* 203–213.

Walsh, R. (1995). Asian psychotherapies. In R. J. Corsini (Ed.), *Current psychotherapies* (5th ed.) (pp. 387–398). Itasca, IL: Peacock.

Weisz, J. R., Rothbaum, F. M., & Blackburn, T. C. (1984). Standing out and standing in: The psychology of control in America and Japan. *American Psychologist, 39,* 955–969.

West, M. (Ed.). (1987). *The psychology of meditation.* Oxford: Clarendon Press.

Counseling and Psychotherapy With Children

Mary E. Stafford
Arizona State University

As we approach the beginning of a new millennium, reflection on ways the world has changed helps set the stage for understanding the paths children must negotiate in order to develop in both physically and mentally healthy ways, as well as how we, as mental health professionals, can facilitate that development. Whether conditions for children today are better or worse than they have been in the past thousand years, or even hundred years, is speculative at best. Simeonsson (1994) argues that the statistics about abuse, suicide, teen pregnancy, poverty, and crime are inconsistent with what should be the best of times, given the advances made by our society.

The Child in Today's World

Vast advances in information technology have both exposed children to images as never before (Simeonsson, 1994) and made us aware of every possible harm that can come to them, giving us insight into the level of complexity that children face today in negotiating every type of developmental milestone. Children are faced with violence and sexually explicit images through television, videos, and the Internet that children fifty years ago never dreamed of seeing. Children are being exploited sexually through child pornography. Although it is difficult to determine whether there is greater **sexual exploitation** today than there was fifty or a hundred years ago, the exploitation, when discovered, is in the public arena. One must question whether the explicit nature of the public airing of discovered abuses provides stimulation for perpetrators to further harm children. Several factors make the child's world today very different from the environment children grew up in fifty years ago, including lack of safety, redefinitions of family, violent **peer influences,** and changing **gender roles** (Mintz

413

& O'Neil, 1990; Orton, 1997; Scher & Good, 1990; Simeonsson, 1994; Thompson & Rudolph, 1996; Zigler, Kagan, & Hall, 1996). These topics will be addressed in the following sections.

Safety

Safety is a fleeting and conditional experience for children. Children are victimized by crimes, family violence, and abduction in greater numbers than adults and are victims of all forms of abuse, including sibling assault (Finkelhor & Dziuba-Leatherman, 1994). Statistics from 1992 indicate that on the average 58.45 children age 12 through 19, compared to 17.85 adults, per 1,000 are victims of assault; 11.53 children age 12 through 19, compared to 4.73 adults, per 1,000 are victims of robbery; 1.6 children age 12 through 19, compared to 0.5 adults, per 1,000 are victims of rape; and 0.09 children age 12 through 19, compared to 0.10 adults, per 1,000 are victims of homicide (Finkelhor & Dziuba-Leatherman, 1994). Statistics further indicate that parent-to-child violence is nearly four times more likely than spouse-to-spouse violence (620 versus 158 per 1,000), and nearly twice as likely in its most severe form (i.e., kicking, biting, hitting with fist or object, beating up, and using or threatening to use a knife or gun; 107 versus 58 per 1,000). The high numbers are influenced in part by children's relative lack of strength and power to fight back, as well as their lack of choice regarding whom they live with. Thus their dependent status makes them more vulnerable for victimization.

Even in the most mentally healthy home environments, random acts of violence can shatter the hope for making the environment safe for children. Drive-by shootings are the norm in many low-income inner-city areas. Additionally, in many mentally unhealthy home environments, children often are physically, sexually, and emotionally abused. Over 3 million children were reported abused or neglected in 1994, a figure about double that of 1984 (Children's Defense Fund, 1996). After the age of 5, boys are more than twice as likely as girls to be physically abused, while girls are more than twice as likely as boys to be sexually abused (Finkelhor & Dziuba-Leatherman, 1994).

Redefinitions of Family

In the 1980s and 1990s approximately 35% of all children experienced divorce, with the majority of parents remarrying (Stevenson & Black, 1996). Divorce rates for remarriages are higher than those for first marriages due to a variety of factors, including the complexity of the newly formed family system (Martin & Bumpass, 1989). Wineberg (1992) found an increased probability of marriage dissolution if there were minor children from previous marriages, and an increased probability of the marriage staying together if children were born to the newly formed union. Finkelhor, Hotaling, and Sedlak (1992) reviewed national police records to examine the extent of child abduction in the United States. Based on police records from a one-year period, the estimated national incidence for children abducted in the United States is 5% to 7%. Most are younger than 7 years of age, and some come from divorced families and were abducted by a family member in a dispute over custody (Finkelhor, Hotaling, & Sedlak). When found, children who have the most difficulty recovering are those who were abused, witnessed violence, or were missing for long periods of time (Stevenson & Black).

In addition to the instability of family structure and custody fights, family mobility and poverty have led to a breakdown in the extended family system. Years ago the extended family system could be expected to be available to children and provide them with support as they met with difficult circumstances. Besides **nuclear families,** now **single-parent families, blended families, step families, foster care, latchkey children,** and **homelessness** comprise the environments within which children live and develop (Orton, 1997; Thompson & Rudolph, 1996). Mobility in our society has played a large part in children's growing up away from grandparents and other relatives who could provide support, care, discipline, and love for the child. Moreover, for most women who are in the workforce, child care is a necessary part of the child's world. When child care is unreliable and of poor quality, parents may experience guilt and stress, leading to further reduction of the quality of family life (Zigler & Gilman, 1996).

Peer Influence

Peer influence has always played an important part in children's identity development. Today, with some of the breakdown of the family support system, gangs provide the support system that draws children in and then takes over their lives. Drugs, alcohol, smoking, and poor eating habits add to the problems that children face today (Crabbs, 1989). Furthermore, violence on school campuses has become an everyday event, and the presence of a police officer assigned to many city school campuses is the norm rather than the exception.

Changing Gender Roles

Another change that has occurred in the past fifty years is the redefinition of gender roles (Scher & Good, 1990). In contrast to a previous time in our society, less specificity exists relative to gender roles. More options are open to males and females now, leading to greater opportunities for all. With greater opportunity comes the need to decide among seemingly unlimited choices. However, attitudes about changing gender roles vary, leaving children with less clear guidelines than have been evident in the past. Additionally, counselors and therapists must examine their own attitudes relative to gender roles and expectations in order to increase their effectiveness in influencing children with whom they work (Mintz & O'Neil, 1990; Thompson & Rudolph, 1996).

Given the nature and conditions of the world that children grow up in today, it is not surprising that there is need for enhanced counseling programs for children. **Prevention** programs, programs that can have an impact on the home and school environments, and individual and group counseling programs are necessary to provide a comprehensive delivery of services. In order to better understand the needs of children, developmental perspectives are presented next, followed by legal and ethical issues, treatment settings, and issues, models, and techniques related to child counseling and psychotherapy.

Developmental Perspectives

Children are not "small adults." Although all humans continue to grow throughout their lifetime, the growth that children experience occurs at a heightened pace over a short time and includes elements of process, content, and context. Growth occurs in several domains, including physiological, cultural, cognitive, language, social, behavioral, emotional, and personality areas. Cognitive, language, social, behavioral, and emotional growth are sub-sumed under the physiological and cultural areas, as all growth and learning require **phys-iological changes** and a cultural system that specifies rules for language, nonverbal sys-tems, behavior, **socialization patterns,** values and beliefs. The various aspects of children's growth will be discussed in the following sections.

Physical Growth

Increases in height and weight, changes in appearance, and strengthened bone structure to support walking and later physical activity are a few of the obvious developmental changes that children undergo in the physical area. As the body grows, children must ad-just how they think about their bodies. Identity and self-image perceptions include ele-ments of how children think about their physiological growth.

The brain also undergoes physiological changes. Within the first year after birth, the brain nearly triples its weight (from about 350 grams to approximately 1,000 grams), then continues to add only about 200 to 400 grams in weight over the remainder of the life-time, mostly during the first 10 to 15 years of life (Kalat, 1995). The growth of the brain parallels the development of cognitive, language, social, behavioral, and emotional growth and other aspects of cultural learning. Without the development of neural connections, no learning or behavior will occur (Carlson, 1995). Likewise, during counseling or psy-chotherapy one attempts to foster new connections, thus new ways of thinking about ex-periences. If the child is able to think about events in new and more adaptive ways, it is because new neural connections are being formed. Thus, of the physiological growth that children experience and adjust to, growth of the brain is the most important element. With-out it, no growth or learning would occur in any other area.

Cultural Learning

Children learn within a context of **cultural norms.** Values, beliefs, rules for behavior, so-cialization patterns, language, nonverbal communication, how space and time are allo-cated and observed, and how we deal with our emotions are a few of the categories in-cluded in cultural learning (Sue & Sue, 1990). Cultural learning occurs primarily through children's observations of and messages from their primary caregivers. People who are reared as part of a defined group tend to have similar views of the world and how one must interact with others. However, within cultural groups there are variations as well. When working with children from an ethnic or cultural group different from one's own, the counselor or therapist must be cautious about assuming that the child's family and cul-tural group have beliefs similar to the counselor's. Being able to help the child necessi-tates understanding the expectations for values, beliefs, and behaviors that the family holds for the child.

Many cultural groups are represented in American society. As children grow, they move through several separate identity processes prior to the development of **self-iden-tity** in adolescence: **gender identity, racial identity,** and **ethnic identity** (Ocampo, Bernal, & Knight, 1993; Phinney & Rotheram, 1987). The ethnic identity process is due as much to recognition that one belongs to a specific group as to recognition that one does not belong to other specific groups. Developing one's ethnic identity is a process rather than an achievement and is influenced both by **enculturation** (i.e., learning one's first culture) and **acculturation** (i.e., adaptation to the dominant culture and its members) (Bernal & Knight, 1993). Thus children experience cultural growth specifically by recognizing that they belong to a larger group of people who share a common culture, and generally by acquiring cognitive, language, social, behavioral, and emotional knowledge and skills as they are viewed by those of their cultural group.

Cognitive Growth

Children's cognitive growth develops along predictable lines. The **stage theory** of **Jean Piaget** (1926/1959, 1932/1968, 1970) explains children's cognitive development and has been the cornerstone of cognitive developmental theories during the past century. Piaget proposed four age-bound stages that children move through in their development (as summarized in Miller, 1989):

1. **Sensorimotor period,** from birth to 2 years of age, during which children modify their reflexes, repeat behaviors over and over as they discover that behaviors have consequences, coordinate schemes of behaviors into meaningful new behaviors, and invent new behaviors because the ability to use mental symbols to represent objects and events is emerging.

2. **Preoperational period,** from 2 to 7 years of age, characterized by egocentrism, rigidity of thought, semilogical reasoning, and limited social cognition.

3. **Concrete operations period,** from age 7 to 11, during which children internalize actions that are part of an organized structure (i.e., operations) that are used for conservation, class inclusion, relations, temporal-spatial representations, and moral judgments.

4. **Formal operations period,** from age 11 to 15, during which thinking along the lines of the scientific method develops.

Moving from one stage to the next is dependent upon children's having reached a state of equilibrium in the first stage between their mental representations and observations in the environment, followed by a state of **disequilibrium** caused by observations that are incongruent with their mental representations. Moving into the higher stage occurs when children try to attain **equilibration** again by changing their mental structures to explain the new observations (i.e., **accommodation**). Piaget's theory continues to provide a basis for understanding cognitive development in children, although research has not supported some of his findings (Miller, 1989).

Jerome Bruner (1973) proposed a three-stage theory of cognitive development that is similar to Piaget's theory. Bruner's three stages are the **enactive stage,** in which the infant learns through actions; the **iconic stage,** in which imagery is developed; and the **symbolic stage,** in which the child uses language to talk about abstract events (Craig, 1989).

In the past 25 years, **information-processing** investigators have made a considerable contribution to understanding cognitive development by studying the flow of information through the cognitive system (Miller, 1989). Rather than focusing on the stages of cognitive development that children go through, information-processing research has focused on how adults mentally process information from the moment that a stimulus is received until a response is given. Better understanding of short- and long-term memory storage has resulted from these studies. More recently, information-processing research has focused on children's memory, attention, comprehension, and problem solving (Miller, offering a greater understanding of what children achieve at different age levels. Space does not permit a full review of findings in this area; however, counselors and therapists may gain a greater understanding of children's abilities at different ages by reviewing findings from information-processing research on children.

Language Growth

As children develop from birth to adulthood, they acquire a language. **Noam Chomsky** (1959) asserted that every child is born with a **universal grammar** (i.e., a common system of principles, conditions, and rules for all languages) and a **language acquisition device,** which is a mental structure that allows the child to receive language from others, process it, and formulate a generative grammar that becomes refined as the child interacts with others in the environment. The process of refining language occurs over time and involves unconsciously intuiting rules about how language is structured, then adjusting one's language to reflect the new rules.

In addition to understanding how children develop language, it is important to understand the relationship between language and thought. Several theories have been offered explaining this relationship, including those of Piaget (1926/1959), Vygotsky (1934/1962), and Whorf and Sapir (Carroll). Piaget believed that development of representational abilities is a precursor to language development, or that thought shapes language. **Benjamin Lee Whorf** proposed both that higher-level thinking is dependent on language and that the structure of one's language influences the way one views the world (Carroll). Whorf and his mentor, **Edward Sapir,** are known for having proposed the **Whorf-Sapir hypothesis,** which states that the language of a culture influences the way members of that culture view the world, or that language shapes thought (Siegler, 1991). **Lev Vygotsky** believed that language and thought begin developing independently but that by the age of 2 they are mutually influencing each other to the extent that thought becomes internalized language. Research findings support **Vygotsky's hypothesis** that language and thought mutually influence each other (Siegler).

Counselors of children must consider the age and cognitive/language abilities of the child in structuring treatment. Use of language that is understood and used by the child is important for maximizing the meaningful communication that must go on for the child to make progress in counseling. Additionally, getting children to communicate what they understand the counselor or therapist to have said will aid the counseling process by providing an opportunity to reinforce accurately received messages and to explain further when accurate messages are not received.

Social and Behavioral Growth

The theories of social learning theorist **Albert Bandura** (1969, 1977) and behaviorist **B. F. Skinner** (1953) provide the basis for understanding the development of children's social behavior. Both believe that children learn by noticing the consequences of their actions and adjusting their behavior. However, Bandura proposed that children also learn through watching others who model a behavior, taking note of the consequences of the behavior, and then imitating the model's actions. Thus, unlike Skinner, Bandura believed that children learn vicariously as well as through direct experience.

Developing socially appropriate behaviors requires appropriate modeling of behavior as well as positive reinforcement when appropriate behaviors are exhibited. Children are exposed to a broader range of models of behavior today. Often when children are referred for counseling it is because they are exhibiting inappropriate behaviors. In order to help the child develop more socially appropriate behaviors, the counselor will need also to provide interventions for the school and home that both address the models the child is exposed to and provide a behavior management program to give the child consistent feedback about his or her behavior.

Emotional and Personality Growth

As children grow they develop personalities and grow emotionally. **Erik Erikson** (1963) provided a **psychosocial stage development theory** to explain personality development. This theory consists of eight stages of psychosocial development and is based in the psychoanalytic tradition. It includes the following stages, with rough guidelines for the approximate ages at which children and adults go through them:

1. **Trust vs. mistrust,** from birth to 1 year, during which children develop a sense of trust for their mother based on her trustworthiness in meeting their needs.

2. **Autonomy vs. shame and doubt,** from 1 to 3 years, during which, through parental support, the child can develop a sense of self-control and autonomy.

3. **Initiative vs. guilt,** from 4 to 5 years, during which the child identifies with parents as powerful and seeks to be like them.

4. **Industry vs. inferiority,** from 6 to 11 years, during which feelings of competence and mastery come from successful experiences.

5. **Ego identity vs. role confusion,** during early adolescence, during which the adolescent blends various identities from earlier stages into a more integrated one.

6. **Intimacy vs. isolation,** during late adolescence and early adulthood, when, following the development of a strong identity, the adolescent develops intimacy with self and others.

7. **Generativity vs. self-absorption** or stagnation, during adulthood, when having children and guiding the next generation become primary goals.

8. **Ego integrity vs. despair,** during late adulthood, when the person accepts his or her lifetime contributions and limitations and has a sense of a larger history, including previous generations and the wisdom of the ages.

Abraham Maslow's (1954) theory of human development arises from humanistic psychology. Maslow proposed a hierarchy of human needs that is comprised of five levels. Each higher level is dependent upon lower levels having been satisfied. His five levels are ranked in order from lowest to highest:

1. **Physiological needs,** i.e., food, warmth, rest.

2. **Safety needs,** i.e., avoiding danger and feeling secure.

3. **Belongingness and love needs,** i.e., to love and be loved, to participate and associate with others.

4. **Esteem needs,** i.e., positive responses from others about oneself.

5. **Self-actualization needs,** i.e., full development of one's potential through searching for truth, justice, love, and beauty.

Children's emotional growth is dependent upon early experiences and the development of consistent, secure attachments with primary caregivers (Shaffer, 1988). As with language, cognitive, and social growth, emotional growth is a process that is dependent upon nervous system connections and growth as well. The point in the process of emotional development that children are at when they are in counseling will vary. To promote emotional growth, counselors and therapists may find it necessary to provide younger children with words to describe their emotions. Additionally, working with primary caregivers to help them develop skills that will enhance the child's emotional development will result in greater gains for the child emotionally.

Legal and Ethical Issues

The rights of children are at the core of ethical and legal practice for counselors and therapists. Compared to adults' rights, less consensus exists about **children's rights** and how to ensure that they are not violated during counseling (Hall & Lin, 1995). In the past, legal systems have extended fewer rights to children than to adults (Hart, 1991), based on the belief that children are incompetent to fully understand what is best for them. However, during the twentieth century, changes both in views and in treatment of children have occurred, culminating in the 1989 UN Convention on the Rights of the Child. This treaty, adopted on November 20, 1989, by the UN General Assembly and placed in force on September 2, 1990, was ratified by twenty member nations (Wilcox & Naimark, 1991). The United States played a key role in drafting the treaty, but remained one of only five UN member nations that had not ratified it by the end of 1996 (Limber & Wilcox, 1996).

Some of children's rights emanating from the UN Convention include the rights to express an opinion in matters affecting them and to be heard; to live with parents or to maintain contact with both parents; to receive protection when placed in alternative care; to receive legal protection of privacy; to be protected from abuse, neglect, and exploitation; to receive rehabilitative care to recover from victimization; and to be educated and to enjoy one's own culture (Unofficial Summary of Articles, UN Convention on the Rights of the Child, 1991). Underlying these rights is the right to the protection of the dignity of the child (Hall & Lin, 1995; Melton, 1991, 1996). Melton (1991) proposed six principles for counseling practice that address children's rights as identified by the UN Convention:

1. The provision of high-quality mental health services for children is of the highest priority.

2. Children are active partners in treatment.

3. Mental health services support and respect family integrity.

4. When children must be removed from the family for their protection, family-like alternatives to residential placement are found.

5. Children are protected from harm when the state has custody of them.

6. The cornerstone of mental health policy for children is prevention.

Given the new focus on children's rights, we will next discuss ethical and legal issues for counseling practice related to informed consent, privacy, confidentiality, and duty to warn and to report child abuse.

Informed Consent

Because children's capacities are in the process of development, clearly defining ethical guidelines for children's capacity to give **informed consent** for counseling is difficult. Being capable of giving informed consent is based on three standards: knowing consent, voluntary consent, and competent consent (Brakel, Parry, & Weiner, 1985). The standard for **knowing consent** is met when the counselor or therapist explains the process of and procedures for treatment and the child is able to understand the concepts and terms well enough to make an informed decision about participating in treatment. The standard for **voluntary consent** is met if the child is able to give consent freely rather than as the result of threat, duress, fraud, or compliant response to authority (DeKraai & Sales, 1991).

The standard for **competent consent** is based on the capacity to give legal consent to treatment (DeKraai & Sales, 1991). Because courts consider children incompetent to consent (Rozovsky, 1990), this standard is difficult for children to meet before the age of 18. A few studies have addressed the competence of children younger than 18 and found that minors 15 and older are as competent as adults to give treatment consent, and 11- to 14-year-old children may be competent depending on individual characteristics (Garrison, 1991; Grisso, 1981; Grisso & Vierling, 1978; Lewis, 1981; Rencher, 1997; Taylor, Adelman, & Kaser-Boyd, 1985; Weithorn & Campbell, 1982).

Since research has shown that children as young as 11 years of age can make competent decisions regarding treatment, current practice suggests that children are capable of and should participate in giving consent for their treatment and in selection of treatment techniques and methods (Hall & Lin, 1995). Legal standards in the United States continue to require that parents give consent for treatment for children younger than 18 years of age. However, the counselor should keep abreast of changes in legal standards, given new perceptions of the rights of children.

Privacy

Right to privacy refers to the client's right to choose what others know about him or her (Thompson & Rudolph, 1996) and to withhold information (Rinas & Clyne-Jackson, 1988). The child's right to privacy is not guaranteed legally, but in order to help protect the right to privacy the counselor or therapist can discuss with the child what generally will be shared with the parents, inform the child that it is not necessary to share information from sessions, and not pressure the child to disclose information that he or she does not want to reveal (Orton, 1997).

Confidentiality

Confidentiality is an ethical consideration and refers to "the professional responsibility to respect and limit access to clients' personal information" (Thompson & Rudolph, 1996, p. 508). Confidentiality in counseling is necessary for the development of the therapeutic relationship, the protection of the client's interest, and the effectiveness of treatment (DeKraai & Sales, 1991). It exists to benefit the client. Confidentiality has been a problematic concept for at least four decades for counselors working with children (Hendrix, 1991). The questions of who the client is (i.e., the parent or the child) and how competent the child is to fully participate in his or her treatment are at the heart of the issue. Varying opinions have been advanced regarding the level of confidentiality offered to the child, with four alternatives emerging (Hendrix): (1) **complete confidentiality**—that is, without consent, no information is shared (Ross, 1958), or information is shared only if someone is in danger of being harmed (Taylor & Adelman, 1989); (2) **limited confidentiality**—that is, at the beginning of counseling the child is told that therapeutically beneficial information will be shared; (3) **informed forced consent**—that is, the child is told that information will be disclosed with or without permission; and (4) no guarantee of confidentiality. As we have discussed, children age 14 and above usually have the capacity to fully understand treatment and offered choices and can be offered the same complete confidentiality as adults. When the child is not competent to fully understand or to make informed decisions, the counselor must act in a way that protects the child's interest by applying an alternative to absolute confidentiality (Hendrix). Current practice indicates that even children under the age of 14 should be asked to give voluntary, informed consent to have information shared with others for therapeutic reasons and should be convinced of the therapeutic benefits of sharing the information with select others (Hendrix; Taylor & Adelman).

Duty to Warn and to Report Child Abuse

Confidentiality is limited by two legal responsibilities: the **duty to warn** and the **duty to report suspected child abuse.** Duty to warn potential victims about the possibility of an attack by a dangerous person is based on the landmark decision of *Tarasoff v. Regents of the University of California* (1976) and is less often applicable in working with children than with adults (Orton, 1997). However, the duty to warn also applies to suicide threats and necessitates that counselors and therapists be able to assess the risk of suicide and warn parents or other authorities of the potential for suicide. In cases of suicide threat, it is important to remain with the child until parents are advised of the potential for suicide, are given options for further care, and take the child or the child is hospitalized. Protecting the child from potential harm is of utmost importance, as is true in any case requiring the duty to warn or to report child abuse.

The duty to report suspected child abuse and neglect is a legal mandate that requires anyone who comes in contact with children in their profession to report actual or suspected cases of child abuse and neglect (Orton, 1997). States may differ on what should be reported, so it is important for practitioners to review current relevant laws in the state in which they practice. With the increasing number of reports of child abuse and neglect, the likelihood is great that you will report at least one incident of child abuse during your career.

Treatment Setting Issues

Counseling of children occurs both in school and in clinical settings. Although the process is similar in both settings, there are differences in the environment, referral process, goals, confidentiality, and termination.

The Environment

The school is a natural, everyday setting in each child's world (Tharinger & Stafford, 1995). Access to educators and peers who interact with the child and the opportunity to observe the child's interactions with others provide the counselor or therapist with rich diagnostic information for both understanding the child and constructing effective interventions. In contrast, in the clinical setting the practitioner is dependent on parental report and observations of the child in early sessions to more fully understand the child and his or her needs.

The Referral Process

Referral for counseling or psychotherapy in clinical settings most often involves parents seeking treatment for their child for a variety of reasons, some of which maintain the privacy of the family (i.e., behaviors that occur only in the family setting and are not open to others' scrutiny). Commitment to the therapeutic process is made by the parent who brings the child for counseling. In schools, referral typically is initiated by the teacher because of behaviors the child is exhibiting that are disruptive to the educational process for the child or for others. The referral and assessment process in schools is inherently intrusive to the family, placing the child's problems in the public arena. Although many parents recognize their children's problems and are cooperative in giving permission for and participating in counseling interventions, some do not agree to having their child and family scrutinized by outsiders.

Goals of Counseling

In the clinical setting, goals of counseling derive from goals found within the mental health system (i.e., promoting emotional functioning that allows the child to progress normally in all developmental areas); in the school setting, however, such goals frequently are an integration of the goals of both the educational and mental health systems, which often are conflicting. The educational and mental health systems share the goal of promoting growth in children, but they have different perspectives and priorities about what it means to promote growth in children. Educational systems focus on academic progress, socialization, and appropriate behavior; thus counselors and therapists working in school systems must focus on developing emotional, behavioral, and social skills and functioning that will lead to the child's full participation in the educational process (Tharinger & Stafford, 1995).

Confidentiality in Schools

Ensuring confidentiality requires constant vigilance in any setting. However, in schools the pressure to share information with others who work with the child is constant (Tharinger & Stafford, 1995). Additionally, teachers and other school personnel do not share the ethical codes that govern the professional behavior of counselors and therapists, and at times they will talk indiscriminately in the halls or teachers lounge about children and their families. The success of treatment efforts requires some communication with those directly involved with the child. Finding ways to share just enough information to ensure the success of a recommended intervention in the classroom without violating the child's confidentiality and privacy is a necessary skill for practitioners working in school settings to develop.

Termination of Counseling

Termination usually occurs when the goals of counseling have been met and the child's emotional functioning is adequate. In schools, however, termination often occurs when the school year ends rather than when the child's goals are met. Children who need continued care through the summer months should be referred to community professionals. However, changing counselors can be disruptive to the therapeutic relationship and at times results in the child's resistance to developing new therapeutic relationships.

Child Treatment Issues

Some aspects of counseling children are different from counseling adults. In addition to noting developmental changes that are ongoing processes with children, Clarizio and McCoy (1983) summarize three unique aspects of counseling children. First, children rarely present themselves voluntarily for counseling. In the school setting they typically are referred for counseling by their teachers, parents, or school administrators, and in clinical settings they usually are brought by their parents. However, the effect of **involuntary submission** for counseling may not be resistance in the same form as it is with many adults who are required to submit to counseling. Behaviors ranging from passive compliance to refusal to go to counseling are possible, but often children will go to counseling because they haven't considered the possibility that they can refuse.

Second, children often lack an explicit understanding of the counseling process, purpose, and goals, and of the role they play in developing more functional feelings and behaviors. Third, children are dependent upon and influenced by their environment, particularly their families and the school. Thus they are vulnerable and in need of protection from potentially harmful influences. This condition provides a challenge to counselors to carefully consider information and advice given to children to ensure that it does not lead them to further conflict with their environments. However, it also provides an opportunity to enhance children's personality development and influence significant others in children's lives (Tharinger & Stafford, 1995).

Models for Counseling Children

There are various models of psychopathology that are used by counselors in dealing with children, including medical, psychodynamic, behavioral, client-centered, and family models (Johnson, Rasbury, & Siegel, 1986). These models influence the way counselors perceive children's problems and approach treatment.

The Medical Model

The **medical model** assumes that certain groups of symptoms are evidence of a particular disease, or mental illness, with an underlying biological cause. When a person has a particular mental illness, therapy is necessary to bring about a "cure" (Achenbach, 1982). Thus counselors using the medical model assume that the problems the child is having are due to a mental illness, may have a biological basis, are beyond the voluntary control of the child, and must have therapy applied in order to achieve a cure. The child is likely to not be viewed as being capable of participating effectively in making decisions about his or her treatment.

The Psychodynamic Model

The **psychodynamic model** relies heavily on the medical model and utilizes psychoanalytic theory (**S. Freud,** 1904/1959) as its treatment focus (Johnson et al., 1986). Assumptions of this model posit a biological or intrapsychic cause to the patient's problems. Works by **Anna Freud** (1946), **Hug-Hellmuth** (1921), and **Melanie Klein** (1932/1960) were the first applications of psychoanalytic theory to child treatment. **Play therapy** is used for younger children, and interpretation of the meaning of children's play and verbalizations provides a basis for understanding their intrapsychic conflicts. Although still used in clinical settings, this model is rarely used in schools, where counseling occurs over a shorter time frame and counseling goals focus on interventions that result in educational progress.

The Behavioral Model

The **behavioral model** focuses on overt behavior and considers environmental factors as determinants of behavior (Johnson et al., 1986). Behavioral excesses or deficits and certain behaviors in inappropriate contexts are considered pathological. Currently, the behavioral model uses principles of classical conditioning (**Pavlov,** 1927/1946), operant conditioning (Skinner, 1953), and observational learning (Bandura, 1969). Behavior management programs (which are based on the assessment of antecedents and consequences of problem behaviors and are applied consistently across settings) and counseling to alter cognitions that maintain behaviors are common interventions using the behavioral model.

The Client-Centered Model

The **client-centered model** is based on **Carl Rogers**'s (1961) methods for adults and **Virginia Axline**'s (1947/1969) methods for children. This model posits that when imposed social and environmental conditions interfere with personal growth, psychopathology results. However, unlike in previous models, client-centered counselors and therapists believe that individuals are capable within themselves of personal growth and adaptive functioning. Treatment requires empathic understanding, unconditional positive regard, and general acceptance of the child as a person. The practitioner focuses on developing the therapeutic relationship and clarifying the child's feelings through reflection (Johnson et al., 1986). Play and verbal interactions form the medium for client-centered counseling.

The Family Model

Drawing heavily on family systems theory, the **family model** assumes that pathology lies in the interactions between family members rather than within the family member who is exhibiting pathological symptoms (Johnson et al., 1986). In this model, which is based on the work of **Murray Bowen** (1976), assessment of dyadic interactions, boundaries between family members and between the family and the outside world, and hierarchical family organization provide the basis for understanding family patterns and coping behaviors of family members. Counseling focuses on all family members developing more mutually beneficial roles and communicating thoughts and feelings more appropriately.

An Integrated, Interpersonal Model for Counseling in Schools

Tharinger and Stafford (1995) proposed a seven-stage **integrated, interpersonal model** for individual school-based counseling which outlines a sequential approach from the referral of the child through termination of therapy, evaluating the counseling intervention, and follow-up to ensure continued progress. Because processes are ongoing, the stages at times are overlapping and activities of one stage may be initiated in previous stages. The model includes the following stages:

1. *Assess appropriateness of referral for counseling.* The referral for counseling is evaluated to judge the appropriateness of counseling as an intervention; alternate interventions are considered; parents are contacted for permission to assess and are interviewed; the child is observed, interviewed, and assessed; a decision is made about initiating individual counseling; and parents are contacted for assessment feedback, input on goals, permission for counseling, and relationship building.

2. *Plan for counseling and construct goals.* Using assessment data, the depth of the counseling intervention is determined, goals are developed and initiated, and methods to be used are determined.

3. *Begin counseling.* The child is educated about counseling, provided feedback about the assessment results, and involved in the planning process; the expectation that counseling will benefit the child is expressed to the child; and rules and confidentiality and its limits are discussed.

4. *Establish a working relationship and implement a plan for change.* A working counselor-child relationship is developed through listening with empathy; making emotional connections; communicating understanding of emotions; offering emotional support; and summarizing, reflecting, and being consistent in setting limits. General progress communication to parents and teachers is maintained, and environmental interventions are proposed as needed. Counselors should monitor their own emotional reactions and seek assistance as needed.

5. *Continue counseling and adjust the plan for change.* The original plan and goals are reevaluated; assessment data are gathered and compared to assessment data from stage 1 to estimate emotional growth and progress toward goals; goals are updated and methods adjusted; and general progress feedback is provided to the child, parents, and teachers.

6. *Assess progress, develop plan for termination, and terminate.* When the child appears to be functioning adequately, posttest assessment measures should be administered and compared to assessment data from stage 1. If there is evidence that counseling goals have been met and functioning has stabilized, termination should be planned, providing

adequate time for ending the relationship. Counseling is terminated and feedback about progress and attainment of goals is provided to parents and/or teachers.

7. *Evaluate effectiveness of the counseling intervention.* The effectiveness of the counseling intervention should be evaluated. A written summary of the initial assessment, counseling goals, course of the counseling relationship, and evaluation of progress should be kept for reference for follow-up with parents and teachers about continued progress and needs.

This seven-stage model provides a guideline for the sequential process of counseling in schools, but also one that can be modified for clinical practice. The theoretical orientation used by the counselor is intended to be an integration of theoretical approaches that best provides both an explanation of the child's difficulty and effective methods for intervention. However, counselors who adhere to one specific theoretical approach (i.e., psychoanalytic, cognitive-behavioral, etc.) can use this model as well, because the model focuses on the process of counseling rather than specific methods for interventions. The use of assessment as a means of evaluating progress in counseling may be objected to by some counselors; however, evaluating progress of counseling fulfills the need for establishing scientific efficacy of counseling interventions as well as establishing accountability in the treatment of the child.

Counseling Techniques for Older Children

Counseling or psychotherapy for older children often requires techniques similar to those used with adults. Use of structured games is often effective in the development of the therapeutic relationships for older children, but because language skills have developed, verbal exchanges are meaningful in bringing about positive changes in cognitions. Play therapy adaptations for adolescent and adult populations are available as well (O'Connor & Schaefer, 1994). The focus of the remainder of the chapter will be on counseling techniques for younger children.

Counseling Techniques for Younger Children

Using the play environment as a background for counseling young children allows the counselor or therapist to have increased communication with the child without increasing the amount of language used in the counseling session. Landreth (1982) refers to play as children's language and suggests that play facilitates expression of thoughts and feelings. Additionally, the use of art, music, books, storytelling, and computers as tools for communication of feelings provides the counselor with a wide range of tools for working with children.

Play as a Medium
The child's natural world consists of play; play is "the child's natural medium of self-expression" (Axline, 1947/1969, p. 9); and the child learns through play. Therefore, play is an excellent medium for communicating with children during counseling. Children's

growth and development in all areas are facilitated by play through exploring their curiosities, developing relationships with others, learning to express their emotions in socially acceptable ways, learning to cooperate and to share, and experimenting with the use of language. The natural progression of play is from spontaneous, unstructured play as toddlers, to structured games with rules between the ages of 7 and 11, to games that require higher cognitive skills in adolescence (Orton, 1997). Various play therapy techniques are discussed in the following sections.

Toys as Tools.   A variety of toys are recommended as staples in the therapeutic playroom, including a dollhouse with furniture and doll family; doll clothes; baby doll with bottle; puppets; building blocks; Legos; toy cars and trucks; toy guns, knives, and swords; stuffed animals; play telephones; crayons, paints, scissors, glue, and paper; play dough; and clothes for playing dress-up (Landreth, 1982; Orton, 1997). Toys should be available that allow children to be creative, to release emotion, to develop insight, to test reality, and to express themes from real life, such as anger and aggression, love and nurturing, and sadness (Axline, 1947/1969; Ginott, 1960; Landreth, 1982; Orton, 1997). When children find it difficult to express their emotions directly, puppets provide effective stimuli for dramatized, symbolic acting out of emotions (Webb, 1991). Toy guns, toy soldiers, play dough, doll families, and drawing and coloring pictures can all be used to encourage expressions of anger and aggression. Baby dolls with bottles can be used to encourage expression of need for nurturance and love. Several sources (O'Connor & Schaefer, 1994; Orton, 1997; Thompson & Rudolph, 1996) provide suggestions for play activities that may be helpful when planning counseling sessions for children, and Kaduson, Cangelosi, and Schaefer (1997) provide suggestions for using play therapy with children who have various internalizing, externalizing, or stress-produced disorders.

Sand and Water Play.   Sand and water are natural media that fascinate children. The sandbox can symbolize the child's environment, allowing the child to build the world of his or her fantasy by using toy cars, building-block houses, and doll figures. The child then plays out themes representative of the conflicts he or she is experiencing. Use of dry and damp sand in separate waterproof trays that are painted blue so that a lake is represented when the sand is pushed aside provide stimuli for the changing themes of children's play (Allan & Berry, 1993). Chaos, struggle, and resolution are common stages that recur in children's **sand play.** Additionally, **water play** has been used for work with overly active and constricted children, providing an outlet for aggression or for relaxation (Hartley, Frank, & Goldenson, 1993).

Therapeutic Activities

Many other therapeutic activities can be used effectively when counseling children. They include the use of art, music, books, storytelling, computers, and physical activity.

Art.   Art has been used for therapeutic purposes for over 30 years since the development (Kramer, 1958) of this technique for working with children. **Art therapy** includes the use of materials such as crayons, paints, clay, and play dough for drawings and sculptures. Techniques used to discover the hidden messages of the child's conflict as revealed through the art include listening to the child's "art talk," observing, intuitive guessing, and interpretation of form and content (Orton, 1997).

Music.   **Music therapy** has been used effectively in counseling to reduce stress and anxiety (Orton, 1997). Bowman (1987) provides a description of various methods incorporating music into counseling for children through eighth grade. Music can enhance the counseling program whether the counselor is musically talented or not.

Bibliotherapy.   **Bibliotherapy,** or the use of literary forms in counseling children, is used widely by elementary school counselors and psychologists as well as other mental health professionals (Pardeck & Pardeck, 1993). Bibliotherapy provides a fun and relaxing activity while children gain insight into human behavior, clarify their values and attitudes, develop understanding of socialization patterns, increase self-awareness, and identify and solve problems (Gumaer, 1984; Orton, 1997). Many books are available that address problems children have. Listings within areas of concern can be found in Orton and Thompson and Rudolph (1996).

Storytelling.   **Storytelling** is a therapeutic technique in which children are asked to tell a story with a beginning, middle, end, and moral (Gardner, 1971). Story plots and characters of stories children tell have been found to parallel the events of children's lives (Kestenbaum, 1985), thus providing the counselor or therapist with insight into inner conflicts the child is confronting and allowing the child the opportunity to gain insight into the events and resolve the conflicts in new ways. Storytelling can be used in conjunction with drawings the child makes by having the child tell a story about the drawing. Metaphors, which provide a form of symbolic communication, have been found to be effective means of communication when working with young children (Lankton & Lankton, 1989). Using age-appropriate vocabulary and the therapeutic goal as a guide, stories can be modified to address specific issues the child must resolve.

Other Techniques.   In the last twenty years, with the dawning of the computer age and video games, the use of computer art and games has been explored as a therapeutic technique that captures the attention of today's youth. Bowman and Rotter (1983) found that there are computer games that enhance cooperation, allow creative activity, and promote social and emotional learning. Additionally, use of physical activity, especially pleasant events, with depressed children has shown therapeutic promise when integrated with other interventions (Stark, Kaslow, & Reynolds, 1987).

Summary

Children growing up in today's world face a complex environment with violent images on television, in movies, and on computers. Gangs, drugs, alcohol, smoking, abduction, drive-by shootings, and violence on school campuses are only a few of the situations to which children may have to adjust. Redefinition of the family, family mobility, custody fights, and changing gender roles provide instability for children and confusion in learning what is expected of them. Interventions by counselors and therapists must address a wide variety of problems that children bring to the table, and necessarily must include prevention programs.

In addition to facing a complex world, children are negotiating the normal processes of development. Physical growth is accompanied by cognitive, language, social, behavioral, emotional, and personality growth, all of which occur within a cultural system. Counselors and therapists must adjust the content and process of treatment to take into consideration the developmental levels of children in these areas.

The rights of children and their competence to participate in treatment decisions must be considered when counseling children. Children's ability to provide informed consent will be dependent upon their developmental levels, but it is wise to seek their consent even when getting the legally designated permission for counseling from parents. Respecting the child's right to privacy and protecting the child's confidentiality are of utmost importance as well. Two limits to confidentiality—the duty to warn and the duty to report child abuse—must be communicated to children at the beginning of counseling. With new directions set by the UN in viewing children's rights, counselors and therapists should stay abreast of new developments in legal constraints relative to children's rights.

Differences exist between school and clinical treatment settings for children. The school provides a more natural environment for the child, as well as access to parents and teachers who make up the child's world. However, the school's referral process is more intrusive to the child and family because it is in a public arena. In addition, the goals of counseling or psychotherapy differ somewhat in the two settings, confidentiality is more difficult to maintain in the school setting, and termination often is time-driven rather than goal-driven in schools. Counselors and therapists working in schools should be aware of these concerns and take measures to maintain high-level ethical practice.

Counseling and psychotherapy is different with children than with adults. Children rarely present themselves for treatment. They often do not understand the purpose, goals, process, or their roles in counseling. Children are dependent on and influenced by their environment and, therefore, more vulnerable. Practitioners should provide protection for children and understand their power in influencing children's lives.

Several models have been presented for counseling children, including the medical, psychodynamic, behavioral, client-centered, and family models. Additionally, a seven-stage model for guiding the process of counseling children in schools was presented. It provides counselors a view of a step-by-step approach to the process as it occurs in many schools. Finally, counseling techniques for use with younger children, including play and therapeutic activities, provide the counselor or therapist with methods that have been used with children as well as sources for further techniques.

References

Achenbach, T. M. (1982). *Developmental psychopathology* (2nd ed.). New York: Wiley.

Allan, J., & Berry, P. (1993). Sandplay. In C. E. Schaefer & D. M. Cangelosi (Eds.), *Play therapy techniques* (pp. 117–123). Northvale, NJ: Jason Aronson.

Axline, V. (1969). *Play therapy*. New York: Ballantine. (Original work published in 1947)

Bandura, A. (1969). *Principles of behavior modification*. New York: Holt, Rinehart & Winston.

Bandura, A. (1977). *Social learning theory*. Englewood Cliffs, NJ: Prentice-Hall.

Bernal, M. E., & Knight, G. P. (Eds.). (1993). *Ethnic identity: Formation and transmission among Hispanics and other minorities*. Albany: State University of New York Press.

Bowen, M. (1976). Theory in the practice of psychotherapy. In P. J. Guerin, Jr. (Ed.), *Family therapy: Theory and practice* (pp. 42–90). New York: Gardner.

Bowman, R. P. (1987). Approaches for counseling children through music. Special issue: Counseling with expressive arts. *Elementary School Guidance and Counseling, 21*(4), 284–291.

Bowman, R. P., & Rotter, J. C. (1983). Computer games: Friend or foe? *Elementary School Guidance and Counseling, 18*(1), 25–34.

Brakel, S. J., Parry, J., & Weiner, B. A. (1985). *The mentally disabled and the law*. Chicago: American Bar Foundation.

Bruner, J. S. (1973). *Beyond the information given: Studies in the psychology of knowing*. New York: Norton.

Carlson, N. R. (1995). *Foundations of physiological psychology* (3rd ed.). Boston: Allyn & Bacon.

Carroll, J. B. (Ed.). (1956). *Language, thought, and reality: Selected writings of Benjamin Lee Whorf*. New York: The Technology Press of M.I.T. and John Wiley & Sons.

Children's Defense Fund. (1996). *The state of America's children yearbook*. Washington, DC: Author.

Chomsky, N. (1959). [Review of the book *Verbal behavior* by B. F. Skinner]. *Language, 35,* 26–58.

Clarizio, H. F., & McCoy, G. F. (1983). *Behavior disorders in children* (3rd ed.). New York: Harper & Row.

Crabbs, M. (1989). Future perfect: Planning for the next century. *Elementary School Guidance and Counseling, 24*(2), 160–166.

Craig, G. J. (1989). *Human development* (5th ed.). Englewood Cliffs, NJ: Prentice-Hall.

DeKraai, M. B., & Sales, B. (1991). Legal issues in the conduct of child therapy. In T. R. Kratochwill, & R. J. Morris (Eds.), *The practice of child therapy* (2nd ed.) (pp. 441–458). New York: Pergamon.

Erikson, E. H. (1963). *Childhood and society* (2nd. ed.). New York: Norton.

Finkelhor, D., & Dziuba-Leatherman, J. (1994). Victimization of children. *American Psychologist, 49*(3), 173–183.

Finkelhor, D., Hotaling, G. T., & Sedlak, A. J. (1992). The abduction of children by strangers and nonfamily members: Estimating the incidence using multiple methods. *Journal of Interpersonal Violence, 7*(2), 226–243.

Freud, A. (1946). *The psycho-analytical treatment of children: Technical lectures and essays* (N. Proctor-Gregg, Trans.). New York: International Universities Press.

Freud, S. (1959). Collected papers. In J. Riviere (Trans.), *Sigmund Freud: Collected papers* (Vol. 1). New York: Basic Books. (Original work published 1904)

Gardner, R. A. (1971). *Therapeutic communication with children: The mutual storytelling technique*. New York: Science House.

Garrison, E. G. (1991). Children's competence to participate in divorce custody decision making. *Journal of Clinical Child Psychology, 20*(1), 78–87.

Ginott, H. G. (1960). A rationale for selecting toys in play therapy. *Journal of Consulting Psychology, 24*(3), 243–246.

Grisso, T. (1981). *Juveniles' waiver of rights: Legal and psychological competence*. New York: Plenum.

Grisso, T., & Vierling, L. (1978). Minors' consent to treatment: A developmental perspective. *Professional Psychology, 9,* 412–427.

Gumaer, J. (1984). *Counseling and therapy for children*. New York: Free Press.

Hall, A. S., & Lin, M. J. (1995). Theory and practice of children's rights: Implications for mental health counselors. *Journal of Mental Health Counseling, 17*(1), 63–80.

Hart, S. N. (1991). From property to person status: Historical perspective on children's rights. *American Psychologist, 46*(1), 53–59.

Hartley, R. E., Frank, L. K., & Goldenson, R. M. (1993). Water play. In C. E. Schaefer & D. M. Cangelosi (Eds.), *Play therapy techniques* (pp. 125–130). Northvale, NJ: Jason Aronson.

Hendrix, D. H. (1991). Ethics and intrafamily confidentiality in counseling with children. *Journal of Mental Health Counseling, 13*(3), 323–333.

Hug-Hellmuth, H. V. (1921). On the technique of child analysis. *International Journal of Psychoanalysis, 2*(3/4), 287–305.

Johnson, J. H., Rasbury, W. C., & Siegel, L. J. (1986). *Approaches to child treatment: Introduction to theory, research, and practice*. Boston: Allyn & Bacon.

Kaduson, H. G., Cangelosi, D., & Schaefer, C. E. (1997). *The playing cure: Individualized play therapy for specific childhood problems*. Northvale, NJ: Jason Aronson.

Kalat, J. W. (1995). *Biological psychology* (5th ed.). Pacific Grove, CA: Brooks/Cole.

Kestenbaum, C. J. (1985). The creative process in child psychotherapy. *American Journal of Psychotherapy, 39*(4), 479–489.

Klein, M. (1960). The psycho-analysis of children. In A. Strachey (Trans.), *The psychoanalysis of children*. New York: Grove. (Original work published 1932)

Kramer, E. (1958). *Art therapy in a children's community: A study of the function of art therapy in the treatment program of Wiltwyck School for Boys*. Springfield, IL: Charles C Thomas.

Landreth, G. L. (Ed.). (1982). *Play therapy: Dynamics of the process of counseling with children*. Springfield, IL: Charles C Thomas.

Lankton, C. H., & Lankton, S. (1989). *Tales of enchantment: Goal-oriented metaphors for adults and children in therapy*. New York: Brunner/Mazel.

Lewis, C. C. (1981). How adolescents approach decisions: Changes over grades seven to twelve and policy implications. *Child Development, 52,* 538–544.

Limber, S. P., & Wilcox, B. L. (1996). Application of the UN Convention on the Rights of the Child to the United States. *American Psychologist, 51*(12), 1246–1250.

Martin, T. C., & Bumpass, L. L. (1989). Recent trends in marital disruption. *Demography, 26,* 37–51.

Maslow, A. H. (1954). *Motivation and personality*. New York: Harper & Brothers.

Melton, G. B. (1991). Socialization in the global community: Respect for the dignity of children. *American Psychologist, 46*(1), 66–71.

Melton, G. B. (1996). The child's right to a family environment: Why children's and family values are compatible. *American Psychologist, 51*(12), 1234–1238.

Miller, P. H. (1989). *Theories of developmental psychology* (2nd ed.). New York: Freeman.

Mintz, L. B., & O'Neil, J. M. (1990). Gender roles, sex, and the process of psychotherapy: Many questions and few answers. *Journal of Counseling and Development, 68*(4), 381–387.

Ocampo, K. A., Bernal, M. E., & Knight, G. P. (1993). Gender race, and ethnicity: The sequencing of social constancies. In M. E. Bernal and G. P. Knight (Eds.), *Ethnic identity: Formation and transmission among Hispanics and other minorities* (pp. 11–30). Albany: State University of New York Press.

O'Connor, K. J., & Schaefer, C. E. (1994). *Handbook of play therapy: Vol. 2. Advances and innovations*. New York: Wiley.

Orton, G. L. (1997). *Strategies for counseling with children and their parents*. Pacific Grove, CA: Brooks/Cole.

Pardeck, J. T., & Pardeck, J. A. (1993). *Bibliotherapy: A clinical approach for helping children*. Langhorne, PA: Gordon & Breach.

Pavlov, I. P. (1946). Conditioned reflexes. In G. V. Anrep (Ed. and Trans.), *Conditioned reflexes: An investigation of the physiological activity of the cerebral cortex*. London: Oxford University Press. (Original work published 1927)

Phinney, J. S., & Rotheram, M. J. (1987). *Children's ethnic socialization: Pluralism and development*. Newbury Park, CA: Sage.

Piaget, J. (1959). The language and thought of the child. In M. Gabain (Trans.), *The language and thought of the child by Jean Piaget*. London: Routledge & Kegan Paul. (Original work published 1926)

Piaget, J. (1968). The moral judgment of the child. In M. Gabain (Trans.), *The moral judgment of the child by Jean Piaget*. London: Routledge & Kegan Paul. (Original work published 1932)

Piaget, J. (1970). Piaget's theory. In P. H. Mussen (Ed.), *Carmichael's manual of child psychology* (3rd ed., Vol. 1) (pp. 703–732). New York: Wiley.

Rencher, L. A. (1997). *Minor's competence to provide voluntary consent for hypothetical psychoeducational decisions*. Unpublished doctoral dissertation, Arizona State University, Tempe.

Rinas, J., & Clyne-Jackson, S. (1988). *Professional conduct and legal concerns in mental health practice*. Norwalk, CT: Appleton & Lange.

Rogers, C. R. (1961). *On becoming a person: A therapist's view of psychotherapy*. Boston: Houghton Mifflin.

Ross, A. O. (1958). Confidentiality in child guidance treatment. *Mental Hygiene, 42*(1), 60–66.

Rozovsky, F. A. (1990). *Consent to treatment: A practical guide* (2nd ed.). Boston: Little, Brown.

Scher, M., & Good, G. E. (1990). Gender and counseling in the twenty-first century: What does the future hold? *Journal of Counseling and Development, 68*(4), 388–391.

Shaffer, D. R. (1988). *Social and personality development* (2nd ed.). Pacific Grove, CA: Brooks/Cole.

Siegler, R. S. (1991). *Children's thinking* (2nd ed.). Englewood Cliffs, NJ: Prentice-Hall.

Simeonsson, R. J. (1994). *Risk, resilience & prevention: Promoting the well-being of all children.* Baltimore: Brookes.

Skinner, B. F. (1953). *Science and human behavior.* New York: Macmillan.

Stark, K. D., Kaslow, N. J., & Reynolds, W. M. (1987). A comparison of the relative efficacy of self-control therapy and a behavioral problem-solving therapy for depression in children. *Journal of Abnormal Child Psychology, 15,* 91–113.

Stevenson, M. R., & Black, K. N. (1996). *How divorce affects offspring: A research approach.* Boulder, CO: Westview.

Sue, D. W., & Sue, D. (1990). *Counseling the culturally different: Theory and practice* (2nd ed.). New York: Wiley.

Tarasoff v. Regents of the University of California, 551 P.2d 334 (Cal., 1976).

Taylor, L., & Adelman, H. S. (1989). Reframing the confidentiality dilemma to work in children's best interests. *Professional Psychology: Research and Practice, 20,* 79–83.

Taylor, L., Adelman, H. S., & Kaser-Boyd, N. (1985). Minors' attitudes and competence toward participation in psychoeducational decisions. *Professional Psychology: Research and Practice, 16,* 226–235.

Tharinger, D., & Stafford, M. (1995). Best practices in individual counseling of elementary age students. In A. Thomas & J. Grimes (Eds.), *Best practices in school psychology III* (pp. 893–907). Washington, DC: National Association of School Psychologists.

Thompson, C. L., & Rudolph, L. B. (1996). *Counseling children* (4th ed.). Pacific Grove, CA: Brooks/Cole.

Unofficial summary of articles, UN Convention on the Rights of the Child. (1991). *American Psychologist, 46*(1), 50–52.

Vygotsky, L. (1962). Thought and word. In E. Hanfmann & G. Vakar (Eds. and Trans.), *Thought and language.* Cambridge: M.I.T. Press. (Original work published in 1934)

Webb, N. B. (Ed.). (1991). *Play therapy with children in crisis: A casebook for practitioners.* New York: Guilford.

Weithorn, L. A., & Campbell, S. B. (1982). The competency of children and adolescents to make informed treatment decisions. *Child Development, 53*(6), 1589–1598.

Wilcox, B. L., & Naimark, H. (1991). The rights of the child: Progress toward human dignity. *American Psychologist, 46*(1), 49.

Wineberg, H. (1992). Childbearing and dissolution of the second marriage. *Journal of Marriage and the Family, 54*(4), 879–887.

Zigler, E. F., & Gilman, E. (1996). Not just any care: Shaping a coherent child care policy. In E. F. Zigler, S. L. Kagan, & N. W. Hall (Eds.), *Children, families, and government: Preparing for the twenty-first century* (pp. 94–116). New York: Cambridge University Press.

Zigler, E. F., Kagan, S. L., & Hall, N. W. (Eds.). (1996). *Children, families, and government: Preparing for the twenty-first century.* New York: Cambridge University Press.

Counseling and Psychotherapy: Multicultural Considerations

G. Miguel Arciniega
Arizona State University

Betty J. Newlon
University of Arizona

A lthough a significant amount of research and writing has addressed the impact of culture on counseling and psychotherapy, very few mainstream textbooks have incorporated **multicultural** themes into their discussions of theories of counseling and psychotherapy. Multicultural counseling is at a crossroads (Ponterotto, Casas, Suzuki, & Alexander, 1995), and in spite of the increased attention it has received, it is still considered to be in its infancy (Ponterotto & Sabnani, 1989).

The existence of **cultural bias** in counseling and psychotherapy has been documented by many authors (Atkinson, Morten, & Sue, 1993; Katz, 1985; LeVine & Padilla, 1980; Pedersen, Draguns, Lonner, & Trimble, 1996; Ponterotto & Casas, 1991; Sue & Sue, 1990). Wrenn (1962) first introduced the concept of the "culturally encapsulated counselor" by pointing out how practitioners protect themselves from the reality of change by "surrounding [themselves] with a cocoon of pretended reality—a reality which is based upon the past and the known, upon seeing that which is as though it would always be" (p. 446). More than 20 years later Wrenn (1985) again addressed the issue of the encapsulated counselor with a broader view that dealt with practitioners who denied the reality of change.

The history and legitimacy of multicultural counseling and psychotherapy have paralleled the sociopolitical movements in the United States. The civil rights efforts of the 1960s, 1970s, and 1980s produced a racial and cultural pride among minority groups, which in turn stimulated their demand for recognition and equality. This movement has pushed mental health professionals to consider cultural issues (Wehrly, 1991).

For the past three decades, writers, researchers, educators, and professionals in the field of counseling and psychotherapy have espoused the need for multicultural and cross-cultural awareness, knowledge, strategies, and approaches in order to serve the increasing number of racial, cultural, and ethnic minorities throughout the nation. The need for a minority perspective in counseling and psychotherapy has become one of the most important topics in journals. Between 1983 and 1988, the major counseling and counseling psychology journals (*The Counseling Psychologist, The Journal of Counseling Psychology, The Journal of Counseling and Development,* and *The Journal of Multicultural Counseling and Development*) published 183 conceptual and empirical articles in this area (Ponterotto & Casas, 1991). *The Journal of Counseling and Development* published a special issue called "Multiculturalism as a Fourth Force in Counseling" (American Association for Counseling and Development, 1991). Numerous researchers have responded to Pedersen's (1991) fourth force in counseling, and a call to the professions has been made to establish multiculturalism as an integral part of counseling (Essandoh, 1996). Even more recently, an unprecedented number of presentations and symposia on multicultural psychology has filled professional conferences from the major professional organizations (Sue, Ivey, & Pedersen, 1996).

Wehrly (1991) states, "In spite of the fact that the United States has been (and is) a nation of immigrants whose values differ, a major theme of Euro-American individualistic psychology seems to have been that of assimilation" (p. 4). She proceeds to point out that writers in the field have been slow to recognize the cultural impact of American ethnic minorities. They have not broadened the theoretical base of counseling or psychotherapy beyond Western thought. Consequently, most training institutions, while they might offer a course on multicultural counseling or psychotherapy, still use theory texts that expound a monoethnic, monocultural theory.

We need to acknowledge that traditional theories are based on Western Euro-American assumptions that are considered to be morally, politically, and ethnically neutral. This foundation has also been perpetuated as culturally fair and unbiased. Atkinson et al. (1993), Ivey (1981, 1983), and Pedersen (1994) have noted that counseling and psychotherapy approaches and theories were developed for the white middle class and traditionally conceptualized in a Western individualistic framework.

To clarify this point, Katz (1985) presented a paradigm for viewing cultural dimensions of traditional therapy in terms of white values and beliefs. Katz concluded that the "similarities between white culture and the cultural values that form the foundations of traditional counseling theory and practice exist and are interchangeable" (p. 619). These monocultural-based theories assume applicability to all populations regardless of minority racial and cultural experiences. While these theories may be well intentioned, they have not systematically integrated the current sociopolitical nature of multicultural populations. They inadequately explain the complexities and experiences of racial/ethnic minority groups, are culture-bound and inflexible, focus on a single dimension of personality, and expound only one worldview—Euro-American (Parham, 1996).

Native Americans, African Americans, Hispanic Americans, and Asian Americans/Pacific Islanders

Because it is not possible in this space to provide a descriptive overview of all American minority groups, we have selected the following four groups because they have been identified for special attention by the American Psychological Association and the American Counseling Association: Native Americans, African Americans, Hispanic Americans, and Asian Americans/Pacific Islanders. In order to understand the current experience of these populations, it is essential that counselors and therapists understand the groups' historical, educational, social, political, and economic development and climate in addition to their basic family characteristics and values. For a more thorough understanding of counseling these groups, see LeVine and Padilla (1980), Pedersen et al. (1996), Sue and Sue (1990), and Atkinson et al. (1993).

It is not our intent to provide a comprehensive analysis of all of the factors impinging on theories of counseling and psychotherapy, but rather to introduce the important social, ethnic, and cultural issues and considerations that practitioners must take into account when applying theory. This chapter addresses the following as they relate to the four previously mentioned racial, ethnic, and cultural groups: definitions, counselor and therapist self-awareness, Euro-American mainstream assumptions, acculturation, demographics, racial and ethnic cultural considerations, and racial and ethnic cultural components. In addition, we present a discussion of theories of counseling and psychotherapy and their appropriateness or adaptability to traditional minority groups. The chapter concludes with a discussion of how multicultural considerations can add breadth to prevailing theories. It encourages the reader to examine very critically the most current theory of multicultural counseling and psychotherapy (Sue et al., 1996).

Definitions

For the purpose of this chapter, we propose the following terms and definitions (Krogman, 1945; Linton, 1945; Rose, 1964):

- **Race:** a group of people who possess a definite combination of physical characteristics of genetic origin that distinguishes them from other groups of humans
- **Ethnicity:** a group classification in which members are believed, by themselves and others, to have a common origin and share a unique social and cultural heritage such as language, religious customs, and traditions that are passed from generation to generation
- **Culture:** the configuration of learned behavior whose components and elements are shared and transmitted by the members of a particular society

It is necessary to point out that these three terms have often been used interchangeably in the literature and are often misunderstood. *Race* refers to a biological concept, while *ethnicity* and *culture* refer to shared and uniquely learned characteristics. Ethnic groups within races differ in their cultural specificity, and people of the same racial background and same ethnic group may differ in their cultural specificity. For example, African Americans may be part of a Hispanic ethnic group but may identify with a number of cultural groups from their country of origin.

Here are some other important terms and definitions (Katz, 1985; Pedersen, 1988):

- **Minority:** a group of people who, because of their physical or cultural characteristics, receive differential and unequal treatment due to collective discrimination

- **Multicultural counseling or psychotherapy:** a situation in which two or more people with different ways of perceiving their social environment are brought together in a helping relationship

- **Stereotype:** rigid preconceptions about members of a particular group without regard to individual variations

- **White culture:** the synthesis of ideas, values, and beliefs coalesced from descendants of white European ethnic groups in the United States

Counselor and Therapist Self-Awareness

The implementation of a theory of counseling or psychotherapy that is more responsive to racial and cultural groups requires that practitioners determine the appropriateness or inappropriateness of their approaches. They must have knowledge of the demographics of these groups and an awareness of their history, sociopolitical issues, communication styles, culture, class, language factors, worldviews, acculturation, and identity. In addition, practitioners must have an awareness of their own biases and beliefs. This requires critical examination of themselves and their theoretical frameworks in order to provide effective and ethically appropriate services.

As the previous list implies, this process is not an easy task. It also requires a **paradigm shift** in thinking—broadening personal realities with other worldviews and integrating them into counseling theory and practice. This paradigm shift gives the counselor or therapist conceptual clarity and provides a framework of thought to explain various aspects of reality (Kuhn, 1962). Midgette and Meggert (1991) propose such a paradigm shift: "Multicultural instruction represents an emergent synthesis—a somewhat new systematic outlook that benefits from knowledge of previously developed philosophies but is not an eclectic composite" (p. 136). Lee (1996) posits that as multicultural counseling continues to emerge as a primary mode of practice, a paradigm shift in the theory of intervention is also needed. Ibrahim (1985) and Sue et al. (1996) propose that effectiveness in cross-cultural counseling or psychotherapy is determined by how well the helpers are aware of their own worldview and can understand and accept the worldview of the client. The power of a dominant, preset paradigm can block the pursuit of knowledge through alternative approaches and thereby create major limitations by closing the system and not allowing further development. These paradigms are the source of basic beliefs and attitudes that are difficult to modify. However, if counselors and therapists are to act with integrity and commitment, they must begin to take steps in shifting their theoretical paradigms to include racial and cultural worldviews.

This paradigm shift requires one to assess his or her personal values and beliefs and determine how others' views can be integrated into one's own. Newlon and Arciniega (1992) proposed a process of cultural integration involving the following (p. 286):

1. Confronting and challenging personal stereotypes held about cultural groups

2. Acquiring knowledge about the groups' cultures and, even more important, about heterogeneous responses of the groups

3. Understanding the traditional institutional interaction between the dominant society and minorities, and vice versa

4. Understanding the effects of institutional racism and stereotypes

5. Acquiring firsthand experience with focus minority groups

6. Challenging normative counselor and therapist approaches and understanding their cultural implications

7. Knowledgeably using a culturally pluralistic model

Sue and Sue (1990) posited similar observations in the form of characteristics of a culturally aware counselor or therapist. These characteristics included "being aware and sensitive to their own values and biases; comfortable with differences between themselves and their clients in terms of race and beliefs; sensitive to circumstances dictating referral; and aware of their own racist beliefs and feelings" (p. 160). This shift offers an opportunity to expand theoretical frameworks (not necessarily to replace them) and to integrate a more comprehensive view of our world.

Sue, Arredondo, and McDavis (1992) developed a set of multicultural competencies that were presented to the American Counseling and Development Association and later refined and operationalized by Arredondo et al. (1996). This list of competencies responds to the aforementioned paradigm shift reflecting a more comprehensive analysis of counselor self-awareness, knowledge, and skills.

Acculturation

Acculturation is an important phenomenon to be considered in the light of counseling theory and practice. It is composed of numerous dimensions, such as cultural values, ideologies, ethnic identity, beliefs, attitudes toward self and majority, language use, cultural customs, practices, and ethnic interaction. It has often been confused with the concept of **assimilation.** For the purpose of this chapter, *acculturation* is defined as the degree to which an individual from a racial or ethnic minority uniquely incorporates, adds to, and synthesizes the values, customs, language, beliefs, and ideology of the dominant culture in order to survive and feel a sense of belonging. *Assimilation,* on the other hand, refers to a "process of acculturation in which an individual has changed so much as to become disassociated from the value system of his/her group or in which the entire group disappears as an autonomously functioning system" (Teske, 1973, p. 7907a).

Each racial or ethnic group has its own distinct acculturation process, even though they all manifest similar concerns. Native Americans, who were here before the white settlers, were forced onto reservations and only later entered the majority mainstream. They differ from the Hispanics and Asians, who came from another country. The history of African-American acculturation also has unique characteristics, including slavery and economic and racial oppression.

Acculturation is not continuous from traditional to mainstream; rather, its origin might be best understood as a multidimensional, multifaceted phenomenon. An individual may learn how to become Americanized, but this does not imply that the person incorporates society's values. These values may be additive and not supplantive. Persons can retain the values of their culture of origin and simultaneously operate with mainstream values. Minority individuals who have retained their identity and who still incorporate American values in a healthy way are those who have come to an understanding of self without losing their cultural self-concept.

Demographics

A century from now, the population of the United States is expected to be closer to the world balance: 57% Asian American/Pacific Islander, 26% white, 7% African American, and 10% Hispanic (Edmunds, Martinson, & Goldberg, 1990; Ibrahim, 1991). Judging from census information, researchers believe that by 2010 the white population will have marginal overall growth, while African-American and Hispanic populations will grow at an accelerated rate. By 2010, whites will represent 76.6% of the total population, down from 80.7% in 1989; African Americans will represent 13%, up from 11.8% in 1989; and Hispanics will represent 10.4%, up from 7.5% in 1989 (U.S. Bureau of the Census, 1989). More recent data, however, indicate that Hispanics will be the largest minority by 2010 (Arce, 1997).

Age-related racial and ethnic group data stem from 1987 and are summarized in the *Statistical Abstract of the United States* (U.S. Bureau of the Census, 1989). Whites are the most highly represented group in the age 45–65 cohort (19.3%) and in the 65-and-over age group (12.4%). Whites are followed by African Americans and then Hispanics in terms of "older group" representation.

Hispanics are the highest-represented group among the two youngest age groups. Almost 11% of Hispanics are under 5 years of age, while 9.4% of African Americans and 7.3% of whites fall in this category. In the age 5–14 category, Hispanics have the highest relative percentage at 19.6, followed by African Americans (18.3%) and whites (13.6%). Unfortunately, more recent age-related data on Asian American/Pacific Islanders and Native Americans are not yet available.

In terms of median age, Native Americans are the youngest, with a median age of 23, followed closely by Hispanics at 23.2 years. Interestingly, when looking across age-group categories, we note that more than 50% of African Americans, Hispanics, and Native Americans are under the age of 25.

Some additional demographic information follows.

Native Americans

Native Americans include American Indians, Eskimos, and Aleuts (Alaska natives). American Indians are geographically dispersed throughout the United States. There are 511 federally recognized native entities and an additional 365 state-recognized American Indian tribes, with 200 distinct tribal languages (LaFromboise, 1988). Theory application must be sensitive to the tremendous heterogeneity and diversity existing among Native Americans. The 1980 national census reported the Native American population as roughly 1.5 million (U.S. Bureau of the Census, 1982), but a more recent estimate has placed the population at between 1.5 and 1.8 million (LaFromboise & Low, 1989). States with relatively high Native American populations include California, Oklahoma, Arizona, New Mexico, North Carolina, and Alaska (Dillard, 1985). According to LaFromboise (1988), only 24% of the population lives on reservations, and that segment is remarkably young, with a median age of 20.4 compared to the U.S. median age of 30.3.

In terms of educational, economic, and political power, Native Americans are at the lowest end of the spectrum. More often than not, they have little influence over what happens in the United States or in their own lives (LaFromboise, 1988).

African Americans

African Americans constitute the nation's largest racial and ethnic minority group. They represent 12.1% of the total U.S. population and number close to 30 million. The African-American population is growing at a faster pace than the white majority, with an annual growth rate of 1.87% as compared to ΰ.06% for whites (Rogler, Malgady, Constantino, & Bluementhall, 1987). The African-American population is spread throughout the United States: 11.3% in the Northeast, 10% in the Midwest, 18.8% in the South, and 5.6% in the West (U.S. Bureau of the Census, 1988).

African Americans as a racial group are represented by numerous diverse ethnic and cultural groups, including Spanish-speaking populations from Cuba, Puerto Rico, and Panama; groups from the Caribbean Islands and northern Europe; and Native American/African Americans (Wehrly, 1991). It is important for counselors and therapists to acknowledge and understand the tremendous diversity within the African-American population in the United States.

The African-American experience in America is unique. This group first arrived in the United States in the 1600s and, unlike immigrant groups who followed, came involuntarily as slaves. The group as a whole has been subjected to continuing majority-group oppression. In no case has the sheer brutality and evil of racism, prejudice, and penetrating hate been so evident and salient as in the white majority's treatment of African-Americans throughout U.S. history.

Hispanic Americans

Hispanics comprise a large, diverse group composed of Mexican Americans, Puerto Ricans, Cuban Americans, South and Central Americans, and others. There is also a great deal of heterogeneity within each specific subgroup. Mexican Americans who have recently arrived in the United States may be quite different in values, behaviors, attitudes, and counseling and therapeutic needs from Mexican Americans who are third-generation citizens and more acculturated. Further, internal diversity among groups of Mexican Americans can also be attributed to geographic region and socioeconomic status.

Hispanics are the fastest-growing racial and ethnic group in the United States, and they make up the second-largest minority group. Of the many Hispanic groups in the United States, Central and South Americans experienced the greatest growth rate during the 1982–87 period: 40%. Given the overall high growth rate of Hispanics in general, it is expected that by the year 2035 they will surpass African Americans as the largest racial/ethnic minority group in the United States (Ponterotto & Casas, 1991). Arce (1997) predicts that by 2010 Hispanics will be the largest racial/ethnic minority group.

Hispanics of Mexican origin comprise the largest segment of the Hispanic population, accounting for 63% of the total. Other Hispanic subgroups are represented as follows: Puerto Ricans at 12%, Central and South Americans at 11%, and Cubans at 5%. A majority of Mexican Americans reside in the Southwest. Puerto Ricans reside primarily in and around New York City, while a majority of Cuban Americans live in southern Florida and in the vicinity of New York City. A number of Central American groups are located in the New York City, Los Angeles, and San Francisco areas (Ponterotto & Casas, 1991). Overall, the Hispanic population is younger, less educated, poorer, and more likely to live in inner-city neighborhoods than the general population (Rogler et al., 1987).

Asian Americans/Pacific Islanders

Asian Americans/Pacific Islanders are represented by a number of major subgroups, including Japanese, Chinese, Filipinos, Koreans, Guamians, Malays, Samoans, and Southeast Asians. This collective heterogeneous group represents the third-largest racial and ethnic minority group in the United States. Asian-American/Pacific Islander groups are growing in rapid numbers, and some projections expect this total population to number more than 9.8 million by the year 2000 (Ponterotto & Casas, 1991).

The Chinese and Japanese were the first Asians to settle in the United States in large numbers. Like other minority groups, they arrived in the hopes of improving their economic conditions, lifestyles, and social and political life (Dillard, 1985). Today, Asian Americans/Pacific Islanders are dispersed throughout the United States. A large percentage are located in urban areas in large cities on the West and East Coasts. Although some Asian-American/Pacific Islander groups have been portrayed as "model minorities" in terms of significant educational and economic success, large percentages of these groups live in poverty and suffer high levels of psychological stress (Sue & Sue, 1990).

Asian Americans/Pacific Islanders also differ from group to group. Again, varying levels of acculturation attest to marked internal heterogeneity within groups. The tremendous heterogeneity both between and within various Asian-American/Pacific Islander groups defies categorization and stereotypic description. This group has been subjected to continuing societal oppression, discrimination, and misunderstanding.

Racial and Ethnic Cultural Considerations

Each of the specific racial and ethnic groups that we have addressed has cultural considerations that must be taken into account by counselors and therapists. These considerations should be evaluated with respect to minority groups' needs, values, and level of acculturation. Newlon and Arciniega (1983) addressed these considerations as "factors" to be considered by practitioners when gathering information and integrating them into counseling theory and process. Racial and ethnic cultural considerations include language, cultural identity, generation, cultural custom styles, geographical location and neighborhoods, family constituency, psychohistorical and religious traditions, and individuality

It should be noted that these are stated in a general sense and must be interpolated with information from each group.

Language

When working with minority clients who still use their language of origin, understanding the language is not enough; the practitioner must consider both content and contextual meaning. In addition, the counselor or therapist must be able to assess the language of the various minority groups: not all members will have the same degree of fluency in the language of origin or in English. Practitioners must be cognizant of the fact that the language of origin is where much of the affect is first learned. Although some minority clients may be fluent in English, the English words may have a different affective meaning from that of the language of origin.

Cultural Identity

Counselors or therapists must be aware of the **self-referent labels** that clients choose. Self-referent labels are a sensitive issue for many clients and may be different even for various members within the family. For example, to individuals of Mexican or Latin American descent, the identifiers may be Mexican American, Hispanic, Chicano, Americans of Mexican descent, or Latinos. For clients of African descent, these may be African American, Negro, black, or West Indian. For Native Americans, identifiers may be American Indian, or important tribal names. For Asian Americans/Pacific Islanders, the identifiers may be Asian, Asian American, Oriental, or specific countries of origin. One of the major contributions from multicultural researchers was the idea of **identity stage development models,** which provided a framework to help counselors understand an identity process that oppressed people experience. For more detailed information see Sue and Sue (1990) and Atkinson et al. (1993).

Generation

The clients' generational factors—that is, first, second, or third generation in this country—should be assessed by the counselor or therapist to assist in a thumbnail assessment of acculturation. First-generation clients may have more ties to the traditional culture, and these ties may be reflected in the nuclear and extended family dynamics. The acculturation process is unique for each minority group and individual. Contrary to some current beliefs, as clients become acculturated they do not drop their former cultural ways but rather add new ones and synthesize both the new and the old in a creative manner.

Cultural Custom Styles

In addition to the obvious cultural customs of food, dress, and traditions, several cultural styles of responsibility and communication have to be considered. For example, the Mexican, Indian, and Asian cultures emphasize the responsibility an oldest child has for younger siblings. An Asian family's expectations for unquestioning obedience may produce problems when family members are exposed to American values emphasizing independence and self-reliance.

The style of communication in traditional Native American and Mexican-American clients stresses patience and personal respect. Clients from traditional families may show respect by looking down and not making eye contact with authority figures. With African-American clients, verbal interaction moves at a faster pace; sensitive confrontation is accepted more readily than with traditional Hispanic, Native American, or Asian families.

Geographical Location and Neighborhoods

Ethnic groups from different geographical locations exhibit distinct geocultural traditions and customs. Practitioners cannot assume that the same customs apply to seemingly similar cultural groups. They should also note rural and urban influences in the client's present situation within the family history.

Neighborhoods where the minority clients reside have a great deal to do with how clients see themselves. Minority clients living in a totally ethnic area have a different view than clients living in an integrated neighborhood or clients residing in a neighborhood where they are the only minority family.

Family Constituency

In most minority families, kinship networks help to satisfy important cultural needs for intimacy, belonging, and interpersonal relations. Extended families, where more than one generation lives in the same household and where formalized kinship relations exist, are common among minority groups. In many Hispanic and Native American families, significant adults may extend to uncles, grandparents, cousins, close friends, and godparents. Family holds a special place for most minority clients. Love, protection, and loyalty to the family are pronounced, creating an environment where members can develop strong feelings of self-worth despite the lingering effects of discrimination and racism.

Psychohistorical and Religious Traditions

The history of the client's ethnic group, along with the history of that ethnic group in the United States, is information that counselors and therapists need. Minority clients reflect the psychohistory of the family through child-rearing practices. Many facets of child rearing are rooted in the history of minority groups and are distinct from the dominant culture in which the clients presently live. For example, Hispanics and Native Americans have been raised in a cooperative mode rather than the competitive mode of the dominant culture.

Spiritual and religious practices traditionally have been strong within most minorities. Religion provides the medium through which minority clients deal with forces and powers beyond their control. It also provides a basis for social cohesion and support. Historically, the church has been a resource for personal counseling and a refuge from a hostile environment. For example, African Americans have traditionally gone to church leaders for advice and direction.

Individuality

The concept of individual responsibility is viewed differently by minority groups. Native Americans, for instance, judge their worth primarily in terms of whether their behavior serves to better the tribe. Tribal culture places a high value on the harmonious relationship between an individual and all other members of the tribe. This concept of cooperation within certain ethnic groups has been documented (Kagan & Madsen, 1971). Responsibility to the family is a major value found in African-American, Hispanic, Native American, and Asian-American clients and should be considered and encouraged. Individual responsibilities are of secondary value, after the family.

Racial and Ethnic Cultural Components

Specific racial and ethnic cultural components that are common to the four racial cultural groups should be clarified, as they are uniquely important to these respective groups. These components have been identified as critical in assessing minority relationships to the various counseling theories. It is important to have knowledge of these components in order to determine whether theories directly or indirectly address these factors and, if not, whether they can be modified or adapted to their theoretical framework.

Racial/ethnic women's issues are not addressed due to space limitations of this chapter. Rather than provide scant information, the authors encourage you to read "The Woman Factor in Multicultural Counseling" (Arredondo, Psalti, & Cella, 1993); *Women of Color: Integrating Ethnic and Gender Identities in Psychotherapy* (Comas-Diaz & Greene, 1994); and "Gender Issues in Multicultural Counseling" (Hansen & Gama, 1996).

These racial and ethnic components are related to some of the cultural considerations discussed in the previous section. However, they are presented here in the light of counseling theory variables as opposed to counselor or therapist variables. This distinction is important in determining whether a theory allows for the extenuating manifestations inherent in each component. In addition, because these components and considerations manifest a holistic view, they have descriptive overlaps.

Language

Aside from the obvious fact that minority groups may retain their language of origin, use black English, or use code switching (words from English combined with language of origin), there are other considerations that need to be taken into account. Counselors and therapists should be competent in the languages of the particular diverse populations, but they must also be cognizant of the fact that affect is learned in the culture of origin through presymbolic and symbolic language at an early age. This affect reflects the minority member's worldview and the inherent assumptions of the culture. Therefore, the theoretical framework employed must be able to allow for these considerations directly or indirectly.

Family and Social Relations

The importance of family is a major consideration for each of the four groups. Extended family kinship ties, respect for elders, defined gender roles, emphasis on the nurturing of children, hierarchical nature of family structure, primary responsibility to family, and identity are closely linked through strong family ties in all four groups. A counseling theory that does not incorporate this multifaceted component has limited value. The theory must be able to address this component in a familial holistic sense because of the minority group's strong sense of belonging to and identity with the family group.

Time Focus

For these four groups, the concept of time is distinct from the majority view, in which the focus is the future: you sacrifice for tomorrow and postpone gratification. The concept of rigid adherence to time is an artifact of Euro-American culture. For the four groups discussed in this chapter, the present and past may be more important than the future, due to cultural or socioeconomic factors. Worldviews that are based on past cultural history still operate in the present. For these minority groups, time is viewed contextually as an artificial concept of mainstream society. Future predictions and time specificity are placed in context of a possibility, not a fact. Social relations and obligations often have a higher priority than specific time-clock appointments. Theories that incorporate a planning of an individual's future behavior may be counterproductive if this is not taken into consideration. In addition, those theories that impose the "fifty-minute hour" at a specific time take a mainstream cultural view that is not responsive to the cultural worldview of these groups. Events or situations that happen to these groups are often viewed as more important than being on time and, consequently, a client's behavior may be misinterpreted as resistance by a majority theoretical view.

Nature–People Relationships

The relationship of people to nature has a distinct and unique value orientation for these four minority groups. Life may be determined by external forces such as fate, God's will, or "that's the way it is." Acceptance of (not subjugation) and harmony with nature—coexisting without control—are part of an inherent cultural view for these groups. People are a reality, and relationships are important and primary. This view is often at cross-purposes with the majority view, which operates in terms of overcoming, controlling, or conquering nature and environment, including one's own behaviors. Counseling theories that assume that the individual is greater than or separate from nature and the environment have limited effectiveness with these groups.

Holistic View

A holistic view for these groups encompasses both a particularistic cultural perspective and a universal view. These groups operate from the interaction of their environment and themselves as a whole. Support of the interrelationship between individual and environment has been documented extensively (Katz, 1985). Therefore, this holistic component has both universal and particularistic (edic and emic) aspects for these minority groups. Life is based on a totality of this interaction and does not fragment and separate. Counseling theories that only address this component from either a universal view or a particularistic view have limitations in their theoretical application.

Human Activity and Cooperation

Common to all four minority groups is the cultural component of cooperation, which includes connectedness and loyalty to their respective groups. This component is part of the groups' socialization and child-rearing patterns, which are manifested in unique complementary roles and tasks in the family and community. These groups emphasize the concept of "being" as sufficient, not of having to become better in order to have status with one's own group. Contribution is seen from a collective view, with members having value simply because of who they are. Counseling theories that emphasize only the growth of the individual, regardless of how it affects a minority individual's group, will meet with obstacles and confusion.

Identity

For these four groups, personal identity cannot be separated from the cultural identity with which each member contends. Theories that address the universal self or identity development alone bypass a very important cultural component. The process of minority identity has been addressed extensively by Sue and Sue (1990). Hall, Cross, and Freed (1971) have elaborated further on minority identity models. Cultural or ethnic identity is in the midst of much research developed by many authorities in cultural identity theory and addresses many other dimensions beyond what was presented here (see, e.g., Bernal & Knight, 1993; Cross, Parham, & Helms, 1995; Helms, 1990; Sue & Sue, 1990). Each minority member may have distinct self-referent labels that vary even within each group, and these labels are related to both negative and positive identity. Additionally, most members struggle with imposed stereotypes from the majority culture, which affect self-esteem and self-worth of each group member. The psychological costs of racism in identity cannot be stressed enough. Counseling theory and process need to be able to address these complex identity components.

Mental Health

Counseling theories address the concept of mental health from the assumption of a universal (emic) Euro-American point of view, to the exclusion of a culture-specific (edic) view. The four minority groups have similarities in their worldview of what constitutes normality and abnormality, a view that is different from mainstream society's. Current theories rarely take into account the cultural mental health views of these groups, who may not separate the physical from their mental states. The goals and processes of a theory are intimately linked with the theoretical frame of reference that assumes all populations are the same. This issue should be one of the most complex and important concerns when practitioners view theory and process as they apply to these groups.

Spirituality and Religion

Each of these four groups deals with unique and distinct spiritual issues as part of their daily lives. Spirituality and religion are an integral part of every group and its members. They have been a source of stability and hope for these groups for many generations and are part of their socialization. Few counseling theories address this component, and consequently they omit a major mainstay and refuge used by these groups in hostile environments.

Responsibility

The concept of responsibility in these four groups is different from the American majority view. For them, a concept of collective responsibility is prioritized: first to family, then to their own group or community, and finally to self. Most theories deal with responsibility according to a different priority: first to individual, then to family, and finally to group and community. Neither approach implies a wrong or right, but when theories operate from the development of responsibility to self and do not consider the consequences of those implications to members of minority groups, they will meet with confusion and resistance. Individually centered theories, with their goal of individual responsibility, may work in counterproductive ways and are apt to discount the values of these groups. While some theories may espouse the concept of universal responsibility, they often fail to address cultural specificity.

Oppression and Racism

All four groups have experienced a history of oppression and racism that has affected them in terms of identity, alienation, and devaluation of their worth. While other American minority groups have experienced oppression, these four groups have distinct physical traits that are more readily identifiable. This factor alone has kept the differentness on the surface, no matter what may transpire within. Because of the United States's melting-pot philosophy, which is still in existence despite the culturally pluralistic views and values of cultural diversity being professed, racism continues to persist and affect these groups. Few counseling theories address this component in their frameworks, and this omission appears to discount their cultural reality.

A note of caution in addressing these components and considerations: the degree of acculturation plays an important role in that it may be possible that many of these people in the groups will be able to operate contextually depending on whether they are in a majority environment or are within their own minority group. Therefore, these components and considerations need to address the context of the individual's own ability to adjust.

Table 17.1 presents a framework to view diagrammatically whether the nine traditional theories presented in this book address the proposed racial and ethnic components and considerations. (It is important that the reader understand that feminist theory was not included in this diagrammatic comparison, as it directs the majority of its emphasis at only one segment of the client population and comparison with more generic theoretical systems would be inappropriate.) It lists the nine theories and identifies racial and ethnic components and considerations at the top, with their respective intercepting boxes marked as follows: (+) theory responds positively; (-) theory is contrary; (0) theory doesn't address; (P) theory responds partially.

Note that the figure has been proposed as an outline to view how the various identified components correspond to the theories. We interject a note of caution here, pointing out that this figure is not intended to be definitive and closed but to facilitate the understanding of the relationship among the theories and the racial and ethnic components. Arbitrary assessments were made after reviewing the theories and are subject to different interpretations.

For the purpose of the figure, we have given consideration to *traditional* racial and ethnic groups where *survival* is primary and where educational level may be lower than the general white population. For many groups, a major segment of the population has less than a high school education. In addition, many of these minority groups still hold on to the culture and language of origin and therefore still reflect different worldviews.

Table 17.1

Counseling theories in terms of racial and ethnic components

Theory	Racial and Ethnic Components										
	Language	Family and Social Relations	Time Focus	Nature-People Relationships	Holistic View	Human Activity and Cooperation	Identity	Mental Health	Spirituality and Religion	Responsibility	Oppression and Racism
Psychoanalytic	-	-	0	-	-	-	0	-	0	-	-
Jungian	0	-	P	0	P	P	0	0	P	-	0
Adlerian	0	+	P	P	+	+	P	+	+	+	+
Existential	0	-	P	0	+	+	P	+	P	P	0
Person-centered	0	-	+	P	+	+	P	P	P	-	0
Gestalt	0	-	P	-	+	-	0	P	-	-	0
Cognitive-behavioral	0	P	+	0	0	0	P	+	0	-	0
Reality therapy	0	P	+	P	0	-	P	0	0	0	0
Family	P	+	P	0	+	+	0	P	0	+	P

+   Theory responds positively   0   Theory doesn't address
-   Theory is contrary   P   Theory responds partially

Summary and Critique of Theories

In the light of the racial and ethnic components we proposed, our results indicate that very few of the theories discussed in this book address those components effectively. Our purpose is not to show the limitations of these theories with racial or ethnic minorities, but to point out that when the theories were developed, populations with differing and complex worldviews were not taken into consideration.

Alderian, existential, person-centered, and family theories, with some interpolation, could respond to specific components. However, such a response would result from counselor or therapist interpretation that is not necessarily inherent in the theory. It could be argued that existential and person-centered theories have much leeway in the universal sense; therefore, important components could be addressed with adaptations. Philosophically, there may be merit in these approaches. However, in relation to the specificity of these components, both theories appear to be lacking. Alderian and family theories hold the most promise with their holistic, sociocultural and family-centered points of view with minority populations.

The appropriateness of cognitive-behavioral theories is subject to a counselor or therapist's awareness and sensitivity rather than inherent in the theory itself. For the most part, the rest of the theories have little relevance when dealing with these minority populations.

Freudian Psychoanalytic Theory

One of the main limitations of Freudian psychoanalytic theory is its focus on intrapsychic conflict as the source of all dysfunction and its failure to consider interpersonal and socio-cultural variables. It ignores social class, culture, ethnicity, and race as variables in the developmental process. The consequences of racism on the intrapsychic process are not addressed, and differential experiences or the values of being different in a white-dominated society are not acknowledged. Psychoanalytic theory is individualistic and does not deal with cultures that are group or family centered. Stage developments are based on a two-parent family, which is not always the case in many minority groups. The theory also involves a process in which clients are expected to be verbal and disclosing, which can be counterproductive and alien when used with such groups as Asian Americans, Native Americans, and Hispanics, who are socialized not to disclose (Okum, 1990). In addition, the anonymous role the counselor or therapist assumes can be restrictive for minority clients and is in direct conflict with minority clients' social framework and environmental perspective.

Most minority clients cannot afford to devote 5 years to intensive treatment when what they want is immediate response to specific issues. The goals of psychoanalytic therapy are not appropriate for minority clients when dealing with the practical concerns in their social environments. This theory, with modification, could have some application with diagnosed borderline minority clients if they were examined from a sociocultural and developmental perspective. Additionally, the diffused sense of ethnic identity could be addressed, but, again, would bring up the issue of long-term therapy. Based on these considerations, this model is inappropriate for the racial and ethnic groups we have discussed (Corey, 1991; Ivey, Ivey, & Simek-Morgan, 1993).

Jungian Analytical Theory

Jungian theory offers limitations similar to those of Freudian theory for racial and ethnic minority groups. Jungian therapy is an intrapsychic process and does not address racism and discrimination as variables in the developmental process. Consequently, all the problems lie within the individual. Jung's mystical approach, with its collective unconscious, archetypes, and unconscious factors, would have little appeal to those minority groups struggling to survive. It also emphasizes a single model of healthy functioning—one that would take years of counseling and therapy and much money. In addition to using impersonal treatment modalities, Jungian counselors and therapists are subject to their own beliefs about and interpretations of the symbols.

The racial and cultural groups we have discussed may have distinct symbols and are not socialized to deal with abstract symbolic articulation as required by this model. The theory does not deal with the influence of either social class or institutional oppression and thus can be misinterpreted by practitioners. The methodology of this model does not provide a reality base congruent with these minority groups. While it is a holistic model and deals with spirituality, it is not culturally specific to these groups. The model would not be very relevant to or effective with these traditional groups.

Adlerian Theory

Strict Adlerian theory would have some limitations for minority clients who want quick solutions, for the clients would have little interest in exploring early childhood, early memories, or dreams. These clients may not see the purpose of dealing with life's problems by going through details of life-style analysis. However, of all the theories we will consider, this one holds the greatest promise because of several characteristics: it focuses on the person in a familial and sociocultural context; it is involved in developing social interest and in contributing to others; it emphasizes belonging, which supports the value system of these minority groups; and its emphasis on the role of the family and culture fits well with the values of these focus minority groups.

Adlerian assumptions that people are equal, social, and goal centered; that they seek cooperation; and that they contribute to the common good of the group are holistic and are congruent with the cultural values of these racial and ethnic groups. The individual's unique subjective interpretation and perception are part of Adlerian theory, and the client's values and views are honored and accepted. Adlerian goals are not aimed at deciding for clients what they should change about themselves. Rather, the practitioner works in collaboration with clients and their family networks. This theory offers a pragmatic approach that is flexible and uses a range of action-oriented techniques to explore personal problems within their sociocultural context. It has the flexibility to deal both with the individual and the family, making it very appropriate for racial and ethnic groups (Sherman & Dinkmeyer, 1987).

Existential Theory

Existential theory is based on the understanding of the individual and allows the freedom to use other systems and techniques that can be made applicable to racial and ethnic groups. The existential notion of **freedom** and **control** can be helpful in assisting clients to clarify their cultural values, identity, and meaning. Ibrahim (1985) has pointed out that an existential approach provides for the concept of "cultural relativity" and "relative objectivity" (p. 635). It is essential in this approach for practitioners to understand their own cultural heritage and worldviews so that they can more effectively help people with other worldviews.

A major criticism of this approach is that it is excessively individualistic; freedom of choice is a focus. Minority clients may not feel they have much choice because of their environmental circumstances. Because these client groups often seek counseling or psychotherapy for specific direction, reflecting on freedom of choice and meaning may create frustration and misunderstanding. Lack of direction in terms of specificity and the concept of individual responsibility can be counterproductive to these focus minority groups (Corey, 1991; Yalom, 1988).

Person-Centered Theory

In many ways, person-centered theory has made significant contributions to practice in multicultural settings. Carl Rogers used this approach in several countries throughout the world. The theory's emphasis is on humanness and the core conditions that place an egalitarian approach into the model.

In addition it allows the clients to explore their own cultural reality, and if the practitioners do not understand, they need to be honest and develop a learning situation (Freeman, 1993). On the other hand, these core conditions are difficult to translate into the cultural framework of Hispanic, Native American, African-American, and Asian-American/Pacific Islander racial and ethnic groups. It is incumbent on the counselor or therapist to go beyond core conditions of humanness and deal with the cultural relatedness of these minority groups.

Because the theory originated in a white, middle-class milieu, it has inherent limitations unless practitioners carefully look at their own beliefs and gain an understanding of other views.

A limitation of person-centered theory is that many racial and ethnic groups want more structure and direction than is inherent in this theory. Person-centered theory values internal focus, while minority groups may still operate on the value of external evaluation—that of the family and group identity. This theory emphasizes **self** and **real self,** which can be counterproductive because it obscures relational and broader environmental issues that are a priority with these minority groups. These clients may focus more on the real world than the ideal (Corey, 1991; Ivey et al., 1993; Rogers, 1980; Sue & Sue, 1990). In addition, the focus on individual development can be at odds with cultural values that stress the common good and cohesion of a person's group. This model provides a foundation for a relationship to be developed if the counselor or therapist integrates cultural factors. Thus, the theoretical framework alone is not important, but rather how it is used by the counselor or therapist.

Gestalt Theory

Because of its emphasis on individual responsibility and techniques that may be too confrontational or out of the realm of reality for these minority groups, Gestalt theory has several limitations. Confrontation and the techniques used may produce intense feelings that minority clients are not ready for or that are not culturally appropriate. Responsibility focuses on the self without connecting to the group relationship, which may have a higher priority for these minority groups. Native Americans, Asian Americans, and Hispanics have strong cultural characteristics that prohibit them from expressing strong negative emotions about their parents and family. Where cooperation is a heavy cultural injunction, these individuating directions for self-responsibility might meet with opposition.

Another theoretical characteristic in Gestalt theory is that of "being in the present." This may not be understood by groups in which connectedness with the past is important to their worldview. Again, the application of the model depends on its sensitive use by the counselor or therapist (Corey, 1991; Okum, 1990; Perls, 1973; Sue & Sue, 1990).

Cognitive-Behavioral Theories

We discuss the various cognitive-behavioral theories together because they are closely related. Although there are some differences in techniques, all hold to a basic cognitive-behavioral belief system. Albert Ellis's rational-emotive behavior theory does not deal with past history. It does address the client's view of the problem, yet only the cognition of specific events or incidents. This has the danger of devaluing the minority group members' feelings of frustration and their cultural view of self. The theory can be confrontational and dismiss the story around the event or incident that is part of the minority's holistic view, thereby devaluing integrity and values.

Inherent in this theory is the tenet that rational and irrational beliefs are the basis of client problems. These beliefs are based on white, middle-class values; hence what is rational or irrational for the counselor or therapist may not be such for the minority client. The issue of how much power counselors or therapists have may be intimidating or even negatively challenging, creating a retreat from the practitioners or, even worse, an acquiescence to their ideas.

This theoretical framework has a firm set of beliefs that are not culturally relevant and could create confusion. The beliefs the minority client holds may be interpreted as being different from those held by members of other racial and ethnic groups, and this may further exacerbate the client's feelings of insecurity. Unless the counselor or therapist deals carefully and sensitively with the client's cultural beliefs and worldview, this model will meet with disaster.

The theory challenges dependency, which to these groups may be counterproductive to their concept of interdependency, an important part of their cultural values and one they view as essentially healthy. The theory does not deal with such factors as racism, sociocultural experience, and family roles, which are conditioned by the groups' culture (Corey, 1991; Okum, 1990).

There are other cognitive-behavioral theories that do not take such a dogmatic approach as Ellis'. Beck (1976) and Meichenbaum (1979) considered the sociocultural determinants more closely. Yet their approaches are basically the same, with the problem being defined as the client sees it. However, Beck's and Meichenbaum's approaches look at the cultural milieu before determining faulty beliefs, and they involve the client in mutually acceptable goals that can be culturally relevant. Structure is still primary; and once goals are determined, the models proceed on their own. Nevertheless, little room is left for people who do not possess mainstream ideas and are less articulate in majority logic. Behaviors and thoughts deemed culturally acceptable by the dominant culture may have unique and different meanings for these focus groups. Such values and meanings are not accounted for in cognitive-behavioral theory (Okum, 1990). Casas (1988) pointed out that cognitive-behavioral theory does not address racial ethnicity and culture in the development of research paradigms. He points out that the basic assumption of this model is that people are responsible for their own anxiety, contribute significantly to it, and can decide responsibly to act. This view may not be congruent with the life experiences of minorities. Casas further stated, "Racism, discrimination and poverty may have created a cognitive mind set antithetical to any self-control approach" (1988, p. 109). The practitioner's value system concerning race and class is eminently important. If it is incompatible with that of a minority group member, it may be imposed on the client and consequently affect him or her inappropriately. "The theory implies that the dominant therapist's value system is the correct one" (Okum, 1990, pp. 200–201).

Reality Therapy Theory

The principles of this model, which incorporate care, respect, and rejection of the medical model, are that behavior is purposive and geared to fulfilling needs. This model has much potential, depending on its application. Reality therapists can demonstrate their respect for cultural values and assist minority clients in exploring how satisfying their current behavior is and collaboratively form realistic plans that are consistent with their cultural values. The focus is on acting and thinking rather than identifying and exploring feelings. It focuses on positive steps that *could* deal with cultural specificity, which would appeal to these minority groups. However, in this theory the responsibility lies totally with the individual. The counselor or therapist does not seek out the support systems and cooperation values that are part of these groups. The model itself does not address the very real aspects of discrimination and racism that limit these groups. If counselors and therapists do not accept these environmental restrictions as real, minority group members may resist and feel misunderstood.

Additionally, many minority group members may be reluctant to state what they need to an institutional counselor or therapist because of real paranoia or because their socialization has not reinforced self-assertiveness. Their socialization has been to think more in terms of what is good for the group than in terms of their individual needs. Again, as in other approaches, the effectiveness of reality therapy is based on the counselor or therapist's ability to be sensitive to cultural aspects rather than on the theory itself (Corey, 1991; Glasser, 1965).

Family Theory

Family theory incorporates several of the leading family systems theorists and principles of holistic thinking. This theory considers the family as the basic social system and that understanding the system's environment is paramount to being an effective practitioner. By definition a system's environment (institutional, societal, cultural) includes all that affects the basic family system. Consequently, this theory has great implications in its application to minority populations. However, in order for the theory to be effective, practitioners have to have a strong training base in multicultural counseling. This theory has the inherent ability to extend itself to racial and ethnic populations and address the cultural issues and considerations.

The basic premises of family theory deal with the individual, whole family system in its sociocultural contexts. It addresses extended family kinships and respects the concepts of cooperative functioning, an approach that would have much appeal to the racial and ethnic groups we have discussed. It sees the family as the basic unit of development and examines the alliances, subsystems, relationships, and cross-generational issues in their relationship to the larger whole. The theorists include Minuchin's structural approach, which has been implemented with several minority groups, therefore making it culturally adaptable. Minuchin and Fishman (1981) have emphasized the reciprocal influences of the family and community and have focused on interventions that address this interdependence. They incorporate a broad worldview and a knowledge that different cultural systems do affect the function of the family and individuals. The systems approach within family theory can be used with an individual or family yet still deal with the extended family system. Although this approach does not directly address the concept of racism and discrimination in the larger sociocultural context, it lends itself well to the issues minority groups encounter.

Special Note

In 1996, a new theory of multicultural counseling and therapy (M.C.T.) was proposed by Sue et al. (*A Theory of Multicultural Counseling and Therapy*). It provides us with a much needed theoretical framework that addresses all of the racial and ethnic considerations and components more comprehensively than those reviewed here. Though this new M.C.T. theory is not one of the theories covered in this text, we strongly encourage you to read this book and consider its ideas and conceptualization. This theory was developed over a period of time by people who have been in the multicultural counseling field for over two decades. Granted, it was developed with the whole concept of multiculturalism that is reflective of the authors' own Zeitgeist and their views. Beside the authors' own chapters on the theoretical framework, comments from leading experts on multicultural theory from various perspectives are presented, including information on specific racial ethnic groups. Although this area still is in its "infancy," the book is timely and well worth reading.

Summary

This chapter discussed some of the multicultural issues facing our profession—in particular, the racial and ethnic considerations impinging on current theories of counseling and psychotherapy. The study of multiculturalism must consider many facets, including demographics, definitions, racial and ethnic cultural considerations, acculturation, and socioeconomic and cultural distinctions. These considerations do not provide a prescriptive analysis for integration into existing theories, nor do they address all issues that are important, such as research, assessment, training, and ethics. But they have been included in this chapter because of their importance to the four focus minority groups. Table 17.1 was developed to facilitate your understanding of this complex interacting phenomenon. We hope our critique of the chart and the general discussion of the theories will provide insight into the dilemma of how theories must be viewed in the light of our changing population. Counseling theories are fundamental to the way in which counselors and therapists deliver services, but they carry inherent assumptions that we rarely question. Nevertheless, we need to critically evaluate them in the light of minority concerns.

Current counseling theories reflect the Zeitgeist of the era and region in which the theorists lived. Therefore, traditional counseling and psychotherapies were developed for white, middle- and upper-middle-class clients (Atkinson et al., 1993; Sue & Sue, 1990). As Katz (1985) noted, these Euro-American theories were developed by white practitioners enmeshed in Western cultural values, and the applicability of these theories to multicultural populations is questionable.

The onus for the development of cultural awareness and applicability has been shouldered by counselors and therapists. Only recently have training institutions begun to provide cross-cultural training, but those practitioners already in the field have had to rely on workshops and their own readings and experiences to obtain this awareness. Many of them have their own ingrained Euro-American theoretical frameworks and have tried to integrate cultural factors, usually by looking for a "prescription."

In addition to the cultural milieu in which theories were developed, one also has to consider the theoretical framework that reflects practitioners' own Zeitgeist. Theory cannot be considered apart from the context of its original background and its filtering through a counselor or therapist's interpretation. This may provide an even more distorted view, not only of the theory but also of its applicability to different cultural groups. Each of the major models of counseling and psychotherapy has this unexamined assumption: it is true and therefore correct. But at best, theory can only lay a foundation from which to view client behavior and development. There is no one *fully acceptable model* that is considered unassailable in today's world.

Most theories reviewed here do not specifically address the racial, ethnic, and cultural considerations of American minority groups. However, it is possible to adapt some theories if certain cultural considerations are taken into account. So before one "throws the baby out with the bath water," it is essential to take a critical look at significant cultural components and adapt them to theory.

Counselors and therapists are facing a critical impasse in the profession. Multiculturalism—what Pedersen (1991) called "the fourth force"—has gained tremendous momentum. Perhaps this fourth force will require a redefinition of current theories with a major integration of multicultural considerations, or a new multicultural theory that will be applicable to all will emerge, such as the one proposed by Sue et al. (1996). Only time, analysis, research, and exposure will tell. In the meantime, a paradigm shift in our thinking about how to deliver services based on a theoretical framework that incorporates multicultural aspects is no longer just an idea but a reality. As counselors and therapists, we need to proceed with diligence and commitment with the information and research we have on hand. The reality of the rapidly changing demographics of our clientele presents our greatest challenge to integrate this information into our own evolving frameworks.

References

American Association for Counseling and Development. (1991). Special issue: Multiculturalism as a fourth force in counseling. *Journal of Counseling and Development, 70,* 4–76.

Arce, C. (1997). *Hispanic marketing and demographics.* A paper presented at National Hispanic Corporate Council Conference, Hartford, CT.

Arredondo, P., Psalti, A., & Cella, K. (1993). The woman factor in multicultural counseling. *Counseling and Human Development, 25,* 1–8.

Arredondo, P., Toporek, R., Brown, S., Jones, J., Locke, D., Sanchez, J., & Stadler, H. (1996). Operationalization of multicultural counseling competencies. *Journal of Multicultural Counseling and Development, 24,* 42–78.

Atkinson, D., Morten, G., & Sue, D. W. (1993). *Counseling American minorities* (4th ed). Madison, WI: Brown & Benchmark.

Beck, A. (1976). *Cognitive therapy and emotional disorders.* New York: New American Library.

Bernal, M., & Knight, G. (1993). *Ethnic identity: Formation and transmission among Hispanics and other minorities.* Albany: State University of New York Press.

Casas, M. (1988). Cognitive behavioral approaches: A minority perspective. *Counseling Psychologist, 16,* 106–110.

Comas-Diaz, L., & Greene, B. (1994). *Women of color: Integrating ethnic and gender identities in psychotherapy.* New York: Guilford.

Corey, G. (1991). *Theory and practice of counseling and psychotherapy.* Pacific Grove, CA: Brooks/Cole.

Cross, W., Parham, & T., Helms, I. E. (1995). Negrescence revisited: Theory and research. In R. L. Jones (Ed.), *Advances in black psychology* (pp. 1–69). Los Angeles: Cobb & Henry.

Dillard, M. (1985). *Multicultural counseling: Ethnic and cultural relevance in human encounters.* Chicago: Nelson-Hall.

Edmunds, P., Martinson, S. A., & Goldberg, P. F. (1990). *Demographics and cultural diversity in the 1990's: Implications for services to young children with special needs.* Washington, DC: Office of Special Education Programs, U.S. Department of Education.

Essandoh, P. (1996). Multicultural counseling as the fourth force: A call to arms. *Counseling Psychologist, 24,* 126–137.

Freeman, S. (1993). Client centered therapy with diverse populations: The universal within the specific. *Journal of Multicultural Counseling and Development, 21,* 248–254.

Glasser, W. (1965). *Reality therapy: A new approach to psychiatry.* New York: Harper & Row.

Hall, W., Cross, W. E., & Freed, W. R. (1971). Stages in the development of black awareness: An exploratory investigation. In R. L. Jones (Ed.), *Black psychology* (pp. 156–166). New York: Harper & Row.

Hansen, L. S., & Gama, E. M. (1996). Gender issues in multicultural counseling. In Pedersen, P., Draguns, J., Lonner, W., & Trimble, J. (Eds.), *Counseling across cultures* (pp. 73–105). Thousand Oaks, CA: Sage.

Helms, J., (1990). *Black and white racial identity.* Westport, CT: Greenwood.

Ibrahim, F. A. (1985). Effective cross-cultural counseling and psychotherapy: A framework. *Counseling Psychologist, 13,* 625–638.

Ibrahim, F. A. (1991). Contribution of cultural worldview to generic counseling and development. *Journal of Counseling and Development, 70,* 13–19.

Ivey, A. (1981). Counseling and psychotherapy: Toward a new perspective. In A. J. Marsella & P. B. Pedersen (Eds.), *Cross-cultural counseling and psychotherapy.* New York: Pergamon.

Ivey, A. (1983). *Intentional interviewing and counseling facilitating development in a multicultural society.* Pacific Grove, CA: Brooks/Cole.

Ivey, A., Ivey, M. B., & Simek-Morgan, L. (1993). *Counseling and psychotherapy: A multi-cultural perspective.* Boston: Allyn & Bacon.

Kagan, S., & Madsen, M. (1971). Cooperation and competition of Mexican, Mexican-American, and Anglo children of two ages under four instructional sets. *Developmental Psychology 5,* 32.

Katz, J. (1985). The sociopolitical nature of counseling. *Counseling Psychologist, 13,* 615–624.

Krogman, W. M. (1945). The concept of race. In R. Linton (Ed.), *The science of man in world crisis* (pp. 38–61). New York: Columbia University Press.

Kuhn, T. (1962). *The structure of scientific revolutions.* Chicago: University of Chicago Press.

LaFromboise, T. D. (1988). American Indian mental health policy. *American Psychologist, 43,* 388–397.

LaFromboise, T., & Low, K. G. (1989). American Indian children and adolescents. In J. T. Gibbs & L. N. Huang (Eds.), *Children of color: Psychological intervention with minority youth* (pp. 114–147). San Francisco: Jossey-Bass.

Lee, C. (1996). M.C.T. theory and implications for indigenous healing. In D. W. Sue, A. E. Ivey, & P. Pedersen (Eds.), *A theory of multicultural counseling and therapy* (pp. 86–96). Pacific Grove, CA: Brooks/Cole.

LeVine, E. S., & Padilla, A. M. (1980). *Crossing cultures in therapy: Pluralistic counseling for the Hispanic.* Monterey, CA: Brooks/Cole.

Linton, R. (Ed.). (1945). *The science of man (woman) in the world crisis.* New York: Columbia University Press.

Meichenbaum, D. (1979). *Cognitive-behavioral modification.* New York: Plenum.

Midgette, T., & Meggert, S. (1991). Multicultural counseling instruction: A challenge for faculties in the 21st century. *Journal of Counseling and Development, 70,* 136–141.

Minuchin, S., & Fishman, C. (1981). *Family therapy techniques.* Cambridge: Harvard University Press.

Newlon, B. J., & Arciniega, M. (1983). Counseling minority families: An Adlerian perspective. *Counseling and Human Development, 16,* 1–12.

Newlon, B. J., & Arciniega, M. (1992). Group counseling: Cross cultural considerations. In D. Capuzzi & D. Gross (Eds.), *Introduction to group counseling* (pp. 286–306). Denver: Love.

Okum, B. (1990). *Seeking connections in psychotherapy.* San Francisco: Jossey-Bass.

Parham, T. (1996). M.C.T. theory and African-American populations. In D. Sue, A. Ivey, & P. Pedersen (Eds.), *A theory of multicultural counseling and therapy.* Pacific Grove, CA: Brooks/Cole.

Pedersen, P. B. (1988). *A handbook for developing multicultural awareness.* Alexandria, VA: American Association for Counseling and Development.

Pedersen, P. (1991). Multiculturalism as a generic approach to counseling. *Journal of Counseling and Development, 70,* 6–12.

Pedersen, P. (1994). *A handbook for developing cultural awareness* (2nd ed.). Alexandria, VA: American Counseling Association.

Pedersen, P., Draguns, J., Lonner, W., & Trimble, J. (Eds.). (1996). *Counseling across cultures* (4th ed.). Thousand Oaks, CA: Sage.

Perls, F. (1973). *The Gestalt approach and eyewitness to therapy.* New York: Bantam.

Ponterotto, J., & Casas, M. (1991). *Handbook of racial/ethnic minority counseling research.* Springfield, IL: Charles C. Thomas.

Ponterotto, J., Casas, L., Suzuki, L., & Alexander, C. (Eds.). (1995). *Handbook of multicultural counseling.* Thousand Oaks, CA: Sage.

Ponterotto, J., & Sabnani, H. (1989). Classics in multicultural counseling: A systematic five-year content analysis. *Journal of Multicultural Counseling and Development, 17,* 23–37.

Rogers, C. (1980). *A way of being.* Boston: Houghton Mifflin.

Rogler, L. N., Malgady, R., Constantino, G., & Bluementhall, R. (1987). What do culturally sensitive mental health services mean? The case for Hispanics. *American Psychologist, 42,* 565–570.

Rose, P. I. (1964). *They and we: Racial and ethnic relations in the United States.* New York: Random House.

Sherman, R., & Dinkmeyer, D. (1987). *Systems of family therapy: An Adlerian integration.* New York: Brunner/Mazel.

Sue, D. W., Arredondo, P., & McDavis, R. J. (1992). Multicultural competencies and standards: A pressing need. *Journal of Counseling and Development, 70,* 77–486.

Sue, D. W., Ivey, A., & Pedersen, P. (Eds.). (1996). *A theory of multicultural counseling and therapy.* Pacific Grove, CA: Brooks/Cole.

Sue, D. W., & Sue, D. (1990). *Counseling the culturally different: Theory and process.* New York: Wiley.

Teske, R. (1973). An analysis of status mobility patterns among middle-class Mexican Americans in Texas. *Dissertation Abstracts International, 42,* 7907a.

U.S. Bureau of the Census. (1982). *Census of the population: Supplemental report. Race of the population by states.* Washington, DC: Government Printing Office.

U.S. Bureau of the Census. (1988). *Census of the population: Supplemental report. Race of the population by states.* Washington, DC: Government Printing Office.

U.S. Bureau of the Census. (1989). *Census population totals for racial and Spanish origin groups in U.S.* Washington, DC: Government Printing Office.

Wehrly, B. (1991). Preparing multicultural counselors. *Counseling and Human Development, 24,* 1–23.

Wrenn, C. G. (1962). The culturally encapsulated counselor. *Harvard Educational Review, 32,* 444–449.

Wrenn, C. G. (1985). Afterward: The culturally encapsulated counselor revisited. In P. B. Pedersen (Ed.), *Handbook of cross-cultural counseling and therapy* (110–126). Westport, CT: Greenwood.

Yalom, I. D. (1988). *Existential psychotherapy.* New York: Basic Books.

Counseling and Psychotherapy: An Integrative Perspective

Loretta J. Bradley
Texas Tech University

Gerald Parr
Texas Tech University

L. J. Gould
Texas Tech University

In previous chapters of this book, the authors discussed a number of discrete theories. Proponents of each **counseling theory** maintain that with a wide range of client problems, the philosophy, principles, and interventions of that theory are preferable and more effective. Despite the many positive contributions of each theory, research has not shown that any one theory is superior to any other (Smith & Glass, 1977). Further, no theory is an island. Beutler and Clarkin (1990) state that the practice of counseling is evolutionary, extending through the realms of experience and knowledge that are incorporated into the still-developing field:

> Every theory is, in reality, an amalgamation of previous viewpoints. When we speak of one theory or another as "a different perspective," we forget that it is derived developmentally from others. When a "new theory" is developed and compared with an old one, the comparison dims one's awareness of the fact that the new theory has incorporated some of the common knowledge to which the earlier theory contributed. (p. 6)

As more theories and research appear, it becomes increasingly difficult for counselors and therapists to defend a strictly **purist view.** The search for a more comprehensive therapy often leads to integration. Smith (1982) captures the essence of the search for a more **integrative approach:** "Counselors and psychotherapists who consider single-theory orientations too provincial in both theoretical concepts and methodological options tend to seek an eclectic alternative. Eclecticism promises the possibility for a comprehensive psychotherapy that is based on a unified and well-organized body of knowledge and strategies" (p. 802).

The main purpose of this chapter is not to judge the merits of the theories described in previous chapters; rather, it is designed to help you translate information from various **counseling knowledge bases** into a **counseling approach** that best fits your style. Specifically, this chapter will assist you in your search for a **counseling model** that integrates your beliefs, experiences, values, and personal characteristics. The integrity of your **personal model** depends, in part, on your ability to explicate the beliefs and assumptions that underlie your approach. You should be prepared to answer any of the following questions:

- Are there common curative factors that have universal applicability, regardless of the client's background or presenting problem?
- What roles should the counselor or therapist be willing to assume as a helper: a teacher, a mentor, a technical expert, an empathic listener, an informed consultant, a role model, or a wise adviser?
- Are problems solved in the same way in which they are developed?

Another step toward **professional integrity** is understanding how your personal experiences have influenced your beliefs. Perhaps a counselor helped you at one time, and you want to offer to others the same ingredients that you found helpful. Perhaps you respect a counselor educator or supervisor and want to incorporate some of that person's ideas into your approach. Becoming aware of your values and their role in your learning is important too. Your values filter and focus your experiences. Those who value family will seek out approaches—systemic approaches, for example—that feature family as the focal point of intervention; those who value concrete results may be drawn to cognitive-behavioral approaches, which emphasize specific behavior change. Finally, being aware of your personal needs and personality style can help illuminate why certain approaches appeal to you. A person-centered approach, for example, might argue with a dominant personality style. Likewise, a rational-emotive approach might not be the best fit for an individual who seeks to avoid conflict.

In this chapter, we define the integrative approach and address its history and its various types. Additionally, we focus on the development of a personal integrative approach, including a consideration of personal philosophy, clients, treatment goals, and theory constructs.

Integrative Counseling Defined

Integrative counseling evolved from a need. Basically, it began with the assumption that a single theory is too limiting or myopic. Proponents advocate that each counselor should be able to construct his or her own model by taking portions from other theories. This approach allows the practitioner to create a model by synthesizing existing theory and practice. In essence, integrative counseling operates on the premise that the counselor can choose the best from among the various theories.

Young (1992) defines **eclecticism (integration)** as a theory that selects what is best from among many theoretical stances. Implied in this definition is the assumption that the counselor has a thorough knowledge of existing theories, including both their strengths and limitations as well as the knowledge of the necessary ingredients for effective theory building. Young also writes that what is best in counseling is that which works, and integrative counseling is a pragmatic approach devoid of a single viewpoint.

Gilliland, James, and Bowman (1994) describe integration as a broad-based approach that makes systematic and appropriate use of the best interventions from all theories. Garfield (1982, 1988, 1994) cautions that the integrative approach cannot be simply a combination of existing theoretical views or the addition of some interventions from one therapy to another. Instead, it denotes a **conceptual synthesis** and pragmatic blending of diverse **theoretical systems** into a superordinate or **metatheoretical model** that includes philosophy, theory, principles, and interventions (Halgin, 1985; Kelly, 1988, 1991; Norcross, 1985, 1990, 1995; Patterson, 1989b; Wolfe & Goldfried, 1988).

In Chapter 2 of this book, the authors discussed the importance of developing a **personal theory.** Counselors and therapists develop their theory based on study, research, and experience in the field in addition to their personal values and view of human nature. The **integrative perspective** allows them to create models that reflect their unique personalities, talents, and experiences. Typically, this approach represents a synthesis of selected constructs and practices espoused by major theories. It offers several advantages. First, ownership is high when counselors expend the effort to develop and explicate their own paradigms, efforts which often result in an enhanced commitment to ongoing model refinement. Second, this approach encourages authenticity and congruence, which are not fostered by unreflective imitation. Third, integrative counseling allows counselors the flexibility to tailor their approach to best fit the population and problems that characterize their practice. For example, counselors who provide short-term, crisis-oriented assistance, as many school counselors do, may want to rely more heavily on problem-solving models, such as the cognitive-behavioral approaches discussed in Chapter 11, than would counselors in private practice, who treat intra- and interpersonal problems over 10 to 20 sessions. However, given the changes mandated by HMOs, the private practitioner may also need to implement a brief therapy approach.

Conversely, the integrative perspective presents challenges that, if unmet, could become disadvantageous to counselors and therapists. Those who fail to develop, articulate, and define a model of counseling can fall prey to the **lazy eclecticism** that Eysenck (1970) has so forcefully denounced. **Single-theory adherence** suits some practitioners, and an attempt to be integrative may argue against their needs. Hackney (1992) notes that counselors using an individual theory are often either new to the field or have been trained in only one theory. Some inexperienced counselors may lack the courage of their convictions or may find it too demanding to invent a model when ready-made approaches are so readily available. Single-theory adherence can be very alluring when it is formalized with institutes and certification because these trappings can impart a sense of belonging, power, and direction to its devotees. Neophytes often want the security of a well-defined, widely endorsed road map as they launch their professional careers.

History

Orthodoxy dominated the early spirit of the counseling and psychotherapy movement. However, early on, Sigmund Freud (Chapter 4) experienced much controversy both from within and outside his theory base of psychoanalysis. Influenced by psychoanalysis, many theorists, such as Jung (Chapter 5) and Adler (Chapter 6), soon began developing or seeking other models. With the rise of schools of therapy that were independent from psychoanalysis, orthodox psychotherapy was challenged. Schools of therapy, including existential (Chapter 7), person-centered (Chapter 8), Gestalt (Chapter 10), and cognitive-behavioral (Chapter 11), emerged as the preeminence of the analytic paradigm waned. Reality therapy theory (Chapter 12), feminist theory (Chapter 9), and family theory (Chapter 13), along with Eastern theories (Chapter 15), have also contributed to new perspectives in counseling. Furthermore, brief therapy (Chapter 14) has become increasingly important due to the role of HMOs in mental health care. Additionally, the need to consider the special requirements of counseling children (Chapter 16) and the client's culture and worldview (Chapter 17) have been documented.

With the development of new paradigms, an increase in innovative methods and interventions emerged. These new methods and interventions were quickly shared by practitioners from the various schools, a group more likely to use the tools of other orientations and less likely to adhere blindly to one theory (Smith, 1982). Beutler and Clarkin (1990) describe the role of borrowing from other therapies: "Given the role of borrowing and assimilation occurring in the natural course of theory development, the exponential increase in the number of discrete theories of psychotherapy, and the necessity of defining both the similarities and differences among applied theories in order to conduct empirical research, the eventual and formal acceptance of eclecticism may have been inevitable" (p. 10). Hackney (1992) agrees with this assessment. He states that an examination of theoretical integrity appears to demonstrate a convergence—humanistic theories contain some classical behavioral interventions, behavioral approaches acknowledge the legitimacy of feelings and affect change, and systemic approaches use many cognitive interventions. Hackney asserts that the choice of interventions tends to be made by relating the intervention directly to the nature or character of the client's problem.

Historically, integrative counseling first appeared when the constructs and principles of one paradigm were used to explain those of another. Dollard and Miller (1950), for example, drew upon learning theory to explain psychoanalytic theory. The principle of reinforcement replaced Freud's pleasure principle. Transference was explained as a special case of generalization. Thorne (1950), frustrated by the ideological confusion of the psychological sciences, wrote *Principles of Personality Counseling,* in which he espoused an integrative approach that he hoped would promote a standardization of counseling practice similar to that of the medical profession. Borrowing heavily from the medical model, Thorne's approach was reeducative. It emphasized rational-intellectual factors and launched the integrative movement.

Major Constructs

Integration is a broad-based approach that makes **systematic and appropriate use** of the best interventions from all theories. A fundamental assumption of the integrative approach is that counseling involves a **relationship** that, as with other theories, stresses the importance of the **rapport** between client and counselor or therapist. A basic inference of this model is that the practitioner is a genuine human being willing and able to establish a **working alliance** with the client. As stated in Chapter 1, this working alliance best begins through the practice of the **core conditions of counseling.** The counselor or therapist must show the client empathic understanding, respect and positive regard, genuineness and congruence, concreteness, warmth, immediacy, and cultural awareness. Without these core conditions, treatment is extremely difficult, if not impossible. The importance of empathy and the helping relationship is even underscored by those who use brief therapy (Kaplan, 1992). Further, the counselor must recognize that the process of counseling is developmental. The **stages of counseling,** like the stages of human development, often do not follow in a one-two-three order; instead, they most often occur in the order of relationship development, extended exploration, problem resolution, and termination and follow-up. A second assumption is that the counselor is cognizant of the **strategies and methods** used in a variety of theories and can differentiate and selectively use them to meet the needs of the client. A third assumption is that counselors will keep current on new developments in the field so that they continually extend and develop their theory base.

In reviewing research on integrative theory, researchers have concluded the following (Brammer, 1969; Dryden, 1986; Garfield, 1973, 1980; Palmer, 1980; Thorne, 1967):

- The counselor must assume that the client's primary need is to achieve and maintain the highest level of functioning; thus, the practitioner must deal with the client's current psychological state.

- The counselor's approach must be scientific, systematic, and comprehensive without an identification with a single orientation.

- The counselor's orientation should be constantly evolving and changing to incorporate new ideas, concepts, interventions, and research. Counselors should not operate on faith, guesswork, emotion, popularity, or special interest; nor should they consider ideological consistency to be an end in itself.

- The theory should be broad enough to organize, comprehend, integrate, resolve, and use the contributions of all other counseling and therapy approaches.

- The counselor must have a repertoire of concepts, skills, competencies, and strategies from which to draw and thus avoid narrow and simplistic treatments.

- The counselor must deal directly with the client as a person (including the client's worldview, developmental level, culture, social interactions, values, and goals).

- Counseling should focus directly on the client's behavior, goals, and problems as opposed to merely talking about them. Counseling should also deal with problems outside the client's control (e.g., poverty or prejudice).

- The counselor must function in a variety of roles as needed, including counselor, teacher, consultant, facilitator, mentor, advisor, and coach.

There are three main thrusts in integrative therapy. First, counselors help clients become aware of the problem situation. Following awareness, they encourage clients to choose consciously—and, to the extent possible, intentionally—to exercise control over their problem behavior. Finally, they assist clients in developing a higher level of personal integration through proactive choice.

Integrative Models

Researchers have described three types of models in integrative counseling: **atheoretical models,** which emphasize commonalities or interventions above theory; **technical models,** which have a single theory base but use a wide variety of interventions from other orientations; and **synthetic models,** which emphasize a blending of two or more theories and a variety of interventions (Alford, 1995; Norcross, 1986, 1995; Stricker & Gold, 1996).

Atheoretical Models

Atheoretical models are those that emphasize commonalities or interventions above theory. There are two major types of atheoretical models: **common factors models** and **phase models.**

Common Factors Models.   The common factors model emphasizes specific common factors responsible for success in counseling regardless of theoretical orientation. In fact, Karasu (1986) states that it is the nature of psychotherapy to have commonalities. All orientations use some combination of affective, experiential, cognitive, and behavioral regulations as agents of change. Frank (1981) posited that six common curative factors are shared by all therapeutic orientations: the strength of the client and counselor relationship, methods that increase motivation and expectations of help, the enhancement of the client's sense of mastery or self-efficacy, the provision of new learning experiences, the arousal of emotions, and the enhancement of opportunities to practice new behaviors. Frank concluded that these six factors exist to varying degrees in different orientations. Beutler and Clarkin (1990) suggest that common treatment ingredients are created and enhanced by (1) the specific and controllable communication patterns inherent in caring counselors, (2) the interventions chosen by caring counselors, (3) the sensitive use of interventions, and (4) the reasonable amount of control that the counselor maintains over the counseling experience.

Building on Frank's common factors model, Young (1992) developed the **REPLAN model,** which is an example of a specific application of the common factors model. Young's model is based on curative factors (megafactors) that are dimensions of the therapeutic process underlying all counseling approaches (Frank, 1981; Yalom, 1985). The curative factors in REPLAN are relationship (R), efficacy and self-esteem (E), practicing new behaviors (P), lowering or raising emotional arousal (L), activating expectations of help and motivation (A), and providing new learning experiences and changing perceptions (N). The model assumes that treatment planning should be organized and structured so that coherent concepts are presented to the client and reasonable and defensible plans for therapy may be developed. Therapeutic goals are defined by the client and counselor, and the treatment plan uses the curative factors to achieve the goals. Interventions are chosen on the basis of client characteristics. Counseling is structured around specific goals in each session to help the client stay on task. REPLAN is a systematic and pragmatic approach suitable for counselors who have single-theory orientations or multiple orientations.

Even in the context of the same theoretical orientation, diversity exists in therapeutic outcomes (Lieberman, Yalom, & Miles, 1973; Luborsky, Singer, & Luborsky, 1975), thus suggesting that common factors, rather than the theoretical orientation, are responsible for success in counseling. While there is agreement that common factors exist, agreement ends and debate begins about the degree to which common factors can become basic ingredients of therapy (Frank, 1973; Garfield, 1973; Lambert, 1986; Parloff, 1986; Wilkins, 1984). Likewise, Fiedler (1950b) and Sloane, Stapels, Cristol, Yorkston, and Whipple (1975) report that inconsistencies exist between the counselor's stated theory and in-therapy behaviors, thus suggesting that individuals with differing theoretical assumptions may behave similarly and use common factors in therapy sessions.

Phase Models.   The basic assumption underlying the phase models is that the therapy process is characterized by marked phases or stages that clients experience during therapy. Common phases include resistance, action, and change. Phase models attempt to identify characteristic phases (stages) of treatment that are linked to a variety of theories. In phase models, counseling interventions are dependent on the phase (stage) of treatment.

The transtheoretical model of Prochaska (1984) and Prochaska and DiClemente (1984, 1986) is an example of a phase model. It is based on a comprehensive study of phases and principles of change prevalent in a variety of theories. Ten processes of change obtained from client self-reports on personal problem solving were described: consciousness raising (interventions that make clients aware of problems), self-liberation (improving self-efficacy and client involvement in the change process), social liberation (freedom from social obligations), counterconditioning (reframing negative situations or outcomes into positives), stimulus control (learning triggers of negative behaviors, feelings, and thoughts), self-reevaluation (methods for evaluation of values and client-action potential), environmental reevaluation (evaluation of environmental demands), contingency management (controlling rewards and punishments), dramatic relief (removal of symptoms), and helping relationships (use of methods committed to client well-being). Within the counseling process, there are three stages of change that are based on the clients' awareness of their problem: precontemplation (the client is unaware of problems); contemplation (the client, through consciousness raising, becomes aware of problems and begins thinking about them); and action and maintenance (change processes occur). Change occurs on five distinct but interrelated levels: symptom or situational, maladaptive cognitions, current interpersonal conflicts, family or systems conflicts, and interpersonal conflicts. In the phase model, the client and counselor work together to determine the level on which interventions will be focused.

Thorne's Model.   Thorne's (1967, 1968) model is a rigidly empirical scientific approach that avoids giving priority to any theoretical viewpoint. Because all existing methods are included, Thorne described his model as the only truly scientific model. Although not a new model, it does present a collection of methods applied rationally according to their indications and contraindications. Because the model posits a specific treatment method for specific disorders, it has been called a medical model of counseling and is an example of another atheoretical model. In operational terms, Thorne's model first requires a compilation of all known counseling interventions. Next, operational definitions are determined by an experimental analysis of the dynamics of each method, with each method being evaluated to establish its indications and contraindications as well as its relation to psychopathology. Therapeutic effects of each method are then determined, and criteria are established. Statistical analysis is conducted on large-scale data to determine validation through prognosis.

Bohart's Model.   Bohart (1992) proposed an integrative model based on process. He suggests that dysfunctional behavior and psychopathology are not primarily the results of misconstruction, distortion, misperception, or inappropriate behavior, but rather result from a failure to learn from feedback, resulting in an inability to modify dysfunctional behaviors, thus perpetuating them. All therapies operate by helping clients "learn how to learn"—in other words, by helping them function more intelligently. The therapy process models the skills clients need in order to learn more creatively by teaching them to master problems by staying with the experience and tolerating and acknowledging unpleasant emotions; continually check abstractions about oneself, others, and life in general, against reality; broaden attention and recognize both internal and external information; and explore and learn by paying attention to the process of struggling with problems rather than to the outcome.

Technical Models

Technical models emphasize the importance of the counselor or therapist as a technician, a skilled master of interventions successful on a practical level without a strict adherence to a guiding philosophy or theory. In this model, the practitioner applies systematic and planned logic to the assignment of treatment for a client. A technical model is not the idiosyncratic and undefined blend that in the past has often been called **eclectic counseling.** It is, rather, a decision-making process for selecting interventions based on the client's symptoms and goals (Beutler, 1983; Frances, Clarkin, & Perry, 1984; Goldstein & Stein, 1976; Held, 1984; Lazarus, 1976, 1981; Norcross, 1986, 1995). Lazarus (1995, 1996) argues that **technical eclecticism** is the most useful of the integrative models because it permits the counselor to select techniques from any discipline without necessarily endorsing the theory from which it is derived. He further states that numerous case examples exist where a borrowed technique has produced a better treatment outcome for the client.

BASIC-ID Model.   Lazarus's (1967, 1973, 1976, 1981) **BASIC-ID** is an example of a technical model. This multimodal approach (B = behavior, A = affect, S = sensation, I = imagery, C = cognition, I = interpersonal, D = drug or alcohol) is broad-spectrum, both in terms of the battery of interventions Lazarus employs and in terms of how he assesses clients' problems. His interventions range from the creative, intuitive use of imagery (1984) to more standard behavioral interventions, such as aversion therapy (1971). Lazarus's multimodal BASIC-ID profile provides a good example of a pragmatic approach that focuses on what is best for the client and methods for resolving problems. The theory base is behavioristic, although a variety of interventions are applied to client treatment without regard for their theoretical origins. The behavioristic basis of the model suggests that client problems have a triggering sequence and that effects in one mode are transferred to other modalities. Thus, interventions are designed for each modality and are implemented simultaneously in a shotgun approach to interrupt the cycle. Lazarus's assessment procedure addresses the areas denoted by the acronym BASIC-ID and includes an innovative inquiry into potential transference phenomena. For example, he asks his clients to imagine what it would be like to be shipwrecked with him on a desert island for six months (1971). Lazarus asserts that clients' responses to this projective intervention help him identify their expectations and clarify their concerns. In our review of Lazarus's publications, it is apparent that he stresses the importance of designing individual strategies for the client and closely monitoring the progress of the interactive efforts in therapy.

Prescriptive Model.   The **prescriptive model** is a specific problem-solving treatment approach addressing various levels of human functioning (biological, intrapsychic, interpersonal) in both theoretical and applied (practical) terms. According to Diamond, Havens, and Jones (1978), the prescriptive model requires "a framework that permits flexibility in the process of individualizing treatment yet does not lose the benefits of information from theory and research in psychotherapy" (pp. 239–240). It is a systematic effort to provide a specific set of treatment procedures for each of several conditions (neurotic disorders, psychopathology, sexual dysfunction, habit disorders, and psychosis) by delineating the relationship between symptom presentation and treatment. The clinical process includes five steps: theory or conceptual superstructure, assessment, goal setting, intervention, and evaluation. The prescriptive model emphasizes the importance of research in the clinical decision-making process and focuses on the client-counselor relationship rather than theoretical positions, although theory is given more importance than in the purely technical model (Diamond & Havens, 1975; Diamond et al., 1978; Goldstein & Stein, 1976; Held, 1984; Norcross, 1990).

Differential Therapeutics Model.   The **differential therapeutics model** combines clinical wisdom from experienced practitioners with a variety of clinical examples to define counseling practice. Diagnostic, character, and environmental variables help define contraindicators and enabling factors for predicting treatment outcome. This model is less specific than other technical models and depends on the use of a cookbook approach to effective intervention (Beutler & Clarkin, 1990; Frances et al., 1984; Perry, Frances, & Clarkin, 1985).

Synthetic (Systematic) Models

Allport (cited in Lewis, 1985) captured the essence of the synthetic model when he insisted that counselors should be systematic rather than syncretic in client treatment, and that each component of the system should be critically evaluated according to coherence and the available evidence. Further, the practitioner must avoid dogmatism and have a flexible theory base.

Allport's model focuses on both technical integration and social persuasion theory (Brehm, 1976; Brehm & Brehm, 1981; Brehm & Smith, 1986; Goldstein, 1966; Strong, 1978). It is difficult to develop decision criteria for assignment of treatment procedures independent of the theories on which the procedures are based. There are three client/problem dimensions (symptom complexity or severity, defensive style, and interpersonal resistance level) that are matched with three complementary aspects of counseling interventions (treatment focused on symptoms or conflicts; on cognitive, behavioral, or affective procedures, and on the degree of directiveness from the counselor). The systematic model stresses the importance of the helping relationship and of matching the needs of the client with interventions that enhance acceptance of change. Six areas of intervention are considered after assessment: insight enhancement, emotional awareness, emotional escalation, emotional reduction, behavioral control, and perceptual change. Treatment is adjusted as client/problem status changes (Beutler, 1983, 1986; Beutler & Mitchell, 1981; Calvert, Beutler, & Crago, 1988).

Adaptive Counseling and Therapy (ACT).   Howard, Nance, and Myers (1986) have developed an interesting synthetic model of counseling that draws upon Hersey and Blanchard's situational leadership theory (1977). Their model, **adaptive counseling and therapy** (ACT), looks at two key therapist dimensions: directiveness and support. A matrix depicting these two dimensions yields four therapist styles: high directiveness–low support (a telling style); high directiveness–high support (a teaching style); low directiveness–high support (a supporting style); and low directiveness–low support (a delegating style). Mainstream models that illustrate these styles are rational-emotive behavioral therapy (REBT) and behavioral therapy for the telling style, reality therapy for the teaching style, person-centered therapy for the supporting style, and psychoanalytic therapy for the delegating style.

ACT attempts to match these four therapist styles with levels of client readiness, which is defined by willingness to change, confidence, and ability or skills to make changes. The assumption of ACT is that the most effective approach to helping is calibrated by matching interventions to synchronize with the client's readiness, and by moving to new interventions as the client's readiness matures. Thus the telling style (e.g., a token economy in an institutional setting) is best suited for the lowest level of readiness. As readiness improves, the styles of best fit, respectively, are teaching, supporting, and delegating. The ACT model has several well-validated measures of therapist styles that hold promise to research the tenets of this model. Likewise, Howard et al. (1986) provide rich guidelines on process and outcome goals that reflect their model. They also incorporate research on power as an ingredient of therapeutic influence into their model. Truly, ACT is a stellar example of responsible integration.

Interpersonal Style Model.   Using Leary's interpersonal diagnosis model, Andrews (1989) analyzed the therapeutic worldviews and intervention styles of several counseling theories in developing his **interpersonal style model.** Viewed from Leary's typology, which is depicted as a circle, Andrews characterized psychoanalysis as hostile-submissive; humanistic-Rogerian therapy as friendly-submissive; and behavioral and cognitive-behavioral therapy as friendly-dominant. Similarly, Andrews used Leary's typology to classify leading counselors. Perls, for example, exemplifies a hostile-dominant therapeutic stance. What is especially relevant about Andrews's article is the thesis that a flexible, integrative approach avoids the limitations of a single vision of reality. More specifically, Andrews states: "To be fruitful, therapeutic interactions must not complement too exactly the client's interpersonal style, or else that style—and the problems associated with it—will be reinforced. . . . When we structure a personal style or therapeutic outlook around a single vision, we risk becoming single-dimensional caricatures" (pp. 806, 812). Thus, integrative counselors modify their interpersonal behavior to challenge the client and to offer an alternative view of reality.

Redecision Model.   Goulding and Goulding's (1978, 1979) **redecision model** is an excellent example of synthetic integration. Combining transactional analysis (TA) and Gestalt, the Gouldings use a group format in a ranch setting to have individuals revisit early childhood decisions. Imagined dialogues allow group participants to rework dysfunctional childhood script decisions. The Goulding's approach promotes intellectual understanding, cathartic release, and behavioral change by mixing the conceptual framework and interventions of an experiential perspective (Gestalt) with a rational-educative perspective (TA).

Strategic Model.   The **strategic model** is based on two primary concepts: constructivism, which states individuals do not discover reality but rather invent it; and the systems view of process, which states individuals are open to variation that stimulates interaction. Interventions are matched to clients by examination of their construction and process orientations. Three components are paramount to the strategic model: (1) viewing the clients' problems from various theory perspectives that address their level of problematic functioning; (2) choosing and applying the theory or theories that best conceptualize the problem in service of counseling goals (theory, client, counselor); and (3) incorporating strategic interventions into therapy to enhance change. The strategic model is a systematic and problem-solving approach that provides multiple theories and methods for understanding the client's problem and interventions needed to maximize change (Duncan, Parks, & Rusk, 1990; Held, 1984). For example, Rigazio-DiGilio (1994) posited that developmental counseling and treatment (DCT) and systemic cognitive-developmental theory (SCDT) represent integrative models that unify the individual, family, and network treatment within a co-constructive-developmental framework. Treatment must consider the social/cultural environment in which individual and family development occur. Treatment strategies are based on the promotion of the client's horizontal and vertical development (Borders, 1994; Rigazio-DiGilio, 1994; Terry, 1994). Claiborn and Lichtenberg (1989) have developed a model for interactional counseling, integrating ideas from Sullivan (1953) and contemporary interpersonal theorists such as Kiesler (1982), the Palo Alto Group, and systems theory.

Actualizing Counseling and Psychotherapy.   Brammer and Shostrom's **actualizing counseling** (1977) draws upon several mainstream counseling models, including Gestalt, person-centered, humanistic, existential, analytic, and behavioral perspectives. They see growth toward actualization in terms of a developmental perspective. Individuals progress through stages that include, in order, dependency, interdependence, role-taking, conformity, transition, synthesis, experimentation, consolidation, involutional, and the evaluation stage. Their model has seven well-defined philosophical dimensions (e.g., human uniqueness and growth through social interaction) and eight well-defined goals (e.g., spontaneity, living in the here and now, being responsible, and achieving independence).

In summary, the atheoretical, technical, and synthetic (systematic) models account for most of the integrative models; however, other examples of responsible integration abound (Beutler, 1983; Diamond & Havens, 1975; Fitzpatrick & Weber, 1989; Garfield, 1980; Held, 1984; Omer, 1993; Prochaska, 1984; Todd & Bohart, 1994), which is not surprising, because research supports its popularity and effectiveness. Examples of the integrative models currently being proposed for use in counseling are attachment theory

(Lopez, 1995; Lyddon, 1995); behavior therapy (Eifert, Forsyth, & Schauss, 1993); cognitive therapy (Alford, 1995; Alford & Norcross, 1991; Beck, 1991); contextual modular therapy (MacNab, 1991); family therapy (Nichols, 1996); psychodynamic integrative therapy (Stricker & Gold, 1996); relationship-centered counseling (Kelly, 1995, 1997); responsive therapy (Gerber, 1989, 1991); and solution-focused counseling (Guterman, 1996). Studies illustrate that integration is the most common theoretical preference of counselors (Garfield & Kurtz, 1977; Jayartne, 1982; Norcross & Prochaska, 1982; Smith, 1982; Watkins & Watts, 1995). Smith and Glass (1977), using meta-analysis, provided indirect support for the importance of curative factors in counseling when they concluded that although no one theoretical school is better than any other, counseling benefits about 80% of those who receive it. Lambert (1986) amplifies this by identifying three common curative factors that account for counseling gains: support, learning, and action. Fiedler's historical research (1950a, 1950b), which suggested that experience rather than theoretical adherence accounted for differences among counselors, may have been the forerunner of these contemporary studies.

Developing an Integrative Approach

Before practitioners decide to use an integrative approach in the practice of counseling or psychotherapy, they must have a clear understanding of the process involved. First, they must recognize the diversity of ideas available in the theories of counseling. They must read, study, and understand the philosophy, constructs, and goals of the various theories so that an informed and systematic choice may be made with regard to their inclusion or exclusion in their theory base. Second, counselors must know their own **personal agenda:** values, beliefs, and perceptions about humanity. Without this knowledge, they cannot properly judge the fit of a theory to their own philosophy. Third, counselors must know the types of clients they will see and where (agency, private practice, school, etc.) they will be working with these clients. Finally, counselors should recognize that combining some theories and interventions may be problematic; thus they should find alternative ways of achieving the intended goals. Examples of how to approach developing an integrated approach abound. A good example is E. W. Kelly (1997), who writes about how he developed a humanistic model of integration. His account of how he reconciled the technical aspects of techniques within a humanistic framework (which has traditionally disavowed the use of techniques per se) illustrates how building a personal theory is a demanding, soul-searching effort.

In the process of developing an integrated theory approach, the first area of consideration is the theory's philosophy. After examining the basic philosophy of the various theories, counselors should move to an examination of the constructs inherent in each theory. These constructs include the focus of the theory, goals for counseling, counselor and client relationship, and applications. Finally, counselors should examine the interventions of each theory and their comfort level in using them with clients.

Philosophy

In searching the basic tenets of the various theories, practitioners should consider their personal belief system. For example, if their basic belief about human nature is that humankind is self-determining, then they will have difficulty integrating psychoanalytic theory, which emphasizes the importance of psychic energy, unconscious motives, and impulses, as well as early experiences determining human behavior. However, depending on other personal beliefs, they might be capable of integrating parts of individual psychology, existential, Gestalt, or person-centered theories, which stress the importance of self-determination in the change process. Counselors who believe that problems arise from poor choices made by individuals might integrate TA, REBT, and reality therapy. Depending on their cognitive bias and attitude toward learning theories, counselors might also consider behavioral therapy and cognitive-behavioral approaches.

Constructs

Within the various theories, several constructs are considered. This section includes discussions of the following: focus on the present or the past, on insight or action, on feelings or cognitions, on counseling goals, on counseling interventions, and on the counseling relationship. An important issue to consider is whether it is more important to focus on the client's present problems or past experiences. Psychoanalytic and analytical psychotherapy stress the importance of the past to the present problems. Gestalt, which is firmly based in the here and now, uses interventions to bring past or unfinished business into the present. Behavioral, cognitive-behavioral, TA, and reality therapy are concerned with present behavior and needed change. Existential, Adlerian, and person-centered theories are concerned with the present and future growth of the individual. **Frey's model** (1972) is helpful in determining the means of integrating counseling goals and classifying differing theories according to the client's needs. The model is a synthesis of two continua for describing counseling theory: a rational-affective dimension conceptualizing the process of counseling, and an action-insight dimension conceptualizing the goals of counseling. The model possesses four quadrants: action-rational (e.g., behavioral therapy); action-affective (e.g., Gestalt therapy); insight-affective (e.g., psychoanalytic therapy); and insight-rational (e.g., Adlerian therapy).

Should counseling focus on insight, or on action? In psychoanalytic theory the focus is on insight; clients are helped to examine their ego defenses and unconscious processes that have resulted in inadequate resolution of psychosexual stage development. Analytical psychotherapy stresses the importance of developing self-knowledge by integrating the conscious and unconscious through the use of archetypes and other symbols within the psyche. Obviously, the insight theories may be difficult to integrate with the action-oriented theories. However, the theories that focus on action—Gestalt, behavioral, cognitive-behavioral, and reality therapy—may be entirely compatible. Adlerian therapy, with its cognitive perspective on motivation and goals, would not blend well with Gestalt, which emphasizes feelings and unfinished business. However, behavioral, cognitive-behavioral, and reality therapy, all with strong emphasis on learning new behaviors, might integrate easily.

Does the counselor focus on feeling (emotion), or on thinking (cognition)? Person-centered, Gestalt, psychoanalytic, and analytical psychology theories are highly focused on feelings and emotional states. Behavioral, cognitive-behavioral, and reality therapy focus on faulty learning and behavior. Another problem concerns the client's preferred way of looking at the world. A client who "thinks" or prefers to focus on the cognitive (intellectual) may be unprepared to deal with feelings in the beginning of counseling. If the counselor moves too quickly into feelings, the client may terminate counseling because of fear. Therefore, the practitioner must pace with the client's lead and use a more cognitive approach initially and, as appropriate, move to a more feeling-oriented approach.

What are the goals of counseling, and what type of change is to be accomplished? Many clients come to counseling in a quest for self-knowledge. Analytical, person-centered, Gestalt, and existential theories focus on this issue. Analytical psychology provides self-knowledge through the understanding of the conscious and unconscious by investigation of dreams and introspective examination of personal symbols of archetypes. Person-centered theory provides a safe haven for self-exploration that allows clients to become more open, spontaneous, and trusting of themselves and others. Both existential and Gestalt stress moment-to-moment awareness and responsibility for change. Change in behavior, the goal of reality therapy, REBT, TA, behavioral, and cognitive-behavioral theories, may be accomplished by connecting thoughts, feelings, and behaviors; or change may be accomplished by focusing on problem-solving and retraining by systematic methods exemplified by behavioral theory. Change in decisions and decision-making processes are found in TA and REBT.

The counseling relationship is important in all theories. Most accept the core conditions of counseling as being essential to building a good client and counselor relationship, but other issues in the therapeutic relationship must be considered. First, what role does the counselor play in the process of counseling? In psychoanalytic theory, where counselors are the object of projection and transference, they are not as open as in existential or person-centered theories, where the practitioner is a partner in a human-to-human encounter. The counselor is a catalyst for helping clients explore their unconscious processes in psychoanalytic and analytical psychology. The counselor plays the role of teacher-trainer in behavioral, cognitive-behavioral, TA, reality therapy, and REBT.

Finally, counselors must consider the applications of various theories. It is important to recognize that the setting in which they will be working and the types of clients that they will be seeing affect the choice of therapy. For example, a school counselor would not use psychoanalytic or analytical psychology because both theories are more suited for adults who are interested in intensive, long-term therapy. The school counselor would be better served by individual psychology, reality therapy, behavioral, cognitive-behavioral, or person-centered theories, depending on the problems of the clients. Counselors who specialize in crisis intervention might consider combining existential, Gestalt, and cognitive-behavioral theories because of the importance each places on personal responsibility and coping mechanisms. Most theories can be applied equally well to individual, group, and family therapy.

Interventions

Integrative approaches have often been criticized on the grounds that interventions are chosen haphazardly by counselors. Before using any intervention, counselors should ask themselves three questions: What will be accomplished by the use of this intervention? Am I comfortable with the intervention's methodology? Is the client psychologically prepared for the possible results? Some interventions are used by virtually all theories—questioning, paraphrasing, summary, clarification, confrontation, and so on. Other interventions are goal specific. For example, behavioral interventions such as operant conditioning, systematic desensitization, and reinforcement would not be useful for clients interested in self-knowledge. However, contracting, cognitive restructuring, modeling, and rehearsal, all of which are behavioral interventions, might help clients in their quests.

Finally, counselors must keep in mind that the client is the prime concern in counseling; it is the client who must be served, not the counselors' personal agendas. To be successful, counselors must calibrate their interventions to account for the developmental and cognitive levels of their clients. Essentially, counselors serve as pacers. Additionally, they must know and abide by the ethical boundaries of the profession, always keeping in mind that the welfare of the client is paramount. The counselor must recognize and affirm the client as a human being.

As stated earlier in this chapter, counselors should not operate on faith, guesswork, emotion, popularity, or special interest. Their theory base should organize, comprehend, integrate, resolve, and use the "best from the best." Further, counselors must have a repertoire of skills, competencies, strategies, and interventions that they are comfortable with using in order to avoid simplistic and narrow treatments.

Strengths and Weaknesses

The integrative approach to counseling has deep roots in tradition and equally deep roots in controversy. Accordingly, this part of the chapter presents the strengths and weaknesses associated with integrative counseling.

Strengths

One of the many strengths of integrative counseling is its broad-based, integrated system capitalizing on the selection of interventions and strategies for their effectiveness rather than for their membership in a particular theory base. Similarly, integrative counseling advocates selectively applying interventions and strategies to meet the specific needs of clients rather than selection based on counselor comfort. Accordingly, Young (1992) concluded that the focus on common factors and the development of specific interventions maximizes the effectiveness of integrative counseling. Researchers describe the integrative approach as especially effective when a specific treatment is recommended for a specific problem, and further stress the value of the counselor's acquaintance with a variety of theories and interventions (Halgin, 1985; Held, 1984; Lambert, 1986; Nelson-Jones, 1985; O'Leary, 1984; Rubin, 1986; Winter, 1985). Another positive feature of the integrative approach is its assumption that counselors are competent individuals capable of selecting, integrating, and applying either part or whole theories appropriately. Because a single theory has not been identified as the best theory, the integrative model has proven as effective as any single-orientation theory (Lambert, 1986).

Other advantages offered by the integrative approach include its flexibility of choice of methods and its multiagency application. Further, it forces counselors and therapists to develop their personal style. The very core of integrative counseling requires practitioners to evaluate and develop their personal view continually, thus avoiding stagnation or dependence on a single theory. A purely separatist viewpoint can preclude a comprehensive vision of client care and can produce a polarization in counseling approaches (Garfield, 1982; Karasu, 1986). In contrast, the integrative approach conceptualizes counseling as evolving from a variety of established theories, thus avoiding polarization. Finally, a primary advantage of the integrative approach is that it allows counselors to develop an internally consistent, coherent rationale for their counseling behavior. Implied in this description is the assumption that they will study various approaches and thus make a theory selection based on critical analysis. Another implication is that the counselor will be forced to consider the whole person in counseling sessions. A further strength, and perhaps one often overlooked, is that the integrative approach can build bridges between incompatible viewpoints (Norcross, 1990).

Weaknesses

While defenders of the integrative approach list its numerous strengths, it also receives its share of criticism. Some researchers have described integrative counseling as a haphazard clinical approach (Garfield, 1982, 1994; Norcross, 1990, 1995; Omer, 1993; Wolfe & Goldfried, 1988), an approach with little theoretical purity (Omer & London, 1988) or research support (Patterson, 1989a). Patterson (1989b) maintains that integrative counseling consists of disparate interventions from many approaches with little attempt at systematic organization or the formation of guiding principles to regulate their use. Eysenck (1970) has referred to integrative counseling as an undisciplined hybrid of systems likely to breed confusion—a "mish-mash of theories, a hugger-mugger of procedures, a gallimaufry of therapies, and a charivaria of activities having no proper rationale and incapable of being tested or evaluated" (p. 140). Kottler and Brown (1992) and Patterson (1986) liken integrative counseling to a technician approach. They state that counselors operating without the philosophy and assumptions of theory are like technicians who can fix what is broken but do not have the in-depth knowledge to understand why. Abroms (1983) concluded that clients are viewed as problems instead of people. Additionally, Kottler and Brown contend that integrative counselors often use a shotgun approach that is more concerned with alleviating symptoms than with resolving underlying problems. Karasu (1986) asserted that without belief in one's own school or orientation, an element of success in counseling that builds confidence and professional identity is missing. McBride and Martin (1990) concluded that the integrative approach does not provide the counselor with the information needed to operate in new and different situations. Patterson (1989b) said that it demonstrates little concern for compatibility or orderly integration of theories; instead, it attempts to include as many methods and interventions as possible. Linden (1984) stated that without a clear grounding in theory, it is difficult to establish goals, provide encouragement, or measure results.

The question of efficacy has surfaced in regard to integrative counseling. Chessick (1985), Linden (1984), Russell (1986), and Stall (1984) concluded that efficacy is diminished by lack of its fundamental bases in theory, concepts, and empiricism. Similarly, Patterson (1989a) criticized the integrative approach because he believes it lacks a metatheory necessary to guide and implement counseling practice and principles. Abroms (1983) described the integrative approach as having connotations of superficiality. Finally, in their discussion of integrative counseling, Kottler and Brown (1992) concluded that there is an inherent difficulty in expecting counselors to learn the technology of all systems and to keep current with the constant changes in the field. They stated that this leads to mediocrity and to generalists who know a little about everything and a lot about nothing.

Conclusion

The integrative approach has many factors in its favor. It advocates a wide-based approach with a large selection of interventions and strategies that have proven effective. It assumes that counselors and therapists are capable of making appropriate use of interventions and strategies. Further, it forces the practitioner to develop a personal style and theory. However, there is no doubt that there are problems inherent in the use of an integrative approach. If the approach is not carefully considered, it can lack guiding principles to regulate the use of interventions and strategies. Too often, it has been a shotgun approach—fixing what is broken without knowing why. Further, for less experienced counselors, an integrative approach may not inspire the confidence or professional identity of a single theory.

Despite the controversy and criticism surrounding integrative counseling, counselors are continuing to opt for the integrative approach. In the 28 years between 1961 and 1989, researchers reported that between 32% and 65% of practitioners indicated multiple school allegiance or designated themselves as eclectic or integrationists (Garfield & Kurtz, 1976, 1977; Goldfried, 1980; Jayartne, 1982; Kelly, 1961; Kelly, Goldberg, Fiske, & Kokowski, 1978; Larson, 1980; Norcross & Prochaska, 1982; Smith, 1982; Swan, 1979; Swan & MacDonald, 1978; Watkins, Lopez, Campbell, & Himmell, 1986). Hart (1983) captures the invasion of integrative counseling when he writes: "Modern psychotherapists are becoming more eclectic in their approach. Schools still exist, but psychotherapists are less likely to have a life-long membership in just one school, and even psychotherapists who affiliate with a single school are likely to borrow ideas and interventions from other schools" (p. 6).

Perhaps this trend towards integration (eclecticism) reflects a maturation within the profession that parallels human growth and development. The profession may be entering its early adolescence, when individuation takes precedence over dependence on a grand master or a grand theory. Perhaps the profession is moving away from those with idealistic adulations toward a greater acceptance of personal responsibility and agency in creating effective practitioners. No doubt, like adolescents, counselors and therapists attempting to find their integrative identity go through periods of awkwardness and uncertainty. Grand masters and grand theories are vital, as are parents; and unlike many adolescents, we acknowledge their contributions to the development of the profession. At the same time, however, this chapter has celebrated individual counselors who dare to discover their own identity through integrating the ideas of others, through personal experience, and through personal exploration. To achieve this integration, the counselor must struggle, take risks, experiment, model, and reflect. This professional development is no less tumultuous than being an adolescent, and it is also no less exciting, rewarding, and meaningful.

References

Abroms, E. M. (1983). Beyond eclecticism. *American Journal of Psychiatry, 140,* 740–745.

Alford, B. A. (1995). Introduction: Psychotherapy integration and cognitive psychotherapy. *Journal of Cognitive Psychotherapy, 9,* 147–151.

Alford, B. A., & Norcross, J. C. (1991). Cognitive therapy as integrative therapy. *Journal of Psychotherapy Integration, 1,* 175–190.

Andrews, J. (1989). Integrating visions of reality: Interpersonal diagnosis and the existential vision. *American Psychologist, 44,* 803–817.

Beck, A. T. (1991). Cognitive therapy as the integrative therapy. *Journal of Psychotherapy Integration, 1,* 191–198.

Beutler, L. E. (1983). *Eclectic psychotherapy: A systematic approach.* New York: Pergamon.

Beutler, L. E. (1986). Systematic eclectic psychotherapy. In J. C. Norcross (Ed.), *Handbook of eclectic psychotherapy* (pp. 94–131). New York: Brunner/Mazel.

Beutler, L. E., & Clarkin, J. F. (1990). *Systematic treatment selection: Toward targeted therapeutic interventions.* New York: Brunner/Mazel.

Beutler, L. E., & Mitchell, R. (1981). Psychotherapy outcome in depressed and impulsive patients as a function of analytic and experiential treatment procedures. *Psychiatry, 44,* 297–306.

Bohart, A. (1992). Un modelo integrador de proceso para la psicopatologia y la psicoterapia. *Revista De Psicoterapia, 3,* 49–74.

Borders, L. D. (1994). Potential of DCT/SCDT in addressing two elusive themes of mental health counseling. *Journal of Mental Health Counseling, 16,* 75–78.

Brammer, L. M. (1969). Eclecticism revisited. *Personnel and Guidance Journal, 48,* 192–197.

Brammer, L. M., & Shostrom, E. L. (1977). *Therapeutic psychology* (3rd ed.). Upper Saddle River, NJ: Prentice Hall.

Brehm, S. S. (1976). *The application of social psychology to clinical practice.* New York: Wiley.

Brehm, S. S., & Brehm, J. W. (1981). *Psychological reactance: A theory of freedom and control.* New York: Academic Press.

Brehm, S. S., & Smith T. (1986). Social psychological approaches to psychotherapy and behavior change. In S. L. Garfield & A. E. Bergin (Eds.), *Handbook of psychotherapy and behavior change* (3rd ed.) (pp. 69–115). New York: Wiley.

Calvert, S. J., Beutler, L. E., & Crago, M. (1988). Psychotherapy outcome as a function of therapist-patient matching on selected variables. *Journal of Social and Clinical Psychology, 6,* 104–117.

Chessick, R. D. (1985). The frantic retreat from the mind to the brain: American psychiatry in mauvaise foi. *Psychoanalytic Inquiry, 5,* 369–403.

Claiborn, C. D., & Lichtenberg, J. W. (1989). Interactional counseling. *Counseling Psychologist, 17*(3), 355–453.

Diamond, R. E., & Havens, R. A. (1975). Restructuring psychotherapy: Toward a prescriptive eclecticism. *Professional Psychology, 6,* 103–200.

Diamond, R. E., Havens, R. A., & Jones, A. C. (1978). A conceptual framework for the practice of prescriptive eclecticism in psychotherapy. *American Psychologist, 33,* 239–248.

Dollard, J., & Miller, N. (1950). *Personality and psychotherapy.* New York: McGraw-Hill.

Dryden, W. (1986). Eclectic psychotherapies: A critique of leading approaches. In J. C. Norcross (Ed.), *Handbook of eclectic psychotherapy* (pp. 353–378). New York: Brunner/Mazel.

Duncan, B. L., Parks, M. B., & Rusk, G. S. (1990). Strategic eclecticism: A technical alternative for eclectic psychotherapy. *Psychotherapy, 27,* 568–577.

Eifert, G. H., Forsyth, J. P., & Schauss, S. L. (1993). Unifying the field: Developing an integrative paradigm for behavior therapy. *Journal of Behavior Therapy and Experimental Psychiatry, 24,* 107–118.

Eysenck, H. J. (1970). A mish-mash of theories. *International Journal of Psychiatry, 9,* 140–146.

Fiedler, F. E. (1950a). A comparison of therapeutic relationships in psychoanalytic, nondirective, and Adlerian therapy. *Journal of Consulting Psychology, 14,* 435–445.

Fiedler, F. E. (1950b). The concept of an ideal therapeutic relationship. *Journal of Consulting Psychology, 14,* 239–245.

Fitzpatrick, M. M., & Weber, C. K. (1989). Integrative approaches in psychotherapy: Combining psychodynamic and behavioral treatments. *Journal* of *Integrative and Eclectic Psychotherapy, 8,* 102–117.

Frances, A., Clarkin, J., & Perry, S. (1984). *Differential therapeutics in psychiatry: The art and science of treatment selection.* New York: Brunner/Mazel.

Frank, J. D. (1973). *Persuasion and healing: A comparative study of psychotherapy* (Rev. ed.). Baltimore: Johns Hopkins University Press.

Frank, J. D. (1981). Therapeutic components shared by all psychotherapies. In J. H. Harvey & M. M. Parks (Eds.), *Psychotherapy research and behavior change* (pp. 175–182). Washington, DC: American Psychological Association.

Frey, D. H. (1972). Conceptualizing counseling theories: A content analysis of process and goal statements. *Counselor Education and Supervision, 11,* 243–250.

Garfield, S. L. (1973). Basic ingredients or common factors in psychotherapy? *Journal of Consulting and Clinical Psychology, 41,* 9–12.

Garfield, S. L. (1980). *Psychotherapy: An eclectic approach.* New York: Wiley.

Garfield, S. L. (1982). Eclecticism and integration in psychotherapy. *Behavior Therapy, 13,* 610–623.

Garfield, S. L. (1988). Commentary on Omer and London. *Psychotherapy, 25,* 180–182.

Garfield, S. L. (1994). Eclecticism and integration in psychotherapy: Developments and issues. *Clinical Psychology: Science and Practice, 1,* 123–137.

Garfield, S. L., & Kurtz, R. (1976). Clinical psychologists in the 1970s. *American Psychologist, 31,* 1–9.

Garfield, S. L., & Kurtz, R. (1977). A study of eclectic views. *Journal of Consulting and Clinical Psychology, 45,* 78–83.

Gerber, S. (1989, March). *Responsive therapy: A better frame than eclectic.* Paper presented at the annual meeting of the American Association of Counseling and Development, Boston, MA.

Gerber, S. (1991, November). *Responsive therapy and personal commitment: Integrative models.* Paper presented at the annual conference of the Western Association of Counselor Education and Supervision, San Diego, CA.

Gilliland, B. E., James, R. K., & Bowman, J. T. (1994). *Theories and strategies in counseling and psychotherapy* (3rd ed.). Upper Saddle River, NJ: Prentice Hall.

Goldfried, M. R. (1980). Some views on effective principles of psychotherapy. *Cognitive Therapy and Research, 4,* 271–306.

Goldstein, A. P. (1966). Psychotherapy research by extrapolation from social psychology. *Journal of Counseling Psychology, 13,* 38–45.

Goldstein, A. P., & Stein, N. (1976). *Prescriptive psychotherapies.* New York: Pergamon.

Goulding, R., & Goulding, M. (1978). *The power is in the patient: A TA/Gestalt approach to psychotherapy.* San Francisco: TA Press.

Goulding, R., & Goulding, M. (1979). *Changing lives through redecision therapy.* New York: Brunner/Mazel.

Guterman, J. T. (1996). Doing mental health counseling: A social constructionist revision. *Journal of Mental Health Counseling, 18,* 228–252.

Hackney, H. (1992). *Differentiating between counseling theory and process.* Ann Arbor: ERIC Clearinghouse on Counseling and Personnel Services.

Halgin, R. P. (1985). Teaching integration of psychotherapy models to beginning therapists. *Psychotherapy, 22,* 555–563.

Hart, J. (1983). *Modern eclectic therapy: A functional orientation to counseling and psychotherapy.* New York: Plenum.

Held, B. S. (1984). Toward a strategic eclecticism: A proposal. *Psychotherapy, 21,* 232–241.

Hersey, P., & Blanchard, K. H. (1977). *Management of organizational behavior: Utilizing human resources* (3rd ed.). Upper Saddle River, NJ: Prentice Hall.

Howard, G. S., Nance, D. W., & Myers, P. (1986). Adaptive counseling and therapy: An integrative eclectic model. *Counseling Psychologist, 14*(3), 363–442.

Jayartne, S. (1982). Characteristics and theoretical orientations of clinical social workers: A national survey. *Journal of Social Science Research, 4,* 17–30.

Kaplan, A. G. (1992). When all is said and done, what is the core of brief therapy? *Counseling Psychologist, 20*(3), 460–463.

Karasu, T. B. (1986). The specificity versus nonspecificity dilemma: Toward identifying therapeutic change agents. *American Journal of Psychiatry, 14,* 687–695.

Kelly, E. L. (1961). Clinical psychology—1960: Report of survey findings. *Newsletter, Division of Clinical Psychology, 14,* 1–11.

Kelly, E. L., Goldberg, L. R., Fiske, D. W., & Kokowski, J. M. (1978). Twenty-five years later: A follow-up study of the graduate students in clinical psychology assessed in the V.A. selection research project. *American Psychologist, 33,* 746–755.

Kelly, E. W., Jr. (1995, August). *Relationship-centered counseling: The integrative interaction of relationship and technique.* Paper presented at the 103rd annual meeting of the American Psychological Association, New York, NY.

Kelly, E. W., Jr. (1997). Relationship-centered counseling: A humanistic model of integration. *Journal of Counseling and Development, 75,* 337–345.

Kelly, K. R. (1988). Defending eclecticism: The utility of informed choice. *Journal of Mental Health Counseling, 10,* 210–213.

Kelly, K. R. (1991). Theoretical integration is the future for mental health counseling. *Journal of Mental Health Counseling, 13,* 106–111.

Kiesler, D. J. (1982). Interpersonal theory for personality and psychotherapy. In J. C. Anchin & D. J. Kiesler (Eds.), *Handbook of interpersonal psychotherapy* (pp. 274–295). Elmsford, NY: Pergamon.

Kottler, J. A., & Brown, R. W. (1992). *Introduction to therapeutic counseling* (2nd ed.). Pacific Grove, CA: Brooks/Cole.

Lambert, M. J. (1986). Implications of psychotherapy outcome research for eclectic psychotherapy. In J. C. Norcross (Ed.), *Handbook of eclectic psychotherapy* (pp. 436–462). New York: Brunner/Mazel.

Larson, D. (1980). Therapeutic schools, styles, and schoolism: A national survey. *Journal of Humanistic Psychology, 20,* 1–20.

Lazarus, A. A. (1967). In support of technical eclecticism. *Psychological Reports, 21,* 415–416.

Lazarus, A. A. (1971). *Behavior therapy and beyond.* New York: McGraw-Hill.

Lazarus, A. A. (1973). Multimodal behavior therapy. *Journal of Nervous and Mental Disease, 156,* 404–411.

Lazarus, A. A. (1976). *Multimodal behavior therapy.* New York: Springer.

Lazarus, A. A. (1981). *The practice of multimodal therapy.* New York: McGraw-Hill.

Lazarus, A. A. (1984). *In the mind's eye.* New York: Guilford.

Lazarus, A. A. (1995). Different types of eclecticism and integration: Let's be aware of the dangers. *Journal of Psychotherapy Integration, 5,* 27–39.

Lazarus, A. A. (1996). The utility and futility of combining treatments in psychotherapy. *Clinical Psychology: Science and Practice, 3,* 59–68.

Lewis, T. T. (1985). Gordon Allport's eclectic humanism: A neglected approach to psychohistory. *Psychohistory Review, 13,* 33–41.

Lieberman, M. A., Yalom, I. D., & Miles, M. B. (1973). *Encounter groups: First facts.* New York: Basic Books.

Linden, G. W. (1984). Some philosophical roots of Adlerian psychology. *Individual Psychology: Journal of Adlerian Theory, Research, and Practice, 40,* 254–269.

Lopez, F. G. (1995). Contemporary attachment theory: An introduction with implications for counseling psychology. *Counseling Psychologists, 23,* 395–415.

Luborsky, L., Singer, B., & Luborsky, L. (1975). Contemporary studies of psychotherapies. *Archives of General Psychiatry, 32,* 995–1008.

Lyddon, W. J. (1995). Attachment theory: A metaperspective for counseling psychology? *Counseling Psychologist, 23,* 479–483.

MacNab, F. (1991). Psychotherapy: Focused and integrated. *Psychoanalysis and Psychotherapy, 9,* 65–84.

McBride, M. C., & Martin, G. E. (1990). A framework for eclecticism: The importance of theory to mental health counseling. *Journal of Mental Health Counseling, 12,* 495–505.

Nelson-Jones, R. (1985). Eclecticism, integration, and comprehensiveness in counseling theory and practice. *British Journal of Guidance and Counseling, 13,* 129–138.

Nichols, W. C. (1996). *Treating people in families: An integrative framework.* New York: Guilford Press.

Norcross, J. C. (1985). Eclecticism: Definitions, manifestations, and practitioners. *International Journal of Eclectic Psychotherapy, 4,* 19–32.

Norcross, J. C. (1986). Eclectic psychotherapy: An introduction and overview. In J. C. Norcross (Ed.), *Handbook of eclectic psychotherapy* (pp. 3–24). New York: Brunner/Mazel.

Norcross, J. C. (1990). Commentary: Eclecticism misrepresented and integration misunderstood. *Psychotherapy, 27,* 297–300.

Norcross, J. C. (1995). A roundtable on psychotherapy integration, common factors, technical eclecticism, and psychotherapy research. *Journal of Psychotherapy Practice and Research, 4,* 248–271.

Norcross, J. C., & Prochaska, J. O. (1982). A national survey of clinical psychologists: Affiliations and orientations. *Clinical Psychologist, 35,* 4–6.

O'Leary, K. D. (1984). The image of behavior therapy: It is time to take a stand. *Behavior Therapy, 15,* 219–233.

Omer, H. (1993). The integrative focus: Coordinating symptom- and person-oriented perspectives in therapy. *American Journal of Psychotherapy, 47,* 283–395.

Omer, H., & London, P. (1988). Metamorphosis in psychotherapy: End of the systems era. *Psychotherapy, 25,* 171–180.

Palmer, J. O. (1980). *A primer of eclectic psychotherapy.* Monterey, CA: Brooks/Cole.

Parloff, M. B. (1986). Frank's "common elements" in psychotherapy: Non-specific factors and placebos. *American Journal of Orthopsychiatry, 56,* 521–530.

Patterson, C. H. (1986, Summer). Counselor training or counselor education? *Spectrum Newsletter,* pp. 10–12.

Patterson, C. H. (1989a). Eclecticism in psychotherapy: Is integration possible? *Psychotherapy, 26,* 157–161.

Patterson, C. H. (1989b). Foundations for a systematic eclectic psychotherapy. *Psychotherapy, 26,* 427–435.

Perry, S., Frances, A., & Clarkin, J. F. (1985). *A DSM-III casebook of differential therapeutics: A clinical guide to treatment selection.* New York: Brunner/Mazel.

Prochaska, J. O. (1984). *Systems of psychotherapy: A transtheoretical analysis* (2nd ed.). Homewood, IL: Dorsey.

Prochaska, J. O., & DiClemente, C. C. (1984). *The transtheoretical approach: Crossing the traditional boundaries of therapy.* Homewood, IL: Dow Jones–Irwin.

Prochaska, J. O., & DiClemente, C. C. (1986). The transtheoretical approach. In J. C. Norwood (Ed.), *Handbook of eclectic psychotherapy* (pp. 163–200). New York: Brunner/Mazel.

Rigazio-DiGilio, S. A. (1994). A co-constructive-developmental approach to ecosystemic treatment. *Journal of Mental Health Counseling, 16,* 43–74.

Rubin, S. S. (1986). Ego-focused psychotherapy: A psychodynamic framework for technical eclecticism. *Psychotherapy, 23,* 385–389.

Russell, R. L. (1986). The inadvisability of admixing psychoanalysis with other forms of psychotherapy. *Journal of Contemporary Psychotherapy, 16,* 76–86.

Sloane, R. B., Stapels, F. R., Cristol, A. H., Yorkston, N. J., & Whipple, K. (1975). *Psychotherapy versus behavior therapy.* Cambridge: Harvard University Press.

Smith, D. S. (1982). Trends in counseling and psychotherapy. *American Psychologist,* 37, 802–809.

Smith, M. L., & Glass, G. V. (1977). Meta-analysis of psychotherapy outcome studies. *American Psychologist, 32,* 752–760.

Stall, R. (1984). Disadvantages of eclecticism in the treatment of alcoholism: The "problem" of recidivism. *Journal of Drug Issues, 14,* 437–448.

Stricker, G., & Gold, J. R. (1996). Psychotherapy integration: An assimilative, psychodynamic approach. *Clinical Psychology: Science and Practice, 3,* 47–58.

Strong, S. R. (1978). Social psychological approach to psychotherapy research. In S. L. Garfield & A. E. Bergin (Eds.), *Handbook of psychotherapy and behavior change* (2nd ed.) (pp. 101–135). New York: Wiley.

Sullivan, H. S. (1953). *The interpersonal theory of psychiatry.* New York: Norton.

Swan, G. E. (1979). On the structure of eclecticism: Cluster analysis of eclectic behavior therapists. *Professional Psychology, 10,* 732–734.

Swan, G. E., & MacDonald, M. L. (1978). Behavior therapy in practice: A national survey of behavior therapists. *Behavior Therapy, 9,* 799–807.

Terry, L. L. (1994). The theory behind the theory in DCT and SCDT: A response to Rigazio-DiGilio. *Journal of Mental Health Counseling, 16,* 79–84.

Thorne, F. C. (1950). *Principles of personality counseling: An eclectic approach.* Brandon, VT: Clinical Psychology Publishing.

Thorne, F. C. (1967). *Integrative psychology.* Brandon, VT: Clinical Psychology Publishing.

Thorne, F. C. (1968). *Psychological case handling: Establishing the conditions necessary for counseling and psychotherapy* (Vol. 1). Brandon, VT: Clinical Psychology Publishing.

Todd, J., & Bohart, A. (1994). *Foundations of clinical and counseling psychology.* New York: HarperCollins College Publishers.

Watkins, C. E., Lopez, F. G., Campbell, V. L., & Himmell, C. D. (1986). Contemporary counseling psychology: Results of a national survey. *Journal of Counseling Psychology, 33,* 301–309.

Watkins, C. E., & Watts, R. E. (1995). Psychotherapy survey research studies: Some consistent findings and integrative conclusions. *Psychotherapy in Private Practice, 13,* 49–68.

Wilkins, W. (1984). Psychotherapy: The powerful placebo. *Journal of Consulting and Clinical Psychology, 52,* 570–573.

Winter, D. A. (1985). Personal styles, constructive alternativism, and the provision of a therapeutic service. *British Journal of Guidance and Counseling, 58,* 129–135.

Wolfe, B. E., & Goldfried, M. R. (1988). Research on psychotherapy integration: Recommendations and conclusions from an NIMH workshop. *Journal of Consulting and Clinical Psychology, 56,* 448–451.

Yalom, I. (1985). *Theory and practice of group psychotherapy* (3rd ed.). New York: Basic Books.

Young, M. E. (1992). *Counseling methods and techniques: An eclectic approach.* Upper Saddle River, NJ: Merrill/Prentice Hall.

Name Index

Subject Index